Proceedings of the 2009 International Conference on

Software Technology and Engineering

ICSTE 2009

Proceedings of the 2009 International Conference on

Software Technology and Engineering

Chennai, India 24 – 26 July 2009

ICSTE 2009

editors

Venkatesh Mahadevan
Swinburne University of Technology, Australia

Jianhong Zhou
Sichuan University, China

Allan Ng
IACSIT, Singapore

World Scientific

NEW JERSEY • LONDON • SINGAPORE • BEIJING • SHANGHAI • HONG KONG • TAIPEI • CHENNAI

Published by

World Scientific Publishing Co. Pte. Ltd.
5 Toh Tuck Link, Singapore 596224
USA office: 27 Warren Street, Suite 401-402, Hackensack, NJ 07601
UK office: 57 Shelton Street, Covent Garden, London WC2H 9HE

British Library Cataloguing-in-Publication Data
A catalogue record for this book is available from the British Library.

SOFTWARE TECHNOLOGY AND ENGINEERING
Proceedings of the International Conference on ICSTE 2009

ISBN-13 978-981-4289-97-9 (pbk)
ISBN-10 981-4289-97-3 (pbk)

Printed in Singapore by World Scientific Printers

IACSIT
WWW.IACSIT.ORG

Honor Chairs

Prof. Ce Zhu, Nanyang Technological University, Singapore

Prof. Kaninda Musumbu, LaBRI - Université Bordeaux 1, France

HOD, Prof. B.B.Biswal, National Institute of Technology, India

Conference General Chairs

Prof. Venkatesh Mahadevan, Swinburne University of Technology, Australia

Dr. Jianhong Zhou, Sichuan University, China

Prof. Allan Ng, IACSIT, Singapore

Program Committee Chairs

HOD, Prof. Peddoju Sateesh Kumar, Balaji Institute of Technology & Science, India

Dr. Srinivasan Alavandar, Indian Institute of Technology, India

Dr. K.S. Cheung, University of Hong Kong, Hong Kong

Prof. Ashwani Kush, IIT kanpur and Kurukshetra University, India

Publication Chairs

Dr. Xiaoxiao Zhou, Nanyang Technological University, Singapore

HOD, Prof. Sekhar Ranjan Bhadra Chaudhuri, Bengal Engineering & Science University, India

Dr. Yi Xie, Cagayan State University, Philippines

Publicity Chairs

Dean, Prof. G.Selvakumar, School of Electrical Sciences, V.M.K.V. Engineering College, India

Prof. Xuesong Zhang, Claremont Graduate University, USA

Dean, Prof. Shishir K.Shandilya, Rukmani Devi Institute of Science and Technology, India

Technical Committees

Prof. Sarat Kumar Patra, National Institute of Technology Rourkela, India

HOD, Prof. Kung Chih-hsien, Chang-Jung Christian University, Taiwan

Prof. K.Chandra Sekaran, National Institute of Technology Karnataka, India

HOD, Prof. V.Saravanan, Dept of Computer Applications, Karunya University, India

Prof. Rafi-U-Zaman, Muffakham Jah College of Engineering and Technology, India

Prof. Jinlong Wang, Qingdao Technological University, China

Prof. S J Wagh, Maharashtra Academy of Engineering, India

Dean, Prof. Taher Omran Ahmed Aljabal Algharby University, Libya

Prof. Qiang Li, Zhejiang University of Science and Technology, China

Dr. Bruce Moulton, University of Sydney Technology, Australia

Prof. Farhat Anwar, International Islamic University Malaysi, Malaysia

Prof. Shinde Subhash Keshavrao, Bharati Vidyapeeth College of Engineering, India

HOD, Prof. Khaleel Ur Rahman Khan, Muffakham Jah College of Engineering & Technology, India

Prof. Haiyan Wu, Zhejiang Gongshang University, China

Prof. Seung-Soo Han, Myongji University, Korea

Prof. Adrian OLARU, University Polytechnic of Bucharest, Romania

Prof. Zheng Quan, University of Science and Technology of China, China

Prof. Nansheng Pang, North China Electric Power University, China

Prof. Hossein Hassanabadi, Azad University of Quchan, Iran

Prof. Neeraj Kumar Nehra, SMVD University, India

Dr. Qian Chen, Columbia University, USA

HOD, Prof. Bhavesh Patel, Shah & Anchor Kutchhi Polytechnic, India

Prof. Sang Ho Lee, Soongsil University, Korea

Prof. Guoai Xu, Beijing University of Posts and Telecommunications, China

HOD, Prof. H.S.Mohana, Malnad College of Engineering, India

Prof. Ying Jin, Jilin University, China

HOD, Prof. H Naganna, S.J.B. Institute of Technology, India

HOD, Prof. D.Balaji, R.V.S. College of Engineering and Technology, India

Prof. Chetto Maryline, University of Nantes, France

Prof. Aamir Saeed Malik, Yeungnam University, Korea

HOD, Prof. Yogendra Kumar Jain, Samrat Ashok Technological Institute, India

Dr. Rubijesmin Abdul Latif, Monash University, Australia

Prof. Hui Peng, Beijing University of Posts and Telecommunications, China

PREFACE

Dear Distinguished Delegates and Guests,

The Organizing Committee of ICSTE 2009 warmly welcomes you to the 2009 International Conference on Software Technology and Engineering (ICSTE 2009), held on July 24-26, 2009 in Chennai, India. ICSTE 2009 is sponsored by International Association of Computer Science and Information Technology (IACSIT), and the conference proceedings are published by World Scientific Press.

If you have attended the conferences sponsored by IACSIT before, you should know that the conferences together report the results of research efforts in a broad range of computer science and information technology. The conference is aimed at discussing with all of you the wide range of problems encountered in present and future high technologies. The ICSTE 2009 is organized to gather members of our international community of Software Technology and Engineering scientists so that researchers from around the world can present their leading-edge work, expanding our community's knowledge and insight into the significant challenges currently being addressed in that research. The conference Program Committee is itself quite diverse and truly international, with membership from the Americas, Europe, Asia, Africa and Oceania.

This proceeding records the fully refereed papers presented at the conference. The main conference themes and tracks are Software Technology and Engineering. The conference aims to bring together researchers, scientists, engineers, and practitioners to exchange and share their experiences, new ideas, and research results about all aspects of the main conference themes and tracks and discuss the practical challenges encountered and the solutions adopted. The main goal of the event is to provide international scientific forums for exchange of new ideas in a number of fields that interact in-depth through discussions with their peers from around the world. Both inward research; core areas of Software Technology and Engineering and outward research; multi-disciplinary, inter-disciplinary, and applications will be covered during the event.

The conference has solicited and gathered technical research submissions related to all aspects of major conference themes and tracks. All the submitted papers in the proceeding have been peer reviewed by the reviewers drawn from the scientific committee, external reviewers and editorial board depending on the subject matter of the paper. Reviewing and initial selection were undertaken electronically. After the rigorous peer-review process, the submitted papers were selected on the basis of originality, significance, and clarity for the purpose of the conference. The selected papers and additional late-breaking contributions to be presented as lectures will make an exiting technical program. The conference program is extremely rich, featuring high-impact presentations.

The high quality of the program – guaranteed by the presence of an unparalleled number of internationally recognized top experts – can be assessed when reading the contents of the program. The conference will therefore be a unique event, where attendees will be able to appreciate the latest results in their field of expertise, and to acquire additional knowledge in other fields. Attendees arriving as specialist expert will thus have the opportunity to leave the conference as enriched scientists, be they from academia or industry. The program has been structured to favor interactions among attendees coming from many diverse horizons, scientifically, geographically, from academia and from industry. Included in this will to favor interactions are social events at prestigious sites.

We would like to thank the program chairs, organization staff, and the members of the program committees for their work. Thanks also go to the World Scientific Press Editors, for their wonderful editorial service to this proceeding.

We are grateful to all those who have contributed to the success of ICSTE 2009. We hope that all participants and other interested readers benefit scientifically from the proceedings and also find it stimulating in the process. Finally, we would like to wish you success in your technical presentations and social networking.

We hope you have a unique, rewarding and enjoyable week at ICSTE 2009 in Chennai India.

With our warmest regards,

ICSTE 2009 Organizing Committees
24-26 July 2009 in Chennai India

CONTENTS

Session 1

COLLABORATIVE WEB BASED CONSTRUCTION INFORMATICS – A LEARNING SCIENCES PERSPECTIVE IN AN INDIAN CONTEXT

SHION GUHA

Documentation Research and Training Centre, Indian Statistical Institute, 8th Mile Mysore Road Bangalore, Karnataka, 560059, India

This paper investigates web enabled construction informatics in India. Literature has been studied to derive the characteristics of the system. A web site which seems to be the first of its kind in India has been designed and launched for learning and application of the system. Existing software for data analysis have been proposed as much as possible. A new MS Project add-on application to connect MS Project to the cost database has been developed. Open source software has been used for web based recording and collaboration. Collaboration facilities have allowed the deployment of sophisticated techniques like Monte Carlo simulation and interactive linear programming for time-cost optimization in practical cases. A full learning module consisting of study material, reference and test have been developed for online learning. A project management wiki has been launched for recording user's experience.

1. Introduction

Construction management is a complex task. It requires inputs from varieties of stakeholders namely owners, consultants, suppliers contractors and outside agencies like financial institutions, regulatory authorities etc. The stakeholders are often separated geographically from one another and from the work site.

Projects by definition are unique tasks. Construction projects cost millions and might run for years. It should be adjusted continuously for efficiency. These traits tend to add up for a large amount of paper work which is to be executed in a collaborative manner by the stakeholders. Web enabled service is appropriate in such condition. The advent of web connectivity prompted the project managers to collaborate through internet.

There are number of web sites and IT consultant firms who offer construction informatics service in the developed world. However, construction activities are intimately related to the economic status of a nation and the methodology varies accordingly. The approach and service level of the developed nation may not be appropriate for the developing world.

In India, internet based project management methodology has not yet become popular. One of the major reasons is the absence of a locally tuned methodology.

In this paper an attempt has been made to develop an appropriate methodology for the Indian scenario. The methodology includes development of the construction informatics and applying it to an example work site.t.

2. Literature Survey

Literature has been consulted for studies about the frame work for project management.

Ma and Qin [1] studied information management systems for construction projects in China. They analyzed major aspects and the evaluation criteria for the information management systems. This method can be used to design and evaluate an effective information management system for construction projects.

Tang [2] studied management systems for the construction industry in the United Kingdom. A questionnaire survey was conducted. The study suggested a guideline which focuses on training and staff participation to adopt an integrated system.

Broomfield [3] edited "ISO 9001-2000 Interpretive Guide for the Design and Construction Project Team". He opined that establishing a construction management system is a challenging task. Tables including examples have been published to set up an ISO quality construction management system.

Amor, Betts et al. [4] investigated the application of information technology (IT) in construction over the last 20 years. Data seems to indicate that there is little formal research in the Indian context in this field. They found that visualization and integration between processes and people is the most important area of current research.

Wetherill M, Rezgui Y et al. [5] studied about development of tools for knowledge management in construction in Europe. They felt that it has not yet been properly developed. They found several obstacles like:

1. Knowledge mainly resides in the individuals.
2. Decision intent is often not properly documented.
3. Data is not properly compiled and collated.

They have recommended development of a web based standardized knowledge management system for the construction industry.

Mervi, Veli et al. [6] studied the multidisciplinary aspect of information management in construction. They felt that finding information is not a problem but sorting it into a useful form is a major issue. They felt that construction is an intensively information processing industry due to the uniqueness of each building project. After a similar literature and software system search Guha [7] proposed a scheme for construction management with the properties mentioned as follows:

1. Website establishment for project management.
2. The web operation should be user friendly.
3. Reports should be generated every fortnight.
4. Web enabled systems should be developed.
5. Active participation of users is essential.
6. Document storage facility should be provided.
7. Collaboration facilities should be provided.
8. Standardized formats should be developed.
9. Security controlled access should be provided.
10. Photo album facilities should be provided.

3. Website Proposal

A website christened www.sssolutionsonline.com has been launched. This project management (PMC) website would be used mainly by project stakeholders. The client outlines the requirements based on which consultants deliver drawings and specifications. Suppliers and contractors deliver the product as per drawings and specifications set by consultants. The business model requires substantial collaborations among team members that are managed online. The web managers' role will be to analyze and deliver PMC advice. In addition, the web manager should maintain the system. The requirements of the stakeholders from the proposed PMC web site as proposed by Guha [8] are presented in Fig 1.

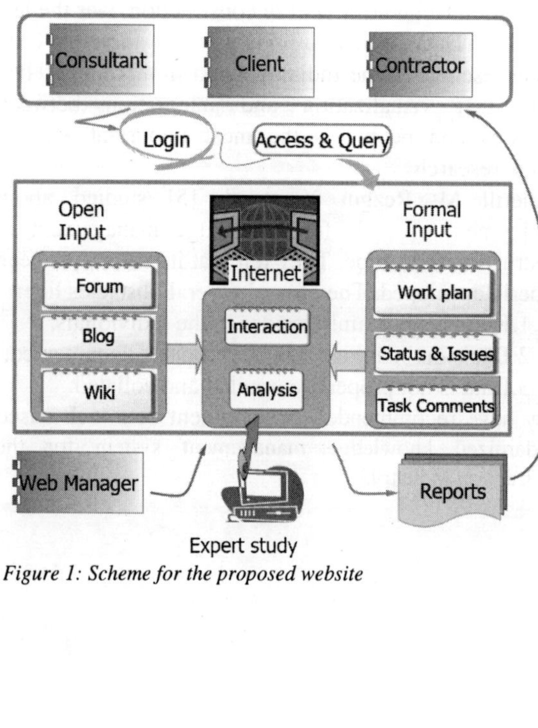

Figure 1: Scheme for the proposed website

The website shall publish reports as presented in Fig 2. Commercial software like Microsoft Project shall be used to generate the reports. The web space shall also be used for collaboration. Open source software has been proposed for collaboration work because source codes would be available for small adjustments.

4. Data Analysis Software

The input data generated in the website is analyzed by varieties of software. The planning for the same are summarized as follows:

1. Open software shall be used wherever possible.
2. Code customization to minimize existing gap.
3. Web enabled databases for online collaboration.
4. Training module to be developed within the site.

The following types of reports shall be generated:

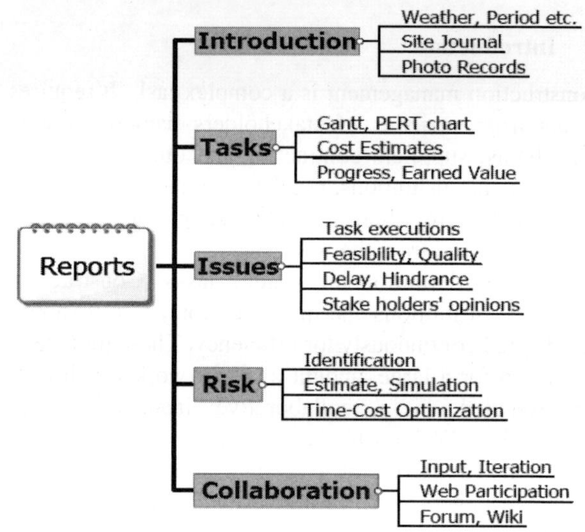

Figure 2: Reports to be published in the website.

Microsoft Project has been taken as the main scheduling software because of its familiarity with the local business community. Moreover, additional open source or otherwise add-ons to MS Project like PERT Chart Expert for primary tracking, WBS Chart for creating Work Breakdown Structure, Project Merlin for assignment lists, Risky Project for simulation and risk analysis etc. have been used.

However, some of the data generated within the website could not be properly processed with the existing software. For instance, costing data cannot be effectively estimated in MS Project scheduling software. Hence, a MS Project add-on christened as REAnalysis [9] has been developed to integrate task scheduling and costing information.

REAnalysis can be used for cost estimating and updating relevant data in MS Project. It executes cost analysis of individual tasks in a manner suitable to the local business practices. Such software was not found in the web survey and hence, the in house product was developed. A screen shot of REAnalysis is provided in Figure 3.

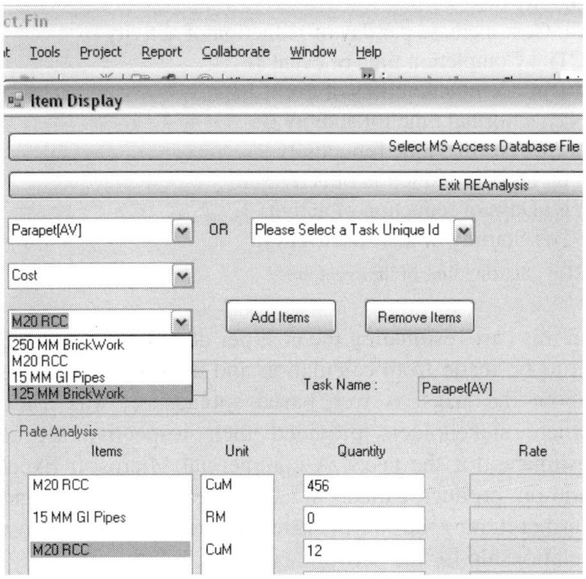

Figure 3: REAnalysis Item Display Screen

Facilities have been provided within the website for collaboration among the stakeholders. Certain open source applications are also used. Since source codes are available minor modifications can be made. Some of the collaboration facilities planned are as follows:

1. Forums for issue wise discussions of stakeholders.
2. Task comments to address daily hindrances.
3. To Do List to track tasks.
4. Editable spreadsheets for stakeholder calculation.

5. Data Analysis Principles

The data has been processed and posted in web site in such a manner that any stakeholder can find usable data with little effort. A PDF volume is published on the website every fortnight. These reports are standardized. Some salient features of these reports may be as follows:

1. Fortnightly volumes are published.
2. Report formats are standardized.
3. Standard formats are adequately explained.
4. Customized Reports for managerial levels.
5. Queries on reports are addressed in the forums.

6. Data Collaboration

The collaboration among stakeholders can be developed as a powerful tool for execution of work and sophisticated management reports. There are several project management techniques that can be practically developed only through collaboration among stake holders. Two such examples that has been actually done in this web site is presented in the following.

Great Eastern Hotel, Kolkata the oldest hotel in India has been taken up for heritage restoration in 2006. The project is an adaptive heritage work. The project scope could not be reliably estimated before starting of construction. Planning and construction is to be executed simultaneously rather than one after another as in normal construction. Collaboration among stakeholders is of more importance in this case. The project is managed through the facilities of the present web site. The existing database and collaboration facilities have been used to develop a simulation and a real time linear programming optimization study.

7. Simulation Example

Monte Carlos' simulation is an operation research tool which is often used for assessing the risk i.e. the variability of outcome of a project. In a simulation study, randomly selected completion time within the assigned limits for each task is assumed and a probable date of completion is estimated from the Gantt chart. It is assumed that the risk of the actual project shall be the same of the derived distribution. A simulation is only good to the extent the individual task boundaries are set. For a project like Great Eastern Hotel Restoration varieties of experts are required to estimate the probable time. Stakeholders who were geographically dispersed collaborated interactively in the web site for assigning time constraints. Guha [10] then traced the relationship between time and probabilities of completion during the design development phase which is presented in Figure 4.

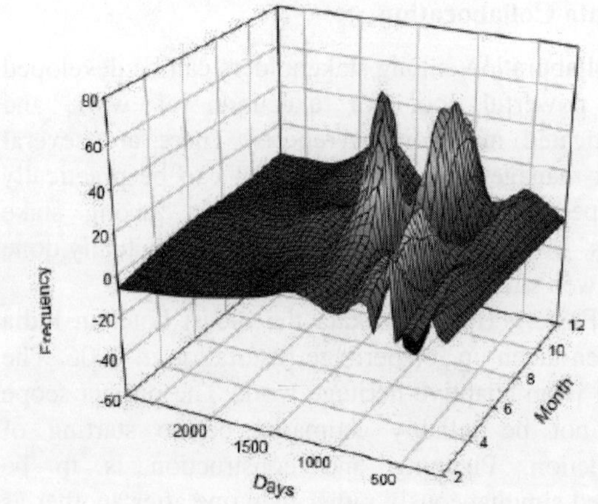

Figure 4: Probabilities of completion during Design Development Phase

In a similar study, Guha [11] extended the estimate to probable distribution of cost which is presented in Figure 5.

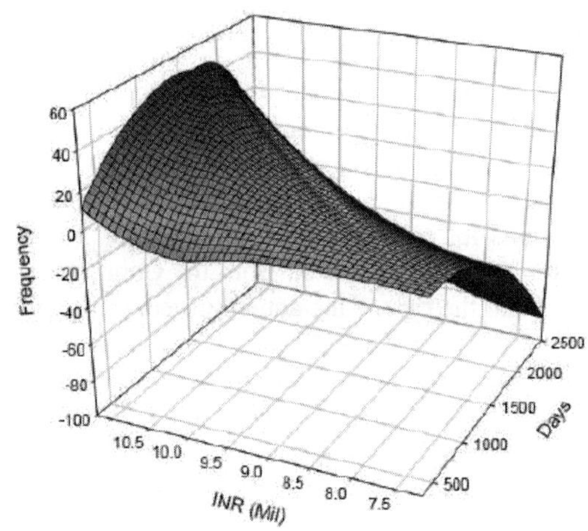

Figure 5: Costing probabilities during Design Development Phase

Such studies could not be practically done without the collaborative system implemented on the said website.

8. Time Cost Optimizing Example

In project management, time-cost optimization of a PERT chart is usually done by linear programming. A network can be represented by a set of linear equations. Once the objective function is known a linear programming model can be formulated as shown in the following example:

Objective function:
Minimize $\Sigma YiCi$
Subject to:

$CTj \geq NTj - Yi + STj$
i *from 1* $\rightarrow$ *nth activity*
$CTjn \geq NTjn - Yin + STjn$

Where,
Yi: No of days of reduction possible by crashing the activity i.
Ci: Cost increase per day of reduction of activity i
CTj_1 : Completion time of event J_1
CT jn: Completion time of event Jn
NTj_1 : Normal time for activity j_1
NTjn : Normal time for activity j_n
Yi_1 : Days of reduction of activity i_1
Yi_n : Days of reduction of activity i_n
STj_1 : Starting time of the event j_1
STjn : Starting time of the event jn

In this case, estimating the cost per day of crashing (Yi) is to be made from calculation and detailed knowledge about the tasks. A web based spreadsheet was made where stakeholders provided their respective set of estimates for the tasks. A commercial Microsoft Excel add-on product called 'What is best' was used and further tuning up were made to arrive at a time-cost relationship for the network as shown in Figure 6.

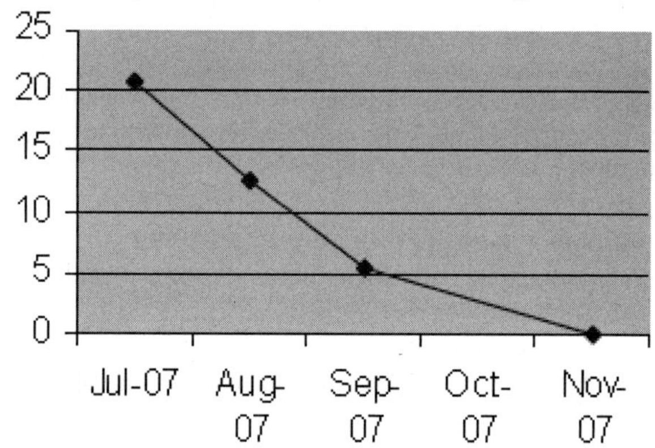

Figure 6: Linear Programming Results

One may note that about 20% cost increase in minimum shall take place by crashing the project for 4 months. Such studies require interactive input from stakeholders and are not practically feasible without the collaborative facility of the web site.

9. Collaboration Benefits

The web based collaboration allowed several consultants to update the data conveniently. As the consultants were filling up the cost estimate for crashing of individual task the Ci values were changing continuously because the contributing factors are changing with time. As a result the plan arrived by linear programming was also varying. In such situation the planning for the tasks that should be crashed to reduce the time most economically would change every month.

10. Training Module

Training is of paramount importance for software application. In this case, a number of stakeholders with different background and computer exposures are required to be involved.

The training and learning processes has been greatly modified with the advent of the web technology. First attempts in personalized, also called adaptive, learning environments appeared in the early 1990s. 1996 is considered as a turning point in the area of adaptive systems [12]. Recent approaches to Web based education try to take into account various dimensions of individual differences, such as level of knowledge, cognitive styles, and learning styles [13]. In line with these approaches, a training module for use of the system and collaborative project management has been integrated in the website.

Usual components of training that are normally used for any academic course or training has been developed as presented in the following:

1. Notes to appraise the reader about the topic.
2. References to provide web links for further study.
3. Query Form for feedback and references.
4. Practice data to practice collaboration concepts.
5. Quiz to take computer graded online tests.
6. Wiki to record experience and improvements.

11. Conclusions

Web enabled technology for construction informatics is relatively a new field in the Indian context. Web enabled project management systems is an efficient system of management as experienced in industrialized countries. The web based collaboration proposed in this study is coined as Enterprise 2.0 by McAfee [14] and many feel that this trend would increase rapidly in near future. The Enterprise 2.0 concept has been further extended to project management learning in this paper.

However, localization is necessary for effective results. The present website is only a starting venture in this direction.

Acknowledgments

The author thanks Professor Shibnath Chakrabarty, Department of Civil Engineering, Jadavpur University, India for his help and support.

References

1. Ma Zhiliang and Qin Liang, (2004) "A Framework of Information Management System for Construction Projects", Department of Civil Engineering, Tsinghua University, Beijing.
2. Tang Jia, (2003) "Corporate Culture and Integrated Management Systems: - A case study of the UK construction Industry" Masters of Science Thesis, University of East Anglia.
3. Broomfield J.R. et al (2003) "ISO 9001-2000 Interpretive Guide for the Design and Construction Project Team", ASQ Quality Press, Mil, USA.
4. Amor R, Betts M et al. (2002) "Information Technology for Construction: Recent Work and Future Directions" in *ITcon* 7, 245-258.
5. Wetherill M, Rezgui Y et. al.(2002), "Knowledge Management for the Construction Industry: The ECognos Project" in *ITcon 7* (2002) 183-196.
6. Mervi L, Veli H et al. (2002), "Multidisciplinary Information Management in Construction Industry, Example of Facilities Management" *ITcon* 7, 213-244.
7. Guha S (2007) "Construction Management Through Web Service in Calcutta, India", International Business Informatics Conference 2007, Dublin City University, Dublin, Ireland.
8. Guha S (2007) "Development of a Web Based Construction Management System", National Conference of Information Technology, New Delhi 2007.
9. REAnalysis (2007) – A MS Project add-on application. http://www.sssolutionsonline.com/reanalysis/
10. Guha S (2007) "Time Estimate of a Heritage Building Restoration Project By Monte Carlo Simulation" International Conference on Modeling and Simulation, CIT, India.
11. Guha S (2007) "Planning with Uncertainties for a Heritage Building Restoration Project in Calcutta, India", IEEE International Conference on Industrial Engineering and Engineering Management, Singapore 2007.
12. Brusilovsky P. "Course Sequencing for Static Courses? Applying ITS techniques in large scale web based education" *Conference on Intelligent Tutoring Systems (ITS 2000)*, Montreal Canada (pp. 625-634), Berling: Springer Verlag.
13. Magoulas G & Chen S (2006) "Web based Education" Information Science publishing.
14. Wikipedia (2007) "Enterprise Social Software", Nov.2007. http://en.wikipedia.org/wiki/Enterprise_social_software

FRAME-BUST PROBLEM & BUST PROTECTIVE ALGORITHM

MR. VISHWAS J RAVAL* †
PROF. AMIT R THAKKAR ** ††
PROF. AMIT P GANATRA*** †††
DR. Y P KOSTA**** ††††

** Lecturer, ** Asst. Professor, Dept. of IT, *** Head, Dept. of CE & IT, **** Principal, Charotar Institute of Technology, Education Campus, Changa – 388421, Ta – Petlad, Dist. – Anand, Gujarat, India*
† vishwas.raval@gmail.com, †† amitthakkar_1981@yahoo.com, ††† amitganu@yahoo.com , †††† ypkosta@yahoo.com

This paper addresses the issue of frame-bust and a probable solution towards it in the form of a bust-protective algorithm. This problem deals with framing in HTML. HTML is Hypertext Markup Language.

1. Introduction

Framing is the concept to divide the window of webpage into several sections. Each section contains a separate frame which displays a different HTML document. Headers and sidebar menus do not move when the content frame is scrolled up and down. The benefit of the frame is, for e.g. if an item needs to be added to the sidebar menu, only one file needs to be changed, whereas each individual page on a non-frameset website would have to be edited if the sidebar menu appeared on all of them. The frames have cross-browser compatibility problem but in such case <noframes> tag can be specified. [1]

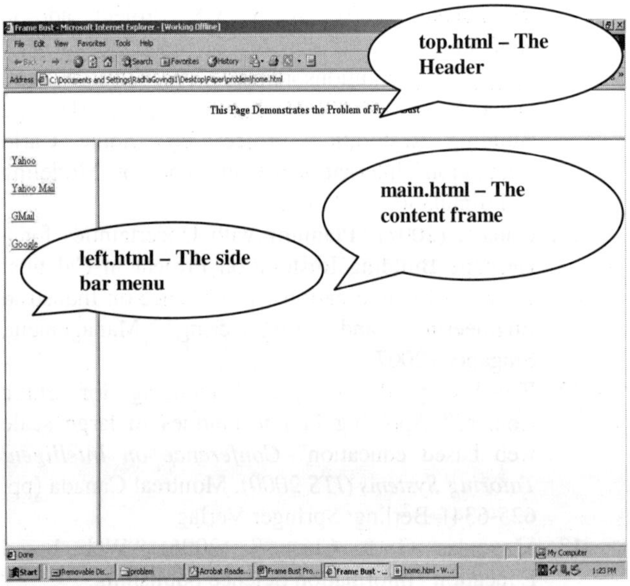

Figure 1. home.html

Figure-1 shows "home.html" page, which has been created using three frames i.e. three html pages - "top.html", "left.html" and "main.html". The side bar menu contains options of Yahoo, Yahoo Mail, Gmail, Google which are expected to be opened in the content frame.

The source code of all pages is given under:

home.html[1]

```
<html>
<head>
<title>Frame Bust</title>
</head>
<frameset rows="64,*">
<frame name="banner" scrolling="no" noresize
target="contents" src="top.html">
<frameset cols="150,*">
<frame name="contents" target="main" src="left.html"
border=0>
<frame name="main" src="main.html">
</frameset>
<noframes>
<body>
<p>This page uses frames, but your browser doesn't
support them.</p>
</body>
</noframes>
</frameset>
</html>
```

top.html[1]

```
<html>
<head>
<title>New Page 3</title>
<base target="contents">
</head>
<body>
```

```
<p align=center><b>This Page Demonstrates the
Problem of Frame Bust</b></p>
</body>
</html>
```

left.html[1]

```
<html>
<head>
<title>Left</title>
<base target="main">
</head>
<body>
<p><a target="main"
href="http://www.yahoo.com">Yahoo</a></p>
<p><a target="_parent"
href="http://www.mail.yahoo.com">Yahoo
Mail</a></p>
<p><a target="main"
href="http://www.mail.google.com">GMail</a></p>
<p><a target="main"
href="http://www.google.com">Google</a></p>
</body>
</html>
```

Main.html[1]

```
<html>
<head>
<title>New Page 4</title>
</head>
<body>
</body>
</html>
```

When a webpage inside frame tries to open a webpage which is located at some remote server; other than the server on which the client application resides. viz. yahoo, google etc., instead of opening the requested page inside the content frame, the page gets opened in a separate window. This problem is called *frame- bust.*

2. Problem Details

The results of some of the experiments performed on home.html given under, would explain the problem in more depth:

2.1. *Yahoo*

When user tried to open the web page of yahoo.com, it got opened into the desired frame. See figure 2.

Figure 2. yahoo.com page into the target content frame.

2.2. *YahooMail*

When user opened link of yahoo mail, the frame got bust and it was opened as if the target had been set as _parent or _top[1]. See figure 3.

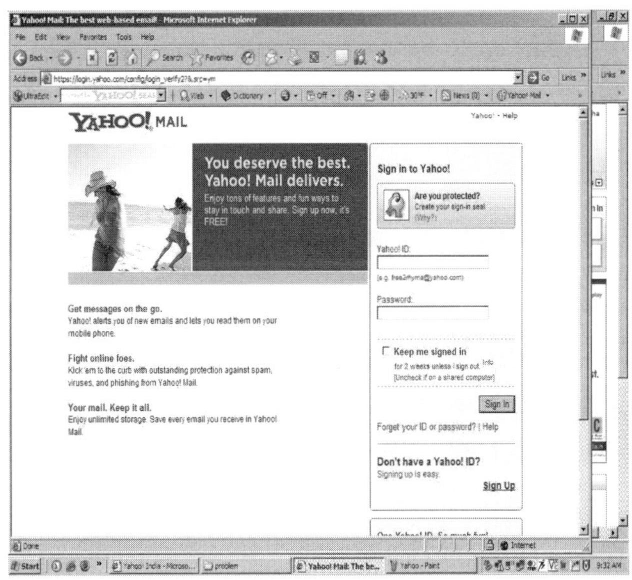

Figure 3. mail.yahoo.com page busts the content frame.

The same scenario happened with the option of Gmail.

2.3. *Google*

With this option the page was opened into the target content frame as desired. See Figure 4.

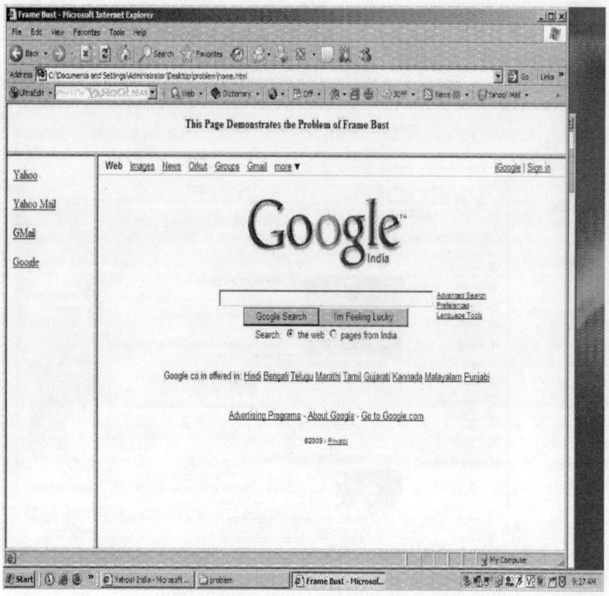

Figure 4. Google.com page into the target content frame.

Figure-4 shows the options available into the page of google.com. Here, user tried to open Gmail link inside the google.com page, the page got opened into the same page i.e into the desired content frame. See figure 5.

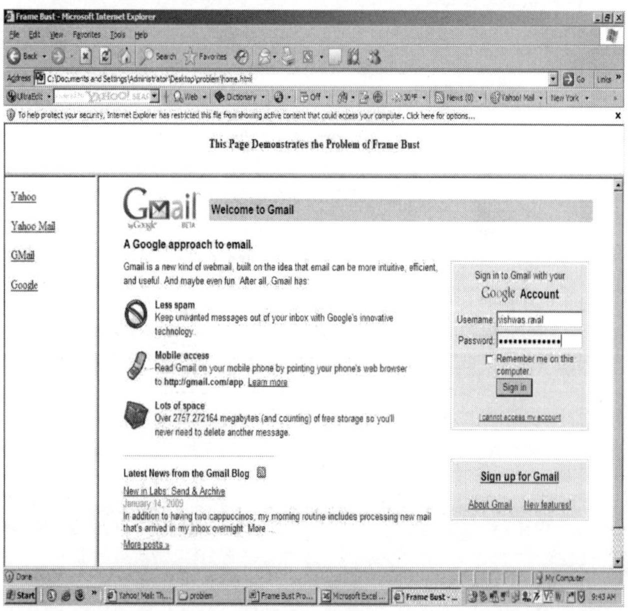

Figure 5. Gmail page into the target content frame.

But when the user logged into Gmail with his usename and password, the content frame again got bust. See figure 6.

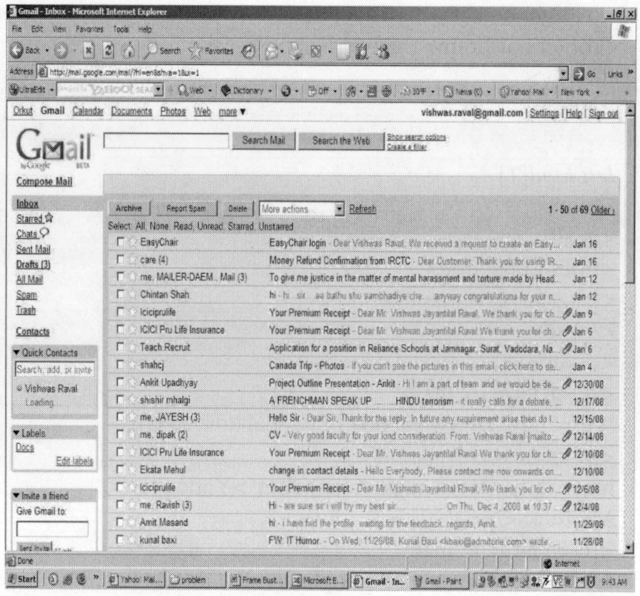

Figure 6. Gmail login after content frame-bust.

3. The Reason

The reason behind this frame bust is the already set target of the called web page's <form> [1] tag.

4. The Probable Solution

Generally to include reference of some other webpage across www, transclusion [2] is used. Transclusion is the inclusion of part of a document into another document by reference [2]. Transclusion in HTML & XML based environment had been proposed, but it is limited [3][4][5][6][7][8]. In the same context, in order to provide the solution to the frame-bust problem, I propose an algorithm. The steps of the algorithm are as under:

1. Extract the contents of webpage received in response to the request made by the user.
2. Create a temporary page using the extracted contents.
3. Display the temporary page into the target frame before user.
4. Repeat the steps 1 to 3 as and when any request is made by the user to access a webpage from other servers.
5. Exit

To protect the webpage from the frame-bust, this algorithm must be invoked after a user makes webpage request and before presenting the requested webpage on to the screen before user. Though this time duration would be too short to work upon but it could be made possible. See figure 7.

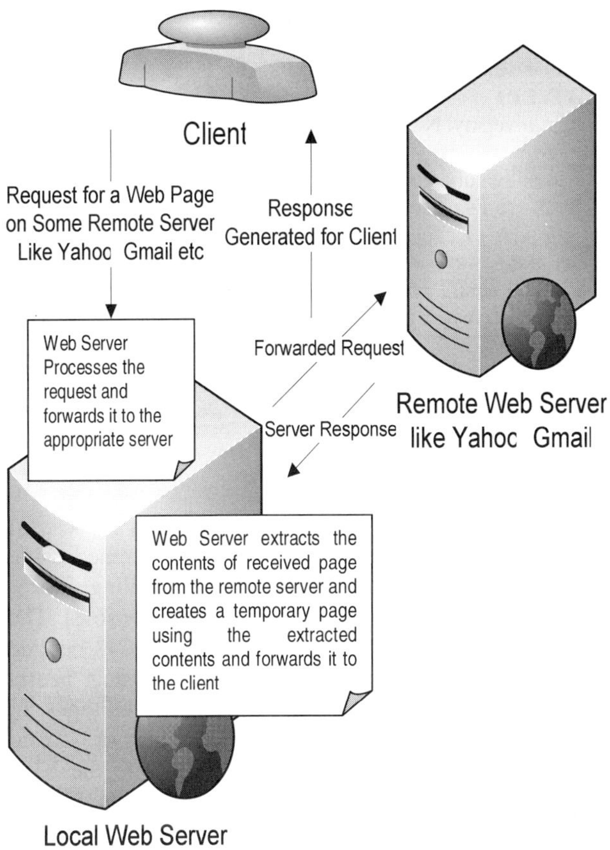

Figure 7. Process of Bust-Protection.

One thing which must be kept in mind that user will get the page as if he/she is accessing the original webpage but it would be a temporary page created by the local server.

Moreover, in the algorithm, I suggested to create a temporary page in step-2 as the pages accessed by user need not to be permanently stored while the user is accessing it; and the temporary page, which is created, will get changed frequently on each request. This could save the memory of the local server and would not cause memory drain.

Acknowledgments

I am thankful to The Omnipotent GOD, who made me able to do something. I am thankful to my parents who brought me on this planet. I express my gratitude to CITC for giving me an opportunity to work there and generously extending support and motivation in writing & presenting this paper. Finally, my acknowledgement can not end without thanking the authors and researchers whose papers helped me to move ahead for this paper.

References

1. Special Edition Using HTML 4.0, MacMillan Computer Publishing
2. Nelson, T. H. (1981). Literary Machines. Mindful Press.
3. Kolbitsch, J.; Maurer, H. (June 2006). "Transclusions in an HTML-Based Environment". Journal of Computing and Information Technology 14 (2): 161–174. doi:10.2498/cit.2006.02.07. http://cit.zesoi.fer.hr/browseIssue.php?issue=25
4. Kolbitsch, J. (June 2005). "Fine-Grained Transclusions of Multimedia Documents in HTML". Journal of Universal Computer Science 11 (6). http://www.jucs.org/jucs_11_6/fine_grained_transclusions_of/
5. Krottmaier, H.; Helic, D. (2002). "Issues of Transclusions" (PDF). Proceedings of the World Conference on E-Learning in Corporate, Government, Healthcare, & Higher Education (E-Learn 2002): 1730–1733.
6. Krottmaier, H.; Maurer, H. (July 2001). "Transclusions in the 21st Century" (PDF, HTML, PostScript). Journal of Universal Computer Science 7 (12): 1125–1136. http://www.jucs.org/jucs_7_12/transclusions_in_the_21st/.
7. Nelson, T. H. (1998). "Transcopyright: Pre-Permission for Virtual Republishing".
8. Pam, A. (1997). "Fine-Grained Transclusion in the Hypertext Markup Language" (Text). Internet Draft

APPLICATION COMPUTATIONAL INTELLIGENCE FOR DEVELOPMENT OF SYNTHETIC PEPTIDE VACCINE FROM HUMAN ADENOVIRUS-5

VIRENDRA GOMASE*
Department of Bioinformatics, Padmashree Dr. D.Y. Patil University, Navi Mumbai, 400614, India
MADHUR MURTI
Department of Bioinformatics, Padmashree Dr. D.Y. Patil University, Navi Mumbai, 400614, India
TEJASHRI GANDHI
Department of Bioinformatics, Padmashree Dr. D.Y. Patil University, Navi Mumbai, 400614, India
NAMRATA GAGNANI
Department of Bioinformatics, Padmashree Dr. D.Y. Patil University, Navi Mumbai, 400614, India
SUNILKUMAR DWIVEDI
Department of Bioinformatics, Padmashree Dr. D.Y. Patil University, Navi Mumbai, 400614, India

Abstract- *Human Adenovirus-5* causes systemic infections leading to be an obligatory step in infection. Peptide fragments of capsid protein can be used to select nonamers for use in rational vaccine design and to increase the understanding of roles of the immune system in infectious diseases. Analysis shows MHC class II binding peptides of capsid protein from *Human Adenovirus-5* are important determinant for protection of host form viral infection. In this assay, we used PSSM and SVM algorithms for antigen design and predicted the binding affinity of capsid protein having 951 amino acids, which shows 944 nonamers. Binding ability prediction of antigen peptides to major histocompatibility complex (MHC) class I & II molecules is important in vaccine development from Human Adenovirus-5.

Keywords- capsid protein, epitope, PSSM, SVM, MHC, peptide vaccine

Abbreviations: Goldman, Engelberg and Steitz, (GES); major histocompatibility complex, (MHC); Position Specific Scoring Matrices, (PSSMs); Support Vector Machine, (SVM)

1. Introduction

Human adenovirus caused infection to small intestine, respiratory illness, common cold, conjunctivitis, croup (or viral laryngotracheobronchitis), bronchitis, pneumoniae and karyomegalic adenoviral nuclear inclusions are present within some enterocytes. Chromagen deposition confirms adenoviral DNA within enterocyte nuclear inclusions [1, 2]. Human adenovirus-5 viral peptides are most suitable for subunit vaccine development because with single epitope, the immune response can be generated in large population. This approach is based on the phenomenon of cross-protection, whereby a plant infected with a mild strain of virus is protected against a more severe strain of the same virus. The phenotype of the resistant transgenic hosts includes fewer centers of initial virus infection, a delay in symptom development, and low virus accumulation. Capsid protein from Human adenovirus-5 is necessary for new paradigm of synthetic vaccine development and target validation [3-5].

***Correspondence**: Dr. Virendra S. Gomase, Department of Bioinformatics, Padmashree Dr. D.Y. Patil University, Plot No-50, Sector-15, CBD Belapur, Navi Mumbai, 400614, India; Mobile- +91-9987770696; Mail- virusgene1@yahoo.co.in

2. Methodology

In this research work antigenic epitopes of capsid protein from Human adenovirus-5 is determined using the Gomase in 2007, Hopp and Woods, Welling, Parker and Protrusion Index (Thornton) antigenicity [6-8]. The major histocompatibility complex (MHC) peptide binding of capsid protein is predicted using neural networks trained on C terminals of known epitopes. In analysis predicted MHC/peptide binding of capsid protein is a log-transformed value related to the IC50 values in nM units. MHC2Pred predicts peptide binders to MHCI and MHCII molecules from protein sequences or sequence alignments using Position Specific Scoring Matrices (PSSMs). Support Vector Machine (SVM) based method for prediction of promiscuous MHC class II binding peptides. SVM has been trained on the binary input of single amino acid sequence [9-14]. In addition, we predict those MHC ligands from whose C-terminal end is likely to be the result of proteosomal cleavage [15].

3. Results and Interpretations

We found binding of peptides to a number of different alleles using Position Specific Scoring Matrix. A capsid protein sequence is 951 residues long, having antigenic MHC binding peptides. MHC molecules are cell surface glycoproteins, which take active part in host immune reactions and involvement of MHC class-I and MHC II in response to almost all antigens. PSSM based server predict the peptide binders to MHCI molecules of capsid protein sequence are as 11mer_H2_Db, 10mer_H2_Db, 9mer_H2_Db, 8mer_H2_Db and also peptide binders to MHCII molecules of capsid protein sequence as I_Ab.p, I_Ad.p, analysis found antigenic epitopes region in putative capsid protein (Table 1). We also found the SVM based MHCII-IAb peptide regions; MHCII-IAd peptide regions; MHCII-IAg7 peptide regions and MHCII- RT1.B peptide regions, which represented predicted binders from viral capsid protein (Table 2). The predicted binding affinity is normalized by the 1% fractil. We describe an improved method for predicting linear epitopes (Table 2). The region of maximal hydrophilicity is likely to be an antigenic site, having hydrophobic characteristics, because terminal regions of capsid protein is solvent accessible and unstructured, antibodies against those regions are also likely to recognize the native protein (Fig. 1, 2, 5). It was shown that a capsid protein is hydrophobic in nature and contains segments of low complexity and high-predicted flexibility (Fig. 3, 4). Predicted antigenic fragments can bind to MHC molecule is the first bottlenecks in vaccine design.

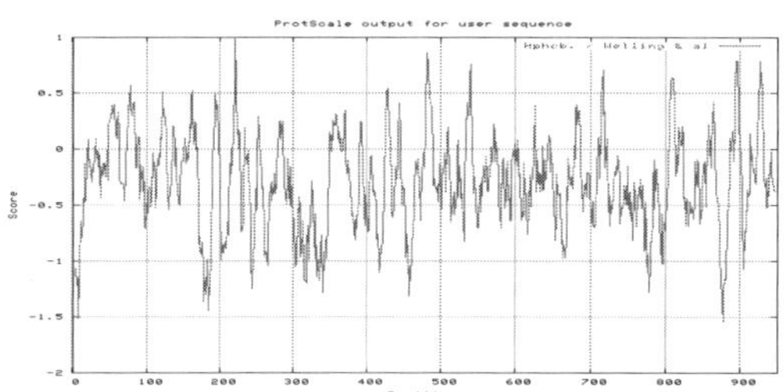

Fig. 1- Antigenicity plot of capsid protein by Welling, et al., scale

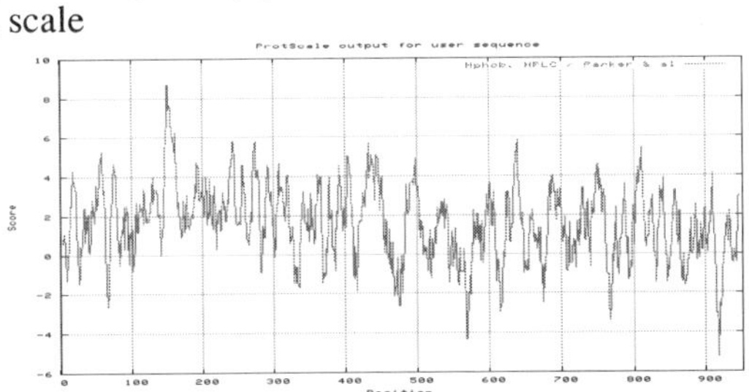

Fig. 2- Antigenicity plot of capsid protein by HPLC / Parker, et al., scale

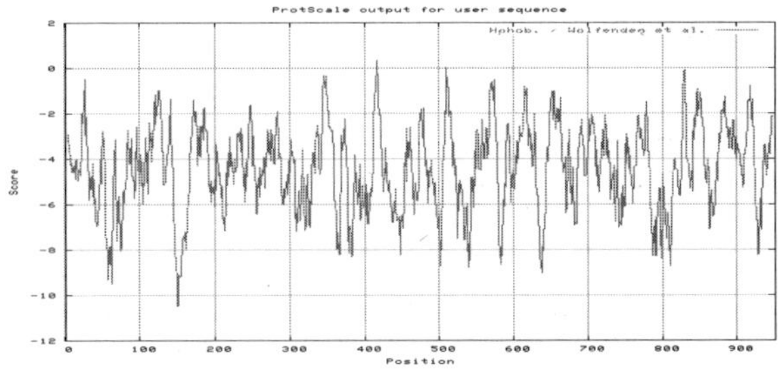

Fig. 3- Hydrophobicity plot of capsid protein by Wolfenden, et al., scale

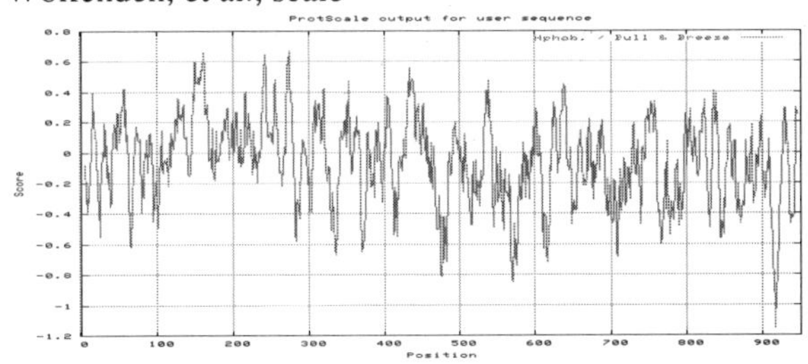

Fig. 4-Hydrophobicity plot of capsid protein by Bull & Breese scale

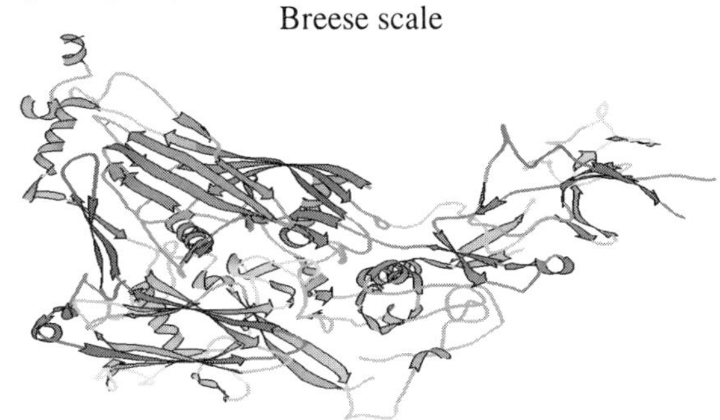

Fig. 5- Capsid protein structure of *Human Adenovirus-5*

4. Conclusion

A capsid protein from *Human Adenovirus-5* peptide nonamers are from a set of aligned peptides known to bind to a given MHC molecule as the predictor of MHC-peptide binding. MHCII molecules bind peptides in similar yet different modes and alignments of MHCII-ligands were obtained to be consistent with the binding mode of the peptides to their MHC class, this means the increase in affinity of MHC binding peptides may result in enhancement of immunogenicity of viral capsid protein. These predicted of capsid protein antigenic peptides to MHC class molecules are important in vaccine development from *Human Adenovirus-5*.

5. References

[1] C.M.Robinson, F. Shariati, J. Zaitshik, A.F.Gillaspy, D.W.Dyer, J. Chodosh, *Virus Res.*,139(1), 122-126 (2009).

[2] Q.L.Matthews, P.Yang, Q. Wu, N. Belousova, A.A.Rivera, M.A.Stoff-Khalili, R.Waehler, H.C.Hsu, Z. Li, J. Li, J.D.Mountz, H.Wu, D.T.Curiel, *Virol J.*, 5, 98 (2008).

[3] A. Joshi, J. Tang, M. Kuzma, J. Wagner, B. Mookerjee, J. Filicko, M. Carabasi, N. Flomenberg, P. Flomenberg, *J. Gen Virol.*, 90(Pt 1), 84-94 (2009).

[4] D. McDonald, L. Stockwin, T. Matzow, M.E. Blair Zajdel, G.E.Blair, *Gene Ther.*, 6(9),1512-9 (1999).

[5] V.S.Gomase, K.V. Kale and K. Shyamkumar, *J. of Proteomics & Bioinformatics*, 1 (4), 188- 205 (2008).

[6] V.S.Gomase, K.V. Kale, N.J.Chikhale, S.S. Changbhale, *Curr. Drug Discov. Technol.*, 4(2),117-1215 (2007).

[7] V.S.Gomase and K.V.Kale, *Int. J. of Applied Computing*, 1(1), 39-46 (2008).

[8] V.S.Gomase and K.V.Kale, *Int. J. of Applied Computing*, 1(1), 33-38 (2008).

[9] V.S.Gomase and K.V.Kale, *Int. J. of Information Retrieval*, 1(1), 11-15 (2008).

[10] V.S.Gomase, K.V. Kale, K. Shyamkumar and S. Shankar, *ICETET 2008, IEEE Computer Society in IEEE Xplore, Los Alamitos, California*, 629-634 (2008).

[11] V.S.Gomase, J.P.Tandale, S.A.Patil, K.V.Kale, *14th International Conference on Advance Computing & Communication, Published by IEEE Computer Society in IEEE Xplore USA* 614-615 (2006).

[12] P.A. Reche, J.P. Glutting, E.L. Reinherz, *Hum Immun.*, 63, 701-709 (2002).

[13] S. Buus, et al., *Tissue Antigens*, 62, 378-384 (2003).

[14] M. Nielsen, et al., *Protein Sci.*, 12, 1007-1017 (2003).

[15] M. Bhasin and G.P. Raghava, *Nucleic Acids Research*, 33, W202-207 (2005).

Table 1- PSSM based prediction of MHC ligands, from whose C-terminal end are proteosomal cleavage sites

MHC-I	POS.	N	Sequence	C	MW (Da)	Score	% OPT.
9mer_H2_Db	566	QKF	FAIKNLLLL	PGS	1026.33	99.0	67.81 %
9mer_H2_Db	417	FPL	GGVINTETL	TKV	884.97	96.0	65.75 %
9mer_H2_Db	271	TTE	ATAGNGDNL	TPK	813.81	95.0	65.07 %
9mer_H2_Db	634	AML	RNDTNDQSF	NDY	1078.06	86.0	58.90 %
9mer_H2_Db	621	FFP	MAHNTASTL	EAM	927.03	86.0	58.90 %
9mer_H2_Db	339	MYY	NSTGNMGVL	AGQ	873.96	85.0	58.22 %
9mer_H2_Db	792	RMY	SFFRNFQPM	SRQ	1155.35	82.0	56.16 %
9mer_H2_Db	594	VLQ	SSLGNDLRV	DGA	942.04	81.0	55.48 %
9mer_H2_Db	445	ATE	FSDKNEIRV	GNN	1089.22	81.0	55.48 %
9mer_H2_Db	305	MPT	IKEGNSREL	MGQ	1027.15	79.0	54.11 %
9mer_H2_Db	820	GIL	HQHNNSGFV	GYL	1021.05	78.0	53.42 %
9mer_H2_Db	547	YRS	MLLGNGRYV	PFH	1004.21	78.0	53.42 %
9mer_H2_Db	317	MGQ	QSMPNRPNY	IAF	1088.21	77.0	52.74 %
9mer_H2_Db	500	PNT	YDYMNKRVV	APG	1169.36	74.0	50.68 %
9mer_H2_Db	736	NDR	LLTPNEFEI	KRS	1057.22	72.0	49.32 %
9mer_H2_Db	451	KNE	IRVGNNFAM	EIN	1003.18	71.0	48.63 %
9mer_H2_Db	873	WRI	PFSSNFMSM	GAL	1029.2	70.0	47.95 %
9mer_H2_Db	808	VDD	TKYKDYQQV	GIL	1154.28	70.0	47.95 %
9mer_H2_Db	471	WRN	FLYSNIALY	LPD	1085.28	68.0	46.58 %
10mer_H2_Db	317	MGQ	QSMPNRPNYI	AFR	1201.37	115.0	52.04 %
10mer_H2_Db	620	TFF	PMAHNTASTL	EAM	1024.15	103.0	46.61 %
10mer_H2_Db	637	RND	TNDQSFNDYL	SAA	1198.21	96.0	43.44 %
10mer_H2_Db	471	WRN	FLYSNIALYL	PDK	1198.44	91.0	41.18 %
10mer_H2_Db	657	PIP	ANATNVPISI	PSR	981.11	85.0	38.46 %
10mer_H2_Db	452	NEI	RVGNNFAMEI	NLN	1132.3	81.0	36.65 %
10mer_H2_Db	388	MWN	QAVDSYDPDV	RII	1090.12	77.0	34.84 %
10mer_H2_Db	840	EGQ	AYPANFPYPL	IGK	1134.32	76.0	34.39 %
10mer_H2_Db	891	GQN	LLYANSAHAL	DMT	1054.22	74.0	33.48 %
10mer_H2_Db	436	GQE	NGWEKDATEF	SDK	1155.22	74.0	33.48 %
11mer_H2_Db	770	VQM	LANYNIGYQGF	YIP	1241.37	99.0	46.70 %
11mer_H2_Db	604	RVD	GASIKFDSICL	YAT	1135.35	97.0	45.75 %
11mer_H2_Db	492	SNV	KISDNPNTYDY	MNK	1311.37	88.0	41.51 %
11mer_H2_Db	451	KNE	IRVGNNFAMEI	NLN	1245.46	85.0	40.09 %
11mer_H2_Db	55	THD	VTTDRSQRLTL	RFI	1271.43	83.0	39.15 %
11mer_H2_Db	327	NYI	AFRDNFIGLMY	YNS	1328.56	74.0	34.91 %
11mer_H2_Db	213	WYE	TEINHAAGRVL	KKT	1162.31	74.0	34.91 %
11mer_H2_Db	745	FEI	KRSVDGEGYNV	AQC	1205.29	69.0	32.55 %
11mer_H2_Db	539	HHR	NAGLRYRSMLL	GNG	1275.54	69.0	32.55 %
11mer_H2_Db	483	LPD	KLKYSPSNVKI	SDN	1258.52	68.0	32.08 %
11mer_H2_Db	75	RED	TAYSYKARFTL	AVG	1302.5	66.0	31.13 %
11mer_H2_Db	820	GIL	HQHNNSGFVGY	LAP	1241.28	64.0	30.19 %
11mer_H2_Db	175	PYS	GINITKEGIQI	GVE	1167.36	64.0	30.19 %

Table 2- SVM based prediction of promiscuous MHC class II binding peptides from capsid protein

MHC ALLELE	Rank	Sequence	Residue No.	Peptide Score
I-Ab	1	RVLKKTTPM	221	1.272
I-Ab	2	GWAFTRLKT	676	1.212
I-Ab	3	TLTKVKPKT	424	1.169
I-Ab	4	GKTAVDSIT	851	1.109
I-Ad	1	SICLYATFF	611	0.819
I-Ad	2	SNFMSMGAL	876	0.746
I-Ad	3	LQSSLGNDL	592	0.698
I-Ad	4	DASEYLSPG	18	0.635
I-Ag7	1	SGTAYNALA	116	2.354
I-Ag7	2	YLSAANMLY	645	1.940
I-Ag7	3	WDEAATALE	134	1.811
I-Ag7	4	INHAAGRVL	215	1.809
RT1.B	1	TTDRSQRLT	56	1.706
RT1.B	2	TTEATAGNG	268	1.252
RT1.B	3	NTELSYQLL	364	0.966
RT1.B	4	LYANSAHAL	892	0.946

APPLICATION OF ROLE ACTIVITY DIAGRAMS IN FINDING PROBLEM FRAMES AND DETERMINATION OF FUNCTION POINTS

KAVITA AGRAWAL
assistant professor, department of CSE, BBDNITM,UPTU
Lucknow, India.
Email id: kavitalucknow@gmail.com ,
Phone number:+ 91-9235794807

DR. S. K. BAJPAI
Prof and ex. HOD ,department of CSE,
IET, UPTU, Lucknow, India.
senior member of IACSIT
Email id : skbajpaiiet@hotmail.com
Ph no:+ 91-9936122089

DR. S. P. TRIPATHI
assistant professor and HOD
department of CSE, IET, UPTU
Lucknow, India.
Email id : tripathee_sp@yahoo.co.in

In the process of software development, it is not easy to capture process information which is useful in effort estimation of the software at that phase. In this paper we have used Role activity diagrams to get complete process information then mapped these to problem frames to get required behaviour and the conditions needed for it. Problem frames then are being used to find out function points which are useful for effort estimation at requirement phase. When Problem frames are used directly to find function points, we find that sometimes we miss out on few function points that are not clearly indicated. When Role activity diagrams are used we are able to locate those function points as well.

1. Introduction

Requirement phase is the most important phase of software development lifecycle [4], [10], [11]. This phase should clearly indicate user requirements and we should be able to use those requirements to further develop our software and provide a measurement useful for cost estimation. Some of the researchers have used use case points to study process [3]. In this paper we have used Role activity diagrams to model our process. This gives us a clear insight into the user requirements and the various aspects of the process. Role activity diagrams when mapped onto problem frames gives us a clear cut required behaviour and the required conditions for it. Problem frames when drawn in isolation are not so easy to draw. We may not be very clear about the domains interacting and the level of interactions, which is clear once we have role activity diagrams.

Functions point analysis requires an indepth insight of the system to be developed. With each point left unevaluated we move further away from the correct estimations. Function point analysis is a technique which relies heavily on the person calculating it [2]. This factor makes it prone to errors as function point for same problem may differ from person to person. In this paper we have tried to remove this discrepancy by introducing role activity diagrams and problem frames in the process. This may resolve this problem to some extent.

To illustrate this we have used an example of sluice gate[6].

1.1 *Role activity diagrams*

We use Role Activity Diagrams a well-regarded process modelling notation. A role activity diagram (RAD) is used to describe business processes that can involve actions and interactions among roles[5]. Roles can be humans as well as software and hardware systems. A RAD has various components.

Roles are drawn as set of boxes; activities are boxes within a role. Interactions are points at which a role interacts with other role to fulfil an objective. Grey activity sends some information to the interacting role.

Choices are represented as linked circles. A state may be explicitly marked by concentric circles.

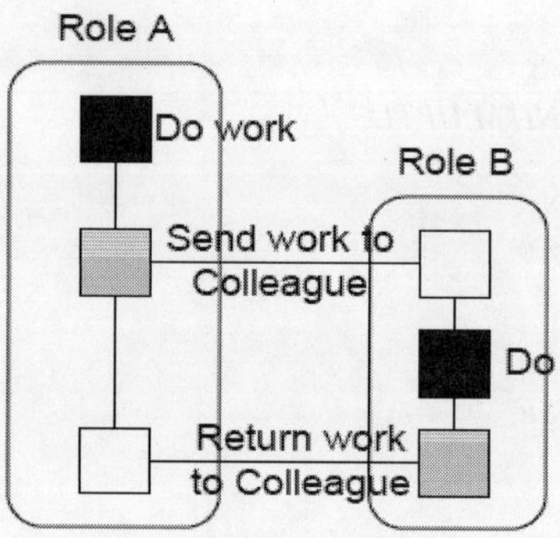

Figure. 1. Elements of a Role Activity Diagram

1.2 *Problem Frames*

Figure 2: A problem frame

The Problem Frames (PF) approach is an approach to be used when gathering requirements and creating specifications for computer software [7], [8], [9]. Its basic philosophy is that the best way to approach requirements analysis is through a process of parallel decomposition of user requirements and user requirements are about relationships in the operational context. The control machine represents the piece of software that the customer requires. The controlled domain is that part of the world in which those effects are perceived by the customer. The Required behaviour are the properties that the customer wants to observe, through the shared phenomena a.Where as b is the interaction between control and controlled machine.

1.3.*Function point analysis*

We will illustrate function points (FP) as our method depends totally on this concept . Since theory of Function point is well known to the reader, we briefly account the necessary parts in the following [1].

The function point measure is done in three steps. Where step one is to classify and count the five user function points namely: external input, external output, logical internal file, external interface file and external inquiry. Each is classified as simple, average and complex with pre specified weights [1]. Unadjusted FP (UFP) is sum of weights of each FP. Next step is to adjust for processing complexity (PC). The degree of influence of each of 14 general characteristics [1] is taken on a scale of 0-5.All influences are summed to get PC and Processing complexity adjustment (PCA) = 0.65+ (0.01 * PC). Last step is to do the function point calculations. Multiply unadjusted function points to processing complexity adjustment. Thus Function Point (FP) = UFP*PCA

2.The mappings

As far as we know some researchers have tried to connect role activity diagrams to problem frames to some extent [5] using a case study in global financial services providing mappings to map a RAD to various components of problem frame. In RAD there are roles which correspond to the domains of interest. One role corresponds to the main machine we want to build other roles correspond to the external domains in the PF. Interactions in RAD correspond to the interface in problem frames. These interfaces lead to external input, external output, external inquiry and external interface files in function points. Required behaviour of problem frames can be derived from actions in role activity diagram. This gives us an insight on internal logical files and external inquiry.

Some researchers have done initial investigations using a simple case study of "sluice gate controller", to provide function point analysis using problem frames [6]. We count each unique user data or user control input that enters the external boundary of the application being measured and classify them as simple, average and complex. Next we count each unique data or user control output that leaves the external boundary of the application and classify it. Then we count each input that produces immediate output. This is classified by taking the greater complexity value of the input and output. In problem frames it is easy to confuse it with external input or external output but the required behaviour will indicate external inquiry clearly. Files passed or shared between domains and is maintained by external domain. Each major user data and control information group in the machine domain is counted as logical internal file type. In problem frames it forms a part of the required behavior.

3. The requirement statement for sluice gate

There is a small sluice with a gate. Gate can be raised or lowered to open or close the sluice respectively. A computer system is needed to lower or raise the gate in response to the command issued by the operator. The gate is opened or closed by screws driven by a motor. There are sensors at the top and bottom of the gate.

3.1 Role activity diagram for sluice gate.

Similar diagrams can be drawn for lowering of the gate and stopping the gate. Only raise will be substituted by lower or stop. Therefore separate diagrams are not drawn.

Domains identified corresponding to the roles are Sluice controller- it is the machine we want to build, Sluice operator and Gate & motor- are external domains

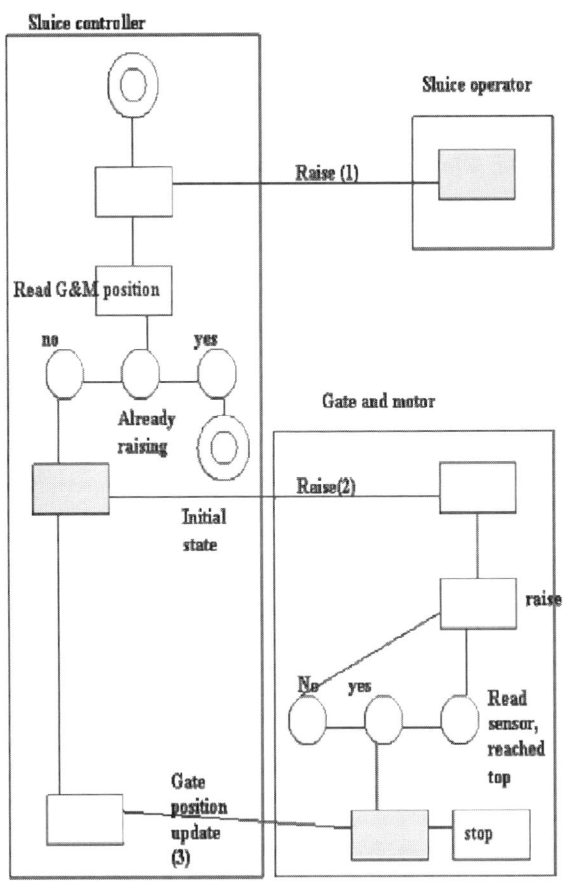

Figure 3: Role activity diagram: sluice gate

3.2.Problem frame for sluice gate

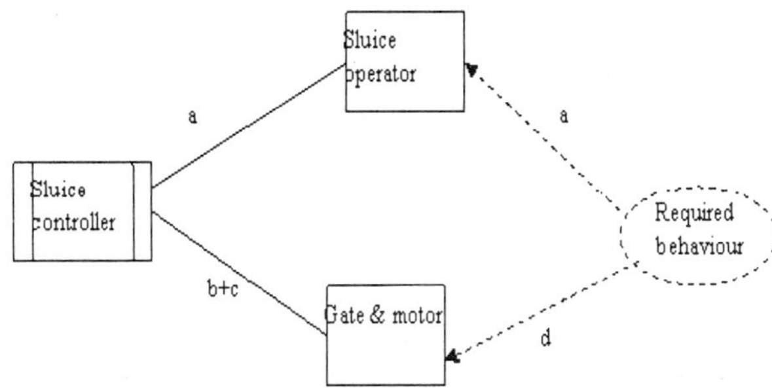

Fig ure4: problem frame: sluice gate

a: Sluice operator to sluice controller: Instruction to raise/lower/stop

b: Gate &motor to sluice controller: Update gate position

c: sluice controller to G&M: Control instruction to raise/lower/stop the gate

d: Open or close gate

D.Required behaviour: To open or close gate as instructed, maintain gate position at G&M, and maintain gate position at sluice controller.

E.Function points

External file= 1 of low complexity since data to be kept require only few fields.

Internal logical file=1 of low complexity since data is of few fields only.

External input=1 of low complexity. This corresponds to (b:) interface because this information is modifying the ILF maintained at the sluice controller. External output=1 of low complexity. This corresponds to (c) interface. This command is also modifying the external file kept at gate & motor.

External inquiry=nil as no input output pairs could be identified.

External files=1*5=5, Internal logical files=1*7=7, External input=1*3=3, External output=1*4=4 and External inquiry=0. Thus UFP=5+7+3+4=19.

Performance =5, Heavily used configuration=5, Online entry=3, Online update=3 and rest are scaled to 0. Therefore Total of influence of 14 characteristics is 16.

PC=.65+(.01*16)=0.81

Function points= UFP*PC =19*0.81 =15.39

4.Conclusion:

This paper presents a means to trace from business process model (role activity diagrams) to function points through problem frames. Attempts have been made to map problem frames to function points directly without the added layer of role activity diagrams but problem frames are sometimes difficult to identify i.e. there are more frames to be discovered. However problem is finite thus number of problem frames is also finite. Starting with RAD and creating Problem frames we arrive to unique outcome. Use of role activity diagrams provides deep understanding of the problem domain, requirements and responsibilities of the machine to be built. Building problem frames based on role activity diagrams ensure that machine to be built has domains behaving according to the requirements.

Another point of departure from previous work to our work is that we arrive to certain function points which were totally missing in the previous work. This will ultimately affect the effort estimation directly.

To measure functional size of the problem to be used for effort estimation we need a clear cut insight into the system. It has been reported that it is easier to measure function points using problem frames.

This paper is an attempt to find functional measurements (function points) of a problem at requirement phase by modelling it in a role activity diagram which is then mapped to problem frames. This approach gives better result than when only problem frames are used to find function points.

References

1. Allan J. Albrecht and J.E. Gaffney, "Software function, source lines of code, and development effort prediction: a software science validation", IEEE transactions on software engineering, SE-9, 6, 639-648, 1983
2. Chris F Kemerer, "Software project management, readings and cases" McGraw hill company,Irwin book team-1997.
3. E.R.Carroll, " Estimating software based on use case points", OOPSLA'05 -2005, California, USA ACM. Pg 257-265.
4. Ian Sommerville, "Software Engineering" , 5th edition, Addison-Wesley
5. Karl Cox , Keith Phalp , A. Aurum , S.J. Bleistein , J.Verner , "Connecting role activity diagrams to problem frames approach", Australian workshop on requirement engineering -2004 pg2.1-2.13.
6. L. Lavazza, V.B. Bianco, "Functional size measurement based on problem frames; a case study",International workshop on applications and advances in problem frames-2008, Germany pg 44-47 copyright 2008 ACM
7. M.A.Jackson, " Software development methods", Chapter 13 of A classical mind: essays in honour of C.A.R.Hoare, A.W.Roscoe", Prentice hall -1994
8. M.A.Jackson , "Problem analysis using small problem frames", South African computer journal 22, Special issue on WOFACS'98, pg47-60, 1998
9. M.Lencastre, J. Araujo , A. Moreira, J.Castro, "Analyzing crosscutting in the problem frames approach", IWAAPF-2006 pg 59-64.
10. Richard Fairley, "Software engineering concepts', Tata McGraw Hill
11. Walker Royce, "Software project management A unified framework", Addison-Wesley.

MACHINE INTELLIGENT APPROACH FOR MAPPING OF MHC CLASS BINDING NONAMERS

VIRENDRA GOMASE*
*Department of Bioinformatics, Padmashree Dr. D.Y. Patil University, Navi Mumbai, 400614, India
ARCHANA KHADE
Department of Bioinformatics, Padmashree Dr. D.Y. Patil University, Navi Mumbai, 400614, India
HANISH KHATRI
Department of Bioinformatics, Padmashree Dr. D.Y. Patil University, Navi Mumbai, 400614, India
ANISH PHADNIS
Department of Bioinformatics, Padmashree Dr. D.Y. Patil University, Navi Mumbai, 400614, India
KARBHARI KALE
Department of CS & IT, Dr. Babasaheb Ambedkar Marathwada University, Aurangabad, 431004, (MS), India

Abstract- Functional analysis of the binding ability of Hpv11 e2 tad protein antigen peptides to major histocompatibility complex (MHC) class molecules is important in vaccine development. Antigenic epitopes of Hpv11 e2 tad protein form Human papilloma virus-11 are important determinant for protection of many host form viral infection. We used PSSM and SVM algorithms for antigen design, which represented predicted binders as MHCII-IAb, MHCII-IAd, MHCII-IAg7, and MHCII- RT1.B nonamers from viral Hpv11 e2 tad crystal structure. These peptide nonamers are from a set of aligned peptides known to bind to a given MHC molecule as the predictor of MHC-peptide binding. Analysis shows potential drug targets to identify active sites against diseases.

Keywords *Tad crystal structure, PSSM, SVM, MHC, epitope, peptide vaccine*

Abbreviations: Goldman, Engelberg and Steitz, (GES); major histocompatibility complex, (MHC); Position Specific Scoring Matrices, (PSSMs); Support Vector Machine, (SVM)

1. Introduction

Human papillomavirus (HPV) is a papillomavirus that infects the skin and mucous membranes of humans, epithelia of humans and animals, where they generally induce benign proliferation at the site of infection. Also, in some cases the lesions induced by certain papillomaviruses undergo malignant progression. There is a strong association between malignant progression of human genital lesions and certain human papillomavirus (HPV) types, such as HPV16. The cervical carcinomas contain and express HPV early genes, and these genes have been shown to have potent transforming and immortalizing activity in cultured cells. The virus is made up of many and varied strains that differ in a number of aspects including host range, symptoms, and means of transmission [1, 2]. The strains of Hpv11 e2 tad protein [*Human papilloma virus-11*] are differentiated on the basis of symptoms on indicator host. Viral capsid protein 11 protein is central to the establishment of viral pathogenesis, and yet relatively little is understood about the structural and functional aspects of capsid protein 11 or about the host factors on which they depend. Capsid protein 11 [*Human papilloma virus-11*] and the genetic material necessary for its production in; an exemption from the requirement of a tolerance is established for residues of the biological viral therapy [3-5].

***Correspondence**: Virendra S. Gomase, Department of Bioinformatics, Padmashree Dr. D.Y. Patil University, Plot No-50, Sector-15, CBD Belapur, Navi Mumbai, 400614, India; Mobile- +91-9987770696; Mail- virusgene1@yahoo.co.in

2. Methodology

Antigenic epitopes of Hpv11 e2 tad protein from *Human papilloma virus-11* is determined using the Gomase (2007), Hopp and Woods, Welling, Parker and Protrusion Index (Thornton) antigenicity methods [6-9]. The MHC peptide binding of Hpv11 e2 tad protein is predicted using neural networks trained on C terminals of known epitopes. In analysis predicted MHC/peptide binding of Hpv11 e2 tad protein is a log-transformed value related to the IC50 values in nM units. MHC2Pred predicts peptide binders to MHCI and MHCII molecules from protein sequences or sequence alignments using Position Specific Scoring Matrices (PSSMs). Support Vector Machine (SVM) based method for prediction of promiscuous MHC class II binding peptides. SVM has been trained on the binary input of single amino acid sequence [10-14]. In addition, we predict those MHC ligands from whose C-terminal end is likely to be the result of proteosomal cleavage.

3. Results and Interpretations

RankPep server predicts binding of peptides to a number of different alleles using Position Specific Scoring Matrix (PSSM). Hpv11 e2 tad protein sequence is 207 residues long, having antigenic MHC binding peptides. MHC molecules are cell surface glycoproteins, which take active part in host immune reactions and involvement of MHC class-I and MHC II in response to almost all antigens. PSSM based server predict the peptide binders to MHCI molecules of Hpv11 e2 tad protein sequence are as 11mer_H2_Db,

9mer_H2_Db, 8mer_H2_Db and also peptide binders to MHCII molecules of Hpv11 e2 tad protein sequence as I_Ab.p, I_Ag7.p, I_Ad.p, analysis found antigenic epitopes region in Hpv11 e2 tad protein (table - 1). We also found the SVM based MHCII-IAb; MHCII-IAd; MHCII-IAg7 and MHCII- RT1.B peptide regions, which represented predicted binders from viral Hpv11 e2 tad protein. The predicted binding affinity is normalized by the 1% fractil. We describe an improved method for predicting linear epitopes (table -2). The region of maximal hydrophilicity is likely to be an antigenic site, having hydrophobic characteristics, because terminal regions of Hpv11 e2 tad protein is solvent accessible and unstructured, antibodies against those regions are also likely to recognize the native protein (Fig. 1-4). It was shown that Hpv11 e2 tad protein is hydrophobic in nature and contains segments of low complexity and high-predicted flexibility (Fig. 5-8). Predicted antigenic fragments can bind to MHC molecule is the first bottlenecks in vaccine design.

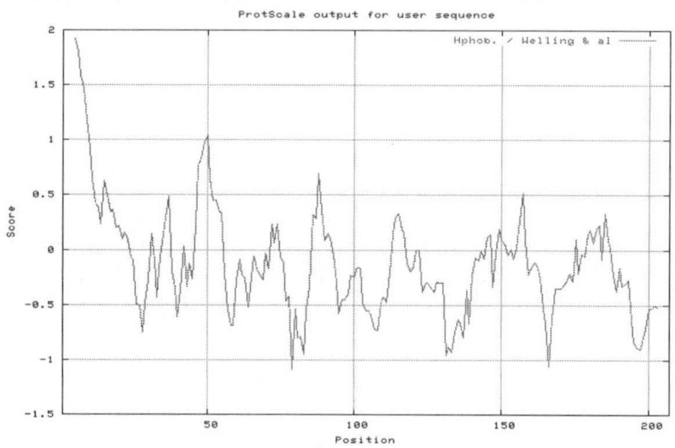

Fig. 1- Antigenicity plot of Hpv11 e2 tad protein by Welling, et al., scale

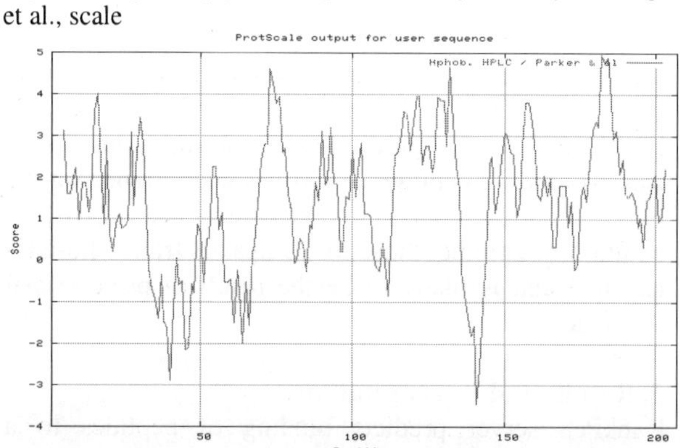

Fig. 2- Antigenicity plot of Hpv11 e2 tad protein by HPLC / Parker, et al., scale

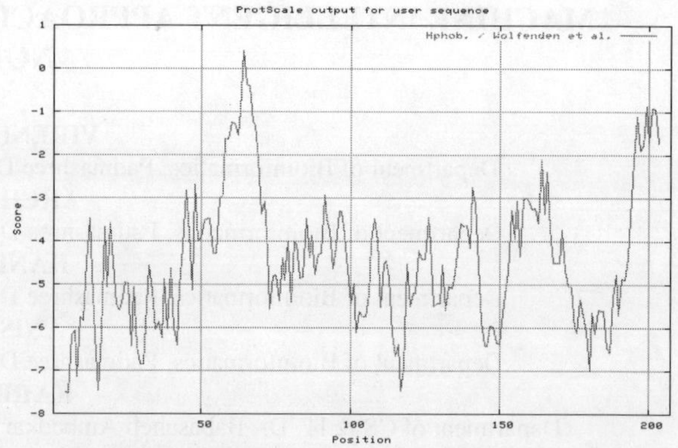

Fig. 3- Hydrophobicity plot of Hpv11 e2 tad protein by Wolfenden, et al., scale

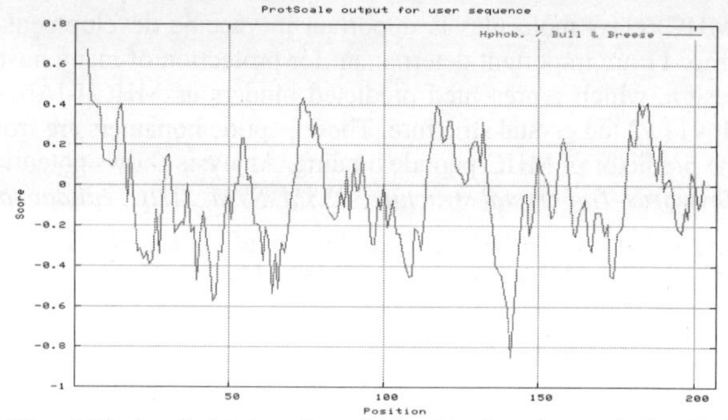

Fig. 4-Hydrophobicity plot of Hpv11 e2 tad protein by Bull & Breese scale

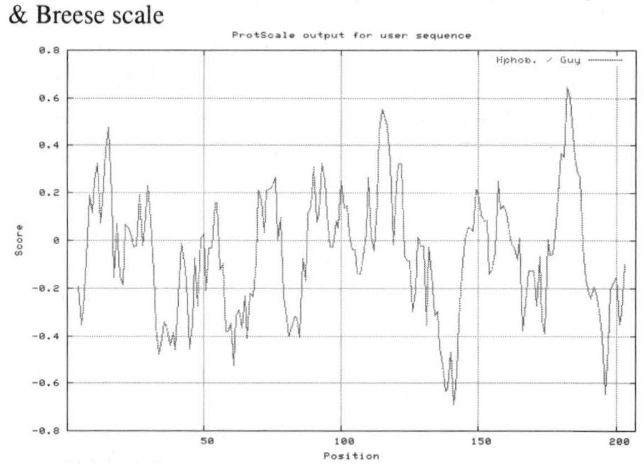

Fig. 5- Hydrophobicity plot of Hpv11 e2 tad protein by Gut scale

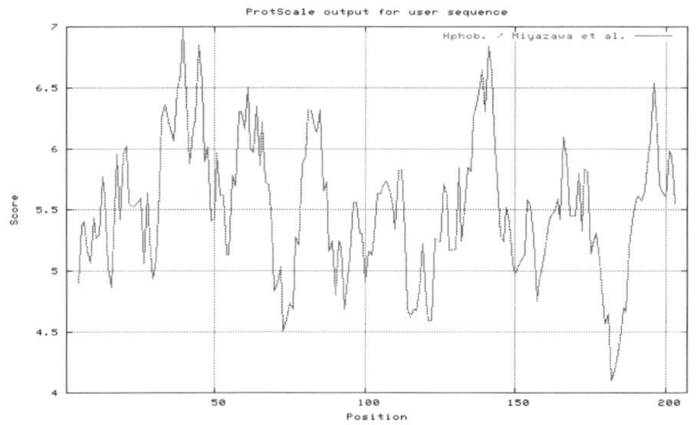

Fig. 6- Hydrophobicity plot of Hpv11 e2 tad protein by Miyazawa et al. scale

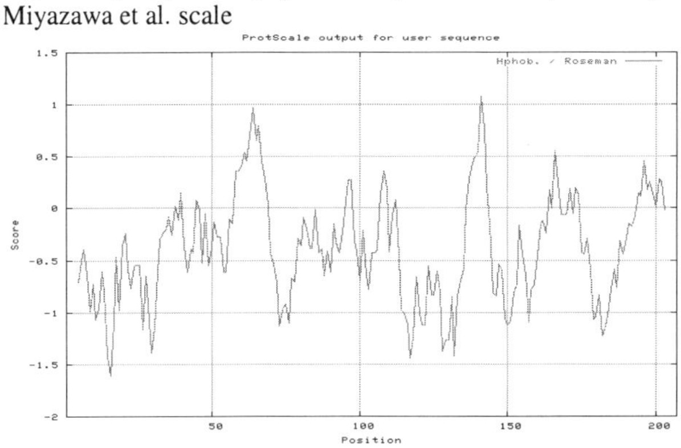

Fig. 7- Hydrophobicity plot of Hpv11 e2 tad protein by Roseman scale

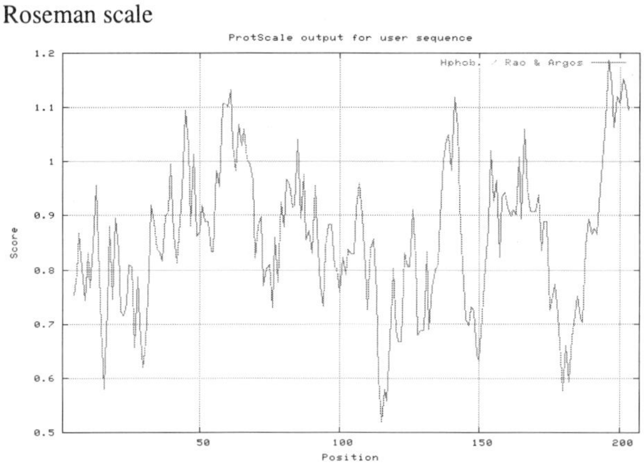

Fig. 8- Hydrophobicity plot of Hpv11 e2 tad protein by Abraham & Leo scale

4. Conclusion

Hpv11 e2 tad protein from *Human papilloma virus-11* peptide nonamers are from a set of aligned peptides known to bind to a given major histocompatibility complex (MHC) molecule as the predictor of MHC-peptide binding. MHCII molecules bind peptides in similar yet different modes and alignments of MHCII-ligands were obtained to be consistent with the binding mode of the peptides to their MHC class, this means the increase in affinity of MHC binding peptides may result in enhancement of immunogenicity of viral Hpv11 e2 tad protein. These predicted of tad protein antigenic peptides to MHC class molecules are important in vaccine development from *Human papilloma virus-11*.

5. References

[1] H. Sénéchal, G.G. Poirier, B. Coulombe, L.A. Laimins, J. Archambault, *Virology*, 358(1), 10-7 (2007).

[2] W. Davidson, G.A. McGibbon, P.W.White, C.Yoakim, J.L.Hopkins, I. Guse, D.M. Hambly, L. Frego, W.W.Ogilvie, P.Lavallée, J. Archambault, *Anal Chem.*, 76(7), 2095-102 (2004).

[3] Y.Wang, R.Coulombe, D.R.Cameron, L. Thauvette, M.J.Massariol, L.M.Amon, D.Fink, S.Titolo, E.Welchner, C.Yoakim, J.Archambault, P.W.White, *J Biol Chem.*, 279(8), 6976-85 (2004).

[4] V.S.Gomase, K.V. Kale and K. Shyamkumar, *J. of Proteomics & Bioinformatics*, 1 (4), 188- 205 (2008).

[5] V.S.Gomase, K.V. Kale, N.J.Chikhale, S.S. Changbhale, *Curr. Drug Discov. Technol.*, 4(2),117-1215 (2007).

[6] V.S.Gomase and K.V.Kale, *Int. J. of Applied Computing*, 1(1), 39-46 (2008).

[7] V.S.Gomase and K.V.Kale, *Int. J. of Applied Computing*, 1(1), 33-38 (2008).

[8] V.S.Gomase and K.V.Kale, Int. *J. of Information Retrieval*, 1(1), 11-15 (2008).

[9] V.S.Gomase, K.V. Kale, K. Shyamkumar and S. Shankar, *ICETET 2008, IEEE Computer Society in IEEE Xplore, Los Alamitos, California*, 629-634 (2008).

[10] V.S.Gomase, J.P.Tandale, S.A.Patil, K.V.Kale, *14th International Conference on Advance Computing & Communication, Published by IEEE Computer Society in IEEE Xplore USA* 614-615 (2006).

[11] P.A. Reche, J.P. Glutting, E.L. Reinherz, *Hum Immun.*, 63, 701-709 (2002).

[12] S. Buus, *et al.*, Tissue Antigens, 62, 378-384 (2003).

[13] M. Nielsen, *et al.*, *Protein Sci.*, 12, 1007-1017 (2003).

[14] M. Bhasin and G.P. Raghava, *Nucleic Acids Research*, 33, W202-207 (2005).

Table 1- PSSM based prediction of MHC ligands, from whose C-terminal ends are proteosomal cleavage sites

MHC-I	POS.	N	Sequence	C	MW (Da)	Score	% OPT.
9mer_H2_Db	117	RCF	KKQGNTVEV	KFD	984.1	71.0	48.63 %
9mer_H2_Db	73	VSE	TKGHNAIEM	QMH	982.11	71.0	48.63 %
9mer_H2_Db	184	AQK	YGSTNHWEV	CYG	1051.11	66.0	45.21 %
9mer_H2_Db	24	LLE	LYEENSIDI	HKH	1077.17	65.0	44.52 %
8mer_H2_Db	118	CFK	KQGNTVEV	KFD	855.93	112.0	62.57 %
8mer_H2_Db	63	IGL	QVVPPLTV	SET	834.02	99.0	55.31 %
8mer_H2_Db	185	QKY	GSTNHWEV	CYG	887.93	87.0	48.60 %
8mer_H2_Db	25	LEL	YEENSIDI	HKH	964.01	78.0	43.58 %
11mer_H2_Db	174	KTY	YVNFNKEAQKY	GST	1385.54	105.0	49.53 %
11mer_H2_Db	184	AQK	YGSTNHWEVCY	GST	1317.43	99.0	46.70 %
11mer_H2_Db	73	VSE	TKGHNAIEMQM	HLE	1241.43	93.0	43.87 %
11mer_H2_Db	155	VKV	TSSVDAKGIYY	TCG	1185.3	72.0	33.96 %

Table 2- SVM based prediction of promiscuous MHC class II binding peptides from Hpv11 e2 tad protein

MHC ALLELE	Rank	Sequence	Residue No.	Peptide Score
I-Ab	1	PPLTVSETK	66	1.110
I-Ab	2	GLQVVPPLT	61	1.011
I-Ab	3	PLTVSETKG	67	0.890
I-Ab	4	RLESVLLHK	43	0.849
I-Ad	1	KQMGLSHIG	53	0.498
I-Ad	2	EAQKYGSTN	180	0.489
I-Ad	3	YEENSIDIH	25	0.466
I-Ad	4	KAKQMGLSH	51	0.454
I-Ag7	1	YYVNFNKEA	173	1.545
I-Ag7	2	SVDAKGIYY	157	1.322
I-Ag7	3	SSVDAKGIY	156	1.254
I-Ag7	4	WLTPPKRCF	108	1.226
RT1.B	1	DACQDQLLE	15	0.826
RT1.B	2	TKGHNAIEM	73	0.724
RT1.B	3	DTSYEMWLT	102	0.713
RT1.B	4	LDACQDQLL	14	0.586

A SYSTEM MODELING AND SIMULATION TOOLS WITH CAPABILITY OF CODE GENERATION USING COLOR-TIMED PETRI NET

TOURAJ MOHAMMADPOUR

Computer Engineering Department
Islamic Azad University, Ayatollah amoli branch, Amol, Iran
E-mail: mohammadpour.touraj@gmail.com

MEHDI YADOLLAHI

Computer Engineering Department
Islamic Azad University, Ayatollah amoli branch, Amol, Iran
E-mail: yadollahi.mehdi@gmail.com

ABOLFAZL TOROGHI HAGHIGHAT

Electronic, Computer and Information Technology faculty
Islamic azad university, Qazvin branch, Qazvin, Iran
haghighat@qazviniau.ac.ir

A vast range of activities has been occurred during the recent years to analyze, simulate and model various systems more quickly and conveniently, one of which is the petri net. In this paper, a Tool called "SimCPN" for modeling, simulation and analysis is presented which uses color-timed Petri net and is capable of generating codes. The generated code is capable of simulating and analyzing a system as an independent software program. The so-called tool has various and more capabilities comparing to the similar tools such as CPN-AMI، EXSPECT, GREATSPN, RENEW, CoopnBuilder and SYROCO. Some of these capabilities are ease of modeling, modeling of vast range of systems and generating codes which are totally object-oriented.

1. Introduction

A vast range of activities has been occurred during the recent years for modeling, simulation and analysis of systems [1, 2]. The purpose of these activities is to model, simulate and analyze the systems as quickly and conveniently as possible. One of the popular methods of modeling is petri net [3-6].

In this respect enormous tools were introduced. PED [2] is a hierarchical petri net editor. CPN [7] is a graphical editor for high level and academic petri net which can be run and executed Macintosh, Linux. CoopnBuilder [2] is a graphical editor which is generated for object-oriented petri net and high level activities. It is executable in Java platform and is capable of code generation. ExSpect [2] is yet another graphical editor for high level and accidental petri net which is commercially produced and is executed on Microsoft Windows. GreatSPN [8] is an academic and graphical editor for high level petri net and is run and executed in Linux and Sun platforms.

In this paper we have presented a new Tool called "SimCPN" for modeling, simulation and analysis of different systems through the use of color-timed petri net. One of prominent features of the afore-mentioned device is the capability of code-generation for particular systems. The generated code is able to simulate and analyzes a system thoroughly. Other features can be as follows: supporting and using a wide gamut of systems for modeling and simulation.

The structure of this paper is as the following: In the section 2 a brief introduction of petri net is given, in the section 3 there is SimCPN description, the experimental results of the comparison of SimCPN with similar tools such as Syroco, CoopnBuilder, Exspect, GreatSPN, Renew, CPN-AMI are depicted in section 4. Lastly, the paper is concluded in Section 5.

2. Petri net

Petri net is a graphical and mathematical modeling device which consists of the four elements of Place, Transition, Arc, and Token. It can be used for systems modeling, timing, simulation, and evaluation. Using petri net will make us get rid of depicting the problem with mathematical formulas [9-11].

Timed- petri net is a type of petri net in which a transition is firing a token after a specific period of time. Color petri net is another ilk of petri net inside FrameMaker and XFig formats. CPN is a graphical

which the transitions can fire the tokens based o the type of tokens.

3. SimCPN description

In this paper, a tool called "SimCPN" for modeling, simulation, and analysis of system through the use of timed-color petri net is presented. This tool described in following section.

3.1. *System modeling*

Using color-timed Petri net, SimCPN is capable of modeling a wide gamut of systems. It enables us to model a system simply by using the pre-defined factors in petri net. The four major components are available in the toolbox, through the use of which every and all systems can be conveniently modeled. Fig. 1 shows the SimCPN toolbox.

Figure 1. Toolbox

The modeling process of a production line system is shown in fig. 2.

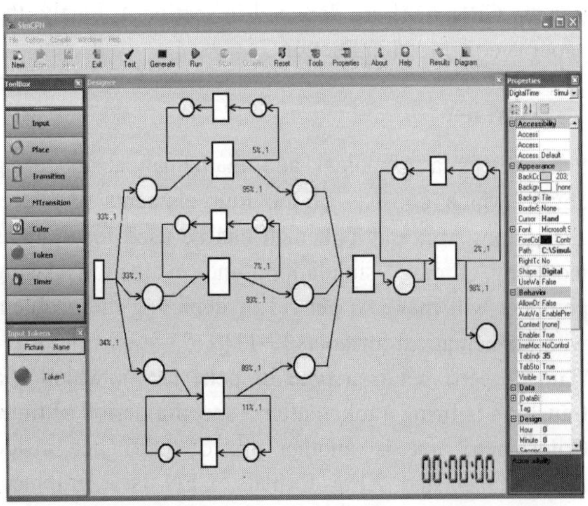

Figure 2. The modeling process of a production line system

3.2. *System simulation and analysis*

The next step to system modeling is the simulation process. In this phase, before activating the simulator, parameters such as the total simulation time, type and number of tokens, input time for tokens and so on should be determined, and after simulator activation, system condition can be dynamically observed. The so called simulator first tests the authenticity and legitimacy of the system modeling, and then the simulation occurs. Fig. 3, described the Simulation algorithms used in the SimCPN in a pseudo code.

Tools Algorithm

```
IF test modeling is false THEN
    Stop procedure
END IF
WHILE simulation time not expire DO
    CALL Input Event Procedure
    CALL Service Terminate Event Procedure
    CALL Active Ready Server Procedure
END WHILE
Show analysis results
```

Input Event Procedure

```
IF time = input time THEN
    Input a token to system
    Input Time := Next Input Time
END IF
```

Service Terminate Event Procedure

```
Find minimum time index in TBL array
Fire the server that its index in TBL array is characterized
Set this server in Passive mode
```

Find Ready Server Procedure

```
FOR each server DO
    IF server is ready THEN
        Set server in Active mode
    END IF
END FOR
```

Figure 3. The simulation algorithms used in the SimCPN tool

Various speeds per millisecond can be chosen for simulation. For example, if the speed is 1000, the simulation is administered in a real time event. The condition of a system and the simulation statistic can be observed dynamically along with the process. Fig. 4

shows the situation of a modeled system in fig. 2 within the second of 309.

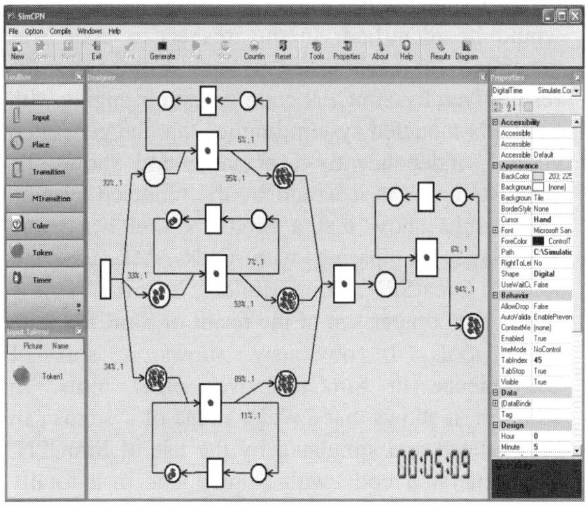

Figure 4. Modeled system situation within the second of 309

After the system simulation , all the statistically information of the final product regarding server activity rate, maximum queue length , total token serviced ,system efficiency, and the output time of the final token are illustrated through the use of diagrams one of the privileges of such simulator is illustrating such statistical data at any moment of simulation process. See fig. 5 and fig. 6.

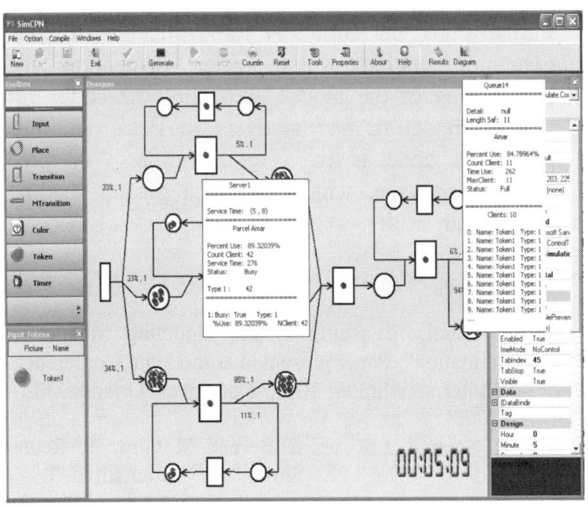

Figure 5. Statistic of modeled system situation within the second of 309

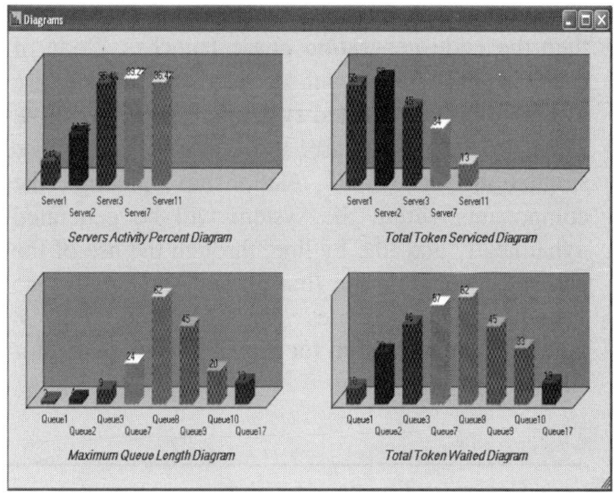

Figure 6. The sample of statistic of system situation

3.3. *Code generation*

One of the major features of SimCPN is having a code generator engine which, based on the modeled system by color-timed petri net, can generate an independently executable code. The generated code with code generator engine is articulated in C#.Net. Such an engine is composed of various sections. Each of which is responsible for a particular course of action. Fig. 7 shows the general structure of the engine.

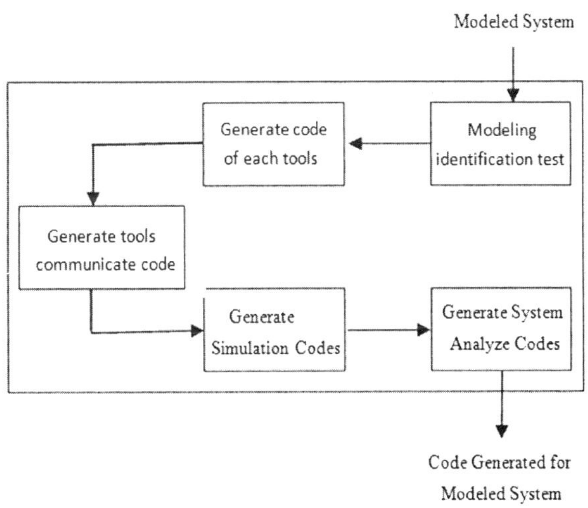

Figure 7. Code generator engine structure

This engine first inspects the modeled system and then the code generation phase launches. Code of each of the component of petri net which are available in the modeled system are generated first. Then, in the next phase, the codes related to the simulation and the relationship among the components within the system will be generated dynamically and line by line, through the use of the generated codes in the first phase. And finally, the systems analysis codes are generated. Fig. 8 describes the algorithm for SimCPN code generator engine.

Code Generator Engine Algorithm

```
IF test modeling is false THEN
    Stop procedure
ELSE
    FOR each component DO
        IF component is Queue THEN
            Generate code for Queue Class
        ELSE IF component is Sever THEN
            Generate code for Server Class
        ELSE IF component is Token THEN
            Generate code for Token Class
        END IF
    END FOR
    Generate code for Simulation Class
    Generate code for Analyze Class
END IF
```

Figure 8. SimCPN code generator engine algorithm

One of the significant features of the so-called generated codes is the capability to simulate and analyze the system independently.

4. Experimental results

Different systems were modeled and simulated with the proposed tools so that its main characteristics would be identified. In this respect, a code was generated for each tested system. Comparing the result given by SimCPN code generator engine with SimCPN modeled system implies that the generated code is independently executable and shows the same statistics as it would by the modeled system. The results show that a SimCPN tool has many advantages comparing with CPN-AMI, Exspect, Renew, GreatSPN, CoopnBuilder, Syroco. Table 1 shows the comparison of the result of SimCPN with other tools. It obviously shows a sort of convenience in SimCPN over other tools. In addition, it shows that a wider range of systems can be modeled and simulated by the use of SimCPN. The generated code with SimCPN is in a totally object- oriented C#.Net language, which entails a greater loading ability with itself.

5. Conclusion

In this paper, a tool called "SimCPN" presented which is used for modeling, simulating, and analyzing system by color-timed Petri net. It is capable of modeling a wide range of systems. After modeling a system in this tool, the simulator takes its course of action and produces the analysis statistics. One of the major advantages of SimCPN is covering and supporting a wide range of systems. Furthermore, the SimCPN tool processes a code generator engine which, after inspection the authenticity of the model, generates the codes for system modeling and analysis in Petri net. The generated code is in a totally object- oriented C#.Net language, which entails a greater loading ability with itself.

References

[1] J. Desel, "Teaching system modeling, simulation and validation", Paper presented at the 32nd Conference on Winter simulation, 10-13 December, Orlando, FL, USA, (2000).

[2] R. Schmid, J. Ryser, S. Berner, M. Glinz, R. Reutemann and E. Fahr, "A Survey of Simulation Tools for Requirements Engineering", (FG 2.1.6) of the German Informatics society (GI), (2000).

[3] P. Bonet, Llado, M. Catalina, R. Puigjaner, Knottenbelt and J. William, "PIPE v2.5: a Petri Net Tool for Performance Modeling", (2007).

[4] N. Akharware,"PIPE2: Platform Independent Petri Net Editor", http://pipe2.sourceforge.net/documents/PIPE2-Report-20050814.pdf, (2005).

[5] S. Heller, S. Greiner and G. Horton, "PENETO: A Petri Net Simulator For Fast Safetyand Quality Analysis And Cost Prediction" , Society for Computer Simulation and Modeling, ESM 2001, Prague, June (2001).

[6] Mortensen and H. Kjeld, "Automatic Code Generation from Coloured Petri Nets for an Access Control System", (2001).

[7] "Implementation of CPN2000", A Post-WIMP Graphical Application. Proc . ACM Symposium on User Interface Software and Technology , UIST 2000, November 2000, ACM Press,(2000).

[8] GreatSPN 2.0, "GRaphical Editor and Analyzer for Timed and Stochastic Petri Nets", http://www.di.unito.it/~greatspn/.

[9] E. Kindler and M. Weber, "The Petri Net Kernel - An infrastructure for building Petri net tools", Software Tools for Technology Transfer (STTT), 3 (4), 486-497, (2001).

[10] G. Maione and M. Ottomanelli, "A Petri Net Model For Simulation Of Container Terminals Operations, Advanced OR and AI Methods in Transportation" , (2005).

[11] D. Gašević, V. Devedžić and N. Veselinović, "P3 - Petri net educational software tool for hardware Teaching", Paper presented at the 10th Workshop Algorithms and Tools for Petri nets, 26-27 September, Eichstätt, Germany, (2003).

Table 1. The Results of comparison between SimCPN and other tools

Tools Name	PN Supported	Components	Environments	Origin
CPN-AMI	High-level Petri Nets Place/Transition Nets	Graphical Editor, Fast Simulation State Spaces, Condensed State Spaces Place Invariants, Transition Invariants Structural Analysis, Interchange File Format services for modular modeling	Linux Macintosh	Academic (free)
CoopnBuilder	Object-oriented PNs	Graphical Editor, Token Game Animation Fast Simulation, Code Generation	Java	Academic (free)
ExSpect	High-level Petri Nets Place/Transition Nets Stochastic Petri Nets Petri Nets with Time Hierarchy in modeling	Graphical Editor, Token Game Animation Fast Simulation Simple Performance Analysis Advanced Performance Analysis Rapid Prototyping Workflow Management System Simulation engine available as COM component	MS Windows	Company
GreatSPN	High-level Petri Nets Stochastic Petri Nets Petri Nets with Time	Graphical Editor, Token Game Animation Fast Simulation, State Spaces Condensed State Spaces Place Invariants, Transition Invariants Structural Analysis Advanced Performance Analysis	Sun Linux	Academic (free)
Renew	Object-oriented PNs High-level Petri Nets Place/Transition Nets Petri Nets with Time	Graphical Editor, Token Game Animation Fast Simulation, Interchange File Format Rapid Prototyping Workflow Management System	Java	Academic (free)
SYROCO	High-level Petri Nets Petri Nets with Time Dynamic instantiation of nets, C++ code associated to transitions and places, priority	Graphical Editor, Structural Analysis Fast Simulation Simple Performance Analysis Advanced Performance Analysis Interchange File Format C++ code generation	C++	Academic (free)
SimCPN	High-level Petri Nets Object-oriented PNs Place/Transition Nets Petri Nets with Time Petri Nets with Color	Graphical Editor, Token Game Animation Fast Simulation, State Spaces Simple Performance Analysis Advanced Performance Analysis Structural Analysis, C#.Net Code Generation Workflow Management System	PC, Linux PC, MS Windows	Academic (free)

QUERY REFORMULATION: AN INTERPLAY OF USER'S REFORMULATION BEHAVIOR AND THEMATIC CONTEXT IN ORIGINAL QUERY

MPS BHATIA
Department of Computer Engineering, Netaji Subhas Institute of Technology, University of Delhi, New Delhi, India

mpsbhatia@nsit.ac.in

AKSHI KUMAR
Department of Computer Engineering, Delhi College of Engineering, University of Delhi, New Delhi, India

akshi.kumar@gmail.com

Formulation and reformulation of queries is one of the most intricate and challenging tasks in users domain, even in the Web Search environment that appears easy to learn and use. Therefore, understanding query behaviors and designing search tools to support those behaviors remains a significant research problem. In order to provide empirical evidence on user's reformulation behavior and to help search engines better handle the query reformulation problem, we propose a Co-information (CI) based algorithm to detect the possible thematic contexts in the original query and analyze the relation between the users' reformulation behaviors to those contexts. We demonstrate that most multiple-term queries include more than one thematic context and users usually reformulate their queries by context instead of terms. The experimental results on query log show that: most users reformulate query at the contextual level; and our proposed CI-based algorithm is a good method to detect thematic context from the original query.

1. Introduction

Query Reformulation is the process of transforming a query into a new query that more accurately reflects the user's information need. It can be seen as a mechanism that recommends query modifications to reduce false positives. Users searching very large information systems, such as those indexing the World Wide Web, often start with naive queries that return too many documents to browse exhaustively. The main problem in modeling an efficient retrieval process is that a user cannot express his information need straightforwardly in a query which is posted to an information repository, i.e. a user's query represents just an approximation of his information need. Consequently such a query should be transformed in order to ensure the retrieval of as much as relevant products. There are three main approaches for improving the initial query formulation: Firstly, the Relevance feedback approaches [1, 2, 3] which are based on feedback information from the user. Query reformulation from relevance feedback, has been shown effective if appropriate feedback (i.e. explicit – this document is/is not relevant; or implicit – through click-through data) is given by the user. Secondly the Local Analysis approaches [4, 5, 6] that are based on information derived from the set of documents initially retrieved (called the local set of documents) and lastly the Global analysis which includes approaches based on global information derived from the document collection.

1.1. *Problems with Query Reformulation*

There are problems with query reformulation, both in principle and in the way it is practiced.

- Query reformulation is **discontinuous**: when the user clicks on a refinement, the information on the screen totally changes, forcing the user, who may just be browsing, to absorb new information and later to resort to backtracking to retrieve the old. Discontinuity leads to an inferior user experience.
- Traditionally, query reformulation quality has not been very good. As a result, either little or **inferior screen space** is devoted to it, so it doesn't get clicked on much because the user's eye is not drawn there. Typically query reformulations are placed at the bottom or the right of the page, which are hardly the places to put top-quality information.
- Access to the **search index** is needed. This means that implementing query reformulation in meta-search mode, where an external search engine is called, is problematic. For example, an external paid-listings provider (Google, FindWhat) might be called in meta-search mode. Since these external

sources aren't pre-processed, the commercial themes reflected there may be absent from the refinements, undermining the chances of seeing click-throughs' to paid listings and hence revenue.

- Since query reformulation involves significant pre-processing, the refinements will **lag** the top search results.
- There is no link between the query reformulation options and the current search results on the screen. Therefore, one cannot easily implement advanced user features which depend on navigating the information **bottom-up**, i.e., from individual search results to groupings (clusters) of them. Vivisimo.com's *Show-in-Clusters* feature is an example of bottom-up navigation.
- If the **query is too long**, then in some implementations no refinements are suggested, even though the returned results are numerous enough for the user to need help in making sense of them.
- Because reformulating a query issues a new search, the user **cannot easily compare** two candidate refinements, short of opening up multiple windows on the screen.

In this research, we present a reformulation strategy addressing the problem of long queries, i.e., multi-term queries. The reformulation process is carried out through the process of *Thematic Context Detection,* by getting the set of all sub-query terms and enriching each sub-query by submitting it into search engine, getting the top N ranked snippets, where for each sub-query set the Co-information value (CI), that measures the degree of one sub-query being a theme, is obtained. Finally, all sub-queries are ordered in a descendant value of Co-information and split it into two parts by the threshold of zero, formulating the list of thematic context words with positive CI value. We validate the algorithm by building a probability space based on the local search results of its all sub-queries from each original query.

1.2. *The need of Context & the Search Process*

New search services that incorporate context, and further incorporation of context into existing search services, may increase the retrieval effectiveness, and help mitigate any negative effects of biases in access to information on the web [7]. It is therefore essential that these systems provide tools for helping users focus their queries.

1.2.1 *Where do we need context?*

- Searching the web happens in context which is unique for any possible single search.
- Users' feelings, thoughts and actions during the course of web searching highly dependent on search context
- Considering the context of search is a pivotal element in understanding users' behaviour.
- Some elements of the search context like time allocation or search importance are more significant in users' judgment about success or failure of the search.
- Context is extremely dynamic and changes constantly even for the same user or during the same search session.

However, context is a relatively vague term. For instance, context can be generated implicitly or explicitly, it can be meant in a thematic way (based on content) or rather in an environmental way (e.g., based on application structures, people worked with, etc.), or it can be seen as a short-term or as a long-term context, etc. One of the current challenges is to elicit the context of a user. End users are aware of the context and prioritize different components in different situations.

1.2.2 *Use of context at different stages of the IR process*

- Query specification: (Query + Context), Retrieval, Presentation.
- Retrieval (matching/ranking): Query, (Retrieval + Context), Presentation.
- Results presentation and interaction: Query, Retrieval, (Presentation + Context).

In order to provide empirical evidence on user's reformulation behavior and to help search engines better handle the query reformulation problem, we propose a Co-information (CI) based algorithm to detect the possible contexts in the original query and analyze the relation between the users' reformulation behaviors to those context. We demonstrate that the information forming the context is usually included as a sub-query in a user's query and it has strong impacts on the quality of search results. This study addresses the following research questions:

1. How to detect the possible context contained in the original user query?
2. Analyze user's reformulation behavior at the contextual level.
3. What are the implications of incorporating this context on retrieval effectiveness?

2. Previous Work

Several kinds of query reformulation methods have been studied in the literature. The Query reformulation involves the following goals:

- Expanding the query with new terms from relevant documents [8, 9].
- Re-weighting the terms in the expanded query [1].

A fundamental problem in Web Information Retrieval (Web IR) is word mismatch [10], which refers to the phenomenon that the users of Web IR systems often use different words to describe the concepts in their queries than the authors use to describe the same concepts in their documents. Thus a gap exists between user's query space and document representation space. The methods for tackling this problem split into two major classes: global methods and local methods [11].

Global methods are techniques for expanding or reformulating query terms independent of the query and results returned from it, so that changes in the query wording will cause the new query to match other semantically similar terms. The basic idea in global analysis is that the global context of a concept can be used to determine similarities between concepts. Context can be defined in a number of ways, as can concepts. The simplest definitions are that all words are concepts and that the context for a word is all the word that co-occurs in document. Similarity thesauri [12] and Phrase Finder [13] are used with those global techniques. Another related approach uses clustering to determine the context for document analysis [14]. Global analysis techniques are relatively robust. However, since the co-occurrence information for every pair of terms in the whole corpus are normally needed, the processing is generally rather computational resource consuming. Moreover, global analysis cannot handle ambiguous terms effectively. It did not show consistent positive retrieval results unless further strategies for term selection could be suggested.

Local technologies analyze only the information in some initial documents, which are retrieved for the original query. Terms are extracted from these documents for query expansion [15]. Local analysis can be further divided into two groups. The first one is called relevance feedback [1], which relies on user's relevance judgments of the retrieved documents. Relevance feedback can achieve great performance if users cooperate well. However, this method is seldom deployed in practice because users are not always willing or able to give sufficient and correct relevance judgment about documents. Local feedback methods [16] are developed to solve this problem. They work without user interaction by assuming the top ranked documents to be relevant. The drawback of these methods is: if the top-ranked documents happen to be irrelevant (this situation is very common in the Web query world), the suggested terms from these documents are also likely to be unrelated to the topic and the query expansion will fail.

3. Query Reformulation Approach

3.1. *Multi-Term Query*

Query, which entails a group of keywords, plays a quintessential role in the Web search paradigm. Recent studies claim that queries involving one or two keywords are most common in Web searches. While most Web Search engines perform very well for a single-keyword query, their precision is not good for query involving two or more keywords because the search results usually contain a large number of pages with weak relevance. Also, the users have a well-defined query re-formulation behavior, i.e., most multiple term queries include more than one context and users usually reformulate their queries by context instead of terms. A context is usually included as a sub-query in a user's query and it has strong impacts on the quality of search results. Thus we focus on how to detect the context of a user query.

Mathematically, we define a *Multi-term query* as:
A query $Q = t_1\ t_2\ \ldots\ t_n$ of n terms, where t_i ($1 <= i <= n$) is the ith term of Q.
Any subsets of $\{t_1, t_2, \ldots, t_n\}$, i.e., any combinations of $t_1\ t_2 \ldots . t_n$ define the sub-queries. The *set of sub-queries* is defined as $SQ = \{sq_k\}$, $1 <= k <= 2^{n+1}-2$.

Our goal is to detect several sub-queries from SQ which could relate and contribute to the context.

3.2. *Local Document Set Analysis*

The analysis is carried out on the basis of the local set of documents as built in the first step. A query typically contains only a few terms, which provide limited information. One straightforward method is to submit a query to a search engine to get the top ranked search pages. Those retrieved results provide some richer information about the query. In other words, we call the retrieved results of query as the local information of this query. Meanwhile, a query has its global information, based on the whole corpus, to provide more information. However, the global based approach can cause high computational complexity and it was shown in [17] that a local based approach outperforms the global based approach. So in this paper, the top ranked search results are utilized to enrich the query.

In the local analysis, we select significant characteristics from each (retrieved and relevant) document and name them 'features', i.e., given the search results for a query, we need to decide what features should be extracted from the search engine to construct the enrichment. Generally, three kinds of features are considered: the title of a page, the snippet generated by the search engine, and the full plain text of a page. We use the top N ranked snippet retrieved by search engine as the local search result of query. A Snippet is a short fragment of text extracted from the document content [18].

3.3. *Co-information Metric*

Feature information interaction or co-information as it was named in [19] is based on McGill's multivariate generalization of Shannon's mutual information. It describes the information that is shared by all of *k* random variables, without over-counting redundant information in attribute subsets. As for a sub-query generated by the original query, the Co-Information between its terms can be used to measure the information bound up in those terms. The more information bound up one sub-query has, the higher possibility to be a context candidate it has. Thus, we define this information-theoretic measure as follows:

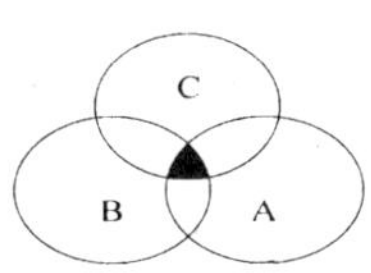

Figure1. How informative are A & B together?

For n events x_{1i}, x_{2j}, ..., x_{nl} we define the co-information, CI, between them I (x_{1i} ; x_{2j} ; ...; x_{nl}) by:

$$I(x_{1i}; x_{2j}; ...; x_{nl}) = \sum_{|v'| \subseteq |T'|} (-1)^{|v'|-|T'|} \log(p(T)) . \tag{1}$$

Another interesting point about Co-information is that it results in positive and negative values, which represent two different types of feature interactions [20]:

- *Positive Co-information: Synergy:* In case of positive co-information the process benefits from an unexpected synergy in the data. Synergy occurs when *A* and *B* are statistical independent, but get dependent in the context of *C*.
- *Negative Co-information: Redundancy:* Negative co-information occurs when attributes partly contribute redundant information in the context of another attribute, which leads to a reduction of the overall dependence.

3.4. *Thematic Context Detection*

To identify the current thematic context of the user we first build the probability space, where each term has probability and joint probability with other terms. Because one sub-query is the joint of terms, the joint probability of several terms can be equal to the probability of the sub-query. In our approach, the probability space of one query is built based on the local results of all sub-queries.

Given a query Q = t_1 t_2 ...t_n, where t_i (1<= i <=n) is the ith term of Q, we obtain the Thematic Context Words as follows:

a) Get the set of all sub-queries, SQ = {sq_k}, 1<=k<=2^{n+1}-2, where 1<=k<=2^{n+1}-2 is the number of all sub-queries and 2^n-2 = $S^1_n + S^2_n + ... + S^{n-1}_n$

b) Enrich each sub-query by submitting it into search engine and get the top N ranked snippets. In this way, we can get (2^n-2). N* snippets for query q. The snippet set is defined as S(Q) = {sn_i}, 1<=i<=(2^n-2). N*, where sn_i is the ith snippet. N* = min(N, N'), where N' is the actual number of retrieved snippets by search engine for each query.

c) The probability of sub-query in S (Q) is defined as:

$$p(sq_k) = \sum_{i=1}^{(2n-2).N^*} (sq_k \text{ can be found in } sn_i)/(2^n - 2).N^* \quad (2)$$

where p (sq_k) is the probability of occurrence of sq_k in collection.

d) As for sq_k , we get its sub-query set, which is defined as:
$SQ_k = \{sq_{k1}, sq_{k2}, \ldots sq_{k2^k-2}\}$. According to the theory of Co- information we mentioned in the previous section, CI value of sq_k is:

$$I(sq_k) = \sum_{|sq_k| - |sq_{kj}|} (-1)^{|sq_k| - |sq_{kj}|} \log(p(sq_{kj})) \quad (3)$$

e) Order all sub-queries in a descendant value of Co-information and split it into two parts by the threshold of zero. In other words, the first part includes the sub-queries with positive CI (Synergy) and the last part includes the sub-queries with negative CI (Redundancy).

f) Finally, the list of context words we detected from SQ is defined as: Thematic Context Words, C = { C_1, C_2, …., C_i,…C_M }, where C_i is one sub-query which has positive CI and M is the total number, and $I(C_i) >= 0$, $I(C_i)>=I(C_{i-1})$, $1<= i<=M$.

4. Query Transformation Statistics

The analysis of query transformation statistics was restricted to web queries as it was assumed that they would show the greatest variety of mechanisms. The queries were recorded in the log in chronological order. Our whole data set, including 8,510,059 query pairs, comes from the query log of a common used commercial search engine. Each query pair contains two queries, where the first one is the original query and the other one is the query reformulated by a user in a session. Three data sets are extracted, corresponding to three categories of reformulations, where Set A contains query term deletion, Set B contains query term substitution, and Set C contains query term expansion. According to the statistical data, the proportions of three categories (A, B and C) are 20%, 32% and 48%. As for each query pair (q, r) in data Set A and Set B, q is used to detect context and r is used to analyze the relation between context and user behaviors. As for each query pair (q, r) in data Set C, r is used to detect context and q is used to analyze the relation between thematic context and user behaviors. After detecting context, three precisions related to the query reformulation are defined as follows:

$$P(A) = \frac{\#\text{user delete or retain context in original query}}{|A|}$$

where P(A) measures the precision of Set A. Similarly, we can measure the precision of Set B, C, and overall. The results of the three Sets and the overall precision are shown in Table 1.

Table 1. Results

	Set A	Set B	Set C	Overall
Precision	0.77	0..81	0.87	0.82

The analysis is as follows:

- 77% users choose to retain the context or delete context when they implement query term deletion. For Example, a query such as "World wide web 2.0" to "World wide web", where "World wide web" is detected as a thematic context using our approach.
- 81% users choose to retain the context or replace it with query term substitution. Such as "aishwarya rai marriage picture" to "indian marriage picture", where "aishwarya rai" and "marriage picture" are detected as two topics by our approach;
- As 87% users' reformulated queries, the original queries were still in context, i.e, users still focus on the original query though some additional information.
- On an average, 82% users reformulate queries at the contextual level.

5. Conclusion

Query Reformulation is an important part for understanding the interplay of Web information retrieval. In this paper, we study the query reformulation problem and provide an empirical evidence to analyze the relation between the user's reformulation behavior and the thematic contexts in the original query. Two major contributions of the research done are: (1) Information-theory based Co-information (CI) metric is utilized to measure the degree of a sub-query being a thematic context word and a context detection algorithm is proposed and validated by building a probability space based on the local search results of its all sub-queries from each original query; (2) we analyze user reformulation behavior based on query log, at the contextual level. The experiments show that on an average 82% user tend to reformulate queries at the contextual level, where the context is detected by our approach. Meanwhile, it also indicates that our CI-based algorithm is a good approach to detect thematic context from the original query.

References

1. J.J. Rocchio, "Relevance feedback in information retrieval", In: G. Salton (ed.), The Smart retrieval system: Experiments in automatic document processing, Prentice Hall, pp. 313-323 (1971).
2. Ruthven, I. and Lalmas, M., "A survey on the use of relevance feedback for information access systems", Knowledge Engineering Review, 18 (2). pp. 95-145. ISSN 0269-8889.
3. Vishwa Vinay, Ken Wood, Natasa Milic-Frayling, Ingemar J. Cox, "Comparing relevance feedback algorithms for web search", Special interest tracks and posters of the 14th international conference on World Wide Web, May 10-14,Chiba, Japan (2005).
4. Pertti Vakkari, Susan Jones, Andy MacFarlane, Eero Sormunen, "Query exhaustivity, relevance feedback and search success in automatic and interactive query expansion", Journal of Documentation, Vol. 60, issue 2, pp.109 – 127, ISSN: 0022-0418, DOI:10.1108/00220410410522016, Emerald Group Publishing Limited (2004).
5. Xu, J. and Croft, W.B., "Query expansion using local and global document analysis", 1996. SIGIR (1996).
6. Xu, J. and Croft, W.B., "Improving the effectiveness of information retrieval with local context analysis", ACM Transactions on Information Systems Vol.18, No.1, Pages 79-112 (2000).
7. Bhatia, MPS, & Khalid, Akshi K. "The Context-driven Generation of Web Search", Proceedings of CISTM, pp 281-287 (2008).
8. Buckley, C., Salton, G. and Allan, J., "The effect of adding information in a relevance feedback environment", Conference on Research and development in Information Retrieval (SIGIR) (1994).
9. Eguchi, K., "Incremental query expansion using local information of clusters", Proceedings of the 4th World Multiconference on systemics, Cybernetics and informatics (SCI 2000), 2, pp 310-316.
10. Furnas, G. W., Landauer, T. K., Gomez, L. M., and Dumais, S. T, "The vocabulary problem in human-system communication", Comunications of the ACM, 30(11), pp. 964–971(1987).
11. Christopher D. Manning, Prabhakar Raghavan and Hinrich Schütze, "Introduction to Information Retrieval", Cambridge University Press. ISBN: 0521865719 (2008).
12. Qiu, Y. and Frei, H. P., "Concept based query expansion", In Proceedings of ACM SIGIR International Conference on Research and Development in Information Retrieval, ACM Press, 160-170 (1993)
13. Jing, Y. F. and Croft, W. B., "An Association Thesaurus for Information Retrieval", In RIAO 94 Conference Proceedings, p. 146-160, New York, Oct. (1994).
14. Crouch, C. J., and Yang, B., "Experiments in automatic statistical thesaurus construction", In Proceeding of ACM SIGIR International Conference on Research and Development in Information Retrieval, pp. 77-88 (1993).
15. R. Baeza-Yates and B. Ribeiro-Neto, "Modern Information Retrieval", Addison Wesley (1999).
16. Buckley, C., Singhal, A., Mitra, M., and Salton, G., "New Retrieval Approaches Using SMART: TREC 4", In Harman, D., editor, Proceedings of the TREC 4 Conference. National Institute of Standards and Technology Special Publication. (1996).
17. iProspect.com, inc., "iProspect Search Engine User Behavior Study" http://www.iprospect.com/premiumPDFs/WhitePaper_2006_SearchEngineUserBehavior.pdf (April 2006).
18. Andrew Turpin, Yohannes Tsegay, David Hawking, Hugh E. Williams, "Fast generation of result snippets in web search", Proceedings of the 30th annual international ACM SIGIR conference on Research and development in information retrieval, July 23-27, Amsterdam, The Netherlands [doi>10.1145/1277741.1277766] (2007).
19. A.J. Bell, "The Co-Information Lattice", 4th Int. Symposium on Independent Component Analysis and blind Signal Separation (ICA2003), pp. 921-926 (2003).

20. Kludas, J., Bruno, E., & Marchand-Maillet, S, "Can Feature Information Interaction help for Information Fusion in Multimedia Problems?", Multimedia Tools and Applications Journal special issue on Metadata Mining for Image Understanding, DOI: 10.1007/s11042-008-0251-y.

BDL – BEHAVIOR DESCRIPTION LANGUAGE

LI WAN
Computer school, Wuhan University,
Wuhan, Hubei, China

GUOQING WU
Computer school, Wuhan University,
Wuhan, Hubei, China

HUAIGUANG WU
Computer school, Wuhan University,
Wuhan, Hubei, China

Formal methods are particular kind of mathematically-based techniques for the specification, development and verification of software and hardware systems. However, the high cost of using formal methods restricts the popularization of formal methods. In this paper, we propose an easily wielded formal description language — Behavior Description Language (BDL). The syntax and semantics of BDL are elaborated. A case study is presented to embody the expressiveness and flexibility of BDL.

1. Introduction

In computer science and software engineering, formal methods are mathematically-based languages, techniques and tools for the specification, development and verification of software and hardware systems [1]. The use of formal methods for software and hardware design is motivated by the expectation that, as in other engineering disciplines, performing appropriate mathematical analyses can contribute to the reliability and robustness of a design.

Over the years, lots of works have been done, with a focus on formal modeling and verification technologies. CSP [1] and CCS [2] are designed for describe concurrent system. Both of them are process algebra. LOTOS is a standard formal description technique used in Distributed System and Communication System [3]. It consists of two parts: abstract data type for dealing with data space and process algebra for handling complexity of concurrency. Z notation is a formal specification language based on set theory and first-order predicate [4]. States are described in terms of mathematical structures such as sets, relations, and functions. The B-Method is a collection of mathematical techniques based on set theory, first-order logic and generalized substitution [5]. Systems are modeled as a collection of interdependent Abstract Machines, for which an object-based approach is employed at all stages of development.

However, it is now widely accepted that formal methods are hard to popularize. The strict mathematical definitions and complex notations of the existing formal methods make it difficult for users to grasp.

In this paper, we propose an easy-to-promote formal description language - Behavior Description Language (BDL). We draw out behaviors of the system and formalize them into BDL. Find out all actions and behaviors of the target system. Describe effective ones into atom behaviors of BDL. Construct atom behaviors into compound behaviors based on a series of rules compound ones if needed. A system could be described by a abstract and compound behavior.

The rest of this paper is organized as follows. Section 2 introduces the syntax of BDL while section 3 details the semantics of BDL. In Section 5, a case study is presented. Conclusions and future works are discussed in the last section.

2. Syntax of BDL

2.1. *Behavior of software*

A behavior is an operation or an action that a subject imposes on an object. The behaviors of software refer to the states transfer when the software is running. The correctness of software behaviors determines whether the software could meet the purpose which it was intended. The properties of the software, such as safety, can be verified by software behaviors. Modeling a requirements model that strictly describes behaviors is beneficial to check varies of properties of software.

Following steps illustrate a general process to build a behavior model from requirements in nature language.

1. Find out all actions and their subjects and objects. We deem an action together with its subject and object as an atom behavior.
2. Filter out ineffective behaviors that are not closely related to requirements.
3. Analysis relationships between behaviors. The relationship could be sequence, parallel, non-deterministic choice or deterministic choice.
4. Construct compound behaviors based on effective atom behaviors and other compound behaviors.
5. A system can be expressed by a behavior expression. A behavior expression is also a compound behavior.

2.2. *Atom behavior*

Atom behavior is the basic element of BDL that cannot be subdivided. We put forward three kinds of atom behaviors:

ABehID: f(SUB , OBJ [&obj_description])
[$(x_1,x_2,\ldots\ldots, x_n)$]
[**WHEN** precondition]
[**INFROM** (ID_i)$(u_1,u_2\ldots..,u_n)$]
[**OUTTO** (ID_o)$(v_1,v_2\ldots..,v_m)$]; (4)

ABehID: IDLE; (5)

ABehID: RETURN ([ABehID]) ; (6)

ABehID is the identification of an atom behavior.

Expression (4) is an executable behavior which describes a requirements process.

f could be a service, an operation or an action that the **SUB** executes and work upon **OBJ**.

SUB is the subject of the behavior. The **SUB** could be a user or an entity in certain domain that executes the behavior. It could also be composite users or entities in the case that the behavior has multiple subjects. Yet the **SUB** should be determined when an atom behavior is declared.

OBJ is the object of the behavior. The **OBJ** could be a user or an entity in certain domain that the effect of behavior is put on it. It could also be composite users or entities in the case that the behavior has multiple objects. When an atom behavior is declared, the **OBJ** could be undetermined, in which case we label it with notation "?" and the parameter list would be empty.

Parameter list $x_1,x_2,\ldots\ldots, x_n$ is data that the current behavior receives from other behaviors. The elements of parameter list are correspond to parameters in **INFORM** clause.

An atom behavior with "**WHEN**" clause represents that the behavior **AbehID** would occur when precondition is true, and would be skiped when precondition is false.

INFROM clause indicates that **AbehID** receives n input parameters u_1, u_2, ..., u_n from **IDi**. According to requirements, **IDi** could be following candidates:

• ABehID: receive parameters from other atom behavior ABehID within viewpoint.

•ABehID.SUB: receive parameters from the SUB of ABehID.

•ABehID.OBJ: receive parameters from the OBJ of ABehID.

•#: receive parameters from storage pool of current viewpoint.

OUTTO clause illustrates that AbehID sends m output parameters v_1, $v_2\ldots..$, v_m to **IDo**. **IDo** includes all candidates of **IDi**, and it could also have the following case:

•#VPID: **AbehID** send parameters to the storage pool of some other viewpoint VPID.

A simple example is given as follow:

Assuming that a requirement item is "Jack gives a book and 10$ to John". The description in BDL could be:

ABehGive: Give(Jack, John)
OUTTO (ABehReceive) (book, 10$);
ABehReceive: Receive(John, Jack)(x, y)
INFROM(ABehGive)(book, money);

Expression (5) defines an empty behavior. While waiting for some event to happen, a compound behavior would stay in **IDLE** behavior.

In expression (6), **RETURN** behavior can transfer the process and jump to ABehID. If the parameter is empty, it just finishes the current compound behavior.

2.3. *Compound behavior*

The following expressions present the syntax of behavior expression.

1. Compound behavior composed of atom behavior.

1) |— ABehID;

2) Sequence behavior:

$$\frac{|-ABehID_1 \& |-ABehID_2}{|-ABehID_1; ABehID_2}$$

3) Parallel behavior:

$$\frac{|-ABehID_1 \& |-ABehID_2}{|-ABehID_1 \| ABehID_2}$$

4) Non-deterministic choice behavior:

$$\frac{|-ABehID_1 \& |-ABehID_2}{|-ABehID_1 + ABehID_2}$$

5) Deterministic choice behavior:

$$\frac{|-ABehID_1 \& |-ABehID_2 \& b \text{ is a bool expression}}{|-If\ b\ Then\ ABehID_1\ Else\ ABehID_2\ Fi}$$

6) Multi-subject behavior:

a. $$\frac{|-ABehID_1 \& ABehID_1'\text{s } sub = sub_1 \wedge sub_2}{|-ABehID_{11}\ \ OP\ \ ABehID_{12}}$$

b. $$\frac{|-ABehID_1 \& ABehID_1'\text{s } sub = sub_1 \vee sub_2}{|-ABehID_{11}\ \ OP\ \ ABehID_{12}}$$

Note: the subject of $ABheID_{11}$ and $ABheID_{12}$ are sub_1 and sub_2 respectively。

OP could be "; ", "||" or "+".

7) Multi-object behavior:

a. $$\frac{|-ABehID_1 \& ABehID_1'\text{s } obj = obj_1 \wedge obj_2}{|-ABehID_{11}\ \ OP\ \ ABehID_{12}}$$

b. $$\frac{|-ABehID_1 \& ABehID_1'\text{s } obj = obj_1 \vee obj_2}{|-ABehID_{11}\ \ OP\ \ ABehID_{12}}$$

Note: the object of ABheID11 and ABheID12 are obj1 and obj2 respectively。

OP could be "; ", "||" or "+".

8) Restrict behavior:

a. $$\frac{|-BehID \& |-ABehID}{|-BehID/ABehID}$$

b. $$\frac{|-BehID \& |-BehID_1}{|-BehID/BehID_1}$$

2. Compound behavior composed of compound behavior.

1) $$\frac{|-BehID_1 \& |-BehID_2 \& .....\& |-BehID_n}{|-BehID_1 + BehID_2 + ... + BehID_n}$$

2) $$\frac{|-BehID_1 \& |-BehID_2 \& .....\& |-BehID_n}{|-BehID_1; BehID_2;...; BehID_n}$$

3) $$\frac{|-BehID_1 \& |-BehID_2 \& .....\& |-BehID_n}{|-BehID_1 \| BehID_2 \| ... \| BehID_n}$$

4) $$\frac{|-BehID_1 \& |-ABehID}{|-BehID_1; ABehID}$$

5) $$\frac{|-ABehID \& |-BehID_1}{|-ABehID; BehID_1}$$

6) $$\frac{|-BehID_1 \& |-BehID_2 \& b \text{ is a bool expression}}{|-If\ b\ Then\ BehID_1\ Else\ BehID_2\ Fi}$$

3. Semantics of BDL

Assuming B and B_i are compound behaviors. ABehID, α and α_i are the notation of atom behavior. We use operational semantics to describe the evolution of a behavior. We present a set of rules below to give a precise meaning to each operator.

1.Sequence behavior:

1)If ABehID is the first atom behavior in B and also ABehID has no parameter, or the object of ABehID is undetermined, or ABehID is the last behavior of compound behavior, we have the following transition:

$$B \xrightarrow{ABehID} B'$$

2)When ABehID(x1,x2,........, xn) is the first atom behavior with parameter in B, we have:

$$B \xrightarrow{ABehID(v_1,...v_n)} B'$$

3)When the first behavior in B is IDLE, we have:

$$B \xrightarrow{Idle} B$$

2.Non-deterministic choice behavior:

1) $$\frac{B_1 \xrightarrow{\alpha} B_1'}{B_1 + B_2 \xrightarrow{\alpha} B_1'}$$

2) $$\frac{B_2 \xrightarrow{\alpha} B_2'}{B_1 + B_2 \xrightarrow{\alpha} B_2'}$$

3.Parallel behavior:

$$1)\ \frac{B_1 \xrightarrow{\alpha} B_1'}{B_1 \| B_2 \xrightarrow{\alpha} B_1' \| B_2}$$

$$2)\ \frac{B_2 \xrightarrow{\alpha} B_2'}{B_1 \| B_2 \xrightarrow{\alpha} B_1 \| B_2'}$$

4.Deterministic choice behavior:

$$1)\ \frac{B_1 \xrightarrow{\alpha} B_1',\ b \text{ is true}}{If\ b\ Then\ B_1\ Else\ B_2\ Fi \rightarrow B_1'{}_1}$$

$$2)\ \frac{B_2 \xrightarrow{\alpha} B_2',\ b \text{ is false}}{If\ b\ Then\ B_1\ Else\ B_2\ Fi \rightarrow B_2'}$$

5.Restrict behavior:

$$1)\ \frac{B \xrightarrow{\alpha} B'}{B/\beta \rightarrow B'/\beta}(\beta \neq \alpha)$$

$$2)\ \frac{B \xrightarrow{\alpha_1 \dots \alpha_n} B'}{B/B_1 \rightarrow B'/B_1}(\alpha_1;\dots;\alpha_n \neq B_1)$$

4. Case study

In order to illustrate how to describe a system in BDL, we provide an example of an Automatic Teller Machine (ATM) system in this section as a case study.

A bank intends to develop an ATM system. The system is composed of a head bank, several ATMs and local banks.

Every user has a bank card which records local bank code and card number. When a user inserts bank card and queries some account information at ATM, ATM will sends card information and password to head bank. The head bank then sends these data to corresponding local bank according to local bank code in card information. After the local bank has finished validated, the head bank will transfer the result from local bank to ATM.

Here we give a description of the head bank:

```
HeadBank   //scenario of head bank.
 BEGIN
ABEH:
 Hbank1:  possess(HeadBank, ATM).
 Hbank2:  compose(LocalBank, HeadBank).
 Hidle :  idle() ;  //wating for request from ATM or
                    //response from local bank.

//receive request from a ATM or response from a local
bank.
Hreceive: ReceiveATMRequest(HeadBank, request of
ATM)
OUTTo  (VPdatacell) (response type))

//receive verification request of ATM
Hresponse: Response (HeadBank, ith ATM)
 OUTTo  (VPdatacell) (ATM number)

// HeadBank receive the card information and password
from ith ATM
Hreceive1: Receive (HeadBank, ATM)(Card Info,
 Password)
 When   ATM number= i
 INFrom (VPdatacell) (Card Info, Password)
//Discern the Local bank number of the card
Discern: Discern(HeadBank,  Card Info)
OUTTo(VPdatacell) (LocalBank number);
//HeadBank sends card info, password and verification
      request to correspond LocalBank.
TranRequest1:  TransRequest(HeadBank, jth
LocalBank)(LocalBank number)
When   LocalBank number = j
INFrom (VPdatacell) (LocalBank number)
OUTTo  (#LocalBank) (Card Info, Password)

//HeadBank receive the verification result
RecRespon1:  Receive (HeadBank,  jth
LocalBank)(Verification Result)
When   LocalBank number= j
INFrom (VPdatacell) (Verification Result);
//HeadBank send the result to ATM
Tranresult1: Send(HeadBank, ith ATM)(ATM number,
LocalBank number)
When   ATM number= i and LocalBank number= j
INFrom (VPdatacell) (ATM number, LocalBank
number)
OUTTo  (#ATM) (Verification result);

//HeadBank receive the business request from ATM
Hreceive2: receive(HeadBank, ith ATM)(Business
 type)
 When   ATM number= i
 INFrom (VPdatacell) (Business type, Business Info)
TranRequest2:  Send(HeadBank, jth LocalBank)
(LocalBank number)
When   LocalBank number = j
INFrom (VPdatacell) (LocalBank number)
OUTTo  (#LocalBank) (Card Info, business type,
Business info)
//HeadBank receive result from LocalBank
RecRespon2:  receive(HeadBank, jth
LocalBank)(Business result)
When   LocalBank number = j
INFrom (VPdatacell) (Business result);
// HeadBank  send result to ATM
Tranresult2: Send(HeadBank, ith ATM)( ATM number,
```

```
LocalBank number)
When   ATM number = i and LocalBank number = j
INFrom (VPdatacell) (ATM number, LocalBank
number)
OUTTo  (#ATM) (Business result);
Returnto:  Return(Hidle);

BEH:
  BEHHeadBank =
   Hbank1;
      Hbank2;
      Hidle;
 If Response type= ATM request type
       Then Behhbank1;
  Else Behhbank2;
 Fi
 Returnto;
  Behhbank1=
      Hresponse;
      If Verification type
       Then Hreceive1;
             Discern;
             TranRequest1;

    Else //Receive business request of ATM
             Hreceive2;
             TranRequest2;
       Fi;

  Behhbank2=
      If Response verification request
 Then //Send result to ATM
 RecRespon1;
      Tranresult1;

    Else //Send LocalBand responds info to ATM
    RecRespon2;
      Tranresult2;
       Fi;
END
```

5. Conclusion

In this paper, we have shown a new formal description language — BDL, which modeling the behavior of the target system directly. We have introduced the syntax and semantics of BDL briefly and proposed a modeling process based on BDL to handle large scale and complex system. A simple example was presented as a case study to show how to use BDL more clearly.

However, there are still several challenges to be tackled in our work. Our short term goal is doing some verification works on BDL. We have proposed a series of verification methods based on BDL, such as behavior legality, behavior consistency, behavior continuity and etc. These works are in progress.

Another further work would be transforming other non-formal models or semi-formal models to BDL, such as data flow chart and state chart in UML. So we can validate these models formally using our model.

Although we have not yet tested our method and BDL in any large industrial setting, the feedback from the case study we have performed has been very encouraging. The BDL has proved useful and convenient to describe a system. Thus, though a number of problems remain to be explored, we believe our work, at the very least, has clarified our research agenda. Acknowledgments

Acknowledgments

This work is supported by Chinese National 863 High-Tech Research and Development Projects, contract number: 2007AA01Z185.

References

1. S. D. Brookes, C. A. R, and A. W. Roscoe, "A Theory of Communicating Sequential Processes", Journal of the ACM (JACM), vol. 31, pp. 560-599, 1984.
2. [2] R. Milner, "A Calculus of Communicating Systems", Springer-Verlag New York, Inc, 1982.
3. [3] T. Bolognesi and E. Brinksma, "Introduction to the ISO specification language LOTOS", Computer Networks and ISDN Systems, vol. 14, pp. 25-59, 1987.
4. [4] J. M. Spivey, "Understanding Z: a specification language and its formal semantics", Cambridge University Press, 1988.
5. [5] J. R. Abrial, "The B-book: assigning programs to meanings",Cambridge University Press, 1996.
6. [6] B. H. Cheng and J. M. Atlee, "Research directions in requirements engineering," FOSE 2007: FUTURE OF SOFTWARE ENGINEERING, pp. 285-303, 2007.

APPLYING SOFL TO CONSTRUCT THE FORMAL SPECIFICATION OF AN AUTOMOBILE DRIVING SIMULATION SYSTEM *

A.RAHMAN MAT

Department of Computer & Information Sciences, Hosei University
Tokyo, Japan

SHAOYING LIU

Department of Computer & Information Sciences, Hosei University
Tokyo, Japan

The SOFL three-step approach to the construction of formal specifications has been proposed and applied in information systems, but its effectiveness and applicability have not yet been demonstrated in developing safety-critical systems. In this paper, we describe an application of the SOFL approach to the construction of a formal specification for the obstacle-avoiding function of an automatic automobile driving simulation system. This case study demonstrates the suitability of SOFL for safety-critical system developments and provides us with an insight into the knowledge of how the SOFL three-step specification approach can be effectively supported.

1. Introduction

The Structured Object-Oriented Formal Language (SOFL) three-step approach to the construction of formal specifications for software systems has been developed and applied in information systems over the last fifteen years [1][2]. Compared to well-known formal methods, such as VDM [3], B method [4] and Larch [5], SOFL has many distinct advantages, mainly because it offers effective ways to integrate formal methods into the entire process of software engineering, which allows practitioners to easily apply formal methods in real software projects. In particular, the SOFL three-step specification approach is one of the many important features of the SOFL method. It emphasizes the fact that constructing a formal specification for design of a system significantly contributes to the quality assurance of the system and the importance of a progressive process for achieving it. According to the progressive process, the formal design specification can be achieved in three steps [1]. The first is to build an informal specification, documenting the major functions, necessary data resources, and constraints (e.g., safety, security, policy). The second is to transform the informal specification to a semi-formal specification which is more precise than the informal one and organized in a modular fashion. The third step is to build a completely formal specification for design on the basis of the semiformal specification by defining the architecture of the system and then defining all the components involved in the architecture using a mathematically-based notation.

While there is sufficient evidence, resulting from many applications, to suggest that the SOFL three-step specification approach be effective in ensuring software quality and reducing development cost for information systems, it has not been sufficiently demonstrated that SOFL is also suitable for the development of safety-critical systems. In this paper, we present a case study applying SOFL to formally specify the obstacle-avoiding function of an automatic automobile driving simulation system [6]. Particularly, we concentrate on the description of how to write the informal specification, how to transform it into the semi-formal specification, and finally how to form the formal design specification based on the semi-formal one. The case study demonstrates the suitability of SOFL for safety-critical system development and provides us with an insight into the knowledge of how the SOFL three-step specification approach can be effectively supported.

The remainder of the paper is organized as follows. Section 2 describes the background of an obstacle-avoiding system adopted in an automatic automobile driving system. Section 3 gives a brief introduction to

* This work is supported by the Ministry of Education, Culture, Sports, Science and Technology of Japan under Grant-in-Aid for Scientific Research (No. 18500027).

the SOFL three-step specification approach which we used in the case study. Section 4 discusses how the SOFL approach is applied in writing the specifications for the obstacle-avoiding system. Section 5 describes our experience and lessons learned from this project. A brief overview of related work is given in Section 6. Finally, in Section 7 we conclude the paper and provide several suggestions for future research.

2. An Obstacle-Avoiding System

Obstacle-avoiding system is required by an automatic automobile driving simulation system (AADSS). Using AADSS we can simulate the situation of an automatic driving automobile on the road. Since there are various possible obstacles on the road, the automatic driving automobile needs to avoid them in order to ensure its safety. Of course, the avoiding system should not merely simply stop the automobile on the road, rather it should allow the automobile to move forward as long as the situation permits. To build a formal specification for such an obstacle-avoiding system to analyze its functional behaviors and safety properties early, we first need to explain the mechanism of the system used in our case study.

2.1. *System Mechanism*

The obstacle-avoiding system contains three distinct types of objects: *MyCar*, *Obstacle*, and *Non-obstacle objects*. MyCar is the main actor of the system. During the journey from the initial location to the destination, MyCar keeps collecting information from its environment, including the road boundary and the distance between the car and any obstacles detected by the sensors installed on MyCar. The information is used to indicate the detection of an obstacle that might prevent the progress of MyCar. Once the sensors have detected an obstacle, the obstacle avoidance system is applied. Furthermore, in the situation where MyCar approaches a corner, for example, and there is no obstacle in the environment, a *route change system* is applied. In this case, MyCar will continue to move normally if no problem arises. An Obstacle can be a static obstacle, such as a big stone, fallen tree, or a broken-down car, or a dynamic obstacle, such as a slow vehicle in front of MyCar or a pedestrian crossing the road. However, objects such as traffic lights, white lines separating lanes on the road, police officers, and road features are classified as Non-obstacle objects. This classification of obstacle information is very useful to MyCar for the purpose of complying with Japanese traffic rule and regulations.

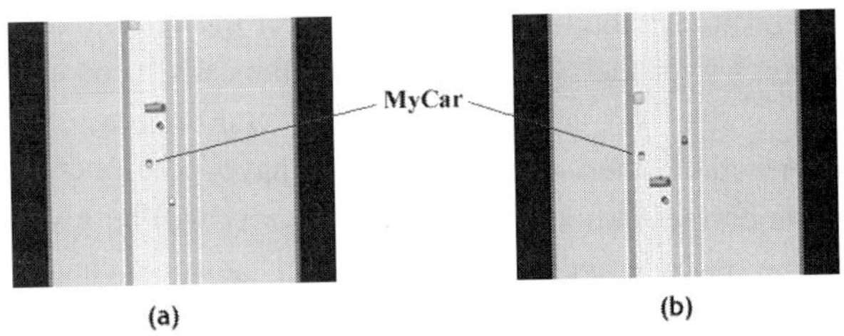

Figure 1. Obstacles on the Road.

2.2. *Avoiding Functions*

The situations where the obstacle-avoiding system, route change system, and acceleration are applied are as follows: (1) when an obstacle is on the road, (2) when traffic lights are installed at a crossing, and (3) when MyCar is turning at an intersection. In the first situation, as shown in Figure 1(a), during driving the sensor installed on MyCar detects an obstacle (e.g., a fallen tree) ahead and sends the information to the obstacle avoidance system to take appropriate action. In judging the situation, the system discovers three points: (1) MyCar has to avoid the obstacle, (2) other sensors have not detected any dangerous obstacle coming from behind or beside MyCar, and (3) once it has confirmed that it is safe to turn, MyCar can change to another lane, avoiding the obstacle, and continue driving. In accordance with Japanese traffic rules, the car should keep left when it is not overtaking, but when meeting an obstacle ahead, it can turn to the left lane if it is applicable. At the same time, the system should also calculate the distance between the obstacle and MyCar. If the system confirms that the distance to the obstacle is sufficiently far, and there is no other obstacle behind, MyCar changes back to the safe lane and keeps on moving forward normally, as shown in Figure 1(b).

In the second situation, as shown in Figure 2(a), when the traffic light is red, MyCar has to stop and wait until the light changes to green. Once the light changes to green, MyCar should use the obstacle avoidance system to turn right, as shown in Figure 2(b).

In the third situation, as shown in Figure 3, when MyCar turns to the left or right (and maybe for U-turns), both the obstacle avoidance system and the route change system will be activated. After the car has turned, there might be a situation in which the car has traveled along various stretches of the road, passed over a white line, and protruded a little from the road. For this reason, it is necessary for the system to calculate the car's speed and the width of the road before approaching the intersection; then, the system will have performed a more correct move with the data. Priority will be given to the obstacle avoidance system over the route change system when both tasks need to be fulfilled at the same time. This means that after the obstacle has been evaded, the route change system will operates immediately.

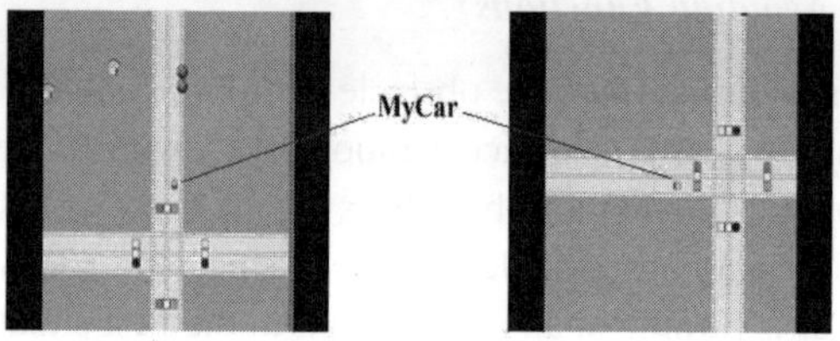

Figure 2. Traffic lights installed at the crossing.

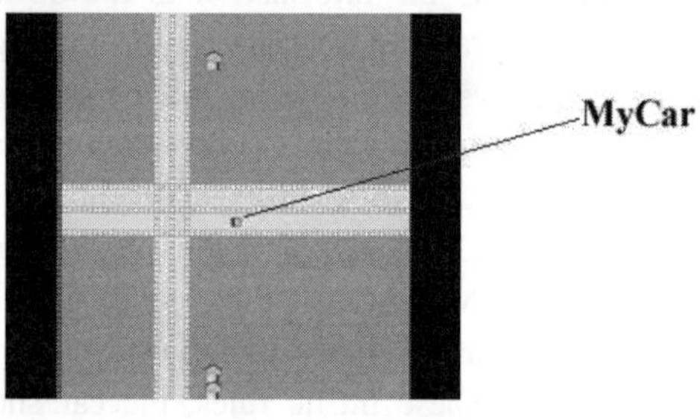

Figure 3. Turning left at an intersection.

3. Brief Introduction to SOFL

SOFL is a formal engineering method that offers a systematic way to develop software systems using an intuitive but formal notation. The notation results from an effective integration of VDM-SL [7], Petri Nets [8], and Data Flow Diagrams [9]. It provides a hierarchical condition data flow diagram (CDFD) as a mechanism for defining system architecture while allowing formal specifications for processes involved in the CDFD to be expressed using pre- and post-conditions in modules. Each level of a CDFD hierarchy is associated with a specification module in which all components of the CDFD, including processes, data flows, and data stores, are formally defined. The diagram remains at a high level of abstraction, describing interactions between processes in terms of data flows and data stores, while the module specification concentrates on the details of the components. To facilitate the process of achieving such a formal specification, SOFL offers a three-step specification approach, which consists of informal specification, semi-formal specification, and formal specification. Each stage of the specification has its own objective and task. In the informal specification, the objective is to enable the developer to fully understand and cover all the desired requirements of the domain problem through communication with the client. Constructing the semi-formal specification allows the developer to clarify the ambiguities in the informal specification and to better understand the relationships among the functions and data resources, as well as the constraints. The formal specification, however, forces the developer to clarify ambiguities in functionality, and serves as a platform for system implementation and verification. For verification and validation, SOFL adopts rigorous inspection [10] and testing [11].

An important feature of the SOFL three-step specification approach is that it defines the specific tasks for each stage of specification. In the first step, an informal specification is written, aiming to reflect the result of an informal requirements analysis on the basis of domain knowledge and available materials. Such a specification consists of three parts: (1) functional description which describes the high-level operations needed for the system, (2) data resources which indicate data items necessary for fulfilling the functions given in (1), and (3) constraints on both operations and data resources. At this stage, the descriptions of the operations, data resources, and constraints are written in a natural language. The second step is to transform the entire informal specification into a semi-formal specification. At this level, all functions, data resources, and constraints are transformed into appropriate expressions in the SOFL specification language, except that all logical expressions, such as type invariants and pre-post expressions for processes, are still kept informal. Finally, the third step is to transform the semi-formal specification into a formal specification. In this step, the system architecture is designed and expressed using CDFDs, and all the informal expressions of type invariants and process specifications in the semi-formal specification are formalized properly.

4. Specifications for the Obstacle-Avoiding System

In this section, we discuss how the SOFL three-step specification approach is applied to the modeling of the obstacle-avoiding system introduced in Section 2.

4.1. *Informal Specification*

The process of developing an informal specification requires continuous communication and interaction between the client and the software developer for better understanding of the domain and requirement analysis. Following the SOFL method, we concentrated on the capturing of desired system functions, necessary data resources, and required constraints.

The construction of the informal specification of the obstacle-avoiding system is based on our own knowledge and experience of driving a car. In general, in order to avoid an obstacle, the car should have a capability to make a decision for appropriate operations which will take place after the car sends a corresponding signal to steering and pedal. Since different countries have different implementation of the traffic rules and regulations, therefore, the constraint of implementing this specification is applicable and based on the Japanese road rules and regulation. In addition, we took an evolutionary process to complete and finalize the specification. It means that, we have to revise and improve the informal specification for several times until it does exactly what is required accordance with the user's agreement.

As a result we completed the informal specification, as shown in Figure 4. There are seven major functions in which function 2 (Change_Lane_Controller), function 4 (Stop_Car_Controller), and function 5 (Reverse_Car_Controller) are decomposed into several lower-level functions: two decompositions each for function 2 and 4, respectively, and three decompositions for function 5. In the data resources part, there are three data items, and in the constraints part, there are three constraints, of which the second is decomposed into four more detailed situations.

Required functional services: Top-level module

1. Operations of Make_Decisions
2. Operations on Change_Lane_Controller
   2.1 Slow_For_Change_Lane
   2.2 Change_Lane
3. Operations of Slow_Down_Controller
4. Operations on Stop_Car_Controller
   4.1 Slow_For_Stop
   4.2 Stop_Car
5. Operations on Reverse_Car_Controller
   5.1 Slow_For_Stop_Reverse
   5.2 Stop_For_Reverse
   5.3 Reverse_Car
6. Operations of Operate_Steering
7. Operations of Operate_Pedal

Data resources

1. Sensors
2. System parameters
3. Data stores

Constraints

1. The decision is made on the basis of the speed and the position of the obstacles detected by various sensors installed in the car.
2. There are 12 sensors installed in the car:
   2.1 If sensors Number 2, 3, and 4 were activated, then the sensors detected an obstacle in front of the car; the car might decide to stop or to change lane.
   2.2 If sensors Number 5, 7, 9, and 12 were activated, then the sensors detected an obstacle on the right side of the car; the car might decides to slow down or stop.
   2.3 If sensors Number 1, 6, 8, and 10 were activated, then the sensors detected an obstacle on the left side of the car; the car might decide to slow down, change the lane, or stop.
   2.4 If sensors Number 10, 11, and 12 were activated, then the sensors detected an obstacle behind the car; the car might decide to increase its speed (if the obstacle is moving toward the car) or stop (if the obstacle is static).
3. The implementation of the specification would follows Japanese Traffic Rules and Regulations.

Figure 4. Informal specification of the obstacle-avoiding system.

4.2. *Semi-formal Specification*

In the construction of the semi-formal specification, we concentrated on grouping the related functions, data resources, and constraints into modules, and clarify ambiguties of the informal expressions by using the SOFL formal notation to define those items. We define several objects including Car, InstalledSensors, SensorsInformation and ObstacleAppearance as a composite types. As shown in Figure 5, MyCar, which is a car, is composed of six fields: the information about the car_speed, and set_speed, car_position for determining whether the car is on the left or on the right lane of the same direction, the information on current_lane and next_lane distance, and as well as the information collected from the sensors. The car has twelve sensors installed at certain positions to obtain information and detect obstacles on the road. The sensors provide three sorts of information: "state" for determining whether the sensors have detected an obstacle or not, "sensor_code" for providing information on which sensors are activating, and "sensor_information" for supplying information on the distance between MyCar and its surroundings. An obstacle may be a human, big_stone, broken_down_car, fallen_tree, animal, or something else.

In this stage, a CDFD is constructed to provide guidelines for formalizing the components of the system. At the same time, the CDFD describes the behavior of the modules in a hierarchical manner. Figure 6 shows the CDFD of the top-level module of the obstacle-avoiding system. In this diagram, once the sensors have detected an obstacle, MyCar has to make a decision: to change lane, slow down, stop or reverse. This decision is made on the basis of the position and speed of the obstacle. Thus the movement of the car will be affected by operating the steering wheel and the accelerator pedal. As an example of a decision on reversing the car, the parameters of back_info, which is information on obstacles behind the car collected by sensors, and speed_for_stop_reverse, which is the speed of the obstacle, would be the input. The result, after some processes inside the Reverse_Car_Controller, would inform the steering wheel and pedal to take actions to effect movement.

```
module Obstacle_Avoidance_Automatic_Car
type

MyCar = set of Car;

Car = composed of
      car_speed: real
      set_speed: real
      car_position: bool   /*true = left, false: right*/
      current_lane: real
      next_lane: real
      sensor: MyCarSensor
      end;

MyCarSensor = seq of InstalledSensors;

InstalledSensors = composed of
     state: bool            /* 1: on , 0: off */
     sensor_code: nat    /* which sensor is activated */
     sensor_info: SensorInformation
     end;

SensorInformation = composed of
     center_x: real
     center_y: real
     sensor_field: real
     width: real
     direction: real
     radius: real
     end;

ObstacleAppearance = composed of
     name: ObstacleName
     speed: real
     position: bool         /* true: left , false: right*/
     end;

ObstacleName = {<Human>, <Big_Stone>, <Other_Broken_Down_Car>, <Tree>, <Animal>,
                <Others>};
```

Figure 5. Partial specification of type definitions in the semi-formal specification

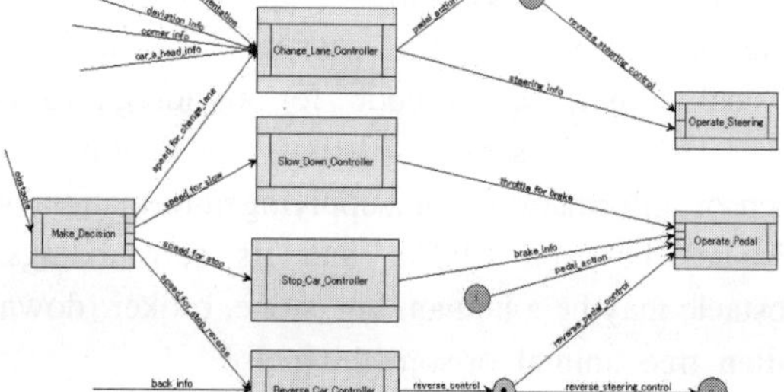

Figure 6. Top-level CDFD of the obstacle-avoiding system

4.3. *A Formal Design Specification*

Once an appropriate CDFD has been created for the design of the sytesm, it may contain new components in addition to the existing components of the CDFDs in the semi-formal specification. The goal of writing a formal design specification is to make the informal expressions in the semi-formal specification percise and to define the meaning of the new components. Specifically speaking, all necessary constant identifiers, types, variables, and invariants in a module must be formally define, a and all processes involved in the corresponding CDFD must be defined using pre- and post-conditions. Such a formal specification is expected to serve as a firm foundation for system validation and implementation.

In the case of our system, we formally specified the module called Change_Lane_Controller, as shown in Figure 7. In this module, two processes are needed: slowing the movement of the car (represented by Slow_For_Change_Lane) and Change_Lane. Since the post-condition of the process of Slow_For_Change_Lane would be equal to the process of Slow_Down_Controller, we could use the keyword "equal", provided by the SOFL language, to express the similarity. The process of Change_Lane needs five parameters as input and produces two outputs. Within this process, we use a condition-based SOFL specification to instruct the steering wheel and accelerator pedal regarding the movement of MyCar. In the case of applying the brake pedal, several parameters would be involved, such as "corner_info" (which represents the distances between MyCar and the left and right barriers), "slow_speed" (which represents the current speed of MyCar after the process of Slow_For_Change_Lane), and "car_a_head" (which represents the distance between MyCar and the vehicle in front of MyCar). Once satisfied, the system will instruct the pedal to brake and the information on braking will appear for notification. On the other hand, in case of MyCar steering to the right, only one piece of information might be needed for consideration (that is car_orientation) and two pieces of information might be needed for consideration, which are "car_orientation" (representing the orientation of the car with respect to the current lane or direction of the road) and "deviation_info" (representing the information on the angle between MyCar and the left and right edge of the road).

```
module Change_Lane_Controller_Decom / SYSTEM_OAAC;

behav CDFD_2

process Slow_For_Change_Lane equal SYSTEM_OAAC.Slow_Down_Controller
end_process

process Change_Lane (car_orientation: nat0 | deviation_info: nat0 | corner_info: real |car_a_head_info: real
                    | slow_speed: real) pedal_action: PedalActionInfo, steering_info: string

post  (if corner_info <= 0.5 and slow_speed >= 10 or car_a_head_info < 2   /* all units in meter */
       then pedal_action = mk_Ops_Pedal(-1, "BrakePedal")
      ) or

     (if corner_info > 0.1 and car_a_head_info > 2
      then pedal_action = mk_Ops_Pedal(1, "AcceleratePedal")
     ) or

     (if car_orientation > 0
      then steering_info = "RightSteering"
     ) or

     (if car_orientation < 0
      then steering_info = "LeftSteering"
     ) or

     (if car_orientation == 0 and deviation_info > 0
      then steering_info = "RightSteering"
     ) or

     (if car_orientation == 0 and deviation_info < 0
      then steering_info = "LeftSteering"
     )

end_process;

end_module;
```

Figure 7. Example of formal specification for Change_Lane_Controller

5. Discussion

With regard to the practical application of the three-step approach in SOFL, we found that the process of writing a formal specification was easier than using pure formal methods, such as VDM and Z [12]. This was because both the informal and semi-formal specifications clearly present the targets for formalization whose process is again guided by the intuitive graphical CDFDs.

Furthermore, the SOFL method, like all other formal methods, is suitable for designing safety-critical systems. Our experience in this case study shows that many important objects, such as the car, road information, obstacles, position, size, and decisions, are required to be thoroughly analyzed, defined, and understood. Compared to natural language, the SOFL formal notation has the power to "force" the developer to examine and express every objects precisely. Such a formal specification allows the developer to analyze, at a detailed level, important properties (e.g., safety, efficiency) of the system and to predicate the potential behaviors of the system. Without it, the analysis and predication would be difficult to perform accurately and efficiently.

On the other hand, we have also found some deficiency in the SOFL tool technology. Currently, there is a prototype tool, known as SOFL GUI Editor, to support the process of formal specification construction in SOFL, but it does not support the entire three-step specification process. In our case study, we used Microsoft Word editor for writing informal specifications and SOFL GUI Editor for writing semi-formal and formal specifications. This proved to be feasible, but difficulties in specification modification, verification, and validation have been encountered. We believe that the SOFL method has set up a solid foundation for developing an effective tool support for the three-step specification approach, and plan the development of the tool as our major task in our future work.

6. Related Work

In this section, we compare our work with other approaches to system development such as iterative models [13] and mural system [14]. An iterative model consists of four phases in sequence: requirement, design, implementation and testing, and final integration and system testing. This model is also referred to as incremental prototyping, because each phase consists of repeating the above four phases in sequence many times to produce a new version of the software. The development begins by specifying and implementing just part of the software, which can then be reviewed in order to identify further requirements. The requirements of the software are gathered and analyzed during the requirement phase. After several iterations, a complete and final specification of requirements is produced. The software solution in which it meets the requirements is designed in the design phase. Again, because of the iteration process, it might be a new design, or an extension of an earlier design. Later, the software is coded, integrated, and tested in the implementation and testing phase. Before the software is released, it will go through the final integration and system testing phase. This is similar to the SOFL three-step approach in which the development of the specification is an evolutionary process. However, an issue arises in the iterative model (but not in SOFL) in that a decision has to be made regarding how long the iteration should continue. In addition, there is no detailed description of the design decision for a flow diagram of the system. In SOFL, on the other hand, the CDFD, with distinct input and output ports, makes the diagram easier to understand. In the case of mural system, the development of a formal specification has three steps: (1) creating the data types and the invariants, (2) creating the specifications by creating the operations and functions, and (3) translating to theory and generating proof obligations. This contrasts with SOFL, which emphasizes the importance of communication between the client and developer in capturing accurate requirements during the first step of developing the specification.

7. Conclusion and Future Work

This case study demonstrates how SOFL can be used as a formal engineering method for writing a formal specification in a safety-critical system application. The process of writing the formal specification involves a three-step approach, consisting of informal, semiformal, and finally formal specification. We have found, based on our experience in the case study, that the use of SOFL is straightforward, easy to follow, and understandable, but when the scale increases, it will require more time and efforts in writing a specification. This problem can be effectively solved by a powerful tool support.

As future work, we will concentrate on the research and development of a powerful tool support for SOFL, studying how artificial intelligence technology can be used to improve the capability of the tool to ease difficulties in choosing appropriate mathematical expressions, reduce efforts in organizing specifications, and shorten the process of constructing specifications.

Acknowledgments

We would like to thank Professor Michael McDonald for checking the English of this paper and Yuichi Oka for implementing the entire automatic automobile driving simulation system.

References

1. S.Liu. *Formal Engineering for Industrial Software Development Using the SOFL Method.* Springer-Verlag, March 2004.
2. S.Liu, M. Shibata, and R. Sato. Applying SOFL to Develop a University Information System. I*n Proceedings of 1999 Asia-Pacific Software Engineering Conference*. IEEE Computer Society Press, December 1999.
3. C.B. Jones. S*ystematic Software Development Using VDM*. Prentice Hall, Second Edition, 1990.
4. J.C. Bicarregui et. Al. Formal Methods into Practice: Case Studies in the Application of the B Method. 144(2), April 1997.
5. J.V. Guttag and J.J. Horning et al. Larch: Languages and Tools for Formal Specification. 1993.
6. 6 Y. Oka. Development of an Automatic Driving Simulation system. Technical report, Hosei University, 2007.
7. J. Dawes. *The VDM-SL Reference Guide*. Pitman, 1991.
8. W. Brauer, G. Rozenberg, and A. Salomaa. *Petri Nets – An Introduction.* Springer-Verlag, Berlin Heidelberg, 1985.
9. E. Yourdon. *Modern Structured Analysis*. Prentice Hall, 1989.
10. S. Liu, F. Nagoya, Y. Chen, M. Goya, and J. McDermid. An Automated Approach to Specification-Based Program Inspection. Pages 421-434, November 2005.
11. S. Liu and Y. Chen. A Relation-Based Method Combining Functional and Structural Testing for Test Case Generation. *Journal of Systems and Software, Elsevier Science Inc.*, 81(2):234-248, 2008.
12. J.M. Spivey. *The Z Notation: A Reference Manual.* Prentice Hall International (UK) Ltd., 1998.
13. C. Larman. *Applying UML and Patterns: An Introduction to Object-Oriented Analysis and Design and Iterative Development*. Prentice Hall, 2001.
14. S. Vadera, F. Meziane, and M.L.L Huang. Experience with Mural in Formalizing Dust-Expert. *Elsevier Information and Software Technology*, (43):231-240, 2001.

APPLICATION OF DATA MINING FOR DEVELOPMENT OF SYNTHETIC VACCINE FROM SCORPION TOXIN

VIRENDRA GOMASE*
Department of Bioinformatics, Padmashree Dr. D. Y. Patil University, Sector-15, CBD Belapur, Navi Mumbai, 400614, India
YASH PAREKH
Department of Bioinformatics, Padmashree Dr. D. Y. Patil University, Sector-15, CBD Belapur, Navi Mumbai, 400614, India
SUBIN KOSHY
Department of Bioinformatics, Padmashree Dr. D. Y. Patil University, Sector-15, CBD Belapur, Navi Mumbai, 400614, India
SIDDHESH LAKHAN
Department of Bioinformatics, Padmashree Dr. D. Y. Patil University, Sector-15, CBD Belapur, Navi Mumbai, 400614, India
ARCHANA KHADE
Department of Bioinformatics, Padmashree Dr. D. Y. Patil University, Sector-15, CBD Belapur, Navi Mumbai, 400614, India

Abstract- *Mesobuthus tamulus* involved multiple antigenic components to direct and empower the immune system to protect the host from infection. MHC molecules are cell surface proteins, which take active part in host immune reactions and involvement of MHC class in response to almost all antigens and it give effects on specific sites. This theme is implemented in designing subunit and synthetic peptide vaccines. In this study we used data mining for sequence analysis method and is allows potential drug targets to identify active sites, which form antibodies against or spider venom infection. The method integrates prediction of peptide MHC class binding; proteosomal C terminal cleavage, TAP transport efficiency and epitopes are important antigenic determinants against the scorpion venom infections.
Keywords- *neurotoxin, MHC, data mining, SVM, PSSM, synthetic vaccine*

1. Introduction

Prediction of Peptide fragments from *Mesobuthus tamulus* involved multiple antigenic components to direct and empower the immune system to protect the host from infection. MHC molecules are cell surface proteins, which take active part in host immune reactions and involvement of MHC class-I & II in response to almost all antigens. The predicted binding affinity is normalized by the 1% fractil. The MHC peptide binding is predicted using neural networks trained on C terminals of known epitopes. In analysis predicted MHC/peptide binding is a log transformed value related to the IC50 values in nM units [**1-3**].

*Correspondence: Dr. Virendra S. Gomase, Department of Bioinformatics, Padmashree Dr. D.Y. Patil University, Plot No-50, Sector-15, CBD Belapur, Navi Mumbai, 400614, India; Mobile- +91-9987770696; Mail- virusgene1@yahoo.co.in

2. Methodology

The Hopp-Woods, Welling and Parkers antigenicity scale was designed to predict the locations of antigenic determinants. Thus beta sheet show high antigenic response than helical region of this peptide, which is highly antigenic in nature [**4, 5**]. We also found the Sweet hydrophobicity, Kyte & Doolittle hydrophobicity, Abraham & Leo hydrophobicity, Bull & Breese hydrophobicity, Guy hydrophobicity, Miyazawa hydrophobicity, Roseman hydrophobicity, Cowan HPLC pH7.5 hydrophobicity, Rose hydrophobicity, Eisenberg hydrophobicity, Manavalan hydrophobicity, Black hydrophobicity, Fauchere hydrophobicity, Janin hydrophobicity, Rao & Argos hydrophobicity, Wolfenden hydrophobicity, Wilson HPLC hydrophobicity, von Heijne Hydrophilicity, Chothia hydrophobicity scales. Theses scales are essentially a hydrophilic index, with apolar residues assigned negative values [**6, 7**]. The MHC peptide binding of neurotoxin is predicted using neural networks trained on C terminals of known epitopes. In analysis predicted MHC/peptide binding of Neurotoxin is a log-transformed value related to the IC50 values in nM units. MHC2Pred predicts peptide binders to MHCI and MHCII molecules from protein sequences or sequence alignments using Position Specific Scoring Matrices (PSSMs). Support Vector Machine (SVM) based method for prediction of promiscuous MHC class II binding peptides. SVM has been trained on the binary input of single amino acid sequence [**8-12**].

3. Results and Interpretation

Neurotoxin protein is 64 residues long, having antigenic MHC binding peptides. MHC molecules are cell surface glycoproteins, which take active part in host immune reactions and involvement of MHC class-I and MHC II in response to almost all antigens.

BepiPrep Server antigenicity determinant shows epitopes present in the *Mesobuthus tamulus* the desired immune response. The region of maximal hydrophilicity is likely to be an antigenic site, having hydrophobic characteristics, because C- terminal regions of Neurotoxin protein is solvent accessible and unstructured, antibodies against those regions are also likely to recognize the native protein (Fig. 1, 2). For the prediction of antigenic determinant site of Neurotoxin protein (*Mesobuthus tamulus*), we got antigenic determinant sites in the sequence. The highest pick is recorded between sequence of AA in the region are '1- GEDGYIADGD -10'. We also found the SVM based MHCII-IAb peptide regions 45-VCWCEDLPT, 49-EDLPTPVPI, 5-YIADGDNCT, 37-DWWVPYGVV, (optimal score is 0.558); MHCII-IAd peptide regions 1-GEDGYIADG, 56-PIRGSGKCR, 17-TFNNYCHAL, 4-GYIADGDNC, (optimal score is 0.543); MHCII-IAg7 peptide regions 17-TFNNYCHAL, 46-CWCEDLPTP, 19-NNYCHALCT, 13-TYICTFNNY, (optimal score is 0.560); and MHCII- RT1.B peptide regions 4-GYIADGDNC, 18-FNNYCHALC, 42-YGVVCWCED, 17-TFNNYCHAL, (optimal score is 1.551) which represented predicted binders from Neurotoxin protein. The predicted binding affinity is normalized by the 1% fractil. The average propensity for the Neurotoxin protein is found to be above 1.0350. All residues having above 1.0 propensity are always potentially antigenic. Further this region form beta sheet. Thus beta sheet show high antigenic response than helical region of this peptide (Fig. 1, 2). A region preferably select peptides lying in loops connecting Secondary Structure (SS) motifs, avoiding peptides located in helical regions. CPHmodels novel method is used for fold recognition/homology modeling, in which a large sequence database is iteratively searched to construct a sequence profile. The predicted segments in Neurotoxin protein identified through this approach tend to be high-efficiency binders, which is a lagers percentage of their atoms are directly involved in binding as compared to larger molecules.

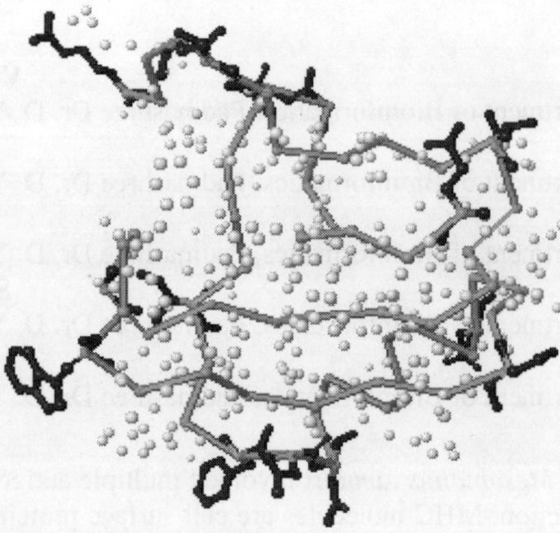

Fig. 1- Structure showing accessible: accessibility > 75% in purple

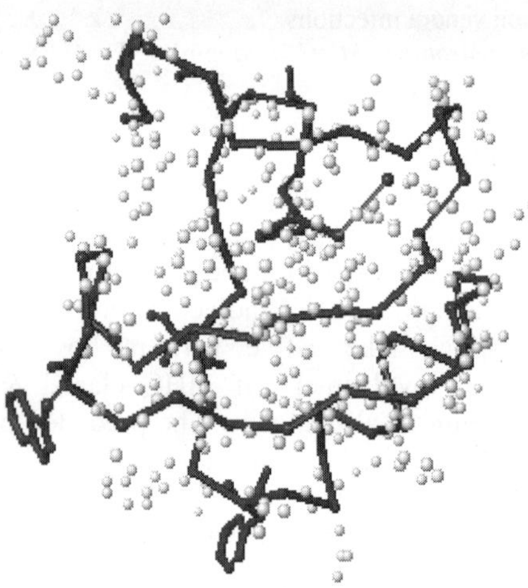

Fig. 2- Structure showing accessible + hydrophobic in Red

4. Conclusion

Data mining techniques are used for development of peptide epitopes which are antigenic in nature. Predicted MHC binding regions acts like red flags for antigen specific and generate immune response against the parent antigen. So a small fragment of antigen can induce immune response against whole antigen. This theme is implemented in designing subunit and synthetic peptide vaccines. The sequence analysis method is allows potential drug targets to identify active sites which form antibodies against plant diseases. The method integrates prediction of peptide

MHC class I binding; proteasomal C terminal cleavage and TAP transport efficiency.

5. References

[1]. R. F. Romi-Lebrun, M.F. Martin-Eauclaire, P. Escoubas, F.Q. Wu, B. Lebrun, M. Hisada, T. Nakajima, *Eur J Biochem.*, 245(2), 457–464 (1997).

[2]. T. Olamendi-Portugal, F. Gómez-Lagunas, G.B. Gurrola, L.D Posan, *Biochem J.,* 315(Pt 3), 977–981 (1996).

[3]. R. Kharrat, K. Mabrouk, M. Crest, H. Darbon, R. Oughideni, M.F. Martin-Eauclaire, G. Jacquet, M. el Ayeb, J. Van Rietschoten, H. Rochat, J.M. Sabatier, *Eur J Biochem.*, 242(3), 491–498 (1996).

[4]. V.S.Gomase and K.V.Kale, *Int. J. of Applied Computing*, 1(1), 39-46 (2008).

[5]. V.S.Gomase, K.V. Kale, N.J.Chikhale, S.S. Changbhale, *Curr. Drug Discov. Technol.*, 4(2),117-1215 (2007).

[6]. V.S.Gomase, K.V. Kale, A. Jyotiraj and R. Vasanthi, *Medicinal Chemistry Research*, 15(1/6), 160 (2007).

[7]. V.S.Gomase, J.P.Tandale, S.A.Patil, K.V.Kale, *14th International Conference on Advance Computing & Communication, Published by IEEE Computer Society in IEEE Xplore USA* 614-615 (2006).

[8]. V.S.Gomase, K.V. Kale, K. Shyamkumar and S. Shankar, *ICETET 2008, IEEE Computer Society in IEEE Xplore, Los Alamitos, California*, 629-634 (2008)

[9]. M. Bhasin and G.P. Raghava, *Nucleic Acids Research*, 33, W202-207 (2005).

[10]. P.A. Reche, J.P. Glutting, E.L. Reinherz, *Hum Immun.*, 63, 701-709 (2002).

[11]. S. Buus, *et al.*, Tissue Antigens, 62, 378-384 (2003).

[12]. M. Nielsen, *et al.*, *Protein Sci.*, 12, 1007-1017 (2003).

RANDOMIZED MULTILEVEL ENCRYPTION: A PROMISE TO BETTER COMPUTER SECURITY

SUDIPTO SARKAR
Department of Computer Science & Engineering, NIT Raipur, G.E. Road Raipur, Chhattisgarh 492010, India

ABHISHEK KUMAR
Department of Computer Science & Engineering, NIT Raipur, G.E. Road Raipur, Chhattisgarh 492010, India

Computers have seen various Operating Systems in olden days, and seeing new developments. But one crucial flaw in their security is that passwords have to be stored somewhere, for user login, which leaves the system open to compromise. Although the encryption algorithms are one way, but with the advent of faster computers and newer techniques in password cracking, they have turned futile. The password storing files store passwords in an encrypted format, and are accessible only to the system and the root users of the systems. Bugs in software allow malicious hackers to gain access to the system with root privileges and they can download the password file(s) and user accounts can be compromised. After gaining the password file, passwords could be cracked. In Randomized Multi-level encryption, password is first encrypted with one algorithm, and the generated hash is encrypted with another, followed by a random number of randomly chosen algorithms. The selection of the algorithms and their sequence is decided, when user account is created. The information about the algorithms used, and their sequences is stored in another file. Now, although this file may be accessible to the hacker, and he/she may be able to get the password file as well, but brute forcing the passwords will be very time consuming. Also, the rainbow tables can not be generated for all possible combinations Even if all combinations are generated by some person, taking into account all encryption algorithms currently used, rainbow tables would still take years to generate, even after using arrays of multiple computers using parallel processing, and by that time, new algorithms would be developed, thereby making their rainblow table databases outdated. Randomized Multi-level encryption is rightly a promise to better computer security. It can not only reduce the chances of account compromise, but also reduce them to null.

1. Introduction

Computers have used various Operating Systems in days gone by, and seeing new developments in the sphere of Operating Systems. But one crucial flaw in their security is that passwords have to be stored somewhere, for matching purposes, while user logs in. But this leaves the system wide open to user accounts' compromise. Although the encryption algorithms are one way, but with the advent of faster computers and newer techniques in password cracking mechanisms, these algorithms have turned to prove themselves futile. The password storing files store passwords in an encrypted format, and are accessible only to the system and the root users of the systems. Bugs in upcoming software programs for example, sendmail (an SMTP daemon), which is also called the buggiest program on Earth, allow malicious hackers to gain access to the system with root user privileges. With root powers, they can download the password file(s), so that individual user accounts or a particular target user account can be compromised. After gaining the password file, passwords could be cracked by dictionary attack, brute force attack or rainbow table attack.

2. Password Cracking Techniques

2.1. *Dictionary attack*

Dictionary attack is the easiest form of password cracking technique. In this technique, a text database of commonly used passwords is used ([10]).

The passwords are compiled from various sources, researching on commonly used passwords. The list could be a few different words or could range from alphanumerals to special characters, depending on how common the password is. At present, the Internet hosts many password dictionaries, many of which are also available in foreign languages, that are no more used. This has increased the chances of success in dictionary attacks. However they are never and will never be very efficient, as it tries to exploit the human side of the password security process, thus failing most of the times.

These passwords are encrypted and compared with the secured encrypted password, for a positive match. This technique has a low rate of success, as the database is never exhaustive.

2.2. *Brute force attack*

The brute force attack technique has been, by far the most widely used technique to crack passwords. Hackers have been using this technique with a high amount of success ([8]).

This technique utilizes another algorithm, which generates all permutations of passwords, that is all possible combinations of strings that can be generated from the keys available on the keyboard. Then each generated string is encrypted with the algorithm that has been used in the encrypted password that has been stolen from the system, and that encrypted hash is compared with the available encrypted password for a positive match.

This technique has an advantage of high rate of success, but it also accompanies a great disadvantage. The amount of time it takes to crack a password is tediously very high. With the advent of more and more complex algorithms like MD5, each encryption takes some notable amount of time, and with the huge amount of strings generated, the time taken for encryption is also huge, which leads to a high amount of time taken to crack a single password, which makes this technique not very usable, when practicality is considered.

Considering an example for both dictionary and brute force attack softwares, John the Ripper is a classic password cracker, coming from the old times of Unix ([6], [7]). John the ripper implements both dictionary based attack through a password dictionary stored in the file wordlist. Alternatively, John provides a brute force algorithm to crack the password in a much more efficient manner. Although this brute force method is very much slow as compared to the dictionary based method, but rate of success has been found to be very much higher. The following is a sample output of John the ripper in a Debian/Linux environment:

```
root@0[john1.6.37]# cat pass.txt
user:AZl.zWwxIh15Q
root@0[john1.6.37]# john -w: password.lst pass.txt
Loaded 1 password hash (Traditional DES [24/32 4K]) example (user)
```

2.3. *Rainbow tables*

Rainbow tables have been the most successful method of password cracking. These rainbow tables are lookup tables, where a hash can be looked up for corresponding plain text passwords ([5]). These have been widely used to crack Microsoft Windows passwords.

Although the rainbow tables can be made futile by utilizing an extra salt ([9]), which is concatenated with the password, before being encrypted, Windows distributions still use unsalted passwords, which leave them wide open to compromise by the use of rainbow tables. Ophcrack would be an example program that uses rainbow tables to crack Windows passwords. The salted passwords can also be cracked, but that will require terabytes of rainbow tables. These rainbow tables are to be generated first. The generation of rainbow tables also requires time and computation power. Thus a salted password would already take a lot of time and space, while unsalted passwords will have much smaller rainbow tables.

Rainbow tables have been known to crack passwords in a matter of seconds, which would take months or even years to crack with conventional brute force technique.

For example, ophcrack is an Open Source password cracker for Microsoft Windows, originally developed in Switzerland, as in [2] and [4]. The company Objectif Sécurité, which is an independent security firm, specializing in IT security had developed this program, as in [3]. This program uses Rainbow tables to crack Microsoft Windows passwords. It comes both as a native Windows executable or Linux native executable. Recently, ophcrack has been made available as a Live Linux CD, which would boot the computer and crack the passwords in the Windows partition. The following is a screenshot of ophcrack:

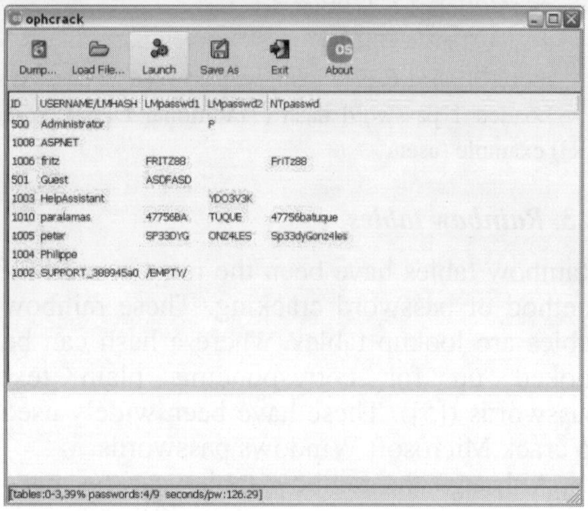

Figure 1. ophcrack screenshot.

3. Randomized Multi-level Encryption

3.1. *Introduction to the technique*

The technique of Randomized Multilevel encryption is simple – to use a random encryption algorithm out of a set A of algorithms, and that too, a random number of times, between 2 to some feasible amount.

The information about the algorithms used, and their sequences is stored in some file on the hard disk, accessible only with root privileges.

3.2. *Working*

In this technique, the password, that has to be encrypted, is first passed through an encryption algorithm, out of which some hash is generated. This encrypted password that is the hash is passed through another algorithm, again chosen from the set A of encryption algorithms, which gives another hash (the hash of the first hash). This hash is again passed through an algorithm, which belongs to A, the set of encryption algorithms. This gives another hash. This hash is then similarly passed through a random number of randomly chosen algorithms, chosen from the set A.

The algorithms used, and the number of encryptions that have to be carried out, are decided during account creation. In case of root user, this is during system installation, and in case of other users, it is during account creation. Also, this process will come into action, while a user requests the system for a password change. In case of Unix systems (and variants), this will be when the passwd program is called.

3.3. *Feasibility*

Since, all this process requires, is some algorithms in the set A, it is entirely feasible. That is, it can be implemented easily. All that is needed to do is apply the number of encryptions by taking into account, the number that is returned by our RNG (random number generator).

The encryption functions can be used with the hash generated by the previous algorithm as the input password. We shall study a sample case below.

3.4. *Implementation*

We take some commonly used algorithms, MD5 (Message Digest 5), and DES (Data Encryption Standard) in the set of algorithms that are to used, i.e. A. These algorithms are used widely nowadays in Unix and variants like Linux. In these Operating Systems, the password and other user information (for all users) is stored in the file /etc/shadow (which was /etc/passwd in earlier systems), accessible only to the root user. DES is an old algorithm that has been in use since years. MD5 is a relatively new algorithm, and is much more secure. DES creates hashes, which are 13 characters in length. Using the native crypt function, would restrict the maximum allowable characters in case of DES to only 8 characters [1]. And, in case of MD5, the hash would contain 32 characters, led by 1 at the beginning. The maximum allowable characters is much more in case of MD5 [1].

In case of our crypt function, the algorithm to be used is decided by the second argument, which is also the salt used with the password. If the salt is a two character string, then DES is used for the encryption. And if the salt is a character string with more than two characters starting with "1", followed by at most 8 characters and optionally terminated by "$", then MD5 is used for the encryption of the password. In that case, the salt would look something like "1<string>$", where <string> is the 8 character long string. The syntax of the crypt function is:

```
char *crypt(const char *key, const char *salt);
```

Our RNG (Random Number Generator) works with a function:

```
int RNG(int lowerlimit, int upperlimit);
```

This is an arbitrary function, and can be developed using other available library functions. The lowerlimit and upperlimit will specify the limits where the generated random number will lie in. That is, the random number would be somewhere between lowerlimit and upperlimit, including the limits.

The RNG function will be used, both to choose the algorithm and to choose the number of times the algorithms will be applied. Let the number of algorithm be denoted by the variable a of type int. If a is 0, then DES is used, and if it is 1, MD5 is used. There are switch cases to select this. We call the function RNG for this purpose as follows:

```
a = RNG(0, 1);
```

The RNG is also used for selecting the number of times the algorithms are applied. In our case study, we consider an upper limit of 10 in this number. Let the variable n of type int denote this number. Then we would call:

```
n = RNG(2, 10);
```

The lower limit is 2, because the lowest number of times the algorithms are used is 2. Below 2, it would be the conventional single time encryption that is used nowadays. A loop runs, which keeps track of how many times the algorithms from set A have been used. The password here, is initially stored in the variable pass, which is of type string, that is char *. The switch cases and loop structure that would be used would have a structure similar to this:

```
n = RNG(2, 10); /*Select the number of
algorithms to be used */
while(n){
      a = RNG(0, 1);
      switch(a){
      case 0:
            pass = crypt(pass, "aa");
            break;
      case 1:
            pass = crypt(pass, "$1$");
            break;
      }
      n;
}
```

The variable pass would store the final hash that is to be stored in /etc/shadow, when setting up a user's password (while account creation or while a password change is requested) or to be matched from that file, when user logs in.

4. Conclusion

Finally, closing the paper, it has to be repeated, that no anti hacking mechanism is fool proof. What matters is how long it takes to be cracked. Taking into account, the cracking time of this technique, using MD5 and DES with rainbow tables, the salt, if used will already increase the database size to terabytes of hard disk space. This rainbow table will take a lot of time to get generated, even after using computers to work in parallel.

If there are multiple algorithms, chosen randomly, and used a random number of times, the rainbow table databases would have to generated for each possible combination, and for all the numbers that are possible for n. That would already take months, or even years to generate. Brute force would not be worth the effort, because time would have to be invested every single time. In case of rainbow tables, the tables would have to be generated for 32 character passwords, because MD5 hashes are 32 characters long.

Considering the trade off, both time and money would have to be invested to crack passwords encrypted with this mechanism, which is definitely not worth the effort. Randomized Multilevel encryption thus seems to be a promise to a better password security.

References

1. Linux developer man pages
2. The ophcrack rainbow table password cracker website. Available: http://ophcrack.sourceforge.net/
3. The Objectif Sécurité website. Available: http://www.objectif-securite.ch/en/index.php
4. Ophcrack on Wikipedia. Available: http://en.wikipedia.org/wiki/Ophcrack
5. Rainbow Table on Wikipedia. Available: http://en.wikipedia.org/wiki/Rainbow_table
6. John the Ripper website. Available: http://www.openwall.com/john/
7. John the Ripper on Wikipedia. Available: http://en.wikipedia.org/wiki/John_the_Ripper
8. Brute force attack on Wikipedia. Available: http://en.wikipedia.org/wiki/Brute_force_attack
9. Salt (cryptography) on Wikipedia. Available: http://en.wikipedia.org/wiki/Salt_(cryptography)
10. Dictionary attack on Wikipedia. Available: http://en.wikipedia.org/wiki/Dictionary_attack

SIMULATION OF FIRE SPREAD BASED ON MULTI-LEVEL PARTICLE SYSTEM MODEL*

YUN KUANG, DEHUI KONG, YONG ZHANG, YANFENG SUN

Beijing Key Laboratory of Multimedia and Intelligent Software Technology, College of Computer Science, Beijing University of Technology, No.100 Pingleyuan, Chaoyang District Beijing, 100124, China

For use of fire prevention and suppression, fire simulations are in demand for virtual reality effects, helping researchers study the dynamics of fire and smoke. In this paper, by extension of particle system hierarchies, we establish a multi-level particle system model (MLPSM) which not only could be top-down controlled to enhance the dynamic simulation, but can be managed in high efficiency to increase rendering speed. Applying this new model, we further formulate a simplified model of fire spread and present a visual system for animating fire and smoke, using OpenGL, based on application requirements. The results show a well balance between rendering effects and real-time display with 10,000 particles, which proves the effectiveness of our multi-level particle system model.

1. Introduction

It is of great practical significance to study how to ensure that people could be evacuated efficiently in the gymnasiums when it is on fire, for gymnasiums are the major gathering places in a city. To set up virtual reality effects for studying this problem, we describe and implement a visual system for animating fire and smoke based on the need of the real-time evacuation planning and application in a gymnasium.

In computer graphics, it is very challenging to simulate fuzzy objects because of their irregular shape and dynamic feature. At present, the most accurate simulation model is based on physical nature of Computational Fluid Dynamics (CFD), but its calculation is too complex to meet the requirements of real-time application. Therefore, researchers of computer graphics have never ceased trying to explore methods and models to simulate fire, smoke, water, clouds, and other irregular fuzzy objects, and have put forward particle systems model, cellular automata model, fractal model, diffusion process model, illumination model, texture mapping model and so on.

Based on the background of the application requirements to reproduce the fire scenes, we focus on the overall visual effect, rendering efficiency and interactive control, rather than a separate burning and spreading flame of extremely physical accuracy. Therefore, in this paper, we use particle systems as the basic model to simulate fire and smoke.

We first set up a multi-level particle system model (MLPSM) based on the classic particle system model. Then, according to the diverse need of application, we apply MLPSM to simulate fire and smoke. In addition, based on this model, we design a simplified model of the fire spread that could generate realistic visual effects of dynamic fire and smoke in the regular paths of gymnasium, laying the foundation for the after evacuation planning.

2. Related Work

W.T. Reeves was the first to model irregular fuzzy objects using particle systems [1]. The basic idea is to treat the object as a dynamic volume composed of a number of primitive particles, and each particle has its individual attributes, such as color, shape, size, lifetime, and speed, which will change with the particle motion so that the modeling object appears as an entirely dynamic system. During the process from creating a particle to destroying it, all the attributes could be definitely or randomly controlled, and they can be complicated set by CFD or simple just as constant. As a result, particle systems have strong flexibility and are so far the most widely used fire model [2].

Many attempts and innovations have been made to model fire using particle systems. Zhang et al. [3] proposed a structured flame model based on particle systems which could generate flames in different degrees of precision. Van der Burg [4] built up advanced particle systems, creating particle manager level above particle system level. Beaudoin et al. [5] put forward a new method for simulating spreading on

* This work is partially supported by the Beijing Municipal fund (4061001) and the Beijing Municipal Education Commission Project (KM200710005017、KM200710005023).

polygonal meshes which consists in using individual flames as primitives to animate and render the fire and setting up a three-dimensional skeleton within the flame. Perry and Picard [6] presented enhanced particle systems to model flame, using dynamic two-dimensional geometry to reduce rendering cost, and they also set up a physically-based model for flame spread which could realistically calculate the boundary between burning and non-burning regions of polygon-defined objects.

The advanced particle system model that Van der Burg [4] created is flexible and fast to simulate a dynamic scene where the particle manager level could manage and update all the particle systems within the scene, but under the only one big group, all of the particle systems are independent to each other and they don't belong to any sub-groups. In this paper, we hope that some of the particle systems could own the same attributes or some of them are related to each other so that they could together show a rendering result in local places, while we need several such small particle systems' groups to distribute in different positions to present the global scene. Therefore, in order to efficiently manage all the sub-groups of particle systems, we extend the advanced particle systems and put forward a multi-level particle system model of which the parameters will be easily top-down controlled. Besides, we use MLPSM in fire spread of preset path simulation which has reached a real-time rendering result.

3. MLPSM: Multi-level Particle System Model

3.1. *Definition and Structure of MLPSM*

We establish relationships between particle systems and the target objects (fire and smoke) which are furthermore extended according to the application background. Based on the definition of particle, particle set, and particle systems by Zhang et al [3], we set up hierarchical definition of multi-level particle systems in order to standardize the process of realization.

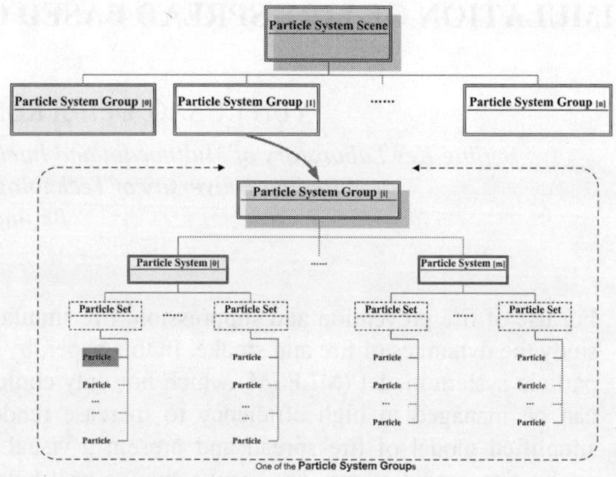

Figure 1. Hierarchical structure of MLPSM.

3.1.1. *Particle*

Particle is defined as an n-dimensional vector R^n ($n \in I$) in real number field, where R^n represents nature and status of a specific particle.

3.1.2. *Particle Set*

Particle set is defined as a finite set of particles, within which each particle has an index with a mapping P: $I \rightarrow R^n$ ($n>=3$, $n \in I$). For the particle with index i, $P(i) = R^n$ represents its nature and status.

3.1.3. *Particle System*

Particle System is considered as a finite set of Particle sets, defining $Q = \{Pt\text{: } It \rightarrow R^n \mid n>=3,\ n \in I,\ t \in \{t0,t1,\ldots ,tm\},\ It \in I\}$, where Pt_k is the state of the particle system at time t_k , Pt_0 is the initial state and Q is a collection of a series of time-dependent state showing a dynamic particle system. On this basis, we define set of particle systems $T = \{Qi \mid i=0,1\ldots n,\ n>=3,\ n \in I\}$.

3.1.4. *Particle System Group*

Particle System Group is known as a finite set of homogeneous (with the same constraints) particle systems, which could present the overall performance of a group of particle systems, defining $Q_{group}(Q_0) = \{Q_i \mid Q_0, Q_i \in T \text{ and } Q_i \backsim Q_0\}$. Operation symbol $\backsim$ indicates that two particle system is homogeneous, which should be regulated in detail to be more concrete during simulation.

3.1.5. *Particle System Scene*

Particle system scene is known as a finite set of particle system group, where each group isn't necessarily homogeneous, so it will show a highly dynamic picture as a whole, defining $Q_{scene} = \{Q_{group(k)} \mid k=0,1\ldots n, n>=3, n\in I\}$.

3.2. *Management of MLPSM*

In this paper, for the given structure (Figure 1) of the multi-level particle system model, we design and implement appropriate roles to achieve multi-level management and orderly hierarchical simulation. The multi-level management could be divided into four grades, which from high to low are management of *Particle System Group* (GroupMgr), management of *Particle System* (ParticleSysMgr), management of *particles* (ParticleSys) and particle self-management (Particle) as showed in Figure 2.

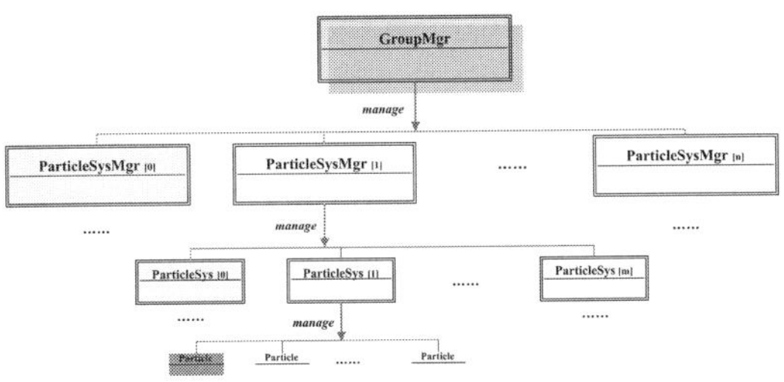

Figure 2. Hierarchical management of MLPSM.

Particle systems within the whole particle system scene can be divided into several groups with different certain tasks and rules, managed by each corresponding ParticleSysMgr, while GroupMgr will manage those ParticleSysMgrs from a higher level so as to effectively control and arrange the overall performance of the particle systems in the scene. We further extend the mechanisms of particle systems realization for the MLPSM shown in Figure 3.

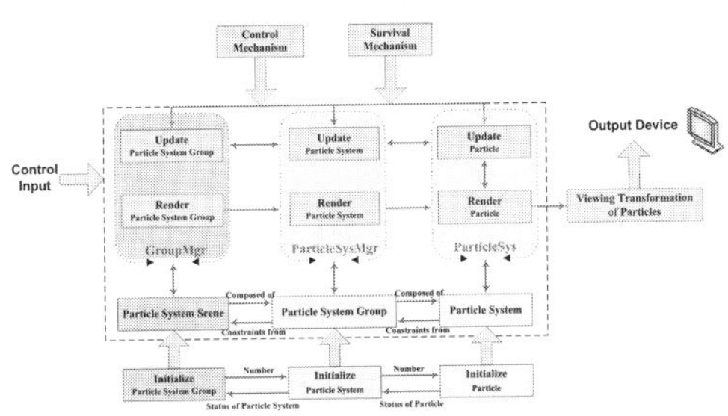

Figure 3. Simulation mechanism of MLPSM.

3.3. *Implementation of MLPSM*

Multi-level particle system model is extensive model of particle systems, and each level takes up its responsibility for specific function. In the process of simulation, parameters of all levels could be set, and top-down initialization, updating and rendering will be operated in order, from Particle System Scene, Particle System Group (GroupMgr in charge), Particle System (ParticleSysMgr in charge) to Particle (ParticleSys in charge). The main steps are as follows:

Step 1: Analyzing both the static and dynamic properties of objects to be simulated, and top-down initializing the entire multi-level particle system.

Step 2: Generating particle systems with structured levels, including the new basic particles with its initial properties.

Step 3: Top-down updating the entire multi-level particle system by the presetting dynamic rules. The procedures displayed in Table 1 show the algorithm in detail.

Step 4: Top-down rendering the entire multi-level particle system.

Table 1. Top-down update MLPSM in order.

```
Procedure GroupMgr_Update()
for all the ParticleSysMgr managed by GroupMgr
    if ParticleSysMgr is alive
        Call ParticleSysMgr_Update()
    else
        Delete all the particle systems in the group
        managed by ParticleSysMgr
    end_if
end_for
Procedure ParticleSysMgr_Update()
TotalTime += IntervalTime
for all the ParticleSys in the group managed by ParticleSysMgr
    if ParticleSys is alive
        if the type of the particle system group is spread-burning
            if TotalTime >= StartTime of ParticleSys
                Call ParticleSys_Update()
            end_if
        end_if
        else if the type of the particle system group is fixed-burning
            Call ParticleSys_Update()
        end_if
    else
        Delete all the particles in the particle system
        managed by ParticleSys
    end_if
end_for
Procedure ParticleSys_Update()
Add IntervalTime of update to the EmitTime
for all the particles managed by ParticleSys
    if particle is alive
        Age += IntervalTime
        if Age >= Lifetime
            Set the particle to dead status
        else
            Percent = Age / Lifetime
            Update all attributes of a particle based on Percent
            and dynamic rules
        end_if
    else if EmitRate>0 and EmitTime >= 1/EmitRate
        EmitTime -= IntervalTime
        Set the particle to alive status
        Particle_Init()
    end_if
end_for
```

4. Fire Spreading Simulation Based on MLPSM

4.1. *Structured Definition of Fire Spreading System*

Based on multi-level particle system model, we have realized real-time simulation of fire spread. Corresponding to MLPSM, the definition of the fire spreading system in separate levels is as follows

4.1.1. *Sparkling particle and smoky particle (Particle)*

Sparkling particles and smoky particles are defined as having three-dimensional position, velocity, acceleration, shape, size, color, brightness, lifetime, and other properties of particles.

4.1.2. *Flame, smoke column and smoky flame (Particle system)*

Particle systems can be used to simulate one flame and one smoke column separately, while one flame and one smoke column could make up one smoky flame if each of them has the same two-dimensional initial position in the particle emission plane (in this paper for the x-z plane).

4.1.3. *Flame system (flames), smoke system (smoke) and fire system (Particle System Group)*

Flame system is composed of groups of several flames which can compare the performance of the overall shape of the fire. Similarly, smoke system is composed of several smoke columns which can display the overall shape of the smoke. Fire system is a general term for the flame and smoke, a unit system in the scene of the fire (see 4.1.4). As a result, there must be a number of flames and smoke included in a fire system, within which there also will be smoky flames, a possible combination of flames and smoke as defined in 4.1.2.

4.1.4. *Fire Scene (Particle System Scene)*

Fire scene is made up of groups of fire system which maintains distinct forms of fire burning and spreading and is set up respectively but related to each other, so it could demonstrate a dynamic scene of the fire with different combinations of fire systems.

4.2. *Initialization*

When we top-down initialize the fire spreading system based on the multi-level mechanism, we must first set up the layout parameters of the fire scene. Then, when initializing the flames and the smoke, it is necessary to set the type of combustion, such as spread-burning using the fire path or fixed-burning using the emission domain, and set the corresponding parameters. For the type of spread-burning, properties related to the spreading interval in time or space and the spreading path are needed to be initialized (see 4.4), while for the type of fixed-burning, properties related to the emission domain of each fire system must be initialized. Finally, many attributes of the classic particle system should be initialized based on characteristics of flame or smoke, including emission angle, the rate of particle emission, the maximum and initial number of particles and lifetime of the whole particle system, as well as velocity, acceleration, color, transparency, shape, size and survival time of each particle within the particle system.

Fire system will be launched in a certain domain of the x-z plane, if its type is set as fixed-burning. There are three types of domain with different shape, including round, rectangular, and linear domain (as shown in Figure 4), and the scope of each domain is controlled by corresponding preset parameters.

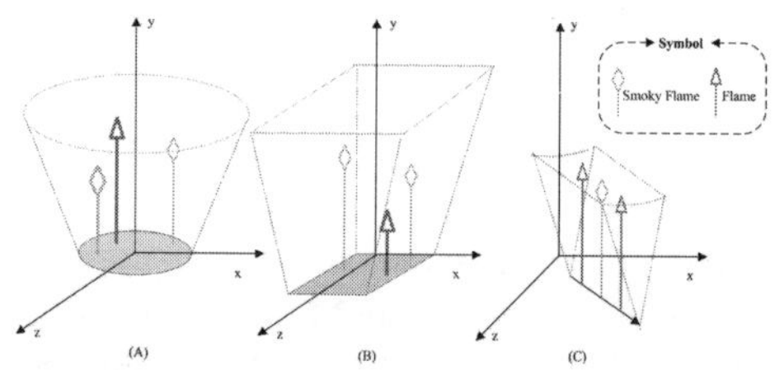

Figure 4. Graphic illustration for emission domain of Fire System.

4.3. *Fire System Dynamic*

Fire system could be top-down dynamically controlled to simulate fire combustion and spread. In the high level, according to the parameters for layout in the fire scene, each fire system will perform well in certain burning type set by its superior level. No matter of the fixed or spreading type, all systems have their own "timetable", as in a particular time to start burning, arising interval between two adjacent particle systems (flame or smoke column), time to make the fire intense, time to put out the fire and so on.

In the middle level, flames or smoke columns within each fire system will adjust their status corresponding to combustion parameters set by the higher level. For example, under the management of ParticleSysMgr, flames and smoke will have their own particular time to start or end the process of particle emission, and they also have chance to increase or decrease the particles within the particle systems (to enhance or diminish combustion) at any time interactively.

In the basic level, to present dynamic effect, attributes of sparkling particle and smoky particle will be constantly changed according to the classic theory of particle systems. Obeying the management of ParticleSys, velocity, position and age of a particle are updated respectively by the following rules: $v(t + \Delta t) = v(t) + a(t) * \Delta t$; $r(t + \Delta t) = r(t) + v(t) * \Delta t$; Age = Age + Δt; other attributes are updated in linear interpolation, that is: Current State = Initial State + Percent * (Final State - Initial State), where the Percent is the growing ratio of a particle, defined as Age / Lifetime. In our systems, particles are given age measured in time, and age will grow as time goes. When the age of a particle reaches the lifetime of its particle system, the particle will be killed, but all the particles within the particle system are to survive in cycles, traversed during each update time. When it is time to emit new particles, ParticleSys will grant revival ability to particles that have been killed before, and then assign each of the initial attributes, making particles enter a new round of life cycle, from generation, activity till extinction.

4.4. *Simplified Model of Fire Spread*

Based on multi-level particle systems model, we design and implement a simplified model of the fire spreading simulation which proves visually realistic. The basic idea is that fire spread could be seen as discrete process by smoky flames defined before. We will set the initially generated time of a group of designated smoky flames in correct order, and then it will show the fire spread effect in a certain direction by the way that consecutive flames are generated one by one in such direction. In accordance with the fire spread model, it applies not only to one-way spread, but good to be used to simulate fire spread in arbitrary directions, as long as the initial time, location of the smoky flames and the spread path are properly designated.

For the need of fire spreading simulation arising from evacuation problems in a gymnasium, the most important is that it can effectively simulate and calculate the direction and speed of spread. Our simplified spreading model is not based on physical nature and can not calculate the real parameters of fire spread, but it can satisfy the current need that it is visually realistic and could be flexibly man-made control. In this model, the direction of fire spreading is known from a given spreading equation and the spreading speed at any moment could be easily calculated through the equation and other related parameters. As a result, this simplified model could help the evacuation planning to some extent. Basic paths of fire spreading are (a) – (d) as follows (as shown in Figure 5):

(a) Linear spreading path: $Z = kX + b$

(b) Conic spreading path: $Z=aX^2+bX+c$

(c) Denary logarithmic spreading path: $Z=k\lg(X)+b$

(d) Semi-circumferential spreading path: $(X-a)^2+(Z-b)^2=R^2$

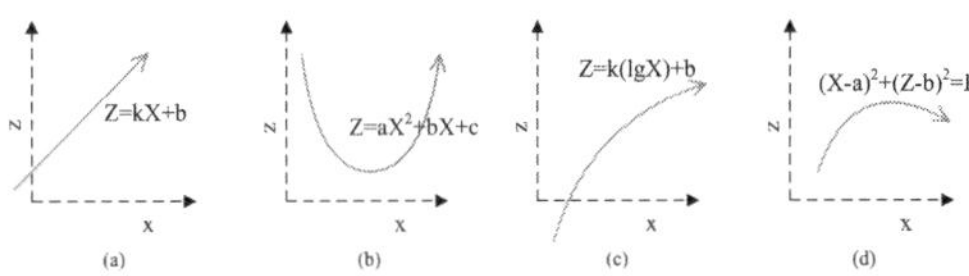

Figure 5. Graphic illustration for basic paths of fire spread.

4.4.1. *Initialization and Calculation*

Set SpreadPos (SPx,SPy,SPz) as the initial spread position of flames, SpreadTime as the starting time. For the two adjacent flames, set Δt and Δx as the generating time interval and distance interval separately.

For all the spreading paths, at time t, we can calculate and obtain the following information of one flame:

(1) Total spreading time:

$$\Delta T = t\text{-SpreadTime};$$

(2) Spreading distance in x direction:

$$\Delta X = [(t\text{-SpreadTime}) / \Delta t] * \Delta x = (\Delta T / \Delta t) * \Delta x;$$

(3) Spreading position in x direction:

$$Xt = SPx + \Delta X.$$

We put Xt into specific equation of spreading path, and compute its spreading position in z direction Zt, and then we can get the spreading distance in z direction: $\Delta Z = Zt\text{-}SPz$. Therefore, it is not hard to further compute the average velocity and velocity at a certain time t when applying different equation path of spread.

4.4.2. *Extension of flame spreading path*

The above four spreading paths can only describe the most basic shapes like which combustible objects will probably be distributed, allowing a flame system spread in a simulative path with the particular shape. On this basis, the basic path can be supplemented and improved. As a result, if there are several flame systems in the fire scene, there would be great diversity of combination to simulate spread as a whole, for each of flame systems could perform distinct spreading process in accordance with their own rules of path.

4.4.3. *Smoke Generation*

The generation and exercise of smoke correlates closely with the fuel and temperature, while in this paper, we simulate smoke without physical consideration, using the same simplified model as flames. Smoky particles in a smoke column (a particle system) can be produced and move according to certain rules until they disperse into space and eventually disappear, thus we simply simulate smoke by the dynamic generation of particle system itself, assigning attributes based on distinct feature of smoke. Moreover, smoke is produced by combustion, so given suitable value of attributes, smoky flames (4.1.2) are usually used to serve the purpose of simulation. As the flames spread, the smoke columns will also be consequently generated according to the spreading path, achieving the horizontal expansion, which can visually present fire spread as a whole.

5. Results

We finally realize simulation of fire spread on the development environment of Visual C++ 6.0 of Microsoft Visual Studio, using texture, blending, and transformation functions of OpenGL graphics interface [7]. To make it more realistic and real-time, we also adopted some rendering techniques, such as texture mapping and billboard skills.

5.1. *Simulation Examples*

5.1.1. *Spread-burning of flames*

There is only one particle system group -- a flame system in the fire scene that adopts spreading path as shown in figure 6. The initial position is (-0.4, 0.0, 0.0); spreading path is $Z^2+X^2=R^2$ (R=0.4); starting time is 0.0, 1.0 second for the time interval; distance interval in x direction is 0.08.

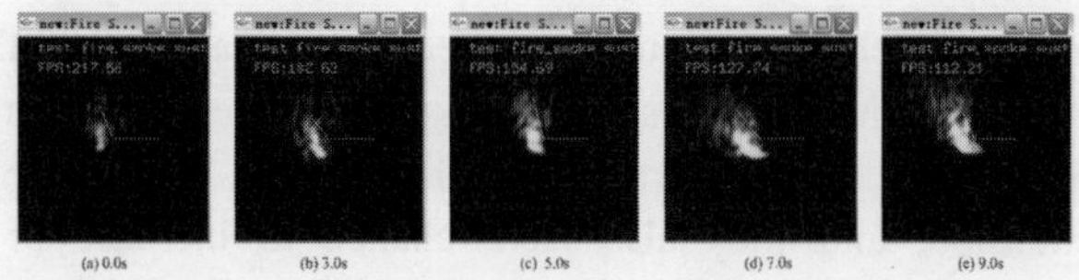

Figure 6. A test example of spread-burning flames.

5.1.2. *Fixed-burning of flames*

Fixed burning can be implemented in two ways. Take flame system for instance. One way is by spreading path. If all the flames arise at the same time, it can simulate flames burning on a combustible object with a certain shape (straight or curved). The other way is by emission domain, which can simulate flames burning in some region, and generating time of flames within the region could randomly set. As shown in Figure 8, the visual effect is based on the rectangular domain, where the starting position for the rectangular field is (0.5, 0.0, 0.5), and the end position is (1.0, 0.0, 1.0).

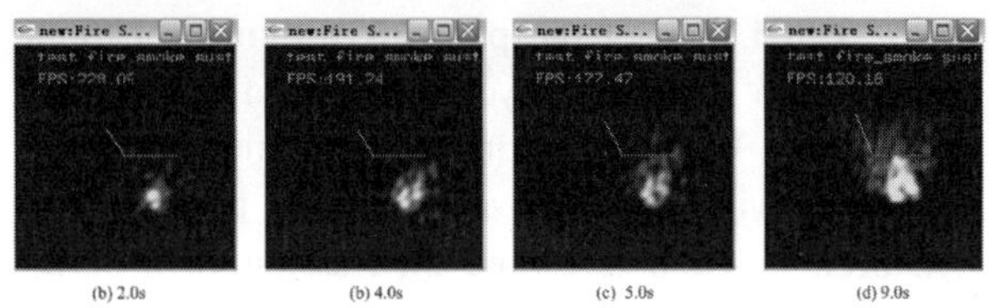

Figure 7. A test example of fixed-burning flames by emission domain.

5.1.3. *Fire systems*

A fire scene is composed of several fire systems, and each of them could be performed according to their own combustion rules, and hence the whole fire spreading system is flexibly displayed with various possible situation and distribution. Figure 8 shows simple overall effects of fire scene, in which part (a) includes one fire system, and part (b) involves four fire systems and each has ten smoky flames.

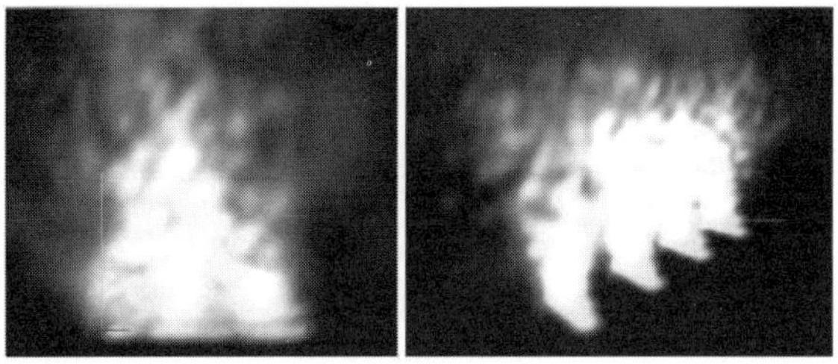

(a) (b)

Figure 8. Simple overall effects of Fire Scene.

5.1.4. *Fire in the gymnasium*

We simulate the fire scene in our three dimensional gymnasium model. As shown in Figure 9, there are six fire systems in the fire scene along the stairway, where the fire is spreading along each row in each fire system.

Figure 9. Fire spreading along each row in one stairway within the gymnasium.

5.2. *Analysis of Visual Effects*

The effects of fire spread depend on attributes setting of multi-level particle system at each level. Through analysis of the role of the attributes played in the simulation (Table 2), we can choose and set the relatively optimal value to those attributes based on needs of different application, in order to achieve expected effects.

Table 2. Influence of the key attributes on fire spreading system.

Attributes	Effects
1. Particle System (Flame or Smoke Column)	
Particle	To Particle System
emission rate	density
emission angle	density / dynamic range
initial velocity	dynamic range / contour
lifetime	height
length / width	partial contour
color	hue
opacity degree	soft degree
texture	quality
2. Particle System Group (Fire System)	
burning type	burning form
number of particle systems	scale
(1) using spreading path	
start time + spreading path	burning area / shape
generation interval of adjacent particle systems	spreading speed
space between adjacent particle systems	density
(2) using emission domain	
type of emission domain	burning area
range of emission domain	density
3. Particle System Scene (Fire Scene)	
number of fire systems	overall scale
start time	signal of fire simulation

5.3. *Performance*

We have run many simulation tests on a 2.8GHz Intel(R) Pentium(R) D system with 1.5GB of main memory and an NVIDIA GeForce 6200 TurboCache(TM) 256MB graphics system.

With the increase of particle number displayed on screen, the real-time performance of simulation decreases. We see in the experiments that when the FPS (frame per second) keeps in at least 10Hz, the rendering effects will maintain continuous and relatively smooth. When the particle number per frame reaches far more than 10,000, real-time results will be affected, and if there are about 8000 particles displayed simultaneously in the system, the frame rate of 20Hz can be maintained as shown in Figure 10. So, supposing that the average emission rate of particles is 20 per second and lifetime of particle is 2 seconds which proves natural enough under test in our simulation system, then we can arrange 20 fire systems in the fire scene, if there are 10 particle systems in each of them on average. All in all, we can adjust every attributes of the system to obtain good balance between rendering effects and efficiency.

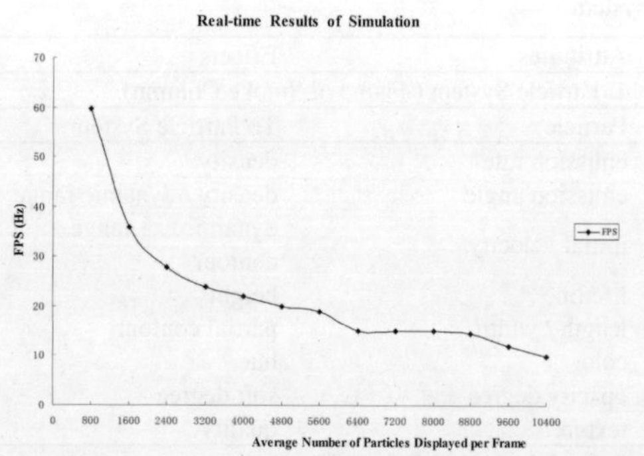

Figure 10. Frames per second vs. average number of particles per frame.

6. Conclusion and Future Work

This paper establishes a multi-level hierarchical model based on the classic particle systems model, including multi-level particle system model, its corresponding multi-level management and multi-level mechanisms for implementation. MLPSM is flexible enough to use due to its top-down control and dynamic combination features. Therefore, in addition to the fire spread, it could be applied to simulate rich multi-level natural scenes of different background.

Applying this new model, we have rendered fire and smoke and modeled their spread in simplified path. From the highest level of the Fire Scene to the most basic particles in the system, every detail in the simulation system could be adjusted according to simulation demand. Therefore, combined with rendering skills, parameters could be appropriately set in order to achieve the effect of rendering and real-time balance, which proves flexible and effective enough to control diverse states of the fire and to simulate the flames spreading process in various preset path. We've applied this visual fire and smoke effect into our three dimensional gymnasium model. Next, we will study behaviors of spectators in the gymnasium when it is on fire, and simulate the integral evacuation scene, including fire and people in the gymnasium.

Considering the limitations of graphical model and complexity of fire spreading process, we still need to take into account physical factors to make our spreading simulation more accurate and acceptable. Besides, simulation speed is not real-time enough when the number of particles reaches the order of magnitude of ten thousands, so we have to further improve our multi-level particle systems approach to meet the more large-scale simulation of fire spread.

Acknowledgments

The authors would like to thank Yaxin Guo and Xiaodong Wu for guidance and advice at the important beginning of this work. Thanks also to Kejia Ye and Kai Wang for encouragement and inspired discussions, especially for the helpful editorial assistance. Finally, thanks to everyone of the graphics project at the Multimedia Laboratory.

References

1. W. T. Reeves, *Particle Systems - A Technique for Modeling a Class of Fuzzy Objects. ACM Transactions on Graphics*, **2(2)**: 91-108 (1983).
2. A. Lamorlette and N. Foster, *Structural Modeling of Flames for a Production Environment. ACM Transactions on Graphics*. **21(3)**: 729-735 (2002).
3. Q. Zhang, H. Z. Wu, J. Y. Xie and Z. J. Zhang, *Study of Particle System Based Flame Modeling and Realization. Journal of Computer-Aided Design & Computer Graphics*. China, , **13(1)**, 78-82 (2001)
4. J. van der Burg, *Building an Advanced Particle System. Game Developer*. **3**, 44-50 (2000)
5. P. Beaudoin, S. Paquet and P. Poulin, Realistic and Controllable Fire Simulation. *No description on Graphics interface 2001*. 159-166 (2001)
6. C. Perry and R. Picard, *Synthesizing Flames and their Spreading. Proceedings of 5th Eurographics Workshop on Animation and Simulation*. 56-66 (1994)
7. OpenGL Architecture Review Board, D.Shreiner, M. Woo, J. Neider and T. Davis, *OpenGL Programming Guide: The Official Guide to Learning OpenGL, Version 1.4. Addison-Wesley Publishing Company*. (2004)
8. D.Q. Nguyen, R. Fedkiw and H.W. Jensen, *Physically Based Modeling and Animation of Fire. ACM Transactions on Graphics*. **21(3)**: 721-728 (2002)
9. Y. Eyman, *Rediscovering Fire: A Survey of Current Fire Models and Applications to 3D Studio Max*, http://www.cs.umd.edu/~mount/Indep/Yulia/fire.html, University of Maryland, Independent Study.

Session 2

EVALUATING USABILITY OF E-COMMERCE SYSTEMS FOR END-USER ADOPTION

ROSHANAK SAFAVI
MBA Center, Multimedia University,
Cyberjaya, Malaysia

The wide spread and relatively easy use of internet and other technologies enables E-commerce to grow exponentially due to reduction of costs, increase efficiencies and improve customer service. E-commerce is a part of human communication and social system, though technical aspects of E-commerce systems are important, there are also social variables which should come to consideration. Any E-commerce system can be viewed from two main view points; Technical and Human/Social. Pure technical solutions can not lead to a successful E-commerce. The main issue of this study is how to create systems and websites which considered being useable. The objective of research is to evaluate variables, both technical and human/social, affecting usability of systems from customers' point of view.

1. Introduction

Today E-commerce is defined as provision of instant access to products and services anytime, anywhere. The medium of internet, which is used widely today, has helped the E-commerce to grow faster, it reduces the transaction costs and gives the suppliers access to global consumers and buyers to global markets. E-commerce offers the opportunity to sellers to provide more information to their customers and educate them. Customers can enjoy the benefit of shop at any time, any where with ease and comfort; so today E-commerce can be called the most cost-effective way of trading.

The critical issue of designing a website is usability. There are two approaches for website usability, a website should be usable for human users and at the same time it should be usable for search engine crawler. The designers should exercise extreme care when they choose the application and navigation schemes. This issue is very critical as the human friendly navigation and search engine friendly navigation are in opposition. If the website wouldn't be recognized with the search engines properly, that would be a negative point for usability and popularity of the web.

Powell (2000) has defined the website usability (based on the international standards organization (ISO)) as "the extent to which a site can be used by a specified group of users to achieve specified goals with effectiveness, efficiency, and satisfaction in a specified context of use". It also implies that usability is user and task dependent, as well as being related to how well the user is able to accomplish what they set out to do, how efficiently the user can do this, and how satisfied the user is during and after the process [6]. Nielsen (2000) states, "Usability rules the Web. Simply stated, if the customer can't find a product, then he or she will not buy it, the web is ultimate customer-empowering environment" [3].

Hoffman and Steenkamp define quality cues as informational stimuli received by a customer prior to purchasing or consuming a product or service. Customers typically use quality cues in choosing between brands. With an e-commerce web site, the first quality cues come from the human interface [2].

Many researches have been conducted to evaluate the importance of usability, for example, Shacklett (2001) asserts that, "Twenty-eight percent of Web site transactions result in consumer failure and frustration....Six percent of users who leave a Web site in frustration say they won't return to the site or patronize the company" [7].

France Belanger et al.(2006) State that In order for a Web site to be deemed successful there must be a match between the firm's Web site objectives, the user's goals when using the Web site, and the Web site's design. Therefore, one way to identify design features is to map Web site goals to consumer goals [1].

The design of a usable and successful site is nit the end of mission, but for maintain the site usable the business should conduct usability testing frequently, Shneiderman (1980), a psychologist and computer scientist, added the need for usability testing that "confirms that an interface satisfies the user's requirements for simplicity, naturalness, or ease-of-use" [8].

2. Objectives of Study:

There are many variables influencing e-commerce website usability. In this study, first, these variables divided into 2 major categories;

✓Technical
✓Human/Social

Technical dimension is fundamental to establish a system, it is important for any e-commerce system to function properly technically but this is not the only issue, E-commerce systems are also a part of the human communication and social system which enable us to send, manipulate and interpret information across global networks, so social dimension must be also considered in developing the system and site.

2.1. *Objective one- Investigation of both technical and human/social aspects on usability of e-commerce websites*

The first objective of this study is to investigate and examine usability of the e-commerce website from two different point of view; Technical and Human/Social. For each aspect relevant variables and sub factors have been identified:

-Technical includes:

- Customer Service: Online Help, FAQ, Call Center and Web site Map
- Security : Network Security and Transaction security
- GUI Design : Page Design, Personalization, Information Presentation, registration &check out, Shopping Cart and payment system
- Feedback : Speed, Accuracy, Responsiveness and Understandability

-Human/Social Includes:

- Privacy : Personal and Financial
- Trustworthiness : Integrity, Authorization, Authentication, Confidentiality and Non-repudiation
- Navigation : Learnability, Searchability, Ease of use, Timeliness, Accessibility and Understanding

2.2. *Objective two- study the influence of website usability factors on online users*

According to this objective, the main goal of this study is to identify the influence of the discussed variables on usability of websites. The survey results indicated that users pay attention to both categories of variables.

3. Findings

The results of this research reinforced that among technical category, Security has the greatest important to users. The e-commerce website must convince the customers that they are working with a secure website and their information and sensitive data would not be revealed. The e-commerce website and system should employ proper hardware/software structure, algorithms and procedures to provide secure transactions. For example, secure e-commerce transactions require web servers and browsers that can handle digital certificates, Secure Socket Layer (SSL) and digital payments.

After security, users are concerned with the feedback returned from the site. Most of the users like to receive an acknowledgement from the site after every task done. For example, when a customer selects a product to purchase, the website should feedback him/her appropriately that the selected product has been added to the shopping cart. Actually users don't like blank pages and inappropriate reaction from the site, while any task is on progress, the user expect an appropriate feedback which convince him everything is in order and his request will be followed. By the way the feedback and acknowledgement must be clear and contain no technical term in order to make it easy for users to understand. Simple examples include highlighting a selection made by the user or filling a field on a form based on a user's selection from a pull down list. Another example is using the sound of a cash register to confirm that a product has been added to an electronic shopping cart. This last feedback feature can be found on Amazon.com, CyberRebates.com, WalMart.com, and other business-to-consumer (B2C) web sites. [4]

Design also plays an important role in attracting customers to the website, though it is not enough to keep customers loyal. The survey result showed that although the design and interface is an important role, but between this feature and trust feature, majority of the respondents voted to trust. By the way, procedures like personalization, registration and shopping cart is nowadays an indispensable part of any website and designers must consider them while designing the site. Personalization helps the system to observe all the activities users have done previously in a glance can help them to decide easily. Personalization gives the website the advantage of discovering buying patterns and other useful information. Some of the recommendations by experts conclude that Audio and video used to attract users, or generated in response to user input should enhance the buyer's experience and not distract from it. Audio sequences and video display segments should be limited to 20-30 seconds. The user should be able to interrupt video, audio, animation, or other multimedia display. Furthermore, the overuse of images, audio and video can increase the time in which a page downloads, which has a negative impact on usability. [4]

Availability of services like call center and online help is obviously proved. Today any website must have such service to satisfy their users in case of any help they need. Other features like website map and FAQ also useful to facilitate working with the website. Website designers can add applications such as chat rooms, Discussion Boards and many other to help buyers share their attitudes and experiences in order to motivate other users to purchase the products offered by the website.

Among Human/Social category, Privacy protection is an essential element in users' minds. The result of the research showed that almost 80 percent of users will terminate the website if they feel that there is not enough privacy protection applied. Web designers and administrators should employ qualified software and algorithm to achieve high level of privacy protection.

After privacy, users are concerned about the way they navigate with the website. Among the sub factors defined for navigation, users were concerned with the level of easiness in working with website. The users expect an interface which is easy to use; the user must be able to recognize all the features of a webpage clearly. The user must be oriented to the business and should not be confused with the design. The company's website must be easy to search and reach. The designer must consider all the elements which are necessary for a website to rank high in search engines operation. Timeliness and fast loading time is another important factor. Users and buyers prefer fast loading pages rather than a webpage with many images and animations but slow and hard to load.

The website must be accessible and reachable from any point. The designer should consider that the webpage must be loaded in any kind of hardware and compatible with all the browsers and operating systems.

The goal of an e-commerce website is to achieve high level of user participation so the website must be completely transparent and easy to understand for users. The designer should avoid using technical and unclear terms and try to make every aspect of the site completely clear and transparent for all the users. All the different parts of the website should follow a similar procedure, this helps users to easily learn how to work with the site and they won't get confused by different algorithms and procedures.

4. Conclusions

As a conclusion for this research, it should be stated that web developers and designers must pay attention to Human/Social variables as well as Technical variables, and they must always keep in mind that to persuade visitors to purchase and make them loyal buyers, only Technical capabilities is not enough.

The designer of the system and the site must define its market target appropriately and design the site accordingly in order to achieve high sale volume, and finally, it should be mentioned that usability testing must be done on regularly basis to order to keep the website always updated.

5. NOMENCLATURE

Shopping Cart: Shopping Cart is a software application that runs on the web server and allows customers to search for specific products and add it to a basket and place order for it.

Authorization: Ensuring authorized uses of systems and performance of business functions by authorized users only [5].

Authentication: Establishing that parties to an electronic transaction or communication are who they claim they are [5].

Integrity: Ensuring data on the host system or in transmission are not created, intercepted, modified or deleted illicitly [5].

Confidentiality: Warranting that data are only revealed to parties who have a legitimate need to know it or have access to it [5].

Non-Repudiation: party to some transaction or communication later denies that it has ever happened; some mechanism is in place to facilitate dispute resolution [5].

Acknowledgments

I would like to express my gratitude and special thanks Mr. T. Subramanian and Dr. G.Marthandan for their kind guidance. Definitely, without the attention and support they have given me, it was not possible for me to complete this research project.

6. References

1. France Bélanger, Weiguo Fan, L. Christian Schaupp, Anjala Krishen, Jeannine Everhart, David Poteet, and Kent Nakamoto, Web Site Success Metrics: 102 Addressing the Duality of Goals, December 2006/Vol. 49, No. 12 COMMUNICATIONS OF THE ACM (2006).

2. Hoffman, D.L. and Steenkamp, J-B. , Marketing and quality. In Hampton, J.J. (ed.) AMA Management Handbook (3rd edition), AMACOM, New York, pp. 2.65-2.68. (1994).

3. Nielsen, J., Designing Web Usability: The Practice of Simplicity, New Riders Publishing, (2000).

4. Norbert J. Kubilus, Designing an E-commerce Site for Users, crossroads, the ACM student magazine

5. Pauline Ratnasingham, The importance of trust in electronic commerce, Internet Research: Electronic Networking Applications and Policy Volume 8 · Number 4 1998 · pp. 313–321, MCB University Press · ISSN 1066-2243 (1998).

6. Powell, T. A., Web Design: The Complete Reference. Berkeley, CA: Osborne/McGraw-Hill, (2000).

7. Shacklett, M., Gauging Web site performance. Credit Union Magazine, 67, 6, 2001, 60-62 (2001).

8. Shneiderman, B., Software Psychology: Human Factors in Computer and Information Systems. Winthrop Publishers, Cambridge, MA(1980).

USING GRAPH TRANSFORMATION TO ANALYZE CONCURRENT RECONFIGURATIONS OF DYNAMIC SOFTWARE ARCHITECTURE*

YU ZHOU, SHUTIAN LÜ, XIAOXING MA, JIAN LÜ

State Key Lab. For Novel Software Technology, Nanjing University
Nanjing, 210093, China

Runtime reconfiguration of component-based systems is an important task in software engineering. In the decentralized settings, as the inherent uncertainty and dynamics introduced from the environments and the requirements, multiple reconfiguration choices might exist at the same time, which are quite possible in conflict. In this paper, we inspect this problem, model the software architectural reconfigurations as graph transformations and present a formal approach for the concurrent conflict and dependency detection based on the critical pair analysis. A scenario is presented to illustrate the feasibility of our approach and a visual IDE tool is developed to facilitate the process.

1. Introduction

Architecture-based runtime adaptation has been proposed as an effective way to increase the continuous availability of component-based software systems in uncertain environments [10,11]. Generally, such kinds of systems have embedded sensors to probe the context information, then propagate the changes to the rule management modules and direct the corresponding dynamic architectural reconfigurations accordingly. In the decentralized and distributed settings, interesting context changes might be reported from place to place, thus it is highly possible that multiple architectural reconfiguration rules are applicable at the same time. As these rules usually address different aspects of concerns, either functional or non-functional, and are not necessarily independent from each other, applying one rule may disable or enable another one. Therefore, in this case, how to detect the potential conflict and dependency relations between the reconfigurations will be an important issue for the efficient adaptation management.

The result set means that the entities in the element tuple are conflicting or dependent. For example, in a component-based software system, the trust management module reports an fraud behavior of a third-party component and the adaptation rule indicates its removal from the system. Meanwhile, a performance monitor reports a low-performance event of another component and the adaptation rule implies an addition of a new back-up component. If the new component relies on the functions of the third-party component stated above, a conflict would happen between these two reconfigurations. Manually assigning each rule with an application-specific priority as commonly adopted leads to an ad-hoc solution which only partly addresses the problem, as the developer may still be unaware of the potential conflicts or the dependency relations between the involved reconfiguration possibilities. Besides, this mechanism lacks a formal treatment of such problems.

Graph notations have been widely applied in software architecture modeling [1,7] due to their unique characteristics. Firstly, graph representation has an advantage of an intuitive visual correspondence to the common practice of box-line notation of software architecture; secondly, the widely recognized importance of connector as a first-class entity can be well captured by the notion of edge attributes; thirdly, by *production*, the graph rewrite techniques can be employed to describe the evolution and to check some interested properties, such as confluence, conflicts, etc., formally.

In this paper, we will focus on the third point listed above and inspect the applicability of graph transformation in the domain of dynamic software architectural reconfigurations. We leverage the theories from the critical pair analysis; inspect the relations of the reconfiguration rules such as dependence, confluence etc, and present a formal approach to analyze the potential conflicts of multiple reconfigurations. The rest of the paper is organized as follows. Section 2 introduces some basic notions relevant to the formalism of conflict analysis and outlines our approach. To illustrate its application and feasibility, a case study is presented with the tool support in Section 3 followed by some discussions on the lessons learned and the limitations of our approach in Section 4. Section 5 reviews some related work. Section 6 concludes the paper.

* This work is supported by the 973 program of China under grant No. 2009CB320702, NSF China under grant No. 60736015 and 863 program of China under grant No. 2007AA01Z178.

2. Reconfiguration Modeling and Analysis

For architecture-based self-adaptation rules, basically they have a spectrum of two layers as in [5], i.e., *goal management layer* and *change management layer*. The first handles the context changes which are usually reflected in the condition part of the rule. It is on the application level. The other deals with the reconfiguration actions which are on the architecture level. For example, a load-balancing rule specifies that when the workload of a component reaches a certain threshold, a backup component will be added dynamically to the system. As the condition part depends on the concrete requirements, it varies across applications. In contrast to this, the architectural reconfigurations are manipulated at the level of constituent components and connectors and can be specified as graph transformation rules [15]. Under such considerations, we will focus on the architecture level rule modeling. It fits in the *change actions management layer* in [5]. To detect reconfiguration dependency and conflicts of dynamic software architecture, their independence relations needs to be modeled and analyzed. In this section, we will first introduce some basic concepts, and then present our approach.

2.1. *Critical pair and dependency*

Critical pair analysis originates from term rewriting and later has been generalized to graph transformation to check whether the transformation system is confluent [12]. Given a graph *G*, a production $p : L \rightarrow R$ and a match $m : L \rightarrow G$, the transformation from *G* to *H* is specified as $t : G \xrightarrow{p,m} H$. A critical pair is a pair of transformations *(P1, P2)* in which $t1 : G \xrightarrow{p1,m1} H1$ and $t2 : G \xrightarrow{p2,m2} H2$ have potential conflicts with the minimal *G = m1(L1)Um2(L2)* to ensure that the critical pair sets for two rules are finite. Intuitively speaking, for two rules both applicable to a Graph *G*, to become a critical pair, at least one rule deletes the common item(s) of their match images in Graph *G* or generates graph objects that violate application conditions, e.g. NAC [4], of the other one.

To analyze critical pairs and dependency, first we need to distinguish the categories of transformation independence. There are two cases for independence, i.e. *parallel independence* and *sequential independence* [13]. Given two *alternative* direct transformations $t1 : G \xrightarrow{p1,m1} H1$ and $t2 : G \xrightarrow{p2,m2} H2$, if *m2(L2)∩m1(L1-dom(p1)) = NULL*, we say the direct transformation *P2* is *weakly parallel independent* of *P1*. If both *t1* and *t2* are mutually weakly independent of each other, the two transformations are parallel independent. In case of two *consecutive* direct transformations $t1 : G \xrightarrow{p1,m1} H1$ and $t2' : H1 \xrightarrow{p2,m2'} X$, we say that *t2'* is sequentially independent of *t1* if *m2'(L2)∩m1(R1-P1(L1))=NULL* and *m2'(L2-dom(P2))∩m1(R1)=NULL.* According to the local Church-Rosser theorem [13], the parallel independence of *P1* and *P2* is equivalent to the statement that there are a graph *X* and direct transformations $H1 \xrightarrow{p2,m2'} X$ and $H2 \xrightarrow{p1,m1'} X$ such that $G \xrightarrow{p1,m1} H1 \xrightarrow{p2,m2'} X$ and $G \xrightarrow{p2,m2} H2 \xrightarrow{p1,m1'} X$ are sequentially independent transformations. In the context of multiple architectural reconfigurations choices, this theorem states if the two (or multiple) reconfigurations are parallel independent, they can be applied in any order, and the transformation sequences will result in the same confluence.

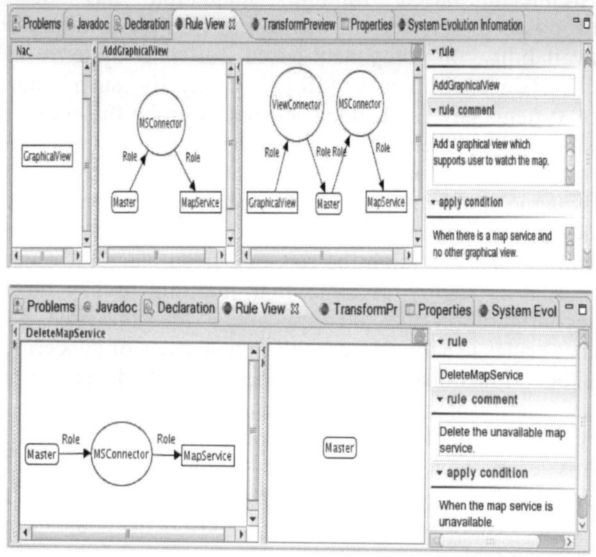

Figure 1. Reconfiguration conflict illustration

Independence is only a subset of the relations between transformation rules. There are other cases, such as the dependency and the conflict. Informally speaking, if the transformation result of one rule enables another one, it implies a dependency. If the application of one rule disables another one, they represent a potential conflict and form a critical pair. As a concrete example, Figure 1 illustrates a conflict situation. The rule *DeleteMapService* denotes a detachment of the map service from the master component. This may happen when the map service component is unavailable or untrustable. While the second rule *AddGraphicalView* adds a graphical interface component to display the map data retrieved from the map data component by the master component. This rule may be invoked when the system developer wants to provide the value-added service or when the network bandwidth is in good state. If the conditions of the both reconfiguration rules are satisfied, applying the *DeleteMapService* rule first would disable the application of the other one, as the left side of the rule *AddGraphicalVew* requires the existence of the *MapService* component. However, if the rule *AddGraphicalView* is applied first, it will not disable the application of *DeleteMapService*. Thus, in this critical pair, there is an asymmetric conflict.

2.2. *Architectural reconfiguration analysis*

We use *AGG* [14] to calculate the relations of graph transformation rules. *AGG* supports the critical pair and dependence analysis. It computes by overlapping the left hand sides of two rules in all possible ways to see whether they constitute a critical pair. *AGG* distinguishes three kinds of conflicts: *delete-use, produce-forbid, change-use attribute*, and three kinds of dependencies: *produce-use, delete-forbid, change-use attribute*. For details, we refer interested readers to [6]. After getting the relations between the pairs of the reconfiguration rules, we classify them into four sets, i.e., *independence, symmetric conflicts, dependency, asymmetric conflicts*. As dependency and asymmetric conflicts are partial order relations, if the concurrent rules belong to these two sets, the first rule of the pairs should be applied first, so as to enable the other one. If the concurrent rules are in the independence set, as it is free of conflicts and dependency, the order of applying them can be set freely. If the concurrent rules are in the symmetric conflicts, applying each one will disable the other one. In this case, human expertise has to be involved to decide which one has the priority. The next step is to map the transformations to the corresponding architectural reconfiguration. As stated previously, architectural reconfigurations can be reduced to the manipulation of the constituent elements of the software architecture. We extracted some primitive commands from Acme [3]. The reason why we use Acme as the underlying elementary commands lies in three considerations: 1, Acme can be used as the common denominator of the existing ADLs, as it provides the most common sets of ADL design concerns; 2, Acme is a general purpose architectural description language itself and can be extended flexibly; 3, there are program libraries which can be integrated in our tool. The basic reconfiguration commands of Acme are: *AttachmentCreateCommand, AttachmentDeleteCommand, ComponentCreateCommand, ComponentDeleteCommand, Connector-CreateCommand, ConnectorDeleteCommand, PortCreateCommand PortDeleteCommand, Role-CreateCommand, RoleDeleteCommand.* Accordingly, we have three graph models, i.e., component model, connector model, and role model. The port and the attachment are implemented as attributes of the component model and the role model respectively.

To facilitate graph transformation-based dynamic architecture modeling and reconfiguration commands generating, we have developed an integrated tool: *Vide*. *AGG* has been embedded as an external utility to analyze the rule relations. *Vide* is implemented in Java and released as an Eclipse plug-in. It supports the graph grammar directed development of software architecture and transformation. In this way, only rule compliant transformations can be applied. It bridges the gap between our previous work on runtime architecture object [8, 16, 17] and the analysis of concurrent transformation rules. The generated command list of the rules can be applied to the architecture object model, and in this way the potential conflicts are eliminated before applying. Figure 1 presents the rule view of the example transformations. A complete description of Vide is out of the scope of this paper, Figure 2 gives a basic overview of the user interface.

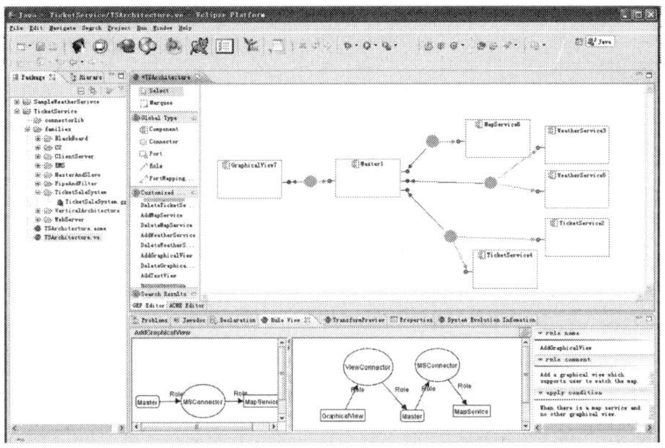

Figure 2. Vide user interface overview

3. Case Study

In this section, we use a simple online ticket-booking system as a running example. The system normally offers online ticket booking services plus other value-added services for example, location service, weather information services, etc. Those services are distributed and integrated from other third parties. It also has a graphical display component depending on the workload condition of the system or other factors. The type graph of the architecture elements is shown in Figure 3. There are three child-types of component type, i.e., *master, slave* and *view*. *Master* component is responsible for receiving the requests from the clients and delegating the work to other components. *Slave* component handles the requests from the master component and further has three different child-types, i.e., TicketService, Mapservice, WeatherService. *View* component is for the result display, graphical or textual. The first two kinds are functional components while the last one addresses non-functional concerns. The connectors interact with the components. Corresponding to their difference, there are four kinds of connectors, i.e., Viewconnector (for view service), WSConnector (for weather service), TSConnector (for ticket service), MSConnector (for map service).

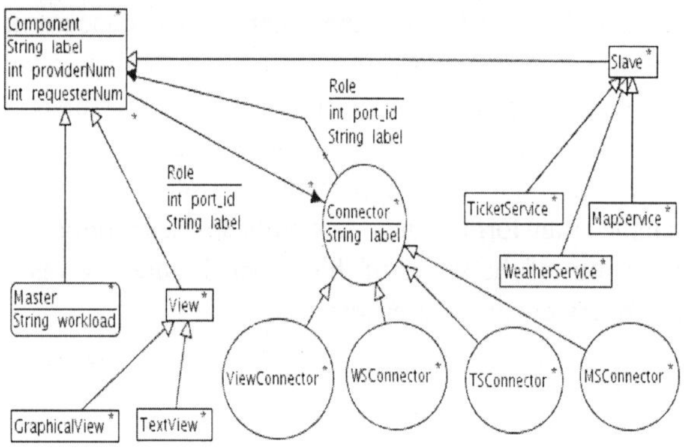

Figure 3. Type graph of the example

Because of the uncertainty and the changes from the dynamic environment, the system is under the pressure to evolve. The developer may identify some reconfiguration patterns. For example, when a new ticket broker is active and broadcasts the online ticket-booking service, it may lead to an AddTicketService rule, while an unavailable service leads to its detachment from the system. Ticket booking and weather broadcasting are two basic services provided to customers, while the map service is a value-added service. Below, we list some common but incomplete reconfigurations.

1. *AddTicketService*: integrates a new ticket service provider. Addition may happen when a new provider is found or the requirements change to add another kind of ticket-booking service;
2. *DeleteTicketService*: detaches a ticket service component from the system. Removal may happen when the service is unavailable or the component is unwanted. There is one *positive application condition* for this rule, i.e., at least one ticket service should exist after the removal;
3. *AddMapService*: integrates a map service into the system. This component provides location services, such as spotting, traffic routing etc. Addition may happen when the map service is available or trustable. In this scenario, we make an assumption that for one system there is only one map service, as the map covers whole interested cities;
4. *DeleteMapService*: detaches the map service from the system. It may happen when the component is unavailable or untrustable;
5. *AddWeatherService*: integrates a weather service into the system to provide weather broadcasting services;
6. *DeleteWeatherService*: detaches the weather service component from the system. Similar to the application condition of the *DeleteTicketService*, at least one weather service should exist after the removal;
7. *AddGraphicalView*: adds a graphical display to the application. This graphical interface displays the map data from users retrieval. Thus graphical view component depends on the existence of the map service component. The addition may happen when the bandwidth is in good condition or the workload of the server is not heavy;
8. *DeleteGraphicalView*: detaches the graphical display component from the system. This may happen when the bandwidth is not enough for graphical display;
9. *AddTextView*: adds a textview to the application. The textual display can save the bandwidth of the network and the workload of the *master* component.
10. *DeleteTextView*: detaches the textual display of the system. As there is only one view component at a time, this may happen when the system switch from a text view to a graphical view.

First, we examine these rules one by one and then check against the results obtained from automated tools. *AddTicketService* should have no conflicts relations with other reconfigurations, since adding a ticket service component will not disable other reconfigurations. Despite deleting a ticket service depends on its existence first, generally these two actions will not happen at the same time. This case holds similar for other Add-Delete pairs.

DeleteTicketService should have no conflicts with other reconfigurations except itself. Thus if multiple deletion reconfigurations of the same ticket service happen, they can be reduced to just one. This case holds similar for other Delete-* reconfigurations.

AddMapService should have causal relation with *AddGraphicalView* and conflicts with itself, as our system assumes that only one map service is needed. *DeleteMapService* should have conflicts with *AddGraphicalView*, since the graphical display are for the location spotting near the destination. The location data come from map service component. Deleting the map service component will disable the addition of a graphical view component.

AddWeatherService and *DeleteWeatherService* are similar to the cases of AddTicketService and DeleteTicketService. *AddGraphicalView* should have dependency relation with AddMapService and conflict with *DeleteMapService* as mentioned above. Besides, it also has conflicts with *AddTextView*, as the system assumes that there is only one view style at a time.

DeleteGraphicalView should have dependency relation with *AddTextView* since the graphical view component and text view component are mutual exclusive. Thus the latter reconfiguration depends on the former one.

AddTextView and *DeleteTextView* are different to the cases of *AddGraphicalView* and *DeleteGraphicalView*. This is because they are not dependent on the map service component. These two reconfigurations should be self-conflicting.

Figure 4 and Figure 5 illustrate the conflict and dependency relations analyzed by AGG. The two tables give a clear view on the relations of the reconfigurations. The obtained results correspond to our expectation. For example, *Add/DeleteTicketService* and *Add/DeleteWeatherService* have similar relationship with other reconfigurations. *AddGraphicalView* has conflicts with *AddTextView* and is dependent on *AddMapService*.

It is noteworthy that reported conflicts and dependencies are often more than there are actually. This is because *AGG* computes pairs by overlapping the left hand sides of the rules in all possible ways. For example, *AGG* reported 13 conflicts within two AddGraphicalView reconfigurations. In fact, all the reported conflicts are kinds of *produce-forbid* conflict. In actual settings, it is possible that there is only one occurrence of the left hand side of the reconfiguration rule in the architectural topology. This scenario is a very simplified version but still has ten reconfiguration patterns. Nevertheless, the proposed approach can capture the essential relations between the reconfigurations.

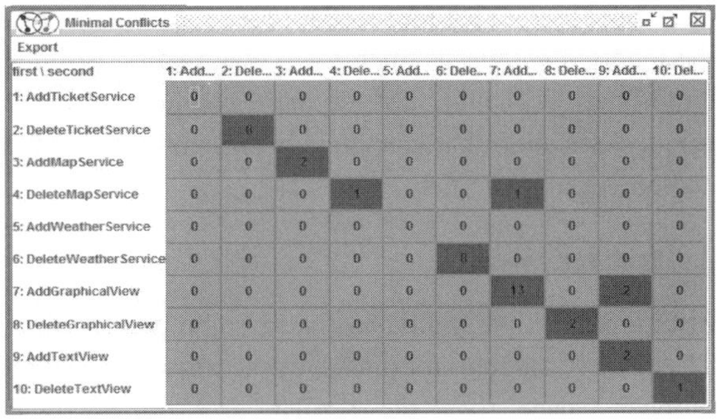

Figure 4. Conflict illustration

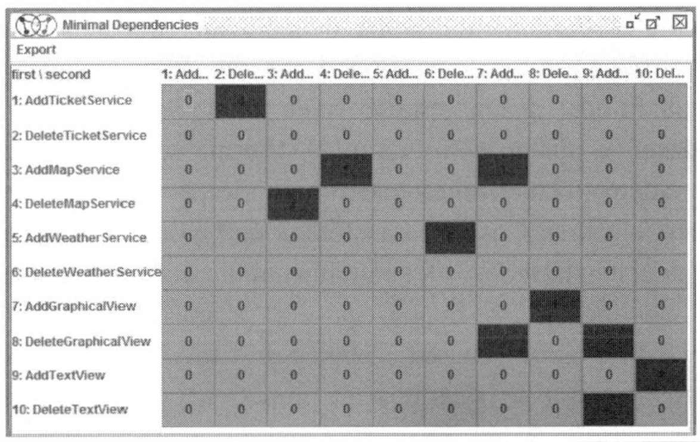

Figure 5. Dependency illustration

4. Discussion

Critical pairs only imply potential conflicts between reconfiguration rules. To decide whether or not they become real ones, other factors are needed to be taken into considerations. The key point is whether the pre-conditions will be fired at the same time.

As those reconfigurations are statically checked, the result can give the developers an insight on how to design the application specific rules. For example, developers can group all the possible reconfigurations into distinguished sets according to their inter-relations, e.g., independent, dependent, and conflicting. When the number of rules increases, the proposed approach can provide a more precise and helpful guidance. Our contributions are two-fold. First we demonstrate the feasibility of the critical pair analysis based approach to modeling and detecting the potential conflicts of concurrent reconfigurations; second, we explore an application domain of conflict and dependency analysis in graph transformations.

Despite we believe our approach has potential use for the effective reconfiguration management, the approach still requires further investigations. Currently, the transformation rule is context free, the critical pair is calculated by overlapping all the possibilities [14]. Thus the reported number is often more than reality. Besides, there is no mechanism for the more complicated graph rule specification that can support existential quantifier and universal quantifier.

5. Related Work

In this section, we briefly overview some related work. These work are relevant in two ways: within the similar problem space, i.e., the similar problem but with different solutions; within the similar solution space, i.e., similar solution but in different application domains.

Le Metayer demonstrated the feasibility of using conditional graph rewrite rules as a coordinator to describe dynamic evolution [7]. Wermelinger and Luiz Fiadeiro further investigated the concept and proposed an algebraic graph transformation based approach (double pushout) for architectural reconfiguration modeling [15]. Baresi et al. proposed a graph transformation based approach to model the architectural style refinement process [2]. But none of the work included the conflict and dependency analysis in case of multiple reconfigurations.

In [4], Hausmann et al. presented a critical pair analysis based approach for the detection of conflicting functional requirements. The theory from graph transformation makes the conflicts and dependency relations of use case models more precise and accurate. It demonstrated the applicability of graph transformation in UML use case models. Mens et al. further widened the application domain of graph transformation, e.g., refactoring dependency and conflict analysis [9]. The methodology is similar to ours. They used the graph transformation rules to specify refactoring or model inconsistency detection/resolution. *AGG* was also employed as the underlying tool.

6. Conclusions and Future Research

For architecture-based self-adaptive software systems, multiple reconfigurations are possible due to the various context changes. Ad-hoc solutions are not satisfactory to address the potential conflicts and dependencies between the involved reconfigurations. A rigorous modeling and analysis is necessary. Throughout this paper, we present a graph transformation based approach. We also developed a tool *Vide* which integrates *AGG* as an external utility to help with the architecture and reconfiguration rules design. Possibilities for the future research include applying the approach to more practical and complicated applications; tailoring the critical pair analysis algorithm to reduce the duplicate conflict or dependency report so as to better fit the problem context.

References

1. L. Baresi and R. Heckel. Tutorial introduction to graph transformation: A software engineering perspective. In Proc. of the First International Conference on Graph Transformation, ICGT 2002.
2. L. Baresi, R. Heckel, S. Th¨one, and D. Varr´o. Style-based refinement of dynamic software architectures. In WICSA, pages 155–166. IEEE Computer Society, 2004.
3. D. Garlan, R. Monroe, and D. Wile. Acme: Architectural Description of Component-Based Systems. Foundations of Component-Based Systems, pages 47–68, 2000.
4. J. Hausmann, R. Heckel, and G. Taentzer. Detection of conflicting functional requirements in a use case-driven approach: a static analysis technique based on graph transformation. In Proceedings of the 24th International Conference on Software Engineering, pages 105–115. ACM New York.
5. J. Kramer and J. Magee. Self-Managed Systems: an Architectural Challenge. In International Conference on Software Engineering, pages 259–268. IEEE Computer Society.
6. L. Lambers, H. Ehrig, and F. Orejas. Conflict Detection for Graph Transformation with Negative Application Conditions. LECTURE NOTES IN COMPUTER SCIENCE, 4178:61, 2006.
7. D. Le Metayer and R. IRISA. Describing software

architecture styles using graph grammars. Software Engineering, IEEE Transactions on, 24(7):521–533, 1998.

8. X. Ma, Y. Zhou, J. Pan, P. Yu, and J. Lu. Constructing self-adaptive systems with polymorphic software architecture. In Proceedings of the 19th SEKE, 2007.
9. T. Mens, G. Taentzer, and O. Runge. Detecting structural refactoring conflicts using critical pair analysis. Electronic Notes in Theoretical Computer Science, 127(3):113–128, 2005.
10. P. Oreizy, N. Medvidovic, and R. N. Taylor. Architecturebased runtime software evolution. In ICSE '98: Proceedings of the 20th international conference on Software engineering, IEEE.
11. P. Oreizy, N. Medvidovic, and R. N. Taylor. Runtime software adaptation: framework, approaches, and styles. In ICSE Companion '08: pages 899–910, ACM.
12. D. Plump. Hypergraph Rewriting: Critical Pairs and Undecidability of Confluence. Term Graph Rewriting: Theory and Practice, 1993.
13. G. Rozenberg. Handbook of graph grammars and computing by graph transformation: volume I. foundations. World Scientific Publishing Co., Inc. River Edge, NJ, USA, 1997.
14. G. Taentzer. AGG: A Graph Transformation Environment for Modeling and Validation of Software. LECTURE NOTES IN COMPUTER SCIENCE, 3062:446–453, 2004.
15. M. Wermelinger and J. Fiadeiro. A graph transformation approach to software architecture reconfiguration. Science of Computer Programming, 44(2):133–155, 2002.
16. Y. Zhou. A runtime architecture-based approach for the dynamic evolution of distributed component-based systems. In Proc. of ICSE Companion '08: ACM Press, 2008.
17. Y. Zhou, J. Pan, X. Ma, B. Luo, X. Tao, and J. Lu. Applying ontology in architecture-based self-management applications. In Proc. of the 2007 ACM SAC, pages 97–103. ACM Press, 2007.

SECURE MULTI-PARTY COMPUTATION PROTOCOL FOR STATISTICAL COMPUTATION ON ENCRYPTED DATA

ROHIT PATHAK*†

Acropolis Institute of Technology & Research, Rajiv Gandhi Technical University (Bhopal), Indore Madhya Pradesh, India

SATYADHAR JOSHI

Shri Vaishnav Institute of Technology & Science, Rajiv Gandhi Technical University (Bhopal), Indore Madhya Pradesh, India

In this paper we have shown how our proposed protocol for Secure Multi-Party Computation (SMC) can be used for Statistical Computations. Statistical computations and surveys involve confidential data from many parties or organizations. As the concerned data is property of the organization or the party, preservation and security of this data is of prime importance. Although the computation requires data from all the parties, but none of the associated parties would want to reveal their data to the other parties. We have shown how our protocol can be used to perform computation on encrypted data. The protocol is called Virtual Party Protocol (VPP). The data is encrypted in a manner that it does not affect the result of the computation. It uses modifier tokens which are distributed among virtual parties, and finally used in the computation. The computation function uses the acquired data and modifier tokens to compute right result from the encrypted data. Thus without revealing the data, right result can be computed and privacy of the parties is maintained.

1. Introduction

1.1. *Recent Works*

Yao has described millionaires' problem and gave the solution by using Deterministic Computations and introduced a view of Secure Computation [1]. We see about collaborative benchmark problem and a proposed solution in which the private shares are changed but in a manner that the sum remained the same [2]. Mikhail *et al.* has provided privacy-preserving solutions to collaborative forecasting and benchmarking that can be used to increase the reliability of local forecasts and data correlations, and to conduct the evaluation of local performance compared to global trends [3]. Wenliang *et al.* has proposed development of practical solutions to SMC problems, a new paradigm, in which we use an acceptable security model that allows partial information disclosure [4]. Linda *et al.* presents a unified approach to multi level database security based on two ideas: a trusted filter and an inference engine [5].

Wenliang *et al.* proposes the privacy preserving cooperative linear system of equations problem and privacy-preserving cooperative linear least-square problem [6]. Ran *et al.* has shown how uncorrupted parties may deviate from the case where even protocol by keeping record of all past configurations [7]. Mikhal *et al.* have given a protocol for sequence comparisons in which neither party reveals anything about their private sequence to the other party [8]. A Secure Supply-Chain Collaboration (SSCC) protocols that enable supply-chain partners to cooperatively achieve desired system-wide goals without revealing the private information of any of the parties, even though the jointly-computed decisions require the information of all the parties is proposed by Atallah *et al.* [9]. The problem of defining and achieving security in a context where the database is not fully trusted, i.e., when the users must be protected against a potentially malicious database is discussed by Ueli *et al.* [10]. We have seen building a decision-tree classifier from training data in which the values of individual records have been perturbed, and reconstruction procedure to accurately estimate the distribution of original data values has been described [11].

1.2. *Problem Statement*

In all we see a lot of work in SMC in past but no one has focused on Statistical Computations. Statistical computations include data from many organizations, and the safety of the data of the organization is of the prime concern. Suppose a statistical calculation is to be performed among several organizations. This calculation includes information related to various person's related to the organization, may it be employees working for the organization or the customers of the organization such as customers of a bank. In this case, information of every person is to be kept secure so as to keep privacy of every individual. Our protocol called the Virtual Party Protocol (VPP) [12] can be used safely to ensure the privacy of individual and preserving the data of the organization as a whole by not revealing the right data and will allow us to reach zero hacking security. In this method we will create some fake data and some virtual parties. Since the calculation is not dependent upon the number of parties, we can create any desired number of virtual parties. Now we will encrypt the data and create modifier tokens correspondingly. This modified data is mixed with fake data. These modifier tokens are related to the modification done in the data and will be used in the final computation to obtain the correct result. Now this modified data and the modifier tokens are distributed among the virtual parties. These parties will send their data to trusted anonymizers. These trusted anonymizers will send the data to un-trusted anonymizers. The un-trusted anonymizers will send this data to Third Party for computation. Third Party will use the data and the modifier tokens to compute the result. The modifier tokens will aid to bring the result obtained by the encrypted data values. The modifier tokens in any manner will not reveal the identity of the party or such. The modifier is a short collection of information which is used in the final computation to ensure the right result. The method of encryption, modifier tokens, encrypted data and the method of computation all are interdependent. With proper configuration zero hacking security is achieved with this protocol.

2. Virtual Party Protocol

2.1. *Informal description*

We have to compute the function $f(a_1, a_2, a_3..., a_n)$ where the function is dependent on the number of data items sent by the organization. There are n parties $P_1, P_2, P_3..., P_n$. Each party P_i has data $X_{i1}, X_{i2}, X_{i3}..., X_{im}$. Each party P_i has some trusted anonymizers $A_{i1}, A_{i2}, A_{i3}..., A_{ix}$. There are z number of un-trusted anonymizers $A_1, A_2, A_3..., A_z$.

For every party P_i we will create some fake trivial data entries $F_{i1}, F_{i2}, F_{i3}..., F_{iq}$, where q is the total number of fake entries. The total number of fake entries q may be different for every party P_i but for the sake of simplicity in explanation it is kept same for every party. The fake data is generated in a manner that it doesn't effects the overall result. We will group this data with original data entries $X_{i1}, X_{i2}, X_{i3}..., X_{im}$. Thus the new group of data having $m+q$ total number of data items, i.e. $D_{i1}, D_{i2}, D_{i3}..., D_{i(m+q)}$. The value of each data $D_{i1}, D_{i2}, D_{i3}..., D_{i(m+q)}$ is encrypted to obtain the encrypted data $E_{i1}, E_{i2}, E_{i3}..., E_{i(m+q)}$.

For every party P_i we will create k virtual parties $P_{i1}, P_{i2}, P_{i3}..., P_{ik}$. Encrypted data $E_{i1}, E_{i2}, E_{i3}..., E_{i(m+q)}$ is distributed randomly among the virtual parties $P_{i1}, P_{i2}, P_{i3}..., P_{ik}$. Modifier tokens $T_{i1}, T_{i2}, T_{i3}..., T_{ik}$ are generated for every party P_i. These modifier tokens are randomly distributed among the virtual parties $P_{i1}, P_{i2}, P_{i3}..., P_{ik}$ such that every virtual party gets one modifier token. Encryption of data and generation of modifier tokens is explained in section III and IV respectively.

Now the virtual parties $P_{i1}, P_{i2}, P_{i3}..., P_{ik}$ distributes their data and modifier tokens randomly among the trusted anonymizers $A_{i1}, A_{i2}, A_{i3}..., A_{ix}$. Trusted anonymizers distribute their data randomly among the un-trusted anonymizers $A_1, A_2, A_3..., A_z$. Anonymizers can take data from multiple parties. The data of the un-trusted anonymizers is sent to third party.

The function $h()$ uses the encrypted data and the modifier tokens to compute the right result. Function $h()$, will vary for different types of computation and will depend highly on $f()$.

Third party will compute the value of function $h(E_{11}, E_{12}, E_{13}..., E_{1j}...E_{i1}, E_{i2}, E_{i3}..., E_{ij}, T_{11}, T_{12}, T_{13}..., T_{1j}...,T_{i1}, T_{i2}, T_{i3}..., T_{ij})$ which is the desired result, same as the result computed by the function $f(X_{11}, X_{12}..., X_{1m}, X_{21}, X_{22}..., X_{2m}, X_{31}, X_{32}..., X_{3m}..., X_{n1}, X_{n2}..., X_{nm})$, and this result is declared publicly.

2.2. *Formal description*

VPP Algorithm

Identifier List:

P_i – parties where i ranges from 1 to n

X_{ij} – Data of party P_i where j ranges from 1 to m

F_{ij} – Fake data of party P_i where j ranges from 1 to q

D_{ij} – total data including the fake and the original data

P_{ij} – Virtual Party of party P_i where j ranges from 1 to k

E_{ij} – Encrypted data associated with party P_i where j ranges from 1 to $m+q$

A_{ij} – trusted anonymizer of party P_i where j ranges from 1 to x

A_y – untrusted anonymizer, where y ranges from 1 to z

TP – third party

Start VPP

- Create k virtual parties P_{ij} for every party P_i
- Create fake data F_{ij} for every party P_i
- Group fake data F_{ij} with original data X_{ij} to get D_{ij}
- Encrypt data D_{ij} to get E_{ij}
- Create modifier tokens T_{ij} for every party P_{ij}
- Distribute the encrypted data E_{ij} among the virtual parties P_{ij}
- Send the data and modifier tokens from party P_{ij} to trusted anonymizer A_{ij}
- Send the data and modifier tokens from trusted anonymizer A_{ij} to un-trusted anonymizer A_y
- Send the data from un-trusted anonymizer A_y to *TP*
- Calculate the result at *TP* using the encrypted data and the modifier tokens
- The result is announced by *TP*

End of Algorithm

3. Application

3.1. *A secure Average*

Suppose we have to compute the average salary of persons among several organizations. We will proceed as follows:

There are n Organizations $P_1, P_2, P_3..., P_n$. The data given by organization P_i is the salaries of its workers, i.e. $X_{i1}, X_{i2}, X_{i3}..., X_{ik}$, where k is the number of workers. The number of workers k may be different for every organization P_i but for the sake of simplicity in explanation it is kept same for every organization.

We will now generate some fake workers and modifier keys correspondingly. The way for average computation is to insert some random number values and their negative values as fake salary data for the fake workers. Like a person having salary 10000 and another having data -10000. The modifier token can hold the number of fake data entries. We can associate one modifier token with every virtual party. Now suppose we have inserted q number of fake workers in the organization then the sum of all the modifier tokens $T_1, T_2, T_3..., T_q$, should be the number of fake workers inserted, i.e. $T_1 + T_2 + T_3 +..., T_q = q$. Now a good way to find out values of $T_1, T_2, T_3..., T_q$ is to generate random values for $T_2, T_3, T_4..., T_q$ and the value of $T_1 = q - (T_2, T_3, T_4..., T_q)$.

Other method's to encrypt data and generate modifier tokens is explained in further sections of the paper.

Now we can alter the salaries, like we can subtract a number from a person's salary and add it to another person's salary thus not affecting the average, but preserving the possibility of leaking the salary of an individual.

Now we will distribute the workers among the virtual organizations and the modifier tokens as well.

These virtual organizations will send their data and modifier tokens to trusted anonymizers. The trusted anonymizers will send this to un-trusted anonymizers, which will then send it to Third Party.

The Third Party will compute the average but with a modified function for average. The modified function for average is $h(G_{11}, G_{12}, G_{13}..., G_{1j}...G_{i1}, G_{i2}, G_{i3}..., G_{ij}, T_{11}, T_{12}, T_{13}..., T_{1j}..., T_{i1}, T_{i2}, T_{i3}..., T_{ij}) = (G_{11} + G_{12} + G_{12} + ..., G_{1j} + ..., G_{i1} + G_{i2} + G_{i3}+..., G_{ij}) / (T - (T_{11}+T_{12}+T_{13}..., T_{1j}..., T_{i1}+T_{i2}+T_{i3}..., T_{ij}))$.

Where T is the total number of workers including the fake workers, as seen by the Third Party. According to our assumptions $T = (k+q) \times n$.

By the above method we get the result which can be announced publicly. As every virtual party approaches the third party individually so if the third party is malicious we can safely send our organizations data. And also we have altered the salary of every worker so we have also preserved the privacy of individual worker. And as we have inserted a number of fake worker profiles we have prevented anyone from knowing the exact number of workers belonging to a particular organization. We have covered almost every aspect of security.

3.2. *A secure Root Mean Square*

Suppose we have n parties $P_1, P_2, P_3..., P_n$ and they all have a number $X_1, X_2, X_3..., X_n$ respectively. Now if we have to compute the root mean square of the numbers from all the parties, then we will proceed as follows.

Every party P_i will make virtual parties $P_{i1}, P_{i2}, P_{i3}..., P_{ik}$, where k is the number of virtual parties made by every party. The number of virtual parties, k may be different for every party P_i but for the sake of simplicity in explanation it is kept same for every party.

We know the formula for RMS is:

$$f(X_1, X_2, X_3..., X_n) = \sqrt{\frac{X_1^2 + X_2^2 + X_3^2 + ...X_n^2}{n}}$$

But the modified function which is to be used for computation on encrypted data is:

Function $h() = \sqrt{\dfrac{\sum_{i=1}^{n}(E_{i1}{}^2 + E_{i2}{}^2 + E_{i3}{}^2 + ...E_{ik}{}^2)}{T - (\sum_{i=1}^{n} T_{i1} + T_{i2} + T_{i3} + ...T_{ik})}}$

Let a function $g(X) = X^2$

Let the encrypted data of each virtual party P_{ij} be E_{ij}.

Now for every Party Pi the encrypted data E_{i1}, E_{i2}, E_{i3}..., E_{ik} should satisfy the following equation:

$g(X_i) = g(E_{i1}) + g(E_{i2}) + g(E_{i3}) + \ldots, g(E_{ik})$

Now every party P_i will generate E_{i1}, E_{i2}, E_{i3}..., E_{ik} satisfying the above equation.

Let the modifier tokens for every party P_{ij} be T_{ij}.

Now for every party P_i the modifier tokens should satisfy the following equation:

$T_{i1} + T_{i2} + T_{i3} + \ldots, T_{ik} = k\text{-}1$

These modifier tokens are generated using any method.

Now the data and modifier tokens by every virtual party is sent to trusted anonymizers and they then send it to un-trusted anonymizers which then send them to the third party for computation. Now the modified function *h()* for RMS, as already defined is used for computation which brings us the right result after computation on the encrypted data.

4. Statistical Computations

Various statistical computation formulas are listed below along with their counter parts to be used in Virtual Party Protocol.

Mean

Original

$$\bar{x} = \frac{1}{n}\sum_{i=1}^{i=n} x_i$$

Virtual Party Protocol Version

$$\bar{x} = \frac{\sum_{i=1}^{i=n}\left(E_{i1} + E_{i2} + E_{i3} + \ldots E_{ik}\right)}{T - \left(\sum_{i=1}^{i=n}\left(T_{i1} + T_{i2} + T_{i3} + \ldots T_{ik}\right)\right)}$$

Variance

Original

$$s^2 = \frac{1}{n-1}\sum_{i=1}^{i=n}\left(x_i - \bar{x}\right)^2$$

Virtual Party Protocol Version

$$s^2 = \frac{\sum_{i=1}^{i=n}\left(\alpha_{i1}^2 + \alpha_{i2}^2 + \alpha_{i3}^2 + \ldots \alpha_{ik}^2\right)}{T - \left(\sum_{i=1}^{i=n}\left(T_{i1} + T_{i2} + T_{i3} + \ldots T_{ik}\right)\right) - 1}$$

Where

$\alpha_{i1} + \alpha_{i2} + \alpha_{i3} + \ldots \alpha_{ik}$ are the secondary modifier tokens

and

$$\left(x_i - \bar{x}\right)^2 = \left(\alpha_{i1}^2 + \alpha_{i2}^2 + \alpha_{i3}^2 + \ldots \alpha_{ik}^2\right)$$

Standard Deviation

Original

$$s = \sqrt{\frac{1}{n-1}\sum_{i=1}^{i=n}\left(x_i - \bar{x}\right)^2}$$

Virtual Party Protocol Version

$$s = \sqrt{\frac{\sum_{i=1}^{i=n}\left(\alpha_{i1}^2 + \alpha_{i2}^2 + \alpha_{i3}^2 + \ldots \alpha_{ik}^2\right)}{T - \left(\sum_{i=1}^{i=n}\left(T_{i1} + T_{i2} + T_{i3} + \ldots T_{ik}\right)\right) - 1}}$$

Where

$\alpha_{i1} + \alpha_{i2} + \alpha_{i3} + \ldots \alpha_{ik}$ are the secondary modifier tokens

and

$$\left(x_i - \bar{x}\right)^2 = \left(\alpha_{i1}^2 + \alpha_{i2}^2 + \alpha_{i3}^2 + \ldots \alpha_{ik}^2\right)$$

Skewness

Original

$$\gamma_1 = \sum_{i=1}^{i=n} \left(\frac{x_i - \bar{x}}{s} \right)^3$$

Virtual Party Protocol Version

$$\gamma_1 = \sum_{i=1}^{i=n} \left(\beta_{i1}^3 + \beta_{i2}^3 + \beta_{i3}^3 + \ldots \beta_{ik}^3 \right)$$

Where

$\beta_{i1}^3 + \beta_{i2}^3 + \beta_{i3}^3 + \ldots \beta_{ik}^3$ are secondary modifier tokens

and

$$\left(\frac{x_i - \bar{x}}{s} \right)^3 = \beta_{i1}^3 + \beta_{i2}^3 + \beta_{i3}^3 + \ldots \beta_{ik}^3$$

Kurtosis

Original

$$\gamma_2 = \sum_{i=1}^{i=n} \left(\frac{x_i - \bar{x}}{s} \right)^4$$

Virtual Party Protocol Version

$$\gamma_2 = \sum_{i=1}^{i=n} \left(\chi_{i1}^4 + \chi_{i2}^4 + \chi_{i3}^4 + \ldots \chi_{ik}^4 \right)$$

Where

$\chi_{i1}^4 + \chi_{i2}^4 + \chi_{i3}^4 + \ldots \chi_{ik}^4$ are secondary modifier tokens

and

$$\left(\frac{x_i - \bar{x}}{s} \right)^4 = \chi_{i1}^4 + \chi_{i2}^4 + \chi_{i3}^4 + \ldots \chi_{ik}^4$$

Conclusion

In this paper we have shown how our proposed SMC protocol named Virtual Party Protocol (VPP) and accompanying algorithm VPP can be used for secure Statistical computations. We have corroborated that we can create fake data and distribute it among the generated virtual parties and send this data along with modifier tokens to carry out computations on encrypted data using an improvised computation method. Anonymizer is used to hide the identity of the parties. VPP is used to perform computation on encrypted data. The protocol and algorithm are highly scalable and optimized for computations of surveys, banking, business etc. It can allow us to reach zero hacking security for a wide variety of applications. An example of the use of protocol has been substantiated. Encryption methods have been built for certain common functions and the process of generating modifier tokens for a collective method has been shown. SMC's are used for many big surveys and large scale statistical calculations. With the use of VPP most of the statistical calculations and other computations can be performed optimally with enhanced security and privacy without revealing the data to other parties and even to the Trusted Third Party.

References

1. Yao, Andrew C., "Protocols for secure computations," Proc. of *The 23rd Annual Symposium Foundations of Computer Science*, pp. 160-164.
2. Mikhail Atallah, Marina Bykova, Jiangtao Li, Keith Frikken, Mercan Topkara, "Private collaborative forecasting and benchmarking," Proc. of *The 2004 ACM workshop on Privacy in the Electronic Society* (2004).
3. Mikhail Atallah, Marina Bykova, Jiangtao Li, Keith Frikken, Mercan Topkara, "Private collaborative forecasting and benchmarking," Proc. of *The 2004 ACM workshop on Privacy in the electronic society*, pp. 103 – 114 (2004).
4. Wenliang Du, Zhijun Zhan, "A practical approach to solve secure multi-party computation problems," Proc. of *The New Security Paradigms Workshop*, (2002).
5. Linda M. Null, Johnny Wong, "A unified approach for multilevel database security based on inference engines," Tran*saction of ACM New York, NY*, USA, Vol. 21 , Issue 1 (Feb 1989).
6. Wenliang Du; Atallah, M.J., "Privacy-preserving cooperative scientific computations," Proc. *14th IEEE Computer Security Foundations Workshop*, pp. 273 – 282 (Jun 2001).
7. Ran Canetti, Uri Feige, Oded Goldreich, Moni Naor, "Adaptively secure multi-party computation," Proc. *The 28th annual ACM symposium on Theory of computing*.
8. Mikhail J. Atallah, "Secure and Private Sequence Comparisons," Proc. *The 2003 ACM workshop on Privacy in the Electronic Society* (2003).

9. Atallah, M.J. Elmongui, H.G. Deshpande, V. Schwarz, L.B., "Secure supply-chain protocols," Proc. *IEEE International Conference, E-Commerce* (2003).
10. Ueli Maurer ETH Zurich, Zurich, "The role of cryptography in database security," Proc. *The 2004 ACM SIGMOD international conference on Management of data* (2004).
11. Rakesh Agrawal, Ramakrishnan Srikant, "Privacy-Preserving Data Mining," Proc. *The ACM SIGMOD Conference on Management of Data* (2000).
12. Rohit Pathak, Satyadhar Joshi, "Secure Multi-party Computation Using Virtual Parties for Computation on Encrypted Data," Proceedings of *The Third International Conference on Information Security and Assurance 2009, Springer Lecture Notes on Computer Science 5576-0412* (June 2009).

Event Driven Architecture Through Nano Computing Models

JOBY JOSEPH
Head, Dept. Comp. Science, St. Anthony's College
Shillong, Meghalaya 793001, India

Dr. A. CLEMENTKING
Head, Dept. of MCA, Loyola College
Chennai, Tamil Nadu 620010, India

This paper is a study on the popular web business model of Event Driven Architecture. In the IT world of business and services, every response of business is dependent on many other related features. In the service related models, one architecture that is winning much appreciation is the Event Driven Architecture. This paper tries to study the Event Driven nature common in business systems and tries to propose a support architecture for such model from the Nano Computing Arena. The model that we propose is by incorporating the Event Driven Nature at both process and design level. Reconfigurable architectures, which are emerging areas of research, seem to be right candidates for this. The paper is an attempt to bring together the ideas of this Event oriented flow at every level of the system.

1. Introduction

Event driven architecture has emerged as one of the most important models in the IT world today. In a complex world of business, driven by the novelties of Information Technology, every decision and direction taken has its implication on other related issues. In every business model, the inner logic of design is an Event-driven one. In an event-driven world, the entity must respond to events within times that are externally determined. They act when the external stimuli changes and not according to any pre-planned order.

Organizations are always event driven in a real world sense. However, the IT systems weren't equally event driven as they were built. But that is not the story today. More and more business models are adapting to a paradigm where responses are based on related events. Today's models are looking at a more Event Driven Architecture at all levels of processing. The reasons for this change are many, viz. the increasing pace of business, the growing IT and On-line responses etc. [1].

Most of such event driven architectures are looking only at the software and level of programs. We could stretch the idea further. One could think of such an Event Driven Hardware too. In such a setup, we can have a multi-layered architecture model that incorporates the *Event-Driven* ideas at the software as well as at the hardware level, as shown below.

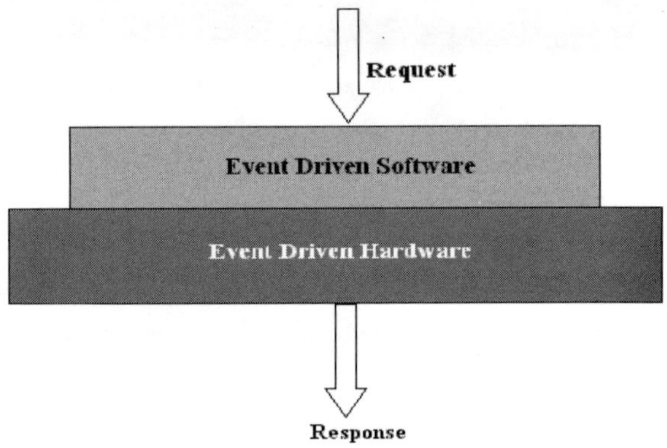

Figure 1. An Event Driven System Model

2. UNDERSTANDING THE EVENT DRIVEN ARCHITECTURE

In an Event Driven Architecture, a specific thing happens inside or outside the business model and that disseminates immediately to all interested parties – both human and automated. The concerned parties evaluate the event and selectively take appropriate action. The event drives an action that my involve a service, the triggering of a business process and/or further information processing. Such an event driven model is extremely loosely coupled and highly distributed. The source of the event only transpires the event and so will not know the subsequent processing associated with the event. This makes such an architecture best suited for asynchronous flows of work and information [2].

2.1. *Event Processing*

In most event processing models, we have a computing process that responds to event objects. The event processing mostly includes creating, reading, deleting, transforming and responding to such objects. Such systems will mostly comprise of two major components: First, a Sensor or a source that senses any event and emits event objects. And secondly, a Responder, that receives and responds to such event objects. Both these actions occur at two layers of the model [3]. Any EDA model will consist of multiple levels of sensors and responders. Each acts in response to a request from the other.

2.2. *Event Processing Styles*

In most EDA, we find three general styles of event processing. They are Simple, Stream and Complex.

2.2.1. *Simple Event Processing*

In such a model an event happens and it initiates many down stream actions. In most real time flow of business systems, such models are used.

2.2.2. *Stream Event Processing*

In such a model, we have both ordinary and notable events happening. This model is commonly used to drive the real time flow of information in and around the enterprise, making decision making in time.

2.2.3. *Complex Event Processing*

Complex Event Processing deals with evaluating a combination of events and then taking the action. There is a high degree of event-correlation possible here. This model will need high degree of matching and processing techniques. This is commonly used in models that need high degree of adaptability, responses and inter-dependencies. [4]

In all these levels of interaction and information flow, there is a need of high degree of data interchange and interconnect. The architectural design of the models will have to be one that supports this at the processing and design levels of the model.

2.3. *Event Flow Layers*

Every event in the model starts with an event being generated at some level and proceeds to any down-stream layers to meet its activity. This involves four logical layers:

2.3.1. *Event Generator*

This is the source that generates an event. The source may be an application, service or a request of any type. In most cases, not all events are generated in the required format for processing. In such cases, they have to be transformed to a format prior to depositing the event into the next stage.

2.3.2. *Event Channel*

The event channel typically is the messaging backbone, which transports standard formatted events between the event generators, the processing engines and the downstream layers.

2.3.3. *Event Processing*

At this layer, once the events are received, they are evaluated against the set of rules for processing and appropriate span out actions are initiated. The actions may include invoking a service, initiating a business process, publishing the event to another system, generating another new event or capturing the event for a later process.[5]. The process is shown below in the diagram.

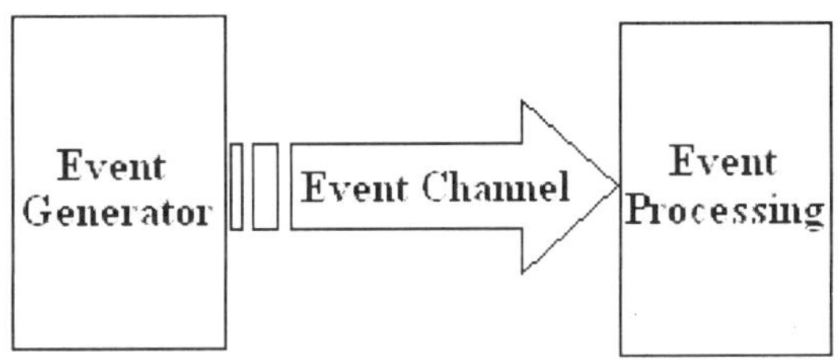

Fig. 2. Event Flow Layers

It is seen that in the processing and information flow of EDA model, there is a high degree of parallelism and data inter connect required. Most models that we have seen have its architectural limitations in its task of information flow. The idea here is to propose a new model that can provide this high level of interconnect at the level of processing and design. Our idea is to propose a new architecture, drawing inspiration from *Nano models*. In the sections that follow, we are going to look at such alternatives that can take the Event Driven Architectures into higher level of processing.

3. Nano Computer Architecture

Most general computing models are based on the "Stored Program" model which relies heavily on media for inter connections and circuitry. We are here shifting our focus. The aim of the nano computer architecture is to shift the focus from the processing arena to the communication level. Using such an architecture we can achieve high degree of parallelism and interconnect and build higher and more efficient business models that can enhance event processing and service.

The basic limitation that make us look up to a higher technology is the from the problem associated with the scaling of CMOS devices. Many nano scale alternatives have been suggested as alternatives to this. Many laboratory experiments have suggested better alternatives and seem to suggest so. Basing on such interconnects, newer architectures have been proposed. But in practice, they all lack real testing and we lack real knowledge to suggest for sure which of these has the potential for robust and efficient realization. [6]

The idea of this paper is to look at an alternative architecture, drawing inspirations from the findings of nano computing, that includes the basic building blocks of the field. We want to enhance the Event Driven Architecture, by incorporating building blocks of Nano Computing.

3.1. Event Driven Nano Architecture

Most research interests in the field of design architectures have been as a response to the challenges offered by computing needs. One of such responses was to look at ways of increasing existing machine resources- be at processor, memory or other peripheral levels. Though these innovations bring about some degree of efficiency and parallelism, very often they run into physical and interconnect limitations.[7] It is here that we come to suggest a paradigm shift in the very architectural nature of the design.

If the system in an Event Driven model needs constant requests and responses between different layers of the system, the process can be made more efficient if the very architecture itself can reconfigure itself to the needs of the request. In the present day systems, most responses are unit dependent and so involve massive interconnections between layers. There are many options that are before us to realize this at the hardware level.

Field Programmable Gate Arrays(FPGA) are thought of as the basic building blocks in this line. They can offer some degree of flexibility and architectural optimization, however, they tend to be inefficient in implementing certain types of operations. The challenge is to find alternative structures that will maintain the flexibility of the FPGA, at the same time minimize the effects of configuration overheads.[8] The model that we propose is a *Defect Tolerant Hardware,* that is *Dynamically Reconfigurable.*

3.2. Defect Tolerant Reconfigurable Architecture

Re-configurability is the key component needed to nano architecture. In such architecture, the nano fabric uses run-time reconfiguration for finding the defect and performs the desired functions. Chemically Assembled Electronic Nanotechnology (CAEN) is a promising technology, which uses self-alignment to construct electronic circuits from nano scale devices that take advantage of quantum mechanical effects. It uses chemical synthesis techniques to construct molecular sized circuitry elements. Such CAEN elements are highly fine grained and allow dynamic re-configurability. The rich inter connect possible is an opportunity for application level implementation. However, the only problem that needs to be overcome is getting around the defects. Proper mappings are available to get around this. [9]

Reconfigurable fabrics offer high performance and efficiency as they can implement hardware matching to each application. If configuration can be created at compile time then one can get rid of complex circuitry. We could stretch our imagination further to adapt the same to an Event Driven Architecture. If the interconnects and circuitry in such an architecture can be realized basing on the Event Generators then the Channels for the Event flow can be dynamically actualized to the best. This allows a lot of possibilities for our field of Event Driven Architecture

- This brings about greater degree of parallelism at all the levels of a business application: instruction, pipeline and bit level
- We Can think of individual functional units that are Event Driven
- Reconfigurability can be used to reduce complex operations and extensive interconnect circuitry.

4. Putting It Together

In this final section, we are proposing a novel model that incorporates all the ideas hereto. We can look at a-four layer architecture. The model proposed here has the elements combined form the Reconfigurability concept and that of Event Driven Architecture. The architectural diagram is shown below:

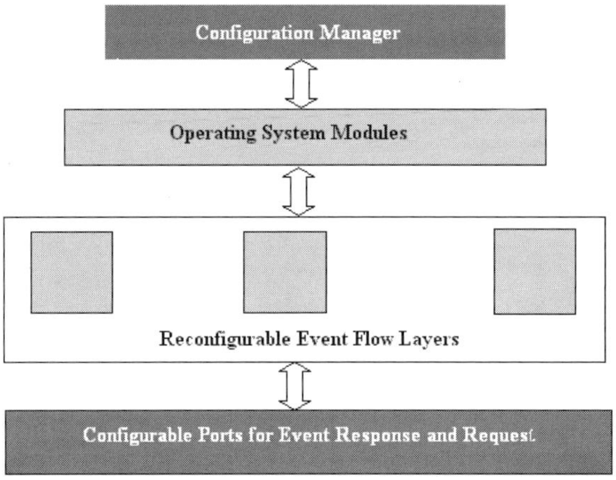

Fig. 3: Event Driven Reconfigurable Architecture

The architecture has four inter-related layers. The autonomous reconfiguration of each layer is based on the adaptation of the software coupled with dynamic reconfigurability at each layer. The top layer of the model is the configuration manager, and it has the role of deciding and monitoring the overall decision making based on events. The layer with OS kernel, must have the provision for two levels of OS: A real time OS Kernel and a Configurable OS Kernel. The former is to take care of critical operations that need fast time responses. The latter is required to control and assist with the mapping and dynamic reconfiguration of the architecture. The development of such an OS kernel is an area needing lot of research. And it is here that Open Source OS have a catch. The Open features of such OS, like Linux, make it an easy interface in this design.[10]

The next layer is where all features of the dynamic nature of nano computing are to be laid out. The event driven model has to be realized through nano structures that support high level of reconfigurability and dynamic interconnect. The realization of the circuitry is realized based on the activation of events at this level. There will have be the upper layer support and overlapping while realizing this.

The base layer is the interface that links and responds to other related event driven systems. There can be some degree of dynamic reconfigurability even at this level. As the interface to the processing environment, this layer is the immediate agent that needs to respond and request for events.

The conceptual idea of the lay out is to bring in the dynamism of reconfigurable nano computing into an Event Driven model. Candidates that can be of great contribution are the elements of Chemically Assembled Electronic Nanotechnology (CAEN).

4. Conclusion

Having presented the entire theme of Reconfigurable Event Driven Architecture, let us now make some concluding remarks. The common criticism that is often raised against EDA is that it is under utilized and most applications fall back on traditional modes of information processing. This is the same that can be put against any novel methods suggested.

The EDA can have higher degree of decision channels and Event- requests and responses if the architecture underlying the model is different. The Nano architecture that we have seen here is a move in this direction. The CAEN reconfigurable elements can act as new building blocks that support the development of such a design. As researches and models are being discovered everyday, we can look at more possibilities that can take Event Driven business models to greater heights.

References

1. Mani K Chandy, Simon Ramo and W Roy Schuttle, "What is Event Driven Architecture(ERD) and Why Does it Matter" © Complex Event Processing Community, (2007). Later referred to as Mani.
2. Mani K Chandy, Simon Ramo and W Roy Schuttle, "What is Event Driven Architecture(ERD) and Why Does it Matter" © *Complex Event Processing Community,* (2007). Later referred to as *Mani.*
3. Brenda M Michelson, "Event-Driven Architecture Overfiew" © *Patricial Seybold Group,* Boston, (2006). Later referred to as *Brenda*
4. Mani
5. *Brenda.*
6. Ibid.
7. Paul Beckett, Andrew Jennings, "Towards Nanocomputer Architecture", © *Australian Computer Society*, Melbourne, (2002).
8. Ibid.
9. Ibid.
10. Seth Copen Goldstein, Mihai BudiuSeth, "NanoFabrics: Spatial Computing Using Molecular Electronics", *Proc. of The 28th Annual International Symposium on Computer Architecture,* Göteborg, Sweden. *June (2001).*
11. Chris Papachristou, Frank Wolff, Robert Ewing "Reconfigurable and Evolvable Hardware Fabric", *Proc. Of MAPLD International Conference,* Washington D. C, (2005).

VISUALIZATION OF WIRELESS AD-HOC NETWORK IN 3D FROM MULTIPLE VIEWS

LIU HONGLEI

School of Information Science & Technology, Northeastern University
Shenyang, China honglei-liu@hotmail.com

LI XIAOCUI

School of Information Science & Technology, Northeastern University
Shenyang, China

ZHANG HONGYU

School of Information Science & Technology, Northeastern University
Shenyang, China

LI ZHE

School of Information Science & Technology, Northeastern University
Shenyang, China

With the development of wireless communications technology, ad-hoc network absorbs more and more concerns. In this paper, the author sets up a 3D simulation system for ad-hoc networks by introducing three-dimensional modeling techniques. The system has functions of three-dimensionally demonstrating the process of network organization and the routing process in multi-view, which makes it intuitive and convenient for researchers to analyze the result of the simulation and make better choices.

Keywords-network simulation; self-organization network; space networks; three-dimensional modeling;

1. Introduction

Ad-Hoc network is composed of wireless nodes that are independent of fixed infrastructures, the most common, such as Mobile Ad -hoc networks and wireless sensor networks. Also, with the development of wireless communications technology, self-organizing network has been used in some special fields, such as space ad-hoc networks. Simulation is an important way of research. At present, there has already been some software for the satellite network simulation, such as the STK (Satellite Tool Kit) from company AGI. As for satellite analysis, STK can be carried out through constellation design, satellite orbit prediction, satellite orbit determination, visibility analysis, posture analysis, communication link analysis, coverage analysis, three-dimensional display, etc, but it cannot be directly applied to the space ad-hoc network, for which a simulation system is needed. In this paper the author sets up a simulation system for demonstrating and evaluating the space ad-hoc network. The system is able to get real-time simulation data from SEP (Self-organization network Emulation Platform) [1] and display the network organization and the routing process[2] multi-view. The observer can not only view the entire network from a point far from the earth but also enter the network and stop to carry out the details of observation.

2. Design of the simulation system

The real-time simulation data can be either directly output or displayed in the form of two-dimensional graphics, but as for space network, it is far from convenience to observe the routing process and the changes of the node location. So, it is necessary to introduce three-dimensional techniques to the user module of the SEP, making it is easier for the researcher to evaluate and analyze the simulation data.

2.1 *Architecture of the simulation system*

Fig. 1 shows the architecture of the simulation system. The simulation system uses a C/S (Client / Server) structure. The clients implement the functions of three-dimensional dynamic simulation while the server does the work such as network design, network performance and data preparing. The C/S structure enables the simulation platform to separate from the user control module making it universal in a certain degree.

2.2 *Design of the functions*

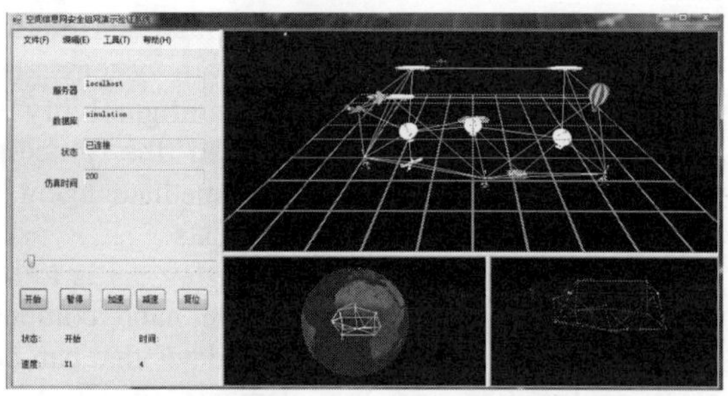

Figure 2. Screenshot of the simulation system

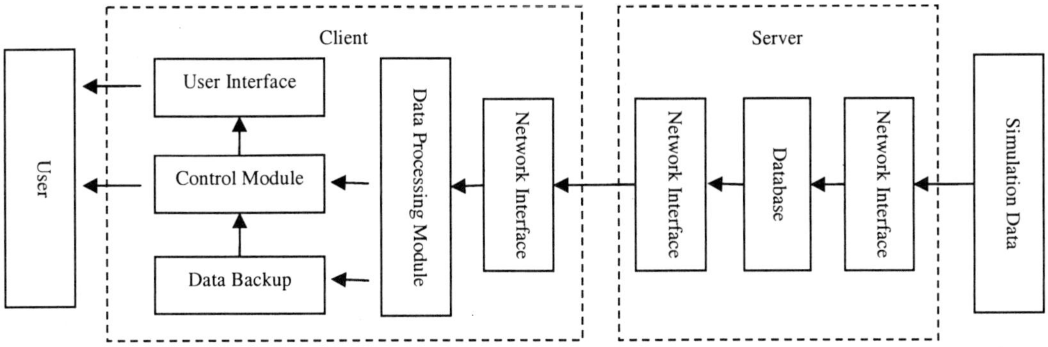

Figure 1. Architecture of the simulation system

a) Getting real-time simulation data from the SEP and display the routing process three-dimensionally.

b) Observing the process in multi-view such as earth perspective, plane perspective and topological perspective.

c) Moving of the observation point.

d) Backup of the simulation data.

e) Playback of the simulation process calling the backup file.

f) Operations such as pause, acceleration, deceleration and reseting when replaying the process.

Fig 2 shows a screenshot of the simulation system.

3. Implementation of the simulation system

The system should be able to get data from the simulation platform and display the routing process based on the processed data, meanwhile, it should have a pleasing and convenient user interface. Taking this into account, we implement the system with .Net Framework and Direct3D techniques.

3.1 *Data processing module*

When simulation begins, the event database will be filled with real-time data which will be processed by the system for display. All these work will be packaged in a class named DataPro.

For the simulation data is real-time, if they are not cached in memory, it would take a lot of time to query the database at a high frequency. This class contains the functions that needed to connect with the event database and cache the data. Table 1 presents the architecture of the event database.

We use the .Net component MySQL Connector Net to make a connection with the database and then get data from it to fill the object of class DataSet named dataset. In this way, the real-time data is cached in memory.

Table 1. Architecture of the event database

Tables	Description
node_data	Locations of the nodes
node_info	Quantity of various nodes
node_link	Link status between every two nodes
node_packet	Communication status between every two nodes
time_syn	Simulation time

Table 2. Members in DataPro

Name	Type	Description
dataset	DataSet	Data cached in memory
SimuTime	int	Simulation time
NodeAmount	int	Amount of all the nodes
Node_Type_Amount	int[]	Amount of a single type of nodes
Node_Id_Type	int[]	Type of nodes corresponding to their id
LinkState_Id_1	int[,]	Link state between nodes
LinkState_Id_2	int[,]	Link state between nodes
PacketState_Id_1	int[,]	Communication state between nodes
PacketState_Id_2	int[,]	Communication state between nodes
NodeLocation	Vector3[,]	Location of nodes

Table 2 lists the members in DataPro. In order to replay the simulation process, the system must have the function of saving the data in the disk when the simulation is finished. As the real-time data has already been cached in memory, we can easily implement the storing function using the method WriteXml from the class DataSet. This function can be activated either through the option ‘save’ in the menu or by the attempt of exiting the system without having saved the data.

3.2 *Three-dimensional Display in Multi-view*

The system can display the simulation process in three-dimension, and more conveniently, in multi-view[3]o explain this, Fig.3 lists the screenshots of the three different perspectives. Lines between the nodes means they are in a connection at this time and the blinking lines means the two nodes are delivering messages. The ideas of designing are as follows:

a) Earth persectives: In this perspective, we can observe the link status between the satellites or zoom in and view the near-earth space network closely. The implemention of this module is packaged in a class named Earth_Device.

b) Plane perspective: Sometimes, the researcher needs to observer the near-earth network only. This module provides excellect supports for that. In this perspective, we can view the whole near-earth space freely. The implemention of this module is packaged in a class named Plane_Device.

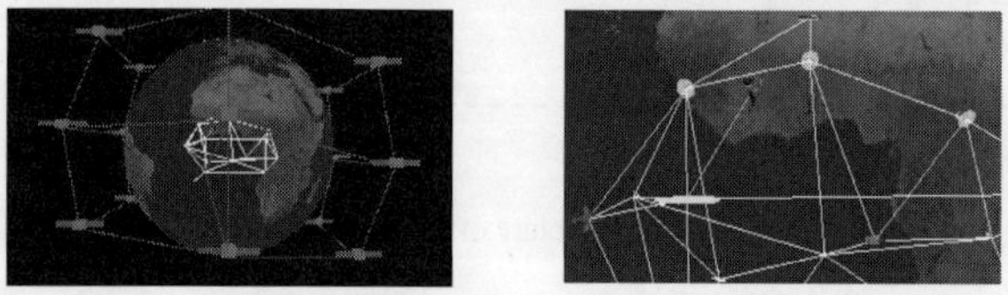

a. Earth perspective when zooming out (left) and in (right)

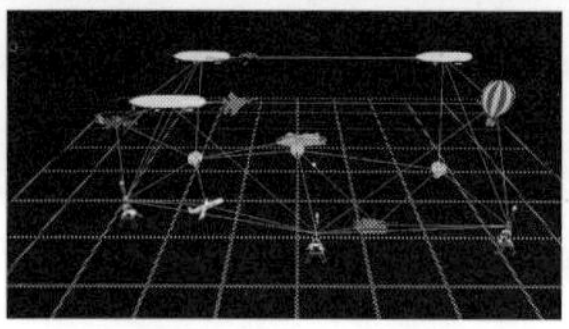

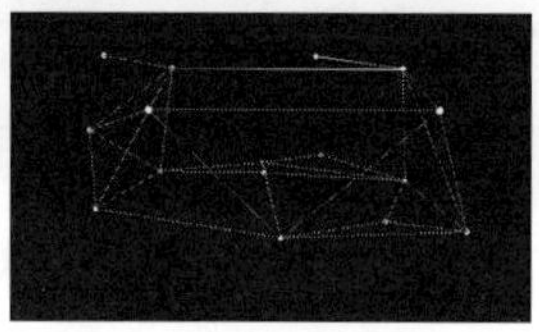

b. Plane perspective c. Topological perspective

Figure 3 Three different perspectives in the simulation system

c) topological perspective: Research of topology structure of networks is of great significance. So in the system there is a special module for this. In this perspective, all the nodes are abstracted into white points so the researcher can get the topology structure easily. The implemention of this module is packaged in a class named Topology_Device .

For there are various kinds of nodes, we can not get this done all by Direct3D programming. So, three-dimensional Modeling[4]needed. Here, we choosed 3DS MAX to build the three-dimensional models each kind of network nodes and convert them to mesh files[5] which are supported by Direct3D programming.

3.3 *Dynamic Display*

During the simulation process, movement of the models and the observation point are two main problems of designing the simulation system. Here, we use geometrical transforms to achieve it. In applications that work with three-dimensional graphics, you can use geometrical transforms to do the following:

- Express the location of an object relative to another object.
- Rotate and size objects.
- Change viewing positions, directions, and perspectives.

You can transform any point (x, y, z) into another point (x', y', z') using a 4 by 4 matrix. As shown by (1):

$$[x' y' z' 1] = [x\ y\ z\ 1]\begin{bmatrix} M_{11} & M_{12} & M_{13} & M_{14} \\ M_{21} & M_{22} & M_{23} & M_{24} \\ M_{31} & M_{32} & M_{33} & M_{34} \\ M_{41} & M_{42} & M_{43} & M_{44} \end{bmatrix} \quad (1)$$

Perform the following operations on (x, y, z) and the matrix to produce the point (x', y', z'). As shown by (2):

$$\begin{aligned} x' &= (x \times M_{11}) + (y \times M_{21}) + (z \times M_{31}) + (1 \times M_{41}) \\ y' &= (x \times M_{12}) + (y \times M_{22}) + (z \times M_{32}) + (1 \times M_{42}) \\ z' &= (x \times M_{13}) + (y \times M_{23}) + (z \times M_{33}) + (1 \times M_{43}) \end{aligned} \quad (2)$$

3.3.1. *Movement of the nodes.* Using geometrical transforms we can achieve the following effects:

a) Scale: The following transform scales the point (x, y, z) by arbitrary values in the x-, y-, and z-directions to a new point (x', y', z').

$$[x' y' z' 1] = [x\ y\ z\ 1]\begin{bmatrix} s_x & 0 & 0 & 0 \\ 0 & s_y & 0 & 0 \\ 0 & 0 & s_z & 0 \\ 0 & 0 & 0 & 1 \end{bmatrix} \quad (3)$$

b) Translate: The following transform translates the point (x, y, z) to a new point (x', y', z').

$$[x' y' z' 1] = [x\ y\ z\ 1]\begin{bmatrix} 1 & 0 & 0 & 0 \\ 0 & 1 & 0 & 0 \\ 0 & 0 & 1 & 0 \\ T_x & T_y & T_z & 1 \end{bmatrix} \quad (4)$$

c) Rotate: The transforms described here are for left-handed coordinate systems.

- The following matrix rotates the point (x, y, z) around the x-axis, producing a new point (x', y', z').

$$[x' y' z' 1] = [x\ y\ z\ 1]\begin{bmatrix} 1 & 0 & 0 & 0 \\ 0 & \cos\theta & \sin\theta & 0 \\ 0 & -\sin\theta & \cos\theta & 0 \\ 0 & 0 & 0 & 1 \end{bmatrix} \quad (5)$$

- The following matrix rotates the point around the y-axis.

$$[x' y' z' 1] = [x\ y\ z\ 1]\begin{bmatrix} \cos\theta & 0 & -\sin\theta & 0 \\ 0 & 1 & 0 & 0 \\ \sin\theta & 0 & \cos\theta & 0 \\ 0 & 0 & 0 & 1 \end{bmatrix} \quad (6)$$

- The following matrix rotates the point around the z-axis.

$$[x' y' z' 1] = [x\ y\ z\ 1]\begin{bmatrix} \cos\theta & \sin\theta & 0 & 0 \\ -\sin\theta & \cos\theta & 0 & 0 \\ 0 & 0 & 1 & 0 \\ 0 & 0 & 0 & 1 \end{bmatrix} \quad (7)$$

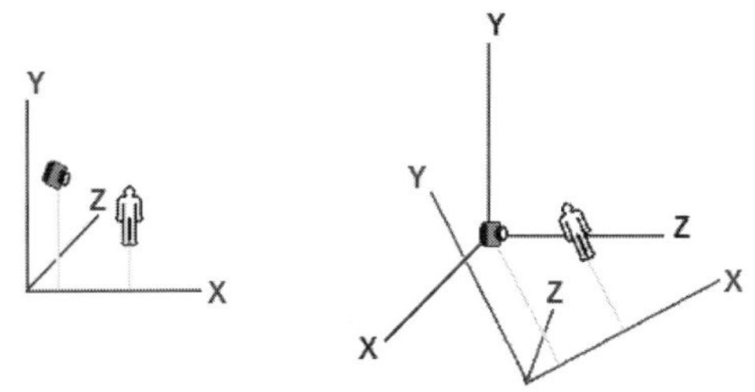

Figure 4. The same object in world space (left) and in view space (right)

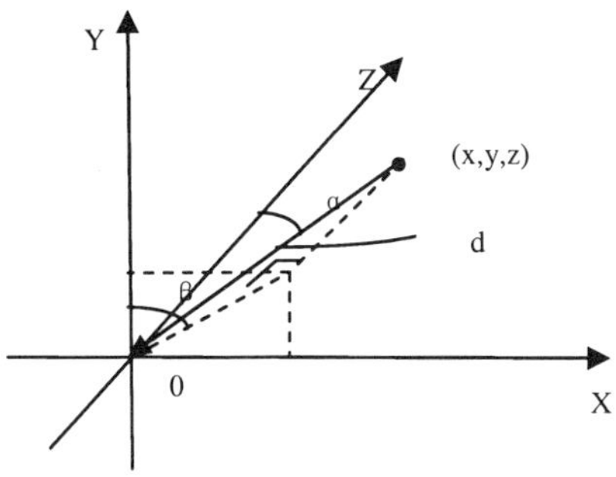

Figure 5. Location of the observation point in earth perspective

3.3.2. *Movement of the observation point.* Condering that the researcher may want to view the link state of a particular node or the whole network, control of the movement of observation point should be convient[6]. In this simualtion system, the user is able to control the movement of obsevation point and the observation distance separately through the movement of the mouse and mouse wheel rolling.

To implement this function, we need to use view transform. View space, sometimes called camera space, is similar to world space in that it is typically used for the entire scene. However, in view space, the origin is at the viewer or *camera.* The view direction (where the viewer is looking) defines the positive Z axis. An "up" direction defined by the application becomes the positive Y axis as shown by Fig.4.

In Direct3D programming, a helper function D3DXMatrixLookAtLH is offered to create a view matrix based on the camera location, view direction and up direction.

Based on the description above, the simulation system offered different solutions in each perspective.

a) In earth perspective: Observation point can be 360-degree horizontal rotation and 180-degrees vertical rotation. At this situation the view direction is （0, 0, 0）, and the up direction is （0, 0, 1）. We assume that the location of the observation point is （x, y, z）, the angle between the view direction and the positive z axis is α, the angle between the projection of the view direction in x-y plane and the positive y axis is β, the distance between the view and the original point is d as shown in Fig.5. From above, we can easily get the following equatons.

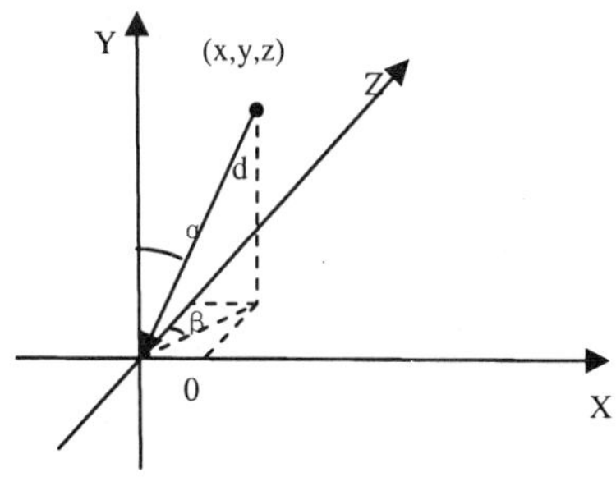

Figure 6. Location of the observation point in pane and topological perspectives

$$\begin{cases} x=d\times\sin\alpha\times\sin\beta \\ y=d\times\sin\alpha\times\cos\beta \\ z=d\times\cos\alpha \end{cases} \quad (8)$$

From (8), we can conclude that α and βcontrols the vertical and horizontal rotation, and d controls the view distance.

b) In plane and topological perspectives: Observation point can be 360-degree horizontal rotation and 90-degrees vertical rotation. At this situation the view direction is （0, 0, 0）, and the up direction is （0, 1, 0）. We assume that the location of the observation point is （x, y, z）, the angle between the view direction and the positive y axis is α, the angle between the projection of the view direction in x-z plane and the positive y axis is β, the distance between the view and the original point is d as shown in Fig.5. From above, we can easily get the following equatons.

$$\begin{cases} x=d\times\sin\alpha\times\sin\beta \\ y= d\times\cos\alpha \\ z= d\times\sin\alpha\times\cos\beta \end{cases} \quad (9)$$

From (9), we can get the same conclusion as in the earth perspective.

Conclusion

In this paper, we design and implement a simulation system for space ad-hoc network. The system gets real-time simulation data and display the routing process three-dimensionally in multi-view. In this way, we create an intuitive and convenient environment for researchers working on space network to test and evaluate their new routing protocol.

References

1. LIU Jun, LI Zhe and YUE Lei, Design and Implementation of the Self-organization Network

Simulation Platform,computer cience , 2008,35(1) p 24-27(in Chinese)

2. Chenna Reddy, P. , ChandraSekhar Reddy, P.,Performance analysis of adhoc network routing protocols, International Symposium on Ad Hoc and Ubiquitous Computing, 2006, p 186-7
3. de la Fraga, L.G. , Vite-Silva, I.,Direct 3D metric reconstruction from multiple views using differential evolution,Applications of Evolutionary Computing. Proceedings EvoWorkshops 2008: EvoCOMNET, EvoFIN, EvoHOT, EvoIASP EvoMUSART, EvoNUM, EvoSTOC, and EvoTransLog, 2008, p 341-6.
4. Stamos, I., Gene Yu,Wolberg, G.,etc,3D modeling using planar segments and mesh elements,Third International Symposium on 3D Data Processing, Visualization, and Transmission (3DPVT'06), 2006, p 8 pp
5. Breckon, T.P. ,Fisher, R.B.,Direct geometric texture synthesis and transfer on 3D meshes, 3rd European Conference on Visual Media Production (CVMP 2006). Part of the 2nd Multimedia Conference 2006, 2006, p 186
6. T. Svoboda, D. Martinec, and T. Pajdla. A convenient multicamera self-calibration for virtual environments,Teleoperators and Virtual Environments, 14(4):407–422, August 2005.

OPTIMIZATION OF THE PRODUCTION COSTS BY SIMULATION [*]

VAŽAN PAVEL [†]
Institute of Applied Informatics, Automation and Mathematics Faculty of Material Science and Technology Slovak University of Technology in Trnava, Hajdóczyho 1, Trnava, Slovak republic

TANUŠKA PAVOL
Institute of Applied Informatics, Automation and Mathematics Faculty of Material Science and Technology Slovak University of Technology in Trnava, Hajdóczyho 1, Trnava, Slovak republic

SCHREIBER PETER
Institute of Applied Informatics, Automation and Mathematics Faculty of Material Science and Technology Slovak University of Technology in Trnava, Hajdóczyho 1, Trnava, Slovak republic

The paper presents the possibilities of production costs minimization by using simulation. The authors have designed solving procedure for optimization of production costs and the other production goals have to be realized simultaneously. The simulation optimization is chosen as the fundamental method for problem solution. The procedure is explained on the example. The simulator Witness was used as the base simulation platform.

1. Introduction

The reduction of the production costs is the important long-time goal of management. Paradoxically a lot of control strategies leads to increase of production costs. It causes a lot of faulty parameters which increase the real costs. Here belong: inappropriate determination of lot size, false input intervals of batches into system, wrong orientation of material flow, incorrect operation schedule, etc. Then these factors break due dates. The management solves this problem by earlier putting into production and this leads to increase flow times and finally the increase of production costs.

It is possible to solve many of these problems via simulation. The simulation tools allow create precise models of production systems and then the management can simulate each decision in advance. The management prefers analytical models but the results of simulation models are more accurate. The data collection is based on occurrence of events during the simulation run. It leads to more accurate and more objective results. Today it is possible to optimize the results of simulation experiments. Simulation optimization allows this process. Optimization packages are standard modules of simulators.

This contribution demonstrates minimization of the production costs by using simulation optimization. The other production goals will be fulfilled at the same time.

2. Problem definition

Modern flexible manufacturing systems are complicated, highly automated, computer controlled integrated systems. Frequent requests on the changes of the types of products and distribution problems especially in batch production, frequently incline to change of production strategies. Production strategies have to respect more production goals at the same time. These production goals are very conflicting, therefore it is very difficult to reach them.

The main goal of the work was to minimize production costs in the manufacturing system. On the other hand the other production goals have to be realized. To these production goals belong:

- to maximize capacity utilization,
- to minimize flow time of manufacturing,
- to maximize the total number of finished parts.

These goals influence a lot of factors. All these factors as number of kinds of parts, input intervals of batches, lot size of batches, cycle times, set up times,

[*] Work partially supported as a part of a solution of projects VEGA 1/0170/08

material flow type, number of workstations, number of storages and their capacities, number of vehicles etc. can be free parameters in simulation experiments.

It is important to decide which parameters solution mentioned above, in defined solution, will be constant or will be changed. The input intervals of batches, lot size of batches will be considered as free parameters in this contribution. They are very important input parameters for management of production process in practice.

3. Costs structure and their calculation

The production cost is computed according to following function:

$$SumCost = \sum_{i=1}^{p} In\_part\_cost_i + \sum_{i=1}^{p} Added\_value_i \quad (1)$$

where: In_part_cost is initial cost for each entered parts
Added_value is gained amount per part in production system
P is number of entered parts

Total added value is calculated:

$$Sum\_Added\_value = \sum_{i=1}^{p} OC_i + SC_i + LC_i + SC_i + TC_i \quad (2)$$

where: OC – operation costs, SC – setup costs, LC – labour costs, STC – storage costs and TC – transport costs.

$$operation\_costs = \sum_{j=1}^{m} t_{Aj} * unit\_costs_j \quad (3)$$

$$setup\_costs = \sum_{x=1}^{s} t_{Bx} * unit\_costs_x \quad (4)$$

where m is the number of machines, tAj is processing time, unit_costs is rate per unit of time, s – number of set up operations, tBx – set up time, unit_costs is rate per unit of time.

$$labour\_costs = \sum_{k=1}^{op} t_{LBk} * unit\_L\_costs2_k \quad (5)$$

where op is number of operations with labour, tLBk is operation time with specific labour, unit_costs2 are rates per unit of time.

$$transport\_costs = \sum_{l=1}^{top} transport\_operation\_costs_l \quad (6)$$

$$storage\_costs = \sum_{n=1}^{NS} t_{Sn} * unit\_costs_n \quad (7)$$

where top is number of transport operations and NS is number of storages.

All functions are calculated in elements of simulation model of production system.

4. Production costs optimization

4.1. *Method*

The solution of optimization of production costs is very complex problem and the using of ordinary optimization methods is impossible in many cases. According to authors the simulation optimization is appropriate method for solving of this complex problem.

Simulation optimization is defined as optimization of outputs from simulation experiments. It is based on optimization of outputs from discrete event simulation models [1].

The value of objective function cannot be evaluated directly but it must be estimated as output from simulation run. It means that optimization via simulation is computationally very expensive. On the other hand the definition of objective function is very simple without complicated mathematical formula. It means that the simulation optimization requires the existence of simulation model.

4.2. *Definition of objective function*

The optimization of the production costs requires the definition of objective function. The function SumCost is growing up with rising of number of finished parts. Therefore it is not proper to use it as an objective function. The function Unit_Cost is designed by the authors as objective function. The objective function is defined inside the simulation model.

This function calculates the production cost per finished part.

$$Unit\_Cost = SumCost/no\_out\_parts \quad (8)$$

where: no_out_parts is the number of finished parts

This function can grow or fall during the time depending on inputs of production system and control strategy of production system.

The management also has to reach the other production goals as was mentioned above. The authors solved the problem of the implementation of the others production goals into the objective function by adding the constant to the objective function, if the specified values of production goals were not fulfilled.

The objective function was defined:

IF No_out_parts () => default value of finished parts AND Machine utilisation () => default value of

machine utilisation AND Flow time () <= default value of flow time
Unit_Cost = SumCost / No_out_parts
RETURN Unit_Cost
ELSE
Unit_Cost = SumCost / No_out_parts+ constant1
RETURN Unit_Cost
ENDIF

It is necessary to mention that the usage of multicriterial optimization was eliminated by this way. It is probably impossible to define the right function with weight coefficients for totally different production goals.

The constrains defined in objective functions can also express different control strategies. The production system can work in two extremes. The management wants to reach high capacity utilization. This is the first extreme. This leads to increasing of flow time and finally to increasing of production costs. On the other hand the production system can also work at low capacity utilization and short flow times, as well as low costs. However this low power causes decreasing of production. We will be oriented to high capacity utilization in our solution. Default values of number of finished parts, capacity utilization and flow time were obtained in the preparatory experiments. Constant1 is ten times bigger than the value of Unit_Costs. This way was defined as the fundament of optimizing scenario.

5. Demonstration of solution

We solved the problem defined above on the selected production system. The simulation model of the production system was created in simulator Witness. The existence of correct simulation model is necessary condition for simulation optimization usage. The word "correct" is needed to be understood in such way that the model has to be validated.

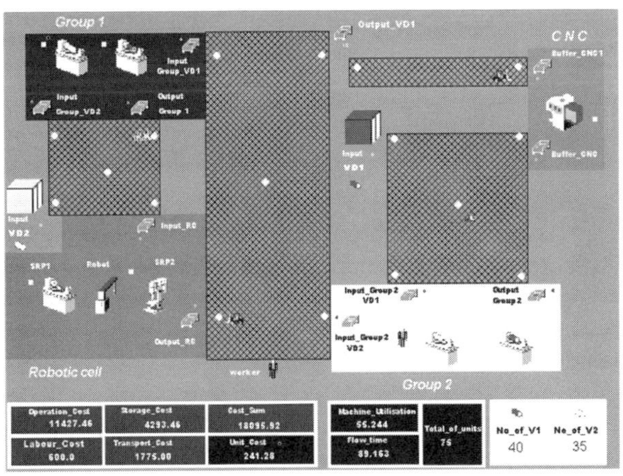

Figure 1: The simulation model of production system

Here is its basic description:

Each workstation of the production system is defined as an independent module (see figure 1). All these modules form the structure of production system according to the following rules:

- 2 compatible machines constitute the Group 1and the Group 2,
- the workstation SRP1 and the workstation SRP2 are the components of the Robotic cell,
- the workstation CNC is an independent module.

Each workstation has its own input and output buffers. The transport system consists of four automated guided vehicles (AGV). There is used a combine storage in the given production system (main storage is also system input and system output of the production system; each workstation as well as FMC has own buffer and there is one emergency storage). Given manufacturing system has been designed to produce two kinds of parts at the same time. They are labeled as VD1 and VD2. The parts were produced in batches.

There is the following material flow:

VD1: input buffer → Grou2 → CNC workstation → Group1 → output

VD2: input buffer → SZP1 → Robotic cell → Group2 → output

6. Simulation optimization

The process of simulation optimization is realized in plug-in module Optimizer. The Optimizer takes over the objective function from simulation model. The values for the quantitative rating of the production goals into the objective function were determined by specially designed experiments. We have decided that we will present the solution, if the capacity utilization is high. We set up capacity utilization on 75%. We would like to point out that the value for batch production is very high.

Default value of flow time was set up for 150 min. and default value of number of finished parts was set up for 1000 pieces.

Simulation optimization typically works in the following way [3]:

1. An initial set of parameter values is chosen and one or more replication experiments is carried out with these values;
2. The results are obtained from the simulation runs and then the optimization module chooses another parameter set to try.
3. The new values are set and the next experiment set is run.

4. Steps 2 and 3 are repeated until either the algorithm is stopped manually or a set of defined finishing conditions are met.

The definition of input variables is the important step. The selection of input parameters is realized in optimizing module. The input intervals of products VD1 and VD2 and their lot size were chosen as input parameters our model. The other factors as cycle times, set up times, number of workstations, number of storages and their capacities, number of vehicles were constant during the all optimization process.

The definition of input variables may be the critical step. It is important to know that the big number of the input parameters and their big range spin out the time for searching of optimal extreme of the objective function. The optimizer has to realize at least one simulation run to get one value of objective function. For example if the number of possible combinations of input parameters is 100000 and we use All combination algorithm and the retrieval of the value of objective functions lasts 1 second (in complex models it lasts longer), the search of the global extreme of objective function will last more than 27 hours. This is probably unacceptable. Therefore it is advantageous to constrain the input parameters. We recommend set up the constraints of input parameters through special designed preparatory simulation experiments. It is important to change the input parameters only to the certain interval to find the system behavior. We recommend set up this interval in such way: the system will be overloaded in its lower line; vice versa in its upper line the system will not be loaded. The best results observed on the output will occurred in the selected input values, in this case it will be guaranteed.

The constraints of the input parameters were determined for the given production system by preparatory experiments:

- Input intervals for parts: VD1∈⟨5,30⟩; VD2∈⟨5,70⟩
- Lot sizes: VD1∈⟨1,10⟩; VD2∈⟨1,10⟩
- It means that the total number of combinations is 171 600.

There is a question how to eliminate the big range of input parameters. The Optimizer offers several possibilities [2]:

- To use the appropriate step of the change of input parameters or to define only chosen values.
- To define constrains with help of functional dependence among input parameters.
- To choose suitable algorithm for optimization

We have selected step 2 for all inputs parameters. The total number of combination in this way was reduced to 17 136.

The selection of the proper algorithm is the important part of this procedure. We can notice that the selection of algorithm has to respect mainly two basic factors:

1. What data will include individual sets of variables – it includes whether we know all data files of given range or whether we only know the min., mean and max. value.
2. Time of optimization process.

The authors have chosen the Adaptive Thermostatistical Simulated Annealing algorithm. This algorithm belongs to so called metaheuristic approaches to the simulation optimization [2].

The optimization process was realized and each simulation run has simulated one week of work of production system. The found value of minimal costs was understandably only near of searching optimal value. It was possible to reduce the range of input variables and also step of the change of input parameters and repeat experiment by using the Adaptive Thermostatistical SA algorithm.

The reduction of input parameters:

- Input intervals for parts: VD1∈⟨4,20⟩; VD2∈⟨4,25⟩
- Lot sizes: VD1∈⟨1,6⟩; VD2∈⟨1,6⟩
  Step 1 for all inputs parameters

The total number of combination in this way was reduced to 13 464.

The new result was found. We have repeated all process of input parameter reduction and finally we have selected All combination algorithm. The best 20 results of optimization process are presented on the figure 2.

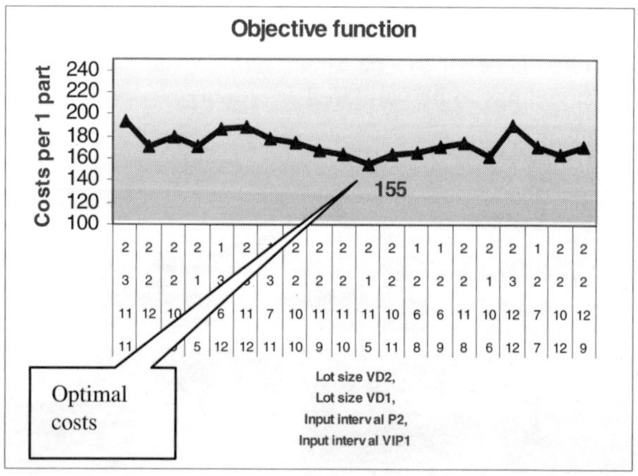

Figure 2: Optimization results

Quantitative parameters of production goals for optimal unit cost:

- Optimal unit costs – 155 SKK

- Total number of finished parts – 1344
- Average machine utilisation – 76,12%
- Average flow time – 42,26 min.

7. Conclusion

The solution procedure of the cost minimization in the dependence on the input intervals of batches and lot size of batches, designed by the authors, has led to the successful solution of the optimization problem when the other production goals were fulfilled. The found solutions and also the other quantitative parameters of the production goals are regarded as balanced in conditions of the batch production. The simulation optimization is very accurate method for costs optimization. It allows respect a lot of factors which influence the production costs in real practice. The best advantage of simulation optimization is very simple definition of objective function. The complex mathematical equipment is not needed. On the other hand the simulation model of production system has to be created. The problems with validation of simulation model can occur.

References

1. Fu C. M. *Simulation Optimization* In: Peters B.A., Smith J.S., Medeiros D.J., Rohrer m.W.:Proceedings of the 2001 Winter Simulation Conference. Arlington, USA, pp. 55-61
2. Važan, Pavol - Moravčík, Oliver - Križanová, Gabriela: *The comparison of selected algorithms of simulation optimization*. In: Annals of DAAAM and Proceedings of DAAAM Symposium. - ISSN 1726-9679. - Vol. 19, No.1. Annals of DAAAM for 2008 & Proceedings of the 19th International DAAAM Symposium "Intelligent Manufacturing & Automation: Focus on Next Generation of Intelligent Systems and Solutions", 22-25th October 2008, Trnava, Slovakia. - Vienna : DAAAM International Vienna, 2008. - ISBN 978-3-901509-68-1, s. 1461-1462
3. Waller A.P. (2006). *Optimization of simulation experiments*, Available from : http://www.dynamic.co.kr/Witness_Training_Center/Articles/White%20paper%20-%20Optimization.pdf Accessed: 2009-02-02

Dynamic Bandwidth Allocation Algorithm Using Fuzzy Logic for Ethernet Passive Optical Network

Nurul Asyikin bt Mohd Radzi
Department of Electronics Communication Engineering
Universiti Tenaga Nasional
Selangor, Malaysia
asyikin@uniten.edu.my

Norashidah bt Md. Din
Department of Electronics Communication Engineering
Universiti Tenaga Nasional
Selangor, Malaysia
norashidah@uniten.edu.my

Intan Shafinaz bt Mustafa
Department of Electronics Communication Engineering
Universiti Tenaga Nasional
Selangor, Malaysia
intanshafinaz@uniten.edu.my

Sajaa Kh. Sadon
Department of Electronics Communication Engineering
Universiti Tenaga Nasional
Selangor, Malaysia
sajaa@uniten.edu.my

Abstract— **Ethernet passive optical network (EPON) is the best candidate for fiber to the home (FTTH) to solve the access network bandwidth problem. In EPON, it is important to control upstream traffic since several optical network units (ONUs) use a single shared medium. In this paper, we propose a new intelligent algorithm of dynamic bandwidth allocation (DBA) using fuzzy logic for EPON that is named as 'Keris' algorithm. We evaluate the performance of this algorithm and compare it with the algorithm created previously. From the simulation result using MATLAB, we have confirmed that our algorithm is more flexible and fairer as compared to the previous algorithm. It can divide bandwidth fairly between voice, video and data traffic within ONUs.**

Keywords- EPON, DBA, fuzzy logic, fairness, MATLAB

I. INTRODUCTION

The rapid development of communication industries in recent years caused the bottleneck problem in the first mile. The most attractive solution to implement broadband access optical fiber to the home (FTTH) is Ethernet passive optical network (EPON) since it can support triple play (voice, video and data) and it has longer transmission distance and higher bandwidth [1].

EPON is a point-to-multipoint optical network which consists of an optical line terminal (OLT) that is connected to multiple optical network units (ONUs) via an optical splitter or coupler. The term 'passive' in Ethernet *passive* optical network means that it employs only passive optical components in the transmission path from source to destination.

EPON carries all data encapsulated in Ethernet frames [2], [3]. In downstream transmission, EPON uses broadcasting, where the OLT will broadcast frames and ONUs will selectively receive frames addressed to them. On the other hand, for upstream transmission, available bandwidth must be shared among all ONUs at the optical splitter to avoid collisions between frames from different ONUs. OLT assigns non-overlapping time-slot to each ONU, and ONUs cannot transmit at the same time. They can only transmit during its timeslot [1], [2]. In static bandwidth allocation (SBA), a fixed amount of time is assigned to every ONU. Therefore, bandwidth cannot be utilized efficiently.

Due to this reason, dynamic bandwidth allocation (DBA) is proposed. DBA is a method to assign bandwidth dynamically using queue state information that is received from ONUs [4]. An efficient bandwidth allocation algorithm is needed in order to enable passive optical networks (PONs) that support DiffServ. Various DBA algorithms have been proposed for EPON networks. For an instance, Chang [5] discusses about Interleaved Polling mechanism with Adaptive Cycle Time (IPACT) protocol. However, IPACT is not suitable for delay, jitter and sensitive services or Service Level Agreement (SLA). In Choi's work [6], the technique used is strict priority scheduling. However, best effort cannot be achieved using this technique and it can also cause starvation of ONUs. Good and fair DBA algorithms should improve the bandwidth utilization.

In this paper, we develop a DBA algorithm that we call as 'Keris' DBA algorithm. This algorithm can support priority queues and fairness among each of the ONUs over EPON. It focuses on dividing bandwidth fairly for voice, video and data traffic within each ONUs. We evaluate the performance of Keris algorithm by comparing it to the algorithm designed by Min [7].

Section 2 gives an overview about Min's DBA algorithm. In section 3, we explain the Keris algorithm where theoretical explanations and implementation issues are described. The performance evaluation and detail analysis are presented in section 4, whereas section 5 gives the concluding remarks.

II. MIN'S DBA ALGORITHM

The following is the DBA algorithm that has been suggested by Min [7]. Let B_{total} be the total bandwidth used and B_{avail} be the available bandwidth. Min also set the biggest limited bandwidth for time division multiplexing (TDM), video, data as follows: S_i^{TDM}, S_i^{video}, and S_i^{data}. Here *i* is the ONU's ordinal number, *n* is the timeslot and *N* is the number of ONUs. R_i is the requested bandwidth for each type of signal, whereas G_{max} is the biggest transfer window as and G_{min} is the minimum transfer window for the ONU bandwidth allocation.

Among the different ONUs, if the total requested bandwidth is: $R_i = R_i^{TDM} + R_i^{video} + R_i^{data}$, then the acquired bandwidth, B_i will be:

$$B_i = \begin{cases} G_{min}, & R_i = 0 \\ G_{max}, & R_i > G_{max} \\ R_i, & R_i \leq G_{max} \end{cases} \quad (1)$$

In each ONU, bandwidth allotment will follow the priority of the business. The high-grade business will first obtain the bandwidth.

Since TDM business is sensitive to delay, each ONU reserves a fixed bandwidth for it. In that case, the surplus bandwidth will be:

$$B_{avail} = \begin{cases} B_{total} - \sum_{i=1}^{N} R_{i,\ n+1}^{TDM} & R_{i,\ n+1}^{TDM} < S_i^{TDM} \\ B_{total} - \sum_{i=1}^{N} S_i^{TDM} & R_{i,\ n+1}^{TDM} \geq S_i^{TDM} \end{cases} \quad (2)$$

ONU allocates the bandwidth for the other two kinds of business as follows:

If $\sum_{i=1}^{N}(B_{i,n}^{Video} + B_{i,n}^{Data}) \leq B_{avail}$, then the allotment bandwidth will be according to their requirement.

Otherwise, the bandwidth allocation follows the SLA below:

$$B_{i,n+1}^{Video} = B_{avail}\left[\frac{S_i^{Video}}{S_i^{Video} + S_i^{Data}}\right] \quad (3)$$

$$B_{i,n+1}^{Data} = B_{avail}\left[\frac{S_i^{Data}}{S_i^{Video} + S_i^{Data}}\right] \quad (4)$$

If there is a surplus bandwidth, it would be allocated between each ONU again using the above algorithm. The surplus is checked using this formula:

$$\sum_{i=1}^{N}(B_{i,n}^{TDM} + B_{i,n}^{Video} + B_{i,n}^{Data}) \leq B_{total} \quad (5)$$

With this algorithm, there is no flexibility between the bandwidth received for voice, video and data. These three traffics will be restricted to their corresponding limitations. For example, if the bandwidth requested for voice is higher than its limitation, but the bandwidth requested for video and data are lower than their limitations, voice will still get only the limited bandwidth.

III. KERIS DBA ALGORITHM

For Keris algorithm, we classify services into three priority categories; high priority, medium priority and low priority [8]. High priority service supports voice traffic that requires bounded end-to-end delay and jitter specifications. Whereas, medium priority service supports video traffic that is not delay sensitive but require bandwidth guarantees. Finally, the low priority service supports data traffic and is not sensitive to end-to-end delay or jitter.

Similar to Min's algorithm, we set the biggest transfer window as G_{max} and the minimum transfer window as G_{min} for the ONU bandwidth allocation. The received bandwidth among different ONUs will be obtained in the same manner as the Min's algorithm with the MATLAB pseudocode as follows. Again, *i* denotes the ONU's ordinal number.

$B_i = G_{min}$ if $R_i = 0$
Else
$B_i = G_{max}$ if $R_i > G_{max}$
Else
$B_i = R_i$ if $R_i <= G_{max}$ (6)

In each ONU, bandwidth allotment will follow the priority of the business. This bandwidth allotment will be done using fuzzy logic. Fuzzy logic regulator is used to regulate bandwidth allocation decision. The regulator comprises of three input parameters and one output parameter as shown in Figure 1. The input parameters are requested bandwidth for voice (rvoice), requested bandwidth for video (rvideo), and requested bandwidth for data (rdata). The output value is the allocation decision whether to adjust voice bandwidth, adjust video bandwidth or adjust data bandwidth.

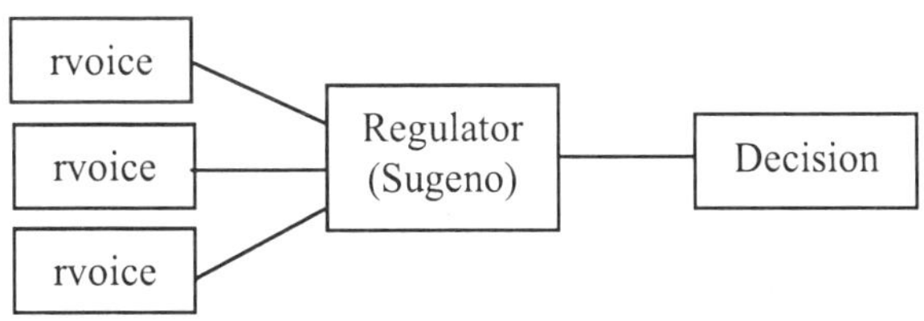

Figure 1. Fuzzy regulator block diagram.

The input membership functions are shown in Figures 2, 3, and 4. The membership functions used are trapezoidal functions, which have been widely used in fuzzy control design for its simplicity and also have been found suitable for real time operations [9]. The trapezoidal functions are used to represent the linguistic truth values, i.e low and high.

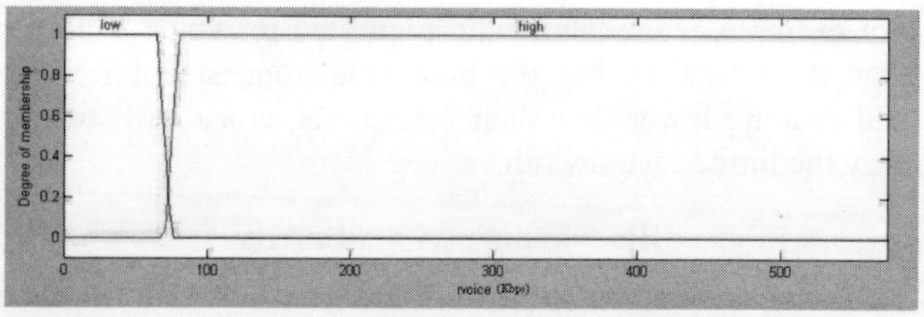

Figure 2. rvoice membership functions.

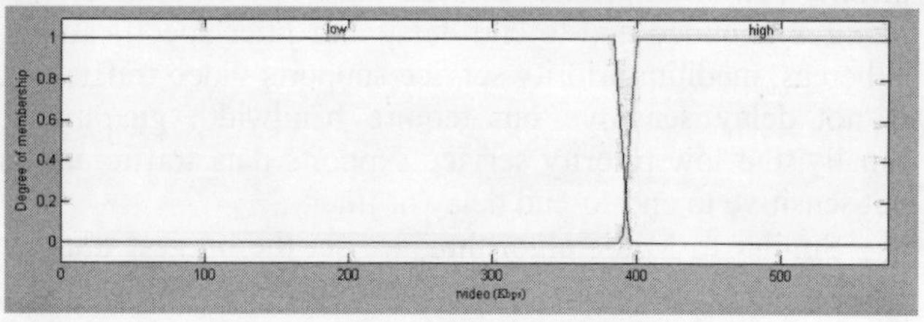

Figure 3. rvideo membership functions.

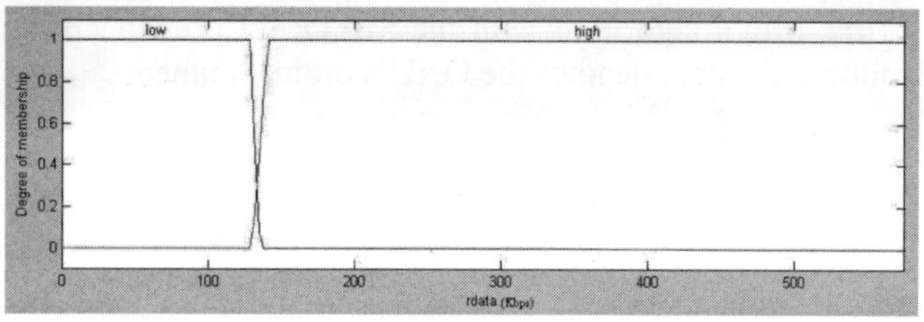

Figure 4. rdata membership functions.

The fuzzy rules are shown in Table I. There are 7 rules that relate the three inputs with fuzzy output. All the rules use "AND" connectives. The construction of the rules is based on logical reasoning of how the system should behave in allocating bandwidth to the ONUs. When all inputs are lower than its limitation (low), the bandwidth requested will be fulfilled and the process flow would not enter the fuzzy regulator. The same set of rules would be triggered everytime the fuzzy regulator is invoked.

TABLE I. FUZZY RULES FOR THE FUZZY REGULATOR

Rule	rvoice	rvideo	rdata	Decision
1	L	L	H	Adjust data(2)
2	L	H	L	Adjust video(1)
3	L	H	H	Adjust data(2)
4	H	L	L	Adjust voice(3)
5	H	L	H	Adjust data(2)
6	H	H	L	Adjust video(1)
7	H	H	H	Adjust data(2)

In order to obtain single crisp solution for the output variable, the Sugeno [9] inference process is used. Figure 5 shows the output singletons based on Sugeno's method where 1 is to adjust video bandwidth, 2 to adjust data bandwidth and 3 to adjust voice bandwidth.

Video bandwidth is adjusted by first, setting the limitation bandwidth for both voice and data. Then, if bandwidth requested for video is low, it will receive all the bandwidth requested. However, if the bandwidth requested for video is high, it can receive up until the surplus bandwidth after allocation for voice and data bandwidth is done.

The same technique applies to adjust voice and data bandwidth. In order to adjust data bandwidth, the limitation bandwidth is set for both voice and video bandwidth, whereas to adjust voice bandwidth, limitation is set for both video and data bandwidth.

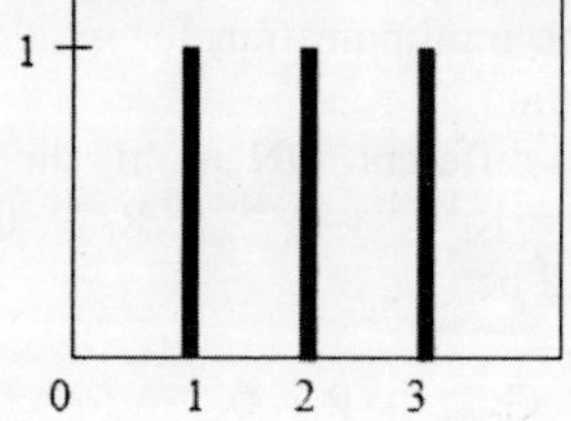

Figure 5. Output singletons based on Sugeno's method.

For defuzzification, the weighted average of the singletons is obtained using:

$$WA = \frac{\mu(k1)k1+\mu(k2)k2+\mu(k3)k3}{k1+k2+k3} \qquad (7)$$

Where μ(k1) the weight associated with each rule, whereas k1 is the membership of the output of each rule.

The fuzzy output range and the corresponding allocation decision are depicted in Table II.

TABLE II. RELATIONSHIP BETWEEN WEIGHTED AVERAGE (WA) WITH ALLOCATION DECISION FOR THE FUZZY REGULATOR

Range of WA	Allocation decision
WA ≤1.5	Adjust video
1.5<WA≤2.5	Adjust data
WA>2.5	Adjust voice

IV. PERFORMANCE EVALUATION

To evaluate the performance of the proposed DBA algorithm, we have compared Keris algorithm to the DBA algorithm presented by Min. Simulation environments are as followed:

- Total number of ONUs is 10
- Maximum transfer window, G_{max} is 576 Kbps
- Minimum transfer window, G_{min} is 0 Kbps
- Each ONU has 3 priority queues (High, medium, low)
- Total bandwidth for each ONU is 576 Kbps
- Limited bandwidth for high priority (voice) traffic is 64 Kbps
- Limited bandwidth for medium priority (video) traffic is 384 Kbps
- Limited bandwidth for low priority (data) traffic is 128 Kbps.

TABLE III. COMPARISON OF MIN'S DBA ALGORITHM AND KERIS DBA ALGORITHM

ONU		1	2	3	4	5	6	7	8	9	10
Bandwidth requested (Kbps)	**Voice**	20	30	40	50	60	200	210	220	230	300
	Video	250	280	300	400	410	350	380	400	410	420
	Data	100	200	300	150	200	120	150	120	200	300
Bandwidth received by Keris DBA algorithm (Kbps)	**Voice**	20	30	40	50	60	106	68	72	64	64
	Video	250	280	300	384	384	350	380	384	384	384
	Data	100	200	236	142	132	120	128	120	128	128
Bandwidth received by Min's DBA algorithm (Kbps)	**Voice**	20	30	40	50	60	64	64	64	64	64
	Video	250	280	402	394.5	387	350	384	384	384	384
	Data	100	200	134	131.5	129	120	128	128	128	128

The two algorithms are simulated using MATLAB. The fuzzy logic part in Keris algorithm is simulated using the fuzzy logic toolbox in MATLAB. After simulating the two algorithms, we can see that both of the algorithms can perform efficient bandwidth assignments. However, Keris algorithm is more dynamic than the algorithm developed by Min. The result is presented in table form and bar chart for easier understanding.

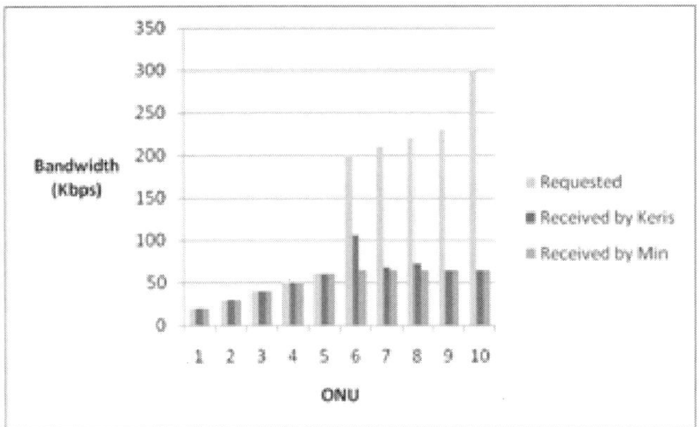

Figure 6. Comparison of voice traffic between Keris and Min's algorithm

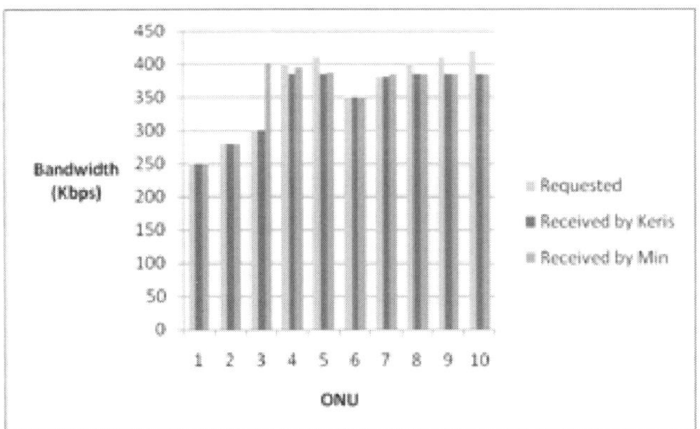

Figure 7. Comparison of video traffic between Keris and Min's algorithm

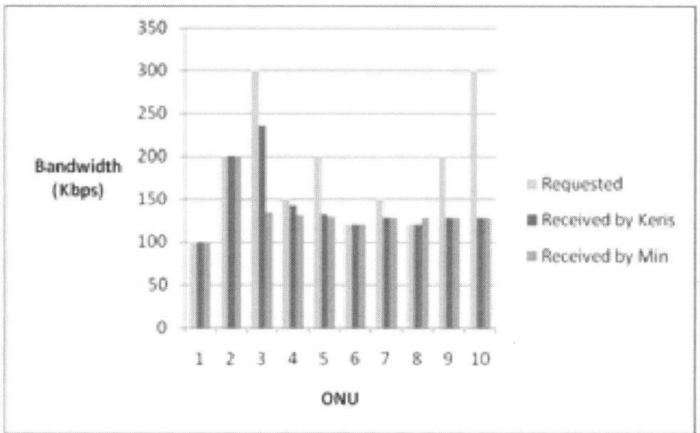

Figure 8. Comparison of data traffic between Keris and Min's algorithm

In the case where the bandwidth requested for the three types of traffic is less than limitation, both DBA algorithms have the same ability in responding to the requirements of the traffics. In another word, we can expand the bandwidth received if we increase the limited bandwidth.

However, when the traffics requested are higher than limitation, the bandwidth received for the two DBA algorithms vary. For Min's DBA algorithm, it can be observed that in any conditions, voice traffic will always received only up until their limitation bandwidths. For example, in the case of the ONU 6 where requested video and data are less than limitation, but requested voice is higher, voice is still restricted by its limitation. Flexibility does not exist. Whereas, with Keris DBA algorithm, voice traffic will received all the surplus bandwidth for that particular ONU; meaning that it can received as close as requested. This condition can be observed in Figure 6 where Keris algorithm will received more bandwidth as compared to Min's DBA algorithm.

Another disadvantage of Min's DBA algorithm is that the bandwidth is not fully utilized. This is proven in the case of ONU 3, where the bandwidth requested for data is higher than the limitation. Since Min is using Service Level Agreement (SLA) that is ratio-based, bandwidth received for both video and data sometimes can be higher than requested. In ONU 3, both video and data requested are 300 Kbps, but ONU 3 will receive 402 Kbps of video and 134 Kbps of data traffic according to the SLA. 102 Kbps of bandwidth is wasted at the video traffic, where supposedly it can be distributed to the data traffic. Keris DBA algorithm overcomes this problem by using fuzzy logic to ensure that bandwidth received is either the same or as close as requested. In the case of ONU 3 for Keris DBA algorithm, bandwidth received is 300 Kbps for video and 236 Kbps for data. Bandwidth is fully utilized here. This condition can be observed in Figure 7 for ONU 3 and ONU 7. It also happens in data traffic where it can be observed in Figure 8, ONU 8.

The result proves that Keris algorithm can receive higher bandwidth than Min's DBA algorithm but will never exceed the requirements. This is to ensure that no bandwidth will be wasted.

We also study the fairness among multiple connections over EPON. The fairness index, f is defined as:

$$f = \frac{(\sum_{t=1}^{p} x_t)^2}{p\left(\sum_{t=1}^{p} x_t^{\,2}\right)} \tag{8}$$

Where p is the number of concurrent connections and x_t is the throughput achieved by timeslot t.

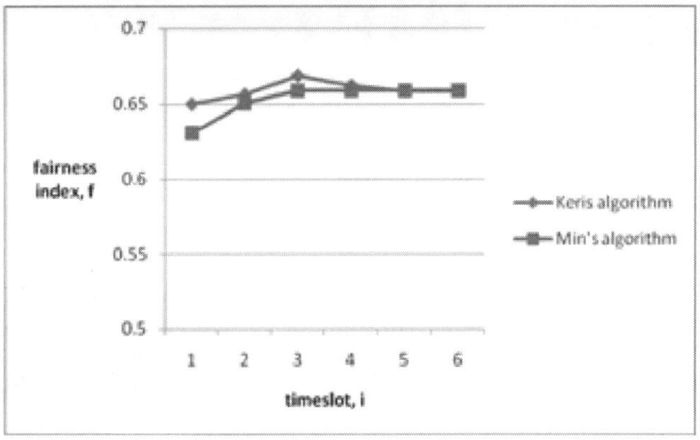

Figure 9. Fairness among multiple connections over EPON.

Figure 9 plots the corresponding fairness indices of multiple connections for both Keris DBA algorithm and Min's DBA algorithm. From the figure, it proves that the bandwidth is more evenly shared for each timeslots in Keris DBA algorithm as to be compared with Min's DBA algorithm.

V. CONCLUSION

In this paper, we propose a novel DBA algorithm in the EPON environment. A comparison study between Min's DBA algorithm and Keris DBA algorithm is presented. For Keris DBA algorithm, the allocation of the requested bandwidth is more flexible than Min's DBA algorithm since it is using fuzzy logic. All the bandwidth allocated in Keris DBA algorithm for a particular ONU will be fully utilized, where all three types of traffic will receive as close as the amount of bandwidth requested. The fuzzy logic replaces the function of SLA in Min's DBA algorithm to ensure that there are no bandwidth wastages. The simulation result using MATLAB fuzzy logic toolbox proves this flexibility and shows that Keris algorithm is fairer through its fairness indices.

REFERENCES

[1] S. Hussain and X. Fernando, "EPON: An extensive review for up-to-date dynamic bandwidth allocation schemes," Canadian Conference on Electrical and Computer Engineering, 2008. CCECE 2008., pp.000511-000516, 4-7 May 2008

[2] D. K. Mynbaev, "Analysis of quality of service provisioning in passive optical networks," 2nd International Conference on Broadband Networks, 2005, pp. 1264-1271 Vol. 2, 3-7 Oct. 2005

[3] IEEE Draft P802.3ah/D1.414, "Media Access Control Parameters, Physical Layers and Management Parameters for subscriber Access Network," Mar. 2003

[4] C. Kim, T. W. Yoo and B. T. Kim, "A Hierarchical Weighted Round Robin EPON DBA Scheme and Its Comparison with Cyclic Water-Filling Algorithm," IEEE International Conference on Communications, 2007. ICC '07. pp.2156-2161, 24-28 June 2007

[5] K. C. Chang and W. Liao, "TCP fairness in ethernet over passive optical networks (EPON)," 3rd IEEE Consumer Communications and Networking Conference, 2006. CCNC 2006. vol.2, pp. 740-744, 8-10 Jan. 2006

[6] S. I. Choi and T. D. Huh, "Dynamic bandwidth allocation algorithm for multimedia sevices over Ethernet PONs," ETRI Journal, vol. 24, pp. 465-468, Dec . 2002.

[7] L. Min, F. Xiaomei, C. Yu and D. Fulei, "New dynamic bandwidth allocation algorithm for Ethernet PON," 8th International Conference on Electronic Measurement and Instruments, 2007. ICEMI '07. pp.3-224-3-227, Aug. 16 2007-July 18 2007

[8] S. H. Jang, J. M. Kim and J. W. Jang, "Performance evaluation of new DBA algorithm supporting fairness for EPON," TENCON 2004. 10 Conference 2004 IEEE Region, pp. 29-32m Vol. 3, 21-24 Nov. 2004

[9] N. M. Din, "Fuzzy logic traffic control for differentiated service-aware generalized multiprotocol label switching network," pp. 55-64, July 2007.

The Applications of Data Mining in Tax Data Warehouse

Wang Tao
Business School, Zhejiang University City College,
310015, Hangzhou City, Zhejiang Province, China,
Guo Ning
Business School, Zhejiang University City College,
310015, Hangzhou City, Zhejiang Province, China,

Abstract

Data warehouse is a big repository of an organization's electronically stored data. It is designed to facilitate reporting and analysis. With the tax data becomes more and more in China, building a data warehouse is necessary to meet the requirements of analysis and inspection. To build the tax data warehouse, firstly, we need to establish the uniform standards and determine the subject, then, we need to construct the data warehouse. Data mining is the process of extracting hidden patterns from data, and many data mining methods can be used. In this paper, we use the rule induction method in tax inspection and find we can improve the prediction accuracy rate of the actual tax inspection to a higher level.

Key words: Data Warehouse, Building, Tax Data, Data Mining, Application

1. Introduction

Data warehouse began to prevail from the 1990's, after quick development in these years, data warehouse technology has become the best solution of information integration, information resource development and decision support in the field of the business and public administration.[1] But in China, data warehouse technology is still in its early stages. With the tax data becomes more and more, the database has been unable to meet the requirements. So, building a data warehouse is a good solution to solve this problem. At the basis of data warehouse, the effective decision-making and tax inspection can be carried out well[2]. In this paper, we will focus on how to build the tax data warehouse, the building steps, the implementation methods, and the applications of data mining technology in the tax data warehouse.

2. Tax Data Warehouse

2.1 The concept of data warehouse

The concept of data warehousing dates back to the late 1980s when IBM researchers Barry Devlin and Paul Murphy developed the "business data warehouse". Data warehouse is a repository of an organization's electronically stored data. Data warehouses are designed to facilitate reporting and analysis.[3]

This definition of the data warehouse focuses on data storage. However, the means to retrieve and analyze data, to extract, transform and load data, and to manage the data dictionary are also considered essential components of a data warehousing system. Many references to data warehousing use this broader context.[4,5] Thus, an expanded definition for data warehousing includes business intelligence tools, tools to extract, transform, and load data into the repository, and tools to manage and retrieve metadata.

In essence, the data warehousing concept was intended to provide an architectural model for the flow of data from operational systems to decision support environments.

2.2 Data warehouse features

According to the meaning of the concept of data warehouse, data warehouse has the following characteristics:[6]

(1) Subject-oriented. The data in the data warehouse is organized so that all the data elements relating to the same real-world event or object are linked together. The so-called theme is that data classification standards, each theme an objective analysis of corresponding areas, such as money supply, loans, savings growth conditions.

(2) Integrated. The data warehouse contains data from most or all of an organization's operational systems and this data is made consistent. The information in the data warehouse is processed through the system, the different data stored in different on-line database, with a variety of application logic bundled together, the duplication and inconsistency.

(3) Non-volatile. Data in the data warehouse is never over-written or deleted - once committed, the data is static, read-only, and retained for future reporting.[7] That is, data warehouses may have a large number of inquiries in generally, but the operations of modification and deletion rarely happened, usually only be required to load and refresh periodically.

(4) Time-variant. The changes to the data in the data warehouse are tracked and recorded so that reports can be produced showing changes over time. The information can be some financial indicators data to the development trend of quantitative analysis and prediction.

2.3 The source of tax data warehouse

The tax data warehouse is a repository of electronically stored tax data. It is very important for tax analysis and inspection, and the sources of tax data warehouse are mainly coming from three aspects:

(1) Levy tax data. This is the main way of data source, including various businesses tax types, tax rates and the amount of such tax information. The monthly data has exceeds one million.

(2) Administration tax data. This source includes the personnel information coming from all levels of State Administrative of Taxation. This way has less amount data than the former

(3) Inspection tax data. This source includes the need to audit object, such as information. This data volume is relatively small.

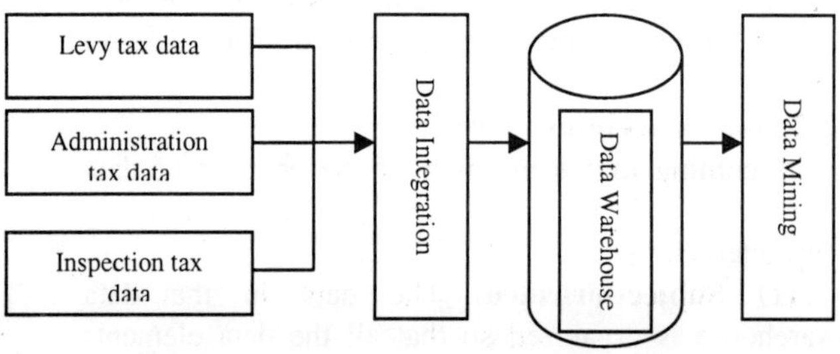

Fig. 1. Tax Data Warehouse Framework

3. Building of the Tax Data Warehouse

3.1 The establishment of uniform standards

In accordance with the integration of tax administration requirements, we should establish the uniform standards to construct the data warehouse. Every application system bears only a simple data acquisition and data analysis, non-cross-platform mission, all the more complex data analysis job completed by the data warehouse system.[8] Designing data warehouse architecture is a key aspect, it consists of three parts: Firstly, obtain information from the internal and external sources; Secondly, establish the data warehouse and data mart; Thirdly, the ways of information show.

3.2 Determine the subject

Before the data warehouse setting up, we need to define the relevant subject. There are many tax data warehouse subjects, and the logic is complex. Subject is an abstract conception which integrates and classifies the data in the information system at a higher level. Each subject is the issue concerned by the policy makers.[9] In particular, subject is the corresponding sector of a macro-analysis involved in the process.

Tax analysis of the subject can be designed as follows:

The first category is "analysis of tax changes in the macro prediction". It's a comprehensive evaluation of the national economy, and can be carried out by macroeconomic analysis and tax analysis. Its aim is to search the potentially running disciplines of the economic tax revenue, and research the impacts of the related economic indicators, providing the first-hand information for the reform of the tax system.

The second category is "tax reporting and query analysis". Its aim is to define or prepare the day-to-day and special statistical statements to satisfy the department's requirements, and to evaluate the tax department as well as the job indicators.

The third category is "auditing, levy and invoice analysis". Its aim is to support the management of checking the election case and levy. In accordance with the needs of user interaction, through analyzing and excavating the abnormal tax act of the taxpayer, the taxpayer lost, we can send the special target information back to the various operating systems and find the tax loopholes of day-to-day operational activities, resulting in early-warning information for the tax service hall staff and specialized member of the taxpayer to make the decision-making judgments more correctly.

The fourth category is "tax assessment and the taxpayer knowledge analysis". The tax assessment usually contains not only the meaning of tax assessment, also includes the tax registration, tax inspectors and other units of the comprehensive utilization of tax-related information. The taxpayer knowledge analysis includes analysis of the taxpayer, the taxpayer acts of identification, taxpayer credibility rating, etc.

3.3 Tax data warehouse architecture

In the planning of tax data warehouse architecture, it needs to design working mode for each part of the system, treating each part as a whole. The tax data warehouse architecture includes three main parts: the tax data acquisition, the tax data storage, and the tax information transfer.

3.3.1 The tax data acquisition

The entire process of tax data acquisition includes the selection of tax-related data sources, the extraction of the information from the data sources, the transfer of the collected data to preparative region, and the preparation of loading data into the data warehouse. We can acquire this data through three ways: the tax department's internal business data (system data, such as integrated levy system and the export tax rebate), external data (including the business tax-related information and other units), and the historical data (previously collected operational data by using the system).[10]

Data extraction, conversion, cleansing and transformation have changed the relevant data in the source system. This turns them into useful information and stores them in the tax data warehouse system. The data from the sources are mainly static data and amendatory data. Static data are generally gotten at the time of the initial filling into the data warehouse. The extraction of amendatory data may be carried out immediately or delayed. Data conversion and cleansing is through the system from the source data format amendment, the conversion unit of measure and key re-build to improve the quality of the data.

At the completion of tax data conversion and integration in the data preparative region, it is necessary to load the preparative region data into the data warehouse. Data loading can be divided into two parts: the initial data loading and daily data loading. Initial data loading is loaded at the completion of design and construction of data warehouse, daily data loading is loaded after the operational data changed, according to the planning to load data into the working data warehouse.

3.3.2 The tax data storage

Tax data storage process is the core of the tax data warehouse environment. It can store the required substantial historical data for analysis, and provide data retrieval support. The prominent advantage is the support for mass data storage and rapid retrieval. Data warehouse organization can be built with top-down approach, bottom-up approach and hybrid design approach. With top-down approach, firstly, it needs to set up an enterprise data warehouse, and then load the data into the various departments and different data mart.

3.3.3 The tax information transfer

This process designs many different ways to transmit information to the user, and enable users to be more convenient access to information from the enterprise data warehouse or an independent data mart. Data flows from the enterprise data warehouse or independent data mart to various types of applicable system. The data warehouse provides the OLAP support. OLAP is powerful. It provides a summary of information, and can also reach a lower level of details. Multi-Dimensional Database loads data from basic data warehouse, and stores information by way of multi-dimensional cube. The user performs these complex multi-dimensional queries through the multi-dimensional database cube. From the rotation of the cube, the user can see the cube in different sections of the page display. The function of multi-level, multi-angle data query can help users understand these tax data better, and make correct judgments and decision-making.

4. Applications of Data Mining

4.1 Data mining

Data mining is the process of extracting hidden patterns from data.[11] As more data are gathered, with the amount of data doubling every three years, data mining is becoming an increasingly important tool to transform this data into information.

Data mining is often used to apply to the two separate processes of knowledge discovery and prediction. Knowledge discovery provides explicit information about the characteristics of the collected data, using a number of techniques (e.g., association rule mining). Forecasting and predictive modeling provide predictions of future events, and the processes may range from the transparent (e.g., rule-based approaches) through to the opaque (e.g., neural networks).

Data mining can be applied to data sets of any size. However, while it can be used to uncover hidden patterns in data that have been collected, obviously it can neither uncover patterns which are not already present in the data, nor can it uncover patterns in data that have not been collected.

At present, the most commonly used data mining methods include artificial neural networks, decision trees, genetic algorithms, nearest neighbor techniques, data visualization and rule induction. Next, we will apply the method of rule induction in the tax data warehouse for tax inspection.

4.2 Application in the tax data warehouse

In order to use the data mining method of rule induction in tax inspection, it is necessary to divide the historical data into training data and test data and use the tax assessment of historical data and the outcome of the election as a guide.[12]

We should take the following four steps: Firstly, use the training data mining models, set up to carry out excavation, and get the rule base. Secondly, test the rule base and amend the rules of the treasury. Thirdly, use the expert knowledge and experience once again, and amend the rules of the treasury. Finally, apply the rules to the current data sets to determine the current assessment and the outcome of the election.

Users can carry out through the rules of the treasury:

- Rules of Management:
- Adjust the rules of the parameters:
- Application of rules

Therefore, the establishment of a flexible rule base can support the correct and timely assessment and case selection.

To set up the rules, the Rough Set Theory (RST) can be used. RST is described by Zdzisław I. Pawlak in 1982 firstly.[13] Concepts of the rough set theory are discussed for approximation, dependence and reduction of attributes, decision tables and decision rides. The applications of rough sets are discussed in pattern recognition, information processing, business and finance, industry, environment engineering, medical diagnosis and medical data analysis, system fault diagnosis and monitoring and intelligent control systems.

Let $I=(U,A)$ be an information system (attribute-value system), where U is a non-empty set of finite objects (the universe) and A is a non-empty, finite set of attributes such that $a:U\rightarrow V_a$ for every $a\in A$. V_a is the set of values that attribute a may take. In words: the information table assigns a value in V_a to each attribute a of each object in universe U.

With any $P\subseteq A$, there is an associated equivalence relation $IND(P)$:

$$IND(P)=\{(x,y)\in U^2 \mid \forall a\in P, a(x)=a(y)\}$$

The partition of U generated by $IND(P)$ is denoted $U/IND(P)$, and can be calculated as follows:

$$U/IND(P)=\otimes\{U/IND(\{a\}) \mid a\in P\},$$

where

$$A\otimes B=\{X\cap Y \mid \forall X\in A, \forall Y\in B, X\cap Y\neq\Phi\}$$

If $(x,y)\in IND(P)$, then x and y are indiscernible by attributes from p. In words: for any selected subset of attributes p, there will be sets of objects that are indiscernible based on those attributes. These indistinguishable sets of objects therefore define an equivalence or indiscernibility relation, referred to as the p-indiscernibility relation.

Application of the above algorithm, we can reduct attributes from the tax data warehouse and extract the relevant rules. After applied these rules in the tax inspector successfully, the prediction accuracy rate of the actual tax inspection can be improved to a higher level.

5. Conclusion

With the tax data in China becomes more and more, the traditional database has been unable to meet the requirements. So, building a data warehouse is a good solution to solve this problem. Through precision processing and mining the mass tax data, extracting potential information, patterns and trends, showing with the visualized form, it can improve the decision-making ability, detect abnormal patterns, and control predictable questions. This is not only an innovative job for tax statistical analysis, but an improvement of internal control. It can establish a tax system in line with the characteristics of China's data warehouse, and can improve the technology systems of China's taxation information by the comprehensive utilization of data.

References:

[1] R. Agrawal et al., *Fast discovery of association rules, in Advances in knowledge discovery and data mining* pp. 307-328, MIT Press, 1996.

[2] Y. Peng, G. Kou, Y. Shi, Z. Chen (2008). "A Descriptive Framework for the Field of Data Mining and Knowledge Discovery". *International Journal of Information Technology and Decision Making,* Volume 7, Issue 4: 639 – 682.

[3] Inmon, W.H. Tech Topic: What is a Data Warehouse? *Prism Solutions*. Volume 1. 1995.

[4] Fox, P. D., "A theory of cost-effectiveness for military systems analysis", *Operations research,* 13(2): 191-201, 1965.

[5] J.Wang, D.Miao, "Analysis on attribute reduction strategies of rough set", *Computer Science and Technology*, 1998, 13(2), pp.189-192

[6] Piatesky-Shapiro, G.; Matheus, C.; Smyth, P.; Uthurusamy, R. 1994, "KDD-93: Progress and Challenges in Knowledge Discovery in Databases," *AI Magazine,* 15(3):77-81.

[7] Bate A, Lindquist M, Edwards IR, Olsson S, Orre R, Lansner A, De Freitas RM. A Bayesian neural network method for adverse drug reaction signal generation. *Eur J Clin Pharmacol.* 1998 Jun; 54(4):315-21.

[8] Yang, Jun. *WareHouse Information Prototype at Stanford (WHIPS).* Stanford University. July 7, 1998.

[9] Yudong Chen, Yi Zhang, Jianming Hu, Xiang Li. "Traffic Data Analysis Using Kernel PCA and Self-Organizing Map". *Intelligent Vehicles Symposium,* 2006 IEEE.

[10] A. Kumar, "New Techniques for Data Reduction in a Database System for Knowledge Discovery Appli", *Journal of Intelligent Information Systems*, 1998, 10(1), pp.31-48

[11] M. Kiang, R. Chi, and K. Tam, "DKAS: A distributed knowledge acquisition system in a DSS," *J. Manage. Inf. Syst.*, vol. 9, no. 4, pp. 59–82, 1993.

[12] Wong KW, Zhou S, Yang Q and Yeung MS, Mining customer value: from association rules to direct marketing, *Data Mining and Knowledge Discovery,* 11, 2005, pp.57-79.

[13] Fang, Schu-Cherng, Lee, Y.-S. and Chiu, N. "Optimal Planning of Parallel Machining Operations", *Handbook of Computational Intelligence in Design and Manufacturing,* CRC Press, 2001, pp.8-1 to 8-33.

Policy based Negotiation for Attracting New Web Services in a Community

Sattanathan Subramanian and Guttorm Sindre
Department of Computer and Information Science,
Norwegian University of Science and Technology (NTNU),
NO-7491 Trondheim, Norway
{sat,guttors}@idi.ntnu.no

Web services are becoming increasingly popular for implementing business software systems, partly due to the flexibility offered as functionality can be dynamically changed or extended by adding or replacing services. A proposed approach to speed up service discovery is to group functionally similar web services into so-called communities. However, the state-of-the-art development protocol of web service communities lacks ability to accommodate web services which do not completely satisfy the expectations of the community. This paper explains why it may be useful to have a more flexible approach where new services may be allowed into a community even if they initially appear not to fully comply with the community's expectations. A policy based negotiation approach is proposed, allowing the community master service to automatically include new services in a flexible manner. The approach is supported by an implemented tool prototype and illustrated by an example.

Keywords: Web service, Community of Web services, Negotiation, Policy.

1. Introduction and Related Work

Web services are considered as the technology of choice to develop B2B and B2C applications.[1] A *Web service* is a URI based accessible application that can be described, advertised, discovered and triggered to satisfy various needs (e.g., weather-forecast) over the network.[2] The technology standards of Web services include WSDL, SOAP, and UDDI. Similar functional Web services are grouped as a community to accelerate the process of service discovery,[3] to support different non-functional requirements of the user,[2] to share the same domain of interest,[4] and to sustain the reliability of service provision[5] including the composition. In simple terms, a *Web Service Community* (WSC) is a collection of Web services with a common functionality, e.g., flight-booking.

The present architecture[6] of WSC is shown in the Figure 1. The main components of WSC are *master* and *slave*. The Master Web Service (MWS) leads and coordinates a WSC. The functions of a MWS include attracting new Web services to the community, providing services through the members of the community, and monitoring the existing members of the community. The Slave Web Services (SWS) follow the orders of MWS, and provide the required services to MWS. The MWS-SWS relationship is regulated using the Contract Net Protocol (CNProtocol) and Web Service Community Development Protocol (WSCDProtocol).[3] The customized Fast Bully Algorithm (cFBA) is proposed in[6] to make the WSC highly available to the customers. This introduces communication among the slave Web services to identify a temporary master for continuing the operations of the WSC (like service provision) when there is any failure with the existing MWS. The cFBA allows the permanent master to take back the administrative controls from the temporary master when it resumes. So far, the topics addressed in WSC are: approach to engineer a WSC,[3] agent based argumentation to improve the performance of a WSC,[7] sustain the high-availability of Web services engaged in composition scenarios,[8] reputation to assess a WSC as perceived by users,[9] and semantic data mediation for the Web services input and output.[10]

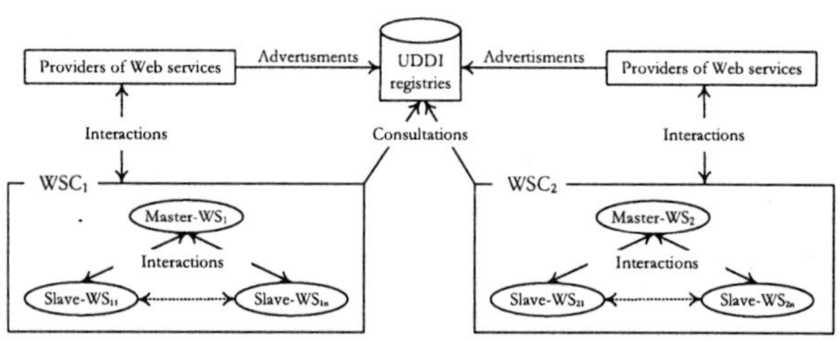

Fig. 1. Overall Architecture of the WSC

The present version of WSCDProtocol[3] cannot attract the new Web services which do not completely satisfy the expectations of a MWS. The master of a Web service community needs to attract such Web services as well for many reasons, some of them are,

- to accommodate the new or varying requirements

of the reputed users,
- to suit the immediate requirements after building or advertising the requirements of the community member,
- to try out the promising yet cost effective Web services, and,
- in general, the business providers are ready to negotiate and compromise many things for the sake of their own business profit or something else.

The above reasons require a flexibility to change the expectations of a community (or a new Web service or both) on the fly, in the process of Web service attraction. The WSCDProtocol protocol misses the required flexibility due to its direct one-time comparison between the expectations of the MWS and the new Web service, while making the decision to take the new Web service as a SWS of the community. A compromising point can be identified when there is a way for open discussions, to reach an agreement. In this paper, we provide a policy based negotiation approach to derive a possible agreement between the MWS and the new Web service which is in the process of attraction. This approach is given by extending the WSCDProtocol. The policy based negotiation approach enables the MWS and new Web service to reach an optimum point, which is beneficial for both. Note that the papers[7,11,12] considered the software agents for raising arguments, whereas this paper considers the Web services and policies for opening arguments.

The organization of the paper is follows. The Section 2 shows the negotiation model with an example. The Section 3 describes the proposed architecture to support negotiations, and provides the definitions of policy including the XML representation. The prototype implementation details are given in the Section 4, before concluding the paper in Section 5.

2. Negotiation Model: An Example

The negotiation is required when there is any conflict between two (or more) entities. In our case, we assume that the conflict happens between the MWS and the New Web Service (NWS) during the Web service attraction process.

(i) The NWS detects the conflict after comparing its expectation with the expectation of the MWS. We consider that the expected contract amount of NWS is higher than the MWS's expectation, i.e., $p \neq q$, where, p is the contract amount advertised by the MWS, and q is the expected contract amount of the NWS. The NWS has an acceptable argument 'a' from its knowledge base k_1 for the contract amount p, which is, 'a' $= r$, $r \rightarrow s$, where, r = present contract amount to work in the community c, and s = contract amount given to other Web service ws_o in the community c, i.e., $s > q$. Here is a conflict since q and s are contradictory. The NWS makes the first move by asserting its acceptable argument 'a' about the change in contract amount.

(ii) The MWS has an argument 'b' in its knowledge base k_2 to attack the argument of NWS, which is, 'b'$= t_1,\ t_2;\ t_1 \theta t_2 \rightarrow u,\ h_1$, where, t_1 = contract amount given to the Web services like ws_o, t_2 = other possible available range of contract amount, θ is an operation that produces a relative contract amount including additional constraints if any, u = contract amount could be given for the NWS, and h_1 is the mandatory time of service provision required from the Web service which receives the contract amount u. Here, u and r are contradictory. The MWS plays the assertion game by advancing the attack move with the argument 'b' including the condition h_1 as a question.

(iii) The NWS has two options at this stage, i.e., either it can accept the argument of MWS or it can attack the MWS with a new argument 'c'. We consider the second option to make our example more interesting. The knowledge base k_1 shows that the condition v of the argument 'b' cannot be satisfied due to the technical limitation of the local server. So, the NWS does not accept the argument 'b'. The new argument 'c' is generated based on the knowledge that the ws_x provides the service to the community c for h_2 time which is less than h_1, so, here h_1 and h_2 are contradictory. Note that the NWS does not attack the contract amount u of 'b' since we assume that there is no further attacking knowledge in k_1.

(iv) The MWS has an attacking argument 'd' in its knowledge k_2, which is, 'd'$=h_2,\ h_2 \rightarrow v$, where, v is the payable contract amount for h_2 time of service provision. Here, $v < u$ and $v < q$. The v and q (and u) are contradictory, hence h_2 of 'c' cannot be acceptable.

(v) Finally, the NWS plays an accept move in which it accepts to work for the contract amount v by providing services for h_2 time.

It is understandable that there is no need of

such negotiation process when the knowledge bases (i.e., k_1 and k_2) are exchangeable and understandable between Web services. Practically, the business providers may not come forward to share their complete knowledge with others due to business profit reasons, although theoretically it may be claimed that it is possible to exchange the knowledge and make it understandable with some semantic specifications (e.g., OWL[a]). This requires the negotiation for sharing parts of knowledge between Web services to make an agreement in the conflicting topics.

3. Architecture

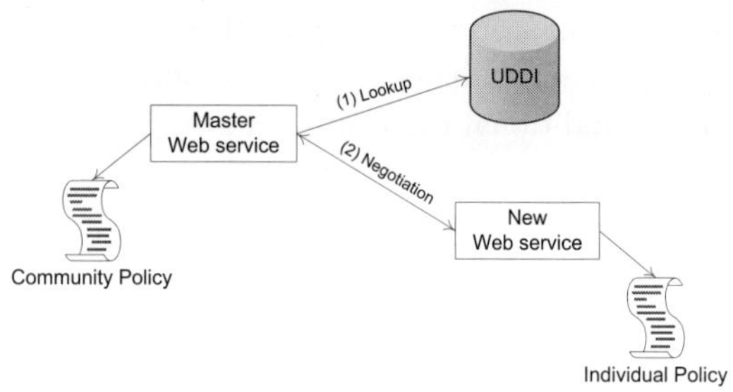

Fig. 2. The Architecture of WS Attraction

The Figure 2 shows the overall architecture of the proposed Web service attraction. The components of this architecture are the UDDI, the Master Web Service (MWS), the New Web Service (NWS), the policy of a community, and the individual policy of a NWS. The MWS uses the UDDI registry to look up the details of Web services that have similar interests of the community. Later, the MWS communicates with the Web services that satisfy the expectations of the community to a certain extent or completely. The negotiation process starts between the MWS and NWS if those expectations differ partially. The existing lookup process of WSCDProtocol is retained as it is in Figure 2. Whereas, the negotiation is introduced newly to the attraction process before making the decision of Web service selection. In the architecture, the knowledge of a Web service community and the new Web service are represented as separate policies, namely *community policy* and *individual policy*. The community policy is attached with the MWS. Similarly, the individual policy is attached with the respective NWS. The negotiation arguments of MWS and NWS are made based on the knowledge available in the respective policy. The following definitions formally define the policy.

[a]`http://www.w3.org/TR/owl-features/`

Definition 1 (Policy Statement) *A policy statement $\mathcal{S}$ is a 5-tuple $\langle n, V, r, L, F \rangle$, where,* - n is the attribute name,
- V is a set of attribute values, an attribute value $v \in V$ can be a single value or a range of values or an array of values.
- r is the relational operator represents the relation between n and $v \in V$, $r \in \{<, \leq, >, \geq, \neq\}$.
- L is a set of logical relations between the attribute name n and other, the possible logical operators are $\vee, \wedge, \sim, \oplus$.
- F is a set of function names that bring additional conditions to satisfy the attribute values V for n, and related attributes.

An example of policy statement is follows: $\langle hours\_of\_service\_requirement\_per\_day, 20, =, \{(\wedge salary\_range\_two)\}, Check\_Availability()\rangle$.

Definition 2 (Policy) *A policy $\mathcal{P}$ is a set of policy statements, i.e., $\mathcal{P} = \{s_1, s_2, ..., s_n\}$,* where, $s_{1..n} \in \mathcal{S}$.

Definition 3 (Community or Individual Policy) *A community or individual policy ($\mathcal{CP}$ or $\mathcal{IP}$) is a set of policies, i.e., $\mathcal{CP}$ or $\mathcal{IP} = \{p_1, p_2, ..., p_n\}$,* where, $p_{1..n} \in \mathcal{P}$.

The sample XML representation of the Web service community policy is given in the Listing 1. This sample is restricted to express the expectations of MWS (on behalf of community) for sake of this paper's focus. We have considered the size of $\mathcal{CP}$ as *one* to meet the restrictions of paper length. The Listing 1 has two logically related policy statements. The first statement (i.e., $hours\_of\_service\_requirement\_per\_day$) states that 20 hours of service is required per day to receive the salary range given in the $salary\_range\_two$. The second statement (i.e, $salary\_range\_two$) states that the salary range of 5000-7000NOK is given if the service provider can provide the service to an certain number of hours per day given in the $salary\_range\_two$. The logical connectivity between the policy statements is $\wedge$.

```xml
<?xml version="1.0" encoding="UTF-8"?>
<Sample_Community_Policy>
 <statement id="1">
  <name>hours_of_service_requirement_per_day</name>
  <value>20</value>
  <rel_op>equal</rel_op>
  <logic_rel>
   <log_op>and</log_op>
   <name>salary_range_two</name>
   <id>2</id>
  </logic_rel>
 </statement>
 <statement id="2">
  <name>salary_range_two</name>
  <value>5000-7000NOK</value>
  <rel_op>equal</rel_op>
  <logic_rel>
   <log_op>and</log_op>
   <name>hours_of_service_requirement_per_day
   </name>
   <id>1</id>
  </logic_rel>
 </statement>
     ...
</Sample_Community_Policy>
```

The sample XML representation of the NWS's individual policy is given in the Listings 2. This also has two policy statements as like the Listings 1. The first statement states that the *salary* is 8000NOK to the service which works in the community of second statement. The second statement states that the community name is $flight\_comm$ which provides the salary of first statement. These two statements are logically connected by $\wedge$. The combination of both statements mean that the salary of 8000NOK is given to the service provider which works for the $flight\_comm$ community.

```xml
<?xml version="1.0" encoding="UTF-8"?>
<Sample_Individual_Policy>
 <statement id="1">
  <name>salary</name>
  <value>8000NOK</value>
  <rel_op>equal</rel_op>
  <logic_rel>
   <log_op>and</log_op>
   <name>community</name>
   <id>2</id>
  </logic_rel>
 </statement>
 <statement id="2">
  <name>community</name>
  <value>flight_comm</value>
  <rel_op>equal</rel_op>
  <logic_rel>
   <log_op>and</log_op>
   <name>salary</name>
   <id>1</id><id>3</id>
  </logic_rel>
 </statement>
     ...
</Sample_Individual_Policy>
```

In addition to the existing functions reported in,[3] and,[6] we introduce the function called *Negotiate* to the MWS and NWS for supporting the arguments exchange in the process of negotiation. *ArgCon* $\leftarrow$ *MWS/NWS-Negotiate(Argument, Context)* allows the MWS/NWS to express its argument including the context for understanding the proposed argument. The *MWS/NWS-Negotiate* is the name of the function. The `NWS-Negotiate` function can be invoked after the *lookup* process. Whereas, the `MWS-Negotiate` function can be invoked after the successful invocation of `NWS-Negotiate`. The *Argument* and *Context* is the incoming message from a NWS to MWS or a MWS to NWS. The data type of the *Argument* and the *Context* are complex. The application designer determines the complete structure of this message. However, the `Argument` is expected to carry one or more policy statements, and the `context` is expected carry the structural and semantic details of the `Argument`. *ArgCon* is the outgoing message from a NWS to MWS or a MWS to NWS. The Data type is complex, and it is determined by the application developer. However, it is expected to carry either the *argument and context* or the *acceptance/rejection* of the received argument.

Note that the `MWS/NWS-Negotiate` function uses the same type of input and output parameters to carry any arguments. Here, the *Context* plays the major role by defining the structural and semantic details of an argument. The structural definitions help the Web service to understand the type of data, whereas, semantic definitions provide a way to understand the meaning of the supplied data.

4. Prototype Implementation

We have developed a prototype to process the usage of negotiations in the Web service attraction. The following technologies and tools are used to develop and execute this prototype. The *Web Service Toolkit* (WTP) of eclipse is used to develop the Web services. The *Java Development Kit* (JDK) is used as a development language. The proposed policies are represented in the form of *XML* for processing. The *Document Object Module* (DOM) is used for parsing the policies. The *Axis* is used as a container for keeping the executable Web services. The *Apache-Tomcat* is used as the software server for deploying the Web services, i.e., the MWS and NWS. The *Eclipse* is used as an Integrated Development Environment (IDE).

The example given in the Section 2 is implemented in this prototype. The server console output of eclipse is shown in the Figure 3. In this, the lookup process is assumed to be completed and a new Web service is identified where there is a conflict in the expectation of salary. The MWS proposes other possible salary after looking the community policy. After reviewing that, the NWS proposes a new argument stating that the ws_x receives 8000NOK for working in the community. The MWS attacks back by saying that it requires 24 hours of service provision per day. Now, the NWS accepts for the 24 hours service provision. Finally, the MWS takes the NWS as a new slave member of the community.

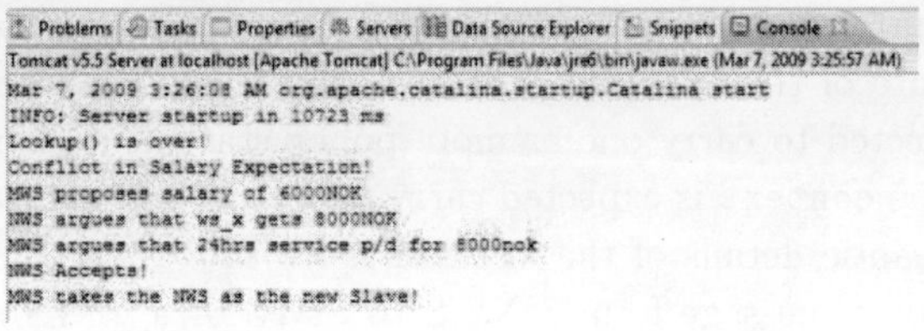

Fig. 3. A Screen-shot of Execution

5. Conclusion

This paper has provided a policy based Web service negotiation approach for attracting new Web services dynamically into the community, even though the expectations of master and the new Web service differ initially. The knowledge of the Web services are represented as policies. Those policies are used for generating the arguments to express the view of the respective Web service. The arguments are communicated through the proposed Web service functions (i.e., `MWS/NWS-Negotiate`) offered by the master and the new Web service for negotiation. The prototype illustrates the process of the proposed policy based negotiation approach for the conflict related to the expectations of salary between the new Web service and the master Web service. Although a prototype has been implemented, we acknowledge that the validation of the approach is so far quite limited, as it has only been tried out on the toy example. A key objective for future work would therefore be to try it out on larger and more complex cases in practical business settings. Also, our future work is in the direction of applying this policy based negotiation approach for different purposes and requirements of the Web service community. For instance, allowing a slave Web service to argue with its master Web service for increasing its benefits.

Acknowledgements

This work was carried out during the tenure of an ERCIM "Alain Bensoussan" Fellowship Programme.

References

1. Q. B. Vo, M. H. R. Kowalczyk and Z. Maamar, *Special issue on Service-Oriented Computing: Agents, Semantics, and Engineering in the International Journal on Agent-Oriented Software Engineering* **3** (2009).
2. B. Benatallah, Q. Z. Sheng and M. Dumas, *IEEE Internet Computing* **7**(January/February 2003).
3. Z. Maamar, S. Subramanian, P. Thiran, D. Benslimane and J. Bentahar, *International Journal of E-Business Research (IJEBR)* **5** (2009).
4. B. Medjahed and A. Bouguettaya, *Distributed and Parallel Databases, Kluwer Academic Publishers* **17** (March 2005).
5. Y. Taher, D. Benslimane, M. C. Fauvet and Z. Maamar, Towards an Approach for Web services Substitution, in *the proceedings of International Database Engineering and Applications Symposium (IDEAS)*, (Montreal, Canada, 2006).
6. S. Subramanian, Highly Available Web Service Community, in *the IEEE proceedings of International Conference on Information Technology New Generations (ITNG)*, (Las Vegas, USA, 2009).
7. J. Bentahar, Z. Maamar, D. Benslimane, W. Wan, P. Thiran and S. Subramanian, *Special Issue on Service Intelligence and Service Science in the Journal of Service Oriented Computing and Applications (SOCA)* **2** (2008).
8. Z. Maamar, Q. Z. Sheng and D. Benslimane, Sustaining Web Services High-Availability Using Communities, in *the proceedings of International Conference on Availability, Reliability and Security (ARES)*, (Fukuoka, Japan, 2008).
9. S. Elnaffar, Z. Maamar, H. Yahyaoui, J. Bentahar and P. Thiran, Reputation of Communities of Web Services - Preliminary Investigation, in *the proceedings of International Conference on Advanced Information Networking and Applications - Workshops (AINAW)*, (Okinawa, Japan, 2008).
10. M. Mrissa, P. Thiran, C. Ghedira, D. Benslimane and Z. Maamar, Using context to enable semantic mediation in web service communities, in *the proceedings of international workshop on Context enabled source and service selection, integration and adaptation (CSSSIA)*, (Beijing, China, 2008).
11. J. Bentahar, Z. Maamar, D. Benslimane and P. Thiran, Using Argumentative Agents to Manage Communities of Web Services, in *the proceedings of International Workshop on Web and Mobile Information Systems (WAMIS)*, (Niagara Falls, Canada, 2007).
12. J. Bentahar, Z. Maamar, D. Benslimane and P. Thiran, *IEEE Intelligent Systems* **22** (2007).

DEALING WITH ANONYMITY: A DESIGN PATTERN FOR PRIVACY-AWARE SYSTEMS

ALBERTO COEN PORISINI PIETRO COLOMBO SABRINA SICARI

Dipartimento di Informatica e Comunicazione
Universit a dell'Insubria
Via Mazzini, 5 - 21100 Varese, Italy
Email: {alberto.coenporisini, pietro.colombo, sabrina.sicari}@uninsubria.itr

Nowadays the wide diffusion of applications that handle data referring to individuals requires the definition of ad hoc mechanisms that aim at protecting citizens privacy. Anonymity is a fundamental requirement for privacy aware systems, which aims at preventing the identification of data owners starting from their data. This paper proposes a design pattern for the definition of anonymity mechanisms built around a previously defined conceptual model for privacy policies..

1. Introduction

Nowadays privacy is a key issue and has received increasing attention from consumers, companies, researchers and legislators. Legislative acts, such as the European Union Directive [1] for personal data, the Health Insurance Portability and Accountability Act [2] for healthcare and the Gramm Leach Bliley Act [3] for financial institutions, require governments and enterprises to protect the privacy of their citizens and customers, respectively.

An important requirement for a privacy aware system consists in introducing mechanisms that aim at protecting the identity of the individuals whose data are handled by the system. Data handled by a system can be categorized into different classes.

Among them, one class includes data that contain information concerning the private life, political or religious creed, behavior of individuals. Another class contains data that describes the identity of individuals (e.g., first name, family name, address, telephone, etc.).

In privacy aware systems only authorized users can view the existing relationship between data belonging to those two classes, while other users may be able to retrieve data belonging to one of the above mentioned classes without viewing the existing relationships.

For example, a hospital information system stores both health related and personal data of hospital patients. For diagnostic purposes a hospital doctor is allowed to access both types of data; while for other purposes such as epidemiology statistics only health related data should be accessed, that is. it should not be possible to retrieve the identity of patients. This kind of problem is know as anonymity.

The aim of this work is to propose a domain independent solution scheme that drives the construction of anonymity assurance mechanisms.

More specifically, we propose a design pattern based on the general UML conceptual model introduced in [4], which drives the definition of mechanisms that guarantee anonymity and which can be used in different application scenarios.

The paper is organized as follows: Section 2 shortly summarizes the most important features of the UML conceptual model proposed in [4]; Section 3 introduces the anonymity pattern; Section 4 presents the application of the pattern to a simple example; Section 5 discusses the related works; finally Section 6 draws some conclusions and discusses plans for future works.

2. The Privacy model

A privacy policy defines the way in which data referring to individuals can be collected, processed and diffused according to the rights that individuals are entitled to. In the following we summarize the UML model proposed in [4] that describes the main aspects of privacy according to the EU directive [1].

A *PrivacyPolicy* is characterized by three classes: *User*, *Data* and *Action*.

User represents an actor either interested in processing data or involved by such a processing. Users are characterized by functions and roles. More specifically, *Function* represents the job performed by a user in an application domain, while *Role* characterizes users with respect to privacy. *Role* is extended by three distinct classes to represent the different roles: *Subject*, which is anyone whose data are referred to, *Processor*

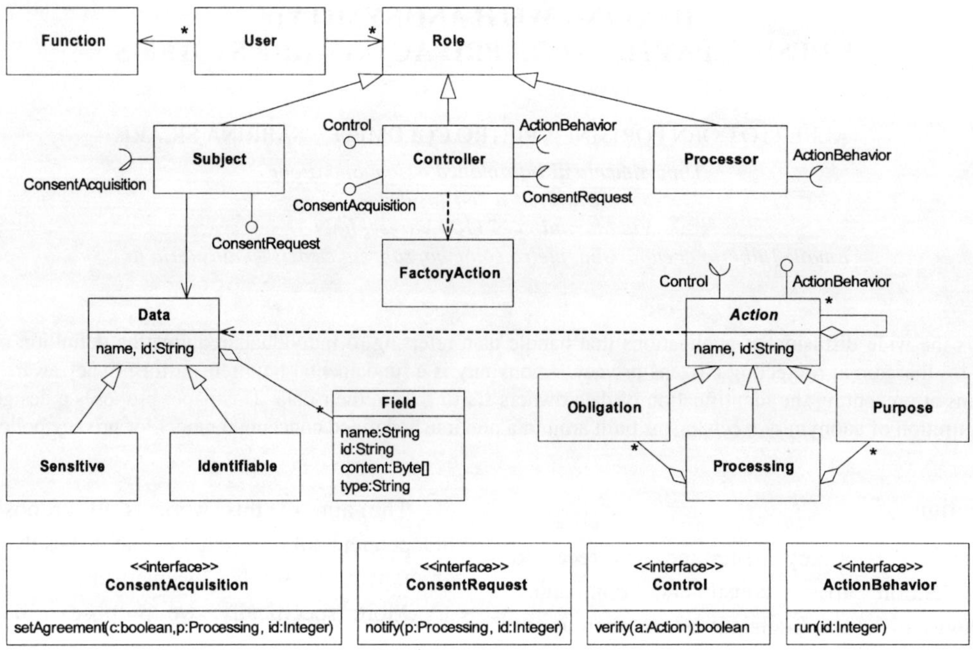

Fig. 1 Privacy Class Diagram

which is anyone who asks for processing data by performing some kind of action on them and *Controller*, which defines the allowed actions that can be performed by the processors.

Data represents the information referring to subjects that can be processed by processors. *Data* is extended by means of *Identifiable* data (e.g., family name, address, phone n.) and *Sensitive* data (e.g.,health, religion). The former represents the information that can be used to uniquely identify subjects, while the latter represents information that deserves particular care and that should not be freely accessible.*Data* is a complex structure composed of basic information unit named *Field*. *Field* is characterized by the attribute *name* that identifies the contained information, which in turn is described by the attribute *content*.

Action represents any operation performed by *User* (usually *Processor*). *Action* has been defined using an abstract class and it is extended by *Obligation*, *Processing* and *Purpose*.

Purpose is the reason for which an authorized processor access data (e.g., marketing, customer satisfaction, evaluate the customer needs). *Processing* is any operation or set of operations which is performed upon data, whether or not by automatic means (such as collection, recording, etc.), while *Obligation* is a set of actions that the processor guarantees to perform, after the data have been processed.

Moreover, each action can be recursively composed of other actions. Since in a privacy aware scenario a processing can be executed under a purpose and an obligation, *Processing* specifies an aggregation relationship with *Purpose* and *Obligation*.

Figure 1 depicts the aforementioned classes along with their relationships. Moreover, classes interact among them exchanging information by means of interfaces.

3. Anonymity

This section illustrates the Anonymity pattern, that is a basic scheme for preventing the identification of individuals, starting from their sensitive data.

3.1. *Requirements*

Several requirements must be taken into account when defining anonymity assurance mechanisms [5].

- Identity masking. Anonymity enabling mechanisms shall mask the identity of subjects.
- Usability. An anonymous data set shall be usable. Extreme solutions such as not releasing any data cannot be accepted. Moreover, anonymity enabling

mechanisms shall not alter the processing actions performed by a system.

- Performance. Anonymity enabling mechanisms shall minimally alter the overall system performances.

3.2. *Solution*

The proposed solution starts from the classification of data and users proposed in the conceptual model.

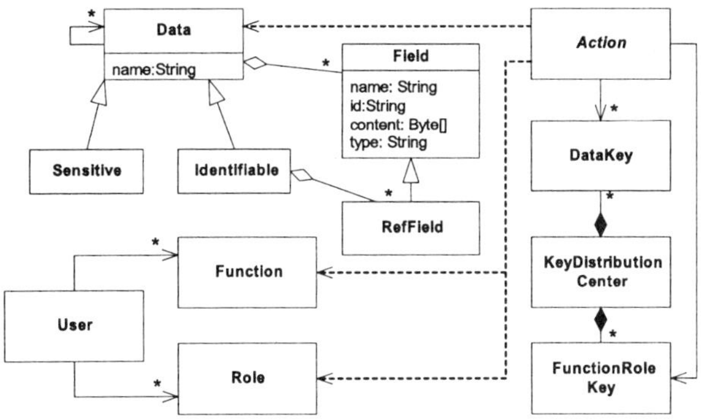

Fig. 2 Extensions of the conceptual model to support anonymity

3.2.1. Data structure

In order to define anonymity, the data handled by a system need to be suitably structured. Data are composed of fields that, depending on their characteristics, are grouped into sensitive and identifiable subsets. Moreover, a data type may be characterized by a hierarchical structure composed of other data types possibly classified as sensitive or identifiable.

In order to keep the link between identifiable and sensitive data we introduce a reference field to the data structure used for identifiable data. This is done by means of class *RefField*, introduced in Figure 2, which extends class *Field* of the conceptual model, as shown in Figure 1. The inherited attributes of class *RefField* are used in the following way: the attribute *name* is set to the name of data to which it refers, while the attribute *content* is set to the value of the attribute *id* of the instance of *Data* to which it refers.

For example, let us consider the definition of a data structure composed of the fields "familyName", "city" and "disease". Fields "familyName" and "city" identify the data owner, while "disease" represents a sensitive information. As a consequence two different data types are defined. The former, named "Person", is composed of the identifiable fields, while the latter, named "Health", contains the sensitive one. Let us consider the following data sets: 1) "Smith", "Milan", "hemicranias"; 2) "Brown", "New York", "gastric ulcer". Therefore, the first triplet is represented by an instance of class *Identifiable* in which the attribute *name* is set to "Person", and attribute *id* is set to "data001", and by an instance of class *Sensitive* in which the attribute *name* is set to "Health" and attribute id is set to"data003".

Moreover, "data001" contains an instance of class *Field* characterized by the attribute name initialized to "familyName", the attribute id initialized to "field001", and the attribute content set to "Smith". It also contains a further *Field* characterized by the attribute *name* set to "city", the attribute *id* initialized to "field002", and the attribute *content* set to "Milan". Finally, "data003" contains an instance of *Field* characterized by the attribute *name* initialized to "Disease", the attribute *id* initialized to "field005", and the attribute *content* set to "hemicranias". In order to represent the link between identifiable data represented by "data001" and the sensitive data represented by "data003", "data001" contains an instance of *RefField* in which the attribute name is set to "Health", the attribute *id* is set to "ref001" and the attribute *content* is set to "data003". A graphical description of the structure of such data is shown by the Composite Structure Diagram of Figure 3.

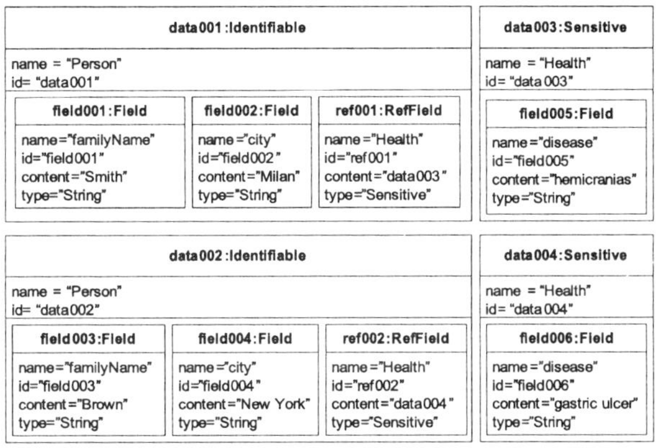

Fig. 3. The Composite Structure Diagram that describes the example

In order to prevent the identification of data owners starting from their sensitive data, instances of *Identifiable* may own references to instances of *Identifiable* or *Sensitive*, while instances of *Sensitive* can own only references to instances of *Sensitive*. In other words, instances of *Sensitive* cannot own any reference to instances of *Identifiable*.

A second issue that must be taken into account concerns the possibility that starting from identifiable data one can access the associated sensitive data, by following the reference fields. However, the system should prevent non authorized users of the system to follow such references, that is there may be some users that can access identifiable data without being authorized to access sensitive data.

The way in which we prevent non authorized accesses to sensitive data is based on cryptography.

Notice that at this level we do not need to choose any particular encryption technique (e.g., public key, symmetric key, etc.), since the needed extensions of the conceptual model are independent from encryption techniques.

3.2.2. Handling cryptography

The way in which we introduce cryptography is based on three new classes (see Figure 2): *KeyDistributionCenter*, *DataKey* and *FunctionRoleKey*. The class *KeyDistributionCenter* manages the generation of the keys usable for encryption purposes. *KeyDistributionCenter* generates keys according to the restrictions imposed by the privacy policy. *FunctionRoleKey* represents the key associated with a specific pair *Function-Role*, while *DataKey* represents the key to encrypt the content of data fields.

In what follows we present the use of the previously introduced concepts for the definition of anonymity mechanisms.

3.2.3. Data encryption

A key, named *DataKey*, is generated to encrypt the value of the attribute *content* of the reference fields that refer to instances of sensitive data. As an example, let us consider that for statistics purposes we need to know how many people living in Milan suffer from hemicranias. As described above, such data types are separately defined and a reference field, named "Health", is defined on "Person". Notice that the attribute *content* of "Health" is encrypted, and therefore it is not possible to access the sensitive data without knowing the key that is required to decrypt such a field. Notice that although the content of sensitive data is not encrypted, such data do not provide any reference to identifiable data.

In order to prevent data inference we assume that all the instances of data types with one (or more) reference field have a non null value associated with attibute *content*. In this way the fact that a person has a reference to a sensitive data element cannot be used to infer that there is some sensitive information in the system (e.g., health condition), since the sensitive data element can be empty.

3.2.4. Actions

Data can be accessed only by means of actions (see Figure 2). Actions are expressly built to be executed by users that belong to a given function-role pair. In order to guarantee that actions once defined can be only executed by the authorized users, an authentication mechanism is introduced. More specifically, a key, represented by the class *FunctionRoleKey*, is generated and released to the authorized users.

FunctionRoleKey instances are handled by *KeyDistributionCenter*, which provides generation and secure communication mechanisms like the ones proposed by Kerberos [6]. Whenever a user-controller defines a new *Action*, two keys are generated. The former key is associated with the pair *Function-Processor* that is authorized to execute the action, while the latter with the pair *Function-Controller* that has to supervise the execution. Notice that the specification of the algorithm to be used for key generation, and of the communication protocol is out of the scope of this pattern.

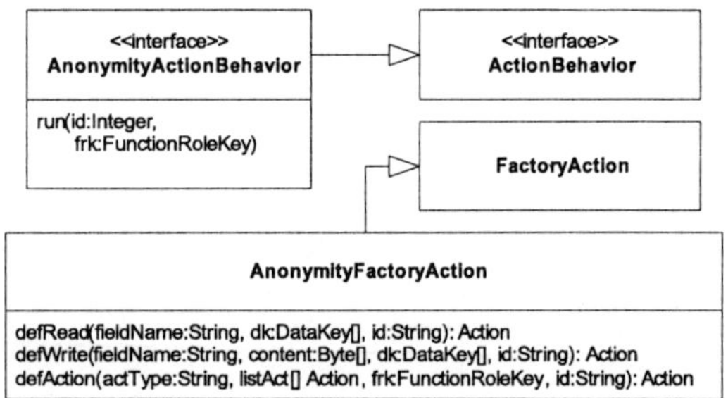

Fig. 4. Extensions of the conceptual model to support actions management

In order to support encryption a new class and a new interface are introduced (see Figure 4).

The class, named *AnonymityFactoryAction*, extends class *FactoryAction*, while the interface, named *AnonymityActionBehavior*, extends the interface *ActionBehavior*.

AnonymityFactoryAction defines three methods: *defRead()*, *defWrite()* and *defAction()*.

defRead()/defWrite() are used to define basic actions that allow one to read/write data. Since data fields are encrypted, such actions use keys to access the data content.

The parameters of *defRead()/defWrite()* specify: the name of the data fields, *dataField*; the data type, *data*; the keys, *kd* that are required to decrypt/encrypt the content of the data fields, and the identifier of the action, *id*. Such actions represent the basic constituent parts of complex actions that can be executed by authorized users. Notice that basic actions cannot be directly executed.

Controller defines executable (complex) actions by means of the method *defAction()*, whose parameters specify the involved basic actions and the users that are allowed to execute the action. In particular the parameters of *defAction()* specify: the action type, *typeId*, which expresses whether the action is a *Processing*, a *Purpose* or an *Obligation*; a list of predefined basic actions, *a[]* ; the *FunctionRoleKey*, *frk* that identifies the authorized users, and the action identifier *id*.

For instance, let us suppose that a researcher who works in a health care institute is interested to know how many people living in Milan suffer from hemicranias. Moreover, suppose that data are organized by means of the structure described in Figure 3. Therefore it is necessary to access the fields "city" and "disease". The controller, in order to create such an action, invokes the method *defAction()* passing as paremeter an instance of class *FunctionRoleKey* associated with the pair *Researcher-Processor* that is authorized to execute the action once defined.

Actions can be executed by invoking the method *run()* (defined by *AnonymityActionBehavior*), providing the key *FunctionRoleKey*, and the *id* of *User*. Notice that users authentication can be carried out in different ways. For example, the first task of the method *run()* may check whether the function-role key provided by the user is the same key that was set at action definition time.

3.3. *Consequences*

The pattern has the following benefits.

- Privacy. The separation of sensitive data from identifiable data, and the adoption of encryption techniques make it more difficult to associate sensitive data with the identity of data owners.
- Minimal user involvement. The users are not required to modify their normal activities.

Notice that the pattern should be applied to only populated datasets, since it cannot guarantee anonymity if the population of the dataset is composed only by a single entry.

A not properly defined implementation of this pattern may suffer from the following weaknesses.

- Usability. A too high granularity level of encryption mechanisms can undermine the usefulness of data. As an example, in the case of database applications, if all the data entries are encrypted, the resultant dataset may be hardly used even by authorized users.
- Overhead and delay. The application of encryption mechanisms requires adequate computational resources. Hence, the overall system performances may worsen, and delays and/or overheads can be generated. In order to guarantee an adequate level of usability and privacy, it is necessary to balance the usage of encryption techniques.

4. Example

This section provides a simple example concerning the definition of a privacy policy for data management in the context of a small neurology department characterized by the functions of neurologist, employee and outpatient:

- Outpatients need to be medically assisted. They request to undergo a medical examination with the neurologist, and once examined they pay the fee
- Neurologists examine outpatients, access and modify their case histories, prescribe therapies or physical examinations.
- Employees perform bureaucratic activities such as registering outpatients, making appointments for medical examinations, preparing purchase orders and so on.

Data processing is regulated by a policy that specifies 1) who is allowed to process data, and 2) what can be done with such data. The system manages different types of data:

- Patient case histories (sensitive data): detailed records on the background of a person under treatment.

- Identifiable data: identifiable data associated with patients such as first name, family name, address, telephone number, etc.
- Administrative data: the status of payments for medical examinations and treatments.

For example let us consider an outpatient who needs to contact the department to request an appointment for a medical examination. The following scenario sketches the involved actors and the actions:

- An employee makes the appointment for the medical examination;
- The outpatient goes to the appointment and is visited by the neurologist;
- The outpatient pays the fee at the payment office.

The main goal of this example is to show how it is possible to exploit the conceptual model and the anonymity pattern for modeling the following requirements:

- The system shall prevent the identification of individuals starting from their sensitive data
- The processing actions can be exclusively executed by authorized users of the department information system.

4.1. *Modeling privacy*

The actors involved in this example are represented by means of instances of classes *User*, *Function* and *Role*.

Employees are instances of *User* characterized by *Function* "Employee" and by the role *Processor*, since employees process data of the outpatients. Similarly, neurologists are characterized by *Function* "Neurologist" and the role *Processor*, while outpatients are the owners of data that will be processed by doctors and employees. Outpatients are characterized by the role *Subject* and no *Function* is associated with them.

Actions can be exclusively executed by authorized users of the information system of the neurology department. We assume the existence of a key distribution center and of a key management service that are able to create and distribute encryption keys to each pair function-role that operates the system.

Actions affect data of subjects, and thus in order to allow processing, the interested subjects have to grant their consent. In what follows we assume that the outpatients provided the explicit consent to access their data. Moreover, we assume the existence of the following actions:

- "Medical examination reservation": performed by employees to reserve medical examinations
- "Update case history": performed by the neurologist to modify the outpatient case history and the prescribed treatment
- "Pay the fee": performed by the employee to record the payment of the fee associated with a medical examination

For space reasons we do not consider the outpatients registration. Hence we assume that the outpatients that require to be examinated are already registered.

At definition time, actions were provided with the name of: 1) the data types and the fields that are accessed; 2) the keys that are needed to access encrypted information (i.e., the references to sensitive data and possibly encrypted further fields), 3) the keys of the pairs *Function-Role* that are allowed to execute them. A more detailed description of the functionalities of such actions is provided later on.

The data managed by the system concern: identifiable information of the outpatients, information on the reservation, the cost, the payment and the case histories of the outpatients (sensitive data).

According to the Anonymity pattern and the proposed conceptual model, in order to prevent the identification of individuals starting from their sensitive data, sensitive and identifiable data are separately modeled by means of the following data types:

- "Person": a data type characterized by fields like " first name", "family name", "birth date", "address", "telephone number", which identify an outpatient.
- "Medical examination": composed of fields like "data", "time", "place", "examination type", "examination report", which provide information on the examination.
- "Price list": characterized by fields such as "examination type" and "price", which describe the price associated with each examination.
- "Case history": sensitive data composed of fields that keep track of the health state of outpatients and the prescribed treatments.
- "Payment information": composed of fields like "total" and "paid" that keep track of the payment of the examinations.

"Person" is an identifiable data type that stores references to instances of sensitive data such as "Medical examination". Moreover, "Medical examination" stores a reference to a sensitive data named "Case history". Instead "Payment information" and "Price list" are neither sensitive nor identifiable data.

We assume the existence of a key management service that generates and stores a new key whenever a new type of sensitive data is introduced. Moreover, similarly to the action management case, we assume that all the previously described data types were defined by an authorized *User* with the role of *Controller*. The generated keys are used to encrypt/decrypt the content of the reference fields to instances of the previously listed sensitive data.

The employee makes an appointment for the medical examination by invoking the action "Medical examination reservation". Such action is a complex processing composed of multiple data writing and data reading basic actions, which affect some of the fields of "Person", "Price list" and "Medical examination". More specifically, the action accesses the fields " first name", "family name", "address", "birth date", "telephone number" of "Person" and the fields "examination type" and "price" of "Price list". The action also defines a new instance of "Medical examination" and initializes its fields "data", "time", "place", "examination type", "examination description". The action is also provided with the keys that are required to encrypt the content of the reference field "Medical examination" of "Person" and of "Payment information", and "Case history" of "Medical examination". Moreover, it integrates the keys associated with the users that are authorized to execute the action, that is those characterized by the pair *Employee-Processor*.

At execution time the employee invokes the method *run()* of the action by specifying, his/her *id*, and his/her *FunctionRoleKey*, the *id* of the outpatient, the type and the description of the medical examination, data, time and place of the examination. The action creates a new instance of "Medical examination", characterized by a certain *id*. The value of *id* encrypted with the key of the sensitive data "Medical examination" is stored in the homonymous reference of the interested instance of "Person". The action creates an instance of "Payment information" and generates a reference to a "Case history" that is stored in "Medical examination". The first data type specifies the total amount due for the examination. Notice that the values of *id* and of the field "total" are initialized. The reference to "Case History" is used to store the results of the examination. Notice that all the other fields are "empty". The values of *id* are encrypted using the key of the sensitive data "Payment information" and "Case History" and the resulting values are stored in the homonymous reference fields of the interested instance of "Medical examination". At the end of the execution, the medical examination is booked.

The outpatient provides the id of the reservation to the neurologist. The doctor, after examining the outpatient, updates his/her case history by means of the action "Update case history". More specifically, the key associated with the couple *Neurologist-Processor* is integrated into the action.

Finally, the outpatient has to pay the fee for the medical examination. Hence he/she provides the *id* of the reservation to the employee. The employee records the payment by invoking the action "Pay the fee". Such action accesses the field "examination type" of "Medical examination" and the fields "examination type" and "price" of "Price list". The value of the field "examination type" of "Medical examination" is used to calculate the price associated with the examination. The resulting amount is used to update the field "paid" of the involved instance of "Payment information".

5. Related works

Anonymity, pseudonymity, unlinkability, informed consent and unobservability are some of the main features of privacy aware systems. Such features can be effectively modeled by means of design patterns, i.e., general reusable design schemes.

Many security patterns were defined to address enterprise, architectural and user-level security [7–10], while, at present only few contributions, concerning the privacy domain, have been defined. Chung *et al.* [10] define privacy patterns for ubiquitous computing domain. Schummer [11] describes the privacy masquerade pattern, i.e., pattern that specifies how it is possible to prevent personal information from being improperly transmitted. Schumacher [12] describes two privacy patterns, named Pseudonymous Email and Protection against Cookies, respectively. The former specifies mechanisms for hiding the sender of an email message; while the latter describes how to control the cookies in a web browser. Romanosky *et al.* [13] introduce privacy pattern for online interactions, distinguishing between pattern for system architecture issues and pattern for end-user support. Hafiz [5] defines anonymity design patterns for various types of online communication systems, online data sharing, location monitoring, voting and electronic cash management.

All these contributions address specific application domain issues, while our solution is general and it can be applied to different contexts.

6. Conclusions

This paper proposed a general solution, based on the conceptual model for privacy policies presented in [4], to implement anonymity. The model provides the conceptual foundations that are required to implement anonymity, such as the separation of sensitive from identifiable data, and the classification of roles and actions. The proposed solution represents a design pattern for anonymity and it consists in concepts and guidelines that drive the modeler towards the definition of privacy aware systems. The solution extends a part of the conceptual model by introducing new concepts that aim at supporting those encryption mechanisms that are necessary for the implementation of anonymity.

A simple example concerning a neurology department illustrated the application of the pattern. The example drives the reader through the classification of users and actions, and shows how it is possible to integrate the encryption mechanisms in order to define anonymity.

Future works concern the evaluation of the scalability of the proposed solution, i.e., we are interested in evaluating the application of the pattern to a case study of realistic complexity. Moreover, we are working on the definition of additional design patterns for privacy aware system. More specifically, at present we are completing the definition of a pattern that drives the acquisition of informed consent of subjects for handling their data.

References

1. Directive 95/46/EC of the European Parliament. Official Journal of the European Communities of 23 November 1995 No L. 281 p. 31.
2. http://www.hipaa.org.
3. http://www.glba.org.
4. A. Coen-Porisini, P. Colombo, S. Sicari and A. Trombetta, A conceptual model for privacy policies, in *Proc. of SEA*, (Cambridge (MS), USA, November, 2007).
5. M. Hafiz, A collection of privacy design patterns, in *Proc. of PLoP*, 2006.
6. http://web.mit.edu/Kerberos/.
7. M. Schumacher, E. Fernandez-Buglioni, D. Hybertson, F. Buschmann and P. Sommerlad, *Security Patterns: Integrating Security and Systems Engineering.* (John Wiley & Sons, 2006).
8. B. Blakley, C. Heath *et al.*, *Technical Guide* .
9. C. Steel, R. Nagappan and R. Lai, *Core Security Patterns: Best Practices and Strategies for J2EE, Web Services, and Identity Management* (Prentice Hall, 2005).
10. E. S. Chung, J. I. Hong, J. Lin, M. K. Prabaker, J. A. Landay and A. L. Liu, Development and evaluation of emerging design patterns for ubiquitous computing, in *Proc. of Designing Interactive Systems*, (New York, NY, USA, 2004).
11. T. Schummer, The Public Privacy–Patterns for Filtering Personal Information in Collaborative Systems, in *Proc. of Pattern Language (CHI 2004 workshop)*, 2004.
12. M. Schumacher, Security Patterns and Security Standards, in *Proc. of EuroPLoP*, 2002.
13. S. Romanosky, A. Acquisti, J. Hong, L. Cranor and B. Friedman, Privacy Patterns for Online Interactions, in *Proc. of PLoP*, 2006.

JNMP2P: AN EVENT DRIVEN ARCHITECHTURE FOR NETWORKED APPLICATIONS

SUBODH MANIVANNAN IYENGAR

Dept. of Computer Science and Engineering, National Institute of Technology, Rourkela
Rourkela, Orissa-769008, India.

In this paper we introduce JNMP2P (Java Network event Model for Peer to Peer applications), a novel event driven architecture for networked application development. We outline our design goals, define the architecture, show how different networked applications can be modeled into the JNMP2P architecture, and discuss an application developed from the initial implementation of JNMP2P in Java. The JNMP2P architecture enforces modularization, making resulting code smaller, understandable and easier to maintain. We qualitatively justify how JNMP2P facilitates the development of applications conforming to the ISO 9126 standard, resulting in production of quality software. At the end we present a road map for the future development of the implementation.

1. Introduction

The growing use of the internet for both commercial and recreational activities has resulted in a greater demand for networked applications. The major challenge faced by an application designer is to coordinate and define the interaction mechanisms between the networked computers. In classical design methodologies, the business logic is so tightly coupled with the interaction mechanisms that the designer is faced with the task of re-inventing the wheel for each application. The design task can become especially complicated in large applications, resulting in convoluted code and poorly defined interfaces which are hard to maintain. It presents a substantial re-engineering effort if modifications need to be made, or the software specification is changed in the middle of development.

The situation presents a need for a software architecture to design networked applications as defined by [1], which decouples business logic and network interaction, supports modularization, and enforces clear definition of interfaces, so that applications are easily extensible. All these factors lead to a quality software development process. The ISO 9126 [2] standard defines software quality with six parameters. Summarized by Barbara Kitchenham et.al., these include Functionality, Reliability, Usability, Efficiency, Maintainability, and Portability [3]. We try to show qualitatively how JNMP2P (Java Network event Model for Peer to Peer applications) facilitates the development of software by enhancing the parameters defined by the ISO 9126 standard.

The structure of this paper is as follows: In Section III we outline our design goals for JNMP2P, Section IV describes the JNMP2P architecture, Section V discusses details of implementation and results, Section VI presents a guide to modeling applications into the JNMP2P architecture and Section VII presents the future work to be done on the framework and concludes the paper.

2. Related Technologies

The functionality of the JNMP2P architecture shows similarities to a technology called Java RMI (Remote Method Invocation), although not inspired by it. RMI enables the programmer to create distributed Java technology-based applications, in which the methods of remote Java objects can be invoked from other Java virtual machines, possibly on different hosts [4].

However, applications created using RMI incur an additional overhead of starting up the RMI Registry outside the purview of the application, and then sending skeleton and stub [4] files to all participating computers. Also, it presents a difficult task to engineer peer to peer applications to suit the architecture of RMI. All requests are compulsorily synchronous, where JNMP2P provides an asynchronous mechanism for communication. JNMP2P enforces modularization of code, thereby simplifying application design.

3. Design Goals

Graphical user interface systems have long since been used by programmers. GUI frameworks use an event driven mechanism to respond to user interaction. Architecture is defined by a three tuple, {Elements, Form, Rationale} [1].

A simple event driven architecture, can thus be defined having the three elements as:

a. Processing element: Event Handler.
b. Data element: Event

c.Connecting element: The framework

An event is a significant change in state [5]. The occurrence of an event, results in an **Event Handler** being called to process the event. The data element, **Event** encapsulates all the information regarding the event, including event source and event type. The event **Framework** is responsible for alerting the Event Handler to the occurrence of the Event. In GUI applications, for example, a mouse click of the user would trigger a MouseClicked event which would result in an **Event Handler** being called. The **Event** data might contain information about the coordinate position of the mouse during the click. The **Event Handler** performs operations based on the data of the **Event** structure.

The Rationale behind an event driven architecture is that in GUI applications, it presents an elegant way to separate business logic from presentation.

In this paper we propose JNMP2P, which introduces event driven architecture to separate business logic from network interaction mechanisms. This philosophy is on similar lines to how GUI applications separate business logic from presentation.

The current implementation for JNMP2P is written in Java, and the network technology is based on TCP/IP. Leveraging the WORA [6] philosophy of Java, JNMP2P thus has a portable nature and can run on any device for which a Java Virtual Machine exists.

The following requirements are set for JNMP2P:

a. It provides a single format (**a message**) to send data between computers and which is used to send any kind of data.
b. It provides a mechanism to connect to other computers and maintain that connection.
c. It provides the ability to create custom events and assign Event Handlers to those custom events.
d. It allows different applications to interact with each other through events by sending messages.
e. It allows multiple computers to cause an event or multiple events simultaneously.
f. It provides for secure communication between the computers and allows users to define a security model for the application.

These goals facilitate development of applications in which designers can specify their own semantics for interaction, and they need not worry about the details of implementation of the semantics. The goals also produce a framework which is excellent for distributed application development as it stipulates that message passing should be done in a fixed format. Since events can be processed concurrently and called upon by multiple applications, JNMP2P produces applications which take on a service oriented architecture. The only difference being, that in the SOA [7], an event is simply referred to as a service.

The JNMP2P architecture facilitates the development of quality software in accordance with ISO 9126 [2], an international standard for software quality.

4. JNMP2P Architecture

The JNMP2P architecture is composed of five components:

a. The JNMP2P server
b. Message Object
c. The Protocol
d. The Event Handlers/service
e. Connection object

The first two components are provided by the framework, the Protocol and the Event Handlers must be defined by the application designer. Fig. 4.1.1 shows a schematic representation of the JNMP2P architecture.

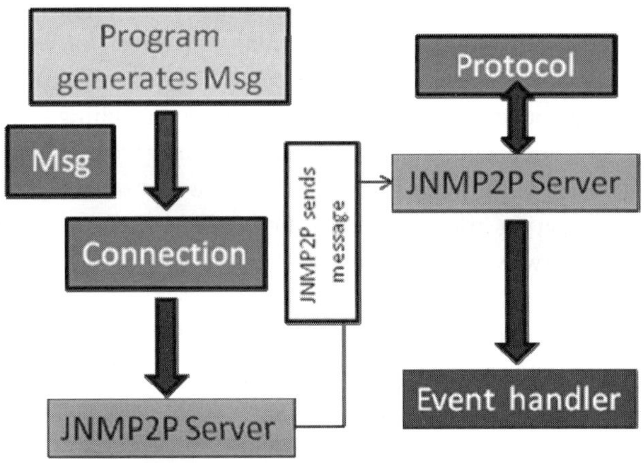

Figure 4.1.1 JNMP2P Architecture

4.1. *The JNMP2P Server*

The JNMP2P server is started by the application before the framework can establish connections and receive events. The JNMP2P server is responsible for:

a. Creating new connections, maintaining existing connections, garbage collecting dead connections.
b. Dispatching events to the event handlers as defined by the Protocol.
c. Receiving message objects and dispatching messages to the event handlers.

d.Enforcing the security model as defined by the user.

The JNMP2P server is bidirectional allowing it to be both server and client. It acts as a connection factory and any connection to another computer is created by invoking a method of the JNMP2P server.

4.2. *Message Object*

The message object forms the interaction mechanism between computers. The message is composed essentially of two parameters, although others are also defined:

1.Message Header

The message header contains the name of the event the message is meant to invoke. A message with the header "hello" thus, results in a "hello" event occurring at the receiver. The handler for the message is decided by the Protocol.

2.Message content

A message can be filled with any Object. Since, in Java, all Classes inherit from System.Object class, the message may be used carry any data structure. This provides incredible semantic flexibility during communication. The message contents can be retrieved using the methods of the Message class.

4.3. *The Protocol*

The protocol represents the mapping between the event name and the event handling method. If defined with only message name, the event handling method is assumed to have the same name as the event. It essentially constitutes a protocol for the event based interaction of the networked application, hence the name.

The protocol must be defined by the application designer prior to starting the JNMP2P server, since the server requires details of the event handling method. Once any event occurs, the protocol is read, and the corresponding event handler for the event that occurred is invoked.

4.4. *Event Handlers*

The event handler contains chunks of business logic which are processed if the event to which the handler is associated occurs. When an event occurs the event handler is passed two parameters as arguments:

1.The connection to the computer which sent the message object which subsequently caused an event and thus called the event handler.

2.A reference to the message object which invoked the event handler.

Since the event handler receives the connection object as an argument, the event handling procedure is generic in nature, that is, the event handler performs the same sequence of operations for all the computers which invoked that event, however, recognizing the difference between the calling machines through the connection object.

4.5. *Connection Object*

The connection object is created from the JNMP2P connection factory. A single connection object represents a persistent end to end connection between two computers. It abstracts the stream, socket and message creation details to make it easy to establish and maintain connections between computers. While the JNMP2P server handles the state of multiple connections, the Connection object handles the state of only a single connection. Connections which time out, or cease to exist, are garbage collected by the JNMP2P server.

5. Implementation and Results

5.1. *Implementation*

The implementation of JNMP2P in Java allows for development of event driven applications. To illustrate the power of JNMP2P, we use an example, **HelloServer,** which sends back whatever string it receives, prefixed with a hello string. Fig. 5.1.1 shows a simple one to one communication situation for a hello server using the classical design methodology.

The JNMP2P version of Hello Server - Fig. 5.1.2.- shows implementation of the event driven architecture. The entire hello server business logic is encapsulated within the event handler method, ***say_hello***. The NodeClient establishes a connection to NodeServer using JNMP2P connection factory. It sends a message with the header **hello** over that connection.

When the JNMP2P framework at NodeServer detects the receipt of the **hello** message, a hello event is said to be thrown. The Protocol uses the addMsgHandler method to assign the ***say_hello*** function as the event handler for the **hello** message. ***say_hello*** gets invoked on the event, getting the arguments as the connection to the machine that sent the **hello** message, and the reference to the **hello** message. The NodeServer sends back a **said_hello** message which is handled by the ***said_hello*** method on NodeClient.

class **Server**{
psvm(String[] args){
ServerSocket s;
Socket cli;
InputStream cliI;
OutputStream cliO;
s=new ServerSocket(11000);
cli=s.accept();
cliI= cli.getInputStream();
cliO= cli.getOutputStream();
String input=cliI.read();
sout(input);
cliO.write("hello "+input);
cliO.flush();
}}
	class **Client**{
	psvm(String[] args){
	Socket serv;
	InputStream servI;
	OutputStream servO;
	String ipAddress;
	String outputString;
	serv=new Socket(ipAddress);
	servI= serv.getInputStream();
	servO=serv.getOutputStream()
	;
	servO.write(outputString);
	servO.flush();
	String reply= servI.read();
	sout(reply);
	}}

Fig. 5.1.1 Java code for Classic Hello Server and Client (Public static void main and System.out.println have been abbreviated)

5.2. *Result*

We show how JNMP2P facilitates development of quality software as specified by the ISO 9126 standard by qualitatively analyzing five quality parameters:

a) Functionality

JNMP2P provides methods to create messages, connect to other computers, send messages in an encrypted and unencrypted format, and assign event handlers to events. Applications communicate by sending messages, thus allowing for diverse communication semantics, while internal communication details are abstracted. Thus JNMP2P provides the application with all the functionality essential for network communication.

b) Reliability

The JNMP2P server allows multiple computers to access the service provided by the event handler. The server garbage collects dead connections so that a network failure will not grind the application to a halt, relieving the programmer from having to introduce network error handling code.

c) Usability

The JNMP2P framework exposes its functionality to the programmer using only standard Java API. Since the architecture is event-driven GUI events can be directly mapped to cause JNMP2P events to occur as described in Section VI.

d) Maintainability

The JNMP2P architecture enforces modularization of code by stipulating that business logic of the application be present in event handlers, resulting in resulting in event handling chunks, which are easily extensible and less susceptible to bugs.

e) Portability

JNMP2P code can run on any machine with an installed JVM. Only the class files need to be imported. As shown in section VI, problems can easily be modeled into the JNMP2P architecture.

class **NodeServer**{
static int port=11000;
psvm(String[] args){
NodeServer n=new
NodeServer();
Protocol p=new Protocol(n);
p.addMsgHandler("hello","sa
y_hello");
jnm=new jnmp2p(p,port);
while (true){ }
}
public void
say_hello(Connection
conn,Msg msg){
Msg outputMsg;
String
input=msg.getContent();
Stringoutput="hello
".concat(input);
outputMsg=conn.createMsg(
"said_hello",output);
conn.sendMsg(outputMsg);
}}
	class **NodeClient**{
	static int port=11000;
	psvm(String[] args){
	Msg msg;
	NodeClient n= new
	NodeClient();
	Protocol p=new Protocol(n);
	p.addMsgHandler("said_hell
	o");
	jnmp2p jnm=new
	jnmp2p(p,port);
	Connection
	conn=jnm.connect(ip);
	msg=conn.createMsg("hello",
	input);
	conn.sendMsg(msg);
	while(true){ }
	}
	public void
	said_hello(Connection
	conn,Msg msg){
	sout(msg.getContent());
	}}

Fig. 5.1.2 Java Code for the server and client code of a JNMP2P HelloServer

6. Applications

6.1. Peer to Peer Applications

Our preliminary implementation of JNMP2P is suited to serve as a platform for P2P applications. The characteristic of P2P applications is that the same code functions similarly on all participating computers. Computers interact only when the user supplies an input either via mouse click or through console input. JNMP2P is perfect for this purpose because the same code can be made to run on all machines modularized as events, and since the architecture is similar to that of GUI, graphical user events can be directly translated as network events and passed on to all connected machines through messages.

Fig. 6.1.1 Procedure for file list request

A file sharing application illustrates the use of JNMP2P. Fig 6.1.1 shows how a FileListRequest function in which a user requests the file list of another user can be designed in JNMP2P. Fig. 6.1.2 shows how the FileDownload function sends a request from user A to user B using JNMP2P and then opens up a parallel channel for transmission of the file from B to A.

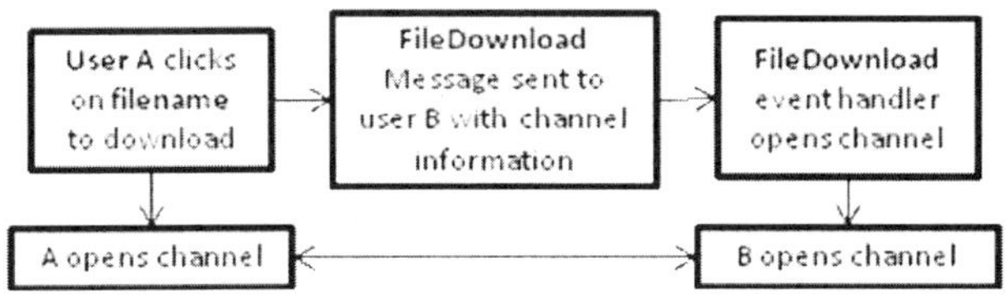

Fig. 6.1.2 Procedure for file download

6.2. Server Client applications

The JNMP2P framework may be used to create server-client applications. By virtue of the JNMP2P framework, event handlers at the server end, in this case take the form of services. The application thus takes on a natural 'service oriented architecture'. Clients send messages to the server in order to invoke services. The server may in turn call upon event handlers in clients. Clients may also provide post-back events for the server to invoke once processing is done. Since the communication is message based, independent of streams, different applications may use the same service and all requests to the service are processed concurrently.

Due to the flexible nature of the JNMP2P architecture, new application interaction mechanisms are easy to develop since all use a common message based calling mechanism. Once the name, address and return format of a service are known, any application can call it using a message object. Depending on the specification of the service to be provided, an event handler can be implemented that provides the service.

7. Conclusion

The event driven paradigm of JNMP2P enforces modularization of code, resulting in decoupling of business logic from details of inter-computer communication and faster application development times. The implementation is completely in Java and requires only an import statement to use the framework, instead of accessing the command line frequently for each build, or writing build scripts to perform the command line activities.

JNMP2P presents a novel architecture for developing network applications. We discuss the design criteria we use while creating the framework specify the components of JNMP2P architecture and we show how applications can be modeled into the JNMP2P architecture and how the JNMP2P development paradigm facilitates the ISO 9126 specification for quality software.

Future work on the JNMP2P framework includes, testing of scalability and performance in comparison with existing techniques, including a service advertising and discovery mechanism, including a security model for JNMP2P, providing methods for secure transmission of message packets and load balancing of jnmp2p server.

8. Acknowledgements

The author wishes to thank Prof. S. Chinara, Department of Computer Science and Engineering, NIT Rourkela, for her inimitable guidance and her valuable advice while writing this paper.

9. References

1. Perry,D.E et.al."*Foundations for the Study of Software Architecture*", Software Engineering Notes, ACM SIGSOFT, vol. 17, no. 4, October 1992.

2. ISO/IEC, "ISO/IEC 9126-1 Software engineering-Product quality- Part 1: Quality model," 2001.

3. Kitchenham, Barbara et.al. (1996), *Software Quality: The Elusive Target.* IEEE Software, Vol 13, No 1 (January 1996).

4. William Grosso, *Java RMI*, O'Reilly publishers, 2001.

5. K. Mani Chandy, *Event-Driven Applications: Costs, Benefits and Design Approaches,* California Institute of Technology, 2006.

6. Herbert Schildt, *Java: The Complete Reference, Seventh Edition*, McGraw-Hill Osborne Media, 2006.

7. Newcomer, Eric et.al., *Understanding SOA with Web Services*. Addison Wesley, 2005.

8. Jim Farley, *Java Distributed Computing*, O'Reilly publishers, 1998.

COMPLEXITY MANAGEMENT OF CUSTOMIZATION REQUESTS ON SOFTWARE PRODUCTS: A VALUE-BASED APPROACH

JOSEPH KIBOMBO BALIKUDDEMBE

Department of Computer Science, University of Cape Town, Private Bag Rondebosch 7701
South Africa

ANTOINE BAGULA

Department of Computer Science, University of Cape Town, Private Bag Rondebosch 7701
South Africa

ULRIKE RIVETT

Department of Civil Engineering, Spatial Data Management, University of Cape Town, Private Bag Rondebosch 7701
South Africa

The pricing of requested customizable product features against existing features remains critical in the software business. The underlying cause being the general lack of adequate techniques that facilitate gauging customer sensitivity to product pricing against vendor profitability derivation on such requests. We propose the Actor Object Dependency Analysis (AODA) technique as an essential capability that can bridge the two perspectives. We illustrate our approach with an industrial case study. Our preliminary results show that profitability on customizable systems requires adequate evaluation and assessment for realization of initial investment made on such products and for ensuring that the products remain profitable in the long run. Our main contribution is in demonstrating that continuous impact assessment of Actor Objects in the system logical model results in greater understanding of different dimensions of the system including determination of development implications that impact upon overall product portfolio value management and enhancement of these portfolios.

Keywords: Software Profitability, Software Customization, Value-Based Software Engineering, Requirements Engineering, Software Economics

1. Introduction

Customizable software products are characterized by high initial process costs and business investment in the short term. Usually, as a long term business strategy, it is often envisaged that these requests will bring about maximized revenue, in a given market segment [1]. However, while the customization business plays a significant role in generating sustainable revenue for most software vendors, it remains a critical concern to ensure that the pricing strategy used for quoting on new requests against existing system features fits the particular operating model [2]. As Kettunen [3] observes, many current decisions taken on customization requests for software products seem to be made from a functional perspective, with little consideration for overall cross-functional implications. This raises key business concerns, for example, sustainable competitiveness in the market-place.

We infer that there are two critical factors for ensuring competitiveness of the product line, namely: implementing the right tools and techniques to meter and measure complexities associated with a given customization request against the overall system functionality; and assessing the business value associated with accepting a given customization request.

As several studies have indicated, for example, [4] and [5], it is imperative to adopt flexible pricing mechanisms that are aligned with the business strategy and which also take into account overall system value and technicalities. Whether the aim is to deliver relatively simple end-user-oriented on-demand applications or to extend sophisticated products into the enterprise software market, cost-effective provisioning and pricing mechanisms still play a vital role.

How can we therefore guarantee that we are quoting and negotiating profitably on customization feature requests, specifically on evolving systems?

The AODA technique of the Complex Adaptive Software Engineering (CASSE) framework developed in this study aims firstly at addressing this business challenge. Secondly, it also aims at ensuring that the pricing approaches utilized for customization requests reflect business value and maximization.

The rest of this paper is structured as follows. Section 1 constitutes this introduction, section 2 addresses related work, section 3 details our engineering approach, section 4 describes the case study results and section 5 of this paper concludes and provides future direction for review.

2. Related work

Over the last couple of years, the area of requirements dependency analysis in general has attracted a great deal of interest within the research community. Although the analysis has proven to be successful in certain cases, it still requires refinement and testing in various areas of the software development cycle.

Past work has shown how this dependency approach can be applied in different ways to the development process. For example, Zhang *et al.* [6] proposed a feature-oriented approach to modeling requirements dependencies which applies a modular way of organizing requirements. Using feature constraints, Zhang *et al.* [7] demonstrate how to use constraint dependencies to facilitate the customization-based reuse of requirements and show how this is applied in designing high-level software architecture. Cho *et al.* [8] propose an object-oriented approach in managing operational dependencies between features. Chen *et al.* [9] propose a feature-oriented approach to the identification of crosscutting requirements based on feature dependency analysis. Lienhard *et al.* [10] propose a technique that precisely identifies dependencies between features based on a fine-grained dynamic analysis which captures details about how objects are referenced at runtime. Lee *et al.* [11] present a feature- oriented approach to managing domain requirements dependencies.

Although these models offer great insight into the feature dependency paradigm, the way they are applied is dependent on the business strategy as well as on the investment involved in establishing and integrating them into the production process. The alternative approach suggested in this study is directed towards the analysis stage of the development life-cycle, addressing a scoping problem rather than an operational need.

3. Our modeling approach

3.1. Underlying assumptions

We base our engineering approach on emergence engineering principles described in [12]. Our underlying belief is in understanding and modeling the entire software product as a complex adaptive system in which patterns of interrelationships emerge from local interrelationships between Actor Objects (AO) and their properties.

The other assumption is that profitability on any software product is shaped by how well the product features are scoped and understood, how well they are ranked and scheduled, how well their progress during implementation is monitored, how well their evolving nature is managed and how well personnel on the project are managed. Thus, overall product value is perceived as a function of the optimized development process as given in equation 1 below,

$$f(x_1,x_2 \text{---} x_n) = a_{x}, + a_2x_2 + \text{------} a_nx_n + b) \qquad (1)$$

where x denotes a feature in the product (where feature implies functional points in the AOs that have to be adjusted so that the client's expected system behavior and requirements are met), which could be new or existing; b is a unit matrix of limited resources, unknown, for example, actual programming time to implement this feature; and a is a constraint, that is, the uncertainty about a value-based coefficient attached to this functional point.

Maximizing profits on any product requires that a vendor understand well how much of the existing functionality will be priced against the new functionality. This is often difficult to determine and quantify, especially during the quotation stages. In order to achieve a breakthrough in this aspect, it is required that viable tuning be made on the unit sale value (S) of each type of functional points (FP) to be priced. This results in a mathematical problem of the objective function, as given in equation 2 below, where unit sale value for a new functional point (X_1) is donated as S_1 and new functional point (X_2) is donated as S_2. Existing functional points could be already-existing libraries or components that a firm has on their project database or they could be open-source libraries that can be interfaced.

$$\text{Max: } s_1\, x_1 + s_2\, x_2 \qquad (2)$$

However, this is subject to various constraints, including

the following.

1. Determining how many resources (z) will be involved in implementing the new functionality and how many are needed to fine-tune the existing functionality to suit the customization request. This results in equation (i) below.

$$\text{i.}\, z_1 x_1 + z_2 x_2 \leq b1$$

2. Determining total optimal time (t) needed to achieve the functionality of a given functional point, resulting in equation (ii) below.

$$\text{ii.}\, t_1 x_1 + t_2 x_2 \leq b2$$

3. Determining total labour cost (c) to complete the functional point. This results in equation (iii) below.

$$\text{iii.}\, c_1 x_1 + c_2 x_2 \leq b3$$

However, existing functional points can never be negative and new functional points can never be negative, thus resulting in equation (iv) as given below.

$$\text{iv.}\, x_1 \geq 0,\ x_2 \geq 0$$

3.1. *Deriving AO properties and relationships*

In understanding and modeling the complexity associated with a given system logical model that will be impacted by a given customization request, several considerations have to be taken into account. These include: the AO properties that will be adjusted; the OA dependency relationships and their extent in relation to other AOs in the model; the critical path position of each AO in the model for optimal scheduling purposes; the explicit risk associated with each AO; how each AO is prioritized in the model; and how this entire complexity is handled in the model.

3.2.1 AO Properties.

Each OA has the following properties. ***Sale Value*** – the amount quoted by the vendor to the client; an ***Implicit Cost*** – the actual cost incurred by the vendor to implement an AO; ***Nature*** of AO – whether it is an existing or new AO; ***Number of resources*** to implement that AO; ***number of functional points*** (FP) in that AO; and ***time*** required to implement that AO. Each vendor decides his implicit cost and sale value respectively based on the costing model he has adopted and on the prevailing market forces. This is often in the form of an hourly rate.

This approach assumes that a vendor has a qualified team to execute a customization request in the shortest time possible or has a contracting pool he can draw from – thus balancing the human resource problems on a given project. The time attribute has a derived value. Total time (T_t) is a product of total number of functional points and the Productivity Factor (*PF*). The relative PF per functional point used in this framework is 7.2. This value has been recommended in [13] as a relative estimation value for an FP.

3.2.2 Analyzing AO dependencies

All functional points are contained in AOs which have specialized dependencies between them. These AOs interact in a specialized fashion using functional points to achieve a given system goal. Thus computing a unit AO's weight, given the number of dependencies it has with other AOs in the model, is imperative for determining its overall priority in the model. The main aim here is to establish how each object relates to each other in the model and what risk factor this weight will give it in relation to its neighbors. The computation used at this stage extends principles of information theory, specifically, weighted network principles proposed in [14].

The value of each dependency link in the model is calculated based on the four relationships described in our earlier work [15]. The value obtained will be between 0 – 1 where 1 is extremely risky and 0 is Low. This results in 3 state classifications for each AO in the model, that is, Low, Medium and High. It is upon these states that belief propagation is learnt in the network and upon which sensitivity analysis is made about the model. This computation results in the determination of each AO risk level, which in this regard is the implicit risk. AO weight is computed as given in equation 3 below.

$$\varpi = \frac{\sum_{i=1}^{n} w_{ij}}{n} \qquad (3)$$

The implicit risk of an AO denoted by ϖ is computed as the total average of all link dependencies denoted by w_{ij} incoming into the AO in the model with *i* starting from 1 to *n* where *n* is the total number of all link dependencies going through an AO in the model.

3.2.3 Calculating the critical path

To calculate the critical path (CP) of the model, a forward pass and a backward pass are used to determine the minimal customization request duration. The algorithm used has a starting object and works on computing 'flag value' for the objects in the model. The flag values represent the longest time for each AO. The AO in the model can be processed in any sequence so long as all preceding objects have flags at each step.
Early start time of the whole model is computed as:

$$ESK = MAX_{j:j \to k}\{EF(j)\} = MAX_{j:j \to k}\{ES(j) + d(j)\}$$

$$EF(k) = ES(k) + d(k) \quad (4)$$

Late start and finish is computed as:

$$LF(j) = MIN_{k:j \to k}\{LS(k)\} = MIN_{k:j \to k}\{LF(j) - d(k)\}$$

$$EF(j) = LF(j) + d(j) \quad (5)$$

An activity on a project, in this case an AO and its properties, is denoted as k and j. Duration of an activity is denoted as d. ***ES*** is the early start time, ***EF*** is the early finish time, ***LF*** is late finish time and ***LS*** is late start time.

3.2.4 Explicit risk of the model

The explicit risk is determined as time required for completing an AO implementation in the model. It is calculated as an average difference of implementation time and slack time as given in equation 6 below,

$$E_r = \frac{t - s_t}{t} \quad (6)$$

where t is the time required to complete an AO implementation in the model and s_t is the slack time.

3.2.5 Prioritization

Prioritization of the AOs in the model is carried out for optimal scheduling purposes and identification of key AOs in the model. The critical path methods together with the complexity-handling module in the framework handle this emergence. These two modules categorize and rank the AOs into three groupings, that is, high to low. *High* would imply very critical AOs required in achieving the overall system functionality. *Medium* would imply AOs that are relatively influential in achieving the overall system functionality. *Low* would imply AOs of least significance in impacting on overall system functionality.

With this approach it is possible to identify key system integration points that will require much attention and often these will form the basis for overall customer acceptance criteria for the envisaged customization request. In both instances, where project time is known and unknown, this option facilitates optimal scheduling and prioritization of system features against time, cost and resource constraint on the project.

3.2.6 Handling complexity in the model

The complexity handling in the logical model is attained with the use of the *Bayesian Belief Network* (BN) as a multi-criteria decision making mechanism. The Bayesian scoring metrics are applied in defining a scoring function for measuring model quality in terms of marginal likelihood or penalized likelihood. A BN is traditionally defined as a directed acyclic graph (DAG) $G = (V,E)$ (where V is a finite set of nodes, and E is a set of edges, that is, $E \subseteq (G \times G)$ together with a joint probabilistic distribution P that satisfies the *Markov condition*, namely that each variable $x \in V$ is conditionally independent of the set of all its non-descendents given the set of all its parents [16].

We apply the L1 Regularized Path algorithm proposed by Schmidt *et al.* [17] to handle the complexity check and management in the logical model, as given in equation 7 below. The goal is to find the DAG G that equivalently minimizes the MDL (Minimum Description Length) cost. Assumption is made that the data is complete and is fully observed and can either be continuous or discrete.

$$MDL(G) = \sum_{j=1}^{d} NLL(j, \pi_j, \theta_j + \frac{|\theta_j|}{2} \log n \quad (7)$$

$$NLL(j,\pi,\theta) = -\sum_{i=1}^{n} \log p(X_{ij} \mid X_{i\pi j,}\theta)$$

Where n is the number of data cases, π_j are the parents of node j in G, $NLL(j,\pi_j,\theta)$ is the negative log-likelihood of node j with parents π_j and parameter θ. $\theta_j = \text{argmin}_\Theta\ NLL(j,\pi_j,\theta)$ is the maximum likelihood estimate of j's parameters. This approach has been used in other studies, for example in [18].

4. Case study for a customizable product

4.1. *Case study description*

In validating our approach, we undertook a feature dependency analysis for the Intelligent Dispensing of Antiretroviral Treatment (iDART) system as our case study. iDART is a customizable mobile patient monitoring system developed by Cell-Life, one of the leading organizations in developing mobile health management systems in South Africa. It is a customizable software solution designed to assist in the Antiretroviral Treatment (ART) patient monitoring as well as the supply chain management of ARV drugs in the public health sector in South Africa. Developed using Java technology and with the capability of providing real-time assessment of a given ARV programme, the system comprises two applications for different functions within the supply chain, that is, *iDART Pharmacy* for pharmacy management and *iDART Clinic* for remote clinic management. This project was developed and released under the General Public License (GNU) as ARV dispensing software in the public health sector in South Africa. Some of the components of this system utilized existing libraries; thus not all AOs on this project were new; rather, they were a combination of existing and new components.

Some of its features include: Patient management, prescription management, dispensing drug management, label printing, report generation, stock management, remote clinic management as well as data export functionalities as illustrated in figure 1 below.

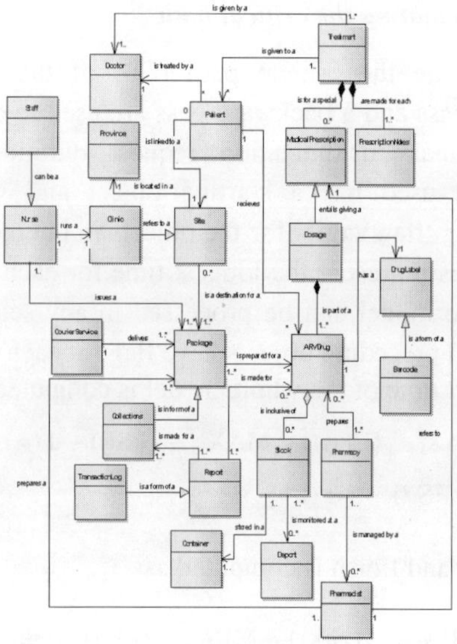

Figure 1: iDART Logical Model

As illustrated in the figure above, these features are managed by the system logical model composed of AOs that have different relationship types and properties. As a Non-Governmental Organization, Cell-Life has to have sufficient funds to run its activities and at the same time stay operational. Therefore, as a mechanism to ensure that there is a stable revenue stream in the organization, it embarked on selling customizable features of the iDART system at a negligible markup price. Frequently, various clients approach this organization requiring customized features of iDART. Clients interested in such features are required to pay customization costs evaluated on the basis of the features and time required to complete these customization requests. Invariably, these customizations have to be profitable as drawn from the organizational operational model. Therefore, while losses are a no-go zone area, achieving break-even is the minimum acceptable status for any customization request.

4.2. *Model analysis*

With Cell-Life's business model in mind, we applied the CASSE framework to the system logical model to assess system dependencies using AOD. We were keen to establish the viable customization base-line of system modules and features. Another point of interest was in determining the relationships and strengths between different AOs in the model. The overall aim was to determine which AOs were critical in providing overall system functionality from the given set of AOs. We also wanted to extract an AO-based value matrix which could be used as a basis for quoting on future customizations on the system and for carrying out system maintenance impact assessments. As an additional benefit, the resultant matrix would highlight module dependencies. This in return would highlight strategic system integration points and eventually form the basis for minimum AO units required for any customization request.

To assess the AO dependencies, we used the logical system model developed in UML as illustrated in figure 2 above. Analysis of the model was done in the framework. Based on the nature of interrelationships, the dependency assessment classified AOs into 3 categories, namely: High (Marked red), Medium (marked Green) and Low (marked blue). This is illustrated in figure 2 below.

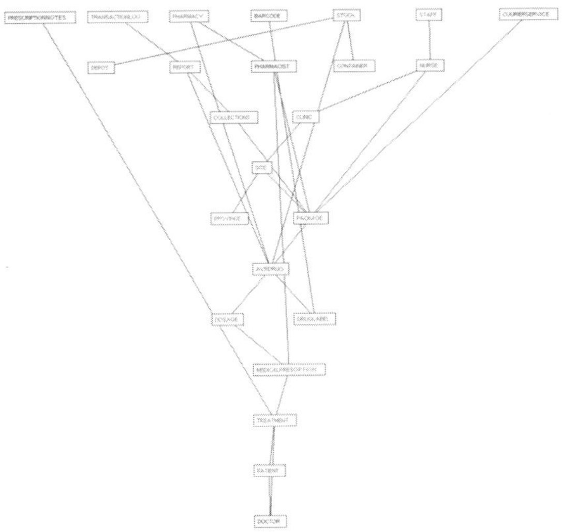

Figure 2: iDART AOD model

The AOD graph above illustrates the complex interdependency of all the AOs in the iDART system. High implies AO with the highest risk in the model. AOs in this category have a high impact on their dependants. Functional points in these high-risk AOs have a high task and causality impact. Certain AOs' tasks are influenced/impacted upon by these high-risk AOs. A high causality dependency in this regard implies that these high-risk AOs cause the tasks of their dependants to be at a medium (or lower) risk level. Therefore, overall functional performance in the model would rely heavily on these high-risk AOs if desired system behavior is to be achieved.

Medium implies AOs which have an averagely significant task and causality impact. However, they do have a high resource dependency with their parent. Resource in this regard implies that these AOs depend on their parent for the same resource. Any changes in their property parameters would not influence the model immensely but would have a significant effect on the overall model outlook.

Low risk implies that AOs in this category have a lower task, causality and resource dependency. Their overall status in the model does not directly impact on overall system behavior. However, any change in any of their properties would change their category classification status, thereby changing their dependency impact and ultimately desired behavior in the system.

Using the complexity check module of the framework, it was observed that this emergence pattern is bound to be propagated through the entire model each time a change is made on the model property. This holds equally true when a new AO is introduced or an existing AO is deleted. With this kind of analysis, it was observed that dependency checks support impact assessment analysis, customization scope base-lining and functional sizing measurement as well as change management implications.

An experimental analysis was done to determine AO dependencies on this system as illustrated in the table 1 below.

Table 1:AO dependencies in iDART system

	Risk Level	Strong Linkages	Dependants
ARVDrug	H	12	Clinic, Collections, CourierService, Nurse, Package, Pharmacist, Pharmacy, Report, Site, Staff, Stock, TransactionLog
Doctor	M	18	ARVDrug, Clinic, Collections, CourierService, Dosage, MedicalPrescription, Nurse, Package, Patient, Pharmacist, Pharmacy, Report, Site, Staff, Stock, TransactionLog, Treatment, TreatmentNotes
Patient	M	17	ARVDrug, Clinic, Collections, CourierService, Dosage, Nurse, Package, Pharmacist, Pharmacy, Report, Site, Staff, Stock, TransactionLog, Treatment, TreatmentNotes, MedicalPrescription,
Treatment	H	16	ARVDrug, Clinic, Collections, CourierService, Dosage, MedicalPrescription, Nurse, Package, Pharmacist, Pharmacy, Report, Site, Staff, Stock

All the AOs in the model were analyzed. However, for illustration purposes, four AOs were considered with emphasis on their dependency magnitude in the model and how they impact on others. This was for AOs ARVDrug, Patient, Treatment and Doctor as given in the table above.

The Framework classified each AO in the model in different categories, that is, Medium - M, High - H and Low - L. The number and names of dependant AOs that strongly depend on this AO are given. The framework revealed that certain AOs have strong relationships with others in the model, yet others do not necessarily have strong relationships with others. Each AO with its associated AOs therefore forms a system package within the system. This kind of packaging would form an aggregated estimation of the number of functional points impacted if a customization request is made. Profitable quotation on either system package therefore holds a maximum macro value of total number of functional points contained within each AO multiplied with the productivity factor of 7.2. Any customization made for less than the maximum hours required per AO therefore would increase project revenue, hence ensuring business continuity on this project. The reverse would be losses on any customization request. For example, any customization request that requires adjustments in functionality in managing or assessing patient responses to ARV drug treatment given by a qualified doctor will impact on the following AOs as illustrated in figure 3 below.

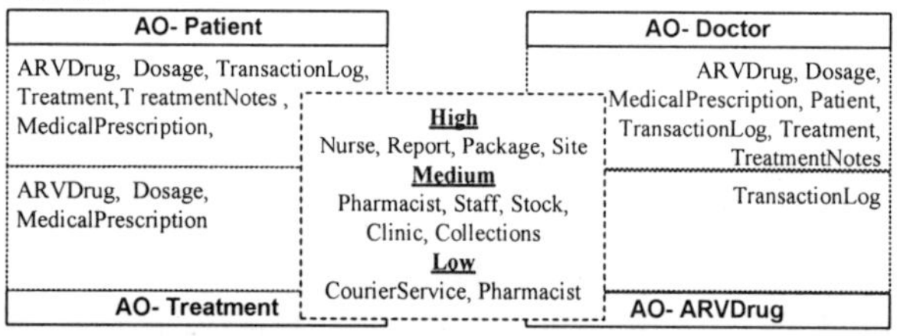

Figure 3.Common AOD scenario

According to the model results, 11 AOs cut across the four packages. Out of these, 4 are of high risk (Nurse, Report, Package and Site), 5 are of medium risk (Pharmacy, Staff, Stock, Clinic and Collections) and 2 are of low risk (CourierService and Pharmacist). This implies that changes made on any of these four AOs in one system package in the model will have to be propagated to the rest of the other packages specifically addressing resources or tasks from the 11 common AOs.

This impact therefore has to be taken into consideration if any customization request is to be made in terms of hours required to achieve overall system behavior and functionality. For a client willing to pay for limited functionality, dependant AO costs also need to be built into the quotation since a change in any of the properties of the model will propagate through other system packages.

The case study results presented here therefore demonstrate that viable quotation of customization products is attainable given the dependency of the AOs in the system logical model. However, for it to be rendered effective, it has to be aligned with the processes utilized in achieving business targets. This approach sets a basis for negotiating on required functionality, since sizing and measurement can be assessed based on complexity involved in comparison with anticipated customization value.

5. Conclusion and future work

The complexity associated with hidden dependencies between product features, if underestimated, poses serious business risks. Therefore, as software vendors, our pricing strategy and decisions must be based on whether our business return warrants the long-term investment incurred in the production of such customizable products. The way we price new features against existing ones determines the value we derive from such requests. Therefore, with lack of adequate techniques to help us identify the intricacies involved with customization management, we are prone to taking on risky and unprofitable business; a likelihood we must guard against.

Successful customization on any product therefore largely depends on addressing the technical complexity allied with the product, market and financial uncertainties, as well as competent manpower availability throughout the customization process. Therefore, in order to improve our business selection processes and the entire software customization processes effectively, it is essential to reduce the level of uncertainty at all levels. The key strategy therefore is continuously to assess the impact of each AO in the model so as to derive different dimensions of system implications. Profitability on evolving systems needs to be well tracked and analyzed, firstly if initial investment made on such products has to be realized, and secondly if the product is to remain profitable in the long run. As we make inroads into certain market niches, we ought to ensure that the we continue to track profitability and assess that our products are maturing and that we are always operating in the profitable business quadrant for competitive advantage purposes.

We strongly believe that this approach paves the way for adopting new requirement engineering techniques which enhance customization request viability assessment and decision-making for stakeholders via feedback control mechanisms. As a direction for future research, more comparisons need to be made to explore how better to align attractive pricing mechanisms with profitability derivation, using the complexity levels embedded within system features.

Acknowledgement

Great thanks to *Cell-Life* for their support both technically and academically.

References

1. M. Katsioloudes, J. Grant, D. S. McKechnie, "Social marketing: strengthening company-customer bonds," Journal of Business Strategy, vol.28, no., 3, pp.56 – 64, 2007.
2. M. M. Helms, M. Ahmadi , W.J. K. Jih and L.P. Ettkin, "Technologies in support of mass customization strategy: Exploring the linkages between e-commerce and knowledge management," Computers in Industry, vol. 59, no. 4, pp. 351-363, April 2008.
3. P. Kettunen, "Adopting key lessons from agile manufacturing to agile software product development—A comparative study, " Technovation, Article in Press
4. H. Karandikar and S. Nidamarthi, "Implementing a platform strategy for a systems business via standardization," Journal of Manufacturing Technology Management, vol. 18, no. 3, pp. 267 – 280, 2007.
5. Y. Liao, "Business strategy and performance: the role of human resource management control," Personnel Review, vol. 34, no.3, pp. 294 – 309, 2005.
6. W. Zhang, H. Mei and H. Zhao, "A Feature-Oriented Approach to Modeling Requirements Dependencies," *in the 13th IEEE International Conference on Requirements Engineering*, 2005, pp.273 – 284.
7. W. Zhang, H. Mei and H. Zhao, "Feature-driven requirement dependency analysis and high-level software design," Requirements Engineering, pp.205 - 220, 2006.
8. H. Cho, K. Lee, and K. C. Kang, "Feature Relation and Dependency Management: An Aspect-Oriented Approach," *in12th International Software Product Line Conference*, pp.3-11, 2008.
9. K.Chen, H. Zhao, W. Zhang and H. Mei, "Identification of Crosscutting Requirements Based on Feature Dependency Analysis," *in the 14th IEEE International Requirements Engineering Conference,"* pp.300 - 303 , 2006.
10. A. Lienhard, O. Greevy and O. Nierstrasz, "Tracking Objects to Detect Feature Dependencies," *in the 15th IEEE International Conference on Program Comprehension*, pp.59-68, 2007.
11. Y. Lee and W. Zhao, "A Feature Oriented Approach to Managing Domain Requirements Dependencies in Software Product Lines," *in the First International Multi-Symposiums on Computer and Computational Sciences,"* pp. 378 - 386, 2006.
12. A. Kossiakoff and W. N. Sweet., Systems Engineering Principles and Practice. USA :John Wiley, 2003.
13. B. Anda, H. C. Benestad and S. E. Hove, "A Multiple-Case Study of Effort Estimation based on Use Case Points," in the 2005 *International Symposium on Empirical Software Engineering*," pp.10, 2005.
14. A. Barrat, M. Barthélemy, R. Pastor-Satorras, and A. Vespignani, "The architecture of complex weighted networks," in the National Academy of Sciences, 2004,pp.3747-3752
15. J.K. Balikuddembe and A.E. Potgieter, "Using Actor Object Operations Structures to Understand Project Requirements Complexities," *in the 2008 Third International Conference on Software Engineering Advances*, pp.290-294, 2008 .
16. R. Neapolitan. Learning Bayesian Networks. Prentice Hall : New Jersey, 2003.
17. M. Schmidt, A. Niculescu-Mizil, and K. Murphy, "Learning graphical model structure using L1-Regularization paths," in the 22nd Conference on Artificial Intelligence, pp. 1278-1283, 2007.
18. M. Y. Park, T. Hastie, "L1-regularization path algorithm for generalized linear models," Journal-Royal Statistical Society - Series B Statistical Methodology, vol.69, no. 4. pp. 659-677, 2007.

Session 3

DESIGN OF AUTOMOBILE COMPREHENSIVE PERFORMANCE TEST STATION BASED ON DISTRIBUTED TECHNOLOGY

HONGJIANG HE

College of Information &Electrical Engineering Hebei University of Engineering Handan, 056038, China

YONGAN LI

College of Information &Electrical Engineering Hebei University of Engineering Handan, 056038, China

A new control and management model is proposed on the basis of automobile comprehensive test station. The core is distributed control and networking management, and this new model realizes full automatic web-based test and evaluation of automobile security, economical efficiency and pro-environment, solves the problem of multi-item, disunity of test time and disperse of detecting station, makes the test station flow and time control easy. It can realize breezily efficient allocation of resources on FPGA, reduce design cost and cut down develop cycle by using the internal embedded NIOS; meanwhile, data collect of FPGA has the advantage of high-frequency and high-precision. Automobile comprehensive performance test station also has advanced data management and remote monitoring program, which realizes all-in-one control.

1. Introduction

With the development of auto detecting technology, for the safety performance of motor vehicles and the comprehensive performance, their individual detection technology is maturing. Currently, for multiple projects detecting simultaneously and automatic control mode, only motor vehicle safety performance test line can be achieved. And vehicle performance test is still in a state of manual or semi-automatic manual. This is mainly because that the comprehensive performances test of motor vehicles include not only security detecting but also detecting of vehicle power, economy, reliability, state of engine technology and emissions performance. Its problem is many test items and not unity of test time beat. Some detection equipment is distributed at various detecting workshops. It will be difficult to meet their needs if still adopting the traditional control mode of security performance test. Therefore, toward the problem of motor vehicles overall performance automatically detecting, on the whole design of control structure and model plan, in addition to absorb automotive safety advantages of automatic detection system and it also be able to adapt to the special requirements of car comprehensive performance test of. In order to solve the above problem, distributed network-based approach must be chosen in the control mode. SOPC technology will be applied to the bottom of detecting positions, with SOPC as the core to design PC to complete signal acquisition, conditioning, transmission, and communication with the host computer. Finally, use the station computer networking to achieve data sharing of detection station.

2. Principles of Implementation

Apart from the completion of the inspection operation, the most important thing of Vehicle test Station is to use detected data to maintain and manage the car, which will extend the service life of motor vehicles and ensure safe driving. Using advanced communication technology and computer network technology can achieve networked management of station; therefore, detection, control and management are set in unity. Briefly, it includes environmental protection, vehicle performance test and fault diagnosis. To achieve above function, the whole detect station is divided into vehicle detection sub-system which achieve fully automatic detection of motor vehicles; data management sub-systems which manage and maintain the information of vehicles, vehicle test data and test line;remote maintenance sub-system which is major to remote maintenance and diagnosis of the vehicle detection line system.

SOPC (System on a Programmable Chip) is a flexible and efficient SOC solution proposed by Altera Corporation. It's a programmable system with flexible design approach that can be trimmed, scalable, upgradeable, and has in-system program functions. The design of SOPC is based on IP core, as sub-level hardware description language for the main description means of the system functions and structure, by means of EDA tools on computer. At aspect of high-speed data collection, FPGA has unmatched advantages compare to single-chip machine and DSP, including high clock frequency, small internal delay and all control logic can be completed by the hardware.

3. Function Implementation of System

As mentioned above, the function of automobile comprehensive performance test station relies on the three subsystems to carry out. Each subsystem can be designed and accomplished independently. Introduction is as follows.

3.1. *Vehicle detection Sub-system (achievement based on SOPC technology)*

Vehicle detection sub-system is the core of whole system and it has lots of test items. It is divided into three parallel work-stations to detict all parameters; each has independent sampling, control and processing function. Data sampling and control system is launched to design with SOPC as the core. Each upper computer interconnects main control machine with network device to build a vehicle detecting sub-system LAN. every item has independent test instrument , detection of axle weight and braking performance are designed to real-time and accurate measurement of the pulse signal and analog signals in accord with the core of SOPC.Station division and test items are shown in figure 1.

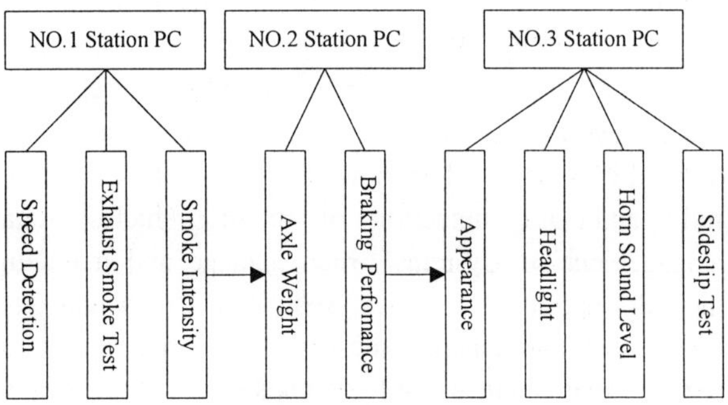

Fig1. Station division and test items

3.2. *Data Management Sub-system*

Data management subsystem is mainly responsible for vehicle information management, international standard information management, detection line business management and system user management. The logic structure of data management is shown in figure 2.

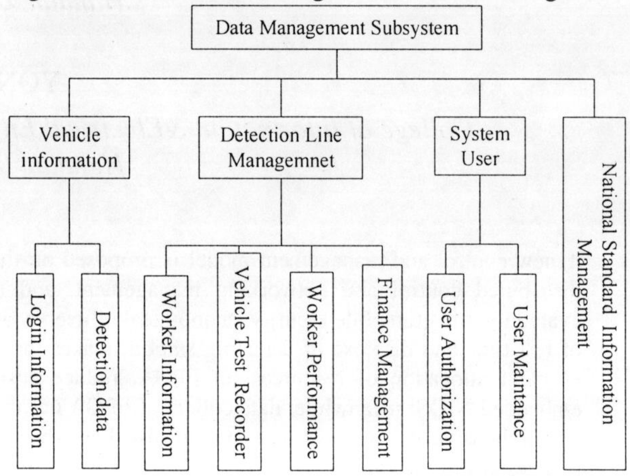

Fig2. Logic structure of data management subsystem

Due to large amount of data and complicated data processing in data management sub-system, it requires that we must be clear about data flow automobile in test line system; otherwise, it is impossible to design a data management subsystem which is suitable for the test line system. Data flow diagram of the system is shown in figure 3.

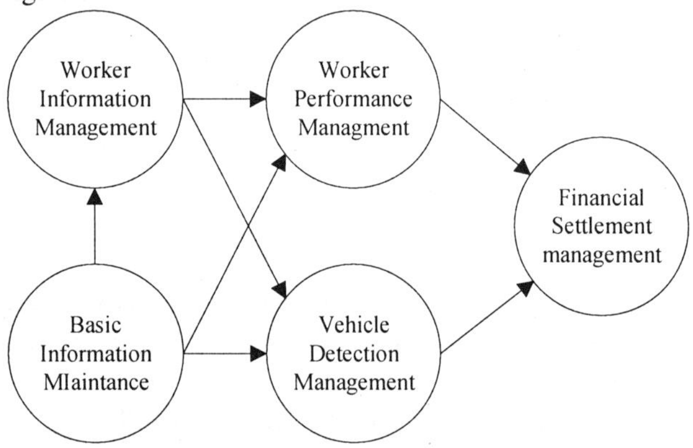

Fig3. Data flow diagram of the system

3.3. *Remote maintenance Sub-system*

Remote maintenance sub-system is carried out by remote control basing on internet. Remote Control allows the development and maintenance personal at different places to show the target computer's desktop environment on your computer monitor through the computer network, and it can be adopted by the local computer to control remote computer as the same of operating your own computer. Network administrator and technical services staff can do remote maintenance operations through the remote maintenance subsystem system for automobile test line. The function is accomplished by remote control software which is based on client/sever mode. It consists of two components, namely client program and server program.

4. The Key Hardware Technologies

4.1. *Analog Signal Acquisition and Processing*

Due to analog signals such as axle weight, wheel speed and braking power, it should be real-time, high precision and high frequency when they are being collected. Besides these analog signals are mV-class weak ones which can't be transmissed for long-distance with normal signal processing method, so it is necessary to isolate amplification, A/D conversion and other treatments.AD202 has been selected in system to tranlate current signal into voltage signal ,chieve the purpose of isolation and amplification. I/V transfer electric circuit is shown in figure4. AD7862 chip which has high-speed 4-channel differential input, low-power dual-job 12 A/D converter is used to carry out A/D transform.

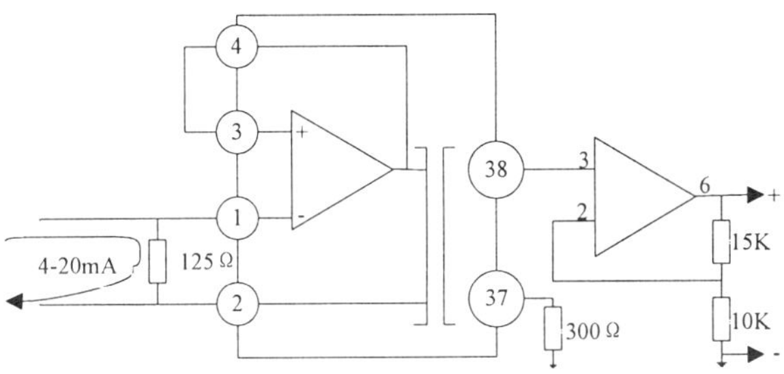

Fig4. I/V transfer electric circuit

4.2. *Serial Communication*

Communication interface circuit uses RS-485 which adopts balancing-sending and difference-receiving to communicate, which has strong ability of anti-common-mode interference. It takes MAX485 as RS-485's transceiver; its highest transfer rate is 2.5Mbps which is completely to satisfy the requirement of communication. RS-485 communication interface circuit is shown as figure5. Separating optical coupler TLP521 is added to FPGA and MAX485 in order to increase its reliability. To avoid level on signal wire be distracted, pull-up register and I/O buffer may be fixed onto input signal wire.

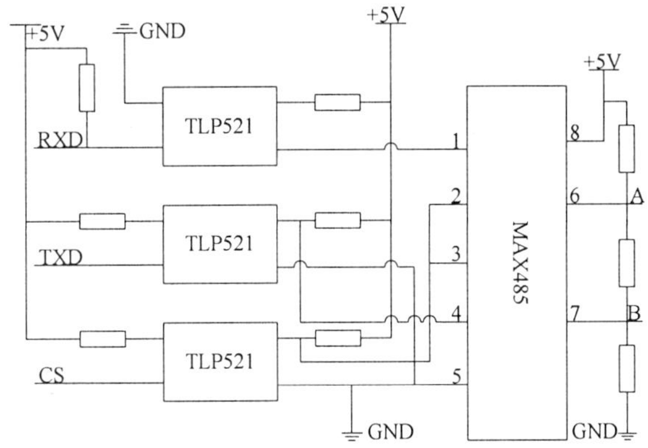

Fig5. RS-485 communication interface circuit

4.3. *Computer Network Technology*

LAN design should take the characteristics of automobile test line into account, select HUB as the center first, use unshielded twisted pair as transmission medium, take normal computer to be interface components, so as to realize internet-working among all station computer. Detecting lines adopt distributed structure, which is composed of four parallel working computers. The system includes one vehicle inspection station; three test station and a central control computer sever. Each test station adopts measurement and control hardware based on BUS, and works independently, control computer in detected position connects with central computer as network sever in order to coordinate the work of every detected position. Division like this will make working load of every station balance and increase test capacity.

WAN connections can be accomplished with special line or Dial-up Network, depending on the specific requirements of inspection station. Put conclusions or acknowledgments here.

5. Data Management Software

Detecting data transmitted from lower computer is written into corresponding database files by PC, then, uploaded to special data sever for master computer querying. Through the effective preservation, collation and analysis to the test data, and with reference to the corresponding national standards, data management software makes an evaluation to automobile comprehensive performance. For achieving the function, in addition to the management of test data, data management software should manage the vehicle information, national standard information; detect line business processes and system users. The system chooses the most common Access data files, *.mdb, which has utilized Microsoft Jet data engine that operating system defaults, so as long as adding a few simple SQL structured query statements in the process system can achieve the requirements of systematic application. To access database successfully, ADO(ActiveX Data Objects) belongs to Visual Basic can be adopted, because ADO is one kind of more effective and more powerful database access method, and it will finally replace any other data access methods.

Part of pseudo-code to illustrate the software implementation process of the data management subsystem is shown.

```
Sub Manipulate Database ()
  If（Not CheckData()）Then
    Exit Sub
  End If
  If（Not CheckData()）Then
    Exit Sub
  End If
  BuildSQL（）
  Err.Clear
  On Error GoTo Errprocess
  BeginTrans
  ExecuteSQL
  CommitTrans
  Exit Sub
ErrProcess：
  RollbackTrans
  Call ErrorProcess
End Sub
```

References

1. GB 7258-2004.The Safe 0peration of the Technical Conditions of Motor Vehicles[S].
2. Cuifeng Fan. Research of Automobile Braking Test Networking System[D].Ji Lin:Ji Lin University，2005.
3. Xingjia Jiang, Caihong Yao. Design of Automobile Comprehensive Performance Test System Based on Distributed Technology [J].Gansu Technology, 2005, Vol 21 NO.3.
4. Zhongfu Liu, Zhongqiang Liu. Research of Integrated Protection System of High-voltage Flameproof Switch Based on Multi-CPU Control[J].Industry and Mine Automation，2008,NO.6.
5. Huanhai Xu，Mingquan Zhu，Yongxing Huan. Distributed Automobile Test, Control and Manage System [J]. Computer and Communications, 2005, NO.2.
6. Xiangmo Zhao. Research and Development of Distributed, Networking and Automatic Test and Control System on Automobile Comprehensive Performance [D].Shan Xi: Chang-an University, 2003.

FAST MODE DECISION ALGORITHM FOR INTRA ONLY SCALABLE VIDEO CODING USING COMBINED SUBBAND/DCT CODING

AMRITA GANGULY

Department of Electronics and Communication Engineering
Indian Institute of Technology Guwahati, 781039 Assam India

A.MAHANTA

Department of Electronics and Communication Engineering
Indian Institute of Technology Guwahati, 781039, Assam, India

In this paper, we propose a fast mode decision algorithm for inter layer intra prediction for intra only scalable video coding. We make use of the inherent spatial scalability in the subband/wavelet approach. It is well known that there is a very strong correlation between the different layers in the scalable video. The LL band of the wavelet decomposition of the video can be directly used for base layer (BL) prediction using the H.264/AVC encoding. The LH, HL and HH bands are used for enhancement layer (EL) prediction. Choice of intra4x4 (I4) and intra8x8 (I8) depends upon the quantization parameter (QP) in the BL and the EL. The candidate modes in the EL depend upon the BL prediction. Intra16x16 (I16) is chosen only if the QP is above a threshold or the resolution is above the CIF resolution. In the trade-off between the complexity and the coding efficiency, there is encoder time saving of 45% to 60% and complexity reduction up to 80% with negligible reduction in the coding efficiency.

1. Introduction

Application of video today ranges from multimedia messaging, video telephony, video conferencing and video over mobile phones, HDTV broadcasting, Blu-ray disc, optical storage media etc. These diverse applications need varying video transmission and storage capabilities. The Scalable Video Coding (SVC) standard [1] is an attractive solution to the problems posed by the modern transmission characteristics. The SVC has been standardized as an extension of the H.264 /AVC video coding standard [2].

The SVC standard gives enhanced coding efficiency but at the cost of higher complexity. Spatial scalability is one the important features required for transmission over variable bandwidth and for various devices over a heterogeneous network [5]. One of the key feature in the SVC standard is the inter layer prediction between different layers. For the intra prediction in the SVC standard, there are three modes namely the I4, I8 and I16 [3]. For each macroblock (MB), the intra prediction requires the calculation of the prediction signals for each of the modes. The I4 and I8 each have nine modes from which the predicted MB is obtained based on the best rate distortion performance. The I16 has four modes from which to form the prediction [4]. The time required for the intra mode prediction and decision is large and is a bottleneck for real-time applications. It is also computationally expensive. Hence it calls for ways to reduce the computational complexity and the time required to perform the prediction of the MB.

Several approaches have been proposed to reduce the complexity and time for the mode decision. There are a number of fast intra coding algorithms [6]. In some of the schemes [7]-[8] suggest that I16 prediction mode be skipped and only the vertical, horizontal and DC modes of I4 are used for prediction. All these approaches speed up the encoding process. However, skipping the modes or using some pre-defined modes actually reduces the overall coding efficiency. To ensure that the encoding process is efficient, we propose a method wherein we retain all the modes. We exploit the inherent scalability offered by traditional wavelet decomposition. We also use the directional features of the different high frequency bands for choosing the candidate modes. There are a number of proposals [9]-[10] where different algorithm are discussed for 3D Subband/DCT based video coding for spatial scalability. The proposed method uses the prediction based on the QP for the BL and the EL. The BL is of QCIF resolution and the LL band is the BL video. The BL chooses the best performer between the I4 and I8 based on the R-D performance. The intra prediction in the EL is constrained to take the corresponding mode of the BL i.e. I4 or I8. The candidate modes for the EL are taken to be the same or similar prediction direction as that of the bands used for the EL prediction. The I16 mode will be chosen if the QP is high or the resolution is higher than CIF.

The paper is organized as follows. Section 2 gives the statistical analysis of the intra prediction modes at different QP and resolutions. Section 3 presents the proposed fast encoding algorithm based on the statistical analysis. Section 4 gives results of the proposed scheme and compares the results with the JSVM8 in terms of coding efficiency, reduction in computational complexity and time.

2. Statistical Analysis of Intra Prediction modes

In this section, we study the statistical correlation between the layers at different resolutions. The experimental setup consists of a BL at QCIF resolution obtained after the subband decomposition of the CIF sequence and an EL at dyadic upsampling resolution namely the CIF resolution. Only spatial scalability has been considered. Intra only encoding is done on standard sequences.

2.1. *BL mode at different QP*

We first conducted a series of experiments for different sequences at the QCIF resolution. We did a rigorous intra prediction search using all the prediction modes namely I4, I8 and I16 at different QP to ascertain the modes. Figure.1 gives the distribution of the prediction modes for the first 50 frames at different QP for two sequences Foreman and Crew. Similar results have also been observed for other sequences namely City, Mobile, Bus and Football.

Observation: From Fig.1 it is clearly seen that for QP up to 24, most of the MBs are encoded in the I4 mode. For values of QP above 24, more and more MBs are encoded in the I8 mode. For QP above 45, almost all the MBs are encoded in the I16 mode.

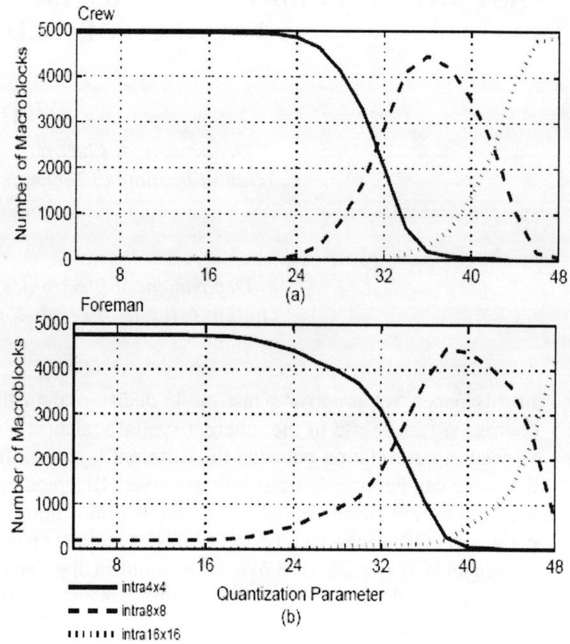

Figure 1. Prediction Mode Distribution (BL QCIF) (a) Crew Sequence (b) Foreman Sequence.

2.2. *EL mode at different QP*

We did a rigorous intra prediction search using all the prediction modes namely I4, I8 and I16 at different QP to ascertain the modes. Figure.2 gives the distribution of the prediction modes for the first 30 frames at different QP for two sequences Foreman and Crew. Similar results have also been observed for other sequences namely City, Mobile, Bus and Football.

Observation: From Figure.2 it is clearly seen that for QP up to 24, most of the MBs are encoded in the I4 mode. The distribution is seen to be similar to the base layer prediction which actually indicates the high correlation between the layers. For values of QP above 24, more and more MBs are encoded in the I8 mode. For QP above 45, almost all the MBs are encoded in the I16 mode.

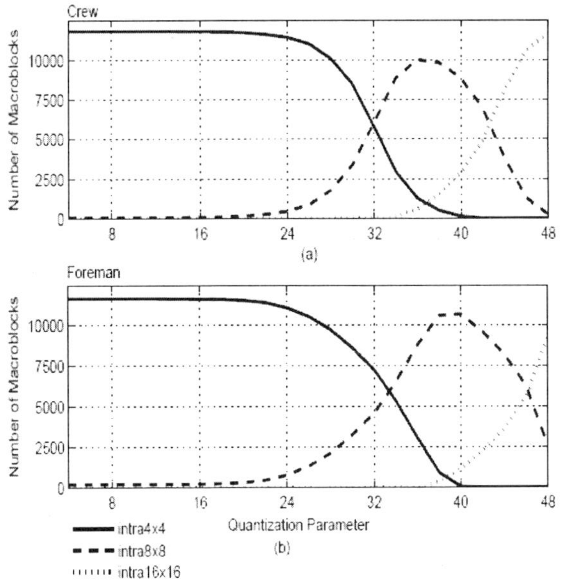

Figure 2. Prediction Mode Distribution (EL CIF) (a) Crew Sequence (b) Foreman Sequence.

3. Proposed Fast Mode Decision Algorithm

The proposed algorithm is based on the observations given in section 2. The different steps for the proposed algorithm are described next.

3.1. *Steps for Fast Mode Decision Algorithm*

Step1: Decomposition of the input video into four subbands

We first decompose the input video which is at a CIF resolution using analysis filter. We get four subbands LL,LH,HL and HH subbands. The LL band which is at the QCIF resolution is directly used for the BL prediction. The transform coefficients of the LH,HL and HH are used for the EL prediction.

Step2: Rigorous BL prediction based on QP

For the BL prediction, if the QP of the BL is below a threshold T_1, rigorous search is performed with only I4 prediction modes. For QP higher than T_1 both I4 and I8 search is performed to identify the best mode. The mode information is stored for future reference.

Step3: EL Intra Prediction

The EL prediction modes have a high correlation with the modes of the BL prediction. The difference between the reconstructed base layer frame and the LL is used for the prediction for the LL subband for the EL. The LH, HL and the HH band are directly used for the prediction since these bands usually have low valued coefficients. The different modes for the prediction for these bands are discussed in section 3.2. Figure.3 shows the block diagram for the encoding and the decoding process for the EL.

Step4: Prediction based on QP

For QP of base layer above threshold T_2, the base layer prediction is too coarse for enhancement layer reference. The enhancement layer intra prediction is done independently without referring to the base layer prediction. The base layer prediction is done using the I16 prediction mode. For the EL, for QP upto T_1, I4 prediction is performed. For QP between T_1 and T_2, both I4 and I8 prediction is done and for QP above T_2, only I16 prediction is performed.

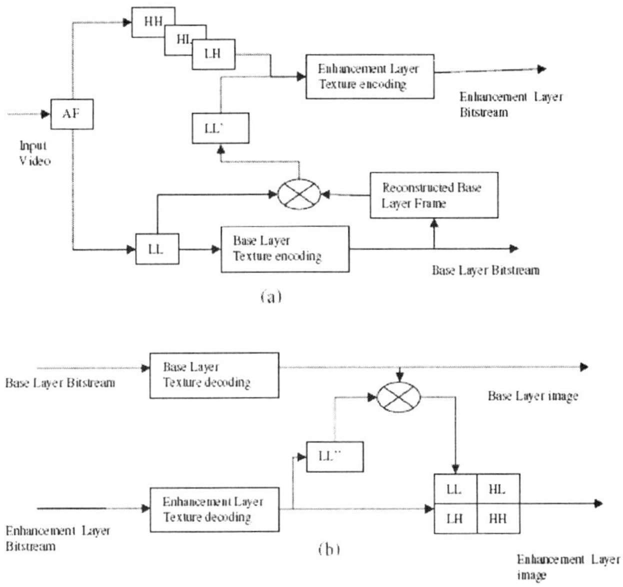

Figure 3. Block Diagram for encoding and decoding of the video sequence.

3.2. *Mode selection for EL prediction*

Since the LL band of the EL is at the same resolution as that of the BL and the BL modes are already obtained from the BL encoding, the BL prediction modes can be used for the prediction in the EL. For the LL band the EL will take the same mode as the candidate mode as the BL mode resulting in one search for each MB. The number of searches is greatly reduced due to this.

The wavelet decomposition can be thought as signal decomposition in a set of spatially oriented frequency bands. The high frequency bands are directed bands. The LH, HL and HH band represents the horizontal, vertical and the diagonal high frequencies respectively. The candidate modes for intra prediction for these bands will have those modes which are inclined in these directions respectively. The candidate modes for the different bands are given in Table1. For each of the three subbands there are four modes from which the best mode is selected based on the best R-D performance. If the QP the base layer is above a particular threshold, then the BL prediction is not taken into consideration and EL is independently predicted. Above this threshold, the BL is predicted in the I16 mode.

Table 1. Look up Table for Enhancement Layer

Bands	Enhancement Layer Modes								
	0	1	2	3	4	5	6	7	8
LH		√	√				√		√
HL	√		√			√		√	
HH			√	√	√		√		

4. Experiments

The proposed algorithm is implemented as per the JSVM8. The CIF sequences FOREMAN, CREW, CITY, BUS, MOBILE and FOOTBALL have been used for the implementation. We employ the Daubechies 9/7 filter set for the subband synthesis of the individual frame. The LL band at QCIF resolution is then directly used for the BL encoding. We have tested the algorithm with dyadic scalability with the EL at the CIF resolution. Referring to Fig.1. and Fig.2., we find that for values of QP upto 24, the prediction mode is I4. So we choose threshold T_1 at 24. Upto this QP, the prediction will be done on I4 mode. As QP increases, more number of MBs use I8 and I16 modes. Thus the second threshold T_2 is set at 45. Between QP values T_1 and T_2, both I4 and I8 prediction is done. Above T_2, only I16 prediction is done. For the EL, we reconstruct the BL frame and the difference between the original LL band and the reconstructed frame is then intra predicted and the residual intra prediction samples are encoded. The LH, HL and HH bands are intra predicted and only the residual is encoded. At the decoder, the LL, LH, HL and HH residuals are decoded and added to the respective reconstructed bands. The output EL image is obtained by applying synthesis filters on the four bands.

Table.2 and 3 lists the performance of the proposed scheme with the JSVM in terms of YPSNR loss, overall saving in the encoding time and reduction in the complexity for the BL and EL in terms of the reduction in the number of searches performed at each layer. The results shown here are with base layer QP=16. The time saving percentage TS(%) and Δpsnr % is calculated according to Equations given below. Complexity Reduction is calculated in terms of the reduction of total number of searches in the proposed scheme as compared to the rigorous searches as per the SVC standard.

$$TS(\%) = \frac{T_{JSVM} - T_{proposed}}{T_{JSVM}} \times 100\%$$

$$\Delta PSNR(\%) = \frac{PSNR_{JSVM} - PSNR_{proposed}}{PSNR_{JSVM}} \times 100\%$$

Table 2. Simulation Results (BL) for different QP

Sequence		Quantization Parameter (Base)				
		8	16	24	32	40
Foreman	Δpsnr %	0.024	0.01	-0.08	0.001	0.01
	TS %	43	42	44	28	26
	CompRed%	22	22	22	5	5
Crew	Δpsnr %	-0.05	0.0	-0.01	0.023	1.58
	TS %	40	41	44	26	27
	CompRed%	22	22	22	5	5
City	Δpsnr %	0.002	-0.01	-0.02	0.0	-0.01
	TS %	38	42	42	24	25
	CompRed%	22	22	22	5	5
Bus	Δpsnr %	0.066	0.02	-0.01	-2.38	-0.11
	TS %	40	42	42	26	25
	CompRed%	22	22	22	5	5
Mobile	Δpsnr %	-0.01	-0.03	-0.74	0.00	0.00
	TS %	42	44	41	23	23
	CompRed%	22	22	22	5	5
Football	Δpsnr %	0.00	0.01	-0.01	0.00	0.04
	TS %)	42	44	45	26	26
	CompRed%	22	22	22	5	5

5. Summary and Conclusions

In this work we have proposed a scheme to reduce the complexity of intra prediction. The scheme chooses the best prediction mode in both the BL and the EL. The analysis filter may be any other spatial down sampler for the BL. When compared to the JSVM, our scheme provides upto 46% time saving at the encoder at the BL and a reduction in the complexity upto 22%. The PSNR loss is negligible and in a few cases there have been a marginal increase in the PSNR value. For the EL at dyadic resolution with respect to the BL, we get a time saving of upto 60% and reduction in complexity in terms of the reduction in the number of search for the different modes upto 80%.There is a negligible PSNR loss. When the QP for the BL is high, the reconstructed picture is too coarse. When used for prediction of the EL, even for low values of QP in the EL, the reconstructed EL picture gives relatively poor picture quality. This is shown in Fig.4 where frame 1 of Football sequence is shown encoded at a low EL QP of 8 and different BL QP of 8 and 40 respectively. The degradation in quality at high QP is clearly visible. Thus the proposed scheme performs fast mode decision for intra only spatial scalable video using the subband decomposition of the input frame.

Table 3. Simulation Results (EL) for different QP

Sequence	Quantization Parameter (EL)					
		8	16	24	32	40
Foreman	Δpsnr %	0.019	0.01	0.08	0.076	0.058
	TS %	55	56	60	59	57
	CompRed%	70	70	24	24	85
Crew	Δpsnr %	-0.05	0.0	-0.01	0.023	1.58
	TS %	54	52	56	56	57
	CompRed%	70	70	24	24	85
City	Δpsnr %	0.002	0.011	0.004	0.005	0.003
	TS %	52	52	56	56	60
	CompRed%	70	70	24	24	85
Bus	Δpsnr %	0.064	0.009	0.061	0.026	0.008
	TS %	53	53	49	56	57
	CompRed%	70	70	24	24	85
Mobile	Δpsnr %	0.621	0.552	0.745	0.045	0.099
	TS %	52	52	48	54	56
	CompRed%	70	70	24	24	85
Football	Δpsnr %	0.004	0.02	0.015	0.009	0.048
	TS %)	55	53	49	50	49
	CompRed%	70	70	24	24	85

References

1. T..Wiegand, G. J. Sullivan, J. Reichel, H. Schwarz, and M. Wien, "Joint Draft 11 of SVC Amendment, Doc. JVT-X201, Jul. 2007.
2. "Draft ITU-T recommendation and final draft international standard of joint video specification ITU-T Rec. H.264/ISO/IEC 14 496-10 AVC," in Joint Video Team (JVT) of ISO/IEC MPEG and ITU-T VCEG, JVTG050, 2003.
3. H.Schwarz, Detlev Marpe and T.Wiegand, "Overview of the Scalable Video Coding Extension of the H.264/AVC Standard", IEEE Trans. CSVT., vol. 17, no. 9, pp. 1103-1120, Sep. 2007.
4. T.Wiegand, Gary.J.Sullivan, Gisle Bjntegaard, and Ajay Luthra, "Overview of the H.264/AVC Video Coding Standard", IEEE Trans. CSVT, vol. 13, no. 7, pp. 560-576, July 2003.
5. C. Andrew Segall, Gary. J. Sullivan, "Spatial Scalability within H.264 AVC Scalable Video Coding Extension",IEEE Trans. CSVT, vol. 17, no. 9, pp. 1121-1135, September 2007.
6. Jongho Kim, Donghyung Kim, Jechang Jeong, "Complexity Reduction Algorithm for Intra Mode Selection in H.264/AVC Video Coding", ACIVS 2006, LNCS 4179, pp.454 - 465, 2006.
7. L.Xiong, "Reducing Enh. Layer Directional Intra Prediction Modes," ISO/IEC JTC1/SC29/WG11 and ITU-T SG16 Q.6, JVT-P041, 2005.
8. L.Yang, Y.Chen, J.Zhai, and F.Zhang, "Low Complexity Intra Prediction for enhancement Layer," ISO/IEC JTC1/SC29/WG11 and ITU-T SG16 Q.6, JVT-Q084, 2005.
9. Shih-Ta Hsiang, "Intra Frame Dyadic Spatial Scalable Coding based on a Subband/Wavelet Framework for MPEG-4 AVC/H.264 Scalable Video Coding", ICIP, Vol. 1, 2007.
10. Randa Atta, and Mohammed Ghanbari, "Spatio-Temporal Scalability Based Motion Compensated 3-D Subband/DCT Video Coding," IEEE Trans. CSVT, vol. 16, no. 1, pp. 43-55, Sep. 2006.

Figure 4. EL reconstructed frame at different QP (BL).

INTERNET ACCESSED COLLABORATIVE LEARNING SOLUTIONS FOR REMOTE EXPERIMENTS USING WEB 2.0 SOCIAL SOFTWARE AND LABVIEW

JAGADEESH CHANDRA A.P

Department of Electronics & Communication, J.S.S Research Foundation
Mysore, Karnataka-570006, India.

R.D SUDHAKER SAMUEL

Department of Electronics & Communication, S.J College of Engineering
Mysore, Karnataka-570006, India.

Remote laboratory facilities have been available on the web for more than a decade. The integration of collaborative learning tools with the remote experiments enhances the effectiveness in computer supported learning. LabVIEW supported virtual instrumentation tools are widely used to create web based automation and control learning environment. The wide-range of experiments can be accessed and monitored due the advancements in data acquisition features supported by the server. The major challenge lies in converting the remote experiment facilities in to professional remote laboratory infrastructure with setups accessible worldwide. The learning management system plays a major role in the implementation of collaborative learning features in remote laboratory. The paper describes one such implementation using Moodle. Moodle is designed to help educators to create online courses and remote experiments along with rich interaction. The learning management system created using Moodle provides platform to integrate multimedia tools along with graphical user interface of remote experiment. The system uses the client-server architecture to access the virtual instruments through the web browser. Internet accessible online environments allow social interaction along with education and training with the participation of globally distributed users.

1. Introduction

Web based learning is becoming more popular with the advent of Internet technologies and the social software tools. The Internet and World Wide Web have given the facilities to educators and instruction designers to develop interactive courseware which can be collaborated with a wide range of users distributed over the network [10]. The collaboration is an important issue in computer mediated learning, because the learning environment consists of minimum two users (server and client). The sufficient collaborative features have been provided by the learning management system of Web 2.0 technologies and can be easily adopted in web education. The possibility of internet accessible remote experimentation extended web education from theoretical learning to laboratory and training activities [3] [7]. The virtual laboratories are developed and the simulation environments are successfully tested using web based tools. The challenges associated with the remote laboratories are with accessing physical equipments, security, high quality GUI (Graphical User Interface), software adoptability to new components, cost-effective design and collaborative learning [4].

The main objective of the remote experimentation is to meet the learners demand and satisfaction. Many times it is said that, the remote laboratory is not an alternative to the existing physical laboratory, but it is the additional support available for learn and practice [2]. Main benefit with the remote experiment facility is that the learner or teacher can access the laboratory set-up anywhere either from home or classroom, which enhances the flexibility in learning.

The integration of collaborative learning management system and multimedia tools with the remote experiments are described in this paper. The important component to create remote experimentation facility is the virtual instrumentation (VI) tools integrated with real hardware to perform tasks in real time. The LabVIEW virtual instruments provide an ideal platform for developing instructional curriculum and conducting scientific experiments. The LabVIEW supports built-in web server where the experiment VI's can be easily published over the web. The virtual learning environment Moodle publishes and manages the collaborative online learning environment where it facilitates number of features to add many resources and activities [5]. The LabVIEW web server is linked with

Moodle to display the experiment GUI along with the course structure for online access and control. The audio/video interface is derived from Webcam XP software and made available online through Moodle server. With the integration of LabVIEW, Moodle and Webcam XP it is possible to find solutions to some challenges in successful implementation of remote laboratory.

2. WebLab Architecture

The system architecture is based on client/server model where the communication uses the standard TCP/IP protocol. The web based remote experiment access structure of electrical engineering system is shown in Fig 1. The remote access and control of experimental system is developed by graphical programming language LabVIEW and National Instruments (NI) data acquisition card (DAQ) PCI 6251 along with NI Educational Laboratory Virtual Instrumentation Suite (ELVIS) workstation, collectively referred as DAQ system. It supports 12 channels of analog input in Referenced Single Ended (RSE) mode, two channels of analog output and 8 channels of independent digital I/O's. The combination of DAQ and ELVIS facilitates to communicate real-time signals to the external hardware through the GUIs developed by LabVIEW [12]. These GUIs are subsequently transformed to dynamic web page and stored in the server. These dynamic web pages are linked with the web application that hosts the remote experiments. The wide-range hardware experiments are interfaced to the network through the custom designed data acquisition hardware. Standard data acquisition systems such as PCI 6251 can be used for low power application interface. If experiments operation range exceeds the standard data acquisition capacity; there is a need to develop interface circuits to convert high voltage and current in to the required range supported by the system.

The server is primarily used for data acquisition of experimental hardware and to create the learning management system (LMS) which supports collaborative education among distributed users. The LMS uses virtual learning environment tool such as Moodle to design course structure suited for remote experiments. The clients can access the experiment through the link provided with LMS along with the multimedia features. The web camera streaming software WebcamXP5 is used for broadcasting audio and video over the web.

Remote experiment hardware consists of custom developed circuits to interface DAQ system with electrical power circuits, which operates the DC Motor environment. The sophisticated controlling and measuring techniques have been developed to conduct remote experiment on high power engineering laboratory experiments through the web browser. It supports features to control fine tuning of input excitation using computer keyboard, load variation and various indicators to online display of experimental parameters. The developed system imitates the real control of experiment hardware, but being operated remotely through Internet.

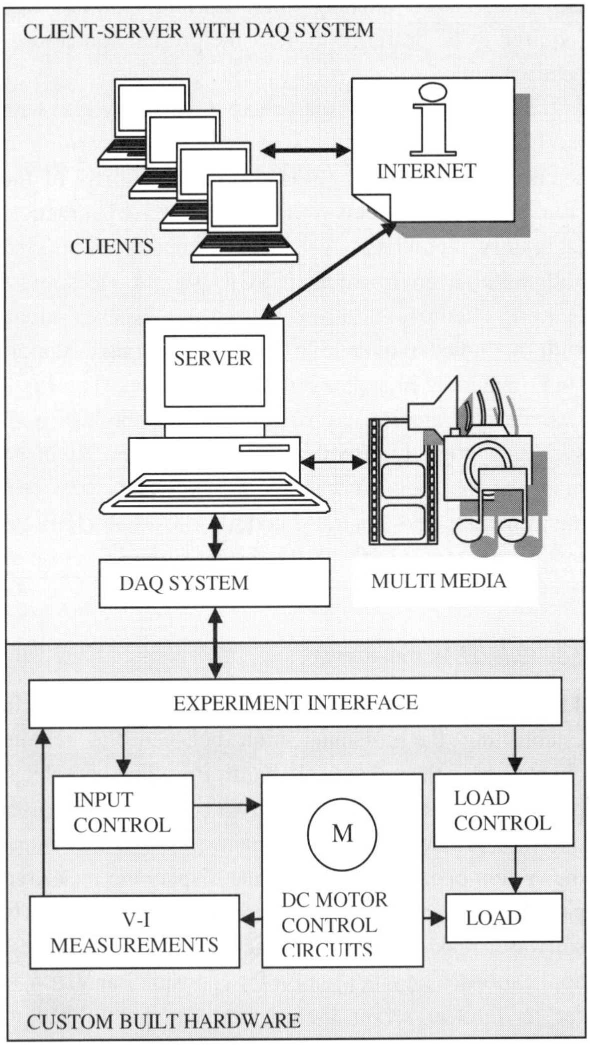

Figure 1. Architecture of web-based remote access of experimental system

3. Software Technologies in Remote Collaborative Learning

The term "Web 2.0" is a second generation of web development and design that facilitates more personalized communication, information sharing, interoperability and collaboration on the World Wide Web. Web 2.0 technology tools are collectively referred as "social software", which encompasses a range of software systems that allow users to interact and share data. Universities are using Web 2.0 where in teachers, researchers and students, started to use social software tools that support group interaction. Learning management system ' (LMS) is responsible for educational interactions at the institutions level by integrating geographically dispersed resources. However, new teaching and learning models are required to be designed to meet the present educational needs [8].

The integration of remote experimental system with the LMS tools gives more scope to distance learning of science and engineering domains. The majority of the courses in these domains are supported by practical laboratory activities. An ideal computer supported collaborative environment (CSCE) should incorporate learning facilities allowing shared workspaces along with multimedia tools. For education, it also support study materials in support of collaboratories. The Fig.2 describes the architecture which integrates the LMS tool such as Moodle to provide learning resources, Webcam management tool WebcamXP to experience the real environment, and control interface uses LabVIEW to make user interaction with the distant system as close as the actual work.

3.1. *LabVIEW web-server*

The LabVIEW web server is the central entity in establishing the communication between the remote clients and the electrical hardware. The graphical programming tool LabVIEW with its intuitive user interface provides the development platform to control the system operation remotely and display the measured parameters in real-time. It is used with the third party software, making it more attractive for remote access applications. The other reason for choosing LabVIEW is for its built-in server facility that can be utilized to publish the GUI for experiment access and control. The LabVIEW programs are called Virtual Instruments (VI), which are developed and converted to HTML page and

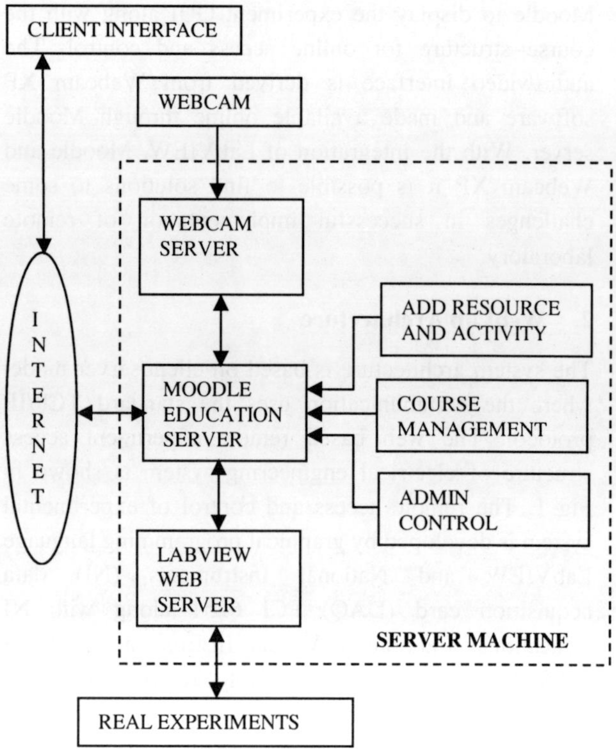

Figure 2. LMS interface with the real experimentation system

stored in the root directory of the server. The VI's of the corresponding experiment is mentioned in the VI access list and the IP addresses of the client machines are mentioned in the browser access list of the server. The graphical interface to the client side is developed by creating a HTML page of the VI, which includes the visual display of control commands, displays for measurement and graphs to record readings of the experiment [1].

3.2. *Webcam Server*

The transmission of audio and video features between the remote user and the server machine are the important objects in the remote learning environment. There are various other easy tools such as chat; email exists to establish communication between the two or more entities. But the audio and visual features are very much essential and are the part of the remote experiment development system. The proposed structure in Fig.2 uses the webcamXP server to transmit audio and video of the hardware experiment to remote clients. WebcamXP is a powerful webcam and IP cameras management and streaming software, which offer features to broadcast multiple video sources on the same computer. It is simple to host internet web-server to transmit video and audio signals over webcamXP tool, just by enabling the broadcast facility and set the machine IP address. WebcamXP allows sharing camera images online by integrating with the preexisting and custom coded website. Thus the live video window allows the users to view the real experimental process using the images captured by single or several web cameras located in the laboratory. The additional functions supported by webcamXP are audio transmission and live chat helps to set-up an online talking space between the client and server entities [11].

3.3. *Moodle Education Server*

Moodle is a widely adopted software package for learning material management through internet. The word Moodle is the acronym for Modular Object-Oriented Dynamic Learning Environment, where all courses and learning materials are organized and delivered to the remote clients using a single data base MySQL. Moodle is open source software under GNU public license. The weblab applications are integrated with the Moodle virtual learning environment using PHP scripts and the components present in the main menu [6].

The developed structure with the Moodle links the different web servers in the learning platform is shown in Fig.2. The different web servers are linked to Moodle through adding a resource by mentioning the location of which the application to be accessed. The LabVIEW web server hosts the application to the remote clients from the location C:\\Program Files\National Instruments \LabVIEW8.5\www and the web page is accessed from the remote users through the admin tools. Similarly the webcam server is linked to Moodle to transfer the real environment of remote site. The Moodle server chooses the default HTTP port 80 and the LabVIEW server is set at port number 918 and the Webcam Server is set to port 8080. A client PC should have Internet explorer and LabVIEW run-time engine (freeware) to perform the task. Fig. 3 describes the web page to access the learning material and various links to remote experiments and webcam interfaces.

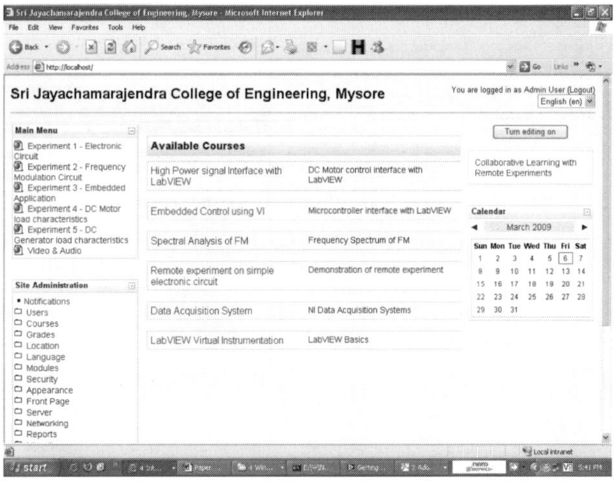

Figure 3. Web page displaying links to courses and remote experiments

4. Remote Access and Control of Experiment

The interface structure is developed to access the experiment remotely using virtual instrumentation tools, operated in web environment. Hardware experimental system is controlled remotely using computer keyboard or mouse. Fig 4 describes the LabVIEW virtual instruments developed to experiment on 1.5kW DC Motor with different load conditions and real-time video window. The input voltage control interface uses the digital control (Boolean) operations to vary the voltage from 0 to 230V in steps of 1V. A dedicated custom hardware is developed to vary the input voltage at the required stages of the experiment. Correspondingly, the voltage and current readings are displayed on virtual meters shown in Fig 4. The virtual meters read the voltage of the range (0-230V) and the current (0-20A) with perfect isolation from high power electrical hardware. The scaling and mapping of the electrical signals are performed to measure the experiment values with minimum error. The experiment load can be varied by operating the digital switches and the observations are made for different working conditions. The speed of the DC motor is measured using non-contact proximity switch by generating a pulse for each rotation of the motor and pulses are processing in DAQ system to produce the RPM of the motor. The system described can be altered for a wide range of experiments in electrical engineering [9].

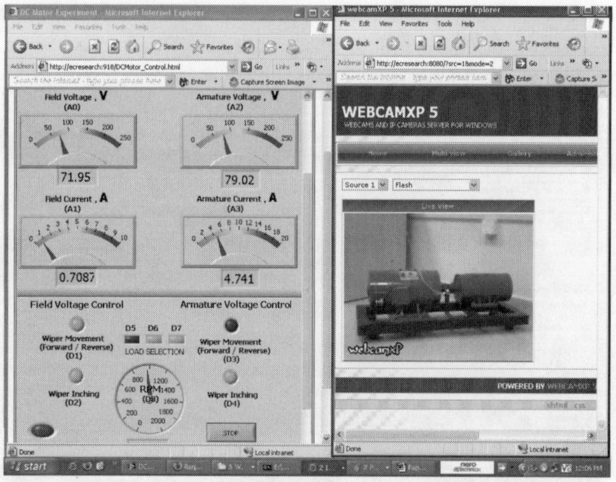

Figure 4. Web accessible LabVIEW virtual instruments along with the live video

5. Conclusion

The paper describes the integration of virtual learning environment with the remote laboratory experiment to enhance the web education in technical environment. The system design consists of combination of software tools and electrical hardware to operate the remote applications with near real-time control features. The LMS tools support collaborative learning in remote laboratory and distributed workspaces. The description of remote operation on complex electrical hardware epitomized by the socially based tools has added more values to the web based applications. The webcamXP software streams live videos on to client's machine without any additional programming. The proposed method of combining LMS tools with LabVIEW for collaborative learning enables the design of a versatile educational environment for science and engineering. The remote hardware experiment is developed in a similar context of real laboratory experiments by designing interface structure which simply extends the local operation to online environment. This methodology gives a collaborative learning solution for remote experiments using social software and graphical programming tool.

Acknowledgments

This paper reports the partial results of a major research on Remote Access Labs funded by the Department of Science and Technology, Ministry of Science and Technology, Government of India, Vide Number: SR/FST/ETI-033/2005.

References

1. C. Mergl. "Comparison of remote labs in different technologies", International Journal of Online Engineering (iJOE), Vol2, No.4, 2006.
2. Jing MA and, J V Nickerson. "Hands-on, simulated, and remote laboratories: A comparative literature review", ACM Computing Surveys, Vol.38, No. 3, 2007.
3. F.M Schaf, C.E Pereira. "Automation and control environment with mixed reality remote experiments architecture", International Journal of Online Engineering (iJOE), Vol3, No.2, 2007.
4. C. Salzmann, D. Gillet. "Challenges in remote laboratory sustainability", International Conference on Engineering Education – ICEE 2007, coimbra, Portugal, 2007.
5. S. Uran, D. Hercog, K.Jezernik. "Remote control laboratory with Moodle booking system", IEEE International Symposium on Industrial Electronics – ISIE 2007, Vigo, Spain, pp2978-2983, 2007.
6. F.M Schaf, D.Muller, C.E Pereira, F.W Bruns. "Computer supported collaborative social environment for education, training and work", International Conference on Remote Engineering an Virtual Instrumentation – REV2008, Duesseldorf, Germany, 2008.
7. Min Wu, Jin-Hua She, Gui-Xiu Zeng, Yasuhiro Ohyama. "Internet-based teaching and experiment system for control engineering course", IEEE transactions on Industrial Electronics, Vol.55, No.6, pp. 2386-2396, 2008.
8. A. Drigas, L. Koukianakis, Y. Papagerasimou. "Advanced methods of web learning", Advances in Blended Learning, Second workshop on Blended Learning, WBL 2008, Jinhua, China, LNCS 5328, pp.16-24, 2008.
9. Jagadeesh Chandra A.P, R.D Sudhaker Samuel. "Design of novel online access and control interface for remote experiment on DC drives", iJOE International Journal of Online Engineering – in press.
10. Timothy K. Shih, Jason C. Hung. "Future Directions in Distance Learning and Communication Technologies" Information Science Publishing, pp.222-242, 2007.
11. WebcamXP, User Manual, revision 1.3, Moonware Studios, 2008.
12. NI ELVIS user manual, National Instruments, National Instruments Corporation, 2006.

ASSESSING CORPORATE ENVIRONMENTAL AND SUSTAINABILITY REPORTS USING TEXT MINING AND BAYESIAN ESTIMATE

JASHUA RAJESH MODAPOTHALA

School of Business and Enterprise, Swinburne University of Technology (Sarawak Campus)
Kuching, Sarawak 93350, Malaysia

BIJU ISSAC

School of Computing and Design, Swinburne University of Technology (Sarawak Campus)
Kuching, Sarawak 93350, Malaysia

Measuring the effectiveness of Corporate Environmental Reports (CERs) is considered to be highly complex. This is due to the fact that they are highly qualitative, less regulated and more diverse in its representation. The performance indicators used in these reports play a vital role and enhance the ability of the stakeholder to perform rational decision-making. This study intends to assess the CERs over the specific performance indicators (organization, environmental and social) using text mining and relevant statistical techniques. A large sample (N=2171) is used for text mining that was implemented in Java, along with Bayesian estimation. The results indicate that the environmental and social performance indicators differ across the industry, where as, organization performance remains the same. Using Bayesian estimation it is found that the correlation between the selected variables and its estimates are highly significant.

1. Introduction

The growing concern of stakeholders towards environmental and social performance of the corporates has forced many managers to adopt and report such performance publicly. Besides providing a competitive advantage, sound environmental management fulfills corporate social responsibility and adds value to the business. In this perspective, environmental report should be seen as a technical document which supports external communication and gives evidence on responsibility and accountability towards environment [1]. Due to the lack of mandatory regulations and no definite rules in spite of greater stakeholder interest, environmental reporting is left to the practice of individual firms - thus limiting the usefulness of the document to the reader. The paper is organized as follows. Section 2 is literature review, section 3 is research objectives and hypothesis, section 4 is methodology, section 5 is results and discussion and section 6 is the conclusion.

2. Literature Review

Greater concern for environment among public and industry is compelling management to build synergy between their economic and environmental policies. Thus, management of environmental resources and their reporting to the stakeholders has become a necessity.

Corporate sustainability as a business approach creates long-term stakeholder value by embracing opportunities and managing risks derived from economic, social and environmental developments. As a strategy it integrates long-term economic, social and environmental aspects of the business while maintaining global competitiveness and green brand equity. Sustainable reporting often being varied makes it difficult for the stakeholders to decide for investment and other decision-making. Numerous methods of reporting were promulgated from time to time which includes, ISO 14031 (1999) [2] and Global Reporting Initiative (2000, 2002) as in [3]. The most prominent reporting guidelines are the Global Reporting Initiative (GRI) Sustainability Reporting Guidelines on Economic, Environmental and Social Performance (GRI, 2000), promulgated in June 2000. These guidelines go well beyond any previous ones in their inclusion of financial and social criteria. This is in addition to those criteria that distinguish ‘sustainability’ reporting from straight environmental reporting.

Surprisingly there was little research made into what types of indicator are being used in Corporate Environmental Reports (CERs). Lober et al. [4] examined types of company reports and, in a generalized, anecdotal manner, looked at types of information provided in CERs. Noci [5] made a deep emphasis on CERs issued by Italian firms and Italy-based multinationals. Prior studies on metrics were done on environmental reporting in SME's [6], internet technologies [7], and text mining approach on selected 10-variables [8].

Unstructured data that are mostly in the form of text files, accounts for 85% of an organization's knowledge data stores, but it's not always easy to find, access, analyze or use such data. Text mining tools allows companies to extract key elements from large unstructured data sets like text files, discover new relationships and eventually summarize the information gathered. Hearst explains that text mining is the discovery by computer of new, previously unknown information, by automatically extracting information from different written resources. A key element is the linking together of the extracted information together to form new facts or hypotheses to be explored further by more conventional means of experimentation [9].

Text mining tasks may include text categorization, text clustering, entity extraction, document summarization, and entity relation modeling. Though there were attempts made earlier in evaluating CERs, it had a limited emphasis on the variables and small sample size. Hence, this study is made to provide a detailed analysis on CERs using GRI sustainability reporting guidelines (2000), with a very large sample and wide demographics.

3. Research Objectives and Hypothesis

The study intends to examine and analyze systematically the CERs in a global perspective. To perform a greater reliable and robust approach, text mining approach is used to perform on a larger data sample. The research objectives are: (1) to construct a text mining and knowledge recovery model for generating frequencies and scorecard for the CERs and (2) to examine which of the selected variables i.e., organizational, environmental, and social performance are most preferred.

Prior studies suggest that the motivation to report would be higher in the sectors with high environmental pressures compared with sectors with low environmental pressures [10]-[11]. On the contrary, KPMG identified the growing desire of low-environment-impact firms to report. Though these studies highlighted the significance of industry based disclosure, little emphasis is made on the aspects they disclose and of their correlation. The hypotheses used are as follows. Hypothesis 1 – 3: The extent of reporting of the selected variables i.e., organizational (H1), social (H2) and environmental (H3) among the various nature of business is similar. Hypotheses 4 (H4): There exists no correlation between organizational, social and environmental variables.

4. Methodology

The assessment technique used in the present study is adapted from questions based on GRI sustainability reporting guideline on economic, environmental, and social performance by Denis et al. [12] using modified criteria that meet the requirement of effective text mining. Only selected variables were used in this study. The data for the study i.e., CERs were extracted from Corporate Register website [13], which is a world directory of published corporate environmental and social reports. To select the relevant data for the study, judgmental sampling was applied in this study. In each of the available categories from the website, where the reports are less than 30 numbers were not considered. All the reports that were under year 2008 category were considered for the initial analysis (of text mining). Thus, the initial sample for the study is 2626 CER documents (inclusive of foreign language).

Text mining and extraction was done by writing a customized Java program. The different criteria that need to be checked were broken down into appropriate keywords. The basic idea was to search for keywords or related words in the reports that were to be analyzed and to check the presence or strength of these keywords. The keywords selected should be appropriate and even strong synonyms can be used for searching. A better approach would be to have the first level search with real keywords and second level searches with synonyms from a dictionary file. The first level searches could be given a higher score weight and second and third level (if any) searches lower weights. The keyword frequency count done was later scaled to be in the range of 0 to 10. The reason for scaling is that it takes range of values and then maps that to a score. So the possible error in the frequency count is lessened.

5. Results and Discussion

After executing the simulated program, the environmental reports that are in foreign languages, i.e., other than English are excluded for analysis. An elimination criterion, with a total frequency of 'less than

10' is applied. Thus the sample size for further statistical analysis is reduced to 2171.

In the present study, manufacturing sector is the major contributor in regard to volume of reports (46.2%), followed by tertiary (42.7%) and primary (11.1%). One-way ANOVA is performed to find whether the extent of reported variables (organizational, environmental and social performance) is of similar across the various industries. The results indicate that organizational performance reported (p-value=0.396, not significant) is similar across various industries where as, environmental performance (p-value=0.000, significant at 0.05) and social performance (p-value=0.000, significant at 0.05) are different. Therefore, null hypothesis will be accepted for organizational performance (H1) and in the case of environmental performance (H2) and social performance, the null hypothesis (H3) will be rejected. In all the sectors of the study as per in figure 1, organizational performance is reported maximum followed by social and environmental performance aspects.

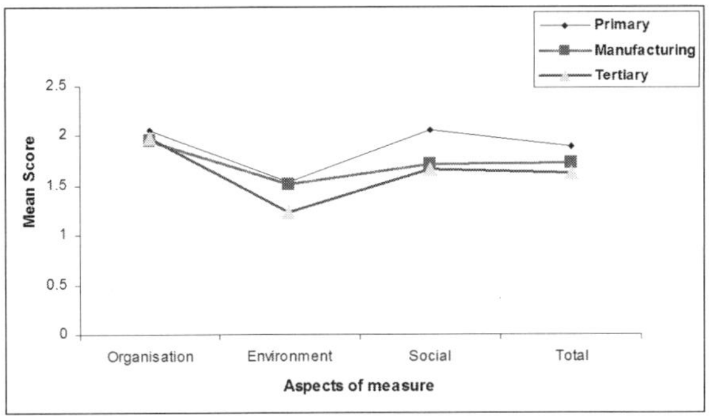

Figure 1. Reported aspects of measure in CERs

This confirms with the findings of one-way ANOVA as the reporting of environmental performance and social performance differ across the industries. The findings in this study are affirmative to the earlier studies by Clemens, Kolk, Martin and Hadley on the extent of environmental and social disclosure but it also confirms the growing need for disclosure in low-environmental-impact sector like tertiary.

To measure the correlation between the selected variables in the present study, we will do this by estimating the variance-covariance matrix under the constraint that organization, environment and social performance variables are uncorrelated. Using AMOS 16.0, the model is tested with co-variance fixed as '0'. The results as shown in figure 2 show significant findings as p-value is 0.000 at 5% (chi-square = 4470.798, df=3).

The estimated means and variances indicate bias or favor towards organizational performance, followed by social and environmental performance respectively. Hence, the null hypothesis (H4) is rejected due to the presence of correlation between the selected variables of study. All the correlation values are significant, with organization performance-social performance (r=0.829) being highly correlated followed by social performance-environmental performance (r=0.756) and environmental performance-organizational performance (r=0.707).

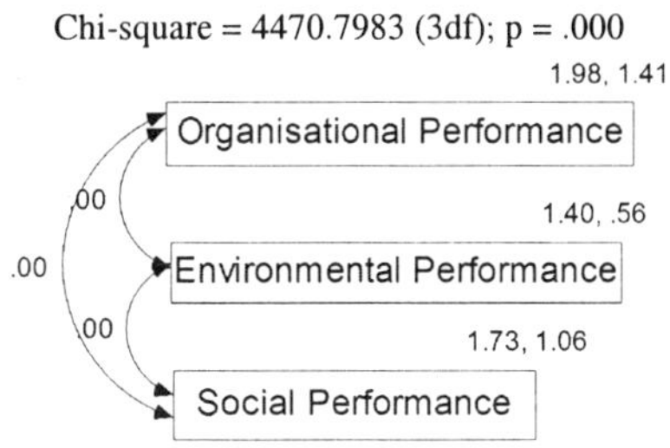

Figure 2. Model testing with fixed co-variance

From Bayesian perspective, if any true model parameters are unknown, it is considered to be random and is assigned a joint probability distribution. The distribution is not to suggest that the parameters are changing in some orderly fashion; but it is intended to summarize what is currently known about the parameters. This distribution observed before the data are seen is called a prior distribution. Upon its observation and by applying Bayes theorem, posterior distribution was drawn which shows a combination of prior belief and empirical evidence [14]. Posterior mean, which is the center or average of the posterior distribution, can be used as a Bayesian point estimate of the parameter, based on the data and the prior distribution. With a large data set, the posterior mean will tend to be close to the maximum likelihood estimate. In this case, as seen in table 1, the two are very close and compare the posterior mean of 0.632 for the *organization-environment* covariance to the maximum likelihood estimate of 0.630 to confirm. A similar close comparison is observed in case of *environment-social* (posterior = 0.586, prior estimate = 0.584), and *organization-social* (posterior = 1.016, prior estimate =

1.020) aspects of reporting. Also the posterior standard deviation, the standard deviation of the distribution, is a useful measure of uncertainty similar to a conventional standard error. In this case, both standard deviation and standard error are very close. Similar observations could be made from the graphical output as shown below.

Table 1. Prior and Posterior Distribution – Bayesian Estimate

Covariances	Prior Distribution				Posterior Distribution		
	Est.	Std Error	Critical Ratio	P	Mean	Std Error	Std Deviation
Avg_org ↔ Avg_env	.630	.023	26.894	***	0.632	0.001	0.024
Avg_env ↔ Avg_soc	.584	.021	28.104	***	0.586	0.000	0.021
Avg_org ↔ Avg_soc	1.016	.034	29.729	***	1.020	0.001	0.035

In this study, the distributions of the first and last thirds of the analysis samples are almost identical (as in figure 3(a), (b) and (c)), which suggests that AMOS has successfully identified the important features of the posterior distribution of the organisation-environment, environment-social and social-organisation covariances. Note that this posterior distribution appears to be centered at some value near 0.63 (org-env), 0.586 (env-soc), and 1.020 (soc-org) which agrees with the mean value for this parameter. Visual inspection suggests that the standard deviation is roughly 0.024 (org-env), 0.021 (env-soc) and 0.035 (soc-org), which agrees with the value of S.D.

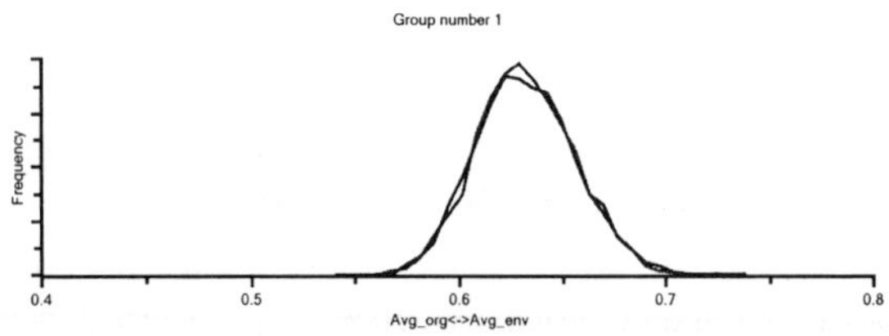

Figure 3 (a). Posterior Graphical Output (First and Last) - Organisation - Environment Performance

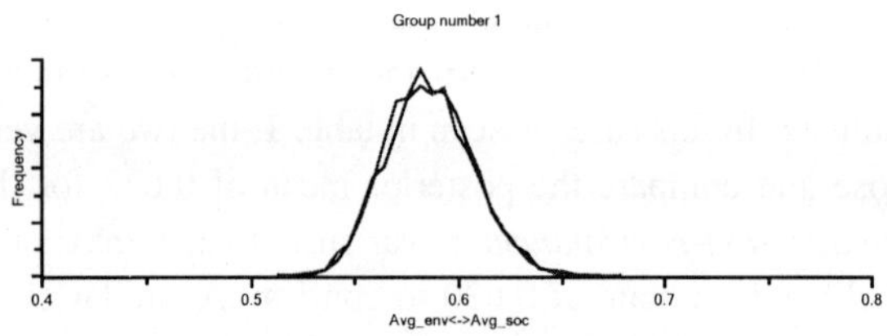

Figure 3 (b). Posterior Graphical Output (First and Last) - Environment - Social Performance

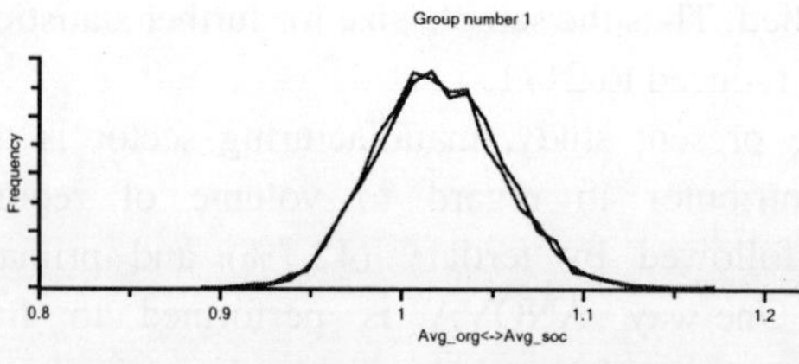

Figure 3 (c). Posterior Graphical Output (First and Last)- Organisation – Social Performance

As most of the sampled values are greater than 0, it provides evidence that the true value of the covariance parameter is positive, and the result is statistically significant i.e., the covariance parameter is greater than or equal to 0, hence null hypothesis (H4) is rejected.

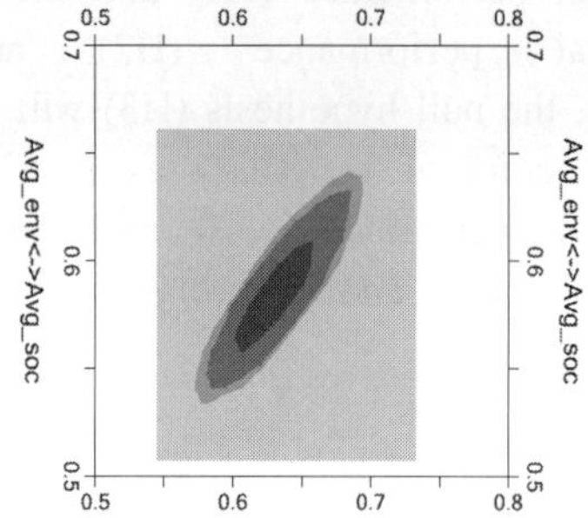

Figure 4(a). Covariances of organizational performance-environmental performance and environmental performance-social performance

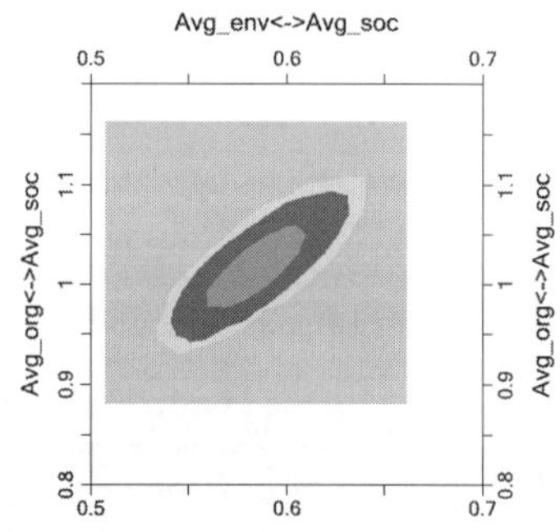

Figure 4(b). Covariances of environmental performance-social performance and organizational performance-social performance

A further investigation is made from marginal posterior distributions. These distributions are of very important nature, but they do not reveal relationships that may exist among the estimands. In a sense, two covariances or regression coefficients may share significance that either one could plausibly be 0, but both cannot. It is evident from the contour bivariate posterior density display that the covariances of organizational performance-environmental performance and environmental performance-social performance is in the credible region of 95% (as in figure 4(a)), where as, the environmental performance-social performance and organizational performance-social performance; and the organizational performance-environmental performance and organizational performance-social performance are in the credible region of 90% (as in figure 4(b) and 4(c)).

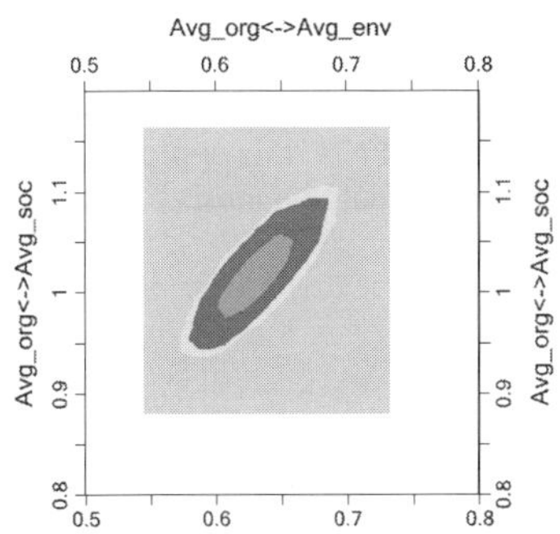

Figure 4(c). Covariances of organizational performance-environmental performance and organizational performance-social performance

6. Conclusion

The study highlight the significance of GRI reporting guidelines by assessing the relational aspects of the selected performance indicators i.e., organizational, environmental and social. The questions used by Dennis et. al [12] were adopted in this study as selected variables and were modified to suit the requirements of text mining. After excluding the foreign language reports, 2171 reports were used for final analysis. Nearly 46.7% of the reports are from manufacturing sector, followed by tertiary and primary sectors. After performing One way ANOVA, the results indicated that organizational performance is viewed uniformly across all the industrial sectors, where as, environmental and social performance is not so. Using AMOS, it is disclosed that the correlation exists between the selected variables and the Chi-square model is proved significant. Bayesian estimation is also performed which confirmed the presence of correlation among the selected variables; and standard error (prior distribution) and standard estimation (posterior distribution) had disclosed similar findings. The co-variances also showed significant credible relationships.

References

1. B. Ing, Developing green reporting systems: Some practical implications. *Green Reporting*, Chapman & Hall, London (1992).
2. International Organisation for Standardization (ISO), ISO 14031 Environmental Management – Environmental Performance Evaluation – Standards and Guidelines, ISO: Geneva (1999).
3. Global Reporting Initiative (GRI), Sustainability Reporting Guidelines on Economic Environmental and Social Performance, Boston, MA: GRI (2000).
4. D. J. Lober, D. Bynum, E. Campbell and M. Jacques, The 100 plus corporate environmental report study: A survey of an evolving environmental management tool, *Business Strategy and the Environment*, 6(3), pp.57–73 (1997).
5. G. Noci, Environmental reporting in Italy: Current practice and future developments, *Business Strategy and the Environment*, 9, pp.211–223 (2000).
6. P. Rao, A. K. Singh, O. Castillo, S. Ponciano Intal Jr., and A. Sajid, A metric for corporate environmental indicators...for Small and Medium Enterprises in the Philippines, *Business Strategy and the Environment*, 17(6), (2006).
7. R. Isenmann, Customized corporate environmental reporting by internet-based push and pull technologies, *Eco-Management and Auditing*, 8, pp.100-110 (2001).
8. J. Modapothala and B. Issac, Evaluation of Corporate Environmental Reports using Data Mining Approach, *Proceedings of International Conference on Computer Engineering and Technology*, Singapore (2009).
9. M. Hearst, What Is Text Mining? SIMS, UC Berkeley, (2003). [Online]: http://people.ischool.berkeley.edu/~hearst/text-mining.html
10. B. Clemens, Changing environmental strategies over time: An empirical study of the steel industry in the United States, *Journal of Environmental Management*, 61, pp.1–11 (2001).
11. A. Kolk,. Trends in sustainability reporting by the Fortune Global 250, *Business Strategy and the Environment*, 12, pp.279–291 (2003).
12. D. M. Hussey, P. L. Kirsop, and R. E. Meissen, Global Reporting Initiative Guidelines: An Evaluation of Sustainable Development Metrics for Industry, *Environmental Quality Management*, pp.1-20 (2001)
13. Online Corporate Register, [Online]: www.corporate register.com [Accessed 20 January, 2009].
14. W. M. Bolstad, *Introduction to Bayesian Statistics*, John Wiley and Sons, Hoboken, NJ (2004).

INTELLIGENT STEAM TURBINE FAULT DIAGNOSIS BASED ON DATA FUSION

XIA FEI, ZHANG HAO, XU LONGHU, PENG DAOGANG †

College of Electric Power and Automation Engineering, Shanghai University of Electric Power,s
Shanghai, 200090, China

Abstract-For enhancing the accuracy of fault diagnosis, an approach of data fusion is proposed in the application of steam turbine with its character. Firstly, performance data which are acquired from sensors of steam turbine are discretization through fuzzy theory. After classified fault symptoms, the corresponding BP neural network is constructed and trained. Finally, supposed the different neural network as the multi-information source, their outputs can be combined by D-S evidence theory. The fusion result shows the correct type of the fault. This method was successfully adopted in the steam condenser fault diagnosis. Compared with the general method of FNN, this approach can enhance the accuracy in the area of fault diagnosis, especially for reducing the uncertainty in the fault diagnosis.

Key words-fault diagnosis, data fusion, steam turbine, multi-information

1. Introduction

The steam turbine is the important equipment on electric power plant [1]. Because of the complexity and the particular operation environment, the equipments is worked under high temperature, high-pressured and high speed revolving. Obliviously, the steam turbine has high fault rate and hazardous breakdown. These breakdowns will make the heavy economic loss and the social consequence [2].

Therefore, the intelligence fault diagnosis of steam turbine which is such a large-scale complex system must be obtained multi-dimensional information about the identical object from various sources which have more reliable and accurate diagnosis. With the development of multi-sensor data fusion technology, data fusion technology [3], as one kind of intelligent data processing technology, can eliminate uncertainty of the system and supply accurate observation result. As a result, it provides a new way for the uncertainty problem of steam turbine fault diagnosis.

As artificial neural networks have many diagnosis characteristic parameters, the network structure is huge inevitably. It caused that the accuracy was reduced and diagnosis reliable was influenced. This paper proposed an approach of data fusion in steam turbine fault diagnosis. Compared with the method of FNN, it raises the rate of accuracy effectively in the application of steam condenser.

2. Theory Fundamental

2.1. *Fuzzy Theory*

In the daily life, many concepts are the fuzzy. It is far insufficient to describe with belonged absolutely or not belong absolutely. Thus, it has the necessity to break the relations of absolutely subordinates. University of California Professor Zadeh has introduced the fuzzy set theory in 1965. The fuzzy set theory develops the ordinary set theory concept, value scope of characteristic function is expanded from gathers {0,1} to [0,1]. Some object of the universe is no longer regarded as belongs to this set or not belong to this set[4].

A fuzzy set which is defined in the universe, its membership function have many different form. Determines the membership function correctly is the foundation for using fuzzy set to describe fuzzy concept appropriately. One

† Work supported by Shanghai Tackling Key Scientific and Technological Project (Grant No. 061111004), Shanghai Dawn Tracking Project (Grant No.06GG13).

basic step of the application of fuzzy mathematics to solve the practical problem is to find one or several membership functions. If this question has been solved, other questions are easily solved.

2.2. *Neural Network*

The neuron is the most basic composition unit of cerebrum nervous system, and it is the foundation for cerebrum to be engaged in the intelligent activity. It is similar with the biological cerebrum nervous system. The basic composition unit of artificial neural network is also a neuron. The multi-inputs, which are widely used, signal output neuron model is shown in Figure 1.

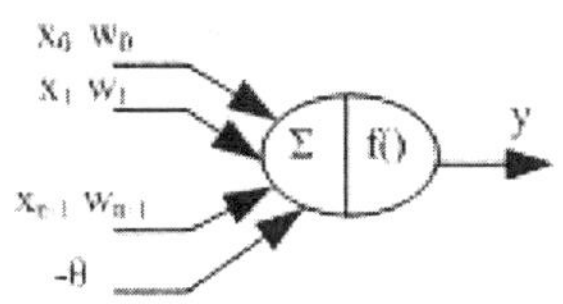

Figure 1. Model of artificial neuron

In the Figure 1, $X=[x_0,x_1,\ldots,x_{n-1}]^T$ is the input of the neural; y is the output of the neural; θ is output threshold, which is acted as a limit valve of determining neural activation state; W_i is the boundary weight between this neural and the upper neural, represent the strength of neural connecting arc; *f()* is activating function, which is often nonlinear function. The output of the neural can be represented as follows:

$$y = f(\sum_{i=0}^{n-1} x_i w_i - \theta) \qquad (1)$$

Single neural model is introduced above. Many neurons can be combined in a certain way to form a network, which is called artificial neural network. In the neural network, knowledge is represented by plenty of neurons inter-connecting and each connecting weight of them. Neural network map identifying approach can achieve the goal mainly by training many samples, and continuously adjusting weights with the help of adaptive algorithm in the network. State recognizer is just hiding on the form of network inter-connection and the weight. During the using of network, as for a particular input pattern, neural network result in an output mode by forward calculating, obtain particular solution by comparing and analyzing output signals.

2.3. *Data Fusion*

There are various methods for data fusion, and D-S evidence theory is adopted here. Evidence theory is an uncertain reasoning method, which can not only better grasp the unknown and uncertainty of problems than the traditional probability, but also provide a useful correlative evidence synthetic method, thus evidence provided by multiple evidence sources can be integrated.

In the D-S reasoning method [5], the basic entity is the identification framework (usually recorded as Θ), which is composed by all incompatible proposition possible values (called Singleton) in a domain. This collection Θ can be defined as (5):

$$\Theta = \{H_n\} \qquad (2)$$

Basic probability assignment function represents precise trust to identification targets H given by a signal source S_j, for every j, there is $j\in[1,Q]$. Q represents the number of the signal source. As for signal source S_j, the corresponding basic probability assignment function can be obtained [6-7]:

$$m_j : 2^{\Theta} \rightarrow [0,1] \qquad (3)$$

It can be proved, this function has following properties:

$$m_j(\Phi) = 0 \qquad (4)$$

$$\sum_{H\in\Theta} m_j(H) = 1 \qquad (5)$$

After obtained basic probability assignment function of each signal sources, according to the composite formula which is provided by D-S evidence theory evidences provided by various evidence sources can be integrated, and thus the final decision result can be obtained.

3. Approach of Fault Diagnosis

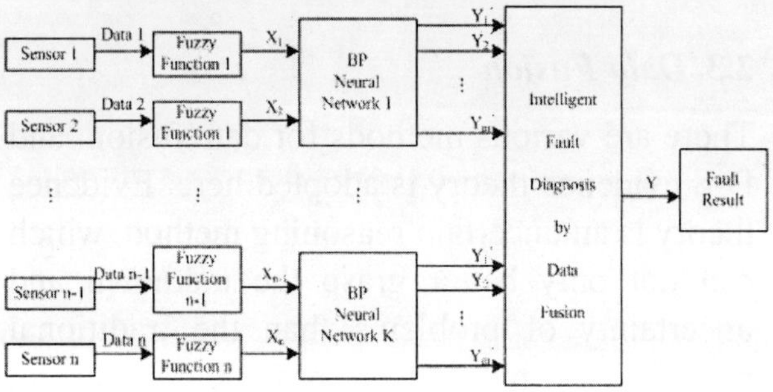

Figure 2. Intelligent fault diagnosis processes

The core of intelligent steam turbine fault diagnosis is as follows. The fault information from multi-sensor is dispersing in the domain of fuzzy theory. The results become the inputs of neural network. With the help of self-learning and non-linear fitting capacity of neural network, sensor information is pre-treated to extend information. Thus, it generates secondary information used in the intelligent fault diagnosis. After that, secondary information should be combined by using data fusion method. The final result is the fault judgement. The diagnosis process is shown in Figure 2.

3.1. *Data Processing*

In order to disperse data from sensors, proper membership function should be constructed. Membership function is the foundation of fuzzy sets applied to practical problems, correctly constructing membership function is the key of properly using fuzzy sets. However there is no mature and effective method in the existing membership functions, they are all determined by experience, and then corrected by experiments or feedback information by computer simulating.

3.2. *Extend Information*

The extending information network is composed by N BP neural networks, whose aim is extending M sensor measuring data network inputs, generating K network outputs in order to provide more comprehensive and more accurate data analysis for fusion fault diagnosis, meanwhile, provide decision analysis for fault diagnosis based on data fusion method. BP network is adopted for neural network.

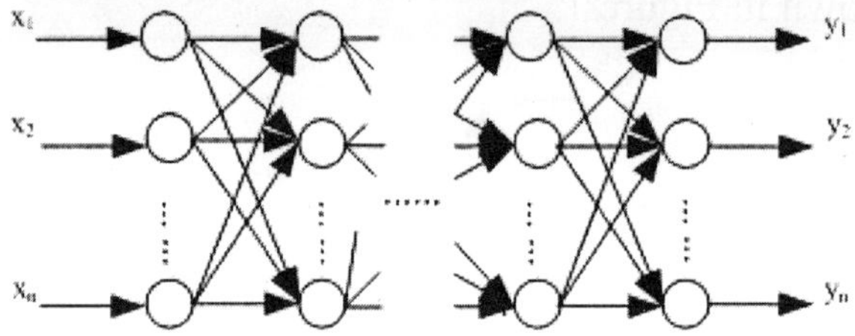

Figure 3. BP neural network structure

In the turbine fault diagnosis, three-level BP network is used. Input nodes of BP network respectively represent key information acquainted by sensor in fault diagnosis; output nodes correspond with other different fault types. Here for simplicity, fault types don't include combined fault.

3.3. *Fault Decision*

The upper outputs of BP network are performed data fusion using D-S theory. It can be known by previous theory introduction that, evidence theory is virtually a process during which new evidence would be formed by different evidences according to evidence composing rules. Whether Evidence provided by every fault symptoms can be combined , the key is constructing basic probability function. The general form of basic probability assignment function is not given in evidence theory. Therefore, specific basic probability assignment function should be constructed according to specific problems in practical applications. In turbine intelligent fault diagnosis, basic probability assignment function of evidence theory is constructed by output of neural network.

According to formula (6), evidence from several sources can be combined [8]:

$$m(H)=\frac{1}{1-k}\sum_{H_i\cap H_j\cdots=H} m_1(H_i)m_2(H_j)\cdots \quad \forall H\in 2^{\Theta} \tag{6}$$

Among which, $k=\sum_{H_i\cap H_j\cdots=H} m_1(H_i)m_2(H_j)\cdots$ reflect the degree of evidence conflict. The coefficient 1/(1-*k*) is called normalization factor, which can avoid non-zero probability being assigned to empty set in the synthesis.

4. Application in Steam Condenser

Fault diagnosis of condenser is mainly discussed in this paper according to previous fault diagnosis methods. In order to carry out fault diagnosis for condenser, fault universe of condenser are divided into three typical fault fuzzy modes through selection combining experience of engineer experts and technicians in this paper, they are Y1:serious fault of cycle pump; Y2:full water of condenser; Y3:not working of condensate pump. Eight symptoms relating with condenser fault are extracted as X1- X8. The details are shown in TABLE I.

4.1. *Fuzzy Function*

According [9], some types of membership functions are applicable to condenser fault symptom. The corresponding symptom of membership function of operating parameters of 300MW unit condenser can be obtained and are shown in TABLE I.

4.2. *BP NN Frame*

After dispersing each fault symptom data using membership function, 3 three-layer BP networks are adopted to extend information. One BP network (is) used to X1 and X2 related to vacuum, which is called neural network 1; then one another BP network is used to X3 and X4 related to condensate water, which is called neural network 2; the last one BP network is used to from X5 to X8, which is called neural network 3. Input of these network input layer are result of blurring the upper corresponding fault symptom. Each BP network output node of output layer belongs to is all these three faults as follows: serious fault of cycle pump, full-water of condenser, not working of condensate pump, output values are corresponding fault probability. Network transfer function adopts sigmoid function. Learning algorithm is standard BP algorithm, and learning ratio is 0.8.

TABLE I. EMBERSHIP FUNCTION OF EACH FAULT SYMPTOM

Fault symptom	Membership function
vacuum declined significantly and sharply（X1）	$\exp[-0.3(x-87)^2]$
vacuum declined slowly and slightly（X2）	$\exp[-0.3(x-97)^2]$
output pressure of condensate pump increased（X3）	$(x-0.5)/3.7$
output pressure of condensate pump decreased（X4）	$\exp[-4(x-3.7)^2]$
temperature rise of cycle water decreased（X5）	$\exp[-0.2(x-8)^2]$
terminal difference of condenser increased（X6）	$(x-3)/3.56$
coldness of condensation water increased（X7）	$(x-2)/0.5$
pressure difference between pumping port and input of extractor decreased（X8）	$\exp[-0.05(x-8.2)^2]$

5. Simulation Experiments

The fault diagnosis of condenser in turbine is simulated with the method proposed.

5.1. *BP NN Training*

Considering the difference of each symptom, real data in power plant should be used when training every BP network [10]. These data are dispersed by membership function shown in table 1. Then the network composed by X1 and X2 is taken as a sample. TABLE II is training data and the probability of three types of fault is shown in TABLE III.

TABLE II. SAMPLE INPUT

	1	2	3	4
X1	0.01	0.01	0.01	0.01
X2	0.58	0.23	0.83	0.57

TABLE III. TARGET OUTPUT

	1	2	3	4
Y1	0.04	0.01	0.01	0.01
Y2	0.26	0.18	0.36	0.17
Y3	0.67	0.3	0.35	0.13

During training, given system target error is 0.001, maximum training time is 1000.The training result is: system error is 0.01565 (average output error of a single node of each sample) .

5.2. *Stimulation Test*

According to the monitoring data of turbine generator unit condenser system in a certain power plant, needed operation parameters are gotten: condenser vacuum is 92.5kPa, condensate pump export pressure is 0.14MPa, cycle pump export pressure is 0.06MPa, the pressure between the pumping port and extractor is 0.03MPa, entrance temperature of cycle water is 28℃, export temperature of cycle water is 36℃, condensate depression is 2.005℃, terminal temperature difference of condenser is 5.306℃.

After blurring these data, three faults basic assignment probability corresponding to each neural network are obtained through three neural networks, which is shown in TABLE IV. Identification framework is $\Theta=\{u_1,u_2,u_3\}$,the value of 0 cannot be obtained by neural network; the initial value is set to zero.

TABLE IV. BASIC PROBABILITY ASSIGNMENT OF FAULT

Information source	$m(u_1)$	$m(u_2)$	$m(u_3)$	$m(\Theta)$
Neural network 1	0.4626	0.2763	0.0919	0
Neural network 2	0.3127	0.4729	0.0077	0
Neural network 3	0.4139	0.3010	0.0877	0

Three neural networks are taken as three information source; the basic assignment probability of three types of condenser fault obtained respectively can do the data fusion by formula (6). Evidence m_1 and m_2 are firstly combined. The whole conflict coefficient k_{12} which caused during the fusion between evidence m_1 and m_2 can be calculated by the following formula:

$$k_{12}=\sum_{u_i\cap u_j=\Phi} m_1(u_i)m_2(u_j)=m_1(u_1)m_2(u_2)+m_1(u_1)m_2(u_3)$$
$$+m_1(u_2)m_2(u_1)+m_1(u_2)m_2(u_3)+m_1(u_3)m_2(u_1)+$$
$$m_1(u_3)m_2(u_2)=0.3830$$

The reliability function value assigned to Y1 can be calculated by the following formula:

$$m_{12}(u_1)=\frac{\sum_{u_i\cap u_j=u_1} m_1(u_i)m_2(u_j)}{1-k_{12}}$$
$$=\frac{m_1(u_1)m_2(u_1)+m_1(u_1)m_2(\Theta)+m_1(\Theta)m_2(u_1)}{1-k_{12}}$$
$$=\frac{0.1447+0.0956+0.0529}{1-0.3830}=0.4752$$

And because the same reason, $m_{12}(u_2)=0.4341$, $m_{12}(u_3)=0.0340$,$m_{12}(\Theta)=0.0567$

According to D-S data fusion rules, TABLE V is obtained. From the calculating result, the fault types can get a certain fusion result after fusion decision. With the value larger than 0.5, the fault of condenser can be diagnosed as Y1 fault.

TABLE V. FAULT DIAGNOSIS RESULT OF CONDENSER

Information source	$m(u_1)$	$m(u_2)$	$m(u_3)$	$m(\Theta)$	Diagnosis result
$m_{12}=m_1\oplus m_2$	0.4752	0.4341	0.0340	0.0567	indefinite
$m= m_{12}\oplus m_3$	0.5175	0.3847	0.0242	0.0184	Y1

5.3. *Compared Experiments*

In order to compare the result obtained by the method proposed in this paper, the same fuzzy function and three-level BP neural network are adopted. The same eight fault characteristics are inputs of the neural network and the same three fault types are the outputs. The probability of Y1 is 0.3765; the probability of Y2 is 0.4275; the probability of Y3 is 0.2817. According to the determining rules, the fault types are indefinite. Furthermore, the above two methods were tested through 30 simulation data.

TABLE VI. COMPARING EXPERIMENT OF CONDENSER FAULT DIAGNOSIS

Diagnosis method	True (%)	Fault (%)	Uncertain (%)
Data fusion	86.7	13.3	0
Fuzzy neural network	63.3	20	16.7

We can see from TABLE VI that method of data fusion can not only decrease the rate of fault in fault diagnosis, but also can avoid the uncertain situation.

6. Conclusion

Steam condenser fault diagnosis is taken as an example to verify the approach of data fusion in steam turbine fault diagnosis. Because multi-information source was combined by data fusion, the uncertainty of fault diagnosis system is decreased sharply. In the future research, this fault diagnosis method can be used in expert system of turbine fault diagnosis, which can improve the intelligent level.

References

1. Y.Diao and K.M.Passinb, "Fault diagnosis for a turbine engine," *Control Engineering Practice*, 1151(2004),.
2. X.Zeng, K.K.Li, W.L. Chan, X, Yin, D.Chen and G.Lin, "Discussion on application of information fusion techniques in electric power system fault detection," *ELECTRIC POWER*, **vol.36**, 8(2003).
3. E.Zhang, H.Zhang and B.Xue, "Steam Turbine Generator Fault Diagnosis Based on Information Fusion Technology," *CONTROL & AUTOMATION*, **vol.23**, 192(2007).
4. J.Zhang, "Research of Algorithm and Application in FNN Model," *Daqing: Daqing Petroleum Institute*, 2002.
5. L.Yang and H.Yu, Theory and Application of Multi-Source Information Fusion, *Beijng : Beijing University of Posts and Telecommunications Press*,2005.
6. G.Niu, T.Han and B.S.Yang, "Multii-agent decision fusion for motor f ault diagnosis", *Mechanical Systems and Signal Processing*, **vol.21**, 1285(2007).
7. B.S. Yang and K.J.Kim, "Application of Dempster-Shafer theory in fault diagnosis of induction motors using vibration and current signals", *Mechanical Systems and Signal Processing,* **vol.20**, 403(2006).
8. Pu Shujin, Yang Shenyuan, Hu Weiwei, A combination rule of evidence theory based on reallocation of the basic probability assigned to conflict, *The 6th World Congress on Intelligent Control and Automation*, 4264(2006).
9. X.Jia, "Fault Diagnosis in Turbine of Condenser," *Haerbin: Harbin Engineering University*, 2004.
10. FeiSi Center of Technology, Neural Network Theory and MATLAB 7 Application, *Beijing: Publishing House of Electric Industry*, 44(2005).

STATIC TASK SCHEDULING IN HOMOGENEOUS MULTIPROCESSOR SYSTEMS BASED ON GENETIC ALGORITHM

MAJID ABOUTALEBI
Islamic Azad University, Sari Branch
Sari, 48164-194, Iran

HAJAR SIYAR†
Young Researchers Club, Islamic Azad University, Sari Branch
Sari, 48164-194, Iran

HAMID HAJ SEYYED JAVADI
Shahed University
Tehran, 18151-159, Iran

ABSTRACT

Static task scheduling in homogeneous multiprocessor systems is an important computing problem, because this problem is an Np-hard problem. Minimizing the execution time of the parallel program is the aim of scheduling. According to dependencies between tasks in the task graph, scheduling must be done so that any task can process with minimum waiting time for processing tasks that dependent to them. In this paper a new method for static task scheduling in multiprocessor systems has been mentioned. That is based on genetic algorithm that gives a priority to the tasks in graph based on set of parameters and then scheduling will be done based on this priorities. This proposed method is simulated and then compared with several alternative scheduling algorithms. Results of simulations are showed that schedule that proposed method is converge to it, has a good performance and behavior in comparison with compared methods.

1. Introduction

Static scheduling in homogeneous multiprocessor systems is an Np-Hard problem [4,5,11,18]. Minimizing the execution time of parallel program is an important goal in task scheduling. Any parallel program consists many tasks and set of tasks of a parallel program forms the task graph [1,13].

The scheduling problem task graph is defined by the tuple (T,E), where T shows a set of *n* tasks and E shows a set of *e* edges in the graph. Each node $t_i \in T$ shows a task of parallel program. The edge $(t_i , t_j) \in E$ shows a data dependency between two tasks t_i and t_j and it means that the execution of t_i must be finished before the execution of t_j is started and data of t_i must set on the processor that t_j will be executed on it. For each edge (t_i , t_j) the value $d_{i,j}$ shows the amount of data that must be transferred from task *i* to task *j* . The task that has no parents is called *entry task* and the task that has no children is called *exit task.* If two tasks t_i and t_j that communicate together with edge e_{ij} are executed in different processors , the communication cost between these two tasks is equal to the weight of edge (t_i , t_j) ,but if these tasks are executed in the same processor, the communication cost between them will be zero [3,7,8,16].

† Corresponding author
Email address: hjrsiar@gmail.com

Many scheduling algorithms are represented for solving scheduling problem with the aim of minimizing the execution time of parallel program and communication cost between tasks in the graph. One important type of this scheduling algorithms are heuristic algorithms [11]. Genetic algorithms is one important type of heuristic algorithms. According to the searching ability of this algorithms, they can represent optimum scheduling in comparison with other types of scheduling algorithms [10,12,14].

Many several methods are represented for task scheduling by genetic algorithms. For example in [15] priority of tasks are determined with the aim of minimizing the length of critical path and communication cost between tasks in the graph. In [6] priority of tasks is determined based on the number of children. In [2] priority of tasks is determined based on height of them. In genetic scheduling algorithm represented in [17], for increasing speed of algorithm, task graph is partitioned to several sections based on divided and conquer technique and then genetic scheduling is separately done on each section. In [14] a mixture scheduling algorithm based on genetic algorithm and learning automata with the aim of minimizing the length of critical path and communication cost between tasks is represented.

In this paper a new method for task scheduling in multiprocessor systems based on genetic algorithm is represented that tasks priority is determined based on three parameters, this parameters consist of tasks height, number of children of each task and execution time of each task, that are gotten from the parallel program's task graph. The encoding method that is represented in this algorithm is different from the method used in [6]. The exit condition from genetic algorithm in this proposed method is convergence to high level of parallelism. Also in this algorithm a new mutation operator have been mentioned to increase the performance and speed of genetic algorithm.

The structure of this paper is as follows. In section two the proposed algorithm, encoding method and genetic algorithm operators are mentioned. In section three, the scheduling algorithm is represented and in section four simulation results that shows the effective performance of proposed algorithm are represented.

2. Proposed Algorithm

This section is shown how proposed genetic algorithm behavior to schedule task graph and then scheduling is represented on a sample graph from [15]. The parallel program task graph is the input of scheduling algorithm.

In the proposed algorithm we assume that processors in the system are homogeneous, also suppose that processors are fully connected to each other, so the communication cost between processors are same and can be ignored from it [7,17]. The aim of algorithm is minimizing the execution time of parallel program and also increasing parallelism level between processors [13,15].

Figure 1 is shown an example of task graph in [15] and in continuance the proposed scheduling will be apply on it.

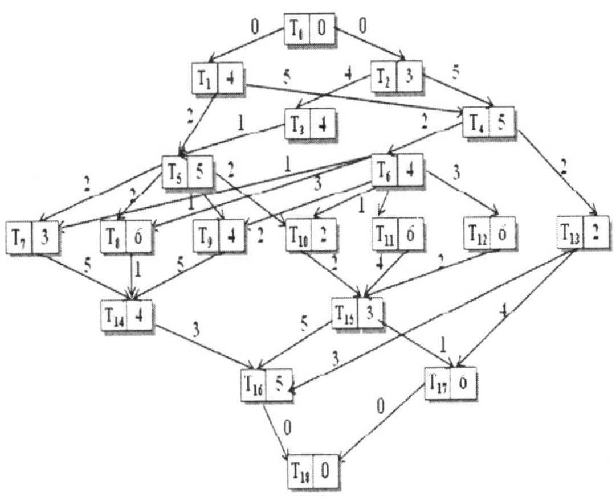

Figure 1. An example of task graph

2.1. *Encoding Chromosome*

Each chromosome shows a possible state of scheduling. In this section the method of encoding chromosome in proposed algorithm is mentioned. In this algorithm each chromosome is represented by the tuple (T,P) that T is shown the set of tasks and P is shown the set of processors in the system. $p_i \in P$ shows a processor that allocated to task $t_i \in T$.

In this method the way of execution of tasks in the processors is generally mentioned and in fact each chromosome shows the sequence of tasks to the processors and also the sequence of execution of tasks. In figure 2 an example of chromosome equivalent to the task graph of figure 1 when there are three processor p0, p1, p2 on the system is shown.

T0	T2	T1	T4	T3	T6	T5	T10	T11	T12	T7	T9	T8	T13	T15	T14	T16	T17	T18
P2	P1	P1	P2	P0	P2	P0	P0	P1	P2	P0	P0	P1	P1	P2	P2	P2	P1	P0

Figure 2. An example of chromosome generated from proposed algorithm based on task graph of figure1

2.2. *Initial Population*

Genetic algorithm first must create an initial population of chromosomes that each chromosome shows a state of scheduling. The more amount of fitness of initial population can effect on the convergence speed of genetic algorithm to the optimal solution and increasing the performance of the scheduling [12].

In this algorithm for creating a chromosome, tasks are take a priority based on three parameters height, number of children and execution time. This parameters value gets from the task graph and the priority of tasks is shown the sequence of execution of them or sequence of scheduling.

The execution time of each task is determined from the weight of each node of task graph. To estimate the value of height and number of children of each task, this algorithm utilize from two functions. The Eq. (1) shows function level(t_i) that determines the height of task t_i and the Eq. (2) is shown function children(t_i) that determine number of children of task t_i.

$$height(Ti) = \begin{cases} 0 & \text{if } PRED(Ti) = 0 \\ 1 + \max\{height(Tj)\} & tj \in PRED(Ti) \end{cases} \tag{1}$$

$$children(Ti) = \begin{cases} 0 & \text{if number of childern } Ti = 0 \\ \sum_{j=1}^{n} children(Tj) & n = \text{number of } Ti\text{'s children} \end{cases} \tag{2}$$

Tasks stand on the priority queue based on their priorities. Whereas for executing each task must attend that whether this task is ready-to-execute or not and if a task is on a lower height the probability that this task can be ready-to-execute is more, so we first attend on the height parameter and choose tasks with lower height for scheduling first. If in each time, only one task have been chosen, this task have the higher priority and stand on the priority queue and then will be removed from height, children number and execution time queues. But if the number of chosen tasks are more than one task, whereas giving priority to tasks based on children number is almost better than giving priority based on height [6], from tasks with same priority tasks that have more children number will be chosen for scheduling, because the task that have more number of children with execution of himself will take the execution possibility to more number of tasks. If only one task is chosen, this task stands in the priority queue and then removed from other queues. But it is possible that more than one task with same children number are chosen, in this time task with lower execution time will be chosen for scheduling from chosen tasks. The reason is that the task with lower execution time will release the processor earlier than other tasks. This task is chosen as optimal task for scheduling and will enter in the priority queue and then will be removed from other queues. But it is possible that there is more than one task with same execution time in this level too, then whereas all chosen tasks are ready-to-execute, the priority of them will be determined randomly and then tasks will be enter in the priority queue.

```
1. Initilalize ready_list to zero
2. Initialize Height_array elements to zero
3. Initialize Children_array elements to zer
4. Initialize Executiontime_array elements to zero
5. For each task t_i in DAG do
     Initialize Executiontime_array(t_i)
   6. For each task t_i in DAG do
        Height_array[i] = height[t_i]
     7. For each task t_i in DAG do
          Children_array[i] = children(t_i)
       8. While there are any task in Height_array
            Initialize minheight_array to zero
            Initialize maxchildren_array elements to zero
            Initialize minexetime_array elements to zero
            For each element in height_array do
              Select nodes with less height and add this element to minheight_array
            End for
            If number of minheight_array elements = 1 then
              Add this element to ready_list
              Remove this task from Heigh_array , Children_array and Executiontime_array
            Else
              For each elements of children_array in min_height
                Select nodes with more children and add this element to maxchildren_array
              End for
              If number of maxchildren_array elements = 1 then
                Add this element to ready_list
                Remove this task from Heigh_array , Children_array and Executiontime_array
              Else
                For each element of executiontime_array in maxchildren_array
                  Select nodes with less execution_time and add this element to minexetime_array
                End for
                If number of minexetime_array elements = 1 then
       Add this element to ready_list
                Else
                  allocate minexetime_array elements randomly to ready_list
                End if
              End if
            End if
          End While
        End for
      End for
   End for
```

Figure 3. Algorithm for giving priority to the tasks

Allocation of tasks to the processors in each scheduling is doing randomly to achieve optimal allocation of tasks to the processors by genetic algorithm.

Figure 3 is shown algorithm used for giving priority to tasks in the proposed method.

Scheduling is done based on tasks priority and in the genetic algorithm execution time, the sequence of tasks priority is not changed but the sequence of allocation of processors to the tasks is variant. The scheduling algorithm will be done until the population is convergent to the determinate fitness value or number of population is further up than the determinate number.

2.3. *Fitness Function*

The aim of the proposed scheduling algorithm is to minimize the execution time of the parallel program. So that the fitness value of each chromosome is determined from the time that processors are processing the tasks, so that processor with more processing time is determinate in each scheduling and this time will be estimated as the fitness value of this scheduling.

Whereas the aim is minimizing the processing time of processors, we can transmute the problem to a maximization problem utilizing fitness function that used in this algorithm and mentioned in Eq. (3). In this way the objective of algorithm is increasing the fitness value of chromosomes.

$$\text{Fitness Cromosome} = \frac{1}{\max\left(\text{CompletationTime}(P_{i,j,\ldots,n})\right)} \qquad 0 \le i,j \le n \quad n: \text{number of processors} \tag{3}$$

2.4. *Crossover Operator*

For selecting more suitable and effective scheduling, in this algorithm, chromosomes are selected based on roulette selection method. Chosen chromosomes from current population are synthesized to each other based on two point crossover operator, to produce next population chromosomes. In synthesizing chromosomes, only offspring processors are supplant to each other to produce children chromosomes of next population. An example of behavior of crossover operator in this algorithm is shown in figure 4.

Parents :

T0	T2	T1	T4	T3	T6	T5	T10	T11	T12	T7	T9	T8	T13	T15	T14	T16	T17	T18
P2	P0	P1	P1	P2	P0	P0	P1	P2	P1	P2	P0	P0	P0	P1	P1	P2	P2	P0

T0	T2	T1	T4	T3	T6	T5	T10	T11	T12	T7	T9	T8	T13	T15	T14	T16	T17	T18
P2	P1	P1	P2	P0	P2	P0	P0	P1	P2	P0	P0	P1	P1	P2	P2	P2	P1	P0

Offsprings :

T0	T2	T1	T4	T3	T6	T5	T10	T11	T12	T7	T9	T8	T13	T15	T14	T16	T17	T18
P2	P1	P1	P2	P0	P2	P0	P1	P2	P1	P2	P0	P0	P1	P2	P2	P2	P1	P0

T0	T2	T1	T4	T3	T6	T5	T10	T11	T12	T7	T9	T8	T13	T15	T14	T16	T17	T18
P2	P0	P1	P1	P2	P0	P0	P0	P1	P2	P0	P0	P1	P0	P1	P1	P2	P2	P0

Figure 4. An example of crossover operator

2.5. *Mutation Operator*

The new mutation operator represented in this algorithm is designed as to convergent speed of algorithm can increase. In this operator, unlike other operators mentioned in this algorithm, tasks in the chromosome supplant to each other so that the first task is selected randomly from the tasks in the chromosome and for preservation the execution sequence of tasks, the selected task is supplanted randomly with one of the tasks with same height with it. If there is no task with same height of it, the task supplant with one task with lower height than it randomly. So the genetic algorithm has the possibility to search in more response area and more states of scheduling can be studied by the algorithm.

3. Scheduling Algorithm

The code of proposed scheduling algorithm is shown in figure 5.

```
1. Create initial population according section 2-2
2. While (completion time of each processor in chromosome are equal
or number of generations is less than given number) do
    for each chromosome in current population do
        compute fitness of each chromosome according to section 2-3
    End for
    while next population is complete do
        select chromosomes with maximum fitness values by
        roulette-selection
        use two point crossover operator to create next generation
        children
        use mutation operator according section 2-5
    End while
End while
```

Figure 5. The proposed scheduling algorithm

As shown in figure 5, the exit condition in this algorithm is reaching to the determinate number of generations and likewise can achieve the processors to the equal processing time too. This condition is utilized to achieve the optimal parallelism goal, because if the processing time of all processors in the system are equal to each other, Whereas the processors are assumed homogeneous, in this mode can deduce that no processor is un active in the system and it can be an optimal mode in the scheduling.

4. Experimental Results

In this section, the results of simulation on the task graph in the [9] are represented. In figure 6 the completion time of each scheduling in the algorithm based on number of runs is shown.

For study the accuracy of results get from algorithm, the results of algorithm are gotten in different thirty runs of the algorithm, the results are shown in figure 7.

The simulation results are shown that the proposed genetic scheduling algorithm is convergent to the optimal scheduling with suitable completion time after repetition several generations.

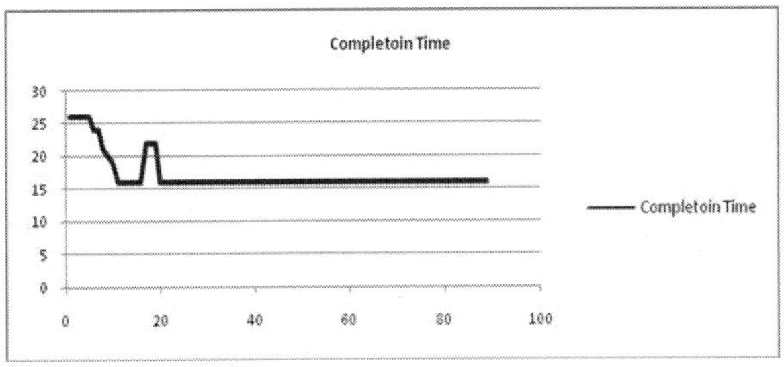

Figure 6 .The proportion between the completion time and number of generations of genetic algorithm

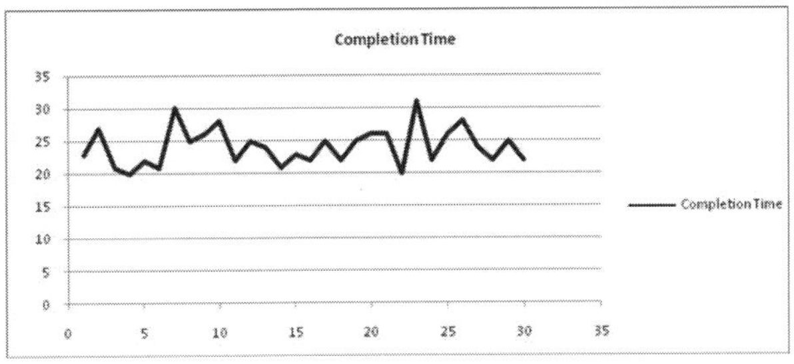

Figure 7. The completion time resulted from thirty runs of proposed genetic algorithm

The figure 8 shows results of comparison of proposed genetic algorithm with standard genetic algorithm and also the genetic scheduling algorithm represented in [15] based on the task graph represented in [15] in thirty different runs. The results are shown that the proposed scheduling algorithm has an effective performance in comparison with standard genetic algorithm, also below figure is shown that the proposed algorithm behavior in proportion of scheduling algorithm represented in [15] is good.

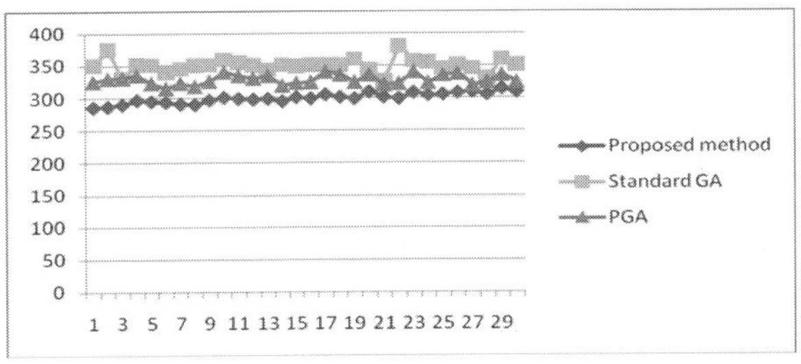

Figure 8. The comparison of proposed algorithm with standard genetic algorithm and algorithm represented in [15], in thirty different runs.

5. Conclusion

Task scheduling in homogeneous multiprocessor systems is an Np-Hard computational problem and so that it has many different solutions. The heuristic methods represented for solving this problem has better performance in comparison with conclusive methods, one of the important heuristic methods are genetic algorithm solutions. In this paper a method for task scheduling based on genetic algorithm is represented. In this algorithm tasks are take a priority based on their height, children number and execution time.

Although with attention to simulation results, proposed algorithm have a good behavior, but this is possible that this method is similar to other scheduling heuristic methods that doesn't get the suitable and optimal solution in some condition of scheduling problem. But with utilizing of algorithm in suitable conditions and with specific number of tasks, this algorithm can display efficient behavior and can be used as a good way for scheduling in many applications.

References

1. D. McLaughlin, Sh. Sardesai and P.Dasgupta. Preemptive Scheduling for Distributed Systems.
2. E.S.H. Hou, N. Ansari nad H. Ren. A genetic algorithm for multiprocessor scheduling. IEEE trans. On parallel and distributed systems. Vol.5, no.2, pp.113-120, February 1994.
3. F. Dong, S. G.Akl. Scheduling Algorithms for grid computing: state of the Art and Open problems. Technicla Report No.2006-504.
4. J. A. Hoogveen, J.K. Lenstra and B. Veltman. Three,four,five,six,or the complexity of scheduling with

communication delays. Operations Research Letters, 16:129-137, 1994.

5. J. K Lenstra, M. Veldhorst and B. Veltman. The complexity of scheduling trees with communication delays. Journal of Algorithms, 20(1):157-173, January 1996.
6. M.Abdeyazdan, A.M. Rahmani, Task scheduling in multiprocessor systems by a new priority genetic algorithm based on children number. 13th national conference of computer society. March 2007. (In Persian).
7. M. I.Daoud, N. Kharma. A high performance algorithm for static task scheduling in heterogeneous distributed computing systems. Journal of Parallel Distributed Computing, 68:399-409, 2008.
8. O. Sinnen, L. A.Sousa. Communication contention in task scheduling. IEEE Transactions on parallel and distributed systems, Vol.16, No.6, June 2005.
9. P. Chaudhuri, J. Elock. Task scheduling in multiprocessor systems using duplication. Journal of System architecture. 54: 519-529, 2008.
10. R. Armstrong, D. Hensgen and T. Kidd. The relative performance of various mapping algorthms is independent of sizable variances in run-time predictions. 7th IEEE Heterogenous computing workshop (HCW'98), pp.79-87, 1998.
11. R. Hwang, M. Gen and H. katayama. A comparison of multiprocessor task scheduling algorithms with communication cost. Computers & Operational research, 35:976-993, 2008.
12. R. L.Haupt, S.E. Haupt. Practical genetic algorithms. Wiley interscience publication. Second edition, 2004.
13. R. Sakellariou, H. Zhao, E. Tsiakkouri and D. Dikaiakos. Scheduling workflows with budget constrains.
14. S. Parsa, H. Eizadkhah, A.Hosseinzadeh, The composition of migration automata and genetic algorithm for task graph scheduling in multiprocessor architecture. 3th international conference of information and knowledge technology. September 2007. (In Persian).
15. S. Parsa, Sh. Lotfi, N. lotfi. An evolutionary approach to task graph scheduling. ICANNGA 2007, Part 1, LNCS 4431, pp. 110-119, 2007.
16. X. Kong, J. Sun and W. Xu. Permutation-based Particle swarm algorithm for tasks scheduling in heterogeneous systems with communication delays. International journal of computational reseach.Vol.4, No.1, pp.61-70, 2008.
17. Y.H. Lee, C. Chen. A modified genetic algorithm for task scheduling in multiprocessor systems.
18. Y.K. Kwok and I. Ahmad. Static scheduling algorithms for allocation directed task graphs to multiprocessors. ACM Computing surveys, vol.31, No.4, December 1999.

OUTLIER DETECTION AND FUZZY LOGIC ALGORITHM FOR PERFORMANCE EVALUATION PROBLEM *

N MEGALA

Business Analyst, CIO Group, Cybernet-SlashSupport, Chennai 600 0017, India,
Email: megalaie@yahoo.co.in

This paper addresses a problem of evaluating the performance of each member in the population having multiple attributes. Outlier Detection algorithm and fuzzy logic algorithm are proposed to find solutions for the Performance Evaluation Problem (PEP). The central limit theorem is used to identify outliers in the metric space define the upper bound and lower bound with respect to each metric. The standardization technique converts metric values of different dimensions into standard scores of dimensionless data space. The fuzzy logic algorithm evaluates the performance index corresponding to the group of metrics. A case study is conducted in technical support department of *Cybernet-Slashsupport* to evaluate the performance of employees and the experimental results are discussed in this paper.

1. Introduction

Performance evaluation of employees has been a major preoccupation of university researchers and management practitioners for a long time [1]. An important part of Business Performance Evaluation is optimizing the operational level activities. In order to understand the performance of the system having a set of monitoring variables, performance metrics have to be mathematically modeled to measure the efficiency of operational activities. The system designer needs to set upper bound (target) and lower bound (acceptance level) for performance metrics. The bound prediction problem becomes complex, if the number of performance metrics becomes more and the data has outliers. The outlier prediction problem has long been handled appropriately by probability theory and statistics. The statistical prediction model determines outliers and the data driven bounds. The reference [2] proposed the Chebyshev outlier detection method that uses the Chebyshev inequality to calculate upper and lower outlier detection limits. Outlier detection in large data sets is an active research field in data mining [3]. The reference [4] proposed distance-based outlier detection and the reference [5] proposed a density-based clustering and outlier detection technique. The difficulty involved in evaluating the performance is arriving at a composite score that involves different metrics. Various techniques have been attempted for performance evaluation problem [6]. Fuzzy logic was introduced by [7] as a mathematical way to represent vagueness in the system. Attempts have been made to include fuzzy logic algorithms in business and management disciplines [8]. The fuzzy approach to Performance Appraisal (PA) allows the organization to exercise professional judgment in evaluating its employees [9]. The present study addresses the problem of performance evaluation. Outlier detection algorithm is proposed to define bandwidth to distribution of data, and fuzzy logic algorithm is proposed to evaluate the performance index corresponding to input metric vector.

2. Problem Description

The solution technique to the Performance Evaluation Problem (PEP) consists of two phases: a outlier detection algorithm to define bandwidth to each metric data space; a fuzzy logic algorithm to compute performance index from the set of metrics. The steps involved in the first phase are as follows: (i) defining the metric functions to be measured for the set of monitoring variables; (iii) determining outliers in the history of data for each metric and defining the upper bound and lower bound; and (iv) defining the transformation function to translate each variable from metric space into a dimensionless standard score space having a uniform bandwidth across metrics. The output metric vector obtained from the statistical model is given as an input to the second phase (i.e., the fuzzy logic system). The output from the fuzzy logic algorithm is the performance index value.

* This work is supported by CIO Group, *Cybernet-Slashsupport* in India.

3. Statistical Models to predict bounds of metric distribution

The n dimensional input data space $\wp^n = \{A : a \in A \& |A| = n\}$ denotes the set of attributes of the population. The n denotes the total number of attributes to be measured for each member in the population. The set of attributes for a member of the population is denoted as $A = \{a : a \in \mathbb{R}\}$. Set of metrics $M = (m_1, m_2 ... m_s)$ are defined to measure the performance of each member given in the population. The number of metrics defined is s. The set of functions corresponding to each metric space is defined as $\Gamma = \{f : for \exists a \in A, f : a \mapsto m\}$. Each member in the population has the set of metric measured by $f : a \mapsto m \; for \forall m \in M$. The input data for each member is collected for the set of time period $T = \{t_1, t_2, t_3 ... t_{pr}\}$ where pr is the number of time period considered for the analysis. From the distribution of input data for $\forall t \in T$ corresponding to each data $a \in A$, the distribution of metric space with respect to each metric can be derived by using the set of function Γ. In order to identify the set of upper bound and lower bound $L^2 = \{(b_u^m, b_l^m) : \forall m \in M\}$ corresponding to each distribution of metric, two data derived bound prediction models are proposed in this paper.

3.1. *Data bounds prediction by using central limit theorem*

In order to define the bounds for the distribution of metric x, ample history of the process is necessary. Most of the time determining the distribution and the parameters of the population are too expensive. The Central Limit Theorem is the foundation for many statistical procedures, including Quality Control Charts to predict the outliers of the data distribution. The Central Limit Theorem is defined as follows: If y is the random variable that is the sum of lots of random variables: $y = y_1 + y_2 + ... + y_n$, then the probability that $z = \frac{y - \mu_y}{\sigma_y}$ is between values k_1 and k_2 (for $k_1 < k_2$) is approximately the same for any such y and is $\approx \int_{k_1}^{k_2} \frac{e^{-z^2/2}}{\sqrt{2\pi}} dz$. The function $\frac{e^{-z^2/2}}{\sqrt{2\pi}}$ is called a normal (called as Gaussian). Central limit theorem proves that approximately 95 percentages of all values of the distribution fall within 2σ of μ of normal distribution. In this present work, the sample $y = y_1 + y_2 + ... + y_n$ is drawn from the population X. The sampling process is repeated for large number of times such that each x appeared at least in one sample. A set of parameters $(\mu_{\bar{x}}, \sigma_{\bar{x}})$ are computed for $\forall x \in X$. The set of parameters are denoted as $\zeta^2 = \{p : (\mu_{\bar{x}}, \sigma_{\bar{x}}) \in p, \; f_1 : x \mapsto \mu_{\bar{x}} \; and \; f_2 : x \mapsto \sigma_{\bar{x}} \; for \forall x \in X\}$. The upper and lower bounds of the distribution of $\forall x \in X$ are defined as $b_u^x = \mu_{\bar{x}} + \frac{2\sigma_{\bar{x}}}{\sqrt{n}}$ and $b_l^x = \mu_{\bar{x}} - \frac{2\sigma_{\bar{x}}}{\sqrt{n}}$. The set of bounds is denoted as $B^2 = \{b^x : (b_u^x, b_l^x) \in b^x, \; f_{ub} : p \mapsto b_u^x \; and \; f_{lb} : p \mapsto b_l^x \; for \forall p \in \zeta^2\}$.

3.2. *Bandwidth selection and Standardization of Metrics*

The data preprocessing plays crucial roles, as each metric space X in the set of metric M are in different units and scale. All metrics $x \in X$ should have the same scale for a fair comparison between them, and derive the performance index. In the present study, standardization technique is used to convert the metric values into standard score: $\int : x \mapsto x' \; for \forall x \in X$. The standard score $x' \; for \forall x' \in X'$ is computed as follows: $x' = \frac{x - \mu}{\sigma}$, the parameter set $\zeta^2 = \{p : (\mu, \sigma) \in p\}$ is the mean and standard deviation of the population. Bounds, $(b_u^{x'}, b_l^{x'})$ for the distribution of standard score x' is defined by computing upper bound $b_u^{x'} = \mu_{x'} + 2\sigma_{x'}$ and lower bound $b_l^{x'} = \mu_{x'} - 2\sigma_{x'}$. In the present study the bandwidth is defined in the range $[l_l, u_l]$. The bounds are mapped into bandwidth as $b_l^{x'} \mapsto l_l$ and $b_u^{x'} \mapsto u_l$, higher the metric value, higher the desirability. Otherwise, the mapping is $b_l^{x'} \mapsto u_l$ and $b_u^{x'} \mapsto l_l$. After mapping the bounds for distribution of x' into bandwidth $[l_l, u_l]$, the standard scores $x' \in X'$ are converted into standardized metric score by using the linear transformation function.

4. Fuzzy logic model for evaluating the performance index

The output from the bandwidth selection and the standardization of metrics is the set of metrics $X' = (x_1', x_2', x_3', ..., x_s')$. A set of metrics $X' = \{x' : |X'| = s\}$ is the input space to be evaluated by using the fuzzy logic algorithm. In the present study, the input space reduction is employed by using the distance based clustering technique to have the upper limit on the size of the input space. The transformed input crisp data space to the system is $\Re=\{r: l_l \le r \le u_l \;\&|\Re|=\mathfrak{A}\}$. The performance index $pi \in PI$ is the output space of the fuzzy logic system. The universe of discourse $[l_l, u_l]$ is considered for $\forall r \in \Re$ on which fuzzy sets are defined to represent the concept of vague classes. The principal elements involved in the fuzzy logic system are as follows: fuzzification of input variables, fuzzy knowledge-base, fuzzy inference engine and defuzzification.

4.1. *Fuzzification Interface*

This fuzzification interface maps the crisp value of the input metric space into fuzzy sets which define linguistic values. The crisp input data space to the fuzzy logic system is $\Re=\{r: l_l \le r \le u_l \; for \, \forall r \in \&|\Re|=\mathfrak{A}\}$. The fuzzy logic system evaluate pi by using the fuzzy knowledge system (i.e., $\Re \mapsto pi$). The fuzzy set (set of linguistic variables) is defined corresponding to each metric $r \in \Re$ as $F^r=\{f_1^r, f_2^r, \ldots, f_c^r\}$. The universe of discourse is defined corresponding to each $f_c^r \in F^r$ as $V^r=\{v_i^r : i=1,2,\ldots,c \text{ and } v_i^r \in \mathbb{R}\}$. The function $\mu_{f^r}(v^r)$ is defined as the fuzzy membership function, where $f^r \in F^r$. The triangular membership function is considered in this paper as follows: $\mu_{f^r}(r)=\max\left(\min\left(\frac{r-a'}{b'-a'},\frac{c'-r}{b'-a'}\right),0\right)$, where $a',b',c' \in v_i^r$. For each value of $r \in \Re$, $\mu_{f^r}(r)$ has value between 0 and 1 for $\forall f^r \in F^r$.

4.2. *Fuzzy Knowledge Base*

This contains IF-THEN rules and fuzzy statements, the meaning of fuzzy rules are specified by using linguistic terms defined by their membership functions. Based on the observation of antecedent variables and consequent variables, the fuzzy implication rules are defined in this study as follows: IF $r_1 \in F^{r_1} \wedge r_2 \in F^{r_2} \wedge \ldots \wedge r_{\mathfrak{A}} \in F^{r_{\mathfrak{A}}}$, Then $\lambda \in \xi$, where $\xi=\{\lambda_1, \lambda_2, \ldots, \lambda_{c'}\}$ is the fuzzy set corresponding to the implication space. The fuzzy rule set is defined as $\vartheta=\{\upsilon_1, \upsilon_1, \ldots \upsilon_\omega\}$ where $|\vartheta|=\omega$. The universe of discourse is defined corresponding to the implication space as $\varpi=\{\kappa_1, \kappa_2, \ldots, \kappa_{c'}\}$. The triangular membership function $\mu_\lambda(r')=\max\left(\min\left(\frac{r'-a'}{b'-a'},\frac{c'-r'}{b'-a'}\right),0\right)$ is defined for the fuzzy set of implication space, where $a',b',c' \in \kappa_{c'}$.

4.3. *Fuzzy Inference Engine*

Fuzzy inference engine employs the fuzzy operators on IF part of the fuzzy rule and generate fuzzy output value corresponding to THEN part of each fuzzy rule. When the fuzzy rules are activated by an input vector $\Re$, the output of each rule υ represents the contribution to the performance index to be measured. Let $\mu_{f^{r_1}}(v^{r_1}), \mu_{f^{r_2}}(v^{r_2}), \ldots, \mu_{f^{r_{\mathfrak{A}}}}(v^{r_{\mathfrak{A}}})$ are degree of membership of a given input vector $\Re$ in the universe of discourse F^r corresponding to fuzzy rule $\upsilon \in \vartheta$. The $\mu_\lambda(\kappa)$ is the membership function in the implication space derived from the fuzzy rule $\upsilon \in \vartheta$. The membership function in the implication space is defined as follows: $\mu_\lambda(\kappa)=\mu_{f^{r_1}}(v^{r_1}) \wedge \mu_{f^{r_2}}(v^{r_2}) \wedge \ldots \wedge \mu_{f^{r_{\mathfrak{A}}}}(v^{r_{\mathfrak{A}}})$, if $F^{r_1}=F^{r_2}$ for $\forall r \in \Re$;

$$\mu_\lambda(\kappa)=\frac{\mu_{f^{r_1}}(v^{r_1})+\mu_{f^{r_2}}(v^{r_2})+\ldots+\mu_{f^{r_{\mathfrak{A}}}}(v^{r_{\mathfrak{A}}})}{\mathfrak{A}}, \text{ otherwise.}$$

4.4. *Defuzzification Interface*

Defuzzification interface transforms the fuzzy output into crisp (nonfuzzy) data. Corresponding to each $\mu_\lambda(\kappa)$ in the implication space, the value $r'(\kappa)$ is measured in the implication space by using the function $\mu_\lambda(r')=\max\left(\min\left(\frac{r'-a'}{b'-a'},\frac{c'-r'}{b'-a'}\right),0\right)$. The centre of area method (COA) is used to find out the crisp output pi corresponding to the input vector $\Omega=\{x': x' \in X' \& \Omega \subseteq X'\}$ to the fuzzy logic system. The crisp output pi is defined as follows:

$$pi=\frac{(\mu_\lambda(\kappa_1)\times r'(\kappa_1))+(\mu_\lambda(\kappa_2)\times r'(\kappa_2))+\ldots+(\mu_\lambda(\kappa_{c'})\times r'(\kappa_{c'}))}{\mu_\lambda(\kappa_1)+\mu_\lambda(\kappa_2)+\ldots+\mu_\lambda(\kappa_{c'})}.$$

5. Case Study

A case study has been conducted in one of the business units of the IT industry, *Cybernet-Slashsupport* (CSS), located at Chennai in India. Business processes of technical executives in the organization are monitored and tracked every day by Call Management System (CMS). The upper bound (i.e., target value) and the lower bound (i.e., acceptable level) are defined based on the past data by running the proposed outlier detection algorithm. The statistical model fixes the bounds with respect to each metric by estimating parameters of past data. The metrics defined for the analysis are as follows: Average Handling Time (AHT); Call Resolution Ratio (CRR); Average Staffed Time (AST); Average Break AUX (ABAUX); Average Call Queue Time (ACQT); First Call Resolution (FCR); Customer Satisfaction (CSAT); Average Staffed Time Deviation (ASTD). The metrics are classified into three groups, namely Time Management (TM), Call Management (CM), and Customer Response (CR). The group of metrics, TM, CM, and CR is the input for fuzzy logic algorithm. Input space for the fuzzy logic system is the set of metrics and the output space is the Performance Index of an employee.

The computational experiment is conducted for three hundred employees. The upper bound and lower bound defined for the metric Average Handling Time by the Central Limit theorem are shown in Figure 1. The distribution of group of metrics corresponding to TM, CM and CR are shown in Figure 2 to 4. The Figure 5 shows the distribution of input space to the fuzzy logic system. The fuzzy logic algorithm obtained the Performance Index (PI) and the distribution of Performance Index is shown in Figure 6.

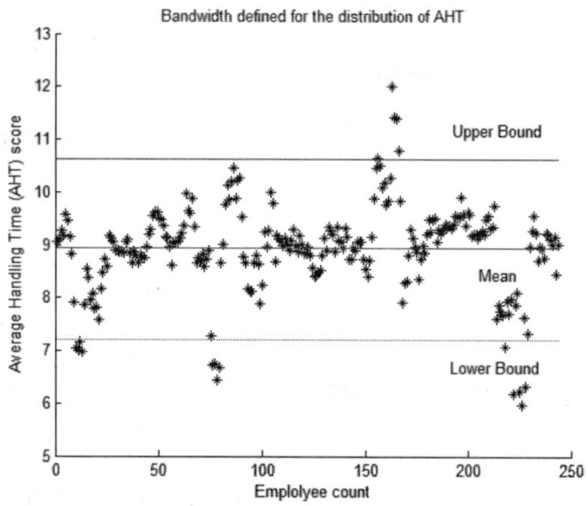

Figure 1. Bandwidth defined by the Central Limit Theorem for the distribution of Average Handling Time

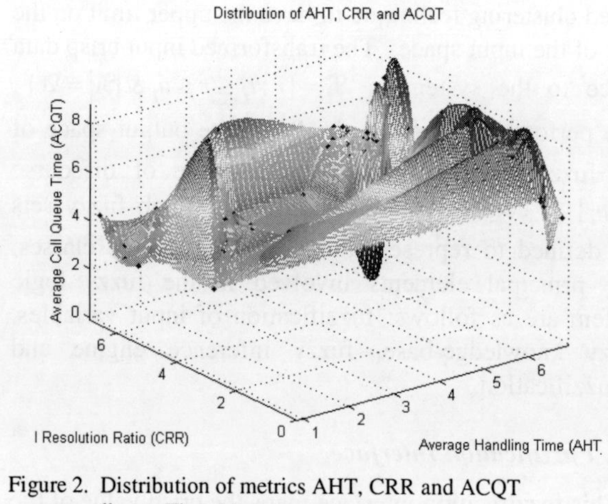

Figure 2. Distribution of metrics AHT, CRR and ACQT corresponding to Time Management

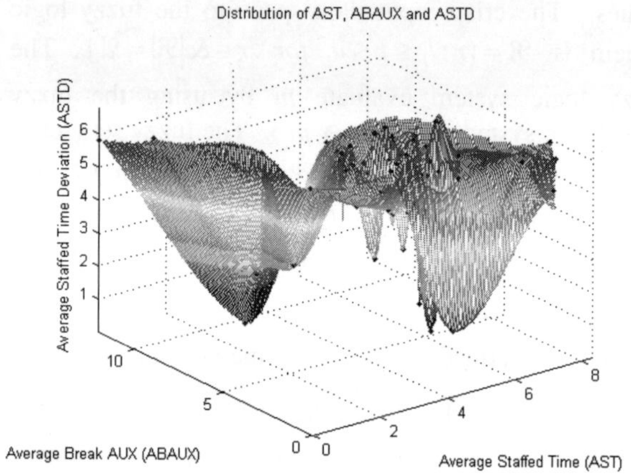

Figure 3. Distribution of metrics AST, ABAUX and ASTD corresponding to Call Management.

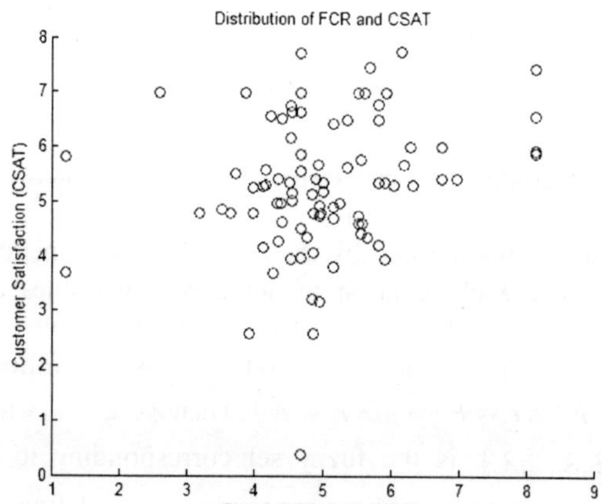

Figure 4. Distribution of metrics FCR and CSAT corresponding to Customer Response.

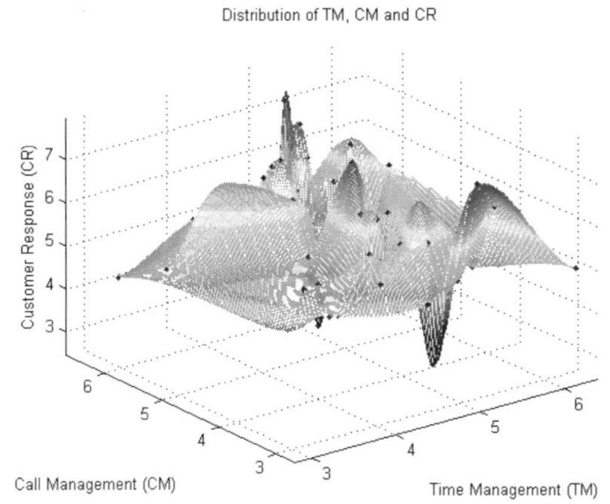

Figure 5. Distribution of metrics TM, CM and CR corresponding to Work Performance.

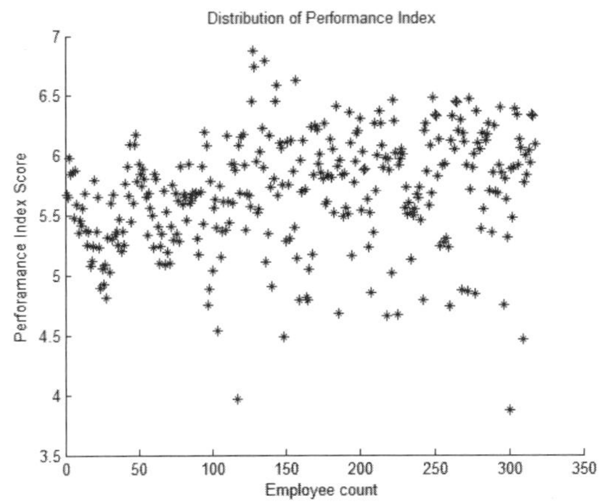

Figure 6. Distribution of Performance Index Score obtained by Fuzzy logic algorithm.

6. Conclusion

The present study proposed an outlier detection algorithm to identify outliers and define bandwidth to the distribution of metric. Standardization technique is used to convert each metric space having different unit and time scale into dimensionless data space. The dimensionless metric space is given as an input for the proposed fuzzy logic algorithm and the fuzzy logic algorithm evaluates the performance index corresponding to the group of metrics. A case study is conducted in technical support department of *Cybernet-Slashsupport,* and a computational experiment has been conducted for 189 employees and the results have demonstrated that the proposed approach is able to predict the performance index from the input data with different unit and time scale. The study can be extended in future to cluster metrics based on the similarity between them and performance index can be evaluated with respect to each cluster.

Acknowledgments

The author thanks Umashankar N, Head of the CIO Group, CSS and Vidyadhar N, Manager of the CIO Group for their support in this research work; Shivi Kalia and Krishnan Rangi, Directors of HR department, CSS for their support in getting data; and Kuamara Raja Singh G, Business Analyst, CIO Group, CSS for his inputs during the research discussion.

References

1. R. Bretz, G. Milkovich and W. Read, "The current state of performance appraisal research and practice: concerns, directions, and implications," *Journal of Management*, vol. 18, pp. 321-352, 1992.
2. B. G. Amidan, T.A. Ferryman and S. K. Cooley, "Data outlier detection using the Chebyshev theorem," *IEEE Aerospace Conference*, Digital Object Identifier 10.1109/AERO.2005.1559688, pp. 3814-3819, March, 2005.
3. J. Han and M. Kamber, *Data Mining, Concepts and Technique*. San Francisco: Morgan Kaufmann, 2001.
4. F. Angiulli, S. Basta, and C. Pizzuti, "Distance-Based Detection and Prediction of Outliers", IEEE Transactions on Knowledge and Data Engineering, Vol. 18, No. 2, pp. 145-160, 2006.
5. T. Yunxin and P. Dechang, "Unifying Density-Based Clustering and Outlier Detection", Second International Workshop on Knowledge Discovery and Data Mining, IEEE Computer Society, pp.644-647, 2009.
6. H. W. Jung, "A linear programming model dealing with ordinal ratings in policy capturing of performance appraisal," *European Journal of Operational Research*, vol. 134, pp. 493-497, 2001.
7. L. A. Zadeh, "Fuzzy sets," *Information and Control*, vol. 8, pp. 338-352, 1965.
8. R. Narasimhan , "A fuzzy subset characterization of a site-selection problem," *Decision Sciences*, vol. 10, no. 4, pp. 618-628, 1979.
9. A. Shaout, and M. A. Shammari, "Fuzzy logic modeling for performance appraisal systems A framework for empirical evaluation," *Expert Systems with Applications*, vol.14, pp. 323-328, 1998.

INFLUENCE OF LEARNING COMMUNITIES AND COLLABORATIVE LEARNING ON STUDENTS' SUCCESS

MUŠIĆ DENIS, AZEMOVIĆ JASMIN

Faculty of Information Technology, University "Džemal Bijedić"
Mostar, Bosnia and Herzegovina

ČATRNJA ELMIR

Faculty of Pedagogy, University "Džemal Bijedić"
Mostar, Bosnia and Herzegovina

FITCS as a faculty platform for students' collaboration and socialization presents very active and attended online community. Its primer goal was to enable and support intensive communication, collaborative activities in small students groups, use of different knowledge archives etc. It was already determined that FITCS fulfils one of its implementation goals – supports knowledge sharing. In order to get more precise conclusion about influence of online community on the students' success, this research has the main goal to find possible relations between a student's grades on a course and his activity inside the online community.

1. Introduction

Application of new technologies in learning environments has considerably changed the forms of education. Usage of WWW (World Wide Web) as instructional medium provides us the possibility to eliminate the time and location constraints and incorporate interactive communication between students and educators. Distance learning, as one of the educational fields that focuses on the pedagogy, technology, and instructional system design that aims to deliver education to students, has become very popular.

As a result of potential demand, FIT (Faculty of Information Technologies) which educates the qualified IT specialists established distance learning study six years ago. Distance learning study made FIT more accessible to adult learners who would otherwise be unable to attend classes or obtain a college degree. In order to support the distance learning educational process, FIT Team (developers from software engineering institute) developed a platform called DLWMS (Distance Learning Web Management System) which integrates the traditional method of teaching based on the following approach: Web-textbooks, audio/video presentations, .pdf (Portable Document Format) document plus tests as the main tool to control the learning process.

By using DLWMS, students are mostly engaged in individual activities and less in collaborative dialogues. However, current studies are mostly focused on the design and implementation of more active and collaborative methods of teaching and learning. Many of these methods (collaborative learning, etc.) are based on constructivist and behaviorist learning theories, and are more aligned with skills needed today and in the future.

After two years of experience in distance learning education, it was clear that DLWMS needs to be additionally strengthened with components for socialization and collaboration. Therefore, FIT Team integrated components called FITCS (Faculty of Information Technologies Community Services) which were primarily designed for knowledge sharing and contain the following elements: forum, blog, gallery, RSS feeds, download/exchange section, Wiki, FITZine (faculty online magazine) etc. FITCS enabled intensive communication, collaborative activities in small groups of students, use of different knowledge archives, critical thinking, etc. FITCS was accessible and used by distance learning and regular (in-site) students.

FITCS was implemented in April 2005. and after four years of existence, system comprises more than 2000 registered users (only students) and more than 145 000 posts. These numbers represent summary in all sections of FITCS which includes global discussions, private messages, anonymous comments, blogs, etc. By visiting FITCS, we can verify the fact that FITCS presents very active and attended community platform. However, attendees and activities can't be a guarantee of knowledge sharing and ensure positive impact on students' success. In order to get more precise conclusion about influence of online community on students' success, this research has the main goal to find possible relations between a student's grade (as one of the success measures) on a course and his activity inside online community. Therefore, in this paper we are trying to prove the hypothesis that: student's activity inside online course group has a positive impact on the student's success.

Although they increase the opportunities to organize student groups, instruct students and support student learning, some authors argue about disadvantages of online learning environments. As one of the main disadvantages, authors [5] indicate the time and energy required of faculty staff to achieve the real potential of online learning environments. Our experience confirms these facts, but we truly believe that the invested time and energy must contribute to students' success. Also, it is important to refer to one research [2] which was conducted with the goal to investigate if FITCS has characteristics of a social network, identify actors in the network according to their roles, and to check if roles of the principal actors are adequate to those they should have in a knowledge sharing community. Aforesaid research tried to check the following hypothesis: H1: educator and technical staff have proper roles as recommended in a knowledge sharing community, H2: stars of the social network are the most successful students, H3: FITCS supports knowledge sharing. Results of this research are not in favor of hypothesis H1, but on the other hand, hypothesis H2 is confirmed. Some of the most successful students, with extrovert personalities, are the stars of the three analyzed networks. Hypothesis H3 was confirmed by the fact that most of the students (85%-90%) have accepted this way of communication, and that there is a very small number of isolated vertices.

2. Data collection and analysis

Our research uses data which are collected from our faculty platforms (DLWMS & FITCS). In order to perform analysis, during data collection we had to apply many filtering procedures. In the last few years we tried to reduce the number of so-called spammers inside online course groups (spammers are students who tend to write posts irrelevant to the course topic). Decrease of spam is made thanks to the significant activities of the educators who monitor students' work and guide them through process of knowledge sharing. During data collection we excluded posts which were made by identified spammers. Therefore, as the object of our research we observed all FITCS registered users' posts made inside forum groups related to the individual courses. Number of observed posts is near to the 70 000. In order to retain the confidentiality of the student we filtered data by student's identification number (ID). Usage of ID number enables us to collect all online community data concerning that student. Demographically, students in the research were predominantly distance learning students (69.2%), but it is important to mention the fact that some of the distance learning students occasionally attend classes.

At the beginning of the research we analyzed two courses by using two different approaches. One of the analyzed courses is held on the first year (Introduction to programming named UPR) and the other on the second year (Introduction to databases named UBP). In order to select appropriate courses for the analysis, we used level of the students' dropout rate. It has been shown that students of the first two years have certain difficulties on these courses.

Table 1. UPR course - student's grades.

	First group		Second group	
grade	*no*	%	*no*	%
5	47	31,3%	60	42,0%
6	37	24,7%	28	19,6%
7	24	16,0%	23	16,1%
8	18	12,0%	15	10,5%
9	14	9,3%	13	9,1%
10	10	6,7%	4	2,8%

Table 2. UBP course - student's grades.

UBP				
	First group		Second group	
grade	*no*	%	*no*	%
5	55	59,8%	57	65,5%
6	7	7,6%	5	5,7%
7	10	10,9%	9	10,3%
8	10	10,9%	15	17,2%
9	7	7,6%	1	1,1%
10	3	3,3%	0	0,0%

Table 3. UPR course – summary of students' activity and grades

Grade	Number of posts	Number of students	Average number of posts
5	902	107	8,4
6	935	65	14,4
7	791	47	16,8
8	489	33	14,8
9	555	27	20,6
10	428	14	30,6

Table 4. UBP course – summary of students' activity and grades.

Grade	Number of posts	Number of students	Average number of posts
5	1002	112	8,9
6	218	12	18,2
7	99	19	5,2
8	223	25	8,9
9	189	8	23,6
10	98	3	32,7

Table 5. Summary of students' grades on six courses

Grade	UPR	UBP	MAT	PR 1	PR 2	DBM S	Average
5	8	9	8	8	8	17	9,67
6	14	19	12	11	13	16	14,17
7	16	5	17	19	21	12	15,00
8	14	9	13	17	13	25	15,17
9	19	'24	22	22	13	10	18,33
10	29	34	30	23	32	20	28,00

2.1. *Analysis – The first approach*

The first approach was to split students in two different groups. The first group was populated with students that posted 5 or more posts, and the second with students that posted less than 5 posts. This way we get two groups that are roughly the same size. Next, for each group we count the number of students that get the same grade. Results for each course are presented in Table 1 and Table 2.

Graphical representations of Table 1 and Table 2 are given on Figure 1. It can be seen that the percentage of students who passed the course is greater among the students who posted more. Although that difference is marginal, it is also worth mentioning that students, who posted more, got top level grades (9 and 10) in comparison to the "less post" group.

Our hypothesis was that students, who post more, have better grades (5-lowest, 10-highest). Thus, there should be a significant statistical difference between these two groups concerning their grades. Using students' T-Test we find out that for UBP $p>0.05$, so there cannot be shown that there is statistically significant difference between these two groups.

It is interesting to mention, that the same conclusion is drawn when other courses are observed. Thus, we decided to try another approach.

2.2. *Analysis – The second approach*

In the second approach we observed the whole group and look at the number of posts that students had concerning their final grade. Results summary for UPR and UBP respectively is shown in Table 3. and Table 4.

By looking at the graphics (Figure 2.) it is easy to see that students who achieved better results (higher grades) posted more. This brings us to a very important question: can we consider this conclusion as a general rule?

Accordingly, we have examined this relationship on wider set of data, and taken into account six courses (UPR, UBP, MAT– Mathematics, PR1– Programming 1, PR2 – Programming 2, DBMS – Database management systems). The same reasoning was drawn as above and average of all of data was taken. Data and the according graph are given in Table 5 and Figure 3. Correlation between grades and average posts was determined, and it is 0.71, which is not a linear correlation, but there is some significance. Based on the calculation results we can conclude that students who posted more get better grades. Once again we emphasize the fact that the term posted relates to knowledge sharing and students collaboration.

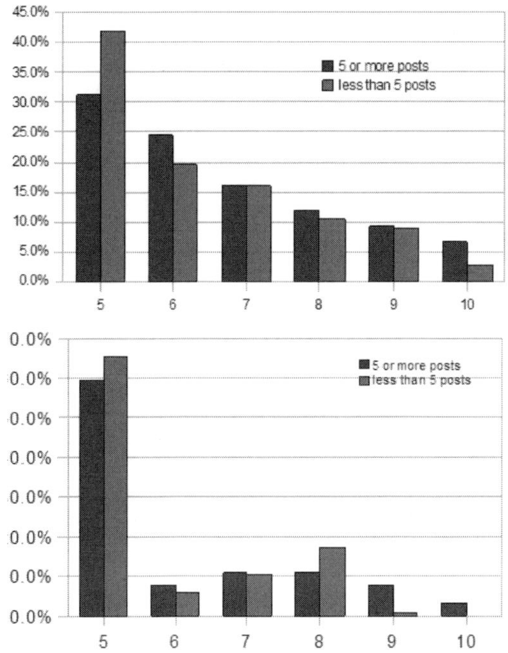

Figure 1. Graphical representation of students' success on UPR and UBP courses.

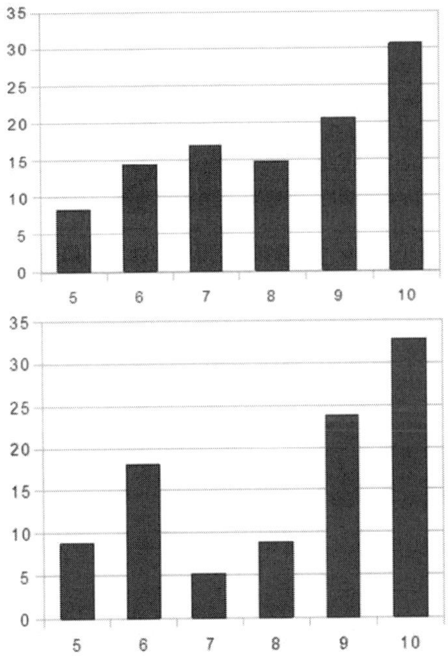

Figure 2. Graphical representation of students' success and number of posts on UPR and UBP courses.

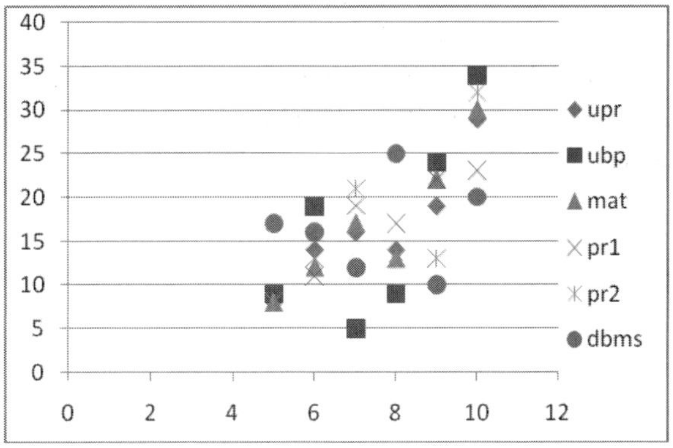

Figure 3. Graphical representation of students' grades and average number of posts on six courses.

3. Conclusion and future work

Although, our research didn't produce very significant results, it can help set some usable bearings for future research. It has shown that there could be some connection between students' grades and number of posts as we saw in the second approach, but this connection is not too strong because there is not statistically significant difference between our two groups, as is shown in the first approach. There is a chance, though, that through adapting of our database and collecting more valuable data, we could get more conclusive results. During this research we have encountered some difficulties.

The first difficulty is that from our database we couldn't make precise distinction between students that scored 5 (negative grade) and students that didn't take the exam at all. Furthermore, the number of fails is not counted at all. It would be interesting to be able to see if students who post more have less fails than students who don't.

The second difficulty is previously stated spam. It would be of great assistance if every post was graded by post readers. That way we could do a research only by using posts that were positively graded.

In any of these cases, adapting the database is easily done, but time is needed to collect reasonable amount of data.

The third difficulty is that we didn't have two independent test groups. It would be ideal if we had one group that used forum and the other that was denied the usage of the collaboration platform (or even a third group that could only read, but couldn't post). The way we "created" control group (students that posted less than 5 posts) was not really scientific, but it was the best we could do, given the data we collected. This obstacle cannot be solved as easy as the previous two because it is not appropriate to deny the usage of forum to some students.

References

1. *Online Learning Communities and Collaborative Learning*; http://www.iienetwork.org/?p=41543
2. I. Hamulić, N. Bijedić, *Social network analysis in virtual learning community at faculty of information technologies* (fit), Mostar, World Conference on Educational Sciences, (2009)
3. Michael K. Swan and Diane H. Jackman, *Comparing the Success of Students Enrolled in Distance Education Courses vs. Face–to–Face Classrooms*, Journal Articles, ISSN-1071-6084, (2000)
4. W.David, *An Analysis Of The Effect Of Distance Learning Site On Student Self-Efficacy Of Junior High School Spanish Students*, Dissertation Prepared for the Degree of Doctor of education, (2004)
5. C. McInnis, *The impact of technology on faculty performance and its evaluation,* New Directions for Institutional Research, 114, pp. 53-61, (2002)
6. R. Hogan, *Analysis of Student Success in Distance Learning Courses Compared to Traditional Courses*, Sixth Annual Conference on Multimedia in Education and Industry, Chattanooga, (1997)

UMLASSURE: A UML PROFILE ASSURING A SECURE SOFTWARE

MANISH THAPER

International Institute of Information Technology, Bangalore
Karnataka 560100, India. E-mail: manish.thaper@iiitb.ac.in

CHANDRASHEKAR RAMANATHAN

International Institute of Information Technology, Bangalore
Karnataka 560100, India. E-mail: rc@iiitb.ac.in

Ubiquity of software systems in human activities has been on the rise since later half of 1970s, which is marked as the early years of personal computers. Present day software solutions are pervasive. From pocket sized mobile phones and desktop solutions to critical controls in a nuclear power plant, all solutions are being complemented with logic coded in software solutions. Though it may not be wrong to vision that software solutions possesses the power to relinquish humans from large number of mundane tasks, the errors and failures in deployed or to-be-deployed software solutions raise question on authenticity of the former vision some times. Modeling languages such as UML, ADL, Formal methods though had (have) empowered software solution architects to model functional requirements of the software correctly; however, modeling solutions still need more attention to correctly interpret non-functional requirements such as reliability, performance and security. In this work, we present a software engineering technique to model a secure software system using UML extension UMLassure. Security models involve three entities called Actors, Assets and Actions. UML extension proposed in this work focuses on entity called Actions.

1. Introduction

There is no denial to the fact that there has been a significant increase in use of software systems in our lives. Automated software systems are taking over the human dominant activities of the past. Software solution(s) are not just catering to the trivial tasks such as preparing to-do lists, publishing documents; software solutions are also aiding humans in efficiently performing the very critical activities such as monitoring a nuclear power plant, controlling air traffic, and executing large financial transactions. At the same time it is vital to note that when a software application which gets deployed in a critical domain malfunctions, then the respective software application may lead to both tangible and intangible losses. Malfunctioning application can cause loss of customers to a business; loss of human trust in technology and in extreme cases, it can turn into loss of human lives. One of the famous examples to cite on failure of software system is Computer Aided Dispatch for London Ambulance Service (LASCAD) in year 1992[a]. Failures of LASCAD reportedly lead to loss of human lives. Another incident of security breach was recorded in January 2009 when the job seekers database maintained by Monster Worldwide Inc. was illegally accessed and job seekers personal information such as social security number was stolen[b]. It is further believed that the defects occurring due to failure to incorporate Non-Functional Requirements (NFRs) properly are difficult and time consuming to correct [1].

Software system requirement(s) can broadly be classified into a set of functional requirements, and a set of nonfunctional requirements. Functional requirements (FR) deal with business logic and Non-functional requirements (NFR) deal with system level properties such as performance, security, safety and reliability. Literature [1] and history in the software engineering illustrates that the failure in software systems may occur due to following -:

1. failure in elicitation of NFR
2. lack in integration of NFR to FR

The functional requirements for a software help us in modeling what needs to be done i.e. in identifying source and destination states to meet a business requirement The non-functional requirements for a software application help us in shaping how to reach the destined state from source state while meeting quality constraints such as usability, performance, security under acceptable limits. Figure 1 illustrates possible

[a] An analysis of the failure of the London Ambulance Service Computer Aided Dispatch system http://www.savive.com/casestudy/londonambulance.html

[b] Security notice to its user by Monster Worldwide Inc. http://help.monster.com/besafe/jobseeker/index.asp

paths [edges], states [SOURCE, DESTINATION] and pseudo state [ps1, ps2] to accomplish a task that is to implement business logic. However, non-functional requirements aid us to mark the set of acceptable states and paths [pseudo states and edges] to implement business logic correctly.

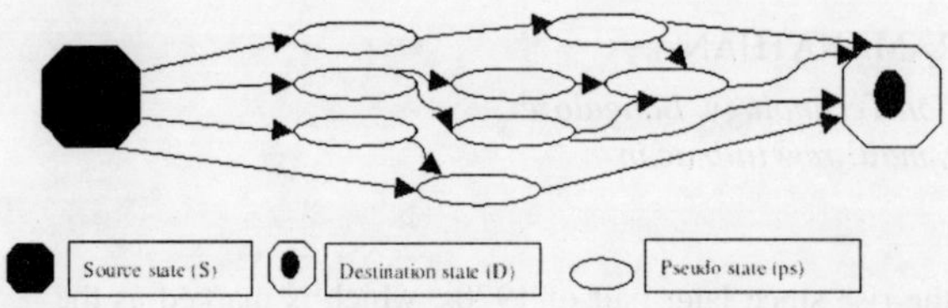

Figure 1. FR and NFR illustration

1.1. *Paper organization*

Section 2 will brief on reasons for choosing UML in this work. Section 3 will outline current state of the art in specifying security requirements using UML and UML extensions. Section 4 explains the approach devised in this work to model security requirements. Our proposed UML profile named *UMLassure* is detailed in Section 5. In Section 6, application of UMLassure using an example is detailed. The main ideas, limitations and future work are summarized in Section 7.

2. Why UML

The reasons for choosing the Unified Modeling Language UML as the modeling language for this work are as follows -:

1. UML is OMGs[c] most-used specification language, and the way global software engineers model not only applications' static, behavior, and architecture models, but also business process and data structures.
2. UML profile is a proven technique to tailor existing UML meta-model subset for business modeling (for example UML profile for software radio) and for a particular technology (for example UML profile for CORBA) [16] and [17].
3. UML, along with MOF (MetaObject Facility)[d] will provide the foundations of Model Driven Architecture [16].

[c] OMG Object Management Group. http://www.omg.org

[d] MetaObject Facility Foundation of industry standard environment by OMG; for model interchange between applications. For more details refer http://www.omg.org/mof/

3. Related Work

UML profile ([12], [13]) helps in extending existing UML modeling capabilities. Examples of related work cited from [9] includes, UML profile developed during CORAS project [5] and [6], which extend use cases to document attack scenarios. A UML profile named as *UMLsec* is described in [7] and [8]. *UMLsec* creates a new set of stereotypes and tagged values to specify security parameters. It uses OCL to add interpretation to the tagged values. *SecureUML* [4] cited from [9] provides a generic language, similar to UML, to specify security policies for the software application.

Cysneiros et al. [1] present an approach to specify NFR and later integrate the modeled NFR to FR. They use LEL (Language Extended Lexicon) to maintain a UofD Universe of Discourse). Using the available or newly added dictionary (UofD), non-functional requirements and functional requirements are modeled. Both NFR and FR are modeled using a common LEL, henceforth the integration of NFR to FR is easier and error minimalist. Pavlovski et al. [2] propose to complement a use case with a control case. The authors explain that the use case describes the functional requirements where-as a control case template expresses the non-functional requirements. An advantage of representing the NFR in control case is the easy-to-understand expressions for NFRs using proposed control case template. Furthermore, a single control case can be linked to a large number of use cases. Howard et al. [3] propose a threat modeling approach to model software security in the design phase. *"...A threat model is a security-based analysis that helps people determine the highest level security risks posed to the product and how attacks can manifest themselves.[3]"* Advantage of using threat modeling approach is that the graphical representation of threats using DFD notations. DFD notations are easily interpreted by software designers globally. However, this approach fails to propose any mechanism to incorporate or map modeled NFR to impacted set of FR's.

4. Proposed Approach

The work done in this paper shares a different approach to model security policies unlike illustrated in existing literature.

There are three active participants in a given security policy of a software system. Referring to Figure 2, participants are named as *Actors*, *Assets* and *Actions* [10]. *Actors* are the end users of the software system, both legal and illegal. *Assets* can be both tangible and intangible goods associated within or outside the system. Customer login information, customer social security number, or cost of equipment such as server, network routers are some examples of assets. *Actions* are the executable methods/procedures or messages. Example of methods may be printPayCheque(), transferMoney() or similar methods in the financial application. Actions are designed and implemented by the system for actors to control/work on assets.

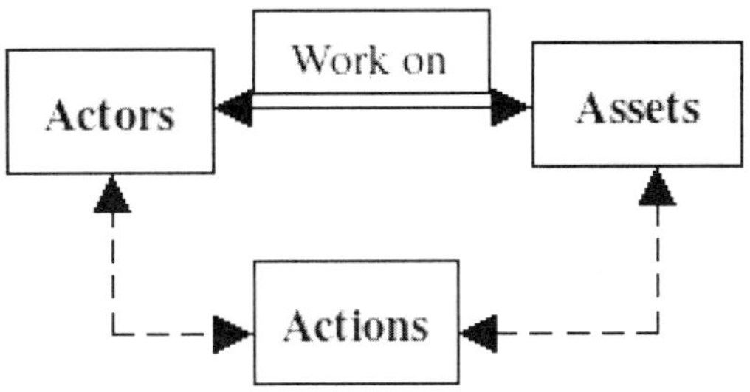

Figure 2. Actor, Assets and Actions relationship

The approach applied in this work is focused on controlling how Actions are modeled, implemented and interacted within a system with motivation to mitigate the security threats for a software system. Sometimes Actions may be less harmful; however because of the low accountability, uncontrolled Actions may cause damages in a software system [10]. The work done in this paper to model secure actions will attempt to meet the following statement as cited in [10]:

"When considering assets, actions and actors; security is concerned with the protection of assets, ensuring the actions are appropriate and holding actors responsible for their actions"

The above statement is the motivation to specify security in design phase and implementing the security models in subsequent phases of the software development in order to deliver a healthy software solution.

5. UML profile *UMLassure*

UMLassure[e] is a UML profile which will add new stereotypes, tagged values to extend existing UML meta-model. UMLassure will use existing UML diagrams such as class diagrams, activity diagrams to model the static and behavioral model for the software application. OCL will be used in defining constraints for easier interpretation of model elements.

5.1. *A brief explanation of stereotypes used*

1. <<bufferoverflow>> : Stereotype to model buffer-flow checks. It has tagged value attribute named 'size' which limits the size of input to an attribute.
2. <<privatesetter>> : Stereotype to prevent access to private class attribute from public methods defined outside the class.
3. <<sqlinjection>> : Stereotype to define a constraint on input text field in a software application which prevents the input field from taking a malicious SQL code as input. Tagged value 'detectRegExSQL' is set to the validating regular expression.
   <<validateXSS>> : Stereotype to define a constraint on input text field in a software application which prevents the input field from taking a malicious XSS scripts as input. Tagged value 'detectRegExXSS' is set to the validating regular expression.

Table 1. UMLassure proposed stereotypes details

Stereotype [Tagged Values]	**Constraints**
<<bufferoverflow>> [attributeName, attributeSize]	Sizeof(attributeName) <=attributeSize

<<privatesetter>> [accessSpecifier]	if((self.attributeName)
	intersection
	(self.BehavioralMethod
	attributeName))==
	"Not Empty" then
	if (readAccessSpecifier
	(self.BehavioralMethod-
	>
	attributeName==
	"Private") then
	self.BehavioralMethod
	.accessSpecifier
	=="Private" else
	return true
	endif
	endif
	
	//Comments
	readAccessSpecifier()
	: will
	determine whether
	parsed attribute

[e] The threats types to be modeled in the profile such as bufferoverflow, sqlinjection and XSS have been chosen from OWASPs official website [14]; top 10 security threats [15].
More on examples of regular expression to detect SQL injection or XSS attacks are available on Security Focus website: http://www.securityfocus.com /infocus/1768
For protection against SQL injection, XSS specifically for ASP.NET read Additional Resources sub-section at http://msdn.microsoft.com/enus/library/ms998271.aspx

	is declared as Private Public or Protected
<<sqlinjection>> [detectRegExSQL]	detectRegExSQL as an input constraint to check against SQL injection attack.
<<validateXSS>> [detectRegExXSS]	detectRegExXSS as an input constraint to constraint to detect XSS attack

6. Case Study

UMLassure is used in modeling a web portal "wearrangeevents.com". This web portal will play the role of a facilitator that will help corporates to determine suitable firms rendering event management services. The web portal will aid in making the best possible pair of corporate and available event management firm(s) to successfully organize an event.

6.1. *Examples*

Usecase: Login

1. User logs in with the given username and password.
2. User may change the login password.

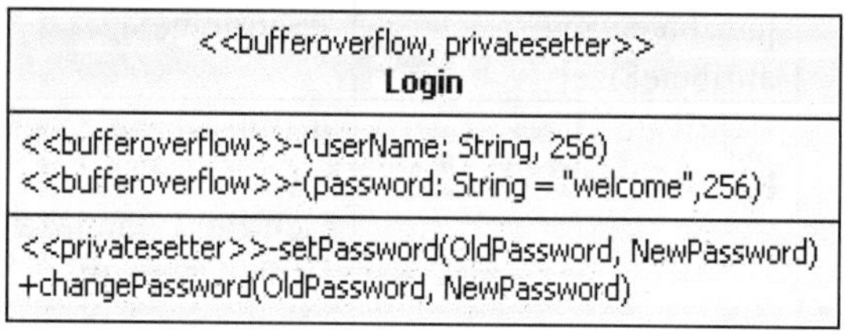

Figure 3. Login class diagram with UMLassure

Description of stereotype applied:

1. << bufferoverflow >> -(username: String, 256) Declares a non-functional constraint on maximum string length of login details i.e. userName and password can be String of 256 character long max.
2. << privatesetter >> - setPassword (OldPassword, NewPassword) Declares that a Class attribute with private access specifier e.g. Loginpassword; cannot be modified using a method with a public access specifier. Hence, ensures that the setter method defined using the private Class attribute can only be called by another method which is declared inside respective Classs body.

Usecase: Create company profile

1. Registered event management firm can create its company profile.
2. The firm can upload company's web link, create media library and add other advertisement details.

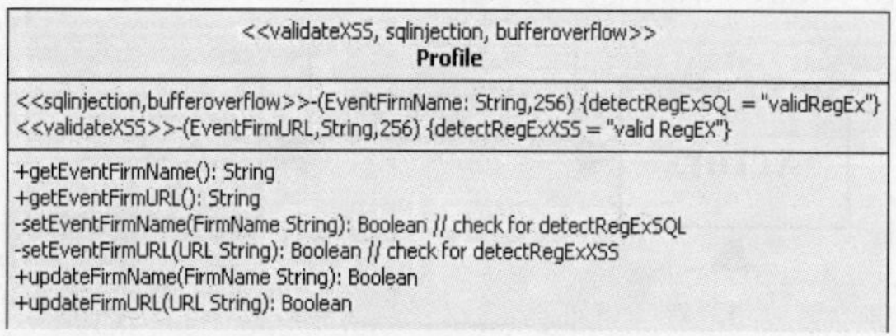

Figure 4. Create Company Profile class diagram with UMLassure

Description of stereotype applied:

1. << sqlinjection >> - (EventFirmName: String, 256) detectRegExSQL tagged value is a typical regular expression to detect SQL injection attack. Applied on attribute EventFirmName to ensure that malicious SQL script could not be entered into the input text field on the web portal.
2. << validateXSS >> - (EventFirmURL, String, 256) EventFirmURL must be validated against detectRegExXSS regular expression. The regular expression ensures that malicious javascript or other forms of XSS script could not be entered as value to attribute EventFirmURL.

6.2. *Benefits of UMLassure*

UMLassure, defined in this work, when applied to software design model will ensure that designers and developers will not end-up writing a poorly implemented code. On the contrary, the software engineers will write *Actions* which will provide a controlled access to expensive *Assets* through *Actors* involved in a software application. When comparing *UMLassure* with existing UML profiles for security, we find that *SecureUML*[4] defines role based access control (RBAC); *UMLsec* [7] and [8] focus on modeling encryption scenarios. Both *SecureUML* and *UMLsec* work on assets and actors whereas *UMLAssure* focuses on actions. *UMLintr* [9] does not specify intrusion constraints using OCL.

6.3. *Potential applications of UMLassure*

UMLassure uses the well understood and standardized techniques to extend UML meta-model, such as UML profiles, and further it uses OCL as its constraint specifying language. Hence, *UMLassure* attempts to map itself to OMGs MDA. *UMLassure* is a UML extension and as we know, extensions defined using UML have the motivation to model a software application closer to implementation level [16] and [17]. Hence, *UMLassure* when applied will help us in modeling secure software system with a step closer to implementation level; thus reducing the gap in *Platform Independent Model* (PIM) and *Platform Specific Model* (PSM) defined as in OMG MDA [11].

7. Conclusions and Future work

This paper introduced *UMLassure* profile as an extension to existing UML. *UMLassure* is unlike other available UML profiles models software security aspects in that this approach uses focuses on *Actions* and uses OCL. UML profile proposed in this paper demonstrates protection against attacks such as bufferoverflow, prevention against private attributes being modified by unintentionally coded public setter methods in a class, detecting SQLinjection and avoiding XSS attacks. Current limitation of the work presented here is that the work on security modeling done is in embryonic stage and captures only a very small set of security threats.

Future work is planned to be finished in different sub-phases. The current phase focused on improving modeling of security aware systems targeting *actions* for software system. An immediate follow up work will be to get automatic flags, code comments based on applied stereotypes to UML diagrams. These would serve as hints to the programmer to start with. Successful implementation of the former will improve code review process. And the later planned milestone is to integrate *UMLassure* to Model Driven Architecture proposed by OMG [11]. Integration to MDA will automatically generate implementation code from the designed models.

References

[1] Luiz Marcio Cysneiros, Julio Cesar Sampaio do Prado Leite. "Using UML to reflect non-functional requirements." *Proceedings of the 2001 conference of the Centre for Advanced Studies on Collaborative research.* p.2, November 05-07, 2001.Toronto, Ontario, Canada.

[2] Joe Zou, Christopher J. Pavlovski. "Modeling Architectural Non Functional Requirements: From Use Case to Control Case". *IEEE International Conference on e-Business Engineering (ICEBE'06).* 2006.

[3] Michael Howard and David LeBlanc. *"Writing Secure Code."* 2nd ed. Microsoft Press, 2003

[4] D. Basin; J. Doser and T. Lodderstedt. "Model Driven Security: From UML Models to Access Control Infrastructures." *ACM Transactions on Software Engineering and Methodology.* Vol.15, No. 1, January 2006, Pages 3991.

[5] Lund, M., Braber, F., Stolen, K., and Vraalsen, F. "A UML Profile for the Identification and Analysis of Security Risks during Structured Brainstorming." *Technical report, SINTEF ICT.* May 2004.

[6] Lund, M., Hogganvik, I., Seehusen, F., and Stolen, K., UML Profile for Security Assessment." *Technical report, SINTEF ICT.* November 2003.

[7] Jurjens, J., "Towards Development of Secure Systems using UML." In H. Hubmann, editor, *Fundamental Approaches to Software Engineering (FASE/ETAPS, International conference).* Lecture Notes in Computer Science, Springer, Genova, Italy, 2001.

[8] Jurjens, J., *"Secure System Development with UML."* Springer-Verlag, 2005.

[9] Mohammed Hussein and Mohammad Zulkernine. "UMLintr:A UML Profile for Specifying Intrusions." *Proceedings of the 13th Annual IEEE International Symposium and Workshop on Engineering of Computer Based Systems (ECBS06).* 2006.

[10] Markus Schumacher et al. *"Security patterns: integrating security and systems engineering."* John Wiley and Sons, Ltd. 2006

[11] "Model Driven Architecture." - http://www.omg.org/mda

[12] "UML Superstructure, OMG Unified Modeling Language (OMG UML), Superstructure." V2.1.2. 2003; http://www.omg.org/spec/UML/2.1.2/Superstructure/PDF

[13] James Rumbaugh, Ivar Jacobson and Grady Booch. *"The Unified Modeling Language Reference Manual."* 2nd ed. Low Price Edition. Pearson Education Inc. 2006.

[14] "OWASP official site." - https://www.owasp.org/index.php/Main Page

[15] "OWASP top 10 threat list." - https://www.owasp.org/index.php/Top 10 2007

[16] "OMGs official UML documentation site." - http://www.uml.org/#Articles

[17] "OMGs UML profile catalogue." - http://www.omg.org/technology/documents/profile_catalog.htm

PROBABILISTIC APPROACH FOR AUTONOMOUS NAVIGATION USING STEREO VISION

PUNEET KUMAR
Student Computer Engineering Dept, Delhi College of Engineering, India
Member IEEE, puneetkumar.dce@gmail.com

NEHA KUMARI
Student BCA, JIMS Rohini, Delhi, India
neha46_dokania@yahoo.co.in

SHIVANGI SRIVASTAVA
Student Electrical Engineering Dept, Delhi College of Engineering, India
Member IEEE, shivangi.dce@gmail.com

This paper concerns an outdoor and indoor autonomous navigation algorithm using stereo vision camera as the environment sensing device. The algorithm integrates binocular stereo vision system along with proposed probabilistic navigation approach to form a robust robotic system for navigation in unstructured environment. We use probabilistic clearance approach to avoid obstacles along with the introduction of speed control function for sharper turning and more time for the navigator to detect additional nearby obstacles. We show stereo vision as a remarkable alternative to active sensing devices such as sonar and laser range finder. Our approach considers 3D point data and thus it is able to avoid hanging obstacles with insufficient ground clearance and chair like obstacles also. We introduce the concept of low cost navigators which is very important for industrial and daily life applications.

The algorithm has been successfully tested on an autonomous robot Lakshya- an Unmanned Ground Vehicle platform at Delhi College of Engineering, India.

Index Terms- Navigation, probabilistic clearance, disparity, triangulation, projection matrix, intrinsic and extrinsic parameters etc.

1. Introduction

Real time autonomous obstacle avoidance is in itself a challenging field of Robotics. Avoiding an obstacle is not a big deal but avoiding an obstacle smoothly and efficiently in both indoor and outdoor environment is what we need. We are interested in high speed operation of outdoor and indoor mobile robots for various applications. The main problem behind autonomous navigation is detecting and locating obstacles and steering between the obstacles efficiently. Here we consider issues related to collision avoidance while navigation so that a robot can avoid obstacles in front of it in sufficient time. Our approach uses stereo vision camera instead of LRF (Laser Range Finder) because most LRFs gives 2D scan data so therefore are unable to detect hanging obstacles and chair like obstacles but stereo vision camera gives 3D data so is capable of detecting hanging obstacles with insufficient clearance and chair like obstacles too. The second reason to replace LRF by stereovision camera is the high cost of good LRFs available in the market. This makes the proposed navigator highly cost effective and is suitable for industrial application.

Stereo Vision system has been used for obstacle avoidance during DARPA Grand challenge 2005 by Terra Max [9]. Real time collision avoidance for mobile robots is a good concept, and a large number of methods have been developed for different applications. In case of indoor robots they move at speeds where we don't bother about the dynamics of the robot [1]. The remarkable methods for these kind of robot navigation are Borestein and Koren's Vector Field Histogram (VFH) [2][8], dynamic window approach [3] and the curvature lane approach [4]. Fajen and Warren have proposed a model for obstacle avoidance by humans [5] which was again modified by Hammer et al [1].

Our approach of probabilistic obstacle avoidance is mainly concerned with the regions having maximum clearance and less angular separation relative to the robots heading. We calculate probabilistic clearance for different regions and we select the most suitable direction for navigation having highest confidence as the region with highest value of probabilistic clearance. The paper is organized as follow. We explain the specification of the navigator used in section 2. Section 3 explains the proposed algorithm along with the block diagram. Results and conclusions of the proposed work are discussed in section 4 and finally section 5 is used to discuss future work related to the proposed method.

2. System Architecture

The algorithm proposed has been successfully tested on an autonomous robot Lakshya- an UGV platform developed at Innovation Lab, Delhi College of Engineering, India under the leadership of Mr. Puneet Kumar (Technical Head) and Mr. Saurav Kumar. The robot is equipped with one bumble bee stereo vision camera, one GPS, two Quick silver servo motors and a Quad core processor. We used PGR library and Intel OpenCV Library along with Microsoft Visual Studio for programming..

3. The Proposed Algorithm

This section includes processing of stereovision data and then converting 3D data into equivalent 2D range data. This 2D range data is further used to calculate probabilistic clearance and finally the velocity control function is calculated after the positive peak removal from the probabilistic clearance data.

3.1. *Processing Stereo Data*

Stereo vision refers to the ability to infer information on the 3D structure and distance of a scene from two or more images taken from different viewpoints [2]. Despite the wealth of information contained in a photograph, the depth of a scene point along the corresponding projection ray is not directly accessible in a single image. With at least two pictures, depth can be measured through triangulation [3].

3.1.1. *Establishing Correspondence and calculating disparity map*

Determining which pixel in the left image corresponds to which pixel in the right image is basically the correspondence problem. The Epipolar constraint greatly limits the search for these correspondences from whole image to single Epipolar line only [6]. In fig 1, M is the object point, x and x' refers to same world point but in left and right images.

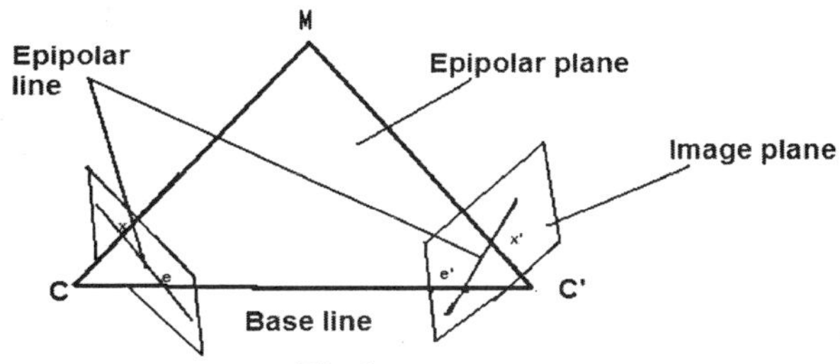

Fig 1

Disparity is the relative separation of the corresponded points. Two camera coordinates are related to each other by the rotation matrix R and translation matrix T.

$$X' = RX + T \qquad (1)$$

Fig 2

The point A_{left} in left image corresponds to the point A_{right} in right image. Cameras are horizontally aligned. Disparity for the feature A will be defined as $D(A) = x(A_{left}) - x(A_{right})$, where $x(A_{left})$ is the x coordinate of point A_{left} in the left image and $x(A_{right})$ is the x coordinate of point A_{right} in the right image.

3.1.2 *3D Location Calculation*

It is the depth information of points. It is calculated from the disparity and camera specifications, through triangulation.

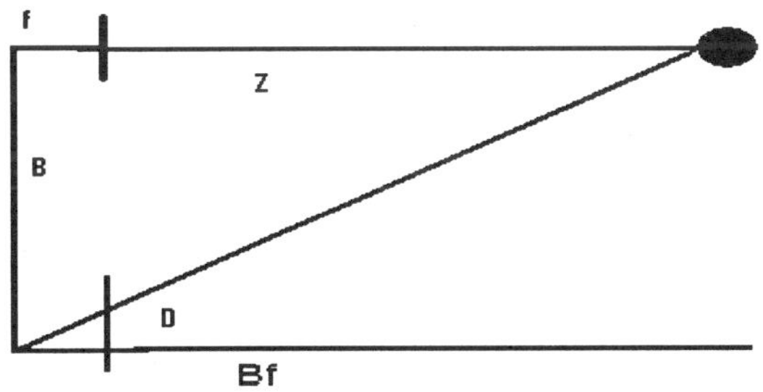

$$Z = \frac{Bf}{D}$$

Fig 3

Fig 3 shows the 1D stereo triangulation where, B is the baseline of the camera, f is the focal length of camera, D is the disparity value and Z is the depth of the point from the camera.

3.2. *Converting 3D depth data into equivalent 2D range data*

This section describes the conversion of stereo depth data into equivalent 2D range data.

3.2.1 *Converting Image coordinate into real world effective coordinate*

We calculate the real world coordinate of the object with respect to camera using cameras projection matrix. We use intrinsic and extrinsic parameters of the camera for this purpose [11]. This gives the coordinates of each space point with respect to camera.
We now select region of interest (ROI). Since the field of view of camera is so large that it's useless to process the whole 3D data. We limit the depth value by drawing an imaginary plane in real world with constant depth value. This can be done by assigning a threshold value of depth. Depth with magnitude greater than the threshold is assigned value equal to the threshold. This decreases the computation burden and makes the algorithm faster.

$$Z = \begin{cases} th, & if\ Z \geq th \\ Z, & else \end{cases} \quad (2)$$

where, th = threshold to decide distance of imaginary Z-plane from the navigator.
We now convert the depth map with coordinates with respect to camera into effective coordinate and effective depth map. For this purpose we create a window of width W. W can be chosen by the user depending upon the environment and the dimension of the robot. For environment with dense obstacles it should be small and for environment with largely separated obstacles it can be large for effective obstacle avoidance and good navigation. Let's say the resolution of the camera is $M \times N$. So we have now $M \times N$ coordinates containing depth information with respect to camera. To reduce the computation we will now convert $M \times N$ coordinates into K effective coordinates containing K depth values only. K is the nearest number obtained after division of number of rows by the window width.

$$K = \left\lceil \frac{M}{W} \right\rceil \quad (3)$$

So for a particular window, effective coordinates can be calculated as:

$$X_{eff} = \frac{\sum_{i=1}^{W} xi}{W} \quad (4)$$

$$Y_{eff} = \frac{\sum_{i=1}^{W} yi}{W} \quad (5)$$

$$Z_{eff} = \frac{\sum_{i=1}^{W} zi}{W} \quad (6)$$

The main benefit of calculating effective depth is that it now contains the depth contribution due to hanging and chair type obstacles too. This is possible because of larger field of view of Camera system. So an obstacle which is hanging above the ground with insufficient clearance can now be avoided by the navigator which is not possible in case of laser range finder if the lasers scan plane does not cut the hanging obstacle plane.

3.2.1 *Calculating alignment with respect to navigator*

Real world alignment of each coordinate with respect to navigator is calculated in this step.

$$\theta z = 90 - tan^{-1}\frac{|(zi - zr)|}{|(xi - xr)|} \quad (7)$$

Where xr and zr are the coordinates of the robot (camera) and xi and zi are the coordinates of desired pixel. While considering camera as origin xr and zr becomes zero and sign of xi and zi can be used to find out whether the angle is in clockwise or anticlockwise direction. In our approach we assume that the range of θz is -80 degrees to +80 degrees. This can also be adjusted by the user according to the situation.

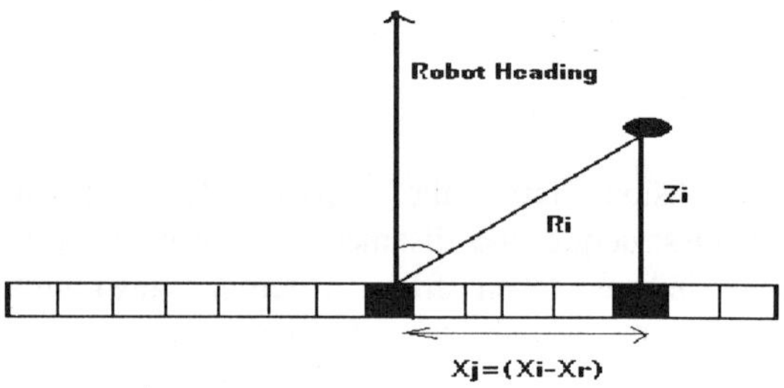

Fig 4

3.3. *Probabilistic Clearance Calculation*

We now calculate probabilistic clearance matrix for each pixel using effective coordinate and alignment values. The probability of clearance for a particular pixel is considered to be directly proportional to the effective range value for that pixel and is inversely proportional to the angle of the obstacle represented by that pixel with respect to the navigator. These two factors are further controlled by two parameters alpha and beta. The concept of these parameters is taken from the ant colony optimization algorithm [7]. These two parameters are very useful and can be tuned based on the environment for sharper and efficient navigation.

$$P_{(xz)} = \frac{(Rz)^{\alpha} (|\cos(\theta z)|)^{\beta}}{\sum_{j\in\Omega} (Rj)^{\alpha} (|\cos(\theta j)|)^{\beta}} \quad (8)$$

$$Rz = \sqrt[2]{Z^2 + X^2} \qquad (9)$$

Where $P_{(X,Z)}$ is the probabilistic clearance for the movement of the navigator to the coordinate (X, Z) with respect to the navigator, Ω represents the other neighbor coordinates, Rz is the range of the coordinate from the camera. We are considering robot at the origin.

We select the final clearest direction with highest confidence for movement as the coordinate with maximum value of probabilistic clearance. The corresponding velocity calculation is explained in section 3.5 of this paper.

Tuning of α and β leads to different possible paths for the same environment and hence can be controlled by the user according to the requirement. This concept makes the algorithm highly flexible.

3.4. *Removing Peaks*

Peaks are sudden changes in any data set. When we plot probabilistic clearance value with depth value, some negative and positive peaks are found. Negative peaks can be avoided as they decrease the probability of movement of the navigator towards them, so decreases the probability of collision. But positive peaks are very dangerous in this situation. Positive peaks basically represent the sudden clearance in the environment. If the window size while calculating effective coordinates is not chosen properly, these positive peaks can lead to collision of the navigator with the obstacles. We can remove the positive peaks by using linear interpolation technique or weighted distance interpolation technique.

3.5. *Velocity Control function calculation*

Velocity control function is basically the function of the distance and the angle of the obstacle from the navigator. We use velocity control function so that vehicle slows down when it gets closer to the obstacle which allows sharper turning and more time for the navigator to detect additional nearby obstacles[1].

The velocity control function used in this paper is directly proportional to the distance of navigator from the obstacle and is inversely proportional to the angular separation between navigator and obstacle.

$$V = \left[\frac{C\,R}{2\,|\cos\varphi|}\right] \qquad (10)$$

The constant C can be changed by the user according to desired speed of the navigator. φ is the angle corresponding to coordinate with maximum probabilistic clearance value, R is the range value of target coordinate from camera.

3.6. *Block Diagram*

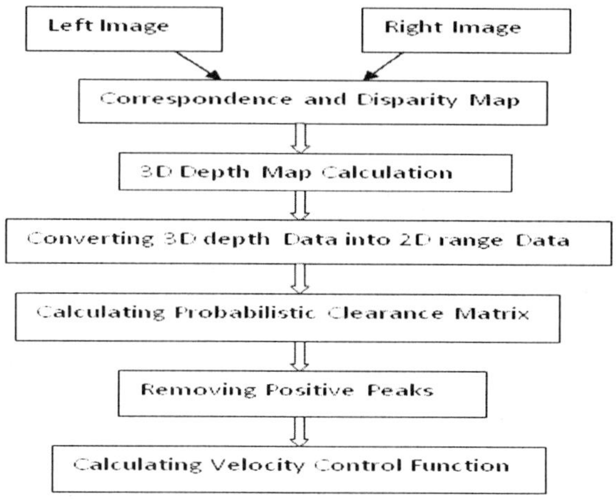

Fig 5

4. Results and Conclusions

The proposed algorithm has been successfully tested in different unstructured environment. The results of the algorithm have been shown in the form of different pose state of the navigator while avoiding an obstacle during autonomous run from figure 6 to figure 9. While using the algorithm for outdoor application the main problems that we faced sometimes was the uneven lighting conditions. Because of ambiguity and correspondence problems in stereovision, the results of navigation deviated sometimes from the expected path. We are still working on these problems.

The algorithm worked well in indoor environment with less varying light conditions.

We discussed different user controlled parameters which makes the algorithm highly flexible for different situations. We used stereo vision camera only as the sensing device which makes the whole navigator highly economical and suitable for industrial applications.

5. Future Work

In future we will use some learning technique so that the control parameters discussed in this paper can automatically get tuned up according to the situation to give the best possible navigation path. Fuzzy approach can also be used to set parameters according to different situations.

Fig 6

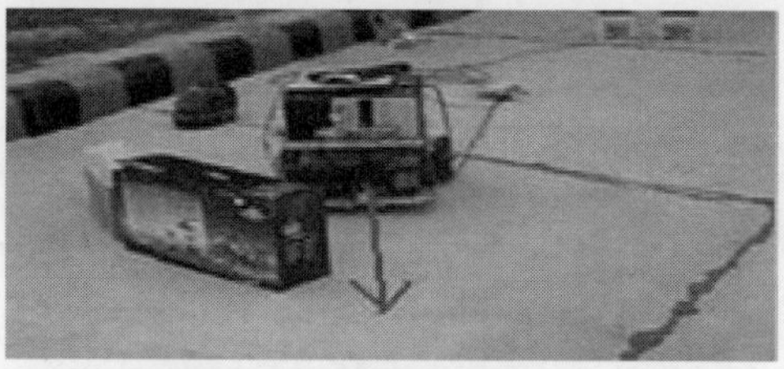

Fig 7

Fig 8

Fig 9

Acknowledgment

Our heartiest thanks to respectable **Prof. P. B. Sharma**, Director, Delhi College of Engineering who always encouraged us towards research.

References

1. Bradley Hamner, Sanjiv Singh, and Sebastian Scherer, "Learning obstacle avoidance parameter from Operator Behavior", Journal of Field Robotics 23(11/12), 1037-1058(2006), Wiley Inter science.

2. The vector field histogram – Fast obstacle avoidance for mobile robots by J. Borenstein and Y. Koren, *IEEE Journal of Robotics and Automation* Vol 7, No 3, June 1991, pp. 278-288.

3. Fox, D., Burgard, W., & Thrun, S. (1997). The dynamic window approach to collision avoidance. IEEE Robotics and automation Magazine 4(1), 23-33.

4. Simmons, R. (1996, April). The curvature-velocity method for local obstacle avoidance. In IEEE International Conference on Robotics and Automation, Minneapolis, MN.

5. Fajen, B., & Warren, W. (2003). Behavioral dynamics of steering, obstacle avoidance, and route selection. Journal of experimental psychology: Human perception and Performance, 29(2), 343-362.

6. Forsyth and ponce, "Computer Vision a modern approach", Prentice Hall; US ed edition (August 24, 2002), ISBN-10: 0130851981, ISBN-13: 978-0130851987

7. O.P.Verma, M Hanmandulu, Puneet Kumar, Shivangi Srivastava, "A Novel approach for edge detection using ant colony optimization and Fuzzy Derivative technique", 2009 IEEE International Advance Computing Conference (IACC 2009) Patiala, India, pp.1427-1433.

8. Borenstein, J. and Koren, Y., "Motion Control Analysis of a Mobile Robot." *Transactions of ASME, Journal of Dynamics, Measurement and Control,* Vol. 109, No. 2, 1987, pp. 73-79.

9. A.Broggie, C.Caraffi ,P.Paolo Porta, and P. Zani, "The Single Frame Stereo Vision System for Reliable Obstacle Detection used during the 2005 DARPA Grand Challenge on TerramMax", in IEEE Intelligent Transportation System Conference, Toronto , Canada, September 17-20 , 2006 .

10. Richard Hartely and Andrew Zisserman, "Multiple View Geometry in Computer Vision", Cambridge University press 2000.

PERFORMABILITY OF LAYERED SYSTEMS – MODELS AND METHODS

ARINDAM DAS
Department of Computer Science and Engineering, York University
Toronto, Ontario, Canada

OLIVIA DAS
Department of Electrical and Computer Engineering, Ryerson University
Toronto, Ontario, Canada

This paper surveys the recent development of a new analytical modeling technique that estimates a combined performance and dependability measure for complex multi-layered client-server-like systems such as telecom, banking, avionics, etc. The novelty of this technique lies in the use of non-state based approach unlike the traditional Markov chain oriented approaches (that are state based). The benefit of this technique lies in the incredibly faster computation of model solution unlike the state-based traditional approaches.

1. Introduction

The increased use of complex mission-critical distributed systems has motivated the study of performance and dependability modeling of such systems in a unified manner, popularly known as performability [1]. Since the failure of such systems incurs high costs, there has been a great emphasis on the formal modeling of their fault-tolerant aspects along with the resource contentions in order to anticipate their expected performability measure. Such systems may be made fault-tolerant by incorporating stand-by servers and a mechanism to re-direct the service requests at the time of failure. They are usually structured in layers, with some kind of operational control or user-interface tasks as the topmost layer, making requests to various layers of servers. Examples of such systems include telecommunication systems, avionic systems, banking systems and airline reservation systems. The purpose of this paper is to describe the incremental advances made in the last decade to develop an analytical model termed as Dependable Layered Queueing Network (Dependable-LQN) [2, 3, 6, 22] that can efficiently predict the performability of such fault-tolerant client–server-like distributed systems.

2. Foundation - LQN Model

A Layered Queueing Network (LQN) model [4, 5] is a performance model for client-server like distributed systems. It was developed by Dr. C. M. Woodside at Carleton University, Canada. It supports nesting of service calls. Its basic components are tasks and request arcs between tasks. A task usually represents a software process abstraction or a device abstraction (e.g. disks). Tasks may send or receive service requests. Each of these service requests are handled by a service handler, known as an "entry", embedded in the task accepting the request. One task may have one or more entries providing various services. Every task is allocated to a processor. Every task and every processor has its own queue. All entries of a single task share the same queue.

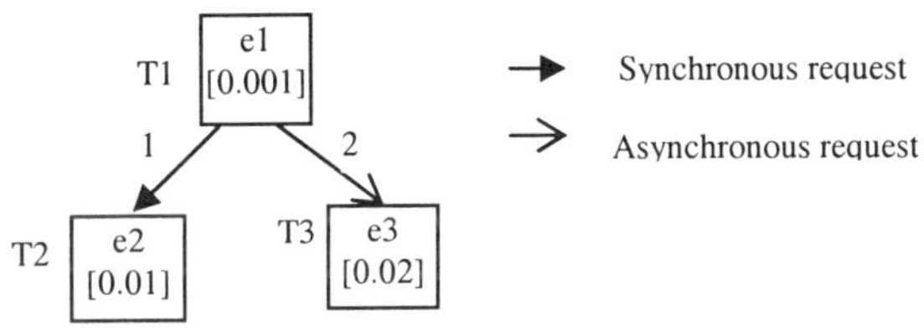

Figure 1. An example LQN model

A task or a processor may be single-server (handling one request at a time), multi-server (refers to multiple copies sharing the same queue) or infinite servers (refers to infinite number of copies that can handle infinite number of requests). A request arc may be synchronous (where the client blocks until the server replies), or asynchronous (where the client proceeds without blocking after sending the request). Figure 1 shows an LQN model with three tasks T1, T2, T3, with one entry each (e1, e2, e3). Each task is running on its own processor. Processors are not shown in this figure.

T1 is the workload generator task. It can have think time associated with it meaning that after receiving a response, a request will be resubmitted by this task after the 'think time'. In this figure, e1 sends 1 synchronous and 2 asynchronous request to e2 and e3 respectively, per invocation. The numbers in square brackets are the execution times of each entry, while those beside the arcs are the mean number of requests made from one entry to another, per invocation.

An LQN model can be solved to obtain various performance measures, e.g. average throughput and utilization of each task, utilization of the processors etc.

3. FTLQN Model

The Fault-tolerant Layered Queueing Network (FTLQN) model [7, 8] was the first incarnation of Dependable-LQN that extends the LQN performance model by adding dependability-related parameters and structure to it, and a calculation of performability figures.

The common approach in performability modeling is to describe the system by a Markov Reward model (e.g., [9-14]) in which the dependability aspects of the system are modeled by a continuous time Markov chain and a reward rate is associated with each of the states of the Markov chain that denotes the performance level in that state. However, for large systems, the state space in a Markov Reward model becomes very large so that to obtain the solution of such models becomes difficult. FTLQN avoids solving large Markov Reward models, and minimizes the number of performance solutions required. The solution strategy for an FTLQN model can be summarized in the following steps:

1. translation of an FTLQN model description of a system into a specialized AND–OR graph,
2. generation of all the possible distinct operational configurations of the system,
3. probability calculation of the system being in each of those configurations, from the AND–OR graph,
4. assignment of a reward rate to each of the operational configurations by applying the layered queueing analysis,
5. determination of the desired performability measures of the system.

The layered structure of an FTLQN model describes the dependencies that determine the service failures, based on service dependencies. In an FTLQN model, we can specify the failure and repair rates for the tasks and the processors. We can also specify various fault-tolerant strategies to be used in case of a failure, e.g. primary-backup, load-balancing. In case of primary-backup strategy, a service request arc may be replaced by a set of alternative arcs with an order of preference. In Figure 2, we have database task-A as well as database task-B. So if database task-A (having priority 1 indicated by #1) fails then the application task will use database task–B (having priority 2 indicated by #2).

An FTLQN model can be solved to obtain various performance measures in presence of failures and repairs for the tasks and processors.

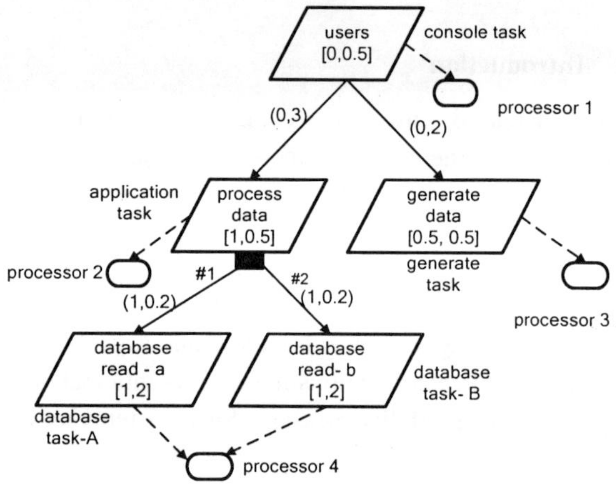

Figure 2. An FTLQN Model

4. Dependable-LQN = FTLQN + Management Architecture

In its second incarnation, the aforementioned FTLQN model formalism is extended to enable the description of a typical fault management infrastructure (in distributed systems) which includes manager processes and agents with various kinds of interactions for monitoring and surveillance of the status of the application software and hardware. The extended model, termed Dependable Layered Queueing Network (Dependable-LQN) [2, 3, 6, 22], accounts for propagation of knowledge of the system state in the management sub-architecture.

The Dependable-LQN work [6] focuses on the following aspects:

1. represents layered systems and their fault-management architectures.

2. captures the failure propagation in layered systems
3. captures the propagation of knowledge about a failure or a repair event in a fault-management architecture
4. presents the performability computation algorithm and compares the effect of coverage of four different fault-management architectures on the expected steady-state reward rate of a system
5. provides an architectural description language for describing the software and the management architecture of a system in a unified way.
6. evaluates the effect of changing the placement of a fixed number of managers in the management model and shows how the modeling technique can be effective in evaluating those placements.

5. Dependability and Software Aging

The FTLQN model was further extended along another direction, different from the Dependable-LQN approach. The extension, known as Rejuvenated-FTLQN [15], captures a software degradation phenomenon known as software aging [16, 17] and a recovery phenomenon known as software rejuvenation [18].

When a fault-tolerant layered distributed system continues its operation despite the presence of component failures, its performance is usually degraded. Its performance can also be degraded if it is executing continuously for a long period of time due to software aging.

Aging related fault refers to the condition where once the software is started, potential fault conditions gradually accumulates with time leading to either performance degradation or transient failures or both. Typical causes of aging are memory bloating or leaking, unreleased file-locks, data corruption, storage space fragmentation and accumulation of round off errors. For example, web browser Netscape, is known to suffer from serious memory leaks which lead to occasional crash/hang of the application.

To prevent unexpected or unplanned outages due to aging, a pro-active technique called software rejuvenation can be employed. This technique involves gracefully terminating an application and immediately restarting it with a refreshed internal state. The work in [15] proposed a model to evaluate the effects of software aging and rejuvenation on performability of the layered systems. Specifically, LQN was used for performance analysis and a Multi State Fault Tree (MSFT) [19] was used for dependability analysis.

In order to evaluate the steady state performability of the fault–tolerant layered distributed systems under the effects of software aging and rejuvenation following steps can be performed:

Step1: Generate a FTLQN model from the system description.

Step2: Add a Continuous Time Markov Chain (CTMC) for every software task (process) to the FTLQN model to take into account the effects of software aging and rejuvenation. CTMC denotes the state of a software task and transitions between states.

Step3: Translate the FTLQN model into the Fault Propagation AND-OR graph. The Fault Propagation AND-OR graph provides a convenient means to model the dependencies of the service failures in a layered system. The Fault Propagation AND-OR graph also takes under consideration the multiple states of the software tasks resulting due to the performance degradation caused by software aging.

Step4: Determine the different operational configurations of the system. Fault-tolerance and software aging gives rise to the different configurations of the system in which the system is operational.

Step5: Evaluate the reward rate for each operational configuration using Layered Queuing Network (LQN) model. Reward rate is the performance measure that will be assigned to every operational configuration to quantify how well the system performs in that particular operational configuration.

Step6: Compute the probabilities of system being in each of the operational configuration using Multi-State Fault Tree's (MSFTs). The input to the MSFT is obtained by solving the CTMCs for the software tasks as well as failure probabilities for processors.

Step7: Combine the probabilities and the rewards for every operational configuration to determine the steady state performability.

6. Dependability and Spatial Mobility of Cellular Clients

Recent advances in mobile computing have enabled users carrying handheld devices to have access to information services regardless of their physical location. Applications using mobile data access include web browser, stock market watcher, video etc. Such an enormous advantage for users has come with its own set of challenges. Unlike a traditional distributed system, in a mobile environment, users and their computers are non-static, connection among devices can change during computation, and there are resource constraints such as limited bandwidth.

Customers expect the same level of service from the mobile applications as with their static counterparts. Meeting the high availability and high performance requirements is one of the most challenging tasks in mobile computing because of several reasons: users want to stay connected while on the move; mobile (i.e. wireless) links are relatively unreliable and currently are slower than the static networks; limited wireless bandwidth; battery life constraints for mobile devices; etc. Modeling is one of the techniques that help us evaluate alternative architectures for a mobile information system in a cost-effective way and decide on the one that meets the quality requirements. Traditional pure performance modeling only considers contention for resources while pure availability modeling solely considers failure and recovery behavior of the system. In case of a distributed mobile system, the performance can be affected by two factors: (i) spatial mobility of clients giving rise to physical nearness or remoteness of data servers resulting in lower or higher latency for data access; (ii) occurrence of software or hardware failures resulting in a system configuration with degraded performance. Thus, ignoring failure-recovery and client mobility in pure performance modeling will generally overestimate the system's ability to do a particular job while ignoring performance characteristics in availability modeling will give conservative results. It is therefore important to develop models and measures considering both performance and availability simultaneously.

Client-server style of communication can be used in mobile systems paradigm. The report [20] has discussed an extended FTLQN model to support the adaptation of mobile systems and applications. In [20], a model-based performability analysis of two possible client-server architectures in the mobile paradigm was proposed. The architectures were adapted from the ideas presented in [21]. The analysis determines all the possible configurations of the system and for each such configuration, (i) it constructs a fault tree to compute its probability of occurrence and (ii) it generates a Layered Queuing Network (LQN) Model to compute its reward rate and (iii) finally, it combines the probabilities with the reward rates to obtain the desired performability measure, e.g. average throughput of mobile clients.

The first FTLQN work in [7, 8] had considered performability analysis for static client-server architectures of traditional distributed systems. However, unlike [20], it did not take into account the issues arising due to mobility of clients, for example, performance hit incurred due to remoteness of client, mobile link failures, and frequency of mobility in the analysis.

7. Conclusions

This research surveyed a recently developed analytical modeling framework and its derivatives. The dissemination of this information is of high importance owing to the framework's ability to avoid state based solutions as well as its scalability unlike traditional techniques.

References

1. J.F.Meyer, On evaluating the performability of degradable computing systems, IEEE Trans. on Computers 29 (8) (1980) 720–731.
2. O. Das and M. Woodside, "Dependability Modeling of Self-healing Client-Server Applications," Architecting Dependable Systems II, LNCS (2004) 266-285.
3. O. Das, "Dependability Modelling of Layered Systems," PhD dissertation, Carleton Univ., Canada, 2004.
4. C.M. Woodside, Throughput calculation for basic stochastic rendezvous networks, Performance Evaluation 9 (2) (1989) 143–160.
5. C.M. Woodside, J.E. Neilson, D.C. Petriu, S. Majumdar, The stochastic rendezvous network model for performance of synchronous client–server-like distributed software, IEEE Trans. on Computers 44 (1) (1995) 20–34.
6. O. Das and C. M. Woodside: Analyzing the Effectiveness of Fault-Management Architectures in Layered Distributed Systems, Performance Evaluation, 56, 2004, pp. 93-120.
7. O. Das, C. M. Woodside: The Fault-Tolerant Layered Queueing Network Model for Performability of Distributed Systems, IEEE Int. Performance and Dependability Symp. (IPDS 98), Durham, North Carolina (1998) 132-141.
8. O. Das and C. M. Woodside: Evaluating layered distributed software systems with fault-tolerant features, Performance Evaluation, 45 (1) (2001) 57-76.

9. J.F. Meyer, Closed-form solutions of performability, IEEE Trans. on Computers 31 (7) (1982) 648–657.
10. R.M. Smith, K.S. Trivedi, A.V. Ramesh, Performability analysis, measures, an algorithm and a case study, IEEE Trans. on Computers 37 (4) (1988) 406–417.
11. A.L. Reibman, R. Smith, K.S. Trivedi, Markov and Markov Reward models transient analysis: an overview of numerical approaches, Eur. J. Oper. Res. 40 (1989) 257–267.
12. G. Ciardo, A. Blakemore, P.F. Chimento Jr., J.K. Muppala, K.S. Trivedi, Automated generation and analysis of Markov reward models using stochastic reward nets, in: C. Meyer, R. Plemmons (Eds.), Linear Algebra, Markov Chains and Queueing Models, Springer, Berlin (1992)
13. K.S. Trivedi, J.K. Muppala, S.P. Woolet, B.R. Haverkort, Composite performance and dependability analysis, Performance Evaluation 14 (1992) 197–215.
14. B.R. Haverkort, K.S. Trivedi, Specification and generation of Markov reward models, Discrete-Event Dynamic Systems: Theory and Applications 3 (1993) 219–247.
15. J. Patel and O. Das: A New Model For Evaluating Performability Under The Effects Of Software Aging And Rejuvenation, in 11th IASTED Int. Conference on Software Engineering and Applications, Massachusetts, USA (2007) 25-30.
16. S. Garg, A. van Moorsel, K. Vaidyanathan, K. Trivedi, "A Methodology for Detection and Estimation of Software Aging," Proc. Ninth Int'l Symp. Software Reliability Eng. (1998) 282-292.
17. K. Vaidyanathan, K.Trivedi, "A comprehensive model for software rejuvenation" IEEE Trans. on Dependable and Secure Computing, 2(2) (2005) 124 – 137.
18. Y. Huang, C. Kintala, N. Kolettis and N. D. Fulton, "Software Rejuvenation: Analysis, Module and Applications", in Proc. 25th Annual Intl. Symp. on Fault Tolerant Computing (1995) 381- 390.
19. X. Zang, D. Wang, H.,Sun, K. Trivedi, "A BDD-based algorithm for analysis of multistate systems with multistate components", IEEE Trans. on Computers, 52(12) (2003) 1608-1618.
20. O. Das and A. Das: Performability Evaluation of Mobile Client-Server Systems. Proceedings of 23rd ACM Symposium on Applied Computing (ACM SAC 2008), Dependable and Adaptive Distributed Systems Track, Ceara, Brazil (2008) 2197-2201.
21. J. Jing, A. S. Helal, A. Elmagarmid, "Client-server computing in mobile environments", ACM Computing Surveys, 31(2) (1999) 117-157.
22. G. Franks, T. Al-Omari, M. Woodside, O. Das, and S. Derisavi, Enhanced modeling and solution of layered queueing networks. IEEE Trans. on Software Engineering (2008) Accepted for publication.

OPTIMIZING RELIABILITY ANALYSIS OF MEMS DEVICES ON AN HPC SETUP USING MULTI SCALE MODELING

ROHIT PATHAK*†

Acropolis Institute of Technology & Research, Rajiv Gandhi Technical University (Bhopal), Indore Madhya Pradesh, India

SATYADHAR JOSHI

Shri Vaishnav Institute of Technology & Science, Rajiv Gandhi Technical University (Bhopal), Indore Madhya Pradesh, India

Powerful Computational have brought new techniques to calculate reliability by multi scale modeling supported by experimental and theoretical methods. These approaches play a crucial role in Micro Electro Mechanical Systems (MEMS) technology where the analysis is based on abstraction level theories and no comprehensive explanation of nano scale phenomenon are proposed. The Reliability modeling contains methods to calculate reliability function, failure rate function, Mean time to failure (MTTF) and Mean Residual time (MRT) are proposed for MEMS technology. It is observed that High Performance Computing (HPC) if used with multi scale optimization library then the reliability calculation and help to accelerate research in reliability of MEMS. In this developed library we can select the various physics at different level and then calculated reliability for better accuracy. It allows the user to perform simulation of a MEMS device in different environments as well as used to compute some aspects of system reliability such as Survival function and failure rate as well as multi scale modeling.

1. Introduction

1.1. *Recent Works*

Recent trends in MEMS and wireless technology together enable remote sensing and also development of Nano-RFID. A wireless sensor node typically consists of three major subsystems: Computation, Communication and Sensing where MEMS devices are extensively used in sensing various parameters as per the need.

MEMS devices offer great potential benefits not only as sensors and actuators but also as antenna in MEMS based RFID. By using and modifying the fabrication techniques originally developed for integrated circuits which are time tested over several decades on ethics and technology based ideologies, microscopic devices can be formed which match or exceed the performance of their conventional counterparts in a smaller volume with lower weight and a greatly reduced cost. There are however considerable challenges in fabricating and packaging such devices and, in particular, there are many yield and reliability issues still to overcome. Some of the failure mechanisms can be studied referring to same in integrated circuits while others are unique to MEMS devices, thus making reliability an issue to be studied in details.

Quantum Mechanical plays a very important role and its calculation for electronic studies has been made easier in recent years by HPC [1]. Optimizing HPC for nanotechnology based computation has been shown by Rohit et al.[21]. MATLAB has tools which provide easy access to utilize HPC resources [2], such as its distributive computing toolbox which allows user to harness the power of a cluster of computers for computational intensive tasks. HPC is being used in many research domains analysis in which remained stagnant for many decades. HPC setup for multi scale modeling in various programming environments has been shown by Rohit et al in [20].In this paper the Reliability modeling codes to calculate reliability function, failure rate function, Mean time to failure (MTTF) and Mean Residual time (MRT) are proposed for MEMS technology, using MATLAB HPC. Modeling and Computation is performed using MATLAB distributed computing toolbox and Sugar MEMS simulation library. This has been done by making a library for MEMS reliability which allows the user to perform simulation of a MEMS device in different environments and compute some aspects of system reliability such as Survival function and failure rate.

1.2. *Reliability Analysis of MEMS Devices and Multi-Scale Modeling*

MEMS are the integration of mechanical elements, sensors, actuators, and electronics on a common silicon substrate through micro-scale fabrication technology thus making nano automation possible with use friendly and reliable techniques. Reliability analysis has been a major challenge in application of MEMS.

Victor has divided MEMS Failure Analysis and Reliability into categories focusing on processing and packaging. Reliability of microfluidic MEMS device to extract Deoxyribonucleic Acid (DNA) from whole human blood and to purify the DNA was studied [3]. Thus OPTIMIZING packaging and fabrication can improve MEMS reliability but it does not predict anything about its failure modeling. Other ways of predicting reliability has been on categorizing MEMS devices on operation as illustrated by Jeremy [4], making it easy to work on solutions. Thus studying failure mechanism can help to improve MEMS reliability but the effects of failure in time domains with strong theoretical backing is still lacking and studying MEMS failure by the use of modeling aspects of causes of failure from multi scale prospective still remains an area to work on. Future Challenges for MEMS Failure Analysis can be classified in categories depending on its application are given in [5] because application gives the main essence of the fabrication and reliability analysis. Accelerated lifetime testing is being used in many areas and its application in MEMS is given in [6]. But in absence of strong theories and modeling, MEMS reliability still remains a challenging field. We know that RF MEMS plays a very important role RFID which are becoming MEMS based and Dielectric Material Impact on Capacitive RF MEMS Reliability affects the overall reliability of a MEMS device [7]. In Reliability-based MEMS System Modeling and Optimization, Nan Liu presented methods for MEMS design to optimize the performance objective function with reliability based constraints [8]. Research in Nano composite material based MEMS devices like Ni-P-CNTs Nanocomposite Film for MEMS Applications [9], [10], makes reliability calculation more complex and thus need for solving complex mathematics emerges. Power and Reliability improvement of an Electro-Thermal Microactuator using Ni-Diamond Nanocomposite [11] is discussed but lacks theoretical backing from reliability engineering and linking it with statistical data. Reliability Analysis on HPC for MEMS devices was introduced by Rohit et.al in [22]. The proposed model developed and discussed in this paper illustrates that device reliability using MATLAB tool can be calculated and understood by using multi scale modeling which may supplementing the development and fabrication of the same.

Some areas of fault modeling and simulation techniques for suspended thermal MEMS has been shown in [20]. The influence of induced stresses, thermal shocks, external vibrations, and pressure can be investigated. Thus allowing new approach of failure mechanisms in a whole system (resonator, optical devices) by understanding of the fatigue phenomenon due to elementary mechanical solicitations. Thus shown is in his work is that statistical modeling of failure mechanisms is an efficient way to optimize the design and the fabrication [22]. Thus Integration of multi scale studies in reliability CAD program will help us to accurately predict failures in MEMS devices.

Neural networks can be used to provide an important mechanism for correlation of MEMS properties to failure probability calculation. Also they have been used to identify desirable MEMS attributes for high reliability has been proposed in [21]. Classical reliability methods take two working states working or failed, but when we take other states such as partially working, partially failed mew dimension are added in MEMS reliability analysis. Thus can be correlated to multi scale modeling for nanotechnology which can be implemented in various ways as shown in [23]. A part of a MEMS device may partially function and still may affect the system in some way which can be mathematically modeled.

Thus each phenomenon of multi scale modeling can be seen by using multi scale modeling to accurately predict the behavior of the device and failure Redundancy is not always the solution in two mode systems.

2. Sugar and Multi-Scale Modeling for MEMS

During the last two decades, the field of MEMS envisaged the progressive path starting from production of simple-function devices to more complex systems that includes many areas which changed wireless communications. They are useful in wide domains and are based on the same manufacturing technology.

Table 1. Table Abstraction layers in Multi Scale setup

Abstraction Scale	Properties
Nano CMOS 30-100nm	Capacitance in CMOS
RF MEMS 100-500nm	Properties of antenna
CNT 10-30 nm	Conductance

Although these tools have been successful in simulating the behavior of simple-function devices but fails when it goes to more complex areas because the physics developed cannot explain accurately all the properties, also they have not been as successful in simulating the behavior of more complex systems on a personal computer (PC) nor within a practical amount of time. Software proves its utility in technological advancements in MEMS by facilitating the design process and reducing the time of computation. Some of the features are packaged in a CAE for MEMS tool called SUGAR [12] which has also been shoed in [22]. Mechanical modeling as from RF-MEMS prospective is given in [24] where MA (Nm) is the reaction moment at the left end, and RA (N) is the vertical reaction at the left end. The equations are:-

$$M_A = -\frac{Pa}{l^2}(l-a)^2$$

$$R_A = \frac{P}{l^3}(l-a)^2(l+2a)$$

Mechanical modeling is an important part of the analysis which can be useful for mechanical failure analysis.

Electrical Modeling it is the physics of 30-100nm, direct-tunneling current is formulated in a Nano CMOS circuit as per [15] is given by

$$J = \frac{q^3}{8\pi h\phi_b\varepsilon_{ox}} C(V_G, V_{ox}, t_{ox}, \phi_b) \exp\left\{-\frac{8\pi\sqrt{2m_{ox}\phi_b^3}}{3hq\,|\,E_{ox}\,|}\left[1-\left(1-\frac{V_{ox}q}{\phi_b}\right)^{3/2}\right]\right\}$$

Equivalent Circuit parameters it's a macro level' is the study of things at abstraction scale. MEMS-Based Inductively Coupled RFID Transponder for Implantable Wireless Sensor Applications has been shown in [23]. This is the part of the code to distribute the computation among various nodes. It is being developed for Microsoft Compute Cluster Server Environment as shown in Fig. 1.

Code 1. Demo code from the developed library

```
Communicator comm = Communicator.world;
        Console.WriteLine("Check from process " +
comm.Rank);
        switch (comm.Rank)
        {           case 0:
            Console.WriteLine("Process " +
comm.Rank + " status: calculating Reaction Moment of
MEMS");
            calcReactionMomentFrmCase();
            break;          case 1:
            Console.WriteLine("Process " +
comm.Rank + " status: calculating Tunneling Current of
nano CMOS");
            calcTunnelingFrmCase();
            break;
          case 2:
            Console.WriteLine("Process " +
comm.Rank + " status: calculating Induced Voltage of
MEMS Transponder");
            calcInducedVoltageFrmCase();
            break;                  default:
            Console.WriteLine("Process " +
comm.Rank + " status: Idle");
            break;
        }           /*All processes join here*/
        comm.Barrier();
        /*All processes completed*/
        if (comm.Rank == 0)
        {                       Console.WriteLine("All
processes finished");           }
```

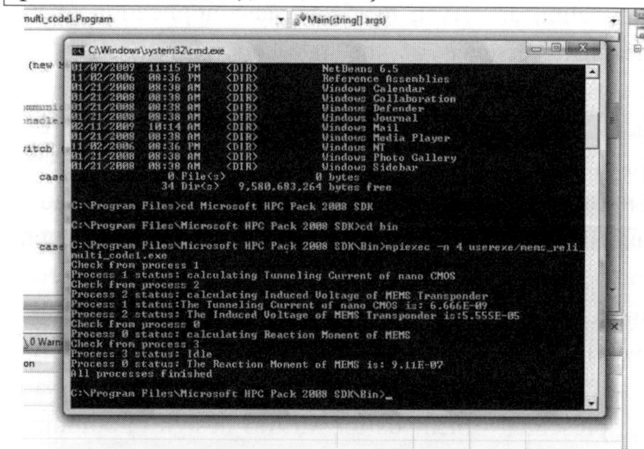

Figure 1. Results of the multi scale computations.

3. Reliability Calculations

We have distributed the 6 functions on reliability to 6 workers and results show that we can achieve considerable speed-up which is shown in our previous

work [22]. In this work we have also worked on the distribution for Multi scale modeling.
Our Investigation was confined to calculation for exponential distribution

$$R(t) = e^{-\lambda t}(t > 0, \lambda > 0)$$

Here we have assumed $z(t) = e^{\frac{-9t}{11}}$ for a single Cantilever of a MEMS device.
The output result of reliability computation on our setup of a node has been shown in Fig. 2.

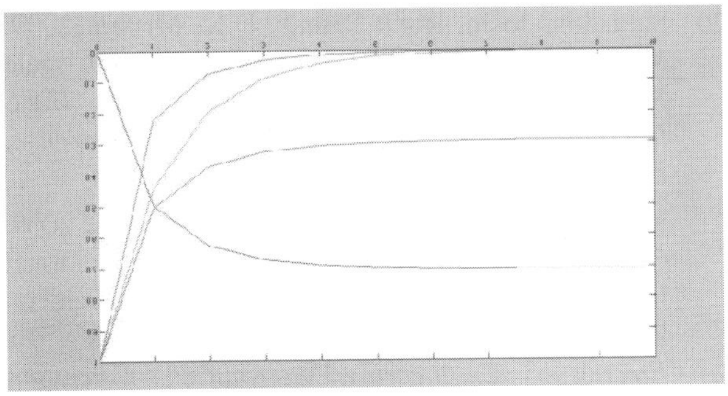

Figure 2. F(t), R(t), f(t) shown for an assumed exponential function.

4. HPC Computation and Optimization

Parallel MATLAB has been used in Signal Processing as shown by Nadya T. to solve many problems [13]. Efficiently use Parallel MATLAB is the key to its proper optimization something regarding which are shown by RON CHOY [14] helps us in optimizing MATLAB for HPC in reliability calculations. Thus we can see that MATLAB provided an excellent platform to work with Distributive computing and HPC. We have calculated the following using MATLAB HPC Distributed computing toolbox. As shown in our last work [22] we can significantly speed up calculations using MATLAB distributive computing toolbox to work on MEMS reliability which is shown in [20].

Future Work and Conclusion

Distributive computing needs to be dissemination and optimized for Nano domain calculation where each problem is studied and solved at some abstraction layers therefore has its own solution which makes multi scale modeling an integral part of Nano domain modeling [16]. Therefore its integration with current MEMS device is an area, which is going to play an important role in realization of Nano Electro Mechanical Systems because in future things are going to integrated with Nano composites and carbon nanotubes. Current status of nanotechnology, its application and advantages in various domains in accelerating research across various areas has been explained by Deepak Srivastava et al. [17]. CNT will be used in many application of Nanotechnology, like CNT nanocomposites in MEMS which shows a significant growth in recent years, the effect of reliability in such case needs to be explored. Nearly realistic simulation for CNT using HPC has been shown by Syogo Tejima et al. that will aid in their development and research which is among the most convincing research in this area[18]. Thus HPC will be used in many areas of Nano and Micro domains.

In this paper we shown a novel way to approach reliability calculations and shown how properties at different levels and types needs to be linked up in an multi scale analysis where HPC can benefit reliability calculations for MEMS devices. We have calculated various parameter of different scale for a MEMS device and proceeded with analysis of reliability using MATLAB distributive computing Toolbox. We have assumed some of the parameters in a multi scale setup hence the reliability and calculated results on an HPC setup. Merging of multi scale properties to calculate the exact failure phenomenon and then with MATLAB remains a major area to work on.

References

1. Miyamoto Yoshiyuki, Takahara Hiroshi. 2007. Nano-Scale Simulation by the Use of Supercomputer Electronic Structure Calculation of Materials. *NEC Technical Journal*. Vol. 2, No. 1 (2007).
2. John Nehrbass, Siddharth Samsi, Juan Carlos Chaves, Jose Unpingco, Brian Guilfoos, Stanley Ahalt, Ashok Krishnamurthy, Alan Chalker, and Judy Gardiner. 2006. Interfacing PC-based MATLAB Directly to HPC Resources. In Proceedings of the *HPCMP Users Group Conference* (2006). *HPSMP –UGC*.
3. Victor Samper, Alastair Trigg. 2003. MEMS Failure Analysis and Reliability. In Proceedings of *IPFA* (Singapore, 2003).
4. Jeremy A.Walraven. 2006. Failure Mechanisms in MEMS. Paper 33.1 In Proceedings of the *International Test Conference* (2006). ITC 2006.
5. Jeremy A. Walraven. 2003. Future Challenges for MEMS Failure Analysis. Paper 33.4 In Proceedings of *International Test Conference* (2003). ITC 2003.

6. Clifford Fung. 2005. Issues of MEMS Reliability and Accelerated Life Time Testing. In Proceedings of the *43rd Annual International Physics Symposium on Reliability* (San Jose, 2005).

7. T. Lisec, C. Huth and B. Wagner. 2004. Dielectric Material Impact on Capacitive RF MEMS Reliability. In Proceedings of the *34th European Microwave Conference* (Amsterdam, 2004).

8. Nan Liu and Souran Manoochehri. 2006. Reliability based MEMS system Modeling and Optimization. In Proceedings of the *44th Annual International Physics Symposium on Reliability* (San Jose, 2006).

9. Guang-Ren Shen, Li-Nuan Tsai, Tzu-Yuan Chao, Y. T. Cheng, T. K. Lin, Wensyang Hsu. 2004. Ni-P-CNTs Nanocomposite Film for MEMS Applications. In Proceedings of the *4th IEEE Conference on Nanotechnology* (2004).

10. Guang-Ren Shen, Yu-Ting Cheng, Member, Li-Nuan Tsai. 2005. Synthesis and Characterization of Ni–P-CNT's Nanocomposite Film for MEMS Applications. *IEEE Transaction on Nanotechnology*. Vol. 4, No. 5, (Sept. 2005).

11. Li-Nuan Tsai, Guang-Ren Shen, Y-T Cheng, Wensyang Hsu. 2004. Power and Reliability Improvement of an Electro-Thermal Microactuator Using Ni-Diamond Nanocomposite. In Proceedings of the *Electronic Components and Technology Conference* (2004).

12. Jason Vaughn Clark, Ningning Zhou, and K. S. J. Pister. MEMS Simulation using SUGAR v0.5. http://www-bsac.eecs.berkel.edu

13. Nadya T. Bliss, Jeremy Kepner, Hahn Kim, Albert Reuther. 2007. PMATLAB: Parallel MATLAB Library for Signal Processing Applications. In Proceedings of the *International Conference on Acoustics, Speech and Signal Processing* (2007). ICASSP.

14. Ron Choy and Alan Edelman. 2005. Parallel MATLAB: Doing It Right. In *Proceedings of the IEEE*, Vol. 93, No. 2 (Feb. 2005).

15. Ban Wong, Anurag Mittal, Yu Cao, Greg W. Starr. 2004. NANO-CMOS Circuit and Physical Design. *Wiley-interscience.*

16. Yoshitaka Tateyama. 2006. Dissemination of Nano simulation Techniques to Promote the Development of Nanotechnology. Science and Technology Trends. *Quarterly Review* No. 20 (Jul. 2006).

17. Deepak Srivastava and Satya N. Atluri. 2002. Computational Nanotechnology: A Current Perspective. *Tech Science Press CMES*. Vol. 3, No. 5 (2002). pp. 531-538.

18. Syogo Tejima, Noejung Park, Yoshiyuki Miyamoto, Kazuo Minami, Mikio Iizuka, Hisashi Nakamura and David Tomanek. 2004. Large Scale Simulations for Carbon Nanotubes. In Proceedings of the *Seventh International Conference on High Performance and Grid Computing in Asia Pacific Region* (2004). *HPCAsia'04*.

19. Microsoft Scholar vs. Scholar Contest 2008. Research Grant

20. Satyadhar Joshi, Rohit Pathak, D.K. Mishra. 2009. MPI & PVM based HPC setup for Multi-scale Modeling. (6-7 Mar. 2009). Proceedings *IEEE International Advance Computing Conference, IACC'09*, (2009).

21. Rohit Pathak, Satyadhar Joshi, D.K. Mishra. 2009. Optimizing HPC for Computational Nanotechnology in MCCS Environment. Proceedings *6th International Conference on Electrical Engineering/Electronics, Computer, Telecommunications, and Information Technology* (ECTI-CON 2009).

22. Rohit Pathak, Satyadhar Joshi, D. K. Mishra. 2009. Distributive Computing for Reliability Analysis of MEMS Devices using MATLAB (23-24 Jan. 2009). Proceedings *ACM International Conference on Computing, Communication and Control-09*, (2009).

23. Lu, H.M.; Goldsmith, C.; Cauller, L.; Jeong-Bong Lee. June 2007. MEMS-Based Inductively Coupled RFID Transponder for Implantable Wireless Sensor Applications. *IEEE Transactions on Magnetics*, Volume 43, Issue 6. 2412 – 2414.

24. Vijay K. Varadan, K.J. Vinoy, K.A. Jose. 2003. RF MEMS and Their Applications. *John Wiley & Sons, Ltd.*

Session 4

A NOVEL INTEGRATED OCR DOCUMENT ACCESS SYSTEM FOR THE SPECIALLY ENABLED

BINDU PHILIP

Department of Electronics and Communication, SJCE, Mysore, Karnataka -560006, India

R. SANJEEV KUNTE

Department of Electronics and Communication, SJCE, Mysore, Karnataka -560006, India

R. D. SUDHAKER SAMUEL

Department of Electronics and Communication, SJCE, Mysore, Karnataka -560006, India

This paper presents a Novel Integration of an OCR system for the specially enabled. It specifically facilitates the visually challenged to access documents and obtain outputs in the form of text read out and/ or Braille print out. This novel system helps to bring reading rooms and libraries to the specially enabled populace. It finds application in all areas where documents need to be accessed. This system designed has an inherent advantage in the sense that it can also be of functional utility to the literate and semi-literate citizen, besides to visually affected persons. Such systems are not presently available for Indian languages. This paper addresses the issues related to the integration of the various subsystems for such applications.

1. Introduction

Information Technology has the potential to revolutionize the way visually challenged people read and write, and make them totally independent for all their reading and writing needs. Compute vision and HCI is a revolution for persons with vision impairment. A computer becomes a basic reading and writing tool for the blind or persons with low vision; thus it means much more to them than it does for persons without vision impairment. This can be made possible by interfacing a scanner as an input device to feed the printed text document after digitization to the which has a software module the OCR (optical character recognition engine) that process the scanned document. The recognized text in the document is then fed to the output interface which is a TTS (text-to-speech) engine and a Braille print out system that enables the specially challenged complete freedom to listen to and print out the required documents in a library or stack of documents. Unfortunately, all this is currently available only in English and other European languages.

The novel system designed here is especially for reading and taking Braille print outs of Indian documents. CDAC Trivandrum has designed NAYANA - Optical Character Recognition System for Malayalam and has also designed SUBHASHINI – A Malayalam TTS, Human Machine Interface System - DRISHTI is an optical character recognition system for Telugu. "Shruti Drishti" is an Integrated Text-to-Speech [TTS] & Text-to-Braille [TTB] System for the for Visually Impaired" using the Information Extraction and Retrieval techniques. Shruti Drishti is a web page browser developed for visually impaired users is considered to provide user-friendly environment, sharing and strengthening of global knowledge by removing barriers and providing equitable access to information for all by the use of Assistive Technologies. JAWS for Windows - Screen Reading Software allows for the text on a screen to be converted to speech, thus enabling a blind individual to hear the information on the computer screen. Kurzweil 1000- it's reading software that makes printed or electronic text accessible to people who are blind or have limited vision. Dhvani - A Text-to-Speech System for Indian Languages.

2. Integration

This section explains the various subsystems for the practical implementation. The system is very user friendly. The user has to place the page onto the scanner. The scanner is so programmed as to give a beep when the page to be scanned is not placed properly on the scanner so as to assist the user to adjust the page to the correct position when ready to be scanned. The scanned /digitized document is then fed to the OCR module where it goes through various stages of preprocessing which include noise removal, Conversion of gray image to binary, skew detection and correction. Then the next important stage within the OCR module is the segmentation process wherein which the digitized text is segmented to first lines then word segmentation and finally character segmentation is performed based on the classical horizontal and vertical projection profiling technique. In this process script identification is also done by different algorithms like Gabor features for differentiation of English from other languages, the techniques used to do the script identification will be explained in the following sections. This step will be used later to supply the recognized text in the document to their respective TTS.

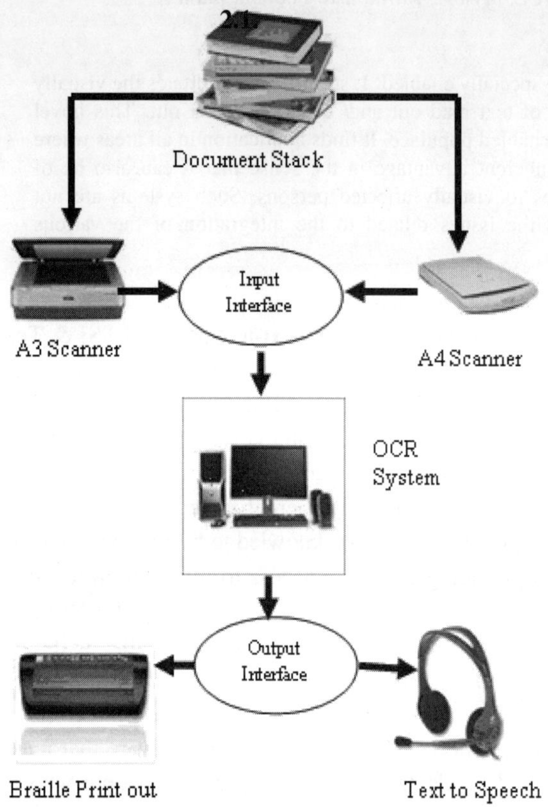

Figure 1. Novel Integrated OCR System.

After the segmentation and script identification stage, this stage is followed by normalization the next important stage in the OCR is the feature extraction is finding a set of feature vectors, which effectively represent the information content of a character. The features are selected in such a way that they help in discriminating between characters. This stage is followed by the final stage of the OCR which is recognition phase which is obtained by proper and most suitable classification techniques. After passing through different stages of the classifier, the character is identified and corresponding character code is assigned. At the end of this stage the scanned images of printed documents is converted to editable text. This editable text is now ready to be fed to a text to speech system which reads out the file also if necessary the text document is further printed out using the Braille Printer in order to be read or preserved by the specially enabled. Thus this fully integrated document access system specially designed for accessing the Indian language documents by the visually challenged. The Figure 1 shows the novel integration of an OCR system. The subsequent sections explain about each module within the system.

2.1. Document Input

The Kodak A3 Flatbed Accessory and Kodak A4 Flatbed Accessory give you the ability to scan exception documents with your Kodak Scanners that are designed to use the flatbed. The cable included with the A3/A4 Flatbed Accessory easily connects your flatbed to the scanner. The document to be scanned is placed face down on the glass platen and align the document in the lower right-hand corner at the corner arrows. Voice assistance is provided for the visually challenged for correct alignment of the documents or some scanners can be programmed to give a beep sound is for misalignment of the document on the glass platen. Close the flatbed cover and start scanning when the Start button on the flatbed is pressed. The associated application in widows is launched. The advantage of scanning using a flatbed scanner is that it supports manual selection in the cropping mode provided the document is properly positioned in the lower right-hand corner of the flatbed.

2.2. Computer Algorithms

The block diagram of the character recognition engine is shown in Figure 2. The stages involved in the development of the model are image acquisition, preprocessing, segmentation, normalization, feature extraction and classification. A printed document containing the Kannada, Telegu, Tamil or Malayalam text is scanned on either a A3 or A4 flatbed scanner at 300 dpi for digitization. The different techniques used to various stages of the optical character recognition system. The preprocessing tasks performed by the first module include noise removal, conversion of grey scale image to binary, skew detection and correction and line, word, and character segmentation. several techniques are used for noise removal which include median filtering technique, connected component based analysis to remove unwanted objects in the image. Thresholding or binarization methods are used to separate foreground object into the image. Most of the threshold techniques can be classified into two categorizes, that is Global thresholding techniques and Adaptive (or local) thresholding techniques. The scanned images in grey tone are converted into two-tone (binary) images using a histogram based thresholding approach (Otsu's algorithm). After binarization the Skew detection is done using the Projection profile based technique. Once the skew angle is estimated the skew is corrected by rotating the image against the estimated skew angle. Boundary growing (BG) and nearest neighbor clustering (NNC) is also used to estimate accurate skew angle for the scanned documents. The BG extracts the boundary characters present in each text line of the document and extracts uppermost, lowermost and centroid coordinates of character components of the scanned document image [1]. The extracted coordinates are then subjected to moments to estimate skew angle of the document image another novel technique for estimation of skew in binary text document images based on linear regression analysis [2]. After preprocessing, segmentation of the text image is done to detect the text lines, to separate the words within the lines and to separate the characters within the words. The text line and words are detected with the help of the horizontal and vertical projections of the image separation of the characters can be done using the connected component analysis and with the help of knowledge based algorithm for Kannada characters depending on their structure and shape. The algorithm also separates the subscripts from the main character [4]. The same technique is used for the segmentation of Telugu, Tamil and Malayalam scripts. A novel segmentation technique is developed for the Malayalam script on the basis of arrangement of sub characters within a Malayalam character added to the connected component analysis for segmentation. On performing segmentation the resultant characters need to undergo normalization [3]. In Kannada, Telugu and Tamil and Malayalam the height of the main characters are almost of the same, the width of the character varies. In the first three scripts the segmented characters are resized to a fixed square image size of 50X50 pixels. But for Malayalam characters the size normalization is applied only with respect to the height of the character while preserving the width of the characters since the width is much greater than the height. The resultant character images are rectangular images of uniform height say ***m1xn*** where ***m1*** is fixed to 50 after many trials.

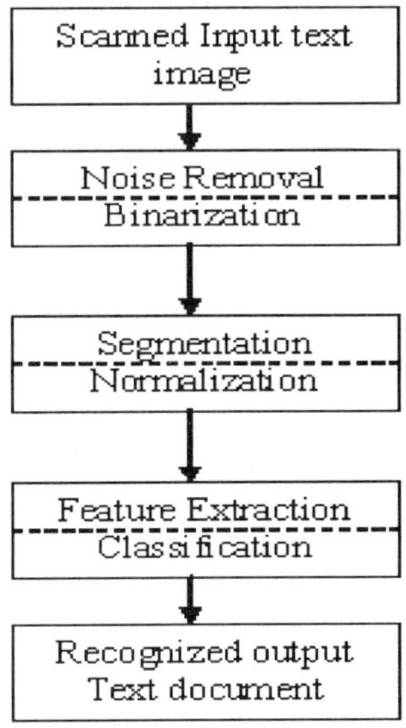

Figure 2. Block diagram of the Character Recognition Engine

The normalized characters are now fed to the next level of OCR, the feature extraction module which is an essential step to pattern recognition and machine learning problems. Classical algorithms of feature extraction essentially are linear techniques for dimensionality reduction. The Principal components analysis (PCA), performs a linear mapping of the data to a lower dimensional space in such a way, that the variance of the data in the low-dimensional representation is maximized. Typical feature extraction methods such as Hu moments, LDA and PCA, for Kannada script the feature extraction in performed in two stages in the first stage the horizontal and vertical histograms of the size normalized character is computed which is feature vectors of 50 elements each. The contours of histograms are considered for the extraction of features for character recognition using wavelet transforms in the second stage of feature extraction module. The technique explained above is applied for Telugu script too and resulted in good recognition rate. Feature extraction for Tamil is performed by considering individual image glyph and features are extracted. First a character glyph is defined by the following attributes; Height and width of the character, total number of horizontal lines present, total number of vertical lines present, total number of circles present, centroid of the image, these features are sufficient to recognize the characters. For Malayalam script marginal frequency of row profiles is extracted as the features as the Malayalam has remarkably distinct lateral variations as compared to many other Indian other languages with a number of curls and twists in the characters. Another very interesting feature of this script is that the number of columns varies from 53 to a phenomenal 347 columns over the entire extended character set of the language. The other feature extraction techniques experimented successfully for printed Malayalam script are, statistical methods like frequency capture, average gap, absorption, other methods like SVD (Singular value decomposition) where a maximum of the top five singular values as features are sufficient to get recognition of the rate of 97.6%. All features extracted in the previous module is stored in the database to be used by the recognizer module. In all the four language scripts experimented a two stage classifier is used in most cases and has proved to be computational simple and very efficient. The conventional Multilayer Perceptrons (MLP) a multilayer feed forward neural networks are used as classifiers for the recognition system. In the first stage the main characters and their combination characters are classified. In the second level of classification vowels, conjunct characters and subscripts are classified by using a second level of MLP [4]. Thus this two stage classification further speeds up the rate of recognition. The same methodology for classification is implemented for Telugu language as it has a very similar character set as Kannada Script. Classification for the Tamil script is done using the features extracted in the feature extraction stage, which corresponds to each character glyph. These features are analyzed using the set of rules and labeled as belonging to different classes. Thus a rule based classification approach [9]. Classification for printed Malayalam script is performed in two stages which further speeds up the rate of recognition. In the first stage, the number of columns of the test image is used to locate the closest subclass of the test characters (coarse classification) while the lp–based classifier (fine classification) uses the test feature vector extracted by applying the lateral analysis to locate the nearest vector in the subclass in order to classify the test character. A two-stage classification is performed to accelerate the rate of recognition and reduce complexity to a great extent. Heuristics is again applied to remove ambiguities in feature vectors lying on the boundaries of the sub classes. An SVM classifier is also used for classification of the printed Malayalam characters. The segmentation stage segments a word into character segments like vowels, consonants, conjuncts, left vowel signs, or right vowel signs and each segment is assigned with a label [12]. The maximum number of segments in a given Malayalam character is not more than three segments. The SVM classifiers are used to label each of the segments. The SVM (binary classifier) is applied to this multiclass character recognition problem by using one-versus-rest type method. The problem now is a *n*-class problem with *n* equal to the number of segments in total, but during training it was found that some of the confusion characters have similar appearance though this problem of similarity is well tackled by using the feature extraction approaches as explained. Hierarchal SVM classifiers are used with the reduction in the search space as shown in Figure 3.

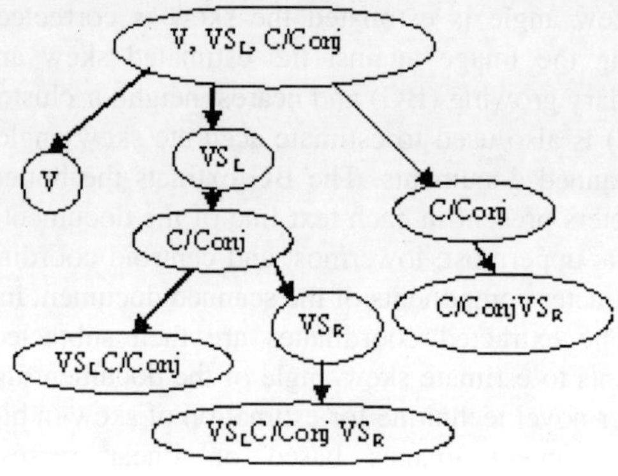

Figure 3. Classification Search Space

2.3. System outputs

The recognized text in the scanned document is then fed to the output interface of both TTS (text-to-speech) engine and the Index Basic Braille Embosser.

2.3.1. The Index Basic Braille Embosser

The Index Basic-D Braille embosser is a great double sided printer which has an excellent range of features. These include double sided printing, speech guidance and tactile graphics reproduction. The Basic-D is a classic and efficient double-sided embosser. The free WinBraille editor makes it one of the most versatile embossers in the market. This Plug and Play embosser is ready for action. It plugs in to the PC via a USB or parallel port. It is also network friendly, with built-in network port (TCP/IP), and printer server supporting DHCP. The Index Basic Braille embosser is operated via an ink and Braille labeled front panel. With the multi lingual speech feedback, it can be installed and operated by blind and sighted users alike. Picture this The Index Basic embosser has a function to emboss tactile images with maximum resolution of 0.5 mm. The image editor is included in WinBraille. The Production Capacity is 340 PPH and a Speed of 97 CPS. The Index Basic Braille Embosser Compatible with Shree Lipi Braille translation software that offers conversion in 12 Indian languages. This is the software used to get the Braille output in different Indian languages here like Kannada, Telugu, Tamil and Malayalam.

2.3.2. The text to Speech Readout System

The backbone of the audio interface is the Indian Language Text to Speech System (TTS). Speech synthesis involves algorithmically converting an input text into speech waveforms and some previously coded speech data. Speech synthesizers can be characterized by the size of the speech units they concatenate, as well as by the method used to code, store and synthesize the speech. The Malayalam Text to Speech system SUBHASHINI™ is Windows based software, which converts Malayalam Text files into fairly intelligible speech output. The TTS is based on Speech synthesis by diaphonic concatenation [13].

3. Conclusion

We have presented a novel scheme for document access through OCR specifically for the needs of the specially enabled. Several algorithmic techniques developed by our pattern recognition research group and others have been integrated to emerge with a complete document stack to read out / Braille print out system. The system has been tested on simple text only bi-lingual documents with a read out accuracy of 98.7 percent and print out accuracy of 97.6 percent. Novel algorithms developed by us in language identification, segmentation of difficult situations, features for different languages, etc have been integrated in the system. The system finds application in libraries, reading rooms, enquiry counters, and tertiary services and so on. The design needs to be extended to multilingual as well as documents with embedded graphics and tables.

Acknowledgment

This work was supported in part by research grants from UGC for Major Research Project in Science and Technology, F.No. 32-113/2006

References

1. V.N.M. Aradhya, G.H. Kumar, and P. Shivakumara, An Accurate And Efficient Skew Estimation Technique For South Indian Documents: A New Boundary Growing And Nearest Neighbor Clustering Based Approach, International Journal of Robotics and Automation, vol.22 (2007).
2. G. Hemantha Kumar, P. Shivakumara, D.S. Guru, & P. Nagab-hushan, A novel technique for estimation of skew in binary text document images based on linear regression analysis. Journal SADHANA, Indian Academy of Sciences, 30, Part 1, February, pp69–85, (2005).
3. A. Vinciarelli and J. Luettin , A New Normalization Technique for Cursive Handwritten Words., Pattern Recognition Letters, vol. 22,no. 9,pp. 1043-1050, (2001).
4. R. Sanjeev Kunte, *et al.*, Neural Network based OCR System for Kannada Printed Text employing Wavelet Features, in the proceedings of the International Conference on Artificial Intelligence in Engineering and Technology, ICAIET (2004).
5. R. Sanjeev Kunte and Dr. R D Sudhaker Samuel, A Two-stage Multi-network Approach for Classification of Large-set of Language Characters, International Conference on Systemics, Cybernetics and Informatics, pp 642-647 (2007)
6. Anand Arokia Raj et al. Text Processing for Text-to-Speech Systems in Indian Languages.
7. Anupam Basu, Debasish Sen , Shiraj Sen and Soumen Chakraborty, An Indian Language Speech Synthesizer – Techniques and Applications, IIT, Kharagpur, December, (2003).
8. O.D.Trier and A.K. Jain,.Goal-Directed Evaluaction of Binarization Methods., IEEE Transactions on Pattern Analysis and Machine Intelligence, vol. 17, no. 12, (1995).
9. Seethalakshmi R., Sreeranjani T.R., Balachandar T., Abnikant Singh, Markandey Singh, Ritwaj Ratan, Sarvesh Kumar, Optical Character Recognition for printed Tamil text using Unicode, Journal of Zhejiang University, pp.1297-1305 (2005)
10. Negi Atul, Chakravarthy Bhagvati and.Krishna B , An OCR system for Telugu. Proc. Of 6th Int. Conf. on Document Analysis and Recognition IEEE Comp. Soc. Press, USA,. pp. 1110-1114 (2001)
11. P. S. Janardhanan. Issues in the development of OCR systems for Dravidian languages - proceedings of Akshara 94., BPB Publications, New Delhi, India (1994).
12. Malayalam standardization report May (2001)
13. http://www.cdacindia.com

METHOD TO ANALYZING SOFTWARE TESTABILITY AFFECTING FACTORS BASED ON TESTABILITY TREE

JIANPING FU, MINYAN LU, SHUNKUN YANG, ZHEN LI
Dept. of System Engineering of Engineering Technology, Beihang University
Beijing 100191, China

To determine the software testability affecting factors systematically an analysis method based on software testability tree is proposed reference to the fault tree analysis approach. Firstly, determine the software to be analyzed. Secondly, select the software testability forms according to the features of software to be analyzed. Thirdly, construct the software testability trees by analyzing the selected software testability forms. Lastly, analyze the software testability trees to find out the software testability affecting factors. The method can not only get the software testability affecting factors roundly and systematically but also help to the follow-up software analysis and design for testability by determining the primary and secondary factors and identifying the factor relationships.

1. Introduction

Software testability is a software quality characteristic which can reflect the difficulty level of software testing. Software testability analysis and design is the research hot spot at present. A number of software testability analysis methods are based on the knowledge of software testability affecting factors. Bruce [1] divided the affecting factors of object-oriented software into three classes: structure factors, communication factors and inheritance factors. Using these factors he calculated the internal testability of the methods, the class testability and the program testability. The ad hoc technique of software design for testability can improve software testability by modifying the design and/or codes [2]. The modification must be carried out under the guidance of software testability affecting factors, too.

Although software testability affecting factors are very important to software testability analysis and design, there is not a sophisticated method which can derive the affecting factors systematically at present. Therefore a new method to analyze the software testability affecting factors is proposed in this paper reference to the fault tree analysis.

2. Fault Tree Analysis

Fault tree analysis (FTA) refers to analyze the hardware, software, environment and man-made factors which may result in product failures and draw the fault tree in order to determine all possible factor combinations and their occurrence probabilities [3]. In 1961 FTA was first applied in reliability study of launch control system of Militia Missile by Bell Labs successfully. FTA was also the main method in the nuclear power plant safety evaluation report of the United States Atomic Energy Commission (WASH-1400) in 1974. Nowadays FTA is applied widely in the field of software. Leveson [4] and Cha [5] used the fault tree to describe the common program structures such as "if-then-else", "while", and so on. AECL applied the software fault tree in a nuclear reactor software risk analysis [6]. Sedo Sohn combined the software fault tree with entropy to measure the testability of the digital security system software [7].

FTA contains identifying top event, constructing fault tree, qualitative/quantitative analysis, etc. Top event is the basis of FTA. Since a different top event may result in a distinct fault tree, an appropriate top event must be selected before constructing a fault tree. The fault tree is a logic causal relationship diagram composed of the events and logic gates. The logic gates link the events to express the logical relationships between the events. When a fault tree is constructed the qualitative or quantitative analysis should be taken to identify all failure mode sets which will lead to the top event or determine the top event occurrence probability.

3. Analysis Method of Affecting Factors

Similar to FTA if we take certain change of software testability as the top event we can construct a tree with the possible factors resulting in the change. Through further analysis we can acquire the software testability affecting factors. Detailed process is as follows:

3.1. *Determine software to be analyzed*

There are a lot of types of software such as communication software, financial software and word processing software. Different software has its own features and may contain different software testability affecting factors. Therefore it is not possible to determine all software testability affecting factors through one analysis. The solution is to conduct a specific analysis to one or certain type of software and determine the affecting factors according to their features.

3.2. *Select software testability forms*

To get the software testability affecting factors the software testability forms (the external software behaviors which can reflect the changes of the software testability) must be determined first. Freedman stated a software component that was "testable" had the following desirable properties: test sets were small and easily generated, test sets were non-redundant, test outputs were easily interpreted and software faults were easily located [8]. Yves Le Traon thought software testability was concerned with three difficulties: generating test sets, interpreting test results and diagnosing faults [9]. Magiel Bruntink distinguished two categories of source code factors in their investigation of class testability: test case generation factors and test case construction factors [10]. In conclusion some acts or indicators in software testing can reflect the software testability and the software testability forms can be derived from the testing process.

Six software testability forms are derived from the process of software testing in this paper: increase of test set (F1), more difficult to generate test case (F2), more difficult to build a test environment (F3), more difficult to impose test input (F4), more difficult to collect test result (F5) and more difficult to explain test result (F6). Because some distinct software testability affecting factors may be derived from the different tree which was constructed according to the different testability form, it is necessary to select appropriate software testability forms considering the software features.

3.3. *Construct testability trees*

After selecting the software testability forms, corresponding trees can be gotten from the analysis of these forms. Because the trees are based on the software testability forms and the purpose of the construction is to obtain the software testability affecting factors, we call them software testability trees. Before constructing a testability tree every kinds of software information are needed such as the requirement specification, design documents and program codes. A testability tree can be constructed from top to bottom based on the software testability form. Because the software testability affecting factor is the software attribute which can be measured directly and will affect the software testability [11], it is not necessary to expand the non-software behaviors and the software behaviors must be decomposed into a direct measure level in the process of constructing a testability tree.

3.4. *Testability tree analysis*

The testability tree analysis includes two steps: identifying the minimal cut sets and determining the software testability affecting factors. Semanderes algorithm and Fussell-Vesely algorithm are two traditional methods to identifying the minimal cut sets:

- Semanderes algorithm. Start from the basic events of a testability tree. Execute event set computing from bottom to up layer by layer. Replace the output event of OR gate with the union of input events and replace the output event of AND gate with the intersection set of input events. In the process of replacement simplify the expression in accordance with the absorption law and idempotence of Boolean algebra. Finally express the top event with the simplest form: the union of the intersection sets of the basic events where each intersection set corresponds to a minimal cut set of the testability tree.
- Fussell-Vesely algorithm. Start from the software testability form of a testability tree. According to the structure of the tree search the minimal cut sets from top to bottom layer by layer. Increase the order of the minimal cut sets (the number of the basic events contained in a minimal cut set) encountering the AND gate and increase the number of the minimal cut sets encountering the OR gate.

After identifying the minimal cut sets, analyze each element in the sets to exclude the non-software behavior one by one. Software testability affecting factors can be derived from the remained software behaviors.

4. Factor Analysis of MC Software

With this paper's method the software testability affecting factors of an aircraft mission computer (MC) software have been analyzed. MC software which resides on the memory of the mission computer belongs to the real-time embedded software and the main function is to load the weapons data, manage the flight data and fire calculation. Considering the difficulty of the real-time embedded software to set up a test environment, impose test inputs, collect and interpret test results four software testability forms were selected: F3, F4, F5 and F6 (see Section 3.2). The testability tree constructed according to F3 is shown in Figure 1.

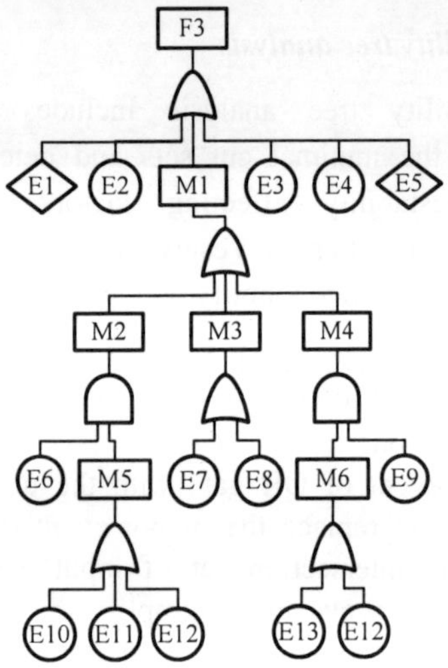

Figure 1. Testability tree of F3

All events in Figure 1 are listed in the following table.

Table 1. Event list of Figure 1

Event ID	Event Meaning
F3	More difficult to build a test environment
M1	Software interface is more complicated
M2	External input interface is more complicated
M3	Internal interface is more complicated
M4	External output interface is more complicated
M5	External input interface complexity increases
M6	External output interface complexity increases
E1	Tester quality declines
E2	Crossing system increases
E3	Coupling between units increases
E4	Unit real-time requirement heightens
E5	Support environment requirement heightens
E6	External input increases
E7	Input parameter increases
E8	Output parameter increases
E9	External output increases
E10	Rate of standard input declines
E11	Dependency set of external input enlarges
E12	Interface type increases
E13	Rate of standard output declines

Fussell-Vesely algorithm was used to identify the minimal cut sets of the testability tree in Figure 1 and the process is shown in Table 2. All minimal cut sets are listed in the table: {E1}, {E2}, {E6, E10}, {E6, E11}, {E6, E12}, {E7}, {E8}, {E13, E9}, {E12, E9}, {E3}, {E4}, {E5}. Because E1 and E5 are non-software behaviors they were not considered in the process of determining the software testability affecting factors. From the rest software behaviors 11 software testability affecting factors were summed up: the number of crossing system (NCS), coupling between units (CBU), unit real-time degree (URT), the number of external input (NEI), the number of external output (NEO), fan-in, fan-out, standard input rate (SIR), standard output rate (SOR), the number of interface type (NIT) and the large of external input dependency set (LEIDS).

Table 2. Process with Fussell-Vesely algorithm

Step	1	2	3	4
Process	E1	E1	E1	E1
	E2	E2	E2	E2
	M1	M2	E6,M5	E6,E10
	E3	M3	E7	E6,E11
	E4	M4	E8	E6,E12
	E5	E3	M6,E9	E7
		E4	E3	E8
		E5	E4	E13,E9
			E5	E12,E9
				E3
				E4
				E5

5. Method Analysis

A method based on casual diagrams is proposed in [11] to analyze the software testability affecting factor. It doesn't need to consider the logical relationships between the events in the same level. This paper's method is a little complicated in determining the logical relationships and looking for the minimal cut sets. However, it has two advantages as follows:

1. Determine primary and secondary factors. According to the order of the cut set it is easy to

judge the importance of the software testability affecting factors. Factors from the cut set with smaller order are more important than factors from the cut set with higher order. For example, in the software testability affecting factors determined prior to NCS which is derived from E2 is more important than SIR which is derived from E10 because the order of {E2} is smaller than the order of {E6, E10}. Affecting factors from the 1-order minimal cut sets should be paid more attention to in the process of software testability analysis and design.

2. Identify factor relationships. Various relationships may exist among the software testability affecting factors. For example, some factors must change simultaneously to affect the software testability and the changes of certain factors could lead to the changes of another part of factors. Identifying the factor relationships is very important to software testability analysis and design. This paper's method pays more attention to the relationship analysis of the events. Therefore it can identify some factor relationships. Because the events in a minimal cut set must occur simultaneously to result in the top event the affecting factors from the same minimal cut set must change simultaneously to affect the software testability. If the factors are correlative (change of one factor can lead to the change of another) they must be derived from the same minimal cut set. According to this principle this paper's method can narrow the identification scope of correlative factors to the minimal cut set although it still cannot identify the correlative factors. Therefore the correlation analysis should only be taken to the factors derived from the cut sets {E6, E10}, {E6, E11}, {E6, E12}, {E13, E9} and {E12, E9} to determine the relevance of the software testability affecting factors prior to.

6. Conclusions

In this paper a method to analyze the software testability affecting factors based on the testability tree is proposed according to the fault tree analysis. The software testability affecting factors can be gotten from the steps of determining the software to be analyzed, selecting software testability forms, constructing testability trees and testability tree analysis. Comparing with other method this paper's method may be a little more complicated. However the method can not only determine the primary and secondary factors but also identify some factor relationships. At the same time it can narrow the factor scope of correlation analysis. Therefore it can provide assist to more accurate software testability analysis and more effective software testability design.

References

1. Bruce W. N. Lo and Haifeng Shi, in *Proceedings of International Conference on Software Engineering: Education & Practice*, Dunedin, New Zealand, 26-29 January, 1998, 330-337.
2. Fu Jian-Ping and Lu Min-Yan, *Journal of Computer Applications* **28**(11), 2915-2918(2008).
3. Zeng Sheng-Kui, Zhao Ting-Di, Zhang Jian-Guo, Kang Rui and Shi Jun-You, *Tutorial of System Reliability Design and Analysis* (Beijing University of Aeronautics and Astronautics Press, Beijing, 2000).
4. N.G. Leveson and P.R. Harvey, *IEEE Transactions on Software Engineering* **9**(5), 569-579(1983).
5. S.S. Cha, in *Proceedings of 10th International Conference on Software Engineering*, Singapore, 11-15 April, 1988, 377-387.
6. AECL, SDSI Software Hazards Analysis Report for Wolsong Nuclear Power Plant, Technical Report, 1994.
7. SeDo Sohn and PoongHyun Seong, *Reliability Engineering and System Safety* **91**, 44-52(2006).
8. Roy S. Freedman, *IEEE Transactions on Software Engineering* **17**(6), 553-564(1991).
9. Yves Le Traon and Chantal Robach, in *Proceedings of International Test Conference*, Washington, DC, 21-25 October, 1995, 710-719.
10. Magiel Bruntink and Ari Van Deursen, *The Journal of Systems and Software* **79**(9), 1219-1232(2006).
11. Fu Jian-Ping, Study of Software Testability Measurement Method, Ph. D. dissertation, Beihang University, Beijing, China, 2009.

PROJECTION BASED FEATURE EXTRACTION PROCESS FOR BANGLA SCRIPT: A MODIFIED APPROACH

M.A. NASER
Dept. of Electrical and Electronic Engineering, Islamic University of Technology (IUT)
Gazipur-1704, Bangladesh

NAFIZ I. B. HAMID
Dept. of Electrical and Electronic Engineering, Islamic University of Technology (IUT)
Gazipur-1704, Bangladesh

M. A. HOQUE
Dept. of Electrical and Electronic Engineering, Islamic University of Technology (IUT)
Gazipur-1704, Bangladesh

Classical projection-based feature extraction has its drawbacks due to lack of scale invariance. In this paper, a heuristic approach is proposed that makes the projection based features scale independent as well as more style invariant. A classifier software is used to classify characters from 12 different types of fonts as well as different characters of same the type of font.

1. Introduction

Projection histograms were introduced in 1956 in a hardware OCR system by Glauberman [1]. It consists of a simple running count of the black-pixels in one direction, i.e. a column or a row. Today, this technique is mostly used for segmentation of lines, words and characters. Segmentation of Bangla characters using projection is discussed by Garain and Chaudhuri [2]. In the process, the document is segmented into lines first, followed by word and character segmentation.

For noncursive handwriting, method proposed by Ohta et al. [3] uses a threshold in projection value for segmentation. Bishnu and B. B. Chaudhuri [4] propose a method for the segmentation of vertically inseparable handwritten Bangla characters which uses zonal information of a character. And this information is provided by projection histogram. Different zones providing structural information across the height of the word are detected. According to this zonal information the words are segmented into characters. They used an approach named recursive contour following to split two touching characters.

However, projection based feature extraction gained a little popularity due to its lack of scale and font style invariance. In this paper, we propose a novel method that will make the projection based feature extraction more reliable for classification.

2. Projection Histogram

Basically two types of projections are used: horizontal and vertical. Horizontal projection is the total number of all black-pixels along a column while vertical projection is the total number of all black-pixels along a row of a character image. For example, if there is n number of rows, then vertical projection:

$$Y = \sum A_{r_i}$$

where A is the value assigned for black-pixel, ri is the row number; i=1,2,3,….,n.

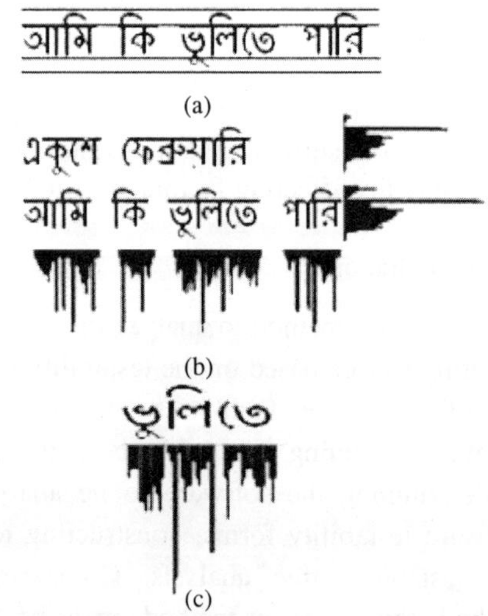

Figure 1. (a) Three zones (b) Horizontal projection for line detection (right) and vertical projection for word detection (bottom) (c) Vertical projection for character detection.

Bangla text can be partitioned into three zones [2], [4]. Presence of a headline (called *matra*) makes it different from English characters. Hence, the portion just above the headline is the upper zone. The headline is detected by counting histogram of the horizontal projection and considering the row of having highest peak. The middle zone contains the characters and the lower zone contains character modifiers. Similarly, the text lines are detected [2] by finding the valleys of the horizontal projection. Rows with larger values have higher probability for the headline of an individual text line; alternatively minimum projection value between two consecutive headlines indicates the boundary between two text lines. Then the words of a text line are distinguished by considering the minimum in vertical projection. Once segmentation up to individual word is done, character segmentation is performed. Since characters in a word are usually connected to each other through the headline, they get disconnected once the headline is erased. Overall process is depicted in Figure 1. After that, features from the characters are extracted. Different techniques [5], [6] are proposed by researchers for this.

Usually projection data are not used as features as it does not provide information about the shape of the character as well as it is highly vulnerable to the variation in shapes. Nevertheless, it is evident that projections are highly scale dependent as number of black-pixels changes with the size of the character. Hence projection value in a particular direction changes with the shape and style of the font (Figure.2).

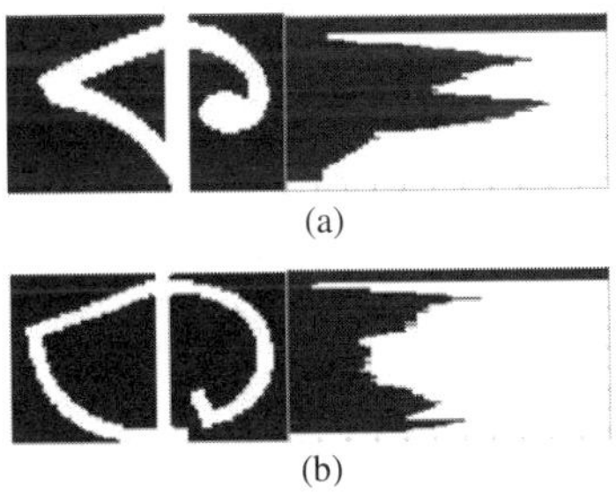

Figure 2. Character KA (a) Font 1 (b) Font 2 with corresponding horizontal projections.

If we can make the projection profile invariant to these variable factors, then the extracted features from projection data can be used to classify characters. In this paper, we propose a technique to make the projection scale and style invariant.

3. Preprocessing for Projection Histogram

To work with a scanned character image, we assume that it is segmented, binarized and inverted.

Then we applied some heuristic techniques. First of all, we take the bounding box of the character. The bounding box represents the smallest rectangle that contains a component, or in this case, a single character, like the one shown in Figure. 2a. This is done to avoid the projection from unnecessary pixels around the character. After that, the characters have to undergo a liner normalization; $f'(r',c') = f(a*r, b*c)$, where $f(r,c)$ is the original image, $f'(r',c')$ is the normalized one and 'a' and 'b' are scaling factors for 'r' rows and 'c' columns. Values are set for a and b such that the character is resized to 80X80.

4. Proposed Method

We have seen that projections change not only with the scaling of the character but also with the character style itself. For example, width of the character changes with font styles. Consequently, same character with different widths or styles gives different histograms. To prevent this we propose to *skeletonize* the character first. Skeletonization is an approach that is used to represent structural shape of the character, yet reducing the feature size.

For skeletonization, typically thinning algorithms are used that iteratively delete edge points of a region, given that deletion of these points does not remove the end points, connectivity is not broken without causing excessive erosion of the region [7]. This is also a very good measure to deal with deformed characters (other than different styles) due to bad scanning condition or effect of noise. There are numerous algorithms for skeletonization, one of them is based on medial axis transform (MAT) proposed by Blum [8]. However, we use the function provided by MATLAB of MathWorks that is based on dilation and erosion. Figure. 3 shows projection histograms of skeletonized characters of different fonts. These projection histograms are more similar to each other compared to Figure. 2. This is because variance in shapes of the characters is reduced now. We have taken the standard deviation between two projections of these two cases. Standerd deviation is calculated by:

$$s = \left(\frac{1}{n}\sum_{i=1}^{n}(x_i - \overline{x})^2\right)^{\frac{1}{2}}$$

where, $\overline{x} = \frac{1}{n}\sum_{i=1}^{n} x_i$; n is the number of elements. It is found that projection histograms without skeletonization have deviated more than the later case.

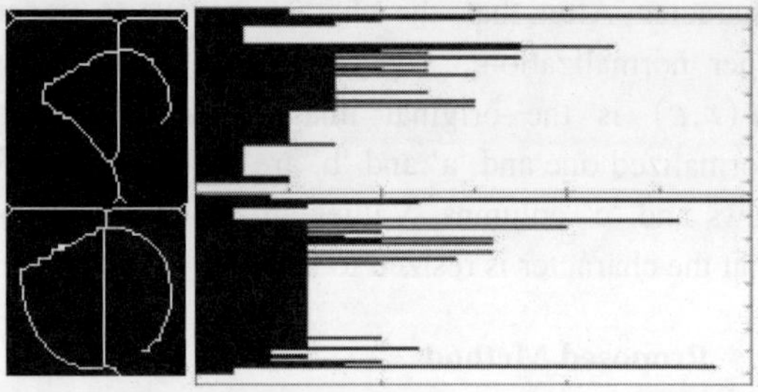

Figure 3. Skeletonized characters and their projections

Even after the techniques employed so far, different characters can have similar projection histogram. Moreover, some Bangla characters shares same features (Figure. 4) which makes them indistinguishable. They generate almost same histograms.

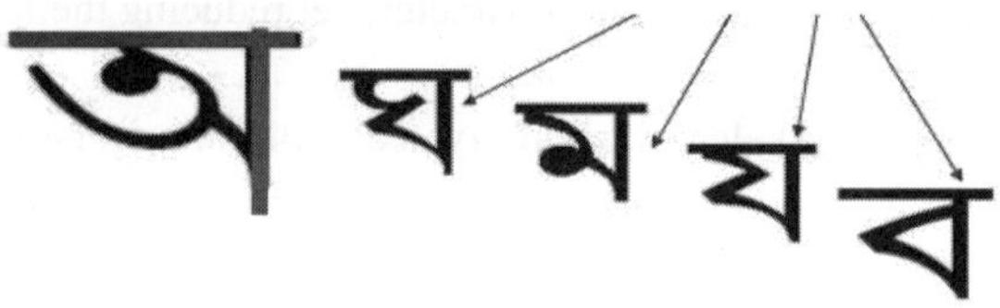

Figure 4. Different characters with similar features

We propose an approach to be adopted to face this problem. We call it Feature Regulation. Here, we eliminate similar features of different characters at the segmentation level. There are several characters that have features like vertical and/or horizontal bars. If we get rid of them at the segmentation level, features of the distinctive part will dominate.

Now, we get back to our main concern; projection based feature extraction. This is how it goes. Regular projection histogram is generated of a character (after character segmentation) as stated in section II. This histogram can be used as features for that character. But due to the drawback associated, projections as features do not get enough ground. Hence, instead of taking horizontal and vertical projections of the whole character, we propose to take projections of the half. In other words, the original character is divided by two parts- horizontally and vertically. From those four pictures, we will obtain two horizontal and two vertical projections. Figure. 5 shows the process.

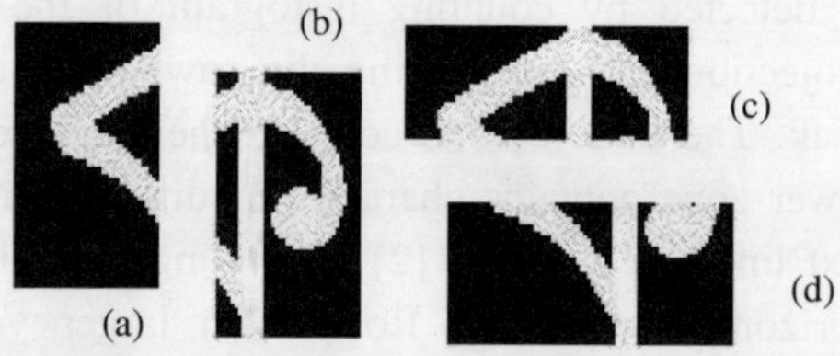

Figure 5. (a) Left half(b) Right half(c) Upper half (d) Lower half

Once we get the histograms, we take ratio of two horizontal histograms as well as that of two vertical histograms. We have seen that this feature is unique for every character. Now these ratios can be used as features for classification purpose instead of histogram itself. As we have resized the image *80X80*, there will be 80 rows and 80 columns. So, we get 80 features in any direction. We have generated projection ratios for 50 characters of Bangla Language from 12 different fonts. There are two types of feature vectors, one is for horizontal and another is for vertical projections. The feature vector for horizontal projection is arranged like in Table 1. This is a *80X12X50* matrix. The other one is arranged in a similar pattern.

Table 1. Arrangement of feature vector

Features	Character 1	Character 2	Character …	Character 50
1	$Ch\ 1_1$	$Ch\ 2_1$	…	$Ch\ 50_1$
2	$Ch\ 1_2$	$Ch\ 2_2$	…	$Ch\ 50_2$
3	$Ch\ 1_3$	$Ch\ 2_3$	…	$Ch\ 50_3$
…	…	…	…	…
N	$Ch1_N$	$Ch2_N$	…	$Ch50_N$

5. Result

Final result is obtained from actual classification performed by classifier software named WEKA, developed by The University of Waikato. It is available in the web [9]. To make our data set compatible to WEKA, we have developed a converter. The user interface of the converter is shown below.

There are many classifiers available in WEKA. We have chosen Neural Network Classifier of Radial Basis function. Details of the classifier can be found in [10]. For simplicity, we have taken only 10 characters out of

50. So, there will be total 120 characters from 12 different fonts. We produced feature tables like Table 1 for all the cases discussed above. After conversion to the desired file format, we fed those to WEKA.

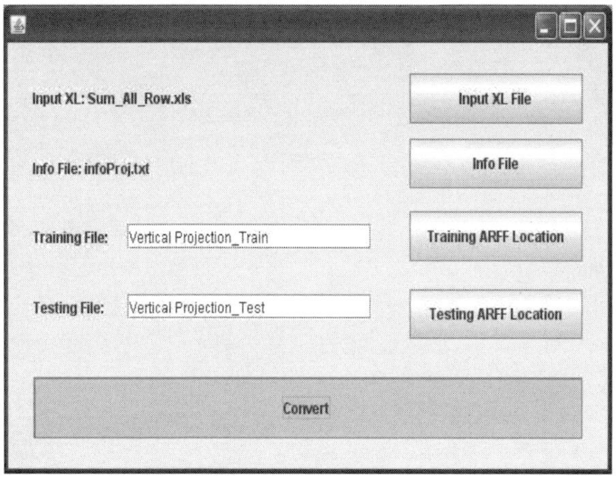

Figure 6. Data file converter for WEKA

The result is given in Table 2. There are two main columns: Accuracy for the projection of whole character and that for characters divided into halves. These columns are sub-divided into two, indicating results for skeletonized and non-skeletonized (i.e. raw input) characters. Since projections are taken from two directions, there are two rows for horizontal and vertical projections. From the table, accuracy is better for our proposed Half-character than classical Whole-character projection. And if we take skeleton, then we get 100% accuracy for both cases. These results are produced by training and testing of same feature set. However, if the feature set is split by 80% and 20% for training and testing respectively, accuracy reduces. But, still skeletonization and Half-character projections have higher accuracy. These results are shown in Table 3.

Table 2. Result obtained using same training and test set.

Type	**Accuracy % (Whole-Character projection)**		**Accuracy % (Half-Character projection)**	
	No Skel	*Skel*	*No Skel*	*Skel*
Horizontal	94.16	100	97.5	100
Vertical	98.33	100	94.16	100

Table 3. Result obtained using different training and test set.

Type	**Accuracy % (Whole-Character projection)**		**Accuracy % (Half-Character projection)**	
	No Skel	*Skel*	*No Skel*	*Skel*
Horizontal	48.78	58.3	53.6	60
Vertical	58	62.5	63.4	68.3

Then, we are interested to see the recognition accuracy after the characters are scaled. We have taken only two types of fonts for simplicity and character size is larger than before. Produced result is tabulated in Table 4. This table is arranged like the previous one. For this table, training set is the one used for previous one. But test set consists of scaled characters. The result shows that scaled characters can be recognized with 95% accuracy if vertical projection of skeletonized Half-character is taken, compared to 85% accuracy, when the same is taken for Whole-character (shown by single star*). Other three entries are satisfactory, except the one marked by four stars *. In this case, usual method gives better results.

Table 4. Recognition accuracy of scaled characters.

Type	**Accuracy % (Whole-Character projection)**		**Accuracy % (Half-Character projection)**	
	No Skel	*Skel*	*No Skel*	*Skel*
Horizontal	95**	92***	95**	90***
Vertical	98.33 ****	85*	85 ****	95*

The effect of feature regulation discussed in section IV is tabulated in Table 5. It is seen that feature regulation gives good result only if characters are skeletonized.

Table 5. Recognition accuracy of feature regulated characters.

Type	**Accuracy % (Whole-Character projection)**		**Accuracy % (Half-Character projection)**	
	No Skel	*Skel*	*No Skel*	*Skel*
Horizontal	92.5	100	95	100
Vertical	98.33	100	93.33	100

6. Conclusion

Projection histograms are very much essential for segmentation. Researchers have been using it considerably for segmenting lines, word and characters. However, in this paper, we have tried to make projection data useful as features for recognition purpose. Results for different types of projections are analyzed. Based on our proposed approach, we conclude with the remark that projection histogram can be considered as one of the feature extraction processes.

Acknowledgement

We would like to thank our teacher A. K. M. Khaled Ahsan Talukder of CIT Dept. for helping us with the WEKA.

References

1. M. Glauberman, “Character recognition for business machines. Electronics”, 29, 132-136.
2. U. Garain and B. B. Chaudhuri, “Segmentation of touching characters in printed Devnagari and Bangla scripts using fuzzy multifactorial analysis”, IEEE Transactions On Systems, Man, And Cybernetics—Part C: Applications and Reviews, Vol. 32, No. 4, November 2002.
3. K. Ohta, I. Kaneko, Y. Itamoto, and Y. Nishijima, “Character segmentation of address reading/letter sorting machine for the Ministry of Posts and Telecommunications of Japan, NEC Research and Development, vol. 34, no. 2, pp. 248-256, Apr. 1993.
4. Bishnu and B. B. Chaudhuri, “Segmentation of Bangla handwritten text into characters by recursive contour following,” Document Analysis and Recognition, 1999. ICDAR apos;99. Proceedings of the Fifth International Conference on Volume , Issue , 20-22 Sep 1999 Page(s):402 – 405
5. M. A. Rahman, A. El Saddik, “Modified Syntactic Method to Recognize Bengali Handwritten Characters”, IEEE Transactions on Instrumentation and Measurement, vol. 56, vol. 6, pp. 2623-2632, December 2007.
6. U. Pall, T. Wakabayashi and F. Kimura, “Handwritten Bangla Compound Character Recognition using Gradient Feature”, 10th International Conference on Information Technology, 2007.
7. R. C. Gonzalez and R. E. Woods, Digital Image Processing, Second Edition, chapter 11, Representation and Description, pp. 648-649, Prentice-Hall of India Private Limited, 2006.
8. H. Blum, "A Transformation for Extracting New Descriptors of Shape", in W. Walthen-Dunn (ed.), Models for the Perception of Speech and Visual Form, M.I.T. Press, 1967, pp. 362-379.
9. http://www.cs.waikato.ac.nz/ml/weka/
10. S. Haykin, Neural Networks A Comprehensive Foundation, Second Edition, Chapter 5,Radial-Basis Function Networks, pp.256-308, Pearson Education

EVALUATION OF AN APPRAOCH FOR DEVELOPING A TOUCH SCREEN UI FOR RESIDENTIAL AGED CARE SERVICES

SEVAG DEMIRJIAN

Faculty of Engineering and IT, University of Technology Sydney
NSW 2007 Australia

ZENON CHACZKO

Faculty of Engineering and IT, University of Technology Sydney
NSW 2007 Australia

BRUCE MOULTON

Faculty of Engineering and IT, University of Technology Sydney
NSW 2007 Australia

VENKATESH MAHADEVAN

Faculty of Higher Education, Swinburne University of Technology
Vic 3140 Australia

This paper explores issues associated with a new approach for developing touch screen user interfaces, and investigates its suitability in the context of residential aged care. The approach draws upon well established human computer interaction principles, with some modifications. The project investigated the suitability of the approach for the development of a specialised software application intended for nurses and caregivers in residential aged care. The case study included usability evaluations and a 3-month field trial undertaken with staff at Concord Community Hostel. The results suggest that the proposed approach is suitable for developing this type of clinical applications.

1. Guidelines

1.1. *Producing Hard Copy Using MS-Word*

Residential aged care services are under increasing pressure to improve efficiencies while providing quality care services for the aging population. The provision of care services is increasingly performed by the private sector. In the USA caring for patients who have chronic illnesses costs approximately US$1.3 trillion per year [1] (which is more than twice the US defense budget [2]). Many organisations competing for a share of this market are increasingly turning to new technologies to achieve greater efficiencies in both administrative and clinical processes [3].

Studies of international best practice suggest that clinical information technology systems can help reduce the time spent by nurses on documentation, and allow more time for direct care or residents [4]. Thus there is considerable motivation for the development of improved clinical applications for residential aged care. The extent to which an application is "usable" is directly related to the approach that is taken for the design of the user interface (UI). Usability refers here to the extent to which a product can be used to achieve specified goals, and relates to effectiveness, efficiency and satisfaction [5]. It has emerged as a key differentiator of modern software [6]. Usability factors contribute to the success (or otherwise) of a software application.

Studies by the Department of Health and Ageing identify that usability is a particularly important issue in the development of systems in aged care, in part because the workforce tends to be older and has mixed levels of experience with computers [7, 8].

Several models and guidelines exist for the development of standard line-of-business software applications. However, few address the design of user interfaces where the primary method of interaction is via a touch screen. Two exceptions are Elo TouchSystems [9] and SAP [10], both of which provide a degree of guidance for touch screen application development. In this paper we describe and evaluate an approach for developing a touch screen user interface that is intended to be suitable for clinical applications in aged care.

2. Background

Requirements elicitation and analysis is widely thought to be among the critical stages of software development. Accordingly, the approach included the adoption of user-centered design [12] and the emerging ISO 13407 standard which relates to human-centered design processes for interactive systems.

Requirements gathering, design and test activities we used for this project include (a) user context analysis, (b) paper-prototyping and computer based prototyping, (c) usability walkthroughs, (d) individual usability evaluations, (d) usability trial metrics (for the three month trial), and (e) subjective assessments using SUS (Software Usability Scale) [14].

2.1. *The User*

A census and survey carried out by the National Institute of Labour Studies provides detailed information about the key characteristics of the residential aged care workforce [13]. The end-users of clinical applications in residential aged care include personal carers/assistants in nursing, enrolled nurses, registered nurses, and healthcare professionals, for example, therapists and doctors.

According to a survey of the computing experiences and competencies of the direct care workforce [3], most registered nurses and allied health professionals use computers at home or work on a frequent (daily) basis. However, personal caregivers as a group (the direct care workforce) tend to be drawn from an older worker population with mixed levels of computer literacy among staff.

Amongst other things, the survey indicated that 25 per cent of the care workforce is not Australian born—some facilities cater for specific ethnic groups tend to employ staff with knowledge in languages other than English. Further, 94 per cent of the care workforces are women, more than half the registered nurses are aged 45 or over, and more than 40 per cent of the care workforce have Year 12 or equivalent schooling. In addition, the results of the survey suggest that personal caregivers on average tended to have a likelihood of feeling less comfortable about the use of computers in their work settings.

While many personal carers indicated that they use a computer at home, only 25 per cent use a computer on a frequent basis. Given these findings, it was decided that workforce characteristics such as these must be taken into consideration when designing an application for aged care.

2.2. *Staff Goals*

The roles and responsibilities of nursing/care staff include a diverse range of activities such as assisting an individual with their personal care needs, assisting with daily living, administering medication, and planning/managing the delivery of complex care. Effective communications between staff and caregivers is of utmost importance, and a large proportion of workplace activities are intended to bring about effective documentation and communication.

2.3. *The Residential Care Workplace*

The usability of a system depends on the context in which it will be used. In an aged care setting, several organisational, physical and technical factors must be taken into consideration when designing any system to be used in the workplace. These include considerations relating to staffing levels, the number of nurse stations, the 24-hour work environment, and the extent to which technical support is available.

2.4. *Evaluation of User Interface (UI) Methods*

A primary consideration in the requirements analysis of the user interface was the capacity to process information at or near the point-of-care. Touch screens and tablet PCs (with touch screens) were considered the most appropriate device (as compared to a desktop PC, laptop, or PDA/Palm) in part due screen size and advanced handwriting recognition capabilities.

3. User Interface Design

The central design strategy was to develop a user interface architecture that would enable highly efficient use by experienced users, while at the same time allow new users to make effective use of the application almost immediately. To achieve this, it was considered important to attempt to make the application user-friendly for older users, highly supportive of users with little or no previous computing experience, intuitive and self explanatory.

Since most users were not expected to have a high level of familiarity with computes, it was essential that the user interface was easy to understand and learn. In particular, three user competency levels were identified: (1) a "learned user", who is able to access the system and read messages; (2) an intermediate user, who is able to perform all clinical tasks using the system, and (3) and advanced user, who is able to perform all clinical and administrative tasks. A goal of the project was that uses with little or no previous computing experience would reach the first level of competency in less than 10 minutes.

3.1. *Framework for the Development of UI Architecture*

The approach made use of Inductive UI standard workbook and wizard models. Inductive UI (IUI) is a set of emerging principles for making software applications simpler to explain and understand. The basic principle of IUI is to break features in to screens or pages that are more self-evident and self-explanatory. Examples of IUIs appear in Windows XP, such as the alternate "category view" found in the control panel. The model combines the standard workbook and wizard models with the task-centric principles of Inductive UI [12] to implement a clinical application that is easy to understand and use.

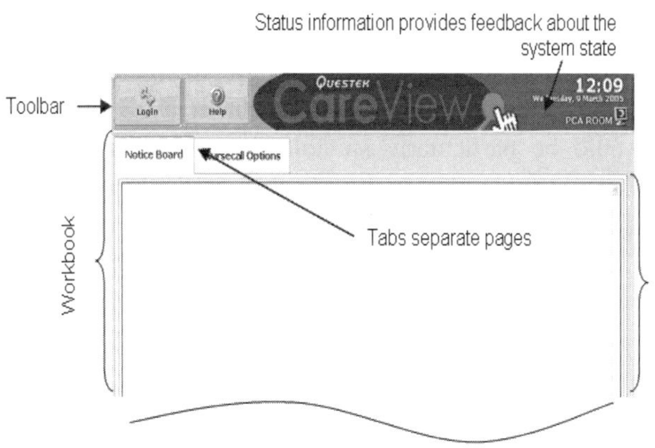

Figure 1. Screen shot which shows toolbar and workbook.

To overcome the limitations of screen real-estate and the problems of "modes", we implement the workbook and wizard models. The workbook model shows a series of tabs that act like pages in a book. It was thought that tabs might make it more convenient to change pages when switching between tasks.

Figure 1 shows that the adopted UI model, in its simplest form, could be reduced to toolbar and a "workbook" of "pages". The workbook hosts all the pages (screens) of the application. Within the workbook there are two types of pages: *(1) Option pages* that organise related groups of common tasks to provide users with a starting point; *(2) Task pages* that focus on a single well defined user goal. A task is something users might think to do, such as view a resident's care plan or write a clinical note.

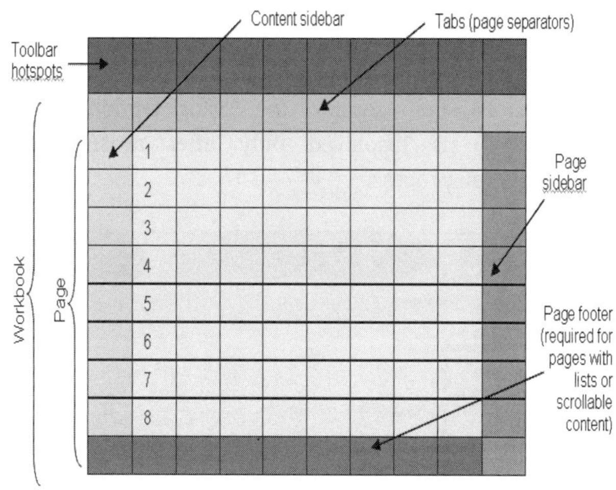

Figure 2. The grid layout that was used.

Viewed as a grid (Figure 2), the interface is partitioned into 10 x 11 target areas (hotspots). We use a minimum button height and width of 15mm (57 pixels at 96DPI), with a minimum spacing of 3mm between hotspots. Hence, given a screen resolution of 1024x768 pixels (15" touch screen monitor) this sizing arrangement can accommodate up to eight list items (vertically) on a page. Common buttons are placed at the edges of the screen (toolbar, page sidebar, page footer, content sidebar). Each page is titled and includes a statement which describes its purpose. The workbook can host several pages at the same time, each denoted by a tab. By using the tabs, a user may switch between reading clinical notes and writing clinical notes, without needing to close one section or open another. It was thought that the ability to check previous while making new entries would be of benefit to the user.

The user's working context is preserved when consulting online help, allowing the user to follow tutorials without loosing track of their progress. Online help is available on another task page.

3.1.1. *Option Pages*

A key element of the design approach is the use of "option pages'. An option page starts a dialogue with the user to provide an instruction or raise a question, by asking the question "What would you like to do?" The purpose of an option page is to allow a user to open additional pages in the workbook (i.e. start a new task) from a set of menu items. Users have access to option pages and menu items based on their role and access permissions. For example, the "Main Options" page (Figure 3) is displayed only after a successful authorisation process.

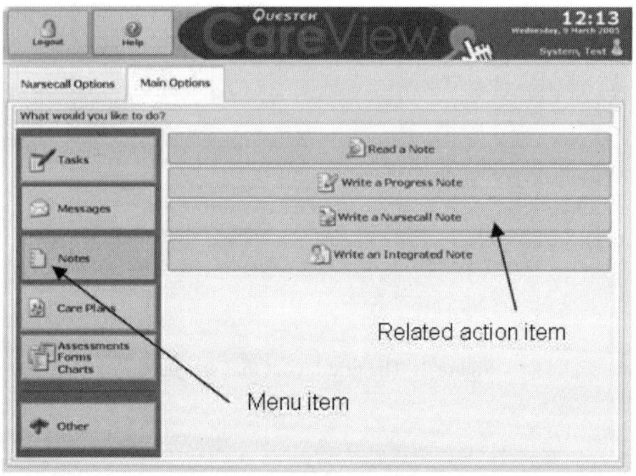

Figure 3. Screen shot which illustrates an option page .

Menu items are grouped and arranged in a two level hierarchy, with progressive disclosure of action items. Each menu item (noun) consists of one or more action items (verbs). For example, the menu item "Notes" prompts the user with four action items including read and write. This enables the user to see what is in effect a sub-menu, at the same time as the main menu.

3.1.2. *Task Pages*

Another aspect of the UI model that was adopted is the use of "task pages". A task page facilitates a conversation between the user and computer, which usually consists of one or more steps to achieve a specific goal. A task page may also launch other related tasks. All task pages include a page sidebar with buttons to navigate between steps (continue/back) and buttons to close or complete/cancel the task. It was thought that this approach would help to reduce screen clutter and eliminate confusion that might have been cased by the introduction of visible but disabled buttons.

3.2. *Approach Taken for the Inclusion of a Touch Screen Tool Set*

The approach taken for the touch screen toolset includes three main components. These components allow users to perform typical actions such as browsing, searching, and data entry.

3.2.1. *Listbox*

Tasks that require the user to select an item from a list include a listbox. Filter and sort operations may also be performed on the list with the help of a listbox sidebar. If the list is long a navigation bar consisting of page up and page down buttons allows the user to scroll the list.

3.2.2. Search Paid

A Listbox with more than eight items is always accompanied with a Search pad. The Search pad uses a keyword search method to progressively restrict the items displayed in the list. It was thought that approach would be particularly suitable for situations where a user has some idea as to what they are looking for, and if it fits the set search criteria.

A simple search may use a single criterion to restrict items (eg. surname), while more complex searches may involve two or more fields joined by a logical OR operation (eg. surname OR first name OR room no.) The intention of this was to make the selection process quick and straight forward.

3.2.3. *Input Panel*

Data input is captured using a variety of methods and technologies. The input panel can accept a combination of text, audio, and image formats to store rich content. It was envisaged that this might be especially applicable for clinical applications where a photo (eg. of a wound or skin tear) can greatly assist in communicating and evaluating the care needs of a resident.

3.2.4. *Onscreen (Virtual) Keyboard*

The approach includes an on screen virtual keyboard. The layout adopted is a cut down version of a typical QWERTY keyboard, and includes a selection of characters/keys caregivers are most likely to need when writing clinical notes. Less frequently used control and special character keys are placed on a secondary "special keys" panel (Figure 4).

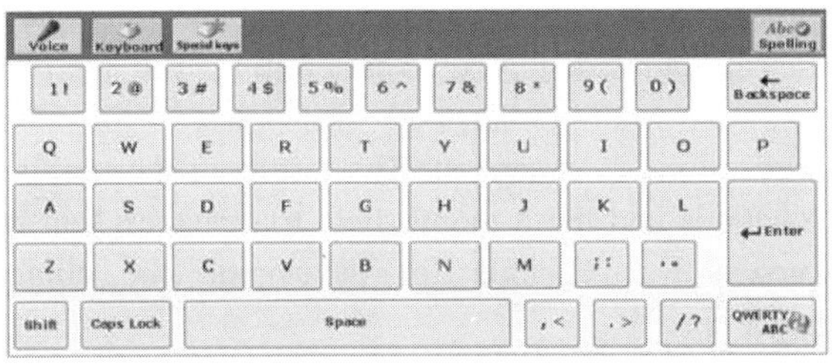

Figure 4. Screen shot which illustrates an option page .

3.2.5. *Audio Recording*

While continuous speech recognition was not implemented within the scope of this project, the audio recording feature provides the ability for users to dictate, so that transcription may be undertaken at a later point in time.

The user interface components (listbox, searchpad, input panel) are the building blocks of task pages, which may be further packaged to form a collection of reusable task steps. For example, the "Select a resident" task step is used in several areas of the application (Figure 5).

Figure 5 provides an example of how the different components can be combined, and shows the *Listbox*, *Search pad* and *Input panel* components together on the one page.

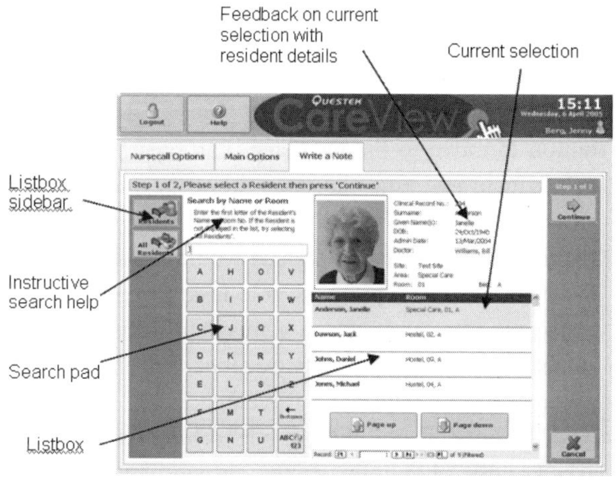

Figure 5. Illustration of different components on a page .

4. Results of Evaluations and Field Trial

Six individual usability evaluations and a 3-month field trial were conducted at Concord Community Hostel (CCH), between May and August 2004. CCH is a modern residential aged care facility that provides low care, high care, and special care services for 62 residents. The typical age of nursing/care staff was 52, ranging from 24-62yrs.

For the usability evaluations, six participants were selected based on their computing experience. Two of the participants had never used a computer before. The evaluations were performed in the staff education room at CCH. At the start of the evaluation session participants were provided with a scripted introduction, followed by a short explanation of the equipment. Participants were required to complete a series of four tasks. The four tasks were (a) finding help; (b) logging in and out (c) reading and writing messages; and (d) reading and writing progress notes.

The evaluation procedure incorporated a "think-aloud" protocol. Data was collected directly by the test monitor. Task completion times and observations were noted. The entire session was also recorded to audio. During the debriefing, participants were asked to complete a usability questionnaire [14] and comment about their experience.

Five of the six participants completed the set tasks within the allocated time (20 minutes). For four of the six participants, the first one or two presses on the touch screen failed to hit the desired target. However, after the first successful hit, each participant's hit ratio improved significantly.

Performance on the login task was poor, as most participants did not locate and press the "Continue" button to move to the next step. Participants were able to navigate and find the tasks from the menu options with little difficulty. When unable to perform the required task, some participants would repeatedly press the page tabs. The progress note task required the user to search for and select a resident; this task was performed without difficulty by all participants.

Participant required an average of 1.3 minutes to type the note "David did not attend bingo today. When asked why, he refused to answer and appeared annoyed". From this it was inferred that an average typing speed of 1.2 characters per second was achieved using the on-screen keyboard. The test monitor formed the opinion that users with no previous computing experience would require some training (approx. 10 minutes) before they could make effective use of the application. After the usability evaluations were completed, several alterations were implemented in an effort to address some of the observed issues prior to the field trial. The field trial was used to collect performance and process metrics, goal being to assess how well the application supported users with the documentation process. The field trial employed a parallel and phased-in approach to introduce features in 5 stages. 13 personal carers were selected to play an active part during the trial. Training was provided (to this group) before each stage in a classroom environment.

Observations recorded during the trial suggested a high level of user acceptance and enthusiasm was shared by nursing/care staff throughout the period of the trial. Figure 6 shows one of the participants using the system during this three month period.

Figure 5. Field trial participant at nurse's station.

Staff reported that they found most things easier and quicker to accomplish, compared to existing paper-based practices. For example, one staff member stated "Finding information is quicker (30 seconds compared to 5mins looking through resident folders)".

An unexpected result was that participants with little or no previous computing experience were among the most frequent users.

The application enabled staff to successfully complete documentation tasks, and in many cases, these tasks were able to be completed in less time using the application, compared with previous processes. The overall findings of the field trial suggested that the development approach is suitable for producing an application that has a high degree of usability.

5. Conclusions

The work undertaken examined the suitability of a new approach for developing a touch screen user interface to be used in a residential aged care setting. The approach draws on well understood principles, with some modifications as described. The results of the usability evaluations and the 3-month field trial suggest that the approach was suitable for developing the clinical application

Acknowledgments

The authors would like to thank all the nursing/care staff at Concord Community Hostel who took part in the usability study, and Questek Australia Pty Ltd. for their support and sponsorship of the project.

References

1. National Coalition on Health Care. "Health Insurance Cost," http://www.nchc.org/facts/cost.shtml [accessed 10.2.2009].
2. The Department of Defense "The Budget for Fiscal Year 2008," http://www.gpoaccess.gov/usbudget/fy08/pdf/budget/defense.pdf [accessed 24.1.2009].
3. Demirjian S, Chaczko Z, Hughes J, 2005, Information Technology and the residential aged care workforce – National survey report, University of Technology, Sydney.
4. Pearson A. et al 2003, *Best Practice Information Sheet.* Joanna Briggs Institute of Evidence – Based Nursing and Midwifery.

5. The international standard, ISO 9241-11.
6. Schaffer E. 2004, Institutionalization of Usability: A step-by-step guide, Addison-Wesley.
7. Clinical IT project – Department of Health & Ageing, http://www.ageing.health.gov.au/rescare/clinitfly.htm, (last accessed 10/3/2005).
8. Albert Research (July 2004), *Results of Research into the Residential Aged Care Industry's use of Computers and the Internet*, Department of Health and Ageing, http://www.ageing.health.gov.au/rescare/racs_itrpt.htm, (last accessed 12/07/2004).
9. Elo Touchsystems, Application tips, http://www.elotouch.com (last accessed 21/4/2005).
10. Interaction Design Guide for touchscreen applications, SAP, http://www.sapdesignguild.org (last accessed 18/4/2005).
11. Jan Miksovsky 2001, Inductive User Interface Guidelines, Microsoft Corporation.
12. INUSE, User-centred Design, NECTAR.
13. Prof. Richardson, S. & Assoc Prof. Martin, B. 2004, The Care of Older Australians, *A Picture of the Residential Aged Care Workforce*, The National Institute of Labour Studies.
14. John Brooke, SUS – A quick & dirty usability scale, Digital Equipment Co. Ltd.

DEVELOPMENT OF A PLATFORM-INDEPENDENT SCADA SYSTEM FOR HOTEL AUTOMATION USING SOAP PROTOCOL

ZENON CHACZKO

Faculty of Engineering and IT, University of Technology Sydney
NSW 2007 Australia

BRUCE MOULTON

Faculty of Engineering and IT, University of Technology Sydney
NSW 2007 Australia

VENKATESH MAHADEVAN

Faculty of Higher Education, Swinburne University of Technology
Vic 3140 Australia

MARCEL CAROLY

Faculty of Engineering and IT, University of Technology Sydney
NSW 2007 Australia

The demand for standards and tools that allow for communication between application components, which might be running on different platforms or frameworks, has been a serious issue in the Information Technology industry. Existing protocols such as HTTP, SMTP, and SOAP are regularly used as a means of solving such interoperability issues. These solutions are particularly seen in large enterprise systems where networked services form applications that are provided across a variety of heterogeneous hardware and software platforms. This paper presents a case study of work carried out by a group of software engineering students at the University of Technology, focusing on the development of a SCADA system for hotel automation.

1. Introduction

The demand for standardized methods of communication between application components across heterogeneous firmware and software has brought about significant levels of research activity within the ICT sector in recent years. Much of the work undertaken to date has focused on the development of standards and standardized protocols relating to Extensible Markup Language (XML) and Remote Procedure Call (RPC) middleware [4, 9].

In the past, many cross-platform IT solutions have made use of CORBA (Component Object Request Broker Architecture) and/or DCOM (Distributed Component Object Model) [9, 11]. However, frameworks such as these can present prohibitive difficulties for software development undertakings, in part due to their reliance on proprietary protocols that are absent from many systems. For example, to make use of CORBA, each machine must ordinarily support the same ORB framework. DCOM, on the other hand, is primarily dependent on the Microsoft Windows platform, although it has been successfully ported to other platforms [5]. Additional difficulties arising from reliance on these frameworks relate to degradation in performance when scaled up. Scalability issues are particularly prevalent in larger systems where machines running different platforms are communicating via an internet, especially when there are firewalls and proxy devices within the network [5]. Another solution that is commonly employed is Java RMI (Remote Method Invocation) [9]. RMI is typically more platform independent than its alternatives. However, a drawback with RMI is that it is reasonably reliant on the java platform and typically incurs extra overhead by way of running a JVM on each machine.

Platform and language independent protocols such as HTTP, SMTP and Simple Object Access Protocol (SOAP) [8] are increasingly being adopted to resolve the inherent interoperability issues associated with the above frameworks. Support for HTTP and SMTP is available in the vast majority of platforms thanks to the popularity of the Internet. SOAP can use SMTP or HTTP (or HTTPS) for transport, thus SOAP can be deployed in almost any platform. In addition, SOAP can make use of Web Services (WS) [6, 13] and XML documents, a structured text format. Given that text files can be transmitted via port 80 (for HTTP) and port 25 (for SMTP), a service using SOAP can be run in a way that is relatively proxy/firewall-friendly.

A "service" is here regarded as a self-contained collection of functions that can operate independently of other services. Service based approaches are often employed in situations where there is a need to pass messages between several networked machines. Web services that use standard protocols are particularly useful for resolving interoperability issues.

This paper reports a case study that makes use of web services within a supervisory application for a wireless sensor network, namely the Hotel Automation SCADA System (HASS) [3], developed at the University of Technology, Sydney, Australia.

2. Background

This section provides background regarding key technologies (XML, SOAP and WSDL) used within the HASS project.

Overview of XML & SOAP protocol

Extensible Markup Language (XML) is an extendable meta-language that uses text to define the structure of (and give meaning to) data [14]. Web services can make use of text based XML documents to describe data by way of XML tags. When combined with standard transfer protocols such as HTTP, data from web services can be transferred in a format that can be understood across different networks, platforms and components. XML allows developers to define custom tags which will be interpreted using an XML Parser. Web Services can make use of XML schemas to describe their interfaces, and transfer data using SOAP/SML [10].

Web Services are typically invoked using an RPC or message passing mechanism as shown in Figure 1.

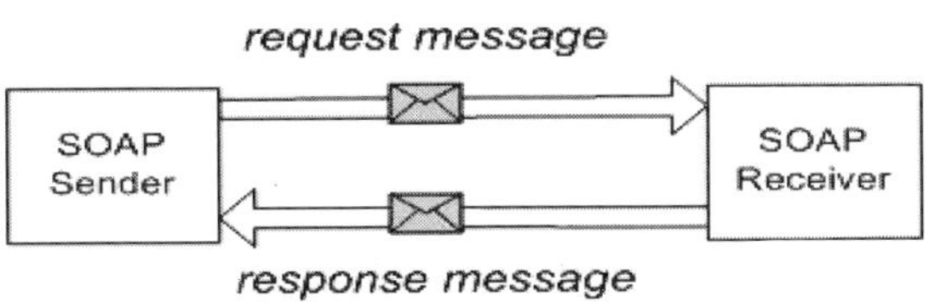

Figure 1. SOAP messaging.

The protocol consists of three main concepts:

- **The SOAP Envelope**, which contains an optional header and a mandatory body that informs an XML parser that the document is a SOAP message. Where present, the SOAP header may contain application specific information such authentication details, whilst the body will contain the SOAP message itself

- **The SOAP Encoding rules** that define how data and messages should be encoded in SOAP packets

- **The SOAP RPC representation**, which defines conventions by which RPC calls and responses will be made.

2.1. *WSDL*

WSDL (Web Services Description Language) is defined as a specification for "networked XML-based services" [12]. WSDL allows for uniform description of data regardless of underlining encoding scheme (MIME) or protocol. In WSDL, a service is defined as a collection of network endpoints which, along with message, are separated by WSDL from their concrete network deployment and data format bindings (Erik, 2001). The data types referred in WSDL have to be understandable by both clients and server. Furthermore, a WSDL document specifies a set of actions (or operations) supported by the service with parameter details.

2.2. *Web services architecture*

The conceptual architecture of web services is described by three main components, the service provider, service broker and service requester and their communication WSDL (Web Service Description Language) which are wrapped in SOAP envelopes. The service broker (directory service) maintains a registry of published web services; this may be provided through the UDDI (Universal Description, Discovery, and Integration) protocol. Service Providers publish their services to a Directory Service through a WSDL descriptor. Service Requesters will query the Directory Service for the definition of the services they require and than use WSDL to communicate with appropriate Provider. Researchers at IBM formally described these three activities as "publish", "find", and "bind" as shown in figure 2 below.

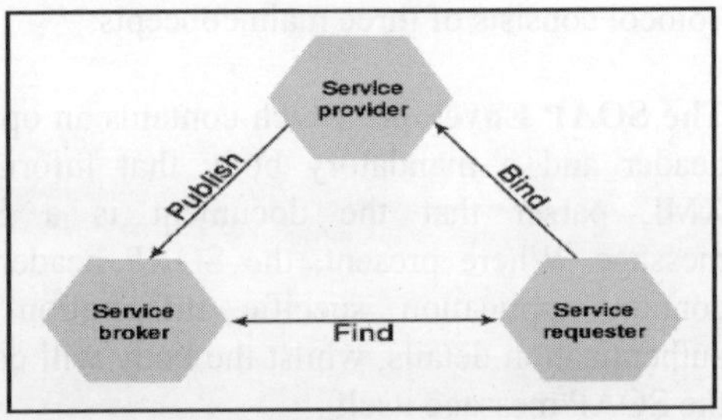

Figure 2. Web service architecture (Source: IBM web services architecture team)

3. The Hotel Automation SCADA Systems

The Hotel Automation SCADA System (HASS) [3] was developed by a group of students the University of Technology, Sydney in Spring 2004 as part of a course in Software Systems Analysis and Design [2].

The HASS was designed with the intention of monitoring the conditions of hardware devices in a hotel and generate alarms whenever a variety of conditions arose that required immediate attention.

3.1. *HASS architecture*

The development team adopted a distributed COTS-based architecture for the development of the HASS. The team made use of a third-party software solution to develop the system, namely Citect™ which supported a variety of functions including:

- Device monitoring
- Alarm management
- Human Machine Interface (HMI) visualization
- Remote Access
- Reporting, and
- Trending

These features fitted in nicely with many of the needs of the client, lacking only a few features that had to be added by the team, namely:

- Remote Contacts & Rosters
- Alarm causality
- Device Driver specific to the hotel's hardware devices

These issues were tackled by developing a number of independent modules (described in Table 1) that operated outside of the central CitectSCADA™ software and communicated amongst each other using Web Services and SOAP. This provided the client with a fully integrated solution that fitted their needs for the HASS.

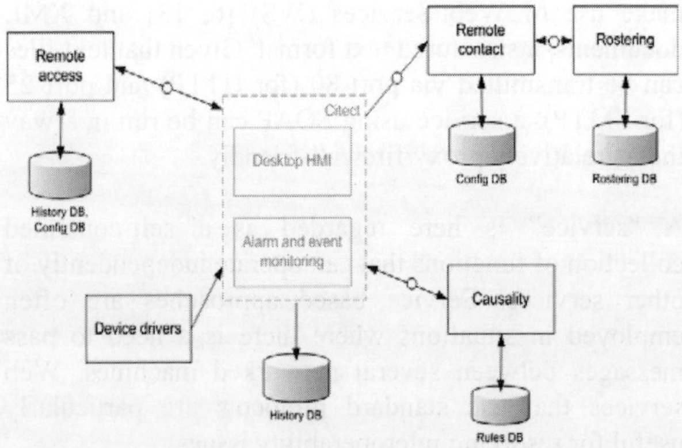

Figure 3. HASS conceptual (Source: Heinietz, S.P. et. Al, SSD)

It was recognized that organizations may make use of a variety of legacy systems or SCADA solutions other than Citect™. The architecture was developed with the principle that each subsystem could be completely independent making use of web services for communication. This approach would allow for easy integration or replacement of module in the system including Citect™.

Table 1. Component responsibility (Source: Heinietz, S.P. et. Al, SSD, A 2004)

Component	Description
Remote access	Retrieves live data from Citect™ for display. Generates reports from the historical data exported from Citect™ Authenticates users for access.
Device drivers	Provides an interface between the devices and Citect™
Citect™	Performs event handling, device monitoring and provides the desktop HMI for monitoring and controlling the devices
Remote contact	Service to contact the on-call operator via some telecommunication channel (e.g. SMS, telephone, email).
Rostering	Allows users to define the list of operators and their working times. Provides a service to determine the current on-call operator
Causality	Allows users to define causality rules for alarms. Accepts requests from Citect™ to apply rules to incoming alarms and returns grouping commands.

3.2. *SCADA Interface*

The conceptual architecture illustrates by figure 3 highlight the distributed nature of the system with sub-systems such as Remote access, Remote contact and Causality connecting through the Citect™ SCADA sub-system. Integration of these distributed subsystems was a critical aspect of the system development requiring the development of interfaces for inter-communication and between external subsystems. This section provides an overview of the approach used to interface the modules with Citect™.

3.3. *Interfacing with Citect™*

Citect™ provided a variety of interfaces to external applications including a ODBC, DDE and a DLL (CTAPI.DLL) for use in C/C++, Visual Basic or Delphi as well as an interface. However, these interfaces only provided access to Citect's tag database. The only interface that provided access to the systems functions such as deleting alarms is the Cicode and Citect VBA interface for scripts that are embedded into Citect. Given these limitations the students had developed the scheme illustrated by figure 4, allowing Citect to interact with the components in our architecture.

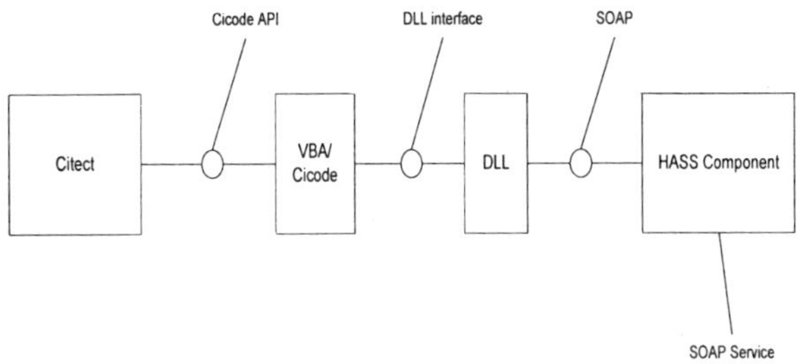

Figure 4. Scheme to interface with Citect™

In this scheme a DLL calls a web service through a SOAP interface which than waits for a response from the service, once the response is received it is sent as a return value back through some Cicode or VBA code.

This mechanism had one disadvantage causing Citect has to wait for response from external component when it could be carrying out other tasks. This would impact on the performance of system especially in situations when there could be a long delay between request and response in the system.

An alternative scheme was used to handle this issue as shown in figure 5. This added an asynchronous messaging mechanism to Citect™ allowing the module to continue on with its primary tasks until a response is received for its request.

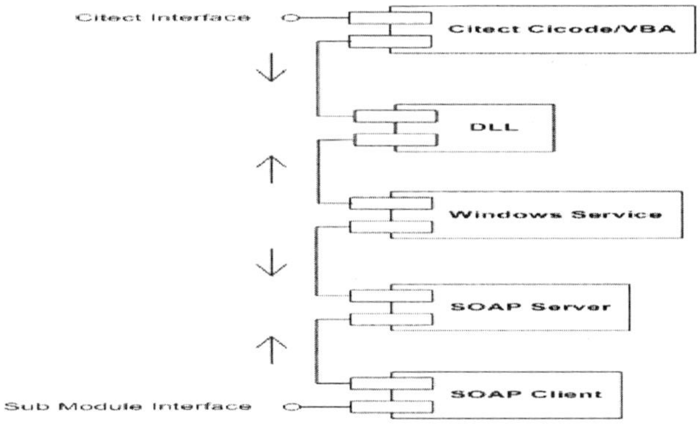

Figure 5. Asynchronous messaging scheme with Citect™

As an example we take a situation where an alarm needs to be sent out to the rest of the system. The process of sending the alarm involves:

- Putting an alarm into the DLL
- The Windows service picks the alarm up
- Windows service sends the alarm to a web service (SOAP server)
- A SOAP client (external sub-system) picks the alarm up from the web service

Once the alarm has been processed the subsystem will return results back to Citect™ through the following steps:

- The sub-system sends results to the web service (SOAP server)
- The Windows service picks the results up
- The Windows service puts the results into the DLL
- Citect picks the results up from the DLL

4. Implementation of the SCADA Interface

The asynchronous communication mechanism provided above operated over a number of different layers. This section provides details on how this interface was established and implemented for use within the HASS project.

In line with the example given above we illustrate the process needed to implement the mechanism in the case of an alarm being sent out to the system.

4.1. *Citect™* to DLL

The process begins with a Cicode function being called that first creates an alarm containing a timestamp and a number of parameters. The function than opens the DLL and places the alarm data as a string into the DLL using the `AddAlarmToQueue()` function.

```
FUNCTION
SendAlarm(STRING time, STRING tag, STRING desc,
STRING category, STRING state)
        INT hadd;
        STRING Result;
        hadd = DLLOpen("CitectDLL.dll",
"AddAlarmToQueue", "CCCCCC");
        Result = DLLCall(hadd, "^"" + time +
"^"" + "," + "^"" + tag +"^"" + "," + "^"" + desc +
"^""+"," + "^"" + category +"^"" + "," + "^"" + state +
"^"");
        RETURN Result;
END
```

Figure 6. Cicode invokes DLL function

4.2. *DLL*

A native windows32 DLL was developed within Visual Studio .NET that implemented an alarm queue that accepts alarms from Citect which can later be read by a Windows service The alarm queue essentially acts as a shared piece of memory allowing two different processes (Citect and the Windows service) to access the information stored within the DLL, this is done by defining a data segment within the DLL as being shared. This also means that a mutex is required to protect the queue from sharing violations.

```
    // string length
    #define SIZE 500
    // Queue length
    #define LENGTH 10000

    // this is the shared memory
    #pragma data_seg("SHARED")
    // for synchronisation
    volatile bool bInCriticalSection=FALSE;
    volatile HANDLE hMutex = CreateMutex(NULL,
FALSE, NULL);
    // alarm queue
    int iWrite = 0;
    int iRead = 0;
    char messages[LENGTH][SIZE] = {0}; // alarm
information
    // results from extern sub-system: causality
    char results[LENGTH][SIZE] = {0};
    int iResultRead = 0;
    int iResultWrite = 0;

    #pragma data_seg()
#pragma comment(linker, "/section:SHARED,RWS")
```

Figure 7. DLL declaration of variables

The add alarm function itself takes in a number of string parameters that are than added to a string that is placed into the alarm queue as illustrated by the code given below.

```
int AddAlarmToQueue(BSTR tag, BSTR time, BSTR desc,
BSTR cat, BSTR state)
{
    Lock();
if ( iWrite >= iRead + LENGTH )
    // the queue is FULL
    {
        Unlock();
return -1;
    }
char message [1000];
strcpy(&message [0], (char*)time);
strcat(&message [0], ";");
strcat(&message [0], (char*)tag);
strcat(&message [0], ";");
strcat(&message [0], (char*)desc);
strcat(&message [0], ";");
strcat(&message [0], (char*)cat);
strcat(&message [0], ";");
strcat(&message [0], (char*)state);

int index = iWrite % LENGTH;
    strcpy(&messages[index][0], (char*)message);
iWrite++;
return iWrite - iRead;
}
```

Figure 9, outlines the code that is used within the DLL to allow the Windows Service to retrieve the alarm from the queue.

```
    BSTR GetAlarmMessage()
    {
        Lock();
    BSTR retVal = NULL;
    if ( iRead < iWrite )
    {
    retVal = ::SysAllocString((BSTR)messages[iRead++ %
LENGTH]);
    }
        Unlock();
    return retVal;
}
iWrite++;
return iWrite - iRead;
}
```

Figure 9. Get alarm from the queue

4.3. *Windows Services*

A Windows service was implemented using Visual Studio .NET. This service continuously polls the DLL to check for incoming alarms using `GetAlarmMessage()` function. When an alarm is received it parsed and encoded into a SOAP envelope that is than sent within a request to a web service.

```
SoapClient::MySoapClient *soapclient = new
SoapClient::MySoapClient();
while (!bStopping)
{
            BSTR message =
GetAlarmMessage();
            if ( message != NULL && level > 0 )
            {
            char *str = (char*) message;
            char *token = strtok( str, seps );
              char *time = token;

              token = strtok(NULL, seps);
              char *tag = token;
              token = strtok(NULL, seps);
              char *desc = token;

              token = strtok(NULL, seps);
              int cat = atoi(token);

              token = strtok(NULL, seps);
              char *state = token;
// this sends alarm to Causality module which only
needs //tag, time and state of the alarm.
              soapclient->SendCSAlarm(tag,
time, state);
            }
}
```

Figure 10. Windows service polls and sends alarm

4.4. *Web Service*

The Causality and Remote Contact alarm web services were written in Java with their underlying platform being JDK 1.4.1_05, Apache TomCat 5.0 and Axis 1.1

In principle, these web services implement the same alarm queue as the DLL with basic functions SetAlarm() and GetAlarm(). SetAlarm() allows a Windows service to send alarms into the queue and GetAlarm() is used by the external sub-systems (Remote Contact and Causality) to extract alarms from the queue.

Below is a code segment of the Causality alarm queue. Note the use of **static** so that calls to the web service shares the same alarm information.

```
public class Causality
{
            private int LENGTH = 1000;
            static String _tags[] = new String[1000];
            static String _timestamps[] = new
String[1000];
            static String _states[] = new String[1000];
            static int iWrite = 0;
            static int iRead = 0;

   public int SetAlarm(String tag, String timeStamp, String
state)
   {
              if ( iWrite >= iRead + LENGTH ) // the
queue is FULL
                return -1;
              _tags[iWrite % LENGTH] = tag;
              _timestamps[iWrite % LENGTH] =
timeStamp;
              _states[iWrite % LENGTH] = state;
              iWrite++;
              return iWrite - iRead;
            }

            public String GetAllAlarmInfo()
            {
              if ( iRead < iWrite )
              {
                int i = iRead++ % LENGTH;
                return
_tags[i]+";"+_timestamps[i]+";"+_states[i];
              }
              else
                return null;
            }
}
```

Figure 11. Alarm queue web service

4.5. *SOAP Client (External Sub-system)*

The SOAP client (or Web service client) was implemented in Java and simply retrieves alarms from the web service's alarm queue. After obtaining an alarm it was parsed to obtain its tag, time and state as shown below.

```
public boolean getAllAlarmInfo()
{
    String endpoint =
"http://causality:8080/axis/Causality.jws";
    try
    {
              String result;
              Service  service = new Service();
              Call    call   = (Call)
service.createCall();
              call.setTargetEndpointAddress( new
java.net.URL(endpoint) );

call.setOperationName( "GetAllAlarmInfo" );

 );
```

```
call.setReturnType( XMLType.XSD_STRING );
                result= (String) call.invoke(new Object[]
{});
                if ( result == null ) return false;
                result = result + ";";
                System.out.println(result);

                // parse the returned string to get tags,
        // times and states
                int begin = 0, end = 0;

                //tag
                end = result.indexOf(";",begin);
                if ( end == -1 ) return false;
                tag = result.substring(begin, end);
                begin = end+1;

                //time
                end = result.indexOf(";",begin);
                if ( end == -1 ) return false;
                time = result.substring(begin, end);
                begin = end+1;
                //state
                end = result.indexOf(";",begin);
                if ( end == -1 ) return false;
                state = result.substring(begin, end);
                begin = end;
                return true;
            }
            catch ( Exception se)
```

Figure 12. Alarm queue web service

5. Conclusion

Web services have emerged as a service oriented framework that allows interoperability across platforms and programming languages. This case study outlines a mechanism used by a group of students at the University of Technology, Sydney to integrate an existing legacy SCADA software solution into a web service based community of distributed systems.

The study focuses on the development of an interface between Citect™ and web services within a distributed system. The techniques and code samples provided by this study illustrate the need for innovation when integrating a legacy system that lacks support for web services into a distributed system that that requires the use of web services.

Acknowledgments

We wish to acknowledge great contributions to the HASS project made by Software Systems Design students in Spring semester 2004. Special thanks go to contributors Nguyen, Hong Son and Do Quang Yen who helped in preparation of notes for this paper.

References

1. Campbell A. T., Coulson Geoff, and Kounavis Michael E. "Managing Complexity: Middleware Explained", IT Professional, Vol. 1, No. 5, September/October 1999.
2. Chaczko Z. et all, 2004, "New Perspectives on Teaching and Learning Software Systems Development in Large Groups." In 5th *Internat Conf on IT Based Higher Ed and Training ITHET '04* p278.
3. Chaczko Z., 2004, "*User Requirements for* a *Hotel Automation SCADA System (HASS)", 48475* Software Systems Analysis, the Faculty of Engineering, UTS, Autumn Semester 2004.
4. Chaczko Z., Caroly M., Lim L., "A Middleware Model for Telecollaboration Systems in Education", In *6th Internat Conf on IT Based Higher Ed and Training ITHET '05*.
5. Chiu, K., Govindaraju, M. & Bramley, R. 2002, *Investigating the Limits of SOAP Performance for Scientific Computing*. Available: http://www.extreme.indiana.edu/xgws/papers/soap-hpdc2002/soap-hpdc2002.pdf [11 September 2004]
6. Karl, G., 2000, *Web Services Architecture Overview*, IBM Architecture Team. [Online]. Available: http://www-106.ibm.com/developerworks/webservices/library/w-ovr/ [4 October 2004].
7. Konigsberg, P. E, B., Francisco, C., 2001, *Web Service Description Language* (WSDL) 1.1, W3C [Online]. Available: http://www.w3.org/TR/wsdl [5 October 2004].
8. Heinitz, S. P. et al, 2004, *Hotel Automation SCADA System - Software Architecture Design,* Software Systems Design, University of Technology Sydney.
9. Mahmoud Q. H., 2004, "Middleware for Communications", West Sussex, Wiley & Sons.
10. *SOAP - Simple Object Access Protocol*, RedHat [Online]. Available: http://rhea.redhat.com/asj/soap/ [09 November 2004]
11. Stonebraker M., 2000, "Too Much Middleware". SIGMOD Records V2.3.
12. Uche, O., 2000, *An Introduction to WSDL for SOAP Programmer*, IBM [Online]. Available: http://www-106.ibm.com/developerworks/webservices/library/ws-soap/?dwzone=ws [5 October 2004].

13. Web Services, Available:http://www-106.ibm.com/developerworks/webservices/library/w-ovr/00,
14. W3G, *Introduction to XML Schema*, [Online]. http://www.w3schools.com/schema/schema_intro.asp [5 October 2004].

IDENTIFYING COVERT MESSAGES INSIDE AN STEGNOGRAPHIC IMAGE USING NEURAL NETWORK

IMRAN KHAN

Technocrat's Institute of Technology (IT Deatartment), Rajiv Gandhi Technical University
Bhopal, Madhya Pradesh, Pincode-462023, INDIA

BHUPENDRA VERMA

Technocrat's Institute of Technology (IT Deatartment), Rajiv Gandhi Technical University
Bhopal, Madhya Pradesh, Pincode-462023, INDIA

ABSTRACT:

Steganographic techniques are being applied across a broad set of different digital technologies. The steganographic method will be used for internet/network security, watermarking and so on. So, the steganography is the process of hiding one medium of communication (Text, Sound, and Image) within another. It can work on JPEG 2000 compressed images & Stir Mark images.

The 'Steganalysis' is the field of detecting the covert messages. Almost all steganalysis consist of hand-crafted tests or human visual inspection to detect whether a file contains a message hidden by a specific steganography algorithm.

The new method of steganalysis based on neural network to get the statistics features of images to identify the underlying hidden data. We first extract the features of image embedded information, then input them into neural network to get the output. Experiment result indicates this method is valid in 'Steganalysis'

The neural network in still images is used to overcome the hurdles by hiding the data indirectly into graphical image using neural network algorithm to get cipher bits, The generated cipher bits are then placed in the least significant bit position of the carrier image. The XOR propagation network model is used which acts as a multilayer perceptron.

Keywords: cipher bits, StirMark filtering, cover image, regression model

Introduction

Steganographic techniques have been used for centuries and being applied across a broad set of different digital technologies. It has been observed that terrorists have been utilizing steganographic techniques within digital images to communicate to the internet[3].

A. Implementing steganography

Secrets can be hidden inside all sorts of cover information: text, images, audio, video and more. However, there are tools available to store secrets inside almost any type of cover source. A possible way of storing a secret inside a text is using a publicly available cover source, a book or a newspaper, and using a code which consists for example of a combination of a page number, a line number and a character number[3].

Hiding information inside images is a popular technique nowadays. An image with a secret message inside can easily be spread over the world wide web or in the newsgroups. The use of steganography in newsgroups has been researched by German steganographic expert, who created a 'scanning cluster' which detects the presence of hidden messages inside images that were posted on the net.

To hide a message inside an image without changing its visible properties, the cover source can be altered in "noisy" areas with many color variations, so less attention will be drawn to the modifications. The most common methods to make these alterations involve the usage of the least-significant bit or LSB, masking, filtering and transformations on the cover image.

The LSB method [4] uses bits of each pixel in the image. When using a 24 bit color image, a bit of each of the red, green and blue color components can be used, so a total of 3 bits can be stored in each pixel.

Masking and filtering techniques usually restricted to 24 bits or grayscale images. These methods are effectively similar to 'paper watermarks', creating markings in an image. This can be achieved for example by modifying the luminance of parts of the image. While masking does change the visible properties of an image, it can be done in such a way that the human eye will not notice the anomalies.

A more complex way of hiding a secret inside an image comes with the use and modifications of Discrete Cosine Transformations (DCT). DCT are used by the JPEG compression algorithm to transform successive 8 x 8 pixel blocks of the image, into 64 DCT coefficients each.

A simple pseudo-code algorithm to hide a message inside a JPEG image could look like this

```
Input:   message, cover image.
Output:  steganographic image containing message.
while    data left to embed do
          get next DCT coefficient from cover image
          if DCT ≠ 0 and DCT ≠ 1 then
              get next LSB from message
              replace DCT LSB with message bit
         end if
         insert DCT into steganographic image
end while
```

'Steganalysis' is the field of detecting these covert messages. Almost all steganalysis consist of hand-crafted tests or human visual inspection to detect whether a file contains a message hidden by a specific steganography algorithm. The process of detecting steganographic messages is known as 'Steganalysis' and a popular Steganalysis technique is called an 'attack'. the 'Steganalysis' is simply : 'Discovering and rendering useless such covert messages is a new art form known as 'steganalysis'. Steganalysis usually consist of brute force attacks using some tools. Brute force attacks usually consist of simply running tools against images.

III. NEURAL NETWORK APPROACH

'Steganalysis' has recently attracted researchers' interests with the development of information hiding (data hiding) techniques. We consider a new method based neural network to get statistics features of images to identify the underlying hidden data. We first extract features of image embedded information, then input them into neural network to get output. And experiment results indicate this method is valid in steganalysis. This method was used for internet/network security,Watermarking and so on.

The positive application of information hiding technology is that it can maintain the owner's legal rights. But there must exist the negative aspect for everything. The Terrorist may be communicated with each other by data hiding technology. US today printed an article "Terror groups hide behind web encryption". In this case, the data hiding in digital media on Internet has proven to be a boon for terrorists. So how to determine whether digital media has hidden information become a emergency problem for social security and stability. This new research area is called as 'Seganalysis'.

A. Information detection based on neural network

The information detection [1] is based on result that host image must be difference with hidden information host image. Maybe because human eye's mask features, we can't find any difference between host images and hidden information host images. But in essentially, data hiding process have to alter host image for embedding data. In other words, data hiding algorithms reveals statistical evidence or traces which can be used to detect the existence of hidden information in still images. Because now popular data hiding methods can be divided into two major classes: spatial domain and transform domain. Spatial domain is simple and easy to implement, but their robustness is weaker than other methods. Transform domain includes discrete Fourier transform, discrete cosine transform, discrete wavelet transform . And in spatial domain, mainly data hiding method is least significant bit (for short writing LSB) including all kinds of improved LSB methods. In transform domain, methods can be divided into several classes, quantization based, LSB based. Because we hope our method is feasible to all kinds of hiding methods no regardless embedding information in spatial or transform domain. So we try our best to consider all kinds' methods' features. But due to methods is too much, so we only consider transforms used in common data hiding methods. we only consider following transforms, DFT, DCT and DWT. Firstly we analysis object digital image according these three different kinds transforms in this method. The object image is algorithm to be able to detect methods as many as possible. These selected features should be significantly impacted by the data hiding processing. But it is difficult to find those features, so we select neural network to process this problem, neural network as the super capability to approximation any nonlinear functions. For these features which have more effected by data hiding process, neural network will assign larger weight coefficients and for these features which have less effected by data hiding process, neural network will assign less weight coefficients.

B. Image features extracting

First we analysis image's discrete cosine transform domain's statistics features. We divide each image into 8×8 sub-block and then take DCT of each sub-block. Based on analysis of Image Quality Measures (IQMs)[2] that depends on image features i.e. the good IQM should be accurate, consistent and monotonic in predicting quality.

We consider following IQMs[2]. We denote multispectral components of an image at the pixel position i, j, and in band 'k' as C_k (i,j) where k = 1….3 for color images. The C(i,j) , $\hat{C}$(i,j) indicate the multispectral pixel vectors at position C(i,j). Use M_i , i=1…10 to describe ten IQM features used in the detector.

a.Minkowsky Measures

The L_γ norm of the dissimilarity of two images can be calculated by taking the Minkowsky average of the pixel differences spatially and then chromatically (that is over the bands)

$$M_\gamma = \frac{1}{K}\sum_{k=1}^{K}\left\{\frac{1}{N^2}\sum_{i,j=1}^{N}\left|C_k(i,j)-\hat{C}_k(i,j)\right|^\gamma\right\}^{1/\gamma} \quad \text{……(1)}$$

γ = 1 corresponds to mean absolute error (M_1) , and γ=2 to mean square error(M_2) , respectively.

c. Correlation Measures

A measure to compare vectors with strictly nonnegative components, as in the case of images, is the Czekanowski distance.

$$M_3 = \frac{1}{N^2}\sum_{i,j=0}^{N-1}\left(1-\frac{2\sum_{k=1}^{K}\min\left(C_k(i,j),\hat{C}_k(i,j)\right)}{\sum_{k=1}^{K}\left(C_k(i,j)+\hat{C}_k(i,j)\right)}\right). \quad \text{……(2)}$$

A correlation-based measure is the statistics of the angles between the pixel vectors of the two images. So, the angular correlation between two vectors $\mathbf{C}, \hat{\mathbf{C}}$, is defined as follows :

$$M_4 = 1-\frac{1}{N^2}\sum_{i,j=1}^{N}\frac{2}{\pi}\cos^{-1}\frac{\left\langle \mathbf{C}(i,j),\hat{\mathbf{C}}(i,j)\right\rangle}{\left\|\mathbf{C}(i,j)\right\|\left\|\hat{\mathbf{C}}(i,j)\right\|}. \quad \text{.(3)}$$

c. Spectral Measures

The Discrete Fourier Transforms (DFT) of the k th band of the original and embedded image be denoted by $\Gamma_k(u,v)$ and $\hat{\Gamma}_k(u,v)$ respectively.

The spectra are defined as:

$$\Gamma_k(u,v) = \sum_{m,n=0}^{N-1} C_k(m,n)\exp\left[-2\pi i m\frac{u}{N}\right]\exp\left[-2\pi i n\frac{v}{N}\right], \quad k = 1\cdots K. \quad (10)$$

……(4)

d. HVS Based Measure

The incorporation of human visual system (HVS) model into objective measures has led to a better correlation with We assume that the human visual system can be modeled as a band-pass filter with a transfer function in polar coordinates.

$$H(\rho) = \begin{cases} 0.05e^{\rho^{0.554}} & \rho < 7 \\ e^{-9\left|\log_{10}\rho-\log_{10}9\right|^{2.3}} & \rho \geq 7 \end{cases}$$

……….(5)

C. Performance Analysis & Experiment Results

From the measured statistics of training sets of images with and without hidden information, the destination is to determine whether an image has been hidden information or not. Because data hiding process is a nonlinear process, if we only use linear classifier to classify images, it is not a good simulation. And neural network has an excellent capability to simulate any nonlinear relation, so we make use of neural network to classify images. so that it uses following regression model, each decision label 'y' in a sample of '*n*' observations as a linear function of the image quality measure scores *x's* plus a random error 'ε'

$$\begin{aligned} y_1 &= \beta_1 x_{11} + \beta_2 x_{12} + \ldots + \beta_q x_{1q} + \varepsilon_1 \\ y_2 &= \beta_1 x_{21} + \beta_2 x_{22} + \ldots + \beta_q x_{2q} + \varepsilon_2 \\ &\vdots \\ y_n &= \beta_1 x_{n1} + \beta_2 x_{n2} + \ldots + \beta_q x_{nq} + \varepsilon_n \end{aligned}$$

………(6)

In this expression, x_{ij} denotes the IQM score, where the first index indicates the i th image, i=1….N . and the second one the quality measure, j=1…..q , q being the total number of quality measures considered. The β_s denote the regression coefficients.

$$\hat{y} = \hat{\beta}_1 x_1 + \hat{\beta}_2 x_2 + \cdots + \hat{\beta}_q x_q \quad \text{..(7)}$$

for $\hat{y} \geq 0$ the image contains watermark, and for $\hat{y} < 0$ it does not.we found that neural network is more feasible to process nonlinear problem, so we take use of BP neural network to train and simulate images. This BP neural network uses three levels: input level, hidden level and output level. In neural network, the important issue is the slow of convergence The following figure shows the three levels of the back propagation neural network.

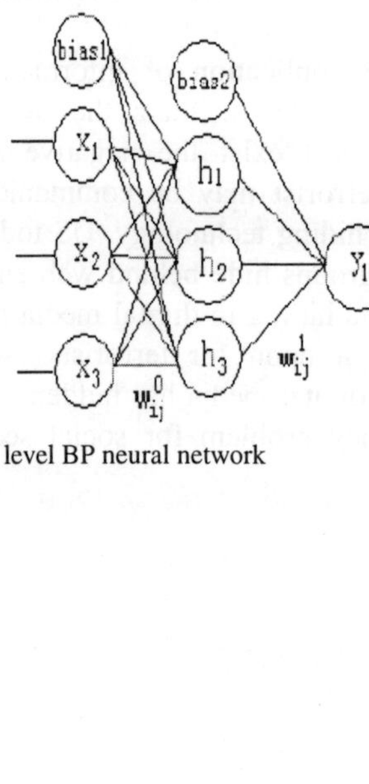

Fig.4 Three level BP neural network

IV. Neural Network Based Camouflaging In Still Images

A. Neural design Architecture

Initially, training the patterns that are formed from the original data and the selected bits from the graphical image produces cipher text. The cipher text is embedded in the LSB of the image and then transmitted to the receiver. The secrecy lies in the design of the neural algorithm that trains the pattern. The neural algorithm has to be exchanged between the sender and receiver through a secure channel. A neural algorithm accepts "n" input pattern that has to be trained, equals to 2^K+1, for an input pattern having k+1 bits. Here 1 bit is selected from the secret message and k bits from carrier image. Input layer is designed with k+1 neurons. The no. of neurons in the hidden layer depends on the problem domain. An "m" bit secret message can be hidden in m pixels of the image and k+1 bit is encrypted at a time.

XOR-Propagation algorithm is implemented in training the bit patterns. On the decryption section, the input patterns bits are formed by the merging of cipher and selected bits from the image. The retrieval process returns back the original graphical image.

Figure 1/Design Architecture

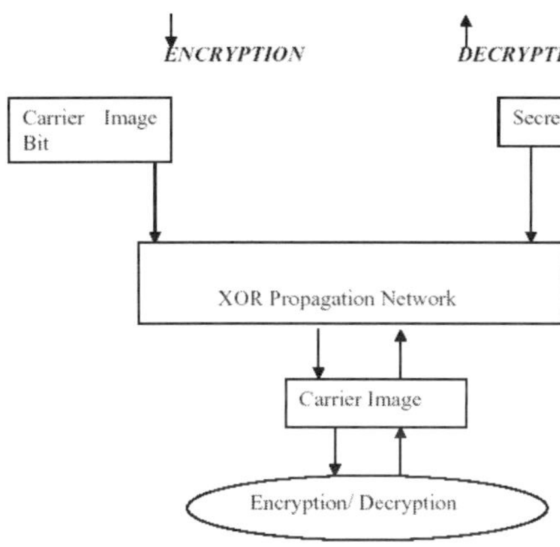

Fig. 5. Design Architecture

B .XOR Propagation Network

The network consists of three-layers with two input units, one unit in the hidden layer and one output unit. The connection weights are shown on links and the threshold of each unit is shown inside the unit. As far as the hidden unit is concerned, the hidden unit is no different from both of the input units, and simply provides another input. Hidden unit's threshold of 1.5 means that it is off unless turned on both the inputs on. The behavior of the network is noted when inputs are off (00), the hidden unit is also off, and there is no net input to the output unit. When the right input only is on (01), the hidden unit does not receive enough net input to turn it on, so it remains off. The output unit sees a net input of +1, which exceeds its threshold, and so it turns it on. The same happens when the left unit only (10) is on. When both inputs are on (11) the hidden unit receives a net input of +2, which exceeds its threshold value, and so it turns on. The output unit now sees a net input of +1 from each of the input units, making +2, and –2 from the hidden unit, making 0 in all. This is less than threshold and so the unit is off.

The hidden unit detects and acts as a feature detector, detecting when both the inputs are on. It can be viewed as recording the basic inputs and mapping of input patterns to output ones.

The neural based steganography is explained by choosing text as a secret message and the graphical image as the carrier medium. The LSB of the 256 Bitmap Picture (bmp) is used as the graphical image. The secret message and the graphical image bits are combined to form the cipher bits, which are referred as trained input patterns. A single bit secret text is combined with single bit graphical image to form possible input patterns. The neural algorithm is designed with respond to binary. The output bits generated called cipher bits embedded in the LSB of the image. Thus secret message is indirectly hidden in the cover.

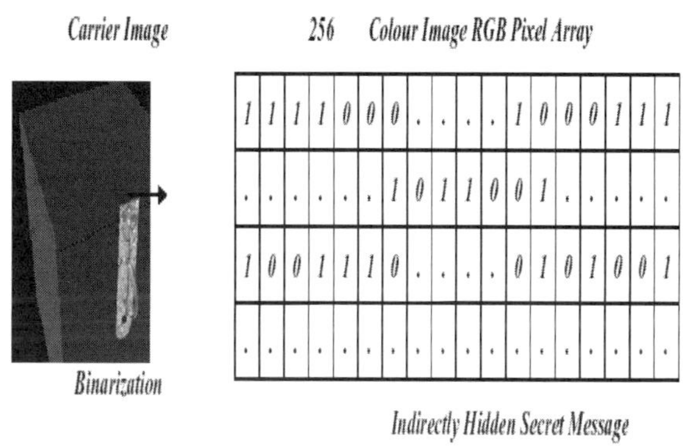

Fig .7. LSB Encoding Symbolic Representation

C. Illustration with an example

A message "Attack Postponed" is converted to binary bits equivalent through the process of binarization.In this example, MSB (Most Significant Bit) of the RGB components are selected bits of the graphical image. The secret data bits and selected graphical image bits acts as input. The neural network for the above example is designed with 2 input neurons, 1 hidden neurons and an output neuron. The training pattern is nothing but the XOR. The weight values are set to train the input pattern with definite thresholds. The trained neural network fires the output neurons (cipher bits) after satisfying the thresholds in the network. The output from the output layer is placed in LSB[4] (Least Significant Bit) of the image placing as 7 bits in a pixel array sequentially in rows.

D. Algorithm

The neural based steganography algorithmic system design as follows.

INPUT: Message Bits, Selected cover image bits

OUTPUT: Stego image.

Step 1: Design Principles of Training Pattern

Form the input pattern by selecting one bit of secret text and k image bit. Choose the number of bits required in the target output pattern.

Step 2: Deign of Neural Network

Design the neural network with the above training pattern by deciding the number of input neurons, middle layer neurons and output neurons.

Step 3: Train the Pattern

While data bits of secret message present do The input is fed into the trained network and the output generated is stored in the LSB of image.

end while

V. FUTURE ENHANCEMENT

Steganography is renewed nowadays merging with different fields like neural network, Fuzzy system, increasing a feasible security and privacy. Using steganographic technique, software can easily transmit private user information without user's knowledge. Steganography is of immense importance and it is indispensable in the fields of digital watermarking, Digital fingerprinting, Internet security, Network security, Authentication, Copyright issues etc.

Since detection can never give a guarantee of finding all hidden information, it can be used together with methods of defeating steganography, to minimize the chances of hidden communication taking place.

In the near future, the most important use of steganographic technique will probably be lying in the field of digital watermarking. Content Providers are eager to protect their copyrighted works against illegal distribution and digital watermarks provide a way of tracking the owners of these materials. Although it will not prevent the distribution itself, it will enable the content provider to start legal actions against the violators of the copyrights, as they can now be tacked down.

Steganography might also become limited under laws, since governments already claimed that criminals use these techniques to communicate. More restrictions on the use of privacy -protecting technologies are not very unlikely, especially in this period of time with great anxiety of terrorist and other attacks.The Steganalysis approaches may be appearing in future in the fields of Artificial Neural Network, Genetic Algorithms, Simulated annealing, other standard signal processing techniques

VI .CONCLUSION

Detection technique development in this area of data hiding will continue. We find image's statistic features are important clues to determine whether hiding information or not from the detection process. So this suggests us to develop more robustness method with statistic features altered as little as possible.

The neural approach to embed information satisfying a secure steganography. Neural approach adds the complexity for the hackers accessing and also presents high potentiality in Defence operations. Neural Steganography is a powerful tool that enables people to communicate without possible eavesdroppers even knowing there is a form of communication.

Steganography, especially combined with cryptography, is a powerful tool which enables peoples to communicate without possible eavesdroppers even knowing there is a form of communication in the first place. The methods used in the science of steganography have advanced a lot over the past centuries, especially with the rise of the computer era. Although the techniques are still not used very often, the possibilities are endless. Many different techniques exist and continue to be developed, while the ways of detecting hidden messages also advance quickly.

Equally important are the ethical concerns of using steganography and steganalysis. Using steganographic techniques, software can easily transmit private user information without the user's permission or knowledge. Watermarks- already an issue in the hosty disputed domain of digital rights management – could be comprised by advanced steganalysis tools. Similar abuses of steganography and steganalysis can easily enumerated.

REFERENCES

[1] Liu Shaohui, Yao Hongxun, Gao Wen "Neural Network based Steganalysis in Still Images" Proceedings of IEEE ICME 2003.

[2] I.Aveibas, N.Memon, B.Sankur. "Steganalysis based on image quality metrics". Multimedia Signal Processing, 2001 IEEE Fourth Workshop on, 2001

[3] Neil F.Johnson and Sushhil Jajodia. "Steganalysis: The Investigation of Hidden Information". Proceedings of the IEEE Information Technology Conference, Syracuse, New York, USA.1998

[4] R.Chandramouli and N. Memon, "Analysis of LSB based image steganography techniques," in Proc. ICIP, Oct. 2001.

The Issues and Challenges for Implementing Web-tools in Malaysian Secondary Schools

RAVICHANDRAN PURUSHOTHAMAN
KOLEJ YAYASAN UEM
LEMBAH BERINGIN, MALAYSIA

The need for using technology in teaching becomes quite clear as the information access through the Web has wide spectrum of resources. What is prevailing among the Malaysian educators, in general, is that they do not have access to tools or skills needed to successfully implement it in their instruction (Mohamed Amin Embi, 2004). Both learners and teachers need Web-tools in order to keep the balance between the technology and pedagogical needs in their classroom. This is because Web-based instruction (WBI) clearly has the potential to offer a rich and stimulating educational environment (Windschitl, 1998). This paper discusses some of the issues and challenges the teachers in secondary schools face while trying to adapt to Web-tools. The findings discussed are based on the quantitative and qualitative analysis conducted in the nine districts of Perak, in two hundred and sixteen secondary schools. Further, findings revel that although majority of the teachers were enthusiastic about infusing technology teaching using Web-tools, time and access seemed to be two predominant factors for the teachers to integrate technology teaching using Web-tools. . What seems even more problematic is that, teachers do not feel sufficiently equipped and prepared to integrate the technology teaching using Web-tools in their classrooms. As a result of this, to a large extent, the kind of teaching that goes on in the classrooms investigated seems to be distinctively different from what is expected from the reformers

1. Background

1.1. *Introduction*

Various agencies within Ministry of Education conduct training for secondary school teachers to use Computers in their classroom teaching. The Curriculum Development Centre also trained a number of teachers in conjunction with the Computer in Education Program. This program started back in 1992, even before the introduction of Smart School. The program focused exclusively on ICT literacy at first, but in last few years, the emphasis has shifted to getting the teachers to use ICT in classroom during lessons. Further, according to Chang, Foong-Mae (2002), the Teacher Education Division has trained at least 55,000 teachers until 2002 and half of these teachers went through in-service training, while the other half were teachers trainees trained in the Teacher Training College.

With all the support having provided by the Ministry of Education in the past decade, it is also worth looking at the research study conducted by the ETD (Educational Technology Division) in 1999, which shows that teachers are not using the computers as expected! Only 17.54 percent of the 4670 secondary and primary schools surveyed used computer for teaching and learning (ETD, 1999). Unfortunately, there was no record of how the teaching and learning was conducted. Also ETD has further surveyed on the amount usage of the courseware (CD titles) provided by them during 2001 and the findings showed that 796 schools surveyed do not use the provided courseware. The reasons given were the courseware were not compatible with the computers in school, teachers did not use the courseware because they were not provided with sufficient training and support were not provided to them after the materials were supplied to the schools (ETD, 2001). Also research conducted by Norhayathi Abd. Mukti (http://www.ejisdc.org), in her findings states that some teachers reported that the level of software provided for them to teach was too sophisticated for their students. They would prefer to use less complicated software with their students at the introductory stage.

Although billions of dollars have been invested in this area to integrate ICT with education, we could clearly notice from the above example that the desired goal of Ministry of Education to impart ICT into education and to prepare today's teachers for tomorrow's demand is a big skepticism. This is also clearly evident from Mohammad bin Hassan, Teacher Education Division of Ministry of education Malaysia, who narrates that, the effective implementation of Smart Schools in Multimedia Super Corridor (MSC) will not be achieved if the focus is only given to the process of improving the level of its physical appearance. What is more important here is to prepare future teachers and teachers who are in service (in other words, trained teachers) with the knowledge and skills in using ICT.

2. Research Methodology

Methodology used in this study to collect data employed both qualitative and quantitative data collection procedures. The respondents for the first phase answered the survey questionnaire. A total of 648 of them teaching form 3 and form 4 in the Perak school districts were involved in this study. After the completion of the quantitative analysis, the qualitative analysis included ten teachers from two school districts of Perak, which included five teachers each from rural and urban schools.

3. Analysis of the results

From the Questionnaires administered to 648 teachers, completed questionnaires were received from 191 schools from 554 teachers, which was 88 percent of all teachers given the questionnaires. The questionnaires were targeted on teachers who handle English, Maths and Science at form 3 and form 4 levels of secondary schools. The sample was 32.3 percent English teachers (N=179), 33 percent Maths teachers (N=183) and 34.7 percent Science teachers (N=192). Descriptive and inferential statistics were used to analyze the quantitative data. The Statistical Package for Social Sciences (SPSS) Version 11.5 software was used to analyze the data for this study.

The percentage of respondents agreeing to the statements reflecting their perceptions of the effectiveness of Web-based teaching was high ranging from 81.9 percent for students' reports can be maintained effectively on the internet for parents to see to 97.5 percent for web-based learning environment will do good as long as they don't misuse it perception on the effectiveness of Web-based teaching in school.

This seemingly overwhelming positive perception of the teachers has to be seen in the light of the fact that the largest proportions of them are only slightly positive about Web-based learning. Those who are strongly positive (strongly agree) account for only 5.3 percent to 8.1 percent. To an extent, there seems to be a realisation among teachers that Web-based learning is good and that they have ICT knowledge, but their conviction about it has not been to the level that it helps a wider adoption of the new teaching transformation. This could be a plausible reason that Web-tools in classroom teaching has not been forthcoming.

Further, it can be seen that respondents collectively agree the most that the speed of the internet may be slow; close to 92.0 percent of them perceive this to be so. About equal percentage (92.0 percent) is of the view that most students will likely replicate the work of others and this makes it difficult for teachers to assess the ability of their students. The third most likely problem perceived is that teaching time is too short for CAI (87.1 percent agreeing). This is followed by most of the computers are old (81.3 percent agreeing); difficult to teach additional subject using computer because most of the time they are involved in meetings, workshops and seminars (80.9 percent agreeing); the school does not provide computer training for students in e-learning (72.8 percent agreeing); the school does not provide sufficient educational software for teaching the subject (61.6 percent agreeing); and most of the software CDs provided do not fit the requirement of the curriculum (55.3 percent agreeing).

On the other hand, slightly more than half (53.1 percent) disagree with the statement that there is no internet connection in the school. That is, 53.1 percent of the respondents agree that there is internet connection in their schools. This means that in the study area, the percentage of schools that still do not have internet connection is still relatively high, and this certainly is not good news to those entrusted to implement e-learning in schools..

It appears that the drive to implement Web-based learning in schools, at least with respect to the study area, will be met with problems, ranging from physical facilities and other management derived constraints to excessive teachers' workload and students' integrity and honesty. However, these problems need not be a permanent stumbling block to the implementation of e-learning in schools for a number of reasons.

Firstly, the largest proportion of respondents perceive these problems to be not that serious as implied by the percentage of those who "slightly agree" with most of the nine statements. Secondly, the lack of physical facilities such as having old computers should not be a problem in the first place because if the authority that be wishes schools to implement e-learning successfully, it must provide sufficient ancillary equipment. Thirdly, some of the perceived problems such as students' integrity (in connection with the tendency to replicate the work of others) and teachers being too involved with meetings, workshops and seminars seem to be perpetual problems in schools with or without e-learning. The authority has to address this problem as part of its overall policy, and not only considers it (teachers being too busy with other non-teaching functions) as problem only of e-learning. Lastly, the unsuitability or the lack of software in schools should be transition in nature as much as the lack of suitable textbooks was initially a problem in conventional teaching in the history of education in the country.

4. Discussion and Findings

The two main issues, which restrict the teachers who adopt technology-based teaching is access and time. Access at school that is limited is not enough to convince teachers to invest time and energy in learning how to teach with technology because there is not reliable access for them. The issue of time in the process of integrating technology into teaching is a very complex procedure. There are several issues that the teachers explained that all seem to boil down to time. From the dialogues taken form the transcripts it was evident that the teachers at the secondary school in Malaysia have lot of hindrance in implementing Web-tools as a teaching and learning tool. This is depicted in a more precise manner as shown in figure1.0.

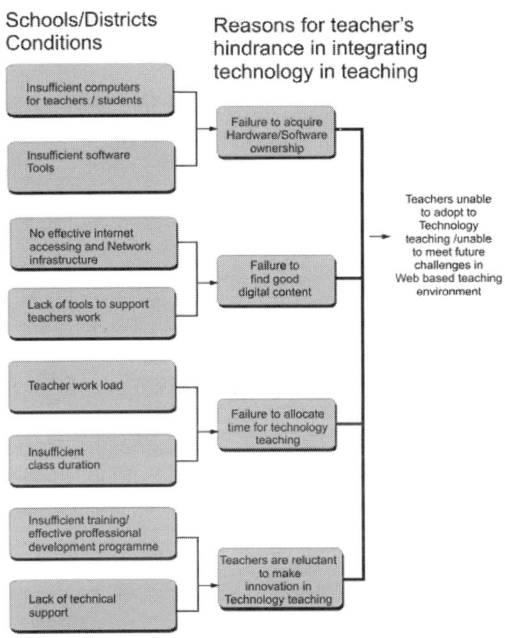

Figure 1.0: Hindrance in implementing Web-tools in secondary schools

From this perspective, it seemed to be necessary to break down the time issues to investigate why it was so prevalent in the teachers' responses. Computers can be effective teaching tools in the classroom. However, they are complex machines and require knowledge and skills to operate them. Knowing how to use Web-tools and how to integrate them effectively into a teaching strategy or method requires an even high skill level. These skills take time to acquire. The time constraint for teachers using computers is a consistent theme in the existing literature (Cuban, 1993; Marcinkiewicz, 1995). Gallo and Horton(1994) identified the necessity for uninterrupted time for teachers to become comfortable with using the internet. For example Knuper (1993) asserts meaningful implementation of computer technology require time; time that is additional beyond the normal teaching day.

Also given that computers have been in use for over a decade, it was interesting to find that staff perceived real difficulties translating their existing teaching programs into Web-based instructions. As previous studies have demonstrated (eg. Tearle et al, 1999, Wolcott, 1997), participants in this study were also unclear about how to integrate technology teaching within existing workload arrangement. For time-related concerns, the teachers expressed many concerns. Some reported that they had to teach other subjects and carry out other responsibilities, so they did not have enough time to prepare lessons that were related to the use of computers. This finding is consistent with the findings by Sheingold (1990) and Plomp and Carleer (1987), whose concerns reported were lack of software, lack of time and lack of training on the use of computers.

In spite of the effectiveness of technology integration in teaching and their benefits have been overall welcomed, still lack of many attributes in effectively integrating technology in teaching has been catastrophic. Understanding how the teachers hone their technology skills to overcome all these hurdles and advance themselves as technologically proficient teachers is important for successful online implementation of teaching. Also, 46.9 percent of the respondents agree that there is no Internet connection in their schools and 92 percent of them collectively agree that the Internet speed is slow. This finding should be seen under the light of the fact about internet access in schools by Samuel, R., & Bakar, Z. (2006, May 31) of University of Malaya, who states that that the broadband access is not consistent and on certain days there is no internet service. The school servers are frequently attacked by virus and there is a need for GITN Sdn. Berhad (Government Integrated Telecommunications Network) to block the virus before they enter SchoolNet. This means that in the study area, the percentage of schools that still do not have internet connection is still relatively high, and this certainly is not good news to those entrusted to bring a Web-based environment in schools.

5. Conclusion

Although teachers in secondary schools in Malaysia are positive about integrating technology in their teaching using Web-tools, they seem to have not adequately prepared to take it to their classroom teaching. Teachers also do not seem to have the opportunities to discuss the innovation with their colleagues and learn in the process. To make this problem even more complicated, there are also no relevant resource materials available, which the teachers could use to read more about infusing technology teaching in a Web-based environment. The few guidelines prepared so far have proved insufficient and yet they are expected to carry out the innovation in their classrooms.

References

1. Chang, Foong-Mae. 2002. Seminar/Workshop on the Promotion of ICT Education to Narrow the Digital Divide, *15-22 Oct, 2002,Tokyo*, Japan.
2. Cuban, L. (1993). How teachers taught: Constancy and change in American classrooms 1880-1990 (2nd ed.), New York: Teachers College Press.
3. Educational Technology Division .(1999). Indicator studies on the use of technology in education. Ministry of Education Malaysia. Not published.
4. Godfrey, C. (2001). Computers in schools: Changing pedagogies. Australian Educational Computing, *16 (2), 14-17.*

MAGNITUDE OF SELF SYSTEMATIZING RESEMBLANCE MEASURES IN KNOWLEDGE MINING

MRS.N.CHENTHALIR INDRA
Lecturer, S.T.Hindu College, Nagercoil, Tamilnadu – 629 001. ncigk@rediffmail.com

DR. E.RAMARAJ
Director, Computer Center,Alagappa University, Karaikudi, Tamilnadu – 629 003 eramaraj@rediffmail.com

In general, knowledge mining is the process of analyzing data from different points of view and summarizing it into useful information for future plan or progression. Clustering is one of the technical parameter of the knowledge mining. A neural network algorithm Self-Organizing Maps (SOM) can be used to cluster data autonomously. An important step in any clustering is to select a distance measure. Instead of distance measure, this paper analyzes the possible similarity resemblance measures with SOM to collect the knowledge by efficient mining. The analysis result produces a new view that similarity measure selection in SOM for mining leads the process to acquire the data knowledge from unkown nodes. Accuracy in learning lend a hand in authentication applications.

1. Introduction

Technically, Knowledge or data mining is the process of finding correlations or patterns among dozens of fields in large relational databases. This information can be used to increase revenue, cut costs, or both. Data mining parameters include Association, Classification, Clustering, Path analysis and Forecasting. Among these parameters, data clustering is a common technique for statistical analysis, which is used in many fields including machine learning, data mining, pattern-recognition, image analysis and bioinformatics. *Clustering* locates and visually documents groups of facts not previously known.

The term *data reduction* in the context of data mining is usually applied to projects where the goal is to aggregate or amalgamate the information contained in large datasets into manageable (smaller) information chunk. Data reduction includes clustering technique. One of the special types of neural network clustering technique is *Self Organizing Maps* that allows the mapping of high-dimensional data onto a smaller dimensional space, making accessible large amounts of data through a visual model. The capabilities of the SOM technique have been extensively explored in different research areas for more than two decades [2]. As in any clustering logics SOM is much influenced by its distance calculation step. Conventional SOM uses Euclidean distance or the dot product as its winning neuron selector for data mining applications. This paper analysis similarity measures in the place of dissimilarity measures to find the better clustering potential in all status of SOM.

This paper is organized as follows: The section 2 goes over the main points of the Self organizing map with its usual distance measure method. Section 3 introduces the resemblance measures which are considered in this paper. Section 4 analysis the efficiency of similarity measures against dissimilarity in SOM and also describes about the best matching similarity measure in color data clustering. The evaluated results are summarized in the section 5.

2. SOM in Data Mining

Self-Organizing Maps (SOM), which continue to influence modern data mining research. SOM learning is accomplished by the application of input data alone; no expected output data is used as a teacher to signal the network that it had made an error. This type of learning is an *unsupervised learning* [3]. The network is therefore allowed to organize itself freely according to connection in the data, resulting in a map containing the input data.

The Self organizing feature map algorithm is primarily a competitive vector quantizer [8]. Competitive learning can generally be viewed as a procedure that learns to group into patterns in clusters in a way inherent to the input data. So competitive learning is closely related to clustering. However, different choices of distance functions have been explored in an attempt to arrive at more meaningful clusters. But the Euclidean distance measure in Eq. (1) is used as a general measure to determine the winner in competitive learning networks.

$$d(x_i, w_j) = \sqrt{\sum_{h=1}^{k} (x_{ih} - w_{jh})^2} \quad (1)$$

where, $x_i = \langle x_{i1},...x_k \rangle$ and $w_j = \langle w_{j1},...w_{jk} \rangle$ are input vector and existing weight vector respectively. In such cases the weight vector at the least distance from the input vector is the winner [6]. After finding winner, SOM modifies the connections to the winning unit and connections to units in its neighborhood with the following weight updating schedule[1]:

$$w_{j(new)} = w_{j(old)} + \alpha(x_i - w_{j(old)} \quad (2)$$

where, α is a gain constant between 0 and 1, that decreases over time. The radius of the neighborhood also does the weight modification as in the same. The finding winner and modifying the weight of wining neuron and its neighborhood neurons repeated until α =0. Self–Organizing Feature Map learning captures the topology and probability distribution of input data [4][5]. Associative connections linking prototypes within SOM based clustering algorithms are generally responsible for their inherent ability to deduce an ordered or topologically conserved mapping of the underlying data space.

The SOM has turned out to be an excellent data-mining tool, suitable for provisional data analysis problems, such as *clustering*, *categorization*, *visualization*, *information compression*, and *hidden factor analysis*. There are many research works which are utilizing learning process of SOM, but with other supporting algorithms like SA Clusters, K_means and fuzzy logics etc. SOM is not yet preferred in the security field. Authentication processes need perfect learning logic. As SOM is an Unsupervised Competitive learner whose winner selector measure requires parallel substitution to make it perfect. This paper handles analysis by using similarity measures and identifies *Jaccard* and *Dice* similarity measures as the suitable one.

3. Proposed Similarity Measures

The similarity measures are well known in the web search engines. The similarity between two tuples t_i and t_j $sim(t_i, t_j)$ in a database D is a mapping from $D \times D$ to the range $[0,1]$.Thus $sim(t_i, t_j) \in [0,1]$.The objective is to define the similarity mapping such that documents that are more alike have a higher similarity value[7]. The characteristics of good similarity measures are:

- $\forall t_i \in D, sim(t_i, t_j) = 1$
- $\forall t_i, t_j \in D, sim(t_i, t_j) = 0$ if t_i and t_j are not alike.

Similarity measures are used in data mining classification techniques where the classes are predefined. But in the case of clustering it is not as simple as the classification because in clustering classes are not known in advance. This paper proposes four types of similarity measures to SOM for its competitive learning. In the following resemblance assessing Eqs.(3), (4) and (5), similarity is evaluated between two vectors $x_i = \langle x_{i1},...x_k \rangle$ and $w_j = \langle w_{j1},...w_{jk} \rangle$.

Cosine coefficient:

$$sim(x_i, w_j) = \frac{\sum_{h=1}^{k} x_{ih} w_{jh}}{\sqrt{\sum_{h=1}^{k} x_{ih}^2 \sum_{h=1}^{k} w_{jh}^2}} \quad (3)$$

Jaccard coefficient:

$$sim(x_i, w_j) = \frac{\sum_{h=1}^{k} x_{ih} w_{jh}}{\sum_{h=1}^{k} x_{ih}^2 + \sum_{h=1}^{k} w_{jh}^2 - \sum_{h=1}^{k} x_{ih} w_{jh}} \quad (4)$$

Dice coefficient:

$$sim(x_i, w_j) = \frac{2\sum_{h=1}^{k} x_{ih} w_{jh}}{\sum_{h=1}^{k} x_{ih}^2 + \sum_{h=1}^{k} w_{jh}^2} \quad (5)$$

The *cosine coefficient* relates the overlap to the geometric average of the two sets. *Jaccard's coefficient* is used to measure the overlap of two sets as related to the whole set caused by their union. *Dice's coefficient* relates the overlap to the average size of the two sets together[7]. The similarity outcome ranges from -1 specifies disimilarity, towards 1 shows exact similarity, with 0 indicating self-determination, and the values in-between indicates a sign of transitional similarity or dissimilarity.

4. Similarity based SOM an analysis

Associative connections linking prototypes within SOM based clustering algorithms are generally responsible for their inherent ability to deduce an ordered or topologically conserved mapping of the underlying data space. The SOM technique has characteristics and capabilities that make it ideal for mining applications. Dissimilarity or distance measures are often used to find the similarity between two vector sets in clustering technique like Self-Organizing Maps. Similarity measures are usually applied in classification techniques.

This is due to the fact that in the clustering the classes are not predefined to compare. SOM uses the distance measure to find winner node which causes the different parts of the network to respond similarity to certain input patterns. The unit whose weight vector is closest to the input vector is allowed to learn [9].

To improve SOM learning accuracy this paper uses similarity measures. Here maximum value indicates the least distance. *But by selecting minimum value, the greatest distance node is treated as a winner in this proposed system*, the same and its neighborhood neurons are also adjusted to learn new knowledge.

Figure 4.1. Input image – (dimension is 75 x 57)

The analysis is carried out with RGB, 3-Dimentional color data which is extracted from an image shown in the Figure 4.1. This similarity based SOM study uses random number as its initial weight. Neighborhood function is set as 1. Threshold value α is set to 1 initially and it is reduced by 0.002 in each iteration. Usually epochs of training is set by the temperament of pattern. This is not fixed in the early SOM.

This paper recommends the column size (or) multiple of the column size of an image dimension value as its epoch value. Epochs mean points of chance remarkable for learning feature of input.

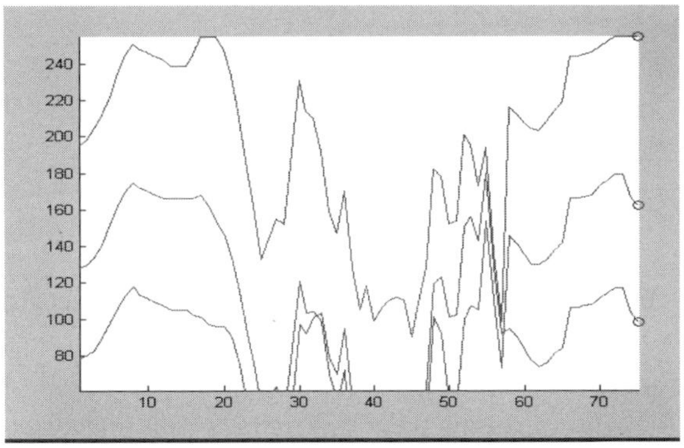

Figure 4.2. RGB data Input vector map

Input image RGB values are extracted and plotted, which is shown in the Fig.4.2. Primary colors of each pixel are ranged from 0 to 255. The dimension of the input image is 75 x 57 x 3. It denotes 75x57 sizes of red, green and blue tints. Traditional SOM acquire the knowledge of input only up to 55.56% at its maximum effort. While matching Fig.4.2 and Fig. 4.3, it explicitly exhibits the fact that the absolute learning is impractical with Euclidean distance method.

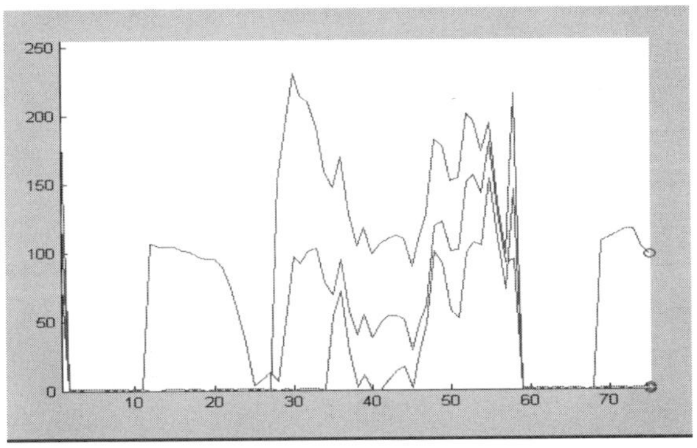

Figure 4.3. Data learned by SOM(Euclidean) 55%

The further experiment results are recorded with the above said similarity measures and the gained self systematizing data are mapped. Cosine coefficient measure using SOM (Fig.4.4) shows unsatisfactory information compilation. It confirms that Cosine as a winner neuron selector in SOM directs it towards improper learning.

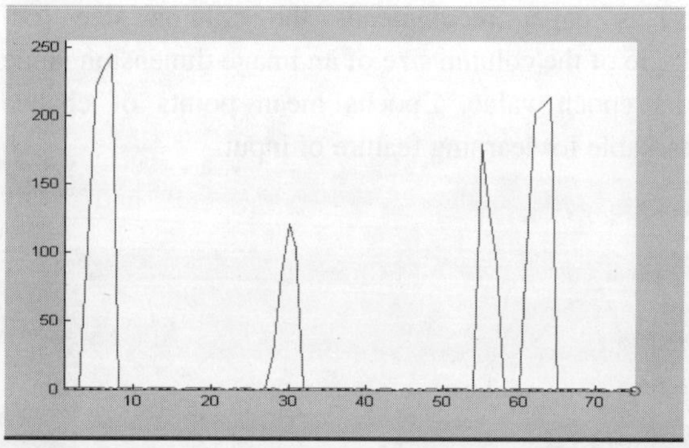

Figure 4.4. Data learned by SOM(Cosine) 9%

Fig. 4.5 and 4.6, are maps of Dice and Jaccard based winner evaluator respectively. Both the measures are acquiring the image information at the maximum of 99.9%. By comparing these two figurers with Fig.4.2 , it is proved that Dice and Jaccard coefficients are mining input data very well and educate the SOM neurons to achieve efficient knowledge. These measures also help the SOM network to learn quickly with limited epochs than existing SOM.

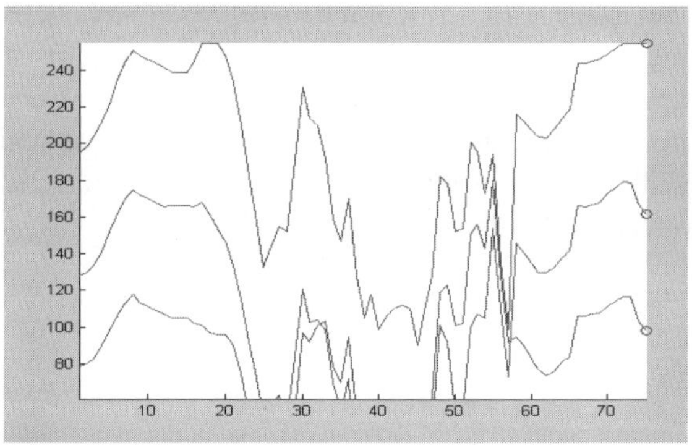

Figure 4.5. Data learned by SOM (Dice) 99%

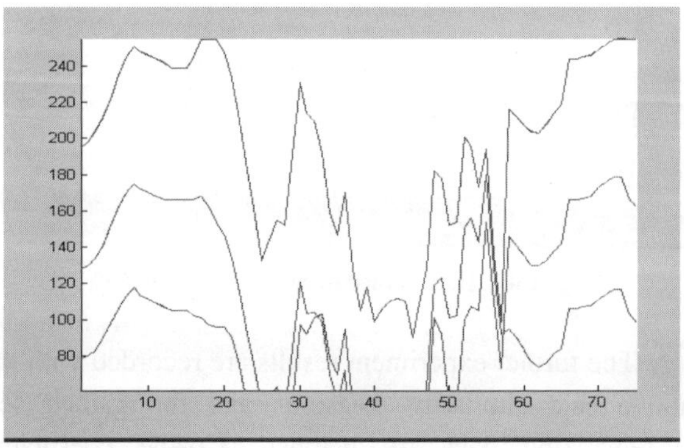

Figure 4.6. Data learned by SOM (Jaccard) 99%

The Table 4.1 explicitly displays the score of distance measure versus similarity measures. The epochs are tuned by the 2's 4's 10's 100's and 1000's multiple of input data's column dimension. Here, input data column size is 75. Euclidean measure assists the SOM to learn only up to 55.56%, and also it takes thousands of epochs. Increasing amount of epochs is directly proportional to the time factor. But in the case of Dice and Jaccard coefficients, 99.9% of self organization is achieved. They lend a hand to learn SOM with minimum epochs. Hence, the time taken for mining is also reduced sufficiently.

Table 4.1. SOM efficiency with proposed measures.

Epoch	SOM learning efficiency(E) in % & time taken(T) in nano seconds with various measures							
	Euclidean		Cosine		Dice		Jaccard	
	E	T	E	T	E	T	E	T
150	7.2	0.2	9	0.3	96	0.1	96	0.1
300	9.5	0.5	6	0.6	99	0.4	99	0.4
750	10	5	6	6.2	83	2.5	82	2.6
7500	55	17	6	25	20	16	19	17
75000	55	28	7	29	4.5	202	3	220

The Table 4.1 explicitly displays the score of distance measure versus similarity measures. The epochs are tuned by the 2's 4's 10's 100's and 1000's multiple of input data's column dimension. Here, input data column size is 75. Euclidean measure assists the SOM to learn only up to 55%, and also it takes thousands of epochs.

Increasing amount of epochs is directly proportional to the time factor. But in the case of Dice and Jaccard coefficients, 99% of self organization is achieved. They lend a hand to learn SOM with minimum epochs. Hence, the time taken for mining is also reduced sufficiently.

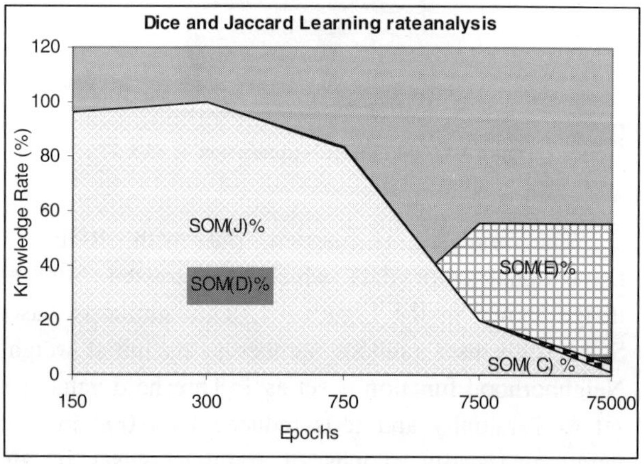

Figure4.7. Competency of Dice and Jaccard

(a) Learned by Euclidean

(b) Learned by Cosine

(c) Learned by Dice

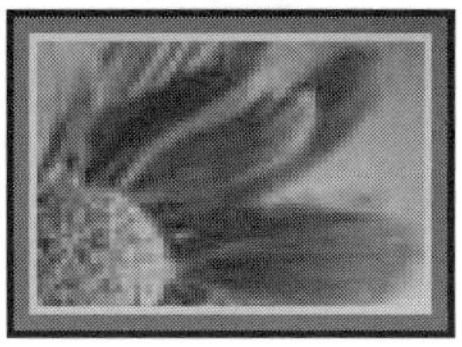

(d) Learned by Jaccard

Figure4.8. Repainted Images from SOM Knowledge with proposed measures

Competency of Dice and Jaccard against Euclidean and Cosine in SOM is publicized through area chart in the Fig 4.7.The reshaped Image is drawn from the SOM learned data are shown in the Fig 4.8. These figures projects efficacy of Dice and Jaccard in SOM.

5. Conclusion

ConventionalSOM and most of the extended SOM are using Euclidean-based distance metrics, where similarity is defined via distance hierarchies. This paper proposes similarity hierarchies to define similarity between two vectors. In SOM procedure, the maximum value of similarity coefficients should be chosen to find winner node. But proposed Similarity based SOM selects least value. In reality it accepts the greatest value node as a winner. This analysis is the evidence for knowledge collection capacity of Dice and Jaccard based measures in SOM. Competitive learning allows the unit whose weight vector is closest to the input vector to learn. But in new similarity based SOM it allows the unit whose weight vector is farthest away to the input vector to learn. The paper suggests two more winner finding measures to SOM. The efficiency of Dice and Jaccard will direct the SOM in security or authentication applications. The future investigation will be carried out with other left over measures like Lee distance measure and Overlap coefficient

References

1. Ananda Rao M., srinivas J., *"Neural Networks Algorithms and Applications."*, Narosa Publishing House.- 2003
2. Dorina Marghescu, MikkoRajanen and Barbro Back, *" Evaluating the Quality of uses of Visual Data Mining Tools "*, 11th European Conference on Information Technology Evaluation -2004.
3. James A. Freeman & David M. skapura, *" Neural Networks Algorithms, Applications and Programming Techniques."*, Pearson Education, 2002.
4. Jorge Pena, Mauricio Vanegas, *"Digital Hardware Architectures of Kohonen's Self-Organizing Feature Maps with Exponential Neighboring Function"*, -2006 IEEE.
5. Kohonen T. , *"Self-Organization and Associative Memory"*, Springer-Verlag, Berlin (3rd ed) (1989).
6. LiMin Fu, *"Neural Networks in Computer Intelligence "*, Tata McGraw-Hill–NewDelhi-2004.
7. Margaret H. Dunham, *"Data Mining Introductory and Advanced Topics",* Pearson Education – 2006.
8. Sathish Kumar, " Neural Networks A classroom approach", Tata McGraw Hill.-2004.
9. Yegnanarayana B, *"Artificial Neural networks"*, Prentice Hall of India, 2001.

DESIGN PATTERNS IN SITUATION CALCULUS*

QIANG LIU

Department of Computer Science and Technology, East China Normal University
Dongchuan Rd. 500, Shanghai, 200241, China

ZONGYUAN YANG

Department of Computer Science and technology, East China Normal University
Dongchuan Rd. 500, Shanghai, 200241, China

YEFEI ZHAO

Department of Computer Science and technology, East China Normal University
Dongchuan Rd. 500, Shanghai, 200241, China

The formalization of design patterns should concern both their structure and behavior. However, many proposed approaches either focused on only one aspect of them or handled them separately using different and incompatible formalisms. To complete and merge the specification of both aspects, we propose an approach based on Situation Calculus in this paper. Firstly, we introduced the core concepts in design patterns and distinguished two types of relations: static relation and dynamic relation, which are capable of modeling pattern's structure and behavior respectively. Then we established a mapping relation between the concepts in design patterns and Situation Calculus, which can serve as a general strategy for translating the informal descriptions of design patterns into their formal correspondences in Situation Calculus. As a case study, we formalized the Observer pattern. Finally we explored the potential uses of our approach by using Projection and Planning in Situation Calculus.

1. Introduction

Design pattern are usually given in informal languages, such as UML diagram with annotations. These descriptions aim for human understanding, not for machine processing. To automate pattern-related application (deployment, reasoning, composition, etc), we need to formalize design patterns.

Formalizing design patterns should concern both their structure and behavior. The structural aspect (e.g. Class A inherits Class B) is static, which cannot be changed during runtime. On the contrary, the behavioral aspect is dynamic, which can be changed by method calls during runtime. However, many proposed approaches [1][3][4] either focused on only one aspect of them or handled them separately using different and incompatible formalisms. To address this shortcoming, in this paper, we initiate an approach based on Situation Calculus. In Situation Calculus, Eternal and Fluent are capable of modeling static and dynamic relations respectively. Furthermore, actions in Situation Calculus are intuitive correspondences of methods in design patterns, whose precondition and post-condition can be captured by the Precondition Axiom and Successor State Axiom in Situation Calculus accordingly. This conceptual mapping relation can serve as a general strategy for translating the informal descriptions of design patterns into the formal specifications in Situation Calculus. Thus, in a natural and seamless way, we combine the structural and behavioral description in Situation Calculus Once design patterns are encoded in Situation Calculus, we can benefit from its reasoning service. It allows us to query about the properties of design patterns as the system evolves.

This paper is organized in the following way. Section 2 is Related Works. In Section 3 we introduce core concepts in design patterns. Section 4 introduces Situation Calculus. In Section 5, the mapping relation is

* This work is supported by Research Fund for the Doctoral Program of Higher Education of China, No. 20060269002.

established and as a case study, we formalized the Observer pattern in Situation Calculus. Section 6 discusses the potential uses of our approach and Section 7 is Conclusion and Future Work.

2. Related Works

The formalization of design patterns was widely studied [1][2][3][4][5][11]. In [3], the authors focus on modeling only static aspect of design patterns using First Order Logic and devoted to graphical representations to facilitate the understanding of system design. [1][4][11] use First Order Logic (FOL) and Temporal Logic of Action (TLA) to describe design patterns' structure and behavior respectively. However, modeling design patterns in two different formalisms is unnatural and inconvenient. To solve this problem, [2] invents a new language BPSL (Balanced Patterns Specification Language) to combine the description of design patterns in a single language. However, this language is rather a combination of FOL and TLA, not a new conceptual model for pattern specification. In this paper, we initiate a way based on Situation Calculus, which is more sophisticated in theory and more practical in application.

3. Design Patterns

Design patterns are originally given in UML diagrams with annotations. Figure 1 is the Observer patterns in UML diagram.

In the domain of Object Oriented Design, we identify four elemental entities: Class, Method, Attribute and Object and a set of elemental relations between these entities. Relations can be represented by predicate symbols in First Order Logic. Table 1 lists some example predicates.

For instance, Inherit(C1,C2) means Class C1 inherits from Class C2, MDefinedIn(M,C) means Method M is defined in Class C, etc.

These relations are static, which are between Class, Method and Attribute. They are defined in source code, hence cannot be changed during runtime. Static relations are meant to capture the structural information of design patterns, though the name and number of the set of relations may be different in proposed approaches [2][3][4]. In this paper we leave this choice open and whenever we use a predicate, we should explain its meaning in annotations.

To complete the specification of design patterns, we use Dynamic relations and Actions to capture the behavioral aspect of design patterns. Dynamic relations are meant to capture relations about Object, which can be changed by performing Actions during runtime. Actions are actually Method Calls. For example, in Table 2 and Table 3, we identify two Dynamic relations and four Actions that characterize the behavior of Observer pattern.

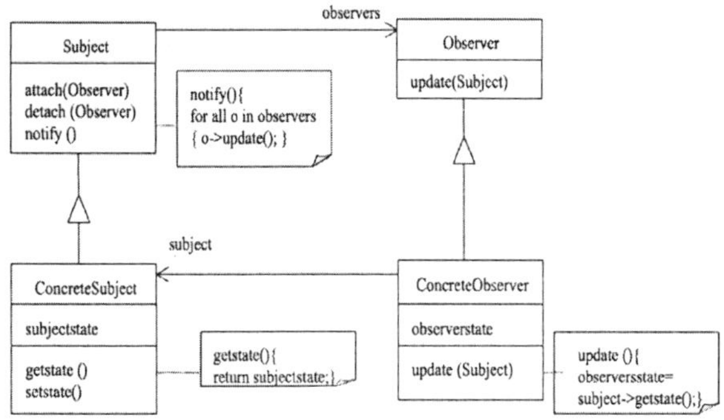

Figure. 1. Observer pattern in UML diagram

Table 1: Some (partial) elemental relations in Object Oriented Design

Static Relations	Domain
Inherit	Class×Class
MDefinedIn	Method×Class
ADefiendIn	Attribute×Class
RefOne	Class×Class
Call	Class×Method× Class×Method

Careful readers may note that the parameters of each action are different from the original description of Observer pattern [6]. We follow the high level abstraction approach as in [1], which aims to specify Observer pattern in an abstract and also rigorous way.

Table 2: Dynamic relations in Observer pattern

Dynamic Relations	Domain
Attached	Object×Object
Updated	Object×Object

For example, in Table 2, Attached(s,o) means Object o1 is attached to Object o2, Updated(s,o) means Object s has updated Object o. In Table 3, method Attach(s,o) sets the Attached relation between Object s and Object o, method Detach(s,o) clears the Attached relation between Object s and Object o, etc.

Generally speaking, Static relations capture the basic concepts in Object Oriented Design, which are shared by all design patterns. Dynamic relations are usually pattern related.

Till here, we have shown the core concepts in design patterns. Next section will introduce the ontology of Situation Calculus.

Table 3: Actions in Observer pattern

Methods	Annotation
Attach	Object×Object
Detach	Object×Object
Notify	Object×Date
Update	Object×Object×Data

4. The Situation Calculus

The core concept in Situation Calculus is action. Actions change world's situation, which are sequences of actions. S0 is used to denote the Initial Situation. The distinguished function do(a, s) returns the successor situation of s. For example: Pickup(r, x) means Robot r pick up an object x.

Relations whose truth values vary from situation to situation are called Relational Fluents. For instance, holding(r, x, S) is a relational fluent represents that robot r is holding x in situation S. Relations whose values do not change by actions are called Eternals. For instance, Robot(r) is an eternal saying that r is a robot, whose value is assumed not change.

Intuitively, actions have preconditions and effects. In Situation Calculus these knowledge about actions are represented by Axioms, which include Precondition axioms and Successor State Axioms.

Precondition Axioms specify conditions that must be satisfied to perform actions. Poss is a distinguished predicate symbol representing Precondition Axioms. For example:

Poss(Pickup(r, x), S) ≡ (z)~holding(r, z, S)

which says whenever possible for robot r to pick up x in situation s, it must not holding anything in situation S.

Successor State Axioms specify how actions change the value of fluents, for instance:

holding(r, x, do(a, s)) ≡

(a = Pickup(r, x)) ∨ holding(r, x, s) ∧ a != Putdown(r, x) which says r will hold x in the next situation if action Pickup(r,x) is performed or r is holding x in this situation and do not perform the action Putdown(r,x).

5. Design Patterns in Situation Calculus

5.1. *The conceptual mapping relation*

Eternals in Situation Calculus are suitable to model structure of design patterns. On the contrary, Fluents in Situation Calculus is suitable for modeling behavioral aspect of patterns. Moreover, Methods in design patterns are mapped to Actions in Situation Calculus; preconditions and postconditions of Methods correspond to the Precondition Axioms and Successor State Axioms (See Table 4).

Table 4: The conceptual mapping relations between design patterns and Situation Calculus

Design Patterns	Situation Calculus
Entities	Eternals
Permanent Relations	Eternals
Temporal Relations	Relational Fluents
Methods	Actions
Preconditions	Precondition Axioms
Postconditions	Successor State Axioms

Table 5: Relations in Observer pattern

Relation Name	Type
Inherit(x, y)	Eternal
MDefinedIn(m, c)	Eternal
ADefinedIn(a, c)	Eternal
RefOne(x, y)	Eternal
RefMany(x, y)	Eternal
Call(c1,m1,c2,m2)	Eternal
Argument(c, m)	Eternal
Object(o, S)	Fluent
Instance(o, c, S)	Fluent
Attached(x, y, S)	Fluent
Updated(x, y, S)	Fluent
StateVal(o, sv , S)	Fluent

5.2. *Observer pattern in Situation Calculus*

In the process of formalizing the Observer pattern, we follow the general steps of specifying a 'system' in Situation Calculus. First, we identify Relations used in the Observer pattern in Table 5.

As mentioned above, Eternals are shared by all the patterns and Fluents are usually pattern related. To obtain a more faithful model, we use fluents Object(o, S), Instance(o, c, S) and StateVal(o, sv, S) which are common to all patterns.

The second step is to enumerate Actions in Observer pattern in Table 6. Note action New(o, c) and Delete(o)

are not specific to the Observer pattern and can be shared by all patterns.

The Precondition Axioms and Successor State Axioms are listed in table 7 and table 8.

Finally, we need to specify the initial situation S0. Generally, we can encode the participants and structure of a pattern in S0. See Table 6 for the encoding of Observer pattern in Situation S0.

Table 6: Actions in Observer pattern

Action	Semantics
Attach(s, o)	Sets the temporal relation Attached between Object s and Object o
Detach(s, o)	Clears the temporal relation Attached between Object s and Object o
Notify(s, d)	Clears the temporal relations Updated between Object s and all the Objects attached to s (in the temporal relation Attached) and reset s' Attribute to d
Update(s, o, d)	Sets temporal relation Updated between Object s and Object o and reset Object o' s Attribute to d
New(o, c)	Sets the temporal relation Object(o, S) and Instance(o, c, S)
Delete(o)	Clears the temporal relation Object(o, S) and Instance(o, c, S)

Table 7: Precondition Axioms

Action	Precondition Axioms
Attach(s, o)	Poss(Act, S) ≡~Attached(s, o, S)
Detach(s, o)	Poss(Act, S) ≡Attached(s, o, S)
Notify(s, d)	Poss(Act, S) ≡ True
Update(s, o, d)	Poss(Act, S) ≡ Attached(s,o, S)Λ~Updated(s, o, S)ΛStateVal(s, d, S)
New(o, c)	Poss(Act,S) ≡ Class(c)
Delete(o)	Poss(Act, S) ≡ Object(o, S)

Once we precisely specify design patterns in Situation Calculus, we can use the main services provided by Situation Calculus: Projection and Planning, to facilitate the understanding and application of design pattern. We will discuss them in next section.

6. Potential usages of Situation Calculus

Based on our encoding of the Observer pattern, we can query whether it is possible to perform certain action in certain situations. For instances:

Axioms |= Poss(Attach(sub, obs1), S0),

Axioms |= Poss(Detach(sub, obs2), S0),

Axioms |= Poss(a, do([Seq], S0)),

where [Seq] is a sequence of actions.

It can also reason properties (Fluent) of system after execution of actions. In the Observer pattern, for instance, we may want to know whether sub and obs2 are attached after following sequence of actions in S0:

[Seq]=Attach(sub, obs1); New(obs3, Subject); Attach(sub, obs2); Detach(sub, obs1).

We can formalize this query in the following way:

Axioms |= Attached(sub, obs2, do([Seq], S0))

The result can be derived from the Successor State Axioms automatically by reasoners such as Prolog.

Table 8: Successor State Axioms

Successor State Axiom
Object(o, do(a, S)) ≡ New(o, c)VObject(o, S)Λa!=Delete(o)
Instance(o, c, do(a, S)) ≡ New(o, c)VInstance(o, c, S)Λa!=Delete(o)
Attached(s, o, do(a, S)) ≡ a=Attach(s, o) V Attached(s, o, S)Λa!=Detach(s, o)
Updated(s, o, do(a, S))≡ a=Update(s,o,d)VUpdated(s,o,S)Λa!=Notify(s, d)
StateVal(o, sv, do(a, S)) ≡ a=Update(s, o, sv)VStateVal(o, sv,S) Λa!=Update(s, o, sv')

Table 9: Formal specification of Oberver pattern

The Structure of Observer pattern
Inherit(ConcreteSubject, Subject), Inherit(ConcreteObserver, Observer), ADefinedIn(subjectstate, ConcreteSubject), ADefinedIn(observerstate, ConcreteObserver), RefOne(ConcreteObserver, ConcreteSubject), RefMany(Subject, Observer), Call(ConcreteSubject, setstate, Subject, notify), Call(Subject, notify, Observer, update), Call(Observer, update, ConcreteSubject, getstate), Argument(Observer, attach), Argument(Observer, detach), Argument(Subject, update)

By using projection, we can keep track of design pattern's behavioral (not only structural) properties as the system evolves. This will facilitate the understanding and reasoning about the system's behavior. Furthermore, projection can help us discover errors in programs at the semantic level. In Object Oriented programming, programs are actually consisted of sequences of method calls, which can be encoded as sequence of Actions in

Situation Calculus. Though we do not have axioms for each method call, however, we can simply ignore the others and extract only pattern related methods from the program. Then we can check whether the sequence of pattern related actions is possible by using the query Poss(a, do([Seq], S0). If the answer is negative, then we have discovered an error in the program without actually running it. This kind of error is at the semantic level, for changing the order of a sequence of method calls is insignificant to compiler as long as they are syntactically correct.

7. Conclusion and Future Work

The formal description of design pattern is fundamental to the understanding and application of design patterns. This paper proposed an approach based on Situation Calculus in Artificial Intelligence. In our approach, the structural and behavioral aspects of design patterns are combined together in a natural and seamless way, which clarify and simplify the specification of design patterns. Furthermore, by representing pattern related knowledge in machine-processable style (Concretely, by Axioms), we paved a way for automatic processing of pattern related problems.

In our future work, the main concern will be exploring and discovering the full potential of the proposed approach in this paper. As discussed above, projection allows us to check semantic level errors in a program statically (without actually run it). We are considering conduct some case studies in Java. To make it practical and efficient, we need to develop a tool that converts sequences of method calls in Java source code to sequences of actions in Situation Calculus. As mentioned above, this tool should filter out unrelated method calls and focus on extracting actions that affect the properties of design patterns. Then with the implementation of Situation Calculus (in Prolog, Coq or other logical engines), the checking can be done automatically.

References

1. Mikkonen Tommi, 1998. Formalizing design pattern. In: Proceedings of the 20th International Conference on Software Engineering, pp. 115–124.
2. Taibi, Toufik, Ngo, David C.L., 2003. Formal specification of design pattern combination using BPSL. International Journal of Information and Software Technology (IST) 45 (3), 157–170.
3. Eden, A.H., Hirshfeld, Y., 2001.Principles in formal specification of object-oriented architectures. In: Proceedings of the 11th CASCON, November 2001, Toronto, Canada.
4. Dong, Jing, Alencar, Paulo, Cowan, Donald, 2000. Ensuring structure and behavior correctness in design composition. In: Proceedings of the 7th Annual IEEE International Conference and Workshop on Engineering of Computer Based Systems (ECBS), April 2000, Edinburgh UK, pp.279–287.
5. Keller, Rudolf K., Schauer Reinhard, 1998. Design components: towards software composition at the design level. In: Proceedings of the 20th International Conference on Software Engineering, pp. 302–311.
6. Gamma, Erich, Helm, Richard, Johnson, Ralph, Vlissides, John, 1995. Design Patterns, Elements of Reusable Object-Oriented Software. Addison-Wesley Publishing Company.
7. Lamport, Leslie, 1994. The temporal logic of actions. ACM Transactions on Programming Languages and Systems 16 (3), 873–923.
8. Jean-Yves Girard, Yves Lafont, and Paul Taylor. Proofs and Types, volume 7 of Cambridge Tracts in Theoretical Computer Science.Cambridge University Press, 1989.
9. Yves Bertot and Pierre Cast´eran. Interactive Theorem Proving and Program Development. Coq'Art: The Calculus of Inductive Constructions. Texts in Theoretical Computer Science. Springer Verlag, 2004.
10. P. Alencar, D. Cowan, and C. Lucena. A formal approach to architectural design patterns. In Proceedings of the 3rd International Symposium of formal Methods Europe, pages 576 – 594, 1996.
11. Jing Dong, Paulo S.C. Alencar, Donald D. Cowan , Sheng Yang. Composing pattern-based components and verifying correctness. The Journal of Systems and Software , pages 1755–1769, 2007.
12. Amnon H. Eden, Yoram Hirshfeld, Rick Kazman. Abstraction classes in software design. IEE Software, Vol. 153, No. 4, pages 163–182, 2006.

AUTONOMIC COMPUTING- SCORE /EROCS

MRS. SHANTA RANGASWAMY
Lecturer, Department of Computer Science and Engineering, R.V. College of Engineering, Bangalore-560059, India.
E-mail:Shanta_suthik@rediffmail.com

"Innovation today is not just product innovation, rather it is about services, processes, business models or cultural innovation." Faced with growing knowledge management needs and its difficulties in organizing and retaining, enterprises are increasingly realizing the importance of interlinking critical business information distributed across structured and unstructured data sources. The structured and unstructured information that are distributed across the organization are automatically combined by the two technologies called EROCS (Entity RecOgnition in the Context of Structured data) and SCORE (Symbiotic Content Oriented information REtrieval)[1]. This enables organizations to generate new contextual and actionable insights to help determine appropriate business decisions. This survey paper highlights the importance and scope of EROCS in the IT industry and in the field of business. A highlight of this technology, which clearly differentiates it from the traditional named-entity recognition systems, is that EROCS identifies an entity even if it is not explicitly mentioned in the document. It exploits the context information present in the document to match and identify entities."

Keywords: Structured Information, Unstructured data, Database, Entity, Transactions

Introduction

An entity is a "thing" of significance, either real or conceptual, about which the relational database holds information [2]. An entity template specifies the entities to be matched in the document and for each entity, the context information that can be exploited to perform the match.

The information content in an enterprise (business) can be structured or unstructured. The structured content could be transaction data, payroll, sales orders, invoice, customer profiles, etc. and unstructured content could be emails, reports, web-pages, complaints, etc. Historically, the structured and unstructured data retrieval technologies have evolved separately.[2] Business analysts are realizing the need to bridge this separation, and are demanding integrated retrieval, management and analysis of both the structured and unstructured content.

EROCS views a document as a sequence of sentences, where a sentence is a bag of terms. Some terms in a sentence are potentially useful since they occur in the database as well, and thus may occur in the context of a candidate entity; other terms are not useful and are filtered out. EROCS uses a part-of-speech parser to identify noun-phrases in a sentence, and filters out the rest; the assumption, which usually holds, is that only nouns appear as values in the database. Further, each noun which is identified is looked up in the database and made note with the database columns it occurs in. [1]

EROCS identifies an entity even if it is not explicitly mentioned in the document; it exploits the available context information to match and identify the entities. As a consequence, while entity matching in named-entity extraction essentially involves a dictionary lookup, entity matching in EROCS involves a significantly more complex search over a multi-table database. Given the large number of candidate entities and the size of context information associated with each entity, it is impractical to appropriately appear and index the entire context of each candidate entity; this appearance would involve expensive joins across multiple tables, and would have high maintenance and storage overheads.

Thus EROCS addresses the problem of linking a document with related structured data in an external relational database. It views the structured data in the relational database as a set of predefined "entities" and identifies the entities from this set that best match the given document. EROCS further finds embedding of the identified entities in the document.[3] These embeddings are essentially linkages that interrelate relevant structured data with segments within the given document.

As an example, consider a retail organization, structured data consists of all information about sales transactions, customers and products.[1] The organization, with a network of multiple stores, has a steady inflow of complaints into a centralized complaint repository; these complaints are accepted using alternative means, such as a web-form, email, fax and voice-mail (which is then transcripted). Each such complaint is typically a free-flow narrative text about one or more sales transactions, and is not guaranteed to contain the respective transaction identifiers; instead, it might disclose, by way of context, limited information such as the store name, a partial list of items bought, the purchase dates, etc. Using this limited information, EROCS discovers the potential matches with the transactions present in the sales transactions database and links the given complaint with the matching transactions. Such linkage provides actionable context to a typically fuzzy, free flow narrative which can be profitably exploited in a variety of ways. In the above example, we can build an automated complaint routing system. Given the transaction automatically linked with the complaint, this system retrieves from the relational database additional information about the transaction (such as type and value of the items purchased, specific promotions availed and the customer's loyalty level), and routes the complaint to an appropriate department or customer service representative based on the same.

Formally, an entity template is a rooted tree with a designated root node. Each node in this tree is labeled with a table in the given relational database schema, and there exists an edge in the tree only if the tables labeling the nodes at the two ends of the edge have a foreign-key relationship in the database schema. The table that labels the root node is called the pivot table of the entity template, and the tables that label the other nodes are called the context tables. Each row e in the pivot table is identified as an entity belonging to the template, with the associated context information consisting of the rows in the context tables that have a path to row e in the pivot table through one or more foreign-keys covered by the edges in the entity template.

Consider an another example, in which the sales transactions entity template, shown in Figure 1 and 2, has the root node labeled by the TRANSACTION table (the pivot table), and the non-root nodes labeled by the CUSTOMER, STORE, TRANSPROD, PRODUCT and MANUFACTURER tables (the context tables) that provide the context for each transaction in the TRANSACTION table[1]. Note that the template definition also provides the information that the SUPPLIER table, though reachable from the TRANSACTION table via both the PRODUCT and STORE tables, carries no contextual information about a given transaction; this is valuable domain knowledge that is hard to figure automatically. Multiple nodes in the template can be labeled with the same table. This is needed to differentiate the different roles a table might play in the context of the entity. Suppose the document mentions product names not only to identify a transaction, but also to identify the store in which the transaction occurred; further suppose it mentions the manufacturer in the former case, but not in the latter[5]. Then, the template in Figure 2 would extend the TRANSACTION→STORE path to TRANSACTION-->STORE-->INVENTORY-->PRODUCT. Now there exist two nodes in the template labeled with the same table PRODUCT representing the two roles the table plays; also, one includes a child labeled with the table MANUFACTURER, the other does not.

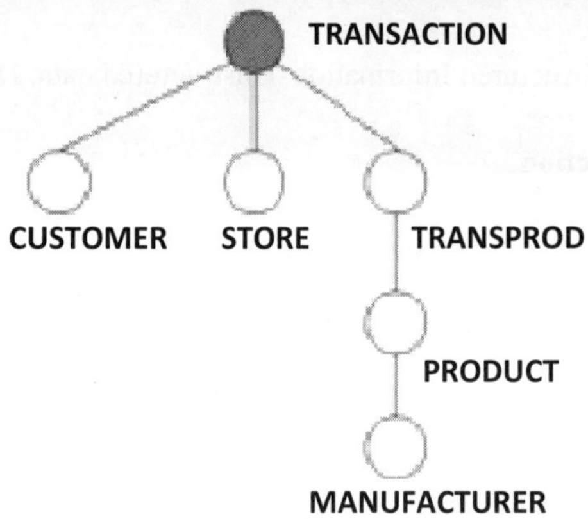

Figure 1: An Entity Template.

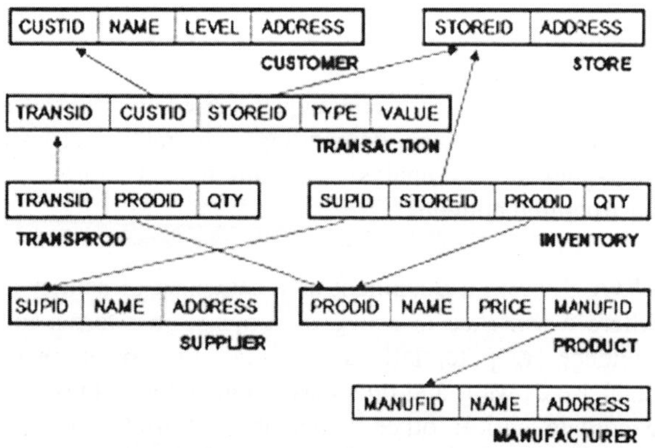

Figure 2: Example of a Relational Database Schema

SCORE (Symbiotic Content Oriented information REtrieval) addresses the problem of consolidated querying of structured and unstructured data, wherein the application specifies its information needs using only a SQL query on the structured data, and this query is automatically translated into a set of keywords that can be used to retrieve relevant unstructured data. At the core of this technology lies a technique for obtaining these keywords from not only the query result, but also from additional related information in the underlying database.

It also works on customer e-mails and transcribed calls and quickly categorizes and manages a wide variety of customer e-mails and calls on numerous subjects, such as complaints, billing questions or other types of inquiries, and enables the identification of specific issues associated with each inquiry.[4] The solution also automatically assesses the sentiment of the customer to determine their level of concern or satisfaction, and identifies the top keywords mentioned throughout the content. These keywords can be used to find the key pain-points of a customer who has a complaint.

Conclusion

SCORE and EROCS technologies provide an organization the ability to generate insights to help enhance customer satisfaction as well as identify new business opportunities. This new technology easily integrates structured and unstructured data, and exploits context information to optimize efficiencies. SCORE /EROCS technology helps enterprises use unstructured data for business intelligence which was till now impossible. It has immense applicability in call centers. By using this technology an enterprise can combine its structured and unstructured information and provide call center agents with a complete history of all customer activity so they are aware of information that has already been shared through previous interactions. Thus these two technologies automatically combine structured and unstructured information that are distributed across the organization, enabling companies to generate new contextual and actionable insights to help determine appropriate business decisions. These technologies are useful for customer information management, targeted marketing, fraud detection and prevention and official compliance.

References

[1] Venkatesan T. Chakaravarthy Himanshu Gupta Prasan Roy Mukesh Mohania, IBM India Research Lab New Delhi, India: Efficiently Linking Text Documents with Relevant Structured Information

[2] Chen, P. P.-S. The Entity-Relationship Model–Toward a Unified View of Data. ACM TODS 1, 1 (1976).

[3] Walker, M. H., and Eaton, N. J. Microsoft Office Visio 2003 Inside Out. Microsoft Press, 2003.

[4] Agichtein,E., and Ganti, V.Mining reference tables for automatic text segmentation.In SIGKDD (2004).

[5] Agrawal,S., Chaudhuri,S., and Das,G. DBXplorer: A System for Keyword-Based Search over Relational databases. In ICDE (2002).

[6] Li,X.,Morie,P., and Roth, D.Semantic Integration in Text: From Ambiguous Names to Identifiable Entities. AI Magazine: Special Issue on Semantic Integration (2005).

[7] R. S. Pressman, "*Software Engineering : A Practitioner's Approach*", 4th Edition, New York: McGraw-Hill, 1997.

ASPECT-ORIENTED CODE OBFUSCATION

KESHNEE PADAYACHEE
School of Computing, University of South Africa, P.O. Box 392, UNISA, Pretoria, 0003
Pretoria, Gauteng 0003, South Africa

This paper reports on an exploratory study investigating the feasibility of using aspect-oriented constructs to instrument objects for the purposes of code obfuscation. With Java programs it is difficult to protect the intellectual property rights and secret information in untrusted environments. Consequently the utilization of software obfuscation techniques has become relevant. It has been found that Aspect-Oriented programming might be abused to overcome advanced code obfuscation used in Java Bytecode. In this paper possible intervention strategy to prevent these types of attacks using aspect-oriented programming language such as AspectJ is presented.

1. Introduction

The aspect-oriented paradigm has been recommended for several design issues, such as security [1], persistence[2] and exception handling [3]. The principal argument supporting the utilization of aspect-oriented programming (AOP) to develop software is that some software requirements tend to crosscut objects, resulting in the code tangling phenomenon. Aspect-orientation has the potential to enhance the implementation of such crosscutting concerns in terms of reusability and extensibility, thereby improving the robustness and maintainability of a system. As the popularity of AOP matures [4], the issue surrounding exploiting aspect-oriented programs for malicious purposes is of critical concern. It has been found that AOP may now be abused for sinister purposes such as, overcoming code obfuscation and thereby modifying software code to render security protection mechanisms ineffective. The aim of this paper is to investigate aspect-oriented tampering and propose a possible intervention to this problem.

A code obfuscator is a tool which converts a program into an equivalent one that is more difficult to understand and reverse engineer [5]. There exist several obfuscation tools for preventing Java bytecode from being decompiled. Most of these tools simply scramble the names of the identifiers stored in a bytecode by substituting the identifiers with meaningless names [6]. It has been found that AOP may expose code obfuscators and render systems vulnerable to malicious purposes [7]. For instance, to extract propriety algorithms, or to subvert protection checks of commercial Java packages. Unfortunately encryption cannot resolve these type of problems since encrypted programs must be eventually decrypted in to executable programs and the adversaries can intercept them in hostile environments [8]. Chen and Chen [7] have shown that is possible for the join point model and the code instrumentation mechanism of aspect-oriented programming to render code obfuscation ineffective for some intended protection. They highlighted the following concern: the 'binary weaving tools of AOP may become a new breed of productivity tools that facilitate the tampering of software integrity and malicious attacks'. The realization of software with tamper-resistance, that is the difficulty to read and modify the software in an unauthorized manner, becomes increasingly important. Software obfuscation transforms a program into a tamper resistant form [8]. This paper presents an exploratory study on aspect instrumentation for the purposes of obfuscation. Zhang and Wen [9] have also considered using AOP to protect Java source code, however they focus on enlarging the range of encryption to protect J2EE applications. It is important to note that although aspect-orientation is a form of instrumentation, it is not instrumentation in the typical sense as the code instrumented may be an essential requirement to the final application such as error handling or exception handling. This type of instrumentation is more formalized than typical instrumentation as it is language-based. It is much more precise and pervasive than traditional methods.

This paper does not present any new techniques for code obfuscation nor is the technique presented evaluated with respect to their *potency* that is, to 'what degree is a human reader confused' [5]. Additionally the author does not negate the need for obfuscators in general. This paper addresses one particular type of attack when code obfuscation may not be adequate. That is specifically when 'malicious users with rudimentary knowledge of Java byte code and cryptography can exploit the join point model and code instrumentation of AspectJ to render code obfuscation and string encryption ineffective for some intended protection' [7]. The rest of the paper is structured as follows. Section 2, elaborates on aspect-oriented programming in general. In Sections 3 and 4 explores how aspect-oriented programming may be exploited for malicious purposes and possible ways to avert to these types of attacks, respectively. Finally, Section 5 concludes, with possible future research opportunities.

2. Aspect-Oriented Programming

The object-oriented paradigm was found to be inadequate in terms of design and implementation of crosscutting concerns, as there is no elegant way of modularising these crosscutting concerns. AOP provides explicit language support for modularising design decisions that crosscut a functionally decomposed program [10], allowing the developer to maintain the code (crosscutting functionality) in a modularised form. It is important to note that aspect-orientation maintains all the benefits of the object-oriented paradigm and should be viewed as an extension rather than a replacement of object-oriented technologies.

An aspect-oriented system consists of two concepts: components and aspects. The components form the atomic and loosely coupled concerns of the system, and the aspects implement the additional crosscutting functionality of the system. According to Kiczales et al. [11], aspects consist of constructs named *pointcuts* and *advices*. A join point is a definable interception point in a system where the aspect could possibly take action. Specifically, join points refer to well-defined points in a program's execution such as when an object is instantiated, when a method is called, or when an exception is thrown, etc. The *pointcuts* are a set of join points described by a pointcut expression. An *advice* defines the functionality to be executed before (i.e. the before advice) or after (i.e. the after advice) a defined join point, or even possibly instead of the defined join point (i.e. the around advice). An aspect weaver is then used to merge components and aspects into a final program.

Aspect-orientation has the potential to reduce the complexity of programs and to improve maintainability of software. However, despite the benefits offered by aspect-orientation, there are some drawbacks. Alexander and Bieman [12] maintain that as a result of the weaving process, the isolation of faults will be difficult, as faults may reside in the source code, the aspect, or the woven code.

Typically when a programmer cannot decipher code, he/she will instrument such code to determine the context. There are several methods of program instrumentation such as binary code transformation, link time manipulation or source code transformation. Typically program analysis tools often rely on profiling information obtained from the programs they analyse. Obtaining such information can be a tedious task and the data achieved may be more abstract and non-specific [13, 14]. The more generic the instrumentation approach, the more abstract is the achievable data. Aspect-orientation resolves this problem, as the code introduced can extract data in more controlled way. However just as AOP may be used for useful purposes, it may be exploited for malicious purposes

3. Using Aspect-Oriented Programming for Malicious Purposes

Soliciting information about software for malicious purposes may be achieved with designing tracing aspects using the pointcut and advice mechanisms of AspectJ. Control flow tracing supplies the calling sequence of Java methods. While data flow based tracing employs field access join points to track where decoding and checking related strings are accessed. Once the exact code segment that reports the check result is located, then one may devise an aspect that will intercept a request to data checking, and a return forged success result. In view of the fact that encryption and decryption of string literals are not a standard service of Java Runtime, at some point the program under attack must decrypt the string literal by itself before they are displayed to the user. Control flow based tracing generates a method call log that will assist a malicious individual with identifying these methods, with the intent of subverting them [7].

These types attack begins with bottom-up control flow tracing and data flow tracing. Both forms of tracing rely on using **thisJoinPoint**, or **thisEnclosingJoinPointStaticPart** variables that are available in AspectJ. These variables are visible in an advice and each is bound to an object that encapsulates some of the context of the advice's current or enclosing join point. (AspectJ has three such variables **thisJoinPoint**, **thisJoinPointStaticPart**, and **thisEnclosingJoinPointStaticPart**.) These variables exist because some pointcuts may pick out very large collections of join points [15] and these variables can be used to differentiate join points. For example, these variables can provide information regarding the methods called and arguments passed at a specific point in the program's execution. If this information trawling exercise were to be prevented in the first instance and obfuscated information returned then further attacks may become much more difficult to realize.

The author recommends that every shipped system should have built in aspect that can not only thwart an attack from any malicious aspect but also return obfuscated information. This aspect which essentially prevents information flow and obfuscates information should not have any impact on the main program and only becomes active when another aspect is attempting to solicit information from the system. As demonstrated in Figure 1, the Obfuscator Aspect sends back obfuscated information to the malicious user thus preventing any further attack.

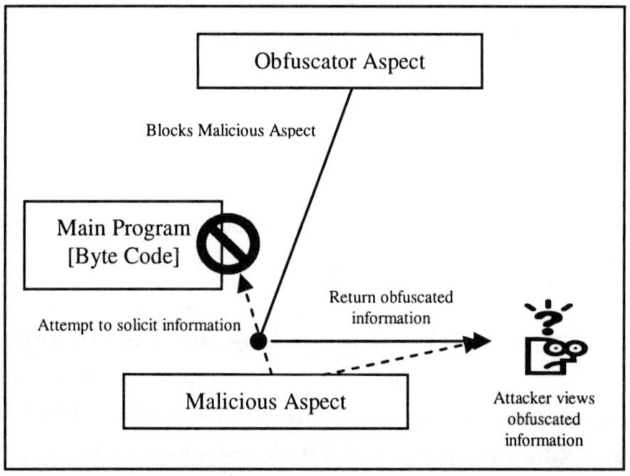

Figure 1. Showing how a Malicious Aspect can be thwarted with obfuscated information

4. Practical example of Aspect-Oriented Obfuscation

A simple program called SJEA which encrypts a file was downloaded from *Google* to demonstrate how encryption methods may be revealed with AOP. SJEA is a simple command-line binary encryption algorithm written in JAVA. As [7] has shown, aspect-orientation may utilized to expose and subvert encryption methods. It found that using an aspect-oriented programming language such as AspectJ, one can easily determine the methods used for encryption. An aspect named Trace was use to trace through SJEA's execution history (Listing 1). It works by exploiting the **thisJoinPointStaticPart** variable, which provides reflective information about the current join point. The method **getSignature()** is used obtain information about this variable. The aspect-oriented paradigm allows a more generic implementation of the Trace aspect through the use of wildcards. Using wildcards eliminates the need for explicit naming [16]. Hence this pointcut will track any method executed in a program's history. Listing 2 shows how the following aspect Trace exposes the methods for encryption in program SJEA.

Listing 1: Aspect Trace

```
public aspect Trace {
before(): execution(* *.*(..)) {
System.out.println(thisJoinPointStaticPart.
  getSignature());
}
}
```

Listing 2: Program SJEA advised by Aspect Trace

```
void enc.main(String[])
SJEA 1.0 ENCRYPT
Usage: java enc <input-file> <password>
Input file size: 10 bytes
> Encrypting...
> Generating checksum...int enc.create(String)
byte[] enc.createChecksum(String)
MD5: 5bdf74912a51c34815f11e9a3d20b609
DONE!
Output file "c:\test\keshnee.txt.enc" created.
File size: 15 Bytes
Checksum file "c:\test\keshnee.txt.md5" created.
Password length: 7 character(s)
```

The solution to this problem was to define an aspect to obfuscate the method names so that is indecipherable to the attacker. Aspect XYZ (Listing 3) was developed to counter this type of "attack". The pointcut risk1 picks out each join point where a getSignature() method is being called. As this is an indication that a joinpoint is being exposed. The keyword within() is used to define scope, in this case pointcut risk1 does not pick joinpoints within aspect XYZ. Once this joinpoint is identified then a method to obfuscate this joinpoint should be used. In order to improve the modularity of the aspect, a method obfuscate() was defined for this purpose. Unfortunately this presented a problem as aspect Trace's pointcut picks up obsfuscate() as a method to expose. This resulted in infinite recursive calls from Aspects XYZ and Trace. If no special precautions are taken, aspects which advise other aspects can easily and unintentionally advise each other recursively. The resolution to this problem was to create another pointcut preventcrosscut which essentially wrapped around the pointcut from Trace and prevented Trace from exposing this joinpoint as well. This pointcut then performed the obfuscation. As this paper does not focus on obfuscation techniques, a rudimentary method was applied where the all method names were given aliases. For example method createCheckSum() was changed to "Rt m(Ar2 x)" which serves the purpose of obfuscation. Name obfuscation is the process of using meaningless or difficult to read string to replace the variable name [9]. However as code defined for obfuscation was separated - other more advanced and verifiable techniques may be substituted. It is plausible that preventcrosscut could be extended to avert all joinpoints picked by aspect Trace, however it could prevent other innocuous aspects that were in the original system from delivering a function that is essential to the system. The around advice for pointcut risk1, obfuscates the joinpoint that Trace was attempting to expose in system. As getSignature() returns a signature, the advice is forced to return the same type of object otherwise the system will throw an exception. The advice for risk1 returns the signature of the joinpoint in aspect Trace instead of the joinpoint in program SJEA. The output produced with both aspects Trace and XYZ advising program SJEA is shown in Listing 4.

Listing 3: Aspect XYZ

```
public aspect XYZ {
pointcut risk1(Object js): !within(XYZ) && call(* *.getSignature(..))
&& target(js);
Object around(Object js): risk1(js){
    obsfuscation(js);
    return thisJoinPoint.getSignature();
}
void obsfuscation(Object obj){
//Do nothing as the Aspect Tracer will pick up this method to advise
}
pointcut preventcrosscut(Object obj): within(XYZ) &&
call( * *.obsfuscation(..)) && args(obj) ;
void around(Object obj):preventcrosscut(obj){
    String s = obj.toString();
    if (s.contains("create")) {
    s = "Rt m(Arg1 x)";}
    if (s.contains("createChecksum")){
    s = "Rt m(Ar2 x)";}
    if (s.contains( "main")){
    s = "Rt. m(Arg3 x)";}
    System.out.println(s);
}
}
```

Listing 4: Program SJEA advised by both Aspect Trace and Aspect XYZ

```
Rt. m(Arg3 x)
Signature org.aspectj.lang.JoinPoint.StaticPart.getSignature()
SJEA 1.0 ENCRYPT
Usage: java enc <input-file> <password>
Input file size: 10 bytes
> Encrypting...
> Generating checksum...Rt m(Arg1 x)
Signature org.aspectj.lang.JoinPoint.StaticPart.getSignature()
Rt m(Arg1 x)
Signature org.aspectj.lang.JoinPoint.StaticPart.getSignature()
MD5: 5bdf74912a51c34815f11e9a3d20b609
DONE!
Output file "c:\test\keshnee.txt.enc" created.
File size: 15 Bytes
Checksum file "c:\test\keshnee.txt.md5" created.
Password length: 7 character(s)
```

The solution presented is simplistic however, attackers could easily rewrite this Trace aspect in other ways to illicit the same information and foil aspect XYZ in more subtle ways. For instance with Java, println statements could be used to expose a joinpoint. There four possible ways of rewriting the same code to gather similar information. We now explore four such cases. We termed these risks. The first risk, is namely using method calls on the thisJoinPoint, thisJoinStaticPart or thisEnclosingJoinPointStaticPart such as getSignature(). Aspect XYZ can easily obfuscate these calls. If method call is made to some other member function such as getSourceLocation(), getArgs() or getKind() then Aspect XYZ would not be able to handle these. However pointcut risk1 (Listing 5) could be expanded to handle all of these cases. Of course the return type will be have adapted accordingly otherwise the system will throw an exception. The next risk occurs when reflective information can be concatenated with string. Currently Aspect XYZ cannot identify this type of attack. For instance, the following statement will be overlooked by aspect XYZ:- System.out.println("thisJoinPoint" + thisJoinPoint)

In this case, incorporating pointcut risk2 to aspect XYZ (see Listing 5) will be one way of subverting this type of statement. Pointcut risk2, essentially checks every string that is passed to a function, which then obfuscates it if is revealing any critical information. This pointcut could also be useful in preventing illegal flows. Information is exchanged among by messages in object-oriented systems. An illegal flow arises when information is transmitted from one object to another object in violation of the information flow security policy [17] .

The next two risks are similar but require two different pointcuts to subvert them. These risks, involve merely passing either thisJoinPoint, thisJoinStaticPart or thisEnclosingJoinPointStaticPart variable to a function which may then expose it. For example:- "System.out.println(thisJoinPoint);". Here two poincuts risk3 and risk4 were developed which essentially tracks down any join point where thisJoinPoint was being passed to any method. Whereas risk4 tracks down any join point where thisJoinPointStaticPart or thisEnclosingJoinPointStaticPart is being passed as an argument.

Listing 5: Pointcuts to be integrated into Aspect XYZ

```
pointcut risk1(Object js): !within(XYZ) && (call(* *.getSignature(..))
|| call(* *.getArgs(..) ) || call * *.getKind (..) ) etc..)
() && target(js);
pointcut risk2(String s): !within(XYZ) && call(void *.*(..)) &&
args(..,s) ;
void around(String s): risk2(s){
    obsfuscation(s);
}
pointcut risk3(JoinPoint jp): !within(XYZ) && call(void *.*(..)) &&
args(jp,..);
void around(JoinPoint jp): risk3(jp){
    System.out.println("risk 3 - output only joinpoint" +jp);
    obsfuscation(jp);
}
pointcut risk4(JoinPoint.StaticPart jp): !within(XYZ) && call(void
*.*(..)) && args(jp,..);
void around(JoinPoint.StaticPart jp): risk4(jp){
    System.out.println("risk4 - outupt only staticpart" +jp);
    obsfuscation(jp);
}
```

5. Conclusion

Obfuscators are a necessary requirement however as shown by Chen and Chen [7], attackers with a rudimentary knowledge of Java byte code and cryptography can exploit the join point model and code instrumentation of AspectJ to render code obfuscation, string encryption and other security mechanisms ineffective for some intended protection. In the worked example, it was demonstrated how a program may be abused. The author then presented an approach to thwart this type of attacks using aspect-oriented programming and obfuscation to prevent reverse-engineering. Chen and Chen [7] suggests that AspectJ should provide a mechanism to "hide" or encapsulate critical join points in a program. However this is subject to whether a programmer deems a point in a program's execution as critical or in fact bears in mind to do so. Unfortunately, incorporating security into software development takes time and developers tend to focus more on the features of the software application. The author does not proclaim this solution could prevent all possible attacks however it is step forward towards trying to prevent this type of attacks. This is analogous to anti-viruses, the attackers will always figure out other ways of defeating anti-virus packages. However this does not negate the need for this type of software. Future research would involve in determining the performance issues relating to aspect-oriented obfuscation.

Acknowledgements

The author acknowledges the use of the Eclipse platform and AspectJ (http://www.eclipse.org/aspectj/) during the development process.

References

1. B. De Win, B. Vanhaute, and B. De Decker, *Informatica* **26**, 141 (2002).
2. A. Rashid and R. Chitchyan, in Proceedings of the 2nd International Conference on Aspect-Oriented Software Development (ACM, Enschede, The Netherlands, 2003), p. 120.
3. M. Lippert and C. V. Lopes, in Proceedings of the 22nd International Conference on Software Engineering (ACM, Limerick, Ireland, 2000), p. 418.
4. K. Padayachee and J. H. P. Eloff, in *Proceedings of the Sixth IASTED International Conference on Modelling, Simulation and Optimization*, edited by H. Nyongesa (ACTA Press, Gaborone, Botswana, 2006), p. 304.
5. C. Collberg, C. Thomborson, and D. Low, *A Taxonomy of Obfuscating Transformation*, in *Technical Report 148* (Department of Computer Science, University of Auckland, New Zealand, 1997)
6. J. Chan and W. Yang, *Journal of Systems and Software* **71**, 1 (2004).
7. K. Chen and J. Chen, in SESS '06: Proceedings of the 2006 international workshop on Software

engineering for secure systems (ACM, Shanghai, China, 2006), p. 19.

8. Y. Sakabe, M. Soshi, and A. Miyaji, *IPSJ Digital Courier* **1**, 349 (2005).
9. X. Zhang and Q. Wen, in Computational Intelligence and Security Workshops, 2007. CISW 2007 (IEEE, 2007), p. 581.
10. R. J. Walker, E. L. A. Baniassad, and G. C. Murphy, in *Proceedings of the 21st international conference on Software engineering* (IEEE, Los Angeles, California, 1999), p. 120.
11. G. Kiczales, E. Hilsdale, J. Hugunin, M. Kersten, and J. Palm, *Communications of the ACM* **44**, 59 (2001).
12. R. T. Alexander and J. M. Bieman, in *ICSE Workshop on Software Quality* (ACM, Orlando, Flordia, 2002).
13. M. Deters and R. K. Cytron, in Proceedings of the OOPSLA 2001 (Workshop on Advanced Separation of Concerns) (Tampa Bay, Florida, 2001).
14. M. Debusmann and K. Geihs, in *Self-Managing Distributed Systems* (Springer, 2003), Vol. 2867, p. 227.
15. *Development Aspects,* http://www.eclipse.org/aspectj/doc/released/progguide/examples-development.html (Last accessed:1/02/2009)
16. G. Kiczales, J. Hugunin, M. Kersten, J. Lamping, C. Lopes, and G. W.G., in *Workshop on Multi-Dimensional Separation of Concerns inSoftware Engineering (ICSE 2000)* (Limerick, Ireland, 2000), p. 1.
17. P. Samarati, E. Bertino, A. Ciampichetti, and S. Jajodia, *IEEE Transactions on Knowledge and Data Engineering* **9**, 624 (1997).

AN OVERVIEW OF CAD METHODS FOR THE DETECTION OF LUNG CANCER

ANITHA MUTHU ASWATHA KUMAR
1,2 -M.S.Ramaiah Institute of Technology, Bangalore .560054 INDIA

UDUPI V
3- Maratha Mandal's Engineering College, Belgaum 591113 INDIA

ABSTRACT -Medical images are the basis for a large number of clinical tasks in the daily routine of healthcare. It is essential to interpret large amount of data efficiently and safely in medical imaging analysis. This paper focuses on how CAD works for lung cancer detection. It critically reviews few diagnostic methods and algorithms. It discusses the suitability of respective methods.

Keywords:- CAD, Diagnostic methods, Lung Cancer and Medical Images.

1. INTRODUCTION

Lung cancer is one of the leading causes of cancer related to death among the people who smoke or who have smoked. It is a great concern to save the lives of the people from mortality by using medical imaging techniques. Tumors can be benign or malignant. Benign tumors can usually be removed and do not spread to other parts of the body [1]. Malignant tumors, on the other hand, grow aggressively and invade other tissues of the body, allowing entry of tumor cells into the bloodstream or lymphatic system and then to other sites in the body. Early detection and treatment of lung cancer can greatly improve the survival rate of patient. Computed Tomography (CT) of the thorax is widely used in CAD system by a radiologist who uses the output from a computerized analysis of medical images as a "second opinion" in detecting lesions and in making diagnostic decisions. The final diagnosis is made by the radiologists.

2. OBJECTIVES OF CAD

There are three main objectives of CAD are represented below

2.1 Diagnostic quality assurance:

By detecting and marking suspicious lesions, CAD can help to avoid potential nodules from being overlooked by the radiologist.

2.2 To increase therapy success by early detection of cancer:

By down staging the typical stage when a cancer is diagnosed; it is hoped that detection at an earlier stage increases the survival rates.

2.3 Reduction of biopsies:

By computation of growth rates and doubling times of lung nodules between follow-up examinations, many of the detected nodules can be evaluated non-invasively to avoid the risks associated with invasive procedures such as needle biopsies.

3. DIAGNOSTIC METHODS

The common methods to diagnose the cancerous tumors are using MRI, CT and chest radiography. Fibre optic bronchoscopy is also used but has limited value for finding nodules other than those in the larger airways. CT offers better contrast than chest radiography between nodule and background, with no overlapping structures, and several studies have shown that CT can detect smaller, earlier stage nodules with a higher sensitivity than chest radiography [2].

4. STAGE WISE CAD PROCEDURE

The various stages of CAD are given in the following sections:-

4.1 Preprocessing

Pre-processing deals with techniques for enhancing contrast, removing noise, and pictures less corrupted by patient motion which can be rectified [3].

4.2 Transformation

The process of transformation is done using the histogram equalization, which is widely used for contrast enhancement in a variety of applications due to its simple function and effectiveness [4]. One drawback of this method can be found on the fact that the brightness of an image can be changed after applying histogram equalization, which is mainly due to the flattening property.

4.3 Segmentation

Segmentation refers to the process of extracting meaningful regions from images. This involves all connected components in the eroded image to be labeled. Then the number of connected components is computed. The labeled components are segmented depending on the region of interest. The area of each segmented components in the image are calculated. Pixel values of the segmented components are also extracted from the preprocessed image. The calculated area and the pixel values extracted from the segmented image are the features given as the inputs to detection phase.

4.4 Detection

Once the lungs have been extracted from the image, the next step is to detect the nodules from the lung regions. The process of lung nodule detection focuses on features like size, location, shape of the nodule and color in terms of brightness, which differentiates the affected nodules from background lungs regions [5]. But the challenge is to avoid the missing of nodules these candidate nodules (nodules, vessels, airways) are extracted from the image. By using the CAD system one has to obtain a high level of true positive detection rate with less number of false positives. In this process the true positives, false positives, true negatives and false negatives are identified as follows: True Positives (TP's) describe, the candidate cells that is classified by the CAD system as cancerous cells, which is true for this cells, and the term False Positives (FP's) describe, the candidate cells that is classified by the CAD system as cancerous cells, but in fact it is not a cancer cells, the true cancer cells that is missed by the CAD are called False Negatives (FN's) and the True Negatives (TN's) refer to the non-cancerous cells that classified by the CAD system correctly.

4.5 Decision making

Knowledge based expert systems is used to formulate the mapping from a given input to an output. This mapping then provides a basis from which decisions can be made. Therefore it is used to recognize the nodule depending on the input, output relationship. The result of the decision-making system represents
(i)The removal of false positive findings.
(ii) The candidate nodule being detected.

5. VARIOUS CAD METHODS

There are several CAD algorithms, which help in detection of cancerous nodules at the early stage. They are as follows:

5.1. Volumetry Detection

The detection starts out from a given seed point selected either manually by mouse click or by the CAD module. The seed point does not necessarily need to be in the centre of the nodule. The region growing first grows into all areas that are spherical or lobular around the current seed point [6]. Then, from all boundary points of the current region expansion, a further seed point is automatically chosen that is closest to the centre of the surrounding mass, and from here the region growing continues into all areas that are spherical or lobular around the current seed point. This iterative scheme involves the growth process which stops only after it has grown far from the original start seed point. Then, a retrospective decision is taken regarding where the optimal cut-off point during the growth process would have been. The cut-off point is chosen such that the structures that are attached to the nodule are cut through at their thinnest connection, or in the case of an attached lung wall, at the strongest inflection.

5.2. Region Detection

The region-based approach is widely used in color image segmentation, because it considers the color information and spatial details at the same time [7]. It creates regions by grouping together similar pixels with higher accuracy than pixel-based segmentation algorithms. This algorithm uses the concept of 8-connected components. It starts searching for individual pixels and merged into the same region if their values are equal to one, after that each tested pixel is compared to its immediate 8-neighboring pixels. If the criterion is fulfilled, then the tested pixel belongs to the same region, else the tested pixel starts as a new region. The process of region detecting is continued until all pixels in the image are belonging to regions as homogenous as possible. The connected - components labeling method is used to identify each region in the outlined image, through assigning a distinguished label to each region in a label matrix

5.3. Rule Based Detection

The main objective of the CAD system is to obtain a high level of true positives detection rate even for small cells and a low number of false negatives [8]. This detection method works on rules which categorize the pixels based on the threshold. Considering the region to be represented by R and the threshold value to be represented by T1….n, the following rules are denoted.

Rule l:

If (R < T1) this cell is a normal cell and is classified as a normal cell. If (T1 < R < T2) this cell is abnormal and is classified as a candidate to be a cancer cell at level-1. If (T2 < R < T3) this cell is abnormal and is classified as a candidate to be a cancer cell at level-2. If (R> T3) this cell is abnormal and is classified as a candidate to be a cancer cell at an advanced stage noted level-3.If (R<<<T1), in this case Rule 1 is not considered, and it is not possible to classify the cell as a normal or abnormal cell, and this happens due to the dispersion of the cytoplasm in the staining process. Special case in Rule 1 appears when more than one cell have connected cytoplasm regions and in this case Rule l will not be accurate to discriminate the normal from abnormal cells. For this reason, we apply the following morphological rule to the nuclei regions.

Rule 2:

Compute the area of the maximum drawable circle (MDC) in the region (A) as follows: Area (MDC) = ∏ x (MDC)2 where ∏= 3.14. Compute the nuclei area of region (A) as follows:

$$\text{Area (A)} = \sum_{A} \text{pixels.}$$

Calculate the absolute value of the deviation (DV) between the two areas, Area (MDC) and Area (A) as follows: DV = |Area (MDC) – Area (A)|.If (DV >T4), then this cell is a candidate at level-3.

5.4 Subtraction Algorithm

A pixel p at coordinate (x, y) has four horizontal and vertical neighbors, whose coordinate are given by (x+1,y), (x-1,y), (x,y+1), (x,y-1). The difference between two images j(x,y) and h(x,y) is obtained. The subtraction algorithm is used to realize the distributing of the pathological tissue [9]. As mention before, an image is denoted by j(x,y) and j(x,y) is sampled so that the resulting image has M rows and N columns. Therefore, g(x,y),h(x,y),j(x,y) can be written in compact matrix form. g(x,y) = f (x,y)-h(x,y) < 0.The value of g (x, y) will be changed as g(x,y) = 0 and when g(x,y) = f (x,y)-h(x,y) >0. The value of g (x, y) will not be changed. Therefore, all cases of known or suspected lung cancer should be initially approached with curative intent.

5.5 Quoit Filter Detection

This method automatically recognizes the candidate regions for the pathological shadows [10].It is composed of two sequential operation named Q trans. and Q Inv. trans. each operation having an interesting characteristics as follows; Q trans. corresponds to extract feature parameter like a matched filter from input image having non ideal isolated shadow and Q Inv. trans. corresponds to restore isolated image using extracted feature parameter.

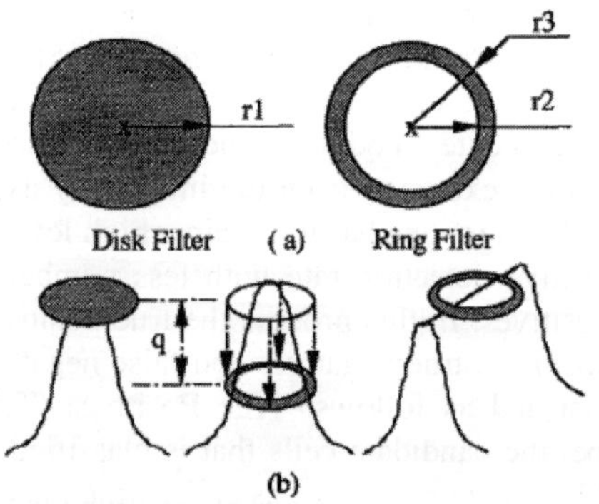

Fig.1.Illustration of Quoit element

Fig.1 shows the concept of the Q- filter which responds selectively only to the isolated shadow. The radius of the filter is labeled r1, r2 and r3 as shown in the figure. Consider the two structural elements shown in Fig. 1(a), i.e., disk and ring types. By applying the elements from upward to the isolated shadow as in the left side of Fig.

1(b), a difference of height q is produced between the two results. Since the ring filter fits well to the isolated shadow, it is called the quoit filter.

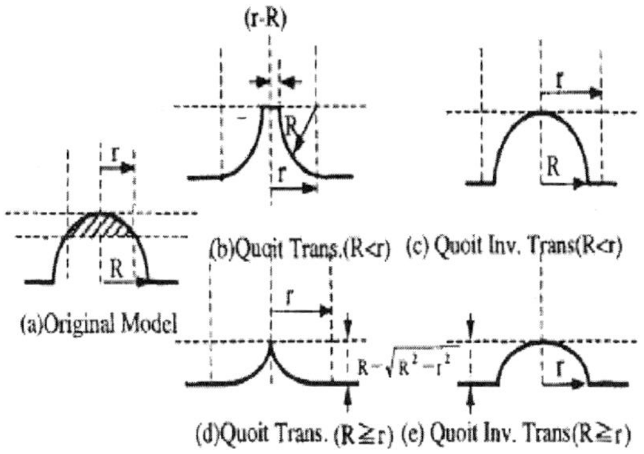

Fig.2 Quoit Trans. and Inv. Trans

On the other hand, the difference of height is not produced if the shadow is not isolated, as in the right side of Fig. 1(b). The processing based on the foregoing property is called Q trans. and Q Inv. Trans as shown in Fig.2.

6. PERFORMANCE OF CAD

SYSTEM

The above mentioned CAD methods are used for early detection of lung cancer. However, an evaluation criterion can be attempted to adopt a reliable CAD system based on the following parameters viz. Sensitivity, Accuracy and Specificity suggested in [17]

Sensitivity = TP / (TP + FN)

Accuracy = (TP+TN) / (TP+TN+FP+FN)

Specificity = TN / (TN + FP)

The above ratios would indicate a reliable CAD system which is able to predict more True Positive and less number of False Negative.

7. CONCLUSIONS

This paper describes the traditional algorithms used to perform CAD on CT images of the lung. One of the apprehensions of using CT for lung cancer screening is the large number of images that need to be interpreted. The increased workload on interpretation of CT studies can be a potential source of fatigue and error in detecting subtle lesions. To overcome this problem of ever increasing burden of image data to be examined, CAD systems can bring several benefits to lung cancer detection. A CAD system may improve the sensitivity of cancer detection, reduce oversight errors, and decrease inter-reader and intra-reader variations. Due to the relatively small size of the existing CT lung nodule databases and the various CT imaging acquisition protocols, it is hard to compare the detection performance among developed algorithms. The present study points out that a sensitivity analysis can be made using performance criteria on various CAD methods.

8. REFERENCES

[1] A. Reeves, et al., "On measuring the change in size of pulmonary nodules,"IEEE Trans. Medical Imaging, vol. 25, no. 4, pp. 435–449, April 2006.

[2] Mathew S. Brown, "Patient specific models for lung nodule detection and surveillance in CT images", IEEE Trans. On Medical Imaging, Vol-20, No.12, Pg.1242-1250, Dec.2001.

[3] Swensen "Lung nodule enhancement at CT: multicenter study", Radiology 2000.

[4] Metin N. Gurcan, Berkman Sahiner, et.al, "Lung nodule detection on thoracic computed tomography images:Preliminary evaluation of a computer-aided diagnosis system", Medical Physics, November 2002.

[5] Goldsmith SJ, Kostakoglu L. "Role of nuclear medicine in the evaluation of the solitary pulmonary nodule", 2000

[6] Fischbach F, Knollmann F,Griesshaber V, Freund T, Akkol E, Felix R. "Detection of pulmonary nodules by multislice computed tomography: improved detection rate with reduced slice thickness", Eur Radiol 2003

[7] J M Gauch."Segmentation and edge detection " in Proc.Chapman and Hall, London, 1998, pp. 163-187

[8]Fiebich M. Wormannas D, Heindel W. Improvement of method for computerassisted detection of pulmonary nodules in CT of the chest.In: Proceedings of SPIE Medical Imaging Conference 2001. SPIE 2001.

[9] Weixing Wang, Shuquang Wu, "A Study on Lung Cancer Detection by Image Proceeding", 2006

[10] M Nakayama,et,Study of 3D morphological filtering applied for automatic detection of lung cancer X-ray CT.Med.Imaging Tech,March,1995

ADVANCED SCANNING SYSTEM FOR VIRTUAL TRY ON

Raghunathan.A
Computer Science and Engineering
Rajalakshmi Engineering College, Chennai
raghucse@ymail.com

Prashant Ranjan
Computer Science and Engineering
Rajalakshmi Engineering College, Chennai
prashanthranjan@gmail.com

The present body scanners for the virtual try on set up are expensive and less accurate in measuring the actual body coordinates. This is a time consuming process and the probability of getting a best fit is rare. In the case of parametric human body modeling for the virtual try on systems, the proposed system of scanning can be easily implemented. The scanning technique that this paper proposes is here after called as 3D illusion scanning. The 3D illusion scanner is used to scan the subjects for getting their body measurements and not for building a 3D model from them. And the calibrated details are given as an input to the parametric body modeling tools· The stored human models are then modified according to the input measurements from the scanner.

Keywords: 3D body structuring, 3D illusion scanner, grayscale cameras, Image processing, laser beam, Virror.

1. Introduction:

Technologies are evolving to make life easier by all means. This paper proposes a new methodology of 3D scanning for the parametric 3D human body modeling [3]. The scanning system we proposed is hereafter referred as 3D illusion scanner in this paper. We choose an application as virtual dressing in shopping malls and textile show rooms to implement the proposed approach. There are three different methods available to model a 3D human body. They are 3D sculpting, parametric modeling and Automatic modeling. Human body modeling by 3D sculpting is an approach where a spherical or a rectangular geometrical mesh is converted into body parts by modifying them with the tools of a general purpose modeling tool. Commercially available 3D software such as Maya, 3Dmax, Softimage are some examples. This approach, although effective, is very time consuming and requires expertise of the software package used. Automatic modeling approaches, on the other hand, usually exploit sophisticated hardware or software to capture data from the bodies of real humans. 3D laser scanning [1] [2], shape from structured light, shape from silhouettes, shape by analysis of images [4] [5] and image sequences [6] [7] are among the techniques employed. Low cost technical devices will always have an edge over the expensive devices, so we propose a relatively low cost scanning method for modeling a 3D human body based on the parametric body modeling.

Section 2 explains the related work, section 3 explains the architecture diagram of the proposed approach, and section 4 describes the working of the 3D illusion scanner. Section 5 explains the applications and advantages of the proposed system.

2. Related Work:

A typical virtual try on set up should consist of 3 main components namely:

1. Body scanner
2. Database.
3. Virtual Fit

Virtual Try on is a technology which takes the body coordinates of the user as the input using a infra red radiation and displays a suitable cloth to the user based on the selections opted by the him.

2.1 Body Scanner:

A three-dimensional body scanner is a device which captures information about the surface of the human body using multiple laser or white lights and grayscale cameras. Electronic circuitry and a microprocessor unload the data which are processed, saved as a file, and visualized as a three-dimensional image on a computer monitor (user interface). A body scanning system should fully scan a person's body or an object from three sides at the same time. By taking advantage of two mirrors, we only require a single grayscale camera and at least one standard line laser, making the system far more affordable than previously possible. Our enhanced measuring procedure consists of three steps:

1. Separate calibration of reflected left, reflected right, and unreflected center Camera.

2. Coarse pose estimation of the left and right mirror plane.
3. Combined fine calibration of the overall mirror-camera setup.

2.2 Database:

A large database of clothes will be maintained in order to provide the users the choice to pick their liked ones. The database will be sorted according to the size of the user and the dress category that they choose. Barcodes will be used to differentiate stocks.

2.3 Virtual Fit:

A method of testing fit by putting a virtual garment on a 3D body image or "dressing" a scanned body image with clothing on the computer screen. Virtual fit provides a method to see cloth fit without actually trying it on.

3. Virtual Try On:

3.1 Architectural Design:

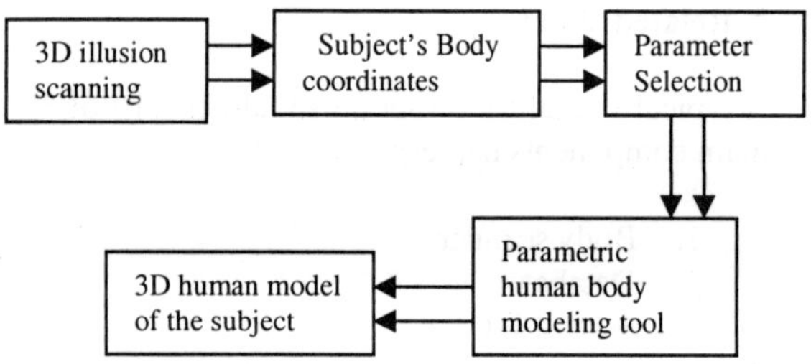

3.2. Working:

The basic working of the Virtual Try on is explained as follow:

The customers are allowed to stand in front of the VIrror and the interface asks the person to enter the waist size in case of pants and shoulder size in case of shirt.

After the size is entered a perspective scan of the person will be taken with the help of scanner. The scanner exactly scans the body of the person standing in front of the VIrror. The main process of the entire setup starts at this point. The scanner takes the body coordinates.

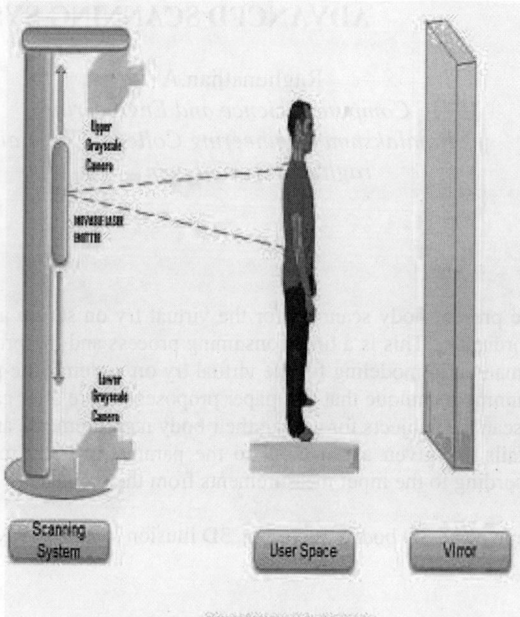

SIDE VIEW OF VIRTUAL TRY ON SETUP

Fig 3.1 Virtual try on set up

Now the user can see a 3d view of his body on the VIrror. The full size image of the user will be taken by a high definition camera placed at the top of the VIrror. The image will be merged with the front side of the 3d pattern of the user's body obtained from the scan. The user now can feel as if he is standing before a mirror.

The user is asked to choose the gender and category. Based on this data types of clothes available will be displayed. The user can then choose category of cloth. The VIrror will now show all the patterns available for the category of cloth chosen by the user based on his/her body coordinates.

As shown in the above illustrative figure the laser beams from the backside of the user will be used to measure the shoulder and waist sizes of the person standing in front of the VIrror. Likewise the various coordinates of the body are captured along with the solid build up of the user's body structure as shown above.

A consumer's body scan is merged with scans of clothes sized for a set of fit models. If the consumer's scanned body is visible beneath the clothes (semi-transparent), it shows that the cloth is tight and loose areas are discernible with the help of image processing the clothes to be tried on is super imposed on the 3d built of the user's body and the user can virtually try the clothes and chooses the best one.

4. 3D illusion scanning:

The scanning technique that we used here is "3D illusion scanning". In order to reduce the cost of the virtual try on set up we propose this idea of 3D image scanning. Here the main components used are as follows:

1. Two ordinary mirrors separated from an angle of 120°.
2. At least two gray scale cameras.
3. Two laser emitting source.
4. Sliding linear frame.

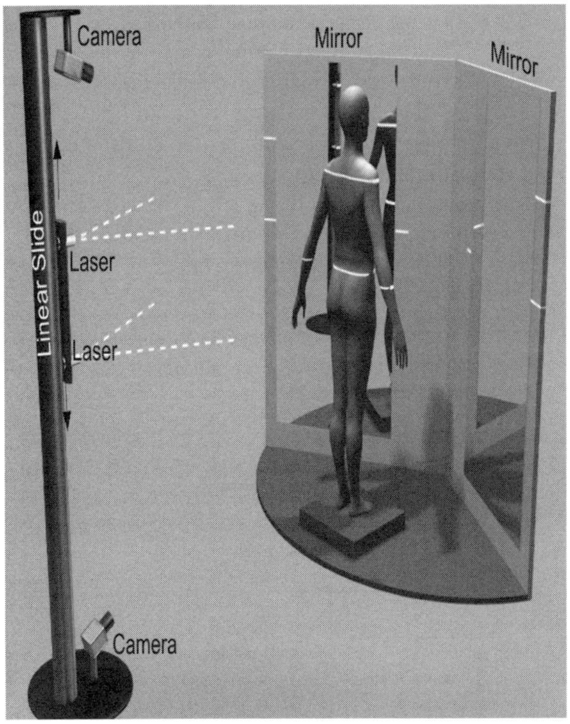

Fig. 4.1.1 3D illusion scanner set up

The subject should stand before the mirror set up as shown above. The laser source mounted in the linear slide starts emitting the laser beam and within a specified interval of time the laser beam will scan the whole body of the user as horizontal and vertical scan lines on the subject's body. Since the subject stands in front of the mirrors separated by 120°, the mirrors get the projected image of the subject. From the view of the gray scale camera mounted at the top and bottom of the linear frame, the subject's side views can also been captured due to the coplanar illumination produced by the mirrors.

After n number of scans taken by the laser beam, the final image from the view of the gray scale camera will look like the one which is illustrated in the figure 4.2.

Computation of surface data consists of two steps:

(1) Extraction of laser line(s) from camera images.
(2) Determination of the laser slide position for each camera Frame.

4.1 Laser Line Extraction:

From each camera image, the laser line(s) need to be extracted for later processing.
In our case an efficient column-wise and row-wise line detection algorithms can be applied, since the laser lines run horizontally and vertically. Since the laser source emitter is placed in a movable slide multiple lines on the same body can be obtained, which will be useful in the later calibration of the subject's body measurement.

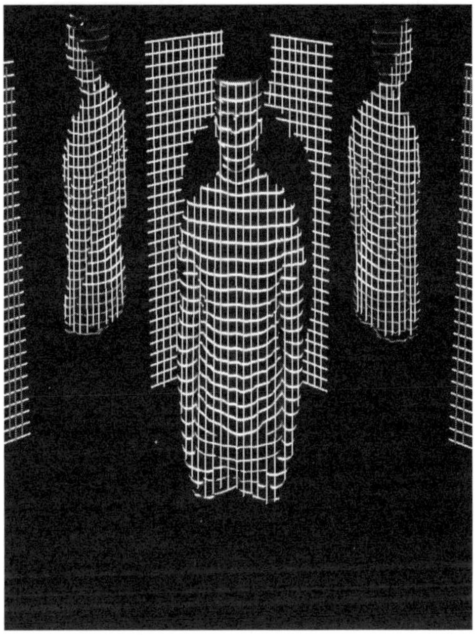

Fig 4.1.2 Wire frame obtained after scanning

As shown in the above illustrative figure the laser beams from the backside of the user will be used to measure the shoulder and waist sizes of the person standing in front of the mirrors. Likewise the various coordinates of the body are captured along with the solid build up of the user's body structure as shown above.
A consumer's body scan is merged with scans of clothes sized for a set of fit models. If the consumer's scanned body is visible beneath the clothes (semi-transparent), it shows that the cloth is tight and loose areas are discernible with the help of image processing the clothes to be tried on is super imposed on the 3d built of the user's body and the user can virtually try the clothes and chooses the best one.

4.2 Parameters choosing from the wire frame obtained:

4.2.1 Front view analysis:

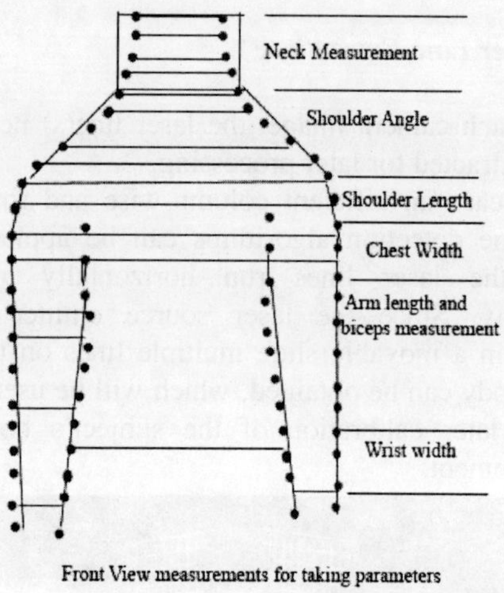

Fig 4.2.1 Front view calibrations

The above diagram shows the modified front view obtained from the wire frame by taking the only the operational points. The measurements of different parts of the body are calibrated separately by determining the starting and finishing edges of that part. Since we have taken only the upper half for the measurement the parts to be considered are neck, shoulder, chest, arm and wrist. There must be more than one point should be taken in between the starting and finishing edge of a body part to get a accurate detail about that particular part. Since the calibrations should be made for each and every physical structure of the human body, the finishing edge of a particular structure will be the starting edge of the next structure. For example, the finishing edge of neck will be the starting edge of shoulder.

From the front view of the human body we can calibrate the following details:

*Neck width.
*Shoulder angle.
*Shoulder length.
*Chest width.
*Arm length.
*Biceps.
*Wrist width.
*Waist size.

For a parametric body modeling tool, these are the parameters to be specified to get a neat front view of the body. The main detail to be specified is the height of the subject, which can be obtained when we combine the upper and lower camera images.

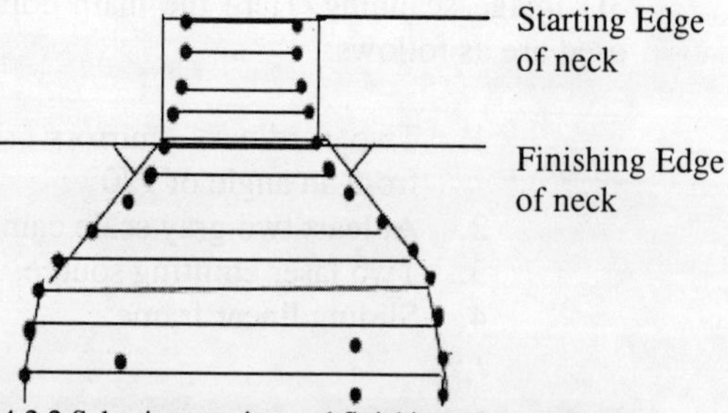

Fig 4.2.2 Selecting starting and finishing edges

The starting and finishing edges are chosen based on the basic starting edge of the wire frame image. It will be taken as the starting edge of the neck. The length of the series of edges is taken into account and the edge whose length varies invariably with the rest of the length of edges is chosen as the finishing edge.

4.2.2 Side view analysis:

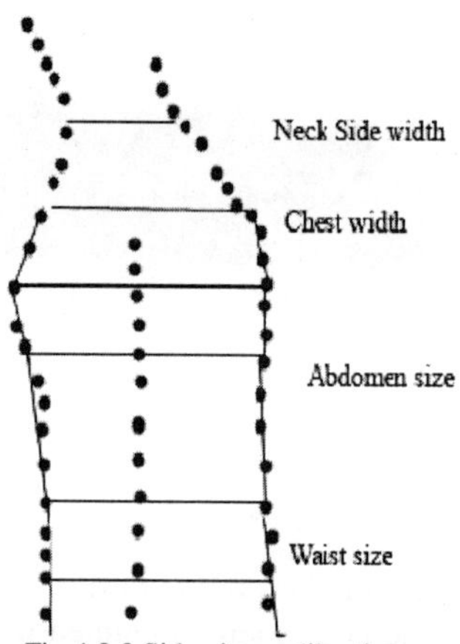

Fig 4.2.3 Side view calibrations

To build a complete 3D model of a human body we require both front and side views of the subject. The length and width requirements of the subject are fulfilled in the front view image calibration, while the thickness or size requirements are taken care by the side view of the wire frame image. The details that we can get from the side view image are,

*Neck thickness.
*Chest thickness.
*Abdomen size.
*Waist size.

Thus the illusion scanning can be used exclusively for parametric body modeling since the calibrations resulted from the illusion scanner can be used as parameters for the parametric human body modeling tools.

5. Applications and Advantages:

The proposed scanning technique can be used for virtual dressing, 3D virtual games, medical and other industry prototype modeling. The major advantages of using the illusion scanner for the virtual try on are listed below:

1. Time consumed in purchasing a cloth and by trying it will be reduced.
2. People will feel it a new experience of trying clothes with best fit assured.
3. The overhead of trying many clothes is reduced.

6. Conclusion: Thus the paper tries to eliminate practical difficulties in having automatic 3D scanners since it is expansive and hence it cannot be used for general applications. Thus the illusion scanning can be used exclusively for parametric body modeling since the calibrations resulted from the illusion scanner can be used as parameters for the parametric human body modeling tools.

References:

[1] B. Allen, B. Curls, and Z. Popovi´c, "The space of human body shapes: Reconstruction and parameterization from range scans," in *SIGGRAPH '03: ACM SIGGRAPH 2003 Papers*. New York, NY, USA: ACM, 2003, pp. 587–594.
[2] H. Seo and N. Magnenat-Thalmann, "An automatic modeling of human Bodies from sizing parameters," in *I3D '03: Proceedings of the 2003 symposium on Interactive 3D graphics*. New York, NY, USA: ACM, 2003, pp. 19–26.
[3]. Bas¸ar U˘gur, Ali Vahit S¸ ahiner A Parametric Human Body Modeling Tool.
[4] W.-S. Lee, J. Gu,. and N. Magnenat-Thalmann, "Generating anima table 3D virtual humans from photographs," in *Computer Graphics Forum (Euro graphics 2000)*, M. Gross and F. R. A. Hopgood, Eds., vol. 19(3), 2000.
[5] A. Hilton, D. Beresford, T. Gentils, R. Smith, and W. Sun, "Virtual people: Capturing human models to populate virtual worlds," in *CA '99: Proceedings of the Computer Animation*. Washington, DC, USA: IEEE Computer Society, 1999, p. 174.
[6] H.-D. Yang and S.-W. Lee, "Reconstructing 3d human body pose from stereo image sequences using hierarchical human body model learning," in *ICPR '06: Proceedings of the 18th International Conference on Pattern Recognition*. Washington, DC, USA: IEEE Computer Society, 2006, pp. 1004–1007.
[7] B. Rosenhahn and R. Klette, "Geometric algebra for pose estimation and surface morphing in human motion estimation," 2004, pp. 583–596.
[8] http://store.sae.org/caesar/.
[9]. Jones, P.R.M., Brooke-Wavell, K., West, G.: Format for human body modeling From 3d body scanning. Int. Journal of Clothing Science and Technology **7**(1) (1995) 7–15.
[10]. Horiguchi, C.: Bl (body line) scanner - the development of a new 3d measurement and reconstruction system. International Archives of Photogrammetry Remote Sensing 32(5) (1998) 421–42.
[11].http://ecommons2.library.cornell.edu/web_archive/explore.cornell.edu/scene5b96.html?scene=The%203D%20Body%20Scanner&stop=3D%20-%20Glossary#3dvisualization.
[12]. http://www.arteven.com.

Session 5

IMAGE BASED HUMAN GAIT RECOGNITION

[1]*D.SHARMILA,MCA,Mphil*, [1]
Lecturer,MCA Dept,
Lord Jegannath College Engineering,
PSN Nagar,Ramanathichanputhur,
Kumarapuram thoppur post,
shamishenai@rediffmail.com.

[2]*Dr.E.KIRUBAKARAN,B.E(Hons),M.E, M.B.A.,Ph.D.(Comp.Sci)*
Dy.General Manager, Outsourcing Department,
BHEL, Trichy. e_kiru@yahoo.com

Human gait is a valuable biometric cue that can be used for human identification besides other biometrics such as faces & fingerprints. The term gait recognition is typically used to signify the identification of people in image sequences by the way they walk. Gait is determined by the physical characteristics of each individual, and so is believed to be as unique to the person as a fingerprint is. Human identification using gait is a challenging computer vision task. Gait is also one of the few biometrics that can be measured at a distance, which makes it useful in surveillance applications as well. In this paper, our objective is to develop robust methods for extracting discriminate gait features automatically and passively from low-resolution video. For this, we explore gait recognition technique of a non-parametric approach that derives its classification feature from the image self-similarity plot of a walking sequence.

1. INTRODUCTION

Biometric characteristics can be divided in two main classes they are physiological and behavioral. Here the first type related to the shape of the body like example finger prints, face recognition, hand geometry, iris recognition and gait recognition. Second type is related to the behavior of a person like signature, keystroke dynamics and voice recognition. Gait is a relatively new and emergent behavioral biometric, that pertains to the use of an individual's walking style (or 'the way they walk') to determine or validate identity. However, it seems unlikely that gait could be used for unique identification in the same way as other conventional biometrics. This is because gait features have poor intra-person reliability due to their dynamic nature, being dependent on various physiological, psychological and external factors (footwear, clothing, surface of walking, mood, illness, fatigue, etc.). Thus it can be used for passive identification of people in surveillance applications, unlike most other biometrics. *Gait recognition* is the typical term used in the computer vision community to refer to automatic extraction of visual cues that characterize the motion of a walking person in video for identification purposes. It is possible to detect and measure gait even in low resolution video.

1.1. MOTIVATION

From a biomechanics standpoint, human ambulation consists of synchronized integrated movements of hundreds of muscles and joints of the body. Although these movements follow the same basic bipedal pattern for all humans, they seem to vary from one individual to another in certain details such as their relative timing and magnitudes, i.e. the kinematics of gait. Gait is hence presumed to be unique to each individual simply because it is determined by the totality of their muscular-skeletal structure. In gait analysis research, gait dynamics are completely characterized by a few hundred kinematics parameters, namely the angular velocities and accelerations at certain joints and body landmarks. In this paper, our goal is to develop robust methods for extracting discriminate gait features automatically and passively from low-resolution video.

1.2. NON-PARAMETRIC GAIT APPROACH

Here we describe a gait recognition technique that takes a correspondence free holistic approach by computing the classification feature directly as a function of the spatiotemporal volume (XYT) of the walking person's image sequence. Specifically, we first compute the self-similarity plot (SSP) as the matrix of self-similarities between each pair of images of the person in the sequence. By properly aligning and scaling the SSP, we then extract normalized feature vectors that we use as input to a standard pattern classifier for gait recognition. Intuitively, the SSP encodes the properties and temporal variations of the person's silhouette shape during the walking, and thus can be regarded as a signature of gait. Furthermore, we contend that the SSP is a projection of the planar gait dynamics, provided that the person is located sufficiently far from the camera.

Assumptions:

This method makes the following assumptions:

- ❖ People walk with constant velocity for about 3-4 seconds.
- ❖ People are located sufficiently far from the camera.
- ❖ The frame rate is greater than twice the frequency of the walking.
- ❖ The camera is stationary.

1.3. OVERVIEW OF METHOD

As shown in the block diagram of Figure 1.1, the method essentially assumes the structure of a general statistical pattern classifier. An image sequence of a walking person (i.e. the input pattern) is processed sequentially by the following steps. First stage in any pattern recognition system is data collection. Second stage is the registration process thus defines the framework in which the system operates so that it knows what to expect as valid input

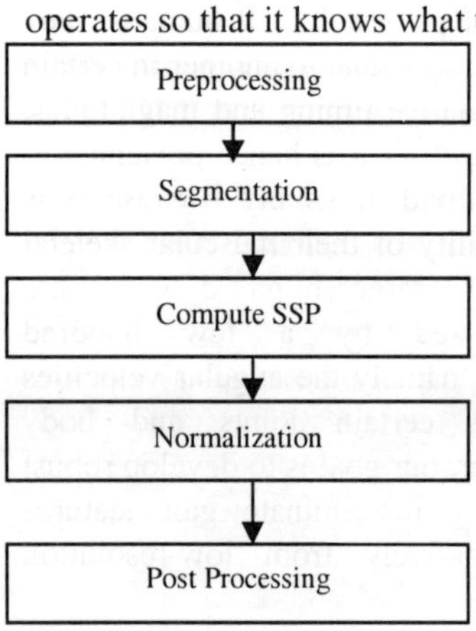

"Fig 1. Overview of Method"

In this first stage the process is data preprocessing. The goal of pre-processing data is to simplify pattern recognition problem with throwing away any important information. Preprocessing can often reduce noise and enhance the signal. Given a sequence of images obtained from the device we detect and track the moving person, and compute the corresponding sequence of motions regions in each frame. First extract four silhouette signatures of a moving person two corresponds to inner edges and other two corresponds to outer edges of each leg.

Once a person has been tracked for N consecutive frames, a sequence of N templates is then computed. Specifically, given the person's blob in each frame, we extract the (rectangular) region enclosed within the bounding box of the blob from either (1) the original color/grayscale image, (2) the foreground image, or (3) the binary image. Thus, three different types of template sequences can in fact be obtained for each person. Clearly, there are competing tradeoffs to using either type of template in measuring image similarity. (When computing the SSP).

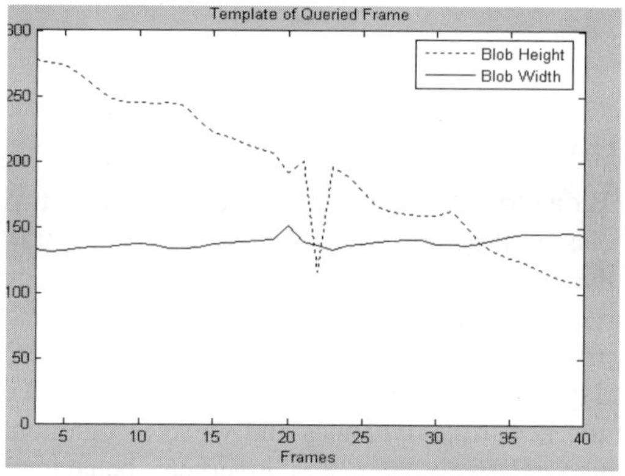

"Fig 2. Template width and height of Input 1"

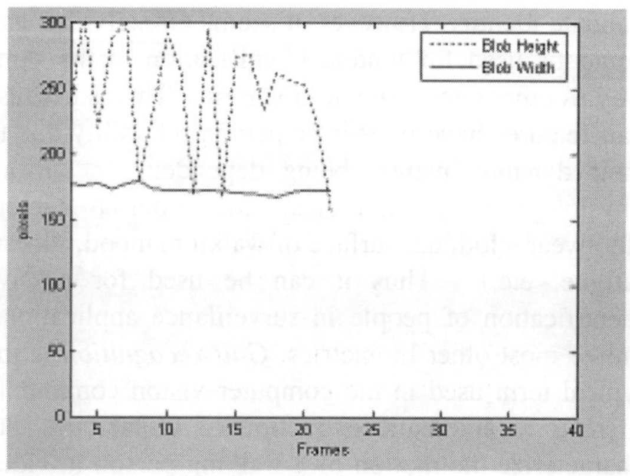

"Fig 3. Template width and height of Input 2"

2. SEGMENTATION

Next process is segmentation. To find out the segmentation errors the rectangular region for each blob is enlarged by a small radius. Motion segmentation is achieved via a non-parametric background subtraction technique that is quite robust to lighting changes. Once detected, foreground objects are tracked in subsequent frames by simple spatial coherence, namely based on the overlap of blob bounding boxes in any two consecutive frames. Here the detection of unusual motions can be achieved by building a representation of the scene background and comparing new frames with this representation. To determine whether a tracked foreground blob corresponds to a moving person, we first compute the gait period (and hence cadence) via periodicity analysis of the width and height of the blob's bounding box. We then verify whether the computed cadence falls within some broad range of normal human cadences. We typically use the range [80,145] steps/minute, which corresponds to two standard deviations around the average cadence.

2.1. NORMALIZATION

Each signature is normalized via spatial and temporal alignment and scaling. These normalized signatures define a spatial temporal sheet over the entire image sequence. Gait consists of repeated steps, and suppose each step takes P frames then we can divide the image sequence into contiguous segments of length P frames.

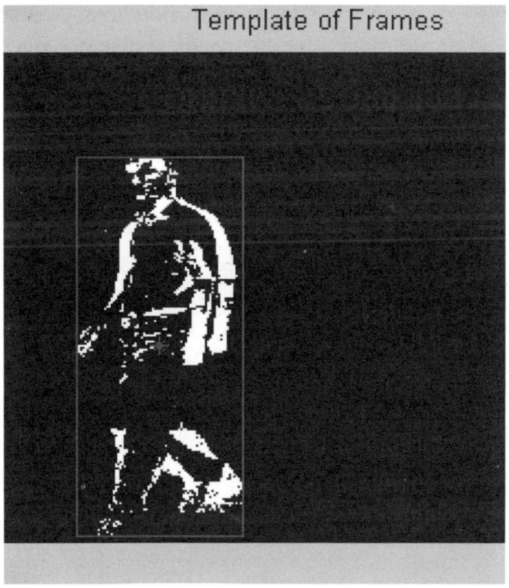

"Fig 4. Template Image of input 1"

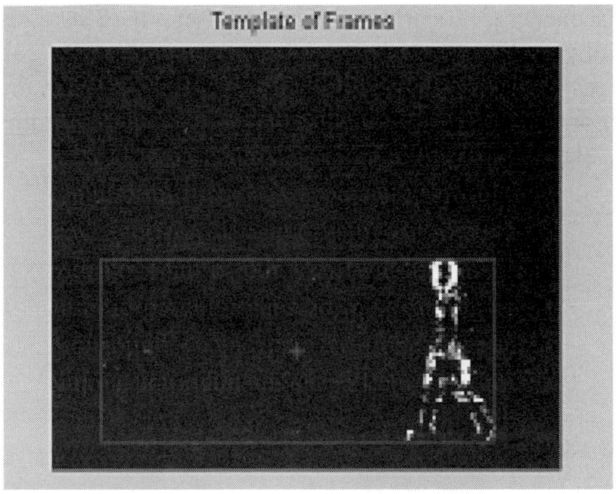

"Fig 5. Template Image of input 2"

The apparent size of s walking person varies at the frequency of gait. Specifically let w(n) and h(n) be the width and height of the n-th image of the person.

$$w(n)=m_w(n)+A_w \sin(wn+\emptyset)$$

$$h(n)=m_h(n)+A_h \sin(wn+\emptyset)$$

where w is the frequency of gait, $\emptyset$ is the phase of gait .$m_w(n)$ is the mean width, and A_w is the amplitude of oscillation. $m_h(n)$ is the mean height.

Here we first computes the normalized cross-correlation of matrices template and A.. The matrix A must be larger than the matrix template for the normalization to be meaningful. The values of template cannot all be the same.

2.2. COMPUTING SELF SIMILARITY PLOT

This step is very important it need to choose which features to extract and how. Given a sequence of a person's N templates (i.e. cropped images) of the walking person, we compute the NxNix of their pair wise correlations, denoted the self-similarity plot (SSP), which we shall use as the basic feature for gait recognition. Self similarity plot S(I,J) is computed as the absolute correlation of each pair of templates li and lj minimized over a small search radius r namely.

Specifically let w(n) and h(n) be the width and height of the n-th image of the person. According to gait analysis literature w(n) and h(n) can be approximated as sinusoidal functions.

Define a Self Similarity Unit (SSU) as the matrix pair wise image similarities of two of the sequences. Clearly a different set of SSU's is obtained for any given starting phase ¢ . We can easily show that for a sequence of K gait periods, the corresponding self-similarity plot contains 2(k(k+1))/2=k(k+1) contiguous SSU's .

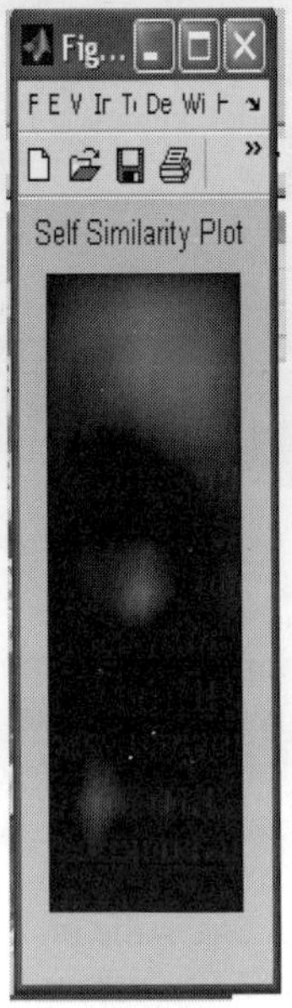

"Fig 6. SSP of input 1"

"Fig 7. SSP of input 2"

2.3. FREQUENCY AND PHASE OF GAIT

Obviously, we need to compute the frequency and phase of gait in order to extract the SSU's. However, there is no simple/straightforward way to estimate the phase of gait based on the width or height of the person in the image sequence. For example, the maxima/ minima of these series correspond to different gait poses depending on the person and the camera viewpoint.

2.4. PATTERN CLASSIFICATION

Classification is the last step after which images can be processed. Here we formulate Fast Fourier Transform approach for classification. Given a set of labeled sequences (the training set), the task is to determine the person corresponding to any novel sequence, based on the ensemble of SSU's derived from the sequences. We herein discuss two statistical approaches to this pattern classification problem: template matching and linear feature extraction. Both approaches fit within the general framework of the pattern classifier. The input pattern, i.e. the SSU, is treated as m^2 dimensional vector, obtained say by concatenating its m rows. Since a sequence typically generates more than one SSU, we treat the SSU's of a training sequence as independent patterns, and those of a test sequence are used collectively to determine the majority label.

Classification is based on the K-nearest neighbor rule, whereby a test pattern (SSU) is assigned to the majority label of the K *closest* patterns to it in the training set where distances are measured in some space in which the patterns are represented. In the template matching approach, distances are measured in the raw SSU-space as the Euclidean distance between the two SSU's. Furthermore, to account for phase alignment errors, we shift one of the SSU's in both directions over a small radius and determine the smallest distance over all possible shifts. In the linear feature extraction approach, we compute the Euclidean distance in a reduced feature space of the original SSU-space.

"Fig 8. Identified Frame of input 1"

"Fig 9. Identified Frame of input 2"

2.4.1 FAST FOURIER TRANSFORM

FFT(X) is the discrete Fourier transform (DFT)of vector X. For matrices, the FFT operation is applied to each column. For N-D arrays, the FFT operation operates on the first non-singleton dimension. FFT(X,N) is the N-point FFT, padded with zeros if X has less than N points and truncated if it has more.

FFT(X[],DIM) or FFT(X,N,DIM) applies the FFT operation across the dimension DIM. For length N input vector x, the DFT is a length N vector X, with elements N.

$$X(k)=\text{sum } x(n)*\exp(-j)*2*pi*(k-1)*(n-1)/N),1<=k<=N. \quad N=1.$$

The inverse DFT is given by N.

$$X(n)=(1/N)\text{sum } X(k)*\exp(j*2*pi*(k-1)*(n-1)/N) \quad 1<=n<=N. \quad k=1.$$

3. CONCLUSION

Here we described a novel holistic gait recognition approach that uses image self-similarity as the basic feature for classification. The method is correspondence-free and works well with low-resolution video and is robust to variation in clothing, lighting. Performance also seems to degrade when camera depth and cadence are significantly changed.

4. Bibiliography

[1] Anderson.A , "An *introduction to Neural Networks"* Addison Wesley ,prentice hall,Inc,1999.

[2] Simon Haykin, "*Neural Networks*" ,Pearson Education,1999.

[3] Donald Hearn,M.Pauline Baker,"*Computer graphics*",Prentice Hall inc,1998.

[4] Anil K.Jain,*Fundamentals of digital Image Processing*",PHI,1989.

[5]Prabhat K.Andleigh, Kiran Thakrar ,"*Multimesia System Design*",PHI,1986.

[6]Earlgose,Richard Johnsonbaugh ,Steve jost,"*Pattern Recognition*",PHI,1997.

[7]Christopher M.Bishop,"*Neural Networks for Pattern Recognition"* ,Chaman Enterprises,India,2004.

[8] Richard A.Johnson "*An Introduction to Java Programming and Object oriented application Development"*,Thomson ,India,2007.

[9] R.K.Gupta "*Audio&video systems principles maintenance and trouble shooting*" Tata 1995.

[10]Dr.Arumugam "*Biomedical instrumentation"* Anuradha pub ,2005.

ENHANCING MIDDLEWARES WITH PARALLEL PROGRAMMING

FARAHNAZ POORFARD
Computer Engineering and IT Department, Amirkabir University of Technology (Tehran Polytechnic), 424 Hafez Ave, Tehran, Iran

HOSSEIN PEDRAM
Computer Engineering and IT Department, Amirkabir University of Technology (Tehran Polytechnic), 424 Hafez Ave., Tehran, Iran

{fz-poorfard, pedram}@aut.ac.ir

Middleware is necessary for distributed systems; in fact all applications in a netware world request their services through a middleware. In modern applications the time for accessing to services through a middleware is important and even critical. Access time not only depends on network speed, but it also depends on runtime of middleware by itself, so we often try to minimize the execution time of middlewares. This paper presents the idea of merging middlewares with parallel programming techniques. We study merging OpenCOM, which is a reflective adaptive middleware, with MPI as a favorite technique in parallel programming. We focus on enhancing the runtime of configuration and reconfiguration operations of this middleware.

1. Introduction

Middleware has emerged as an important architectural component in supporting distributed applications. The role of middleware is to present a unified programming model to application writers and to mask out problems of heterogeneity and distribution [4]. Today, we know that doing this task has been very hard for a middleware than previous, although we have had great progresses in the network world, but this means that there are many newer services like multimedia, real-time, wireless and mobile, that a well-developed middleware should be able to support. In addition because of increasing number of application domains requiring distribution, and the consequent increase in distributed-systems requirements, users might need to extend or restrict a distribution model [18]. It is an aspect of *flexibility*, especially in configuration and reconfiguration operations.

Generally, to apply any changes to a middleware we need *adaptivity* in our model. The need for adaptation comes from the fact that the environment in which distributed applications are executed, changes continuously [1]. The term “changes” in an environment sees all different aspects.

Today, more important roles of a middleware are: *adaptivity*, *(re)configurability* and *flexibility*. Hence, we are looking for some models in middleware that help us to have well-developed and ubiquitous applications. One of the useful models that offer this goal is the *component-based model*. The component-based model has a rich adaptivity feature. In this model, a middleware is just composed of a few components, each of which does a few tasks, and composition of these tasks can make the proposed aims of the determined middleware. Activation of components must occur in real-time, which means that component initialization must not become a bottleneck. Thus, on-demand linking/unlinking mechanisms are necessary to (re)configure component implementations dynamically. The lifecycle for linking/unlinking of these components must be optimized using reflective middleware techniques to minimize footprint, prolong battery life, maximize extensibility, and meet key application QoS requirements more adaptively [25].

Thus, we need an additional feature for our model: *reflection*, which defines the rules for cooperating among components to do the whole task. Clearly, we will need operations to generate and delete component(s), and (un)establish connections among components to reach a complete model.

Reflection refers to the ability of a system to reason about and act upon itself. More specifically, a reflective system is one that provides a representation of its own behavior which is amenable to inspection and adaptation, and is casually connected to the underlying behavior it describes. Casually-connected means that changes made to the self-representation are immediately mirrored in the underlying system's actual state and behavior, and vice-versa [23].

Not only the new and progressive features of a middleware, but also the speed of accessing to its services especially in real-time and/or critical applications, is very important. This is the main reason that encouraged us to work on enhancing middleware's runtime. We decided to apply such enhancement by adding parallel programming to middleware. The remaining of this paper is organized as follows: In the next section, a survey of related works is presented. In section 3 we describe two main tools for our inspection, named OpenCOM and MPI. In section 4 there is an explanation of our experiments. We also present our main results in section 5 and conclude the paper in section 6.

2. Related Works

There are different works to make progresses on middleware, obviously each of them consider different aspects of middlewares. For example in [15] a combination of aspect oriented programming (AOP) with reflective middlewares has been explored. This combination can put together the advantages of customizing a middleware implementation (by AOP) and the ability to alter runtime behavior (by reflection).

Ref. [21] introduced DAJ, a system for encapsulating middleware services to mask invasive and pervasive middleware functionality. This technique can help to increase a middleware design process.

Javier Fernandez et al. introduce GridExpand, a new approach to data access in computational grids. It is a parallel I/O middleware that integrates heterogeneous data storage resources in grids [9].

There are also some individual designs of middlewares, e.g. Jgroup which is a middleware system that integrates group technology with distributed objects. It supports a programming paradigm called object groups and enables development of dependable network services based on replication [22].

ProActive is a Java middleware library for parallel, distributed and multithreaded computing. It is a programming model to simplify the programming and execution of parallel applications on multi-core processors, distributed Local Area Network, clusters and Data Center Servers, and GRIDs [24].

Al-Jaroodi et al. in [17] introduce a middleware infrastructure that provides software services for developing and deploying high-performance parallel programming models and distributed applications on clusters and networked heterogeneous systems. Their middleware infrastructure utilizes distributed agents residing on the participating machines and communicating with one another to perform the required functions.

Among all these trends there is not a direct combination of middlewares with parallelism. We show in this paper that this kind of combination can result in better execution time.

3. Background

In section 1 we enumerated typical features of new generation of middlewares. In studying different existing models, we have chosen the OpenCOM [19] which is a general-purpose and language independent component-based systems building technology [2]. We first tried to evaluate it, so we did some experiences for measuring the runtime of its different operations and considering these timings against each other, for evaluating the overhead/benefit trade off. After all, we tried to join OpenCOM with some existing mechanisms for parallel processing in order to reduce the main timing overheads, if it does. MPI has been used for this.

The following subsections provide a quick review on OpenCOM and MPI respectively.

3.1. *OpenCOM*

OpenCOM is a lightweight and efficient in-process component model, built atop a subset of Microsoft's COM [5]. A core of COM has been used as: the binary-level interoperability standard (vtable); the Microsoft's IDL; COM's GUIDs; and the IUnknown interface.

OpenCOM has been built by using this core and considering three additional concepts: explicit dependencies among components; mechanism-level functionality for reconfigurations, such as mutual exclusion locks; and intercepting on component operations, as pre-method call or post-method call.

Fig. 1 shows the main concepts in OpenCOM: *interface*, *receptacle* and *binding*.

The architecture of OpenCOM is very simple and straightforward. OpenCOM uses two types of components: One (and only one) OpenCOM runtime component that is the header component for other components in an address space, and some other components which can exist in an arbitrary number. The operations and connections between these later components make our middleware environment and its functionality.

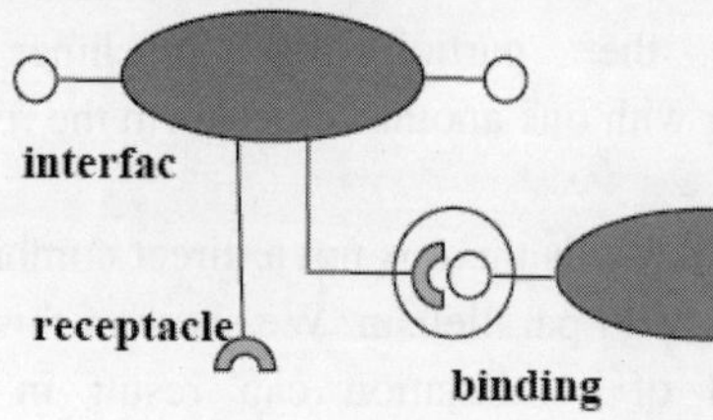

Figure 1. Main concepts of OpenCOM [3]

In addition, it is possible to encapsulate some components in a *component framework* (CF) for applying security and control policies, simplifying the design and maintenance of middleware, and also increasing the speed of reconfiguration by using more coarse grained components in design process (an advanced form of CFs than its primary one, with IAccept interface, has been shown in [10]). Each CF can also accept additional *plug-in components* that change or extend its behavior. In OpenCOM, components or CFs can be connected hierarchically, but we are able to have a layered approach for our design by applying the necessary restrictions. This layering which is just a virtual view for actual hierarchies helps us understand the middleware operations better. We choose layering since it matches our networks architectures (for more details see [5] and [6]).

By using components (and CFs) as major entities in OpenCOM, we can use *reflection*: using different combinations of components and using different interfaces of them which reflects different views of our middleware infrastructure. OpenCOM has been used as an infrastructure layer for some more progressive middlewares too, like GridKit ([12] and [13]), RUNES ([7] and [8]) and ReMMoC ([10] and [11]).

3.2. *MPI*

Parallel programming is a well-known way for enhancing the efficiency of programs' runtime. We can use parallel programming by distributing the run of different parts of program on *separate processes/threads on one CPU,* or even on *separate processes/threads on several separate CPUs*. Different tools for parallel programming have been built and among them is MPI (Message Passing Interface). MPI supports both point-to-point and collective communication operations. The primary goals of MPI are efficient communication and portability [16]. In addition, MPI has a rich library for both primary and complex operations and its library has been prepared for many alive programming languages such as C, C++ and Fortran. MPI can be installed on a wide range of hardware/software platforms, so now we are able to use MPI on all systems from super computers to PC clusters. It is also simple and straightforward to develop and debug a program on it [16], [20] and [14]. For all these, to enhance the timing of (re)configuration phase in our middleware, we chose MPI (more accurately saying, MPICH) as our parallel programming tool.

4. Experiments

In studying the OpenCOM, we did some timing evaluations and noticed that at the configuration phase of middleware and at each reconfiguration operation, there is a time overhead. We measured time for different operations accurately and noticed that it is the creation of the components that contributes mainly to this overhead. It is of note that we should directly create different instances of our proposed components/CFs and define their connections for creating our middleware. Similarly, at each reconfiguration operation, we may have to create some new components/CFs. To reach some equilibrium, we tried to apply a parallel programming technique on our middleware.

First, by expanding the OpenCOM's demo, we measured time for creating and activating some sample components. Then we defined some considerations for ourselves: 1) we did not consider the 'CoInitialize' operation, because it runs just once; 2) we did not consider the creating and activating operations for the main runtime OpenCOM component; 3) to create a component, we used 'createInstance' function and to activate it we obtained its ILifeCycle interface and then called 'startup' function; 4) we consider a *createInstance* operation as an atomic operation.

5. Results and Discussion

In this section we will describe and discuss our results especially considering the speedup. The main goal is to reduce the runtime and increase the speedup. Our experiments are basically divided into two modes: *uniprocessor-multiprocess* and *multiprocessor*.

In our experiments we have 6 components, for two of them we called two more interfaces than just ILifeCycle interface, but the effect of this is negligible. The results are presented in the next two subsections.

5.1. *Uniprocessor-multiprocess*

In the first phase, we ran the merged OpenCOM and MPI middleware on a single processor system, and then increased the number of processes one by one. In this case, as we expected, increasing the processes, increases the total time of initiating the middleware. The growth will continue until the number of processes would be equal to the number of components. The reason is for the atomicity of the *createInstance* operation.

We then applied in two phases some complexity in generating components and considered the results. By increasing the complexity the results would be better especially on one processor. We call these 3 modes of complexity as: 1) *normal complexity*, 2) *a few more complexity*, 3) *more complexity*.

Fig. 2 shows the results for these three modes of complexity on one processor.

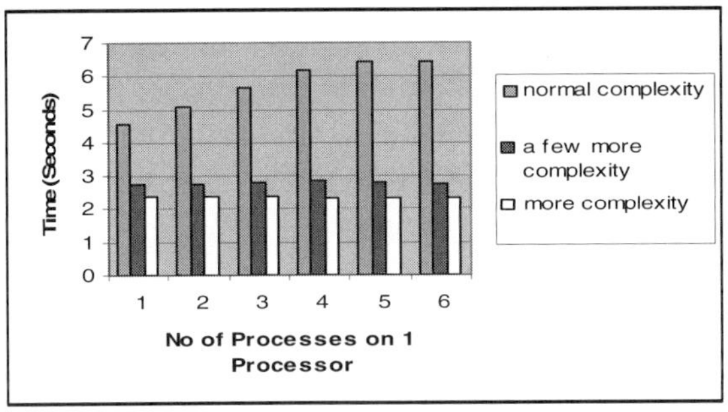

Figure 2. Results for parallel processes on one processor

Afterwards, we first did the experiments with 2 processors, and then increased them to 6. The results are shown in the following subsection.

5.2. *Multiprocessor*

With 2 processors we obtained more interesting results. As before, we started with all 6 components on one processor and continued first by adding a second processor. After adding the second processor we increased the number of processes one by one, up to six. In each step we tried with all different number of processes on our 2 processors, for example when we reached to 2 processors and 4 processes we examined 3 cases separately:

- 1 process on the first processor and 3 processes on the second,
- 3 processes on the first processor and 1 process on the second,
- 2 processes on each processor.

Then we selected the best results (minimum timings). We did all experiments for our previous three modes: "components with normal complexity" (mode 1), "components with a few more complexity" (mode 2) and "components with more complexity" (mode 3). Fig. 3 shows the results. As it is seen:

- There is a sudden enhancement in fig. 3 for distributing all components between processes. Of course, our two processors were not homogeneous.
- Although both mode 2 and 3 have acceptable shapes, mode 2 has greater speedup (2.734/1.391 =1.965) than mode 3 (2.368/1.386=1.709), so it is better to control the complexity of components from being too expensive.

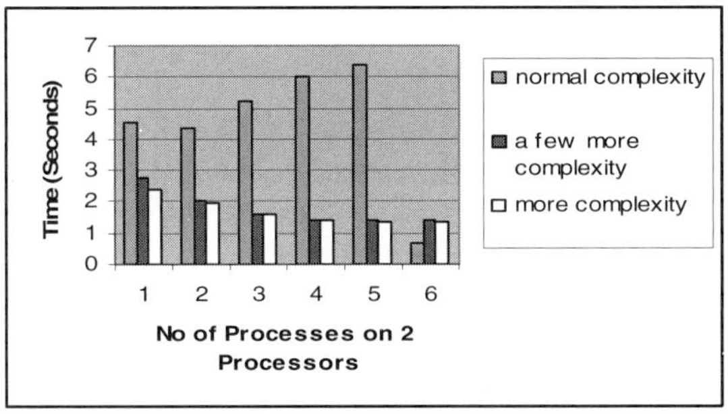

Figure 3. Results for parallel processes on two processors

By increasing the number of processors to 6, we see a considerable decrease in complete distribution mode (6 processors), (depicted in the following figures) which is very similar to complete distribution of components among 6 processes on 2 processors with normal complexity mode (mode 1). Figures 4, 5 and 6 are the integration of 1, 2 and 6 processors and are respectively for our three familiar modes of complexity. The similarity of decreasing runtime with full distribution on 2 and 6 processors in the following figures shows that in distributing components, the best case is a complete distribution (not partial).

Speedups for 6 processors are: 3.121 / 0.771 = 4.048 for mode 1, 2.367 / 0.47 = 5.036 for mode 2, and 2.347 / 0.463 = 5.069 for mode 3, that is a bit greater than 5.036, but we believe that it is not considerable compared to the cost of complexity. In the other word, we vote to a middle complexity ("a few more complexity" mode).

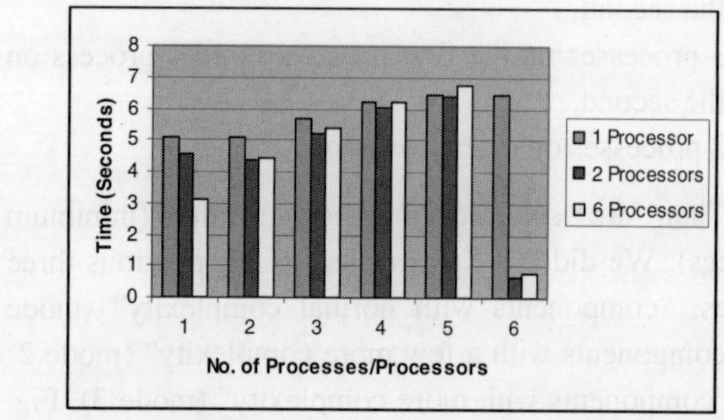

Figure 4. Results for "normal complexity" mode

As it is shown, the best results belong to multiprocessor mode. Both the 2 processors-multiprocess mode and the 6 processors-uniprocess mode have acceptable functionality, but just when all components have been distributed (full distribution).

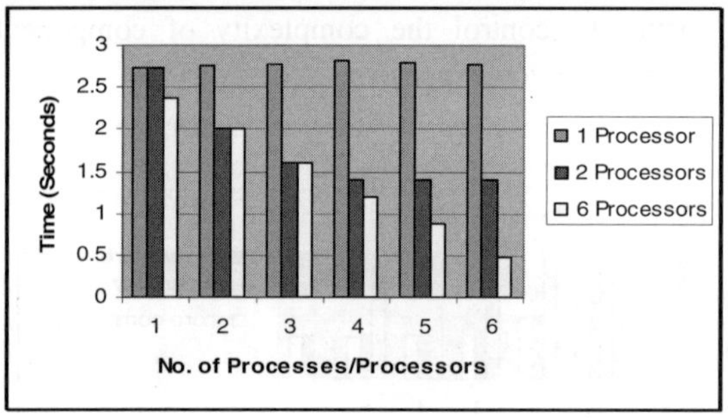

Figure 5. Results for "a few more complexity" mode

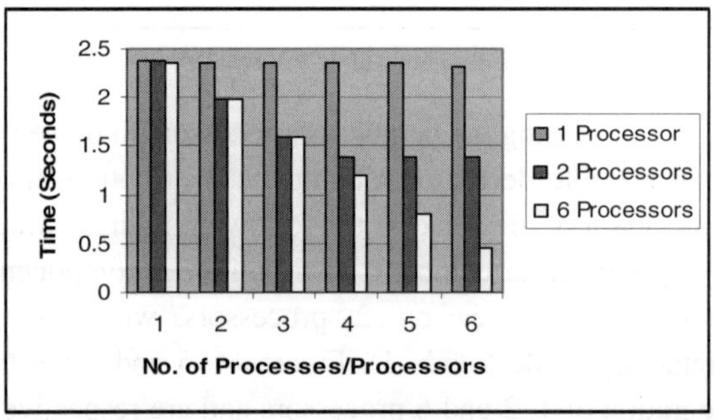

Figure 6. Results for "more complexity" mode

Fig. 7 shows the speedups according to our 3 modes of complexity. We see that results for 6 processors seem better because of their both better speedup and more stability in variation of speedups. But if the usage of "more complexity" mode (mode 3) would not be acceptable for its complexity and time, we suggest the "a few more complexity" mode (mode 2).

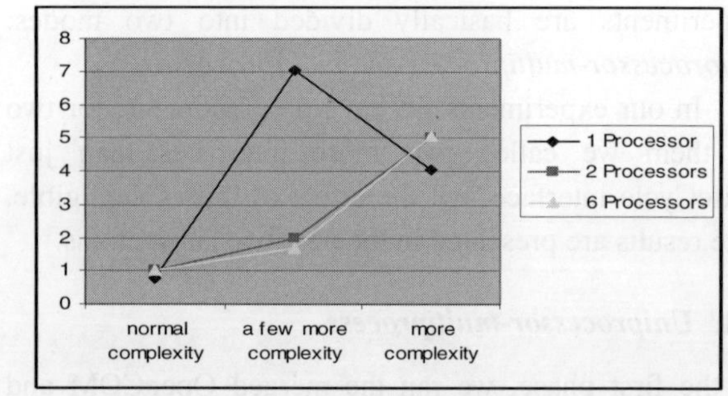

Figure 7. Comparing the speedups according to complexity

6. Conclusion

In this paper, we proposed the idea of distributing the operation in the middlewares aiming lower execution time.

We showed that providing a middleware with parallel processing can enhance the runtime of (re)configuration operation. In selecting a suitable mode for parallelism degree, consideration of speedup can help us. According to our experiments a middle complexity level leads to a better speedup.

Acknowledgments

We would like to specially thank Gordon Blair and Paul Grace, Lancaster University, for their feedback, insights and help.

We also thank Ehsan K.Ardestani, University of California Santa Cruz for reviewing the paper and for his feedbacks and truly help.

References

1. A. S. Tenenbaum and V. S. Maarten, *Distributed Systems (Principles and Paradigms),* Prentice hall (2002).
2. N. Bencomo, G. Blair, G. Coulson and T. Batista, "Towards a Meta-Modelling Approach to Configurable Middleware", *The 2nd ECOOP'2005 Workshop on Reflection, AOP and MetaData for Software Evolution,* RAM-SE Glasgow, Scotland (2005).
3. N. Bencomo and G. Blair, "Genie: a Domain-Specific Modeling Tool for the Generation of Adaptive and Reflective Middleware Families", *In submitted to 6th OOPSLA workshop on Domain Specific Modeling,* Portland (2006).
4. G. S. Blair, G. Coulson, P. Robin and M. Papathomas, "An Architecture for Next Generation Middleware", *In Proceedings of the IFIP International Conference on Distributed Systems Platforms and Open Distributed Processing* (1998).

5. M. Clarke, G. S. Blair, G. Coulson and N. Parlavantzas, "An Efficient Component Model for the Construction of Adaptive Middleware", *Lecture Notes in Computer Science,* vol. 2218, pages 160--?? (2001).
6. G. Coulson, G. S. Blair, M. Clarke and N. Parlavantzas, "The Design of A Configurable and Reconfigurable Middleware Platform", *OpenCOM Documents:* http://www.comp.lancs.ac.uk/computing/research/mpg/reflection/tutorials.php (2002).
7. P. Costa, G. Coulson, C. Mascolo, G. P. Picco and S. Zachariadis, "The RUNES Middleware: A Reconfigurable Component-based Approach to Networked Embedded Systems", *In Proceedings of (PIMRC05),* IEEE, Berlin, Germany (September 2005).
8. P. Costa, G. Coulson, R. Gold, M. Lad, C. Mascolo and L. Mottola, "The RUNES Middleware for Networked Embedded Systems and its Application in a Disaster Management Scenario", *Fifth Annual IEEE International Conference on Pervasive Copmuting and Communications,* 2007, percom '07, pages 69-78 (March 2007).
9. J. M. Pérez Menor, F. García, J. Carretero, A. Calderón, J. Fernández, et al., "A Parallel I/O Middleware to Integrate Heterogeneous Storage Resources on Grids", *Across Grids 2003,* Springer-Verlag, Berlin Heidelberg, LNCS 2970, pp. 124–131 (2004).
10. P. Grace, G. S. Blair and S. Samuel, "ReMMoC: A Reflective Middleware to support Mobile Client Interoperability", *International Symposium on Distributed Objects and Application,* Catania, Italy (November 2003) (to appear).
11. P. Grace, G. Blair and S. Samuel, "A Higher Level Abstraction for Mobile Computing Middleware", *In Proceeding of workshop on Communication Abstractions for Distributed Systems,* Paris, France (November 2003).
12. P. Grace, G. Coulson, G. Blair, L. Mathy, W. K. Yeung et al., "GRIDKIT: Pluggable Overlay Networks for Grid Computing", *To appear in Proc. Distributed Objects and Applications (DOA'04),* Cyprus (October 2004).
13. D. Hughes, P. Greenwood, B. Porter, P. Grace, G. Coulson et al., "Using Grid Technologies to Optimise a Wireless Sensor Network for Flood Management", *In Proceedings of the 4th ACM Conference on Embedded Networked Sensor Systems, Boulder,* Colorado, USA (October 31-November 3, 2006).
14. W. Gropp, E. Lusk and A. Skjellum, "Using MPI: Portable Parallel Programming with the Message-Passing Interface" (1999).
15. P. Grace, E. Truyen, B. Lagaisse and W. Joosen, "The Case for Aspect-Oriented Reflective Middleware", *Proceedings of the 6th international workshop on Adaptive and reflective middleware: held at the ACM/IFIP/USENIX International Middleware Conference,* Newport Beach, CA, Article No. 2 (2007).
16. "HP-MPI User's Guide", *Hewlett-Packard Development Company,* 10th Edition (June 2007).
17. J. Al-Jaroodi, N. Mohamed, H. Jiang and D. Swanson, "Middleware infrastructure for parallel and distributed programming models in heterogeneous systems", *Parallel and Distributed Systems,* IEEE Transactions on. Volume 14, Issue 11, Page(s): 1100 – 1111 (November 2003).
18. F. Kordon and L. Pautet, "Toward Next-Generation Middleware?", *IEEE Distributed Systems Online,* vol. 6, issue 3 (March 2005).
19. Next Genaration Middleware @ Lancaster University: http://www.comp.lancs.ac.uk/computing/research/mpg/reflection/index.php.
20. E. Lantz, "Windows HPC Server 2008", *Using Microsoft Message Passing Interface (MS MPI) – white paper,* Microsoft Corporation (June 2008).
21. C. A. Maffort and M. T. de Oliveira Valente, "Modularizing Communication Middleware Concerns Using Aspects". *Journal of the Brazilian Computer Society,* v. 13, n. 4, p. 81-95 (2007).
22. A. Montresor, R. Davoli and O. Babaoglu, "Middleware for Dependable Network Services in Partitionable Distributed Systems", *Technical Report UBLCS-99-19* (October 1999; Revised April 2000).
23. R. J. Peris, M. P. Martinez and E. M. Jordan, "Decentralized Web Service Orchestration: A Reflective Approach", *Proceedings of the 2008 ACM Symposium on Applied Computing,* Fortazela, Ceara, Brazil, Pages 494-498 (2008).
24. http://proactive.inria.fr/.
25. N. Wang, M. Kircher and D. C. Schmidt, "Applying Reflective Middleware Techniques to Optimize a QoS-enabled CORBA Component Model Implementation", *24th International Computer Software and Applications Conference (COMPSAC 2000),* Taipei, Taiwan (25-28 October 2000).

METRICS FOR WEB APPLICATION DEVELOPMENT

MS. M. KIRUTHIKA

Asst. Professor, Computer Engineering Dept.,
Fr.CRIT, Vashi, Navi Mumbai, Maharashtra venkatr20032002@gmail.com

MS. SUKHWANT KAUR

Asst. Professor, Computer Engineering Dept.,
Fr.CRIT, Vashi, Navi Mumbai, Maharashtra. sukhwantsagar@gmail.com

MS. K.V. SANTHILATA

Lecturer, CS & IS Group, BITS-Pilani, Goa Campus,
Zuarinagar, Goa, santhilata@bits-goa.ac.in

The software development techniques have been evolved ever since its existence. The structural programming technique was replaced by the Object Oriented Design and programming technique and then moved to Component-Oriented Programming and software design. Each level of this progression was seemingly built on the top of the other paradigms. It is important to evolve the techniques of measuring the software quality to suit the approach, design and implementation to ensure the robustness and adaptability of the software product. Here, in this paper, some of the metrics that are suitable to measure the quality of the product using Component Technology in web applications are presented.

Key words - web applications, web servers, web engineering

1. INTRODUCTION

The metrics gauge project quality as well as design complexity during the design phase and implementation phase. The primary objective to employ the metrics is to identify troublesome modules, or stress points, in the structure of the software. The software designer can then make changes in the software design that make the resulting product less error-prone as well as easier to understand and maintain[2].

To corroborate the effectiveness of the metrics as predictors of fault-proneness, the Design Metrics Team reexamines the software when error reports are available to determine to what extent the stress-point modules were indeed fault-prone.

The quality of a design is heavily influenced by a system's relationships amongst the modules. Loosely coupled and highly cohesive modules are qualities of any well-designed application. So a good place to begin assessing design is by evaluating module relationships.

Objectively measuring a system's degree of reusability and maintainability can serve as valuable feedback in determining the quality of software's structure.

The paper is organized as follows: Section 2 depicts the framework for web engineering. Section 3 illustrates the metrics for design modules which are discussed in the framework for web engineering. Finally, Section 4 draws the conclusions.

2. FRAME WORK FOR WEB APPLICATIONS

The web engineering process model is similar to the Spiral model for the software product development which is shown in figure 1.

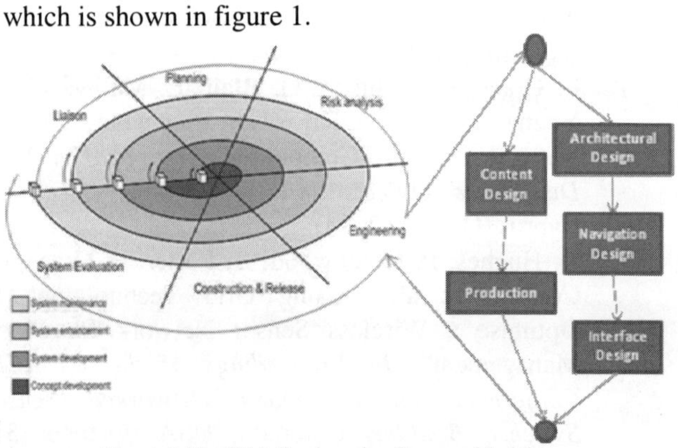

Figure 1.The Web Engineering Process Model

- The web engineering process begins with the *Formulation*- an activity that identifies the goals and objectives of the web applications and establishes the scope for the first increment.
- *Planning* estimates overall project cost, evaluates risks associated with the development effort, and defines a finely granulated development schedule for the initial web application increment, with a more coarsely granulated schedule for subsequent increments.
- *Analysis* establishes technical requirements for the web applications and identifies the content items that will be incorporated.
- However, the *Engineering* activity of this model incorporates two parallel tasks illustrated on the right side of the figure 1.
- *Content design and production* intends to design, produce and /or acquire all the content related to text, audio, video etc. which are to be integrated into the web application. Similarly, a set of technical design tasks is carried on parallel which includes architectural, navigation and interface design.
- *Architectural design* focuses on the definition of overall hypermedia structure and the application of design patterns and constructive templates.
- *Navigation design* concentrates on defining navigation paths that enable a user to access web application content and services. To achieve this, identification of the semantics of navigation for different users of the site is essential and also defining the mechanics of achieving the navigation.
- *Interface design* focuses on a well designed interface which would project the content or services provided by the site.
- *Page generation* is a construction activity that makes heavy use of automated tools for web application creation.
- *Testing* exercises web application navigation; attempts to uncover errors in applets, scripts and forms that are used and ensure that the web application will operate correctly in different environments. Each increment produced as part of the web engineering process is reviewed during *Customer Evaluation.*

3. METRICS FOR DESIGN MODULES OF WEB ENGINEERING

Metrics are invariably proposed in the context of techniques for improving the quality and usefulness of information on the Web. A study of these metrics is a starting point for developing these models, which can eventually aid Web content providers in enhancing web sites and predicting the consequences of changes in certain attributes. We discuss some of the metrics for each of the design modules of web engineering as depicted in Figure 2.

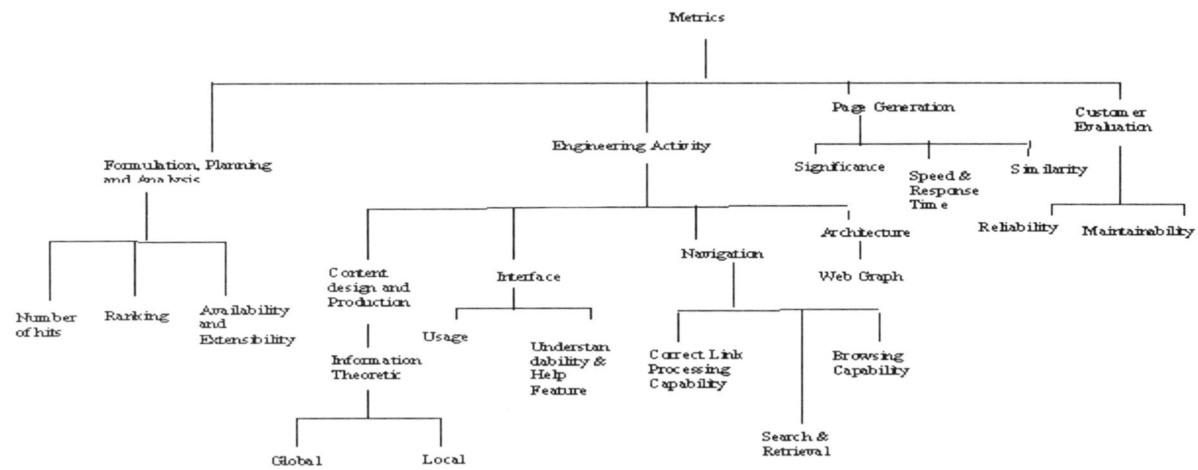

Figure 2 Metrics for Design modules of Web Engineering

3.1 Formulation, Planning and Analysis

3.1.1 Number of Hits:

The number of hits to a web application can be a measure to check whether the objective of the web application is achieved. Also, the proportion of overall hits followed by the user per search engine is a measure of the market share.

3.1.2 Ranking:

Relevance and quality metrics are taken up together by several search engines (e.g. Google) for ranking the results. So, ranking can be one of the measures to check whether the web application has been planned and developed. In general, the good web application is expected to be ranked within top ten results.

3.1.3 Availability and Extensibility:

Basically technical requirements of a web application can be classified into two: Hardware and Software requirements. We always presume hardware to be active (i.e. available all the time).There can be two metrics to check whether the analysis and requirements module have been done properly. They are Software availability meaning the web application should always be available and page fault should not occur due to the non-availability of the application. The other is Software extensibility meaning the application should support any incremental modules.

3.2 Engineering Activity

3.2.1 Content Design and Production

3.2.1.1 Information Theoretic:

Information theoretic metrics capture properties related to information needs, production and consumption. We consider the relationships between number of regularities observed in information generation on the Web.

3.2.1.1.1 Global:

This metric is to measure whether overall (global) content is considered and presented.

3.2.1.1.2 Local:

This metric is to measure whether local content whichever is acquired is considered and presented without any irregularity.

3.2.2 Architecture

Web Graph: We can represent the World Wide Web as a graph structure where web pages represents nodes and hyperlinks denote directed edges. Graph- based metrics can be a measure of structural properties of the web which would reflect the structural organization of the hypermedia. Poorly organized web sites often cause user disorientation leading to the "lost in cyberspace" problem.

3.2.3 Navigation

3.2.3.1 Search and Retrieval:

These metrics evaluate and compare the performance of web search and retrieval services. Information retrieval techniques can also be employed. Their retrieval effectiveness or the quality of results returned in response to the user query can be measured to reflect the Navigational design.

3.2.3.2 Browsing Capability:

The above metric can be a measure to reflect the correctness of the mechanisms used to achieve navigation.

3.2.3.3 Correct Link Processing Capability:

This metric can be used to measure the correctness of semantics of navigation.

3.2.4 Interface

3.2.4.1 Usage:

The way users browse defines the patterns and regularities. This metric gives a measure of user behavior which can also be used to improve web content, organization and presentation of web application.

3.2.4.2 Understandability and Help Feature:

This measure can be a measure which reflects the description of the interface design i.e. whether the interface is understandable by the user.

3.3 Page Generation

3.3.1 Significance:

This metric can be used to check the 'quality' and 'relevance' of web pages retrieved with respect to the information needs of users. Relevance means relevance to a specific information need and quality means search and retrieval irrespective of particular user requirements. A WWW page is considered to be relevant to a user query if, by accessing the page, the user can find resource (URL) containing information pertinent to the query, or the page itself is such a resource. Quality metrics use link information to distinguish frequently referred pages from less visible ones.

3.3.2 Speed and Response Time:

The above two metrics can be used to measure performance which is given by

Performance = Average response time for each service for a query

3.3.3 Similarity:

This metric quantifies the extent of relatedness between web pages. The above can be classified into Content-based and Link-based. Content based similarity is measured by comparing the text of the retrieved documents. Link based similarity mainly relies upon the hyperlink structure of a web graph to obtain related pages. The above metrics would help in grouping the pages or users into meaningful clusters that can further aid in better organization and accessibility of web application.

3.4 Customer Evaluation

3.4.1 Reliability:

This metric is a measure to check how reliable is the web site from the customer point of view with respect to user input validation, recovery and quality.

3.4.2 Maintainability:

This metric gives a measure of how well a web application is tuned for correction, perfection, adaptability and extendibility.

4. CONCLUSION

Web metrics give the indication of the quality of the web site developed and hence develop the business opportunities. Therefore it is very much necessary to test the web application with the above said metrics thoroughly. Several third party tools are available for free or for a nominal price.

Some of the tools are

1. Google rankings - Keyword Performance [5]
2. Quantcast - Traffic Monitoring [6]
3. Marketleap - Link Popularity Checker [7]
4. Webalizer - Web Statistics [8]
5. Awstats - Web Statistics [9]
6. Thumbshots – SEO ranking [10]
7. Google-Yahoo-Ask – SEO ranking [11]
8. Rank Position - – SEO ranking [12]
9. Google Rankings – SEO Rankings [5]
10. Yahoosearchrankings –SEO Rankings [13]

In this paper, we have tried to discuss some of the metrics which would be helpful in assessing design by evaluating modules of web engineering process model. This discussion is fundamental and we do not claim that the focus is complete and acknowledge any omissions. However, the experimentation is under process for best, average and worst case categories of web applications. We hope that this would serve as a starting point for further evolution of new metrics for Web Application Development focusing towards the design.

REFERENCES

1. A Survey of Web Metrics, Devanshu Dhyani, Wee Keong Ng, And Sourav S. Bhowmick, ACM Computing Surveys, Vol. 34, No. 4, December 2002, pp. 469–503.
2. Software Engineering: A Practitioner's Approach, 6/e by R.S. Pressman
3. Quantitative Metrics for Measuring Web Accessibility, Markel Vigo, Myriam Arrue, Giorgio Brajnik , Raffaella Lomuscio, Julio Abascal http://citeseerx.ist.psu.edu/viewdoc/summary?doi =10.1.1.81.5453
4. Web Search Using Automatic Classification, Chandra Chekuri, Michael H. Goldwasser, Prabhakar Raghavan
5. http://www.googlerankings.com/
6. www.quantcast.com
7. www.marketleap.com/publink/deafult.htm
8. www.webalizer.com
9. http://awstats.sourceforge.net
10. http://ranking.thumbshots.com/
11. http://www.jux2.com/
12. http://www.prsearch.biz/
13. http://www.yahoosearchranking

SIMULATION ON ERROR MINIMIZATION USING LINEAR MMSE CHANNEL EQUALIZATION FOR DIGITAL MODULATION SCHEME

JAYMIN BHALANI [1]
V. T. Patel Dept. of Electronics & Communication, C.I.T.-Changa
Dist-Anand, Gujarat, India.

Y.P.KOSTA [2]
Principal, C.I.T.-Changa
Dist-Anand, Gujarat, India.

A.I.TRIVEDI [3]
Dept. of Electrical Engg., Factulty of Tech. & Engg., M.S.U., Baroda
Gujarat, India.

Channel equalization technique uses to remove ISI (Inter symbol Interference) and reduce the errors. In this paper we have adopted $\pi/4$ DQPSK digital modulation system using first-order low pass channel. We have applied Linear MMSE (minimum mean square error) criterion to compensate ISI and the error, which introduce due to non-flat frequency response of channel. As mentioned above, the minimum mean square error channel equalization technique was studied and MATLAB was utilized to evaluate the performance through rigorous simulations. The results of simulation clearly depicted a considerable improvement in the M.S.E. (Means square error) and the percentage error rate against the specified values for E_b/N_o that can be observed through eye diagrams and constellation diagrams. Thus through our study we can advocate that minimum mean square technique is very useful to reduce ISI and errors considerably in present digital communication.

1.0 Introduction to theoretical approach for Minimum Mean Square Error criterion:

It well documented in theory [1] that zero forcing equalization may although remove the ISI, but does not give the best error performance in a digital communication system, mainly because it does not take into account the noises encounter in the communication channels. One investigative approach is to consider a more realistic situation where the noises in counted in the digital communication channel is dealt with, this help us to correctly quantify and get a better approximation analysis of the channel performance. This is done by suitably choosing the mathematical functions such as MMSE to take care of the noises in the channel. In the modeling of Noise in our digital communication channel uses the MMSE make the following suggestive assumptions

- The input symbols are temporally uncorrelated, (i.e.), E {An, An+j} =δ(j)
- The input symbols are uncorrelated with noise.

Under the above conditions the input channel equalizer tap weights are expressed mathematically as

$$Yeq(n) = \sum_{i=-M}^{M} A_k \Pr(n-k) + N(n) \quad (1)$$

and the output of the equalizer will be

$$Yeq(n) = \sum_{i=-M}^{M} w_i Y(n-i) \quad (2)$$

The equalizer output at the sampling times are given by,

$$Yeq(n) = \sum_{i=-M}^{M} w_i [\sum_{k=-\infty}^{\infty} A_k \mathrm{P_r}(n-i-k) + n(n-i)] \quad (3)$$

The quantity to be minimized mean square error (MSE) is given by,

$$MSE = E\{(A_n - Y_{eq}(n)\}^2 \quad (4)$$

final expression of MSE is

$$MSE = \sigma_A^2(1 - 2\Pr^T w + w^T T w) \quad (5)$$

Where σ_A^2 Represents the average signal power

$$\Pr = [\Pr(M), ..., \Pr(0), ... \Pr(-M)]^T \quad (6)$$

Is the received pulse value.
T is a matrix whose (i,j)th element is

$$\gamma(i,j) + (\sigma_N^2 / \sigma_A^2)\rho(i-j) \quad (7)$$

$$w = [w_{-M}, ... w_0, ... w_{+M}]^T \quad (8)$$

Represents equalizer tap-weights.
Differentiating above equation with equalizer tap weights Wi and setting above equation to zero,

$$\Pr = Tw \quad (9)$$

If input noise is uncorrelated or white the above equation will be

$$\Pr = (R + \frac{\sigma_N^2}{\sigma_A^2} I)w \quad (10)$$

Where R is autocorrelation matrix of the unequalized pulse value and I is identity matrix.. The equalizer tap weights can be computed from above equation as

$$w = (R + \frac{\sigma_N^2}{\sigma_A^2} I)^{-1} \Pr \quad (11)$$

Recognizing the fact that

$$(\sigma_N^2 / \sigma_A^2) = SNR \quad (12)$$

we have rewrite above equation

$$w = (R + \frac{1}{SNR} I)^{-1} \Pr \quad (13)$$

The above equation can be used to visualize the *trade-off* between Noise and ISI in the design of the LMMSE equalizer. If the receiver is operating in an almost noise-free condition (*SNR tends to infinity)*, the second term in the T matrix goes to zero and the solution approaches the zero-forcing equalizer solution. In all other cases, the noise term is weighed appropriately (based on the *SNR*).

1.1 Existence of an optimal solution:

The existence of an optimal solution basically rests with the ability to invert the Covariance T matrix. In general, the Covariance matrix is symmetric non-negative definite. The definiteness of the matrix is strengthened by the additive white noise component that provides a strong diagonal component, thus preventing singularity.

1.2 Residual MSE.

The Residual MSE after the equalization can be computed using the expression,

$$MSE = \sigma_A^2[1 - \Pr^T T \Pr] \quad (14)$$

The value of the signal to noise ratio is computed from Eb/No as

$$SNR = \frac{1}{8}(E_b / N_o) \quad (15)$$

It is observed that as Eb/No is decreased, MSE is increasing and this is expected as Eb/No decreases the noise increases and hence the MSE increases. Also the weights and the MSE for zero noise case were found to be very close to the Zero forcing equalizer.

2.0 Generation of I and Q components of $\pi/4$ DQPSK scheme in MATLAB:

The In-phase (I) and Quadrature Phase (Q) components of $\pi/4$ DQPSK can be expressed as:

$$I(i) = I(i-1) * \cos(\Delta\theta i) - Q(i-1) * \sin(\Delta\theta i)$$
$$I(i) = I(i-1) * \sin(\Delta\theta i) + Q(i-1) * \cos(\Delta\theta i)$$
$$s(i) = s(i-1) * e^{j\Delta\theta i}$$

Where I(i) and Q(i) are in phase and Quadrature phase components, while S(i) stands for the modulated symbol and Δ(θ) is phase difference between symbols of I and (I-1) signaling intervals.

2.1 Phase Shift Mapping:

The Phase shift $\Delta(\theta)_i$ depends upon the *input symbol* { 00,01,11,10 }. Thus, the information bits that constitute the input symbol are encoded and transact into one of the 4 possible phase transitions, as defined in the table-1 below:

Table 1: Phase transitions.

b_{i1}	b_{i2}	$\Delta\theta_i = f(b_{i1}, b_{i2})$
0	0	$\pi/4$
0	1	$3\pi/4$
1	0	$-3\pi/4$
1	1	$-\pi/4$

Where bi_1 and bi_2 are information bits.

3.0 Experimental Results:

Our simulations carried out here are specific for the Minimum Mean Square Error Channel Equalizer Algorithm against the selected modulation scheme π/4 DQPSK. For this scheme, we have used rectangular pulse convolved with first order low pass channel. We have calculated channel impulse response after which algorithm was applied to the samples of the channel impulse response in order to calculate the associated individual weights for the realized equalizer filter. This is followed by the calculation of the mean square error (MSE) values and the percentage errors in equalized modulated sequences associated with various values of E_b/N_o in dB. The simulated results are shown below

Table 2: E_b/N_o Vs M.S.E. (Mean Square Error) and the percentage error.

EB/No (dB)	M.S.E (Mean Square Error)	Percentage Error in equalized modulated sequences.
00.00 dB	0.1529	11.91 %
10.00 dB	0.0183	1.37 %
16.98 dB	0.0037	0.28 %
18.75 dB	0.0025	0.18 %
20.00 dB	0.0019	0.14 %
26.98 dB	3.7493e-004	0.028 %
37.78 dB	3.2815e-005	0.0023 %
38.45 dB	2.8370e-005	0.0020 %
38.69 dB	2.6929e-005	0.0019 %
Noise free	1.6993e-006	0.00 %

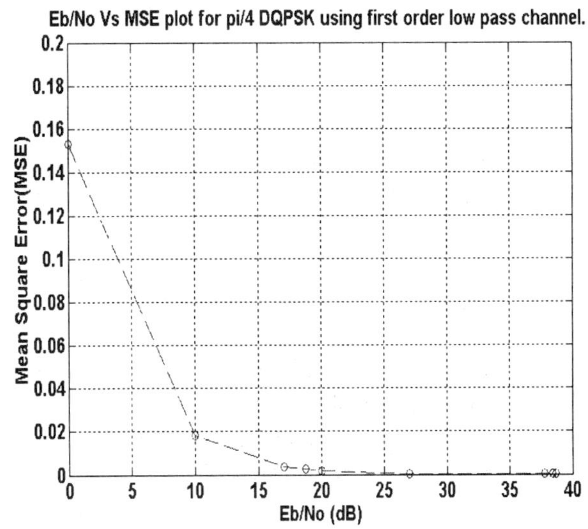

Figure 1. Plot of E_b/N_o Vs M.S.E.

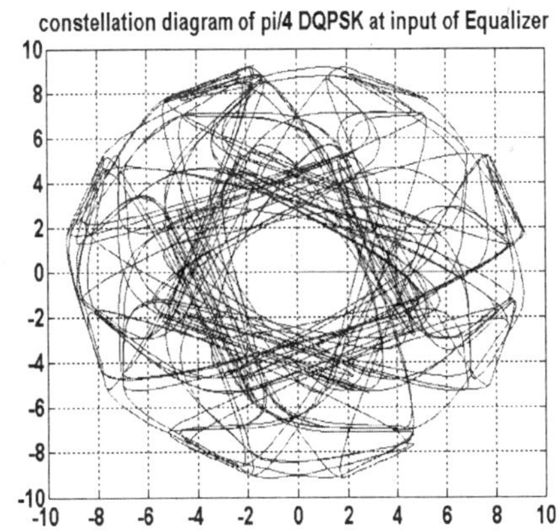

Figure 2. Constellation diagram of the π/4 DQPSK at input of the equalizer

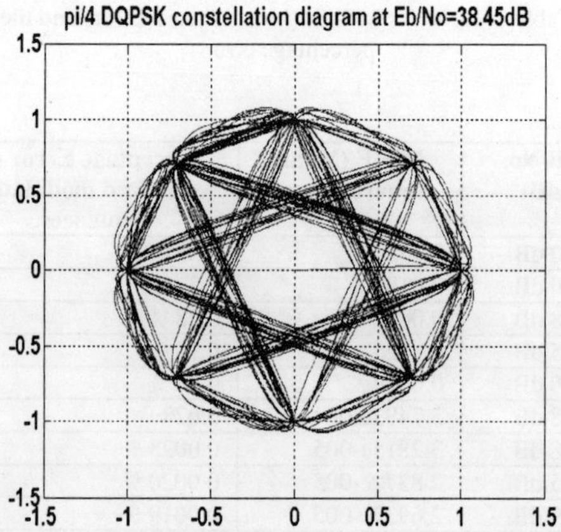

Figure 3. Constellation diagram of the $\pi/4$ DQPSK at 38.69 dB.

4.0 Conclusion:

From the results of MATLAB simulations, it depicts that ISI and errors in equalized modulated sequences reduces against increased values of Eb/No in dB using MMSE (Minimum Mean Square Error) channel equalization technique hence improvements in eye diagrams and constellation diagrams of equalized $\pi/4$ DQPSK modulated sequences. . Thus through our study we can advocate that MMSE channel equalization could be utilized in the present digital communication channels to reduce the ISI and the errors considerably that are depicted in the eye diagrams and constellation diagrams respectively

Reference:

1. John G. Proakias, Fellow IEEE, "Adaptive Equalization for TDMA mobile Radio", IEEE transaction on vehicular technology, Vol. 40,No 2, May 93.
2. K. Abend and B.D. Fraanhankan" Statically detection for communication Channels with intersymbol interference" Proc. IEEE pp-779-789, May 70.
3. Digital Communication by J.G.Proakias, McGraw-Hill edition.
4. B.P.Lathi, Principles of analog and digital communication.
5. Digital Signal Processing, A Computer Based Approach, Sanjit Mitra.
6. Theory of Digital Communication by Wong Lok.
7. Wireless Digital Communication by Kamilio Feher.
8. Mobile Cellular Communication by W.C.Y Lee, Mac-graw Hill edition.

USING PROCRUSTES ANALYSIS TO DETERMINE VERIFIABLE CONJECTURAL LAYOUT OF A FAMOSA FORTRESS, MALAYSIA

M. IZANI , A. BRIDGES
Department of Architecture, University of Strathclyde,
131 Rottenrow G4 0NG UK
E-mail : (mohamad.zainal-abidin , a.h.bridges)@strath.ac.uk)

A. RAZAK
Faculty of Information Technology,Multimedia University,
Cyberjaya, Selangor Malaysia
E-mail: aishah@mmu.edu.my

The "A Famosa Fortress" is one of the oldest partially extant European buildings in Malaysia. It was built in 1511 by the Portuguese and was largely destroyed during the British occupation in 1824. With the subsequent overbuilding of the site by Melaka city today, it is impossible to fully reconstruct this fortress in its physical context. Thus we proposed a 3-D digital model as a way to preserve this historical fortress. The biggest challenge in this research is to determine fortress layout based on various textual descriptions and old drawings and plans. This is due to the lack of any authoritative documentation pertaining to the fortress. In this paper we present our approach in verifying the layout based on several selected old plans of the fortress. Such plans as exist not only differ in their depiction of the fort, but also use various ancient measurement systems. We have adopted procrustes analysis as method to identify the similarities of the plan. We have used the layout constructed from reliable textual documentations as the reference figure. Based on the result, we have identified the plan which is most reliable for our reference in modeling the 3D model of A Famosa.

1. Introduction

Historically, Melaka's strategic position in South East Asia has made it as an important centre of commerce [1]. The traders used to trade various items such as spices, cloth, silk and many more. These traders came from India, China, Borneo, Arabia and Europe. Melaka's popularity attracted the Portuguese to expand their power in commercial dealings, military occupation and religion. The Portuguese believed that by controlling Melaka, they could monopolise spice trading which was a very valuable item in Europe and expand their military power. One said that whoever is lord of Melaka has his hand on the throat of Venice [2]. Besides, one of the Portuguese's objectives was to expand the influence of Christianity in this region and this could only be done by seizing Melaka. In 1511, the Portuguese, with fifteen small and great sails and with sixteen hundred fighting men laid siege to Melaka [3]. With advanced strategy and weapons, the Portuguese managed to capture Melaka within three weeks and, on August 10th, 1511 Melaka fell into Portuguese hands [4]. Albuquerque was the captain for the new Portuguese government in Melaka. He immediately ordered a fortress to be built for defensive purpose [5]. With this success, it also attracted the Dutch with the monopoly of the trading in South East Asia. The fortress of Melaka continued its architectural development over this time. Prior to the occupation of the Dutch, they heavily bombarded the fortress which has critically destroyed part of the fortress. After they succeeded to conquer Melaka in 1641, the Dutch carried out major reconstruction on the fortress as part of their strategy to strengthen their power. This reconstruction involved the extension of the fortress walls and bastions [6]. When the British took over the Dutch's position in 1824, the British captain in Melaka, William Farquhar instructed the fortress to be destroyed. As the result, the only evidence left today is a gate to access the fortress which is known as Porta de Santiago (Figure 1).

Figure 1. Remnant of the fortress, Porta de Santiago [7]

Recently, the Ministry of Culture, Arts and Heritage in Malaysia has allocated more than RM 12 million to excavate and do research on this heritage following the discoveries of some of the fortress walls foundation. However, work to uncover more of the buried wall, despite its historical significance and potential to draw more tourists into the area, may not be feasible as it would involve tearing up the major road that links the old town with the new commercial area. Hence, only certain part of the fortress can be reconstructed. In order to solve this problem, we propose to digitally reconstruct this fortress in form of 3D model which can be navigated in the virtual world. Since the fortress itself has faced several changes in its design and layout, by reconstructing it in 3D allows the researchers to investigate and study the development of these changes from architectural and historical aspects.

2. Fortress layout determination approach

The biggest challenge in this research is to determine fortress layout based on various textual descriptions and old drawings and plans. This is due to the lack of any authoritative documentation pertaining to the fortress. In our first approach, we have tried to construct the layout based on the report of Governor Balthasar Bort in Malacca dated 1678 [8] and description given by Manuel Godinho De Eredia in 1604 [5]. A detail analysis has been done to compare and verify the given data [9]. Based on the findings, we have constructed the A Famosa layout as in Figure 2.

However, the point to point measurement that we get from figure 2 varies slightly than those given in both sources. This variation is caused by several ambiguities in the sources such as:

1. Both sources [8 &5] did not specify whether the measurement of the outermost line include the size of the bastions. There is also no explanation on the size of the fortress or any visual information on the shapes.
2. Balthasar report is from Dutch era, where some modifications have been done to extend part of the fortress compares to the original fortress during Portugese era as explained in [8].

Even though our previous findings conclude that the measurement of Figure 2 is consistent with both sources, however, the findings are based on textual descriptions of the fortress only. Thus further analysis should be done to compare this result with our visual description and verify the consistency of both mediums.

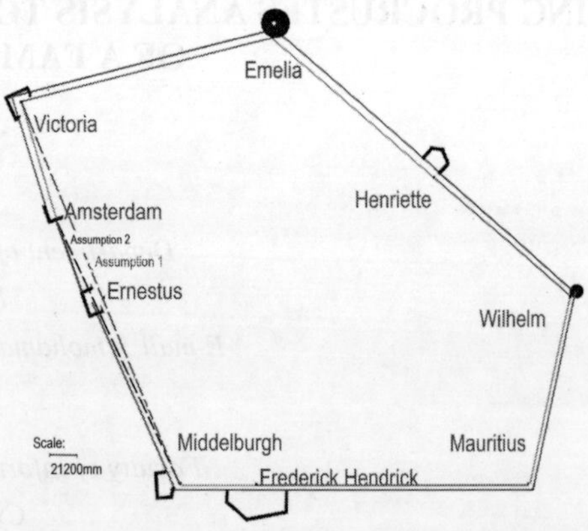

Figure 2. Complete visualization of innermost polygon and the outermost line of A Famosa including the bastions

2.1. *Procrustes analysis.*

To compare the layout that we have constructed in Figure 2 with the visual data that we have collected, we decided to apply Procrustes analysis approach. Procrustes analysis is a rigid shape analysis that uses isomorphic scaling, translation, and rotation to find the "best" fit between two or more landmarked shapes. In our case, we perform a least-squares orthogonal generalized procrustes analysis (least-squares orthogonal mapping). It applies nonlinear mapping algorithm to find best fit, i.e. to find a reference cluster of landmarks, so that the distance of each reference landmark to it's corresponding experimental landmark is minimized. Before we proceed with this analysis, we have to first identify and select appropriate drawings for our visual data.

We have extracted and collected a lot of visual data related to A Famosa from books, journals and even direct from the national archives. Among them are old drawings dated from year 1500 to 1700 recorded by various artists, draftsmen and architects from the Portuguese era until the British era. For the purpose of analysis, we have categorized it into two types which are not to scale drawing and scaled drawings.

2.1.1. Not to scale drawings

All drawings from Portuguese era are not to scale. Even we managed to get some drawings with scale, they are very brief and seemed questionable. Most drawings are in the form of painting and perspective drawings. The drawings are strongly related to the skills of the draftsmen or artist, development of the art movement in that era and availability of the architectural technology during that time. Unfortunately, data from not to scale drawings are not very reliable for extracting the measurement of the fortress. However, it can be used to illustrate data such as shape, materials, surrounding, elements, location and position of the fortress.

2.1.2 To scale drawings

Most of the drawings during Dutch era are scaled drawings. They are in the form of plans, drawn according to scale with specific measurement unit. However, the measurement unit used are old units such chain, rod, furlong and fathoms which are no longer used nowadays. Besides that, even the same unit might use different conversion value such as listed in Table 1.

Table 1: Conversion of old units [10]

Name	Conversion (1 unit equivalent)
Dutch foot	11 Dutch inches 11 3/8 English inches
English foot	12 inches
Dutch rod	Sometimes 11,12 13 Dutch feet
English rod	16.6 English feet

To proceed with this analysis, we have identified 12 plans to be compared to our constructed layout. The plans selected are mostly from the Dutch era because it is drawn according to scale. This is very important to eliminate inconsistencies/variations which are caused by improper drawings. The plans selected are listed in Table 2. From each selected plans, we extract the A Famosa shape and identify 34 landmarks on each shapes as given in Figure 3.

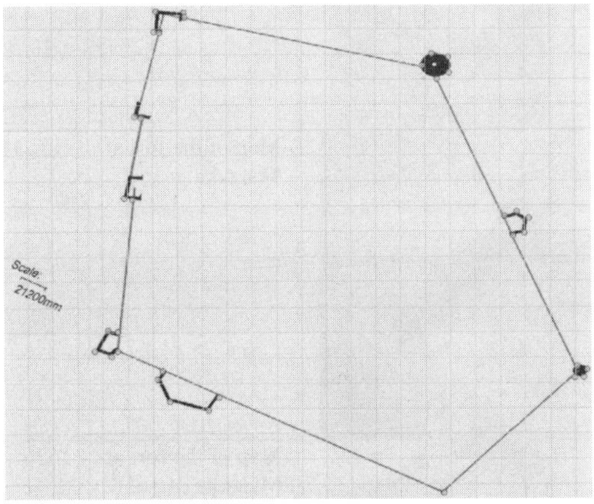

Figure 3. 34 identified landmarks on each experimental shapes

3. Results and analysis

Figure 4 presents the average and standard deviations calculated on the distance of the procrusted plans to the reference figure. Based on the result of figure 4, it is shown that Plan 1 and Plan 7 have the minimum average and standard deviation for the distance with the reference figure, followed by Plan 3 and 6. Thus we decided to run further analysis on these 4 plans. To further verify the consistency of these plans to our reference layout, we projected the innermost polygon that is shown in Figure 2 into plan 1,3,6 and 7. Table 3 presents the result of this projection.

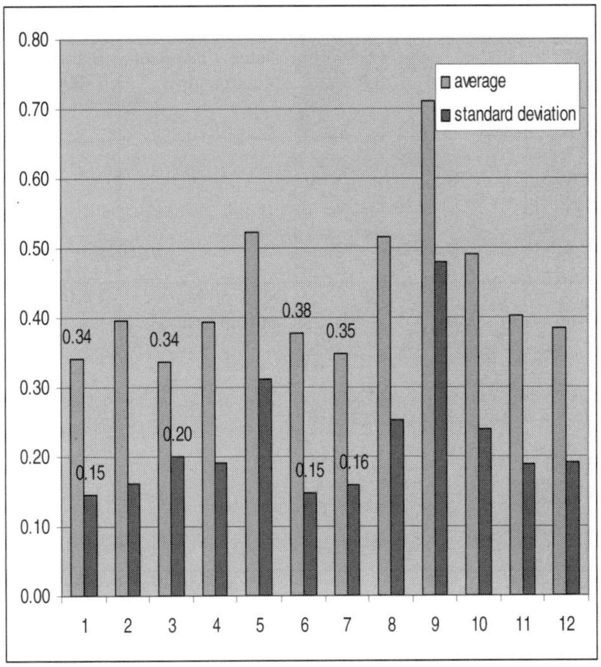

Figure 4. Average and standard deviation of the procrusted plan to the reference figure in Figure 3

From the result in Table 3, we identified that there are 3 innermost polygon angles which clearly indicate some inconsistencies with the outermost line. These angles are identified as angles involving the bastions of Middleburgh, Victoria and Emelia. The reason for these variations might be due to the fact that there has been some modification done during the Dutch era compared to the original during the Potugese era. In Balthasar's report [8], he reported that some modifications were done on the fortress during his time such as the bastion of Victoria was extended to 1/3 of it's original size and the addition of Middleburgh bastion, which does not exist during the Portuguese era. Even though there is no modification made to the bastion of Emilia, but since it is linked to the bastion of Victoria, thus some variation might be observed. Plan 3 and Plan 6 shows further inconsistencies in the angle for Mauritius and Whilem, thus we decided to discard these maps and use Plan 1and Plan 7 as the most reliable visual representation of A Famosa.

Table 2. 12 selected plans for procrustes analysis

No	Plan	Title	Year
1	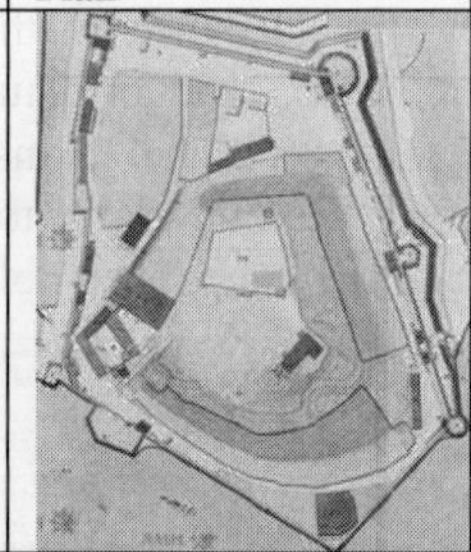	Map of the city and fort at Malakka	1780
2	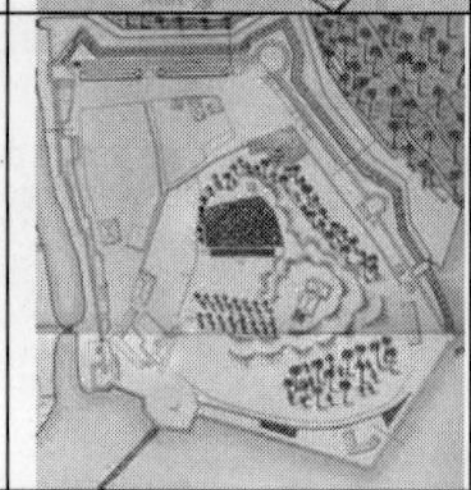	Dutch map of Malacca town	Before AD 1800
3	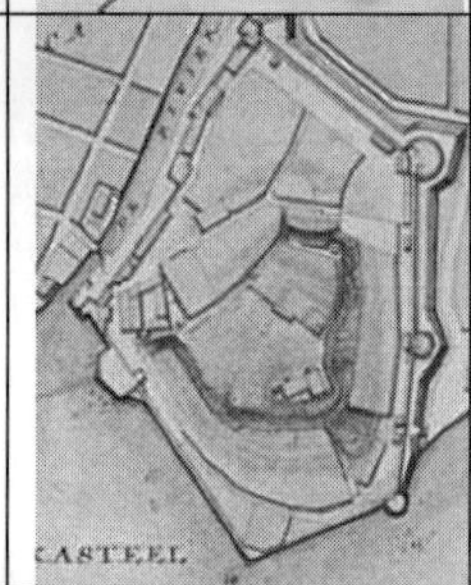	Map of Malacca and environs	1750-1796
4	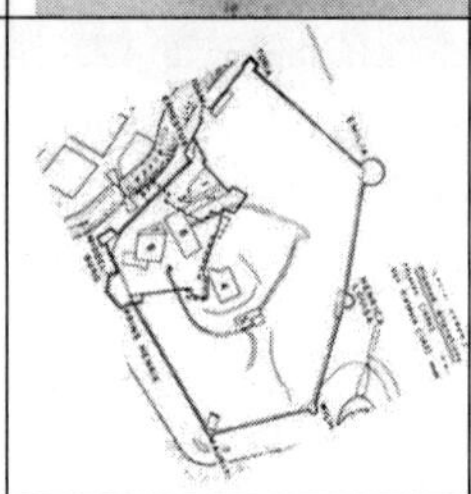	Malacca fort 1660	1660
5	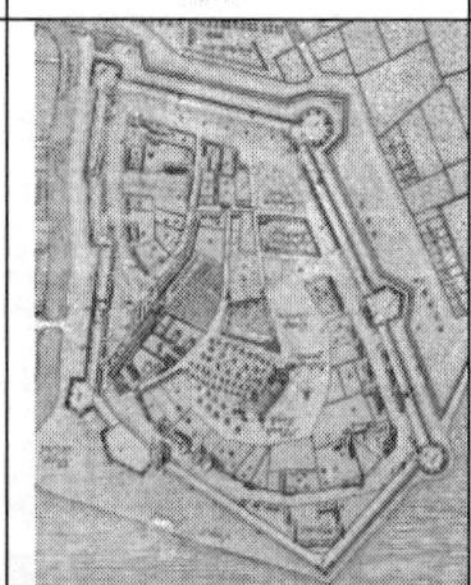	Map of Malakka	1735 - 1744
6	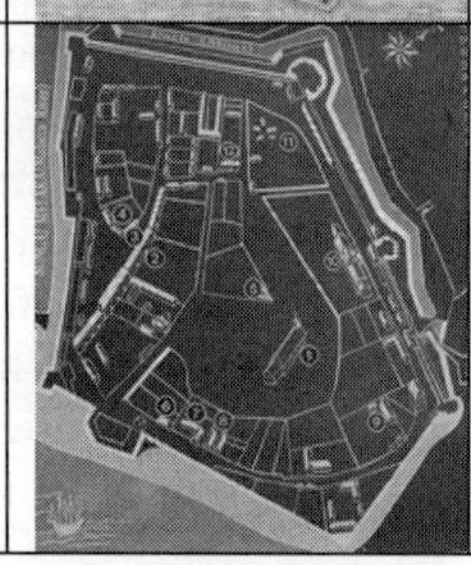	Melaka fortress based on 1744	1744
7	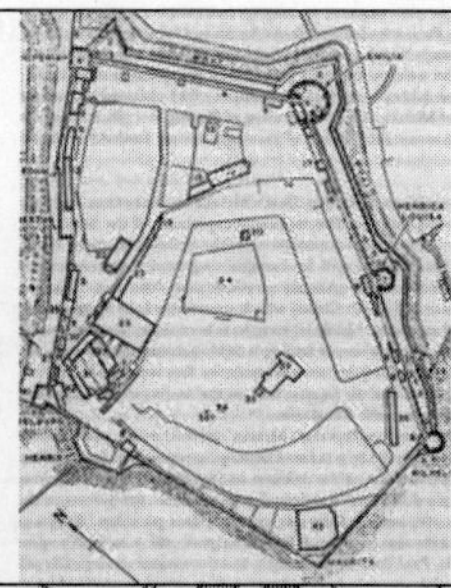	Plan of Malacca fort, ca. 1792, (after Reimer and Elias)	1792
8	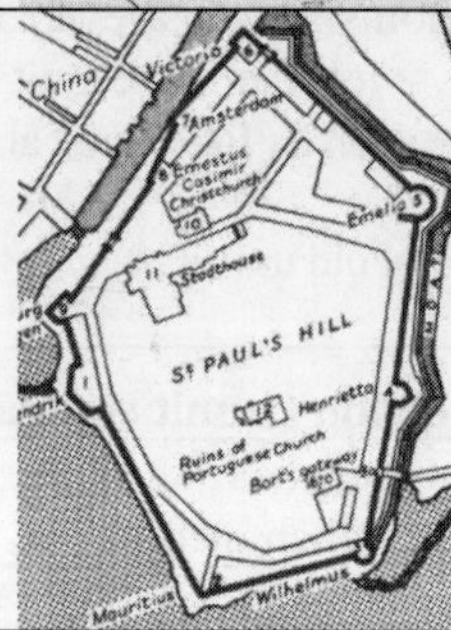	Plan of Dutch fort at Malacca	
9	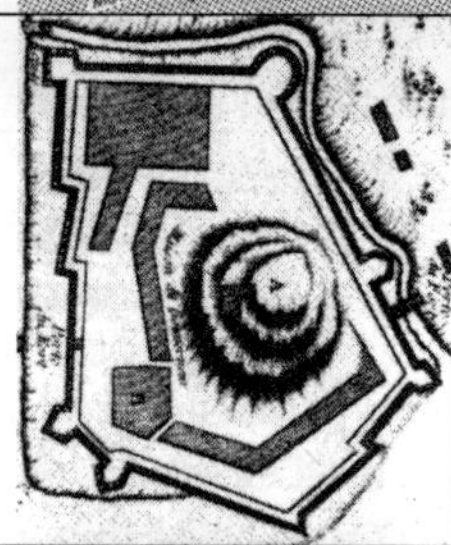	Plan de la ville de Malacca	1764
10	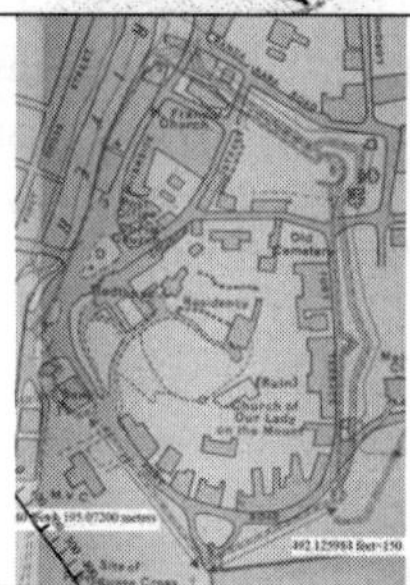	Malacca town: Showing position of old fortifications	
11	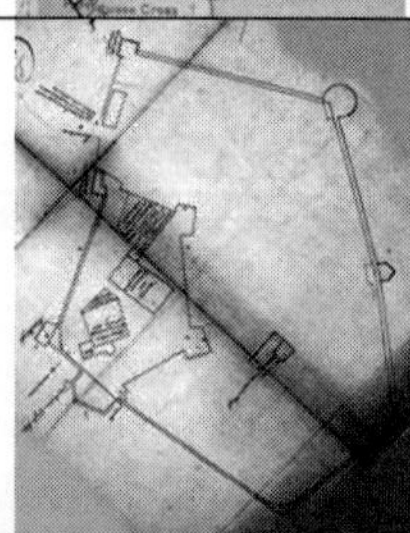	Map of the fort at Malakka	Nov 1663
12	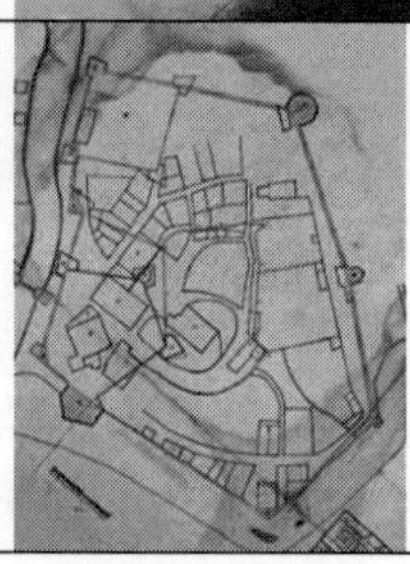	Map of the fort at Malakka ca 1656	1656

Table 3. Projection of innermost polygon onto Plan 1,3,6 and 7

<table>
<tr><th>Plan no.</th><th>Procrustes analysis</th></tr>
<tr><td>1</td><td>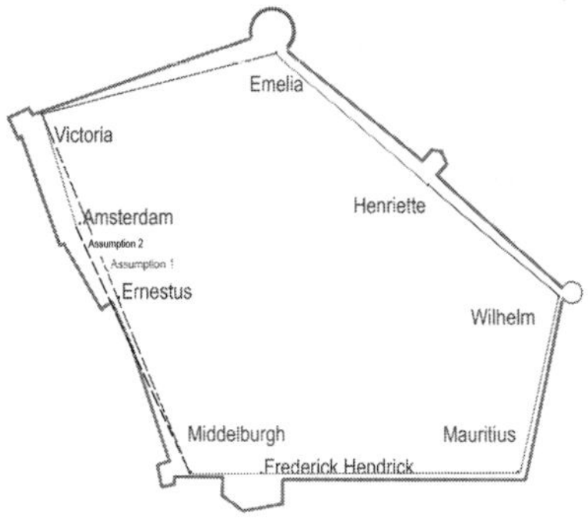</td></tr>
<tr><td>3</td><td>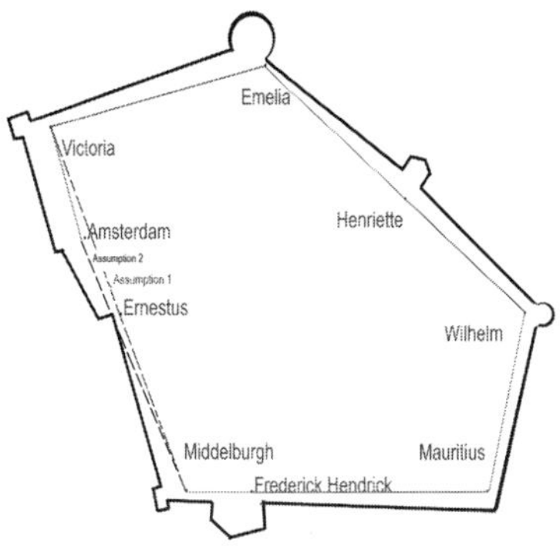</td></tr>
<tr><td>6</td><td>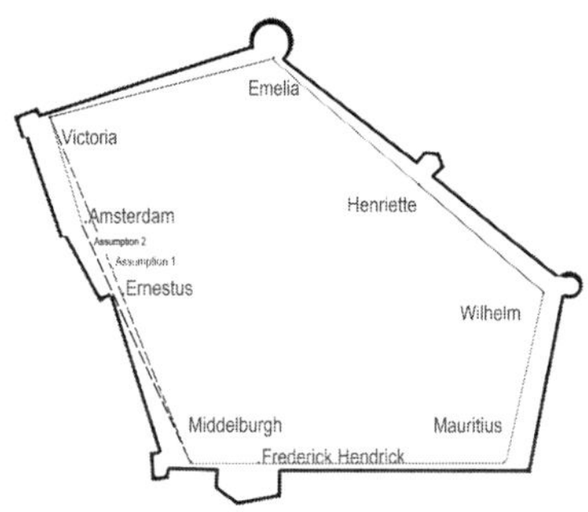</td></tr>
<tr><td>7</td><td>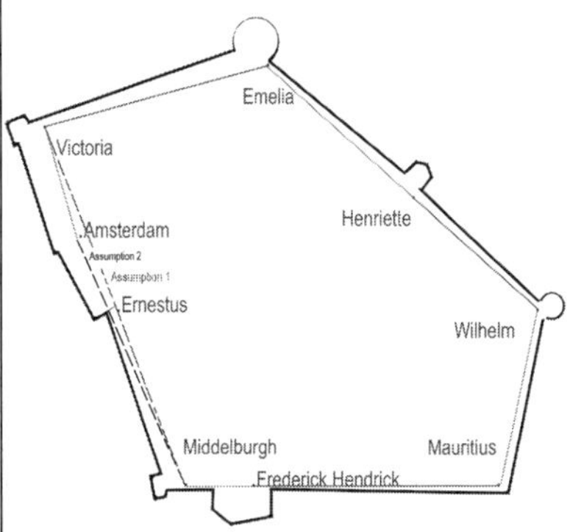</td></tr>
</table>

4. Conclusion and future works

Based on the result from Procrustes analysis, we decided to use Plan 1 and Plan 7 as the main visual reference in our attempt to model this fortress in 3D. Visual information is very helpful in providing the information which is not given in the textual report such as the bastion actual shape, the fortress layout and other details. However, the visual data, might not give the most accurate information in terms of measurement [11 & 12]. Thus in the next step, we intended to compare point to point measurement of the visual data (Figure2, Plan 1 and Plan p 7) to the textual data [5 & 8].

References

[1] Thomaz, Luís Filipe F. R., and Manuel Pintado. 2000. Early Portuguese Malacca. [Macau]: CTMCDP/IPM, pp. 19.

[2] Pires, T., & Rodrigues, F. (1944). The Suma oriental of Tomé Pires, an account of the East, from the Red Sea to Japan, written in Malacca and India in 1512-1515, and The book of Francisco Rodrigues, rutter of a voyage in the Red Sea, nautical rules, almanack and maps, written and drawn in the East before 1515. London: The Hakluyt Society.

[3] Ryan, N. J. (1960). Malaya through four centuries an anthology, 1500-1900. London, Oxf. Univ. Press, pp. 6

[4] Noonan, L. A. (1989). John of Empoli and his relations with Afonso de Albuquerque. Lisboa: Ministério da Educação, Instituto de Investigação Científica Tropical.

[5] Godinho de Eredia, M., & Mills, J. V. (1997). *Eredia's description of Malaca, Meridional India, and Cathay.* Kuala Lumpur, Malaysia: Malaysian Branch of the Royal Asiatic Society.

[6] Leupe, P. A., & Hacobian, M. (1936). The siege and capture of Malacca from the Portuguese in 1640-1641: extracts from the archives of the Dutch East Indies Company. [Singapore, Malayan]

[7] Asia Explorers., 2003. Article on Exploring the Porta de Santiago (A Famosa) Remains of old Portuguese fort, Malacca, Malaysia. http://www.asiaexplorers.com/malaysia/ porta_de santiago.htm (accessed 02 Jun. 2008)

[8] Bort, B. (1927). Report of Governor Balthasar Bort on Malacca, 1678. Singapore: Malayan Branch, Royal Asiatic Society.

[9] Izani, Bridges & Razak, A (2009a), *Determination of the plan of the A Famosa Fortress, Malaysia,* to appear in proceeding of International Conference on Computing and Informatics 2009, June 2009

[10] Murray Hoffman (1862). Treatise Upon the Estate and Rights of the Corporation of the City of New York, E. Jones & Co

[11] Lefe'vre, W. (2004). Picturing machines 1400-1700. Cambridge, Mass, MIT Press.

[12] Goldthwaite, R. A. (1980). The building of Renaissance Florence: An economic and social history. Baltimore: Johns Hopkins University Press.

A SECURED WEB PORTAL FOR RURAL ADMINISTRATION SYSTEM

P.M.ARUNKUMAR, D.DURAIPANDIYAN
Dept of IT, Sona College of Technology, Salem, TamilNadu, India

P.PABITHA
Asst.Professor, Sona College of Technology, Salem, TamilNadu, India, pabithap@gmail.com

DR.R.LAKSHMIPATHY
Professor, St.Peter's Engineering College, Chennai, TamilNadu, India

The Rural administration system is one where the people of specific region and the municipal authorities coordinate together in order to provide the certificates of birth/death, property tax payment bill and handling the general complaints of the public. At present all these activities have done in manually and there is lots of drawbacks .In the Municipal offices information in Manual records is difficult to maintain. There will be longer service fulfillment duration and delay in issuing/approvals in certificate. So, we need a web portal for rural administration system. The rationale of this project is to get the credentials in the Portable Document Format (PDF) through online. Another essential need to implement a successful e-Government web application is security. We propose a secured web portal for Rural Administration system that uses HiWAF for security.

1. Introduction

The online rural administration system is to reduce the workload of the municipal officers and people. The online rural administration System has following four modules: Birth certificate, Death Certificate, Property tax bill and Administrator services. The public can get their certificates through online thereby avoids contacting the person to the concerned offices. This system facilitates citizens with easy & quick access to the department information and services. The System is mainly concerned to perform the Municipality operations automated and widely accessible throughout the closed and open network of Tamilnadu state government. This automated application provides a complete and sophisticated means of Municipalities operations. Information updates can be done automatically and secure from the unauthorized parties. Complaints made by an individual can also be recorded by the concerned authorities through online.

2. Literature Survey

The basic literature survey was done at the Municipal Corporation of Salem, Tamilnadu and also various municipalities in and around Salem by referring the concerned authorities for collecting details for implementing.

3. Existing System

At present all the administration activities in our state municipalities are done manually. Some of the issues they face are as follows:

- Information in Manual records – difficulty in maintenance and retrieval of information.
- Longer service fulfillment duration and delay in approvals/issuing the certificates.
- Cumbersome processes in tax calculations.
- Inefficient mechanism to track the citizen grievances.
- Scope for illegitimate activities being unnoticed.
- Lack of transparency in service fulfillment.
- Tedious manual file movement processes.

The drawbacks of the existing system are that user is confused with larger number of links. The user may be in different site by clicking some of the links." Lost of sight is lost of mind".

4. Proposed System

The system initiates automation of critical processes and services which lead to the development of Rural Administration System. The Municipality officers can perform the Advertisement Tax, Assert and Inventory System, Birth and Death Registration, Property Tax and Administrator Services. Fig 4.1 gives the overview of the system.

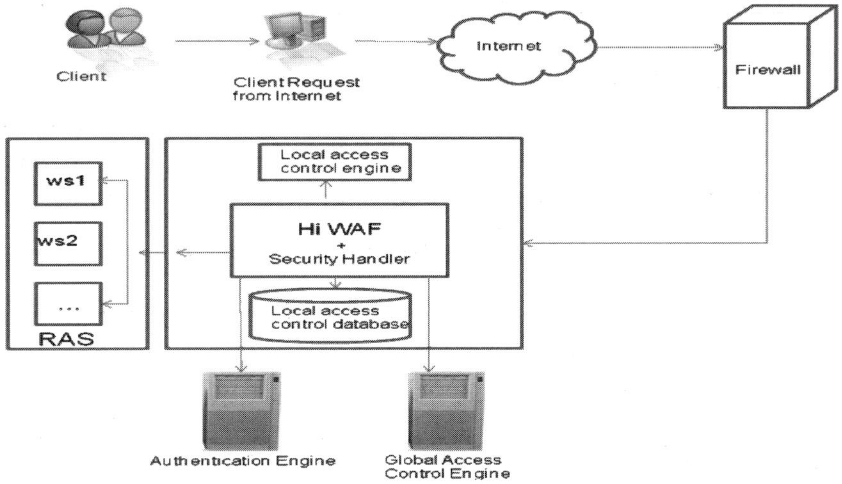

Fig 4.1 Overview of the system

The following working scenario demonstrates the process of requesting the access to a specific Web service by a client:

1) The client system prepares the necessary Web service request, with the digital identification of the client. The request will be submitted.
2) This request will be intercepted by the security unit of the e-Government Provider; which includes the proposed HiWAF web application firewall and a Security Handler.
3) The security handler will filter the request (which is either HTTP or HTTPS message) using positive and negative based filtering. If the request does not acquire the satisfactory conditions of the security handler using HiWAF, then it will be rejected, otherwise; the control over the request moves to the Security Handler.

4.1. *Types of Users*

4.1.1 Normal User or Citizens

The figure 4.2 explains as follows:After the user logins into the system,he can create the request for the birth certificate,death certificate,property tax and administration tax. After creating the request the user can enter the details in the application form which are stored in the database.

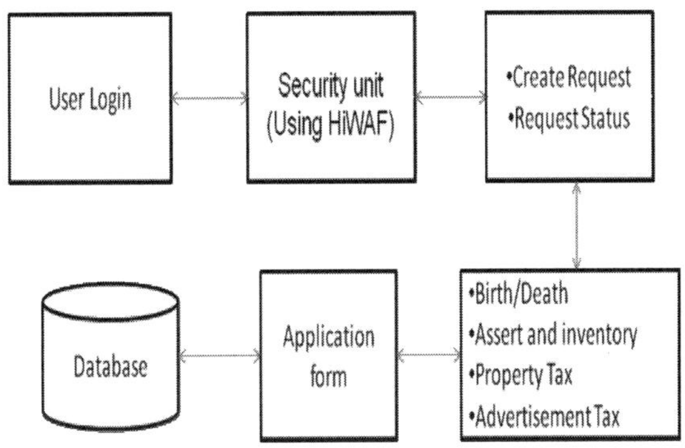

Fig4.2 Basic Flow Diagram For Users

4.1.2 Municipal officers

Fig 4.2 gives the flow diagram for Municipal Officers. The VAO or RI or Thasildar can enter into the login with the appropriate username and password provided by the administrator.

First when the VAO enters into his account he checks his database whether he had received any request from the user. If he received any request from the user he verifies the records. After verifying the record he sends to the RI. The similar process is carried out by RI and Thasildar. After all the verification is made the certificate can be downloaded.

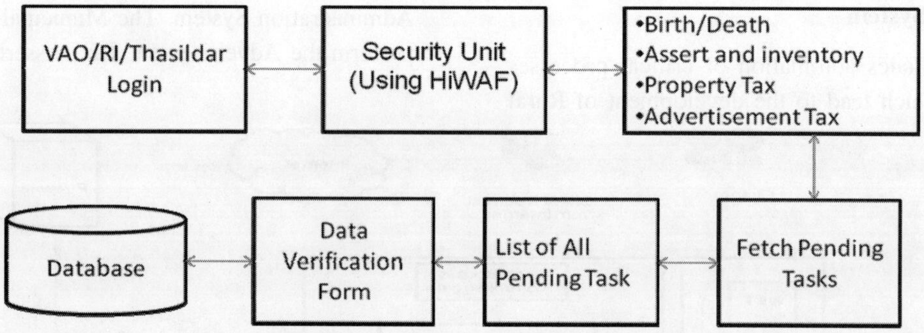

Fig 4.3.Basic Flow Diagram for Municipal Officers

4.2. *Filtering mechanisms*

Positive logic filtering allows valid requests based on a signature set detailing what types of communications protected servers know-how to handle; it prevents any requests not known to be valid from reaching secured servers. To minimize the performance overhead of a filtering engine utilizing positive logic, the set of valid requests is normally defined in some optimized format such as through the use of regular expressions. Valid Method-URL-Parameter combinations can be defined, as can appropriate parameter value ranges, e.g. month should have a value between 1 and 12.

Negative logic filtering relies on signatures of known attacks and allows security systems to prevent any requests that appear to match the attacks' signatures from reaching protected servers. Filters rely on negative logic are quite accurate at preventing known attacks, but are powerless when it comes to shielding against unknown exploits. They also require regular updates to their signature sets.

Session based filtering (also called event-driven dynamic rules) utilizes positive logic based rules but allows the inclusion of variables in the rule set. The values of the variables are set dynamically during user sessions. The capability to utilize variables in positive logic rule sets allows for the creation of extremely strict rules (and tight
security) – for example, a user's name can be included in a URL path – and even after authentication, every request to reach the application firewall will be checked to ensure that the username on the URL matches the authenticated user.

4.3. *Functionalities of the proposed system*

Some of the functionalities of the proposed system are Login, asset & Inventory System, Birth & death registration, Administrator services, Advertisement tax and property tax.

i. Advertisement Tax:

The purpose of this Advertisement Tax module is to specify the requirements of the Advertisement Tax System .It depends upon the area, Advertisement period and size of the Advertisement board. This System is also applicable for Company/Organization Advertisement Tax.

ii. Asset and Inventory System:

Asset and Inventory Module facilitates with the Purchase/Acquisition of Assets, Calculating Depreciation, Sale of Assets, and Purchase/Issue of products, processing of issue returns, purchase returns and wastage of products.

iii. Births & Deaths Registration:

This System automates the citizen's Birth, Still Birth and Death details, issuing of Birth, Still Birth and Death Certificates, service charge details, inclusion of child name at a later date, Issuing of Non-Availability Certificates.

iv. Property Tax:

This module covers Calculation of Property Tax, Issue of Special Demand Notice for New or Revised Tax, Revision Petition, Issue of demand notice, Collection of tax, Collection of Penalties, Tax Payments, Half Year wise updates.

v. Administrator Services:

The Administrator Services are some reusable components for the MAS and common services like User authentication, User-Service-Role Mapping and User Management.

4.3.1 Login

Every user have to login in order to get service from the website. Depending upon the user type the corresponding screen will be displayed.

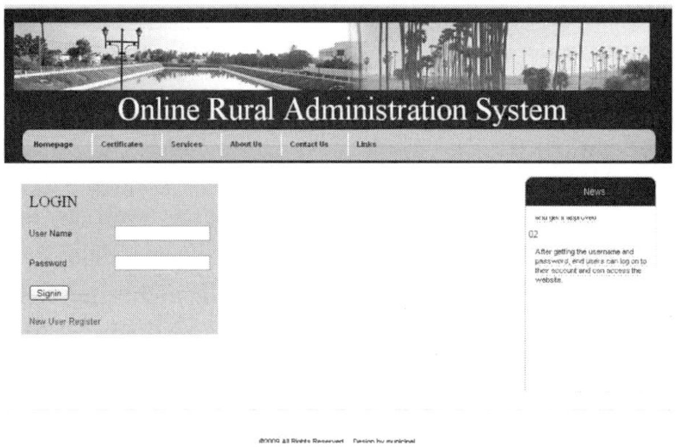

Fig 4.4. Login Page

```
<%--    Document   : intex1    Created on : Feb 28, 2009,
9:33:27 AM <%      Connection con = null;    Statement stmt
= null;    ResultSet rs = null; String ch = null, str;    String
strName1 = request.getParameter("UserName");
      String strName2 = request.getParameter("Password");
      session.setAttribute("name","");
      session.setAttribute("logid", "0");
      session.setAttribute("person","");    int h = 0, g = 0;
try { Class.forName("sun.jdbc.odbc.JdbcOdbcDriver");
        con = DriverManager.getConnection("jdbc:odbc:s", "",
""); stmt = con.createStatement();
        String str1 = strName1.substring(0, 3);
        session.setAttribute("person", str1);
        if (str1.equals("RI_")) {
          h = 1;    rs = stmt.executeQuery("select
userid,pass,firstname,lastname from RI_USER where
userid='" + strName1 + "'");   } else if (str1.equals("VAO")) {
h = 2;  rs = stmt.executeQuery("select
userid,pass,firstname,lastname from village where userid='" +
strName1 + "'"); } else if (str1.equals("THA")) {    h = 3;  rs =
stmt.executeQuery("select userid,pass,firstname,lastname from
taluk where userid='" + strName1 + "'");       }else
if(str1.equals("ADM")) {h=4;
        rs = stmt.executeQuery("select userid,pass from
admin"); }       else { rs = stmt.executeQuery("select
userid,password,name from user_profile where userid='" +
strName1 + "'");        }  rs.next();    String username =
rs.getString(1);          String password = rs.getString(2);   if
(strName1.equals(username) && strName2.equals(password))
{
          session.setAttribute("logid", "1");
          session.setAttribute("user_id", strName1);
if (h == 1) {  session.setAttribute("name", rs.getString(3) +
rs.getString(4));
```

Fig 4.5 Program for Login page

4.3.2. Birth/Death Certificate

The user can sign up the system with new register form or he can sign in the system with existing username and password. After signing in the System, the user can enter into birth certificate module. Here the two options for user, one is to create his request and the other one is to view the status of the previous request. Using the registration no provided by the authorities with necessary details the user can create his request for the birth certificates.

After the request is completed the request ID is provided for each user. Using this request ID user can check his status whether it is pending or verified by VAO or RI or Thasildar.

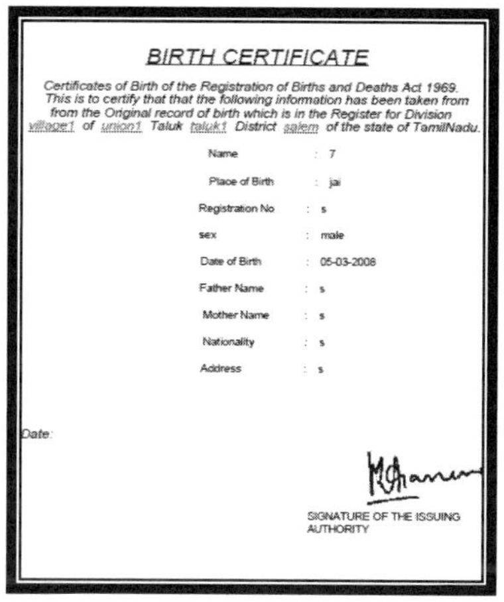

Fig 4.8. Birth Certificate in PDF format

Once all the verification is over, the birth certificate will be generated in PDF format which the user can print.

4.3.3. Property Tax

The user can sign up the system with new register form or he can sign in the system with existing username and password. After signing in the System, the user can enter into property certificate module. Here the user can be authenticated with the survey number. After verifying the survey no the user is allowed to fill up the details in the registration form. According to number of floors the property tax is calculated. Here the user can enter his

DD number of the bank to pay the property tax through online. The property tax paid by the User is verified by the VAO or RI or Thasildar. The proprietor who had paid the tax has been examined once in a six months. After verification by the concerned authorities the bill will be displayed in online. If the bill amount is insufficient then it will be rejected by the administrator.

4.3.7. Asset System

The user can sign up the system with new register form or he can sign in the system with existing username and password. After signing in the System, the user can enter into asset certificate module. The **user** can be authenticated with the survey number. After verifying the survey no the user is allowed to fill up the details in the registration form. According to number of floors the asset system is calculated. Here the user can enter his DD number of the bank to pay the property tax. The Asset System paid by the User is verified by the VAO or RI or Thasildar. The proprietor who had paid the tax has been examined once in a six months. After verification by the concerned authorities the bill will be displayed in online. If the bill amount is insufficient then it will be rejected by the administrator.

4.3.8. Administrator Services

Here the administrator updates the website such as news, other links etc. The administrator overviews the VAO or RI or Thasildar database. If any error occurs in the website the administrator overcomes the error. Here the administrator maintains the signatures of the VAO or RI or Thasildar.

4.3.9.Advertisement tax

The user can sign up the system with new register form or he can sign in the system with existing username and password. After signing in the System, the user can enter into advertisement tax module. According to highest tax payer to the ground, thasildar gives approval to the concerned person. Also the approval is given by the concerned authorities.

4.3.10.Complaints

Here the user can register the complaints regarding the birth, death certificate, property tax certificate, advertisement tax. After registering complaints it was viewed by the concerned authorities.

4.3.11.Security Handlers

WAFs work in different modes depending on the web traffic filtering approach used, such as positive security mode, negative security mode, session-based mode, or mixed modes. The proposed WAF, which is called (HiWAF), is a web application firewall that works in three modes: positive, negative and session based security modes. The artificial neural networks and fuzzy logic concepts will be used to implement a hybrid intelligent web application firewall that works in three security modes.

5. CONCLUSION AND FUTURE WORK

The Municipal Administration System is designed to simplify the work load of the public as well as the Municipal Officers. It helps to reduce time delays in issuing certificates by the concerned authorities. In future, after the certificate can be verified by the concerned authorities a SMS or email will be sent to the concerned persons. The websites are designed in such a manner that they can be accessed through cell phones and websites. By using this project the workload of the Municipal Officer is very much reduced and updates are made easy. This system facilitates citizens with easy & quick access to the department information and services from anywhere in the state. It infuses transparency in providing services to citizens. The client requests a Web-based application on the system. This application requires e-Government's Web services.

6.0. REFERENCES

1. Assad Moosa, Enanas Muhsen Alsaffar "Proposing a Hybrid-Intelligent Framework to Secure e-Government Web Applications".
2. Steve Harris, Jeremy Gibbons,jim Davies, Andrew Tsui and Charles Crichton "Semantic Technologies in Electronic Government"
3. Cristiano Codagnone and Maria A. Wimmer (Eds.) "Road mapping e-government Research".
4. http://hdr.undp.org/nhdr1/docs/Toolkit_files/checklist_eng.pdf
5. White Paper on Municipal Service Partnerships (MSPs). Government Gazette. Vol. 418, No.21126, 26 April 2000. Notice 1689 of 2000. South Africa.
6. World Bank. 2002. World Development Report 2003. Washington, D. C.: World Bank. Worley International Ltd. *Strategic Municipal Asset Management*. Municipal Background Series No. 5. World Bank. April 2000.

SURVEY ON RELIABILITY EVALUATION WITH UML MODELS

MARTIN JEDLICKA

Faculty of Materials Science and Technology in Trnava, Slovak University of Technology, Paulínska 16, 917 24 Trnava, Slovak Republic

OLIVER MORAVCIK

Faculty of Materials Science and Technology in Trnava, Slovak University of Technology, Paulínska 16, 917 24 Trnava, Slovak Republic

PETER SCHREIBER

Faculty of Materials Science and Technology in Trnava, Slovak University of Technology, Paulínska 16, 917 24 Trnava, Slovak Republic

PAVOL TANUSKA

Faculty of Materials Science and Technology in Trnava, Slovak University of Technology, Paulínska 16, 917 24 Trnava, Slovak Republic

Today's software systems are developed and targeted for satisfying sometimes very critical functions. Reliability is considered to be one of the most important nonfunctional quality attribute of such software systems. The aim of reliability estimation in early stages of software development process – analysis and design – should reduce the future costs for possible failure repairing through increasing the reliability before the construction of the software system. Because, the Unified Modeling Language (UML) becomes the standard for software system's specification, the last works done in architecture based reliability estimation and assessment use UML as the base for software architecture specification. In this paper, we discuss the existing approaches with critical overview and outline the directions for future research.

1. Introduction

The role of satisfying of nonfunctional requirements is at least important as it is for functional requirements. The nonfunctional requirements are often evaluated in the end of the whole software development process which might cause the additional costs and also the inevitable requirement for redesigning the whole system architecture. Therefore, the evaluation of nonfunctional requirements at software architecture level should be the reason which could not be.

One of the most important non-functional requirements, which cannot be missed out when designing software system, is the reliability. The software reliability is the probability that a software system is performing successfully its required functions for the duration of a specific mission profile [5]. In the past years there were introduced several approaches to evaluate reliability of software systems. [5] The [7] presents that evaluating the reliability at the architecture level is possible.

2. UML and reliability

Unified Modeling Language (UML) becomes the standard for software system's specification. UML provides tools for modeling the software system architecture which is not dependent on programming language, programming techniques and human factor.

UML provides several types of diagram to model the software behavior and architecture. For the reliability evaluation purposes these following diagrams were used in the past:

1. Use Case diagram,
2. Sequence diagram,
3. Deployment diagram,
4. State chart diagram.

2.1. *Approach of Cortellessa et al.*

The approach [2] provides quite complex approach which evaluates the reliability of the whole system using Use Case diagrams, Sequence diagrams and Deployment diagrams.

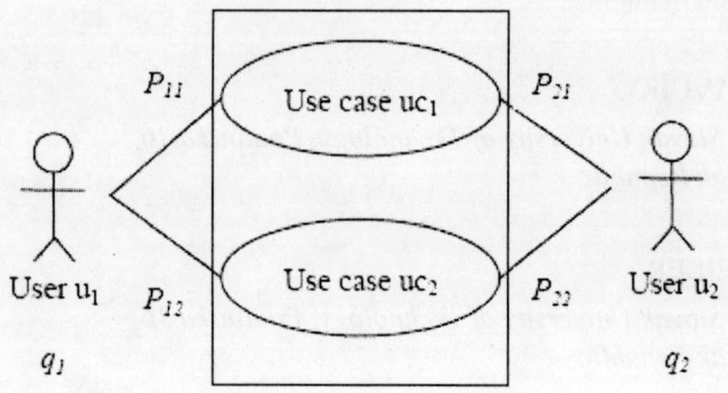

Figure. 1. Annotated Use Case Diagram

The approach presents the Use Case diagram is annotated as follows:

q1 and q2 represent the probabilities of requesting services from system for users u1 and u2

P11 and P12 represent that user u1 requests the functionality f1 represented by use case uc1 or f2 represented by use case uc2.

Then the probability of executing general use case x is:

$$P(x) = \sum_{i=1}^{m} q_i * P_{ix} \tag{1}$$

where m is the number of user types.

Then there is the assumption that for each use case there are specified all relevant Sequence Diagrams representing main scenarios each use case. These sequence diagrams have the non-uniform probability distribution according to following equation:

$$P(k_j) = p(j) * f_j(k) \tag{2}$$

where $f_j(k)$ is the frequency off the *k-th* overall the sequence diagrams referring to the j-th use case and parameter $P(k_j)$ represents the probability of a scenario execution.

In sequence diagram, the approach focuses on the interval where the component is busy. For example, in Figure 2 the interval, when component C_3 is busy, is between the moment when interaction l11 enters the component and interaction l_{22} leaves the component. The total number of busy periods off component C_3 is 2.

Then the estimate of the probability of failure θ_{ij} of the component C_i in the scenario j represents the next equation:

$$\theta_{ij} = 1 - (1 - \theta_{ij})^{bp_g} \tag{3}$$

where bp_{ij} the number of busy periods that component C_i has in the scenario j.

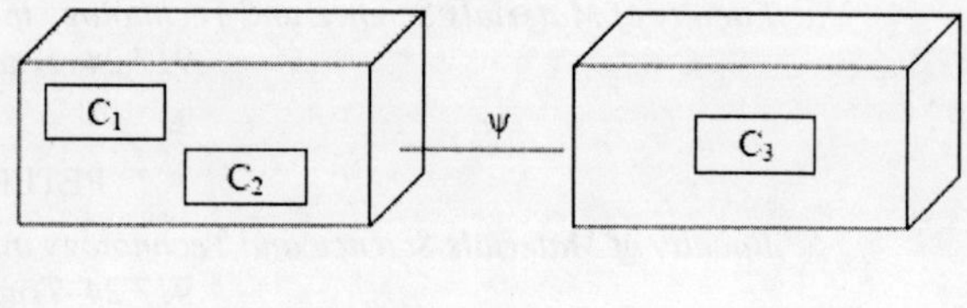

Figure. 2. Annotated Deployment Diagram

The deployment diagram in Figure 2 includes the same components from the sequence diagram. The subject of failure probability ψ_i is every communication between components *(l, m)* through the connector *i*. and *|Interact(l, m, j)|* represents the number of interactions between components l and m from the scenario (sequence diagram) j. e.g. there exist 2 interactions exchanged between C_2 and C_3 but only 1 interaction between C_1 and C_2.

Then the contribute ψ_{lmj} to the reliability of communication between all these components over the connector i in the scenario j is:

$$\theta_s = 1 - \sum_{j=1}^{K} p_j \left(\prod_{j=1}^{N} (1-\theta_{ij})^{bp_g} \cdot \prod_{lj} (1-\psi_{lij})^{|\mathit{interact}(lij)|} \right) \tag{4}$$

3. Approach of Rodrigues et al.

This approach can also be used in early stages of software development lifecycle for component-based systems. As basic modeling techniques, the scenarios and a Message Sequence Charts (MSC) are used [4]. The framework of the approach shows the Figure 3.

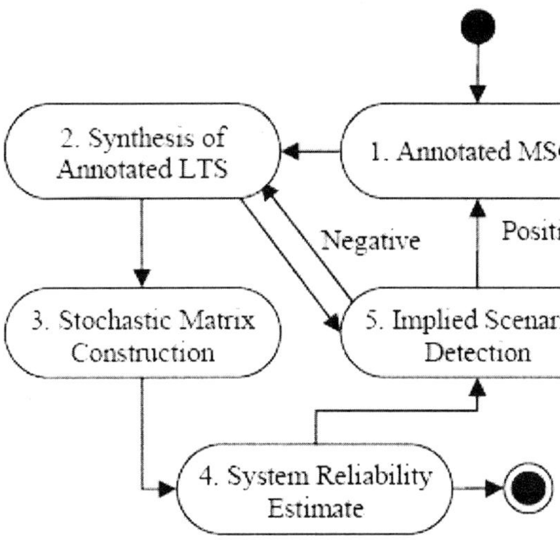

Figure 3. Framework

First step is annotation the MSCs with two kind probabilities:

Probability of transitions between scenarios PTSij

Reliability of the components RC.

PTS is simply the probability that scenario S_j will be executed after executing scenario S_i which value comes from an operational profile for the system [3]. It is annotated on High-level Message Sequence Charts (HMSC).

The component reliability R_C is the probability that component C will successfully perform its service which is invocated by message from another component. The execution time of the service is not significant for component reliability assessment. Component reliability is annotated on Basic Message Sequence Charts (BMSC).

Second step is to made synthesis of Labeled Transition System (LTS) from annotated scenarios. This step consists of several sub-steps to construct the architecture model of the system.

In the third step the architecture model is interpreted as Markov model. First the mapping of the probability weights from architecture model into a square transition matrix is constructed.

In the fourth step the Cheung approach [1] is used to determine the reliability prediction of the whole system.

In last step, the implied scenarios are searching. These scenarios can be found as the result of the fact that in the system there can exist such set of components that don't communicate exclusively through the interfaces described and that can exhibit via unspecified traces when running in parallel [6]. Founding of these scenarios has impact on step 1 and 2 of the approach's framework.

4. Conclusions

When comparing these 2 approaches, the first approach [2] evaluates the reliability of the system as whole, while the second one concern only the reliability of a component of the system. Both approaches take into account just little operational profile.

The present research made in this area shows that UML modeling techniques are applicable for reliability assessment of software.

We made also some thesis and assumptions:

- Sequence diagrams will be the core modeling technique for system architecture and behavior
- We assume that developing of new UML extensions will be necessary for reliability assessment
- Our new approach will combine traditional reliability techniques with UML modeling
- The whole process of our reliability assessment approach will be automatic as much as possible
- The new tool which will cover our approach will be developed
- The approach will be developed with focus on control systems software

In this paper we discuss the area of software reliability and its support in UML. We also introduce the today's main approaches and concepts in this area, make the short evaluation of them and outlook the basis of our future work in this area.

References

1. R. C. Cheung, *A User-Oriented Software Reliability Model,* IEEE Transactions on Software Engineering, vol. 6(2), pp. 118–125. (1980)
2. V. Cortellessa,, H. Singh, B. Cukic, B., *Early reliability assessment of UML based software models*, Proceedings of the 3rd international workshop on Software and performance, Rome, Italy, (2002).
3. J.D. Musa, *Operational profiles in software-reliability engineering*, IEEE Software, vol. 10, no. 2, pp. 14-32, (1993)
4. G.N.Rodrigues, D.S.Rosenblum, S. Uchitel, *Reliability prediction in model-driven development*, Proceedings of the 8th international conference

MoDELS pp. 339-354, Montego Bay, Jamaica, (2005).

5. M. Shooman. *Software Engineering Design/Reliability/Management.* McGraw-Hill, (1983).
6. S.Uchitel, J.Kramer, J.Magee, *Incremental Elaboration of Scenario-Based Specifications and Behavior Models Using Implied Scenarios*, ACM Transactions on Software Engineering and Methodologies, 2004, vol. 13, pp. 3785
7. A. Zarras, V. Issarny, *Assessing Software Reliability at the Architectural Level*, Proceedings of the 4th International Software Architecture Workshop (ISAW-4), Ireland, (2000).

MODELING MEASUREMENT FRAMEWORK WITH FEATURE ORIENTED FRAMEWORK MODELING LANGUAGE

TIANGE ZHANG XIAOCHUN XIAO HUAN WANG LEQIU QIAN

School of Computer Science, Fudan University
Shanghai, 200433, China

Object-oriented framework is recognized as an efficient reuse mechanism in software development, but for its intrinsic abstract and complex, it is still difficult to develop for framework designer. This is mainly due to the lack of framework modeling language that can guide the framework developer, user and tool builder. We introduce a feature oriented framework model language (FOFML) to provide an expressive way to model framework. Measurement systems are wildly applied and of increasing importance in various industry area. Most of measurement systems share much commonality with each other, so it is possible to build an object-oriented measurement framework for this domain. FOFML is used in modeling a measurement framework in this paper.

1. Introduction

A framework is a skeleton of set of applications that is directly related to a specific domain [1], it is an ideal reuse technology provides components that can be easily connected to make a new system. Framework technology has been successfully applied in several application domains [11][8], such as cellular communications, user interfaces, real-time avionics, and typical business applications. Automatic measurement as an important application domain, it is possible to build a measurement system framework.

The problem with framework is that development and framework instantiation are challenging. There are still few tools supporting framework development due to lack of formal framework model language. This paper introduces a feature oriented framework modeling language (FOFML) as an extension of UML metamodel. Framework can be modeled in a modular and compositional way. FOFML is based on our previous work [2] on Z notation based framework model. This model is further used to model a measurement framework.

Automatic measurement [11] and diagnoses is of increasingly importance for life-critical equipment. Data is first collected from running equipment through various sensors, measurement system will then analysis these data, report status of equipments. Most of measurement system have much in common and are expensive to construct, so it is necessary to reuse existing measurement system to improve productivity. There are several ways to improve the reusability of software system, among which framework is the most promising one.

The rest of the paper is organized as follows. In the next section gives the definitions for basic conceptions such as framework, feature, role etc. Section 3 gives the example of measurement framework modeled in FOFML. Finally we exams some related work in this area and summarize this paper.

2. FOFML Metamodel

FOFML is a metamodel defined by MOF [4] meta-meta model. It is an extension of UML metamodel [4], which makes it easy to integrate industry standards and reuse existing tools. Framework developer can define a framework feature model using UML and FOFML, then application developer can define instantiation model as instance of framework feature model. The instantiation model can be serve as input of a generator, be transformed to the final application source.

Figure 1 shows the metamodel of FOFML. Grey colored boxes are meta-classes from UML metamodel.

Framework Feature. Feature model [9] is one of domain analysis method wildly accepted in product-line software engineering (PLSE). PLSE Feature is defined as a prominent and distinctive user visible characteristic of a system. It is building block of feature model. It provides a parameterize mechanism for modeling product family. Framework is similar to product line software in that they all try to identify commonality and variability in a domain, but PLSE feature is not sufficient for framework modeling because more complicated parameterize mechanism is necessary in framework modeling case. Here we adopted a modified feature concept named as framework feature. It contain important framework specific concepts, such as hot-spots [7], role [12].

A framework Feature is a subclass of Classifier from UML metamodel. It describes structure of roles and properties. Each role performs some specialized functions necessary for the feature, and each property specifies some properties of the feature, they collectively specify some desired functionality of the framework.

Framework feature can also reuse other framework features form same or different framework by extension them or declaring references to them.

Sub-Feature. Features can be further organized in a hierarchy structure for modularity purpose. Feature can have sub-features. For example, a Calculator can own a sub-feature named as Guard that indicate whether it has a lower and upper value.

Framework. Framework is defined as subclass of Package from UML metamodel. So it can be container of other Packageable model elements such as classes, interfaces and their relationships. It can also contain properties necessary for its instantiation, such as title, deployment descriptors and so on, so framework is also defined as a subclass of Classifier which can own properties.

The most important part of a framework is that it can own framework features.

Framework need to be integrated with one another in large scale application development, so FOFML support frameworks import mechanism.

Role. A Role performs a specialized function for a feature. The concept of collaboration role is widely adopted by most of works on framework and design pattern modeling[4][6][12]. Type of role should be MetaType which is defined below.

Meta Type. Instance of a MetaType is a normal type from UML metamodel. It is associated with a collection of types. ClassifierType is used to model role type as a specific MetaType, whose instance is subclasses of a Classifier. Because MetaType and MetaClassifier will be used heavily, we introduce a symbol @ into our concrete syntax to represent them, where @[Integer, Float] define a type whose instance is an Integer type or a Float type, and @Thread define a type whose instance is one of sub-class of Thread, @Object represents all classes in an object-oriented language system.

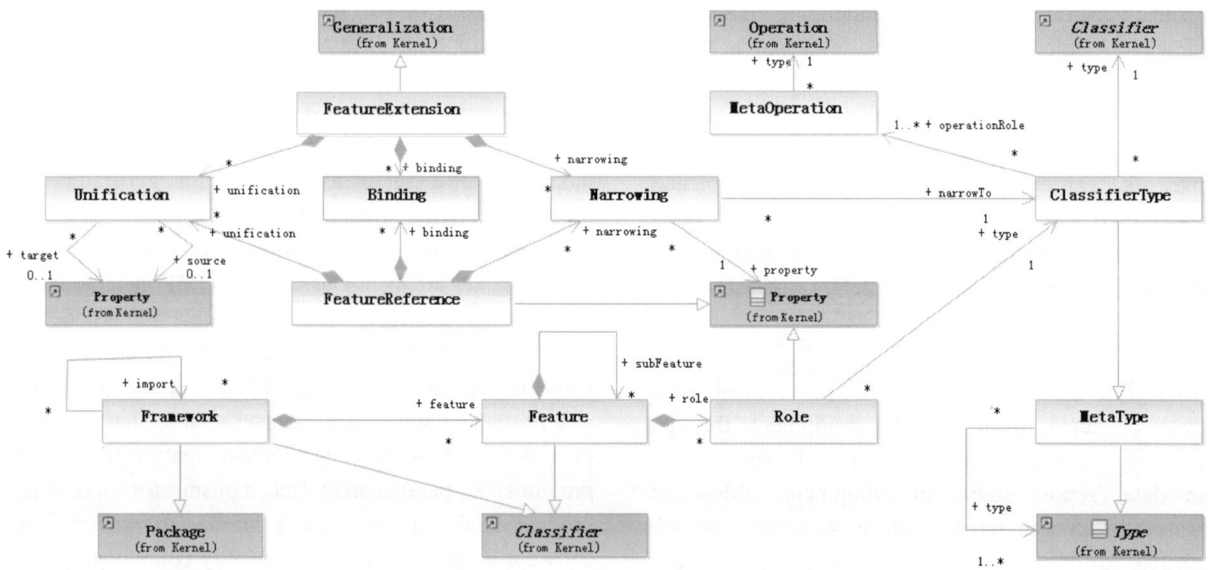

Figure 1. FOFML Metamodel

Meta Operation.- Hot spots are modeled by MetaOperation in our model. They are owned by MetaClassifier. An instance of MetaOperation is an implementation of an operation. For example, @AClassifier.anOperation is a type whose instance is implementer of operation with signature AClassifier::anOperation. Instance of @Thread.run is an operation that overrides run operation declared in class Thread.

Narrowing. As we had defined, @AClassifier is a type whose instance is one of subclasses of AClassifier. Sometimes, a property of @AClassifier should be further restrict to a more concrete type, for example, @BClassifier, where BClassifier is a subclass of AClassifier. We use narrowing operation to define this constraint.

A narrowing specifies that a type should be 'narrow to' a new type which is more concrete than the original one. We use notation □* to represent narrowing constraint in concrete syntax. Here is an example:

calculator : @ICalcuoator;

calculator □ @IQuerableCalculator;*

The original type of calculator is @ICalcuoator, narrowing expression will constraint its type from @ICalcuoator to @IQuerableCalculator. IQuerableCalculator should be subclass of ICalculator.

Narrowing is usually used in framework feature extension.

Binding. Assigning a role or a property to a value or instance of the corresponding type is a binding. If each role and property of a feature is bind to its instance, it is a full binding. Otherwise, it is a partial valued feature. A partial valued feature is still a feature which is to be instantiated by additional binding operation.

We use normal assignment to represent binding operation. Here is an example:

calculator = FrictionCalculator

It means that the calculator role will be played by concrete class FrictionCalculator which is an implementer of IQuerableCalculator.

Unification. Binding a role or property to another role or property is an operation called unification. The unification operation role1 = role2 states that the values of role1 and role2 should be equal.

We use normal assignment to represent unification too, just same as binding does. Here is an example:

```
Feature Device{
   name:String;
  persister: ClassMapping [ (1)
     tableName = this.name; (2)
   ];
}
```

Feature Device will reference another feature named as ClassMapping(1) to implement its functionality. (2) is unification operation come along with this feature reference. It states that tableName property of referenced feature should be unified with name of Device feature.

Narrowing, binding and unification can be used to redefine a feature before reuse it. Just as had said, we support two kinds of reuse: reuse by extension and reuse by reference.

Feature Extension. Framework users (application developers) may want to extend the existing framework for their specific requirements. We model Feature Extension as a subclass of Generalization from UML metamodel. So the semantics of feature extension is same as class generalization concept except that it can include additional constraints such as binding, unification or narrowing.

Feature Reference. A feature can reference to other features as its properties. Just as normal property, property of feature type can use multiplicity to specify the allowable cardinalities for an instantiation of this feature, such as optional [0..1], mandatory[1] or collection[0..*] etc.

3. Modeling Measurement Framework With FOFML

Measurement systems [11] are a class of systems used to measure the relevant values of equipment. A measurement system is used for quality control on produced products that can then be used to separate acceptable from unacceptable products or to categorize the products in quality categories. In some systems, the results from the measurement are stored in case in the future the need arises to refer to this information.

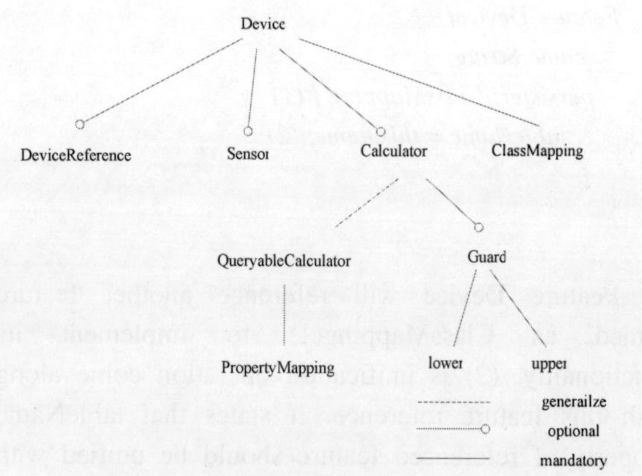

Figure 2. Feature model for measurement framework

As descript above, we adopted a modified feature model to descript high level abstraction of framework. Figure 2 is a feature model diagram providing an outline view for measurement framework. A Device can contain parts or sub-devices which are modeled as DeviceReference, and some Sensors can be installed on the device to collect their running data. Calculators are responsible to calculate running status of a part or whole device. QueryableCalculator is a generalized Calculator which will be persisted to external database for later use.

Normal feature model is typically used in product-line modeling. It provided a parameterize mechanism for decrypting product family. Application of a product-line can be assembled from existing components, but application of a framework is usually constructed by building missing components. It is not sufficient for framework modeling because more complicated parameterize mechanism is needed. For example, when MeasurementFramework is instantiated, we should not only decide what kind of Calculator should be included in a device, but also implement the ICalculator interface following corresponding constraints.

So the feature model should be further enriched by model elements defined in FOFML introduced in section 2. Following is measurement framework defined in FOFML.

```
Framework MeasurementFramework{                    1
    Import Persistence as p;                       2
    Feature Device{                                3
        name:String;
        device: @IDevice;
        sensors[0..*]:Sensor;
        parts[0..*]: DeviceReference;
        parameters[0..*]: Parameter;
        persister: p.ClassMapping [                4
            tableName = this.name;
        ];
        calc[0..*]: Calculator;
    }
    Feature DeviceReference{
        device: Device;
        lower: Integer;
        upper: Integer;
    }
    Feature Sensor{
        sensor: @ISensor;
        parameters[0..*]: Parameter;
    }
    Feature Calculator{
        id: String;                                5
        desc: String;

        type: @[Float, Float[0..*]]                6
        calc: @ICalculator[id=this.id]{            7
            object getValue();                     8
        };

        parameters[0..*]: Parameter;               9
        targetDevice:Device;
        SubFeature Guard[0..1]{                    10
            lower[0..1]: Float;
            upper[0..1]: Float;
        }
    }
    Feature QueryableCalculator extends Calculator[   11
        calc →* @IQuerableCalculator;                 12
    ]{
        persister: p.PropertyMapping[
            persister.column =id;
            persister.property.owner = device.persister;
            persister.property.name=id;
            persister.property.type=type;
        ];
    }
    Feature Parameter{
        name: String;
        type: @[Integer,Float];
    }
    Interface ICalculator{                         13
        id: String;
        object getValue();
        boolean isViolated();
    }
    Interface IQuerableCalculator{
        void save();
        void load();
    }
    Interface Sensor{
    ......
    }
    Interface IDevice{
    ......
    }
}
Framework PersistenceFramework{                    14
    Feature ClassMapping{
        target : @Object;
        tableName: String;
        propertyMapping[0..*]: PropertyMapping;
    }
    Feature PropertyMapping{
        owner: ClassMapping;
        column:String
        description:String;
        property:@Property;
    }
}
```

There are two kinds of elements in a feature oriented framework model (1): framework import (2) and feature definitions (3). Because FOFML is an extension to UML, it can contain UML elements such as interfaces and classes definitions as well (13).

A framework feature contains properties (5,6), roles (7), sub-features (10) and feature references (9). Hot spots are defined by MetaOperation (8) contained in MetaClasifier (7), which means that instance of a Calculator should implement interface IClaculator and its operation getValue().

Feature can be extended (11) to contain new properties and functionalities. Constraints such as narrowing or unifications(12) can be defined to refine the extension.

Feature can reference features defined in other frameworks. In our example, Device feature reference a ClassMapping feature (4) that is defined in an imported PersistenceFramework(14). Framework importing can make it possible to reuse other frameworks and tools of associated with these frameworks, such as generators, wizards.

A measurement system for well elevating conveyor had been successfully built based on the measurement framework model.

4. Conclusion & Related Work

This paper introduces an extension of UML metamodel for feature oriented framework modeling, a case study on measurement framework is provided. A number of works have been adopted for this field.

Mohamed E. Fayad et al collected many examples of framework in industry in [8]. Jan Bosch [11] studied measurement framework in his work. These examples show how application frameworks are used in various industry areas. But most of these works focus on frameworks construction using low level OO techniques, such as hot-spots, design pattern. High level modeling language is necessary to model complex frameworks.

Nadia Bouassida et al.[3] propose a language as an UML extension for frameworks modeling, its formal semantic is defined using Object-Z. They focus on the modeling of the hot-spots, which is first introduced by Wolfgang Pree[7]. Hot-spots are implemented through hook classes and hook methods, which are modeled by MetaClassifier and MetaOperation in our work.

Antkiewicz, M. et al[13] present a framework-specific modeling language approach to modeling and instantiation framework, it use feature model to descript functional requirements of framework. Some works using use case diagram in [3]. We chose feature model and make it a compositional unit to define new features.

Roles are often used in describing patterns [4][6] and frameworks [12]. Role in our model is modeled as MetaType in out model.

Overall, this work contributes a modular and compositional way to model important concepts for object-oriented framework, Tools can be built based on it to guide the development and instantiation of framework.

References

1. Ralph E. Johnson: ‘Components, Frameworks, Patterns’, Proceedings of the 1997 symposium on Software reusability
2. Tiange zhang, ‘Modeling Object-Oriented Framework with Z’, 2008 International Symposium on Computer Science and Computational Technology (ISCSCT 2008)
3. N. Bouassida,H. Ben-Abdallah,F. Gargouri,A. B. Hamadou, ‘Formalizing the Framework Design Language F-UML’, Proceedings of the First International Conference on Software Engineering and Formal Methods (SEFM'03)
4. Meta Object Facility (MOF) Core Specification, V2.0 , OMG, 2006
5. Unified Modeling Language(UML), Superstructure, V2.1.2, OMG, 2007
6. [6]Gamma, E., Helm, R., Johnson, R., and Vlissides, J.: ‘Design patterns: elements of reusable object-oriented systems’ , Addison-Wesley, 1995
7. W. Pree, ‘Hot-Spot-Driven Framework Development’ , http://www.softwareresearch.net/site/publications/J016.pdf
8. Mohamed E. Fayad,Ralph E. Johnson, ‘Domain-Specific Application Frameworks: Frameworks Experience by Industry’, John Wiley & Sons, 2000
9. Kwanwoo Lee,Kyo Chul Kang,Jaejoon Lee, ‘Concepts and Guidelines of Feature Modeling for Product Line Software Engineering’, Proceedings of the 7th

International Conference on Software Reuse: Methods, Techniques, and Tools,2002
10. Peter Van Roy, Seif Haridi: 'Concepts, Techniques, and Models of Computer Programming', MIT Press, 2004
11. Jan Bosch,'An Object-Oriented Framework for Measurement Systems', Research Report, Blekinge Institute of Technology
12. Dirk Riehle,Thomas Gross, 'Role Model Based Framework Design and Integration', ACM OOPSLA' 98, Pages:117-133
13. Antkiewicz, M., Czarnecki, K.: 'Framework-Specific Modeling Languages with round-trip engineering', MoDELS, Lecture Notes in Computer Science, vol. 4199, pp.692-706 (2006)

PERFORMANCE ANALYSIS OF ELLIPTIC AND HYPERELLIPTIC CURVE CRYPTOSYSTEM

GANESAN R

Senior Lecturer, Department of MCA, PSG College of Art and Science, Coimbatore-14, Tamilnadu, India.

DR. VIVEKANANDAN K

Faculty Member, Govt. College of Technology
IBRA, Sultanate of OMAN

It has recently been reported that elliptic and hyperelliptic curve cryptography are the two public key cryptographic techniques used to implement the cryptosystems more efficiently and effectively. Many researches are being done to implement these in both hardware and software fields. In this paper, we discuss the basic concepts of elliptic and hyperelliptic curves. We describe the algorithms for private key, public key generation, encryption and decryption for both elliptic curve and hyperelliptic curve cryptosystem. Also, the performance of both elliptic and hyperelliptic curve cryptosystem are demonstrated. Finally, the comparative study between these two is analyzed.

1. Introduction

1.1. *Producing Hard Copy Using MS-Word*

Cryptography is the branch of cryptology dealing with the design of algorithms for encryption and decryption, intended to ensure the secrecy and/or authenticity of messages. This cryptography is classified into symmetric and asymmetric cryptography based on the number of keys involved in it. The former is the one form of cryptosystem, where the encryption and decryption are performed using the same key which is otherwise called as secret key. The latter one is the another form of cryptosystem, where the encryption and decryption are performed using two different keys in which one is referred to as the public key and another one is referred to as the private key.

In this paper, we mainly deal with the public key cryptosystem. There are many algorithms which are designed based on the public key cryptography. Some of them are RSA algorithm, Diffie-Hellman Key Exchange, Elliptic Curve Cryptography (ECC) and Hyperelliptic Curve Cryptography (HECC). Many researches are still going on based on the ECC and HECC. This paper mainly deals with the ECC and HECC.

2. What is Elliptic Curve?

We start with a principal definition of the concept of an elliptic curve. An Elliptic curve E over a field K denoted by E/K is given by Weierstrass equation **[1]**

$$E: y^2 + a_1xy + a_3y = x^3 + a_2x^2 + a_4x + a_6$$

here the coefficients $a_1, a_2, a_3, a_4, a_6 \in K$ are such that for each point (x_1,y_1) with coordinates on $\overline{K}$ satisfying the above equation , the partial derivatives $2y_1 + a_1x_1 + a_3$ and $3x_1^2 + 2a_2x_1 + a_4 - a_1y_1$ do not vanish simultaneously. The last condition says that an Elliptic Curve is non-singular or smooth. A point on a curve is called singular if both partial derivatives vanish.

2.1. *Elliptic Curve Over Finite Field F_p*

In this subtopic, the author considers elliptic curves over finite prime fields. As they should be used in cryptographic applications, assume p to be large, hence at least p>3. In characteristics p > 3, one can always take for E, an equation of the form **[10]**

$$\mathbf{E: y^2 = x^3 + a_4x + a_6}$$

Where a_4 , a_6 are in F_p . Choose 2 non-negative integers a_4 and a_6, less than p that satisfy $4a_4^3 + 27a_6^2 \pmod p \neq 0$. The $E_p(a_4,a_6)$ denotes the elliptic group mod p whose elements (x,y) are pairs of non-negative integer less than p satisfying $y^2 \equiv x^3 + a_4x + a_6 \pmod p$ together with the point at infinity **O**. Consider the total number of points together with the point at infinity as #**N.**

3. Arithmetic of Elliptic Curve Defined Over F_p

The rules for addition over $E_p(a_4,a_6)$ can be stated as follows for all points $P,Q \in E_p(a_4,a_6)$: **[10]**

i) $P + o = P$

ii) if $P = (x,y)$ then $P + (x, -y) = o$. The point (x,-y) is the negative of P denoted as –P . Observe that (x,-y) is a point on the elliptic curve.

iii) If $P=(x_1,y_1)$ and $Q=(x_2,y_2)$ with $P \neq -Q$ then $P+Q = (x_3,y_3)$ is determined by the following rules:

$$X_3 = \lambda^2 - x_1 - x_2 \pmod p$$
$$Y_3 = \lambda(x_1-x_3) - y_1 \pmod p$$
Where $\lambda = y_2-y_1/x_2-x_1$ if $P \neq Q$
$$\lambda = 3x_1^2 + a / 2y_1 \text{ if } P = Q$$

iv) Multiplication is defined as repeated addition.

4. Keys generation (Public Key /Private Key) in ECC

In order to generate keys, first we have to find out one Base Point (G) from the group of Elliptic Curve Points. The Base Point can be generated as follows: **[8]**

- Find out the large prime factor (k) for the total number of points (**#N**) in the elliptic curve group $E_p(a_4,a_6)$.
- Compute kP where P is the elliptic curve point in group $E_p(a_4,a_6)$.
- If kP = o then one can consider that P as a Base Point (G) for the key generation process.

4.1. *Algorithm for Keys generation: [4]*

Input : Public parameters (G , E , p)
Output : Public key P_A and private key a_A

1. $a_A \in_R N$ [choose a_A as random prime number in N]
2. $P_A \longleftarrow [a_A]G$ [The form of P_A is a Point in the group $E_p(a_4,a_6)$]
3. return P_A and a_A

For the random prime number generation in step 1, one can apply the Rabin-Miller Primality Test **[9]** or AKS Primality Test algorithm **[3]**.

5. Elliptic Curve Encryption/Decryption

In this section, the first task is to encode the plain text message m to be sent as a (x,y) point P_m . It is the point P_m that will be encrypted as a cipher text and subsequently decrypted. Note that we cannot simply encode the message as the x or y coordinate of a point, because not all such coordinates are in elliptic curve group $E_p(a_4,a_6)$. For encryption and decryption, we are considering ElGamal techniques **[4]**. This technique requires some global parameters. Base Point G and an Elliptic group $E_p(a_4,a_6)$ are the global parameters for the encryption. To encrypt the message, the technique works as follows:

To encrypt and send a message to B, A performs the following steps.

- $k \in_R N$ (choose k as a random positive prime number)
- $Q \longleftarrow [k]G$
- $P_k \longleftarrow [k]P_B$ (P_B is receiver's public key)
- $C_m \longleftarrow \{ Q , P_m + P_k \}$ (C_m is the Cipher Text and sent as a Point)

To decrypt message, the ElGamal Decryption technique works as follows:

To decrypt the Cipher Text C_m , B extracts the first coordinate 'Q' from the cipher text then multiply with its Private Key (a_B) and subtract the result from the second coordinate. This can be written as follows,

$$P_m + kP_B - a_B(Q) = P_m + kP_B - a_B(kG) = P_m + kP_B - k(a_B G) = P_m + kP_B - kP_B = P_m$$

In order to perform the above process, we need to apply the various operations like multiplication of points, addition of points, and negative of a point.

A has masked the message P_m by adding kP_B to it. Nobody but A knows the value of k, so even though P_B is a public key, nobody can remove the mask kP_B. For an attacker to remove message, the attacker would have to compute k from the given G and [k]G i.e. Q, which is assumed very hard.

6. What is Hyperelliptic Curve?

For cryptographic purpose we concentrate on imaginary quadratic hyper elliptic curve given by an equation **[6]**
$C : y^2 + h(x)y = f(x),\ h,f \in K[x], deg(f)=2g+1, deg(h) \leq g$*, f is monic*

where genus (g) = (deg(f)-1)/2 is called a hyper elliptic curve of genus g over K if no point on the curve over the algebraic closure of K satisfies both partial derivatives 2y+h=0 and f′- h′y=0. The last condition ensures that the curve is non-singular. The negative of a point P=(x,y) is given by –P=(x,-y-h(x)). Elliptic curves are Hyper elliptic curves of genus 1. Hyper elliptic curves exist from genus 1 to infinity. For Hyper elliptic curves of genus $g \geq 2$, there is no natural groups law on C(K). We can't add points like we do on an elliptic curve as the points on hyper elliptic curve don't form a group. A group law is defined via the **Jacobian** variety of C over a field, which is **finite abelian group**.

Hyper Elliptic Curve Over Finite Field F_p is defined as follows,

$C: y^2 + h(x)y = f(x) (\text{mod } p)$, $h, f \in K[x]$, $\deg(f)=2g+1, \deg(h) \leq g$, f is monic, where genus (g) = $(\deg(f)-1)/2$ is called a hyper elliptic curve of genus g over Finite Field p.

7. Jacobian of Hyper Elliptic Curve

The Jacobian of the curve C **[2]** is the quotient group $J=D°/P$, where D° is the set of Divisors of degree zero, and P is the set of Divisors of rational functions. The equivalence classes of the Jacobian are each represented by a unique reduced divisor upon which we perform group law. The Hyper elliptic curve Discrete Logarithm problem is then: Let F_q be a finite field with q elements. Given 2 divisors, D_1 and D_2 in the Jacobian, determine $m \in Z$, such that $D_2=mD_1$.

MumFord representation **[6]**: Let C is a hyperelliptic curve and g is a genus of C. Each nontrivial divisor class over K can be represented via a unique pair of polynomials u(x) and v(x), $u,v \in K[x]$, where

- u is monic
- $\deg v < \deg u \leq g$
- $u | v^2+vh-f$

Let $D=\Sigma_{i=1..r} P_i - rP_\infty$, where $P_i \neq P_\infty$, $P_i \neq P_j$ for $i \neq j$ and $r \leq g$. Put $P_i = (x_i, y_i)$. Then the Divisor class of D is represented by

$u(x) = \pi_{i=1..r} (x-x_i)$ and if P_i occurs n_i times then $(d/d_x)^j [v(x)^2+v(x)h(x)-f(x)]=0 | x=x_i$, for $0 \leq j \leq n_i - 1$.

A divisor at most g points in the support satisfying $P_i \neq P_\infty$, $P_i \neq P_j$ for $i \neq j$ is called a reduced divisor. The first part states that each class can be represented by a reduced divisor. The second part means that for all point $P_i = (x_i, y_i)$ occurring in D we have $u(x_i)=0$ and third condition guarantees that $v(x_i)=y_i$ with appropriate multiplicity. We denote the class D represented by u(x) and v(x) by [u(x),v(x)]. This Divisor (D) can be act as a generator for the following key generation process like base point (G) in ECC.

8. Keys (Public Key/Private Key) generation in HECC:

Algorithm for keys (Public key/Private key) generation **[4]**:

Input: The public parameters are Hyperelliptic curve C, Prime p and Divisor D

Output: The Public key P_A and Private key a_A

1. $a_A \in_R N$ [choose a_A as random prime number in N]
2. $P_A \longleftarrow [a_A]D$ [The form of P_A is (u(x),v(x)) representation]
3. return P_A and a_A

For the random prime number generation in step 1, one can apply the Rabbin-Miller Primality Test or AKS Primality Test algorithm.

9. Hyper elliptic Curve Encryption / Decryption

In this section, the message 'm' to be sent will be encoded as a (u(x),v(x)) representation. The encoded message is referred as E_m. For the encryption and decryption process, we are again going to consider the ElGamal Encryption/Decryption technique **[4]**. The ElGamal encryption technique works as follows: To encrypt and send a message to B, A performs the following steps.

- $k \in_R N$ (choose k as a random positive prime number in N)
- $Q \longleftarrow [k]D$ (D is the Divisor of the HEC & the form of Q is (u(x),v(x)))
- $P_k \longleftarrow [k]P_B$ (P_B :(u(x),v(x)) is receiver's public key)
- $C_m \longleftarrow \{ Q, P_m + P_k \}$ (C_m :(u(x),v(x)) is the Cipher Text)

To decrypt message, the ElGamal Decryption technique works as follows:

To decrypt the Cipher Text C_m, B extracts the first coordinate 'Q' from the cipher text then multiply with its Private Key (a_B) and subtract the result from the second coordinate. This can be written as follows,

$P_m + kP_B - a_B (Q) = P_m + kP_B - a_B (kD) = P_m + kP_B - k(a_B D) = P_m + kP_B - kP_B = P_m$

In order to perform the above process, we have to apply the various operations like Divisor Multiplication (nD), Divisor Addition (D_1+D_2), Negation of a Divisor (-D). In the above process, A has masked the message P_m by adding kP_B to it. Except A, nobody knows the value of k, so even though P_B is a public key, nobody can remove the mask kP_B. For an attacker to remove message, the attacker would have to compute k from the given D and [k]D i.e. Q, which is assumed very hard.

10. Applications and Reasons for ECC and HECC

Nowadays, the need for ECC and HECC are widespread in the applications like e-commerce, m-commerce and embedded systems where the security plays a vital role.

The following are the reasons for why ECC and HECC are required and why it can be the best alternative compared to RSA.

- Both ECC and HECC are based on Discrete Logarithm Problems (*DLP*) which is very hard to break
- The length of the key size for performing the encryption and decryption is very minimal compared to any other public-key cryptographic techniques. The following table shows the recommended key size for the various cryptographic techniques which is suggested by the National Institute of Standards Technology (*NIST*).

Table 1: NIST Recommended Key sizes

Stallings [10] states that the computational complexity for breaking the elliptic-curve cryptosystem for an elliptic curve key size of 150 bits is 3.8 x 10^{10} MIPS (Million Instructions Per Second years). From table 1 it

Symmetric Key Size (bits)	RSA Key Size (bits)	Elliptic Curve Key Size (bits)	Hyperelliptic Curve Key Size (genus=2) (bits)
80	1024	160	80
112	2048	224	***
128	3072	256	***
192	7680	384	***
256	15360	521	***

is clear that HECC is better than ECC and RSA in terms of key sizes. The HECC asymmetric-key cryptography with 80 bit key length performs well and provides more security when compared to the RSA's 1024 bit key length and ECC's 160 bit key length.

11. Performance Analysis of ECC and HECC

Performance of ECC and HECC as asymmetric key cryptography technique is tested by designing a digital envelope which comprises AES as symmetric key cryptography along with either ECC or HECC as asymmetric cryptography. Table 2 provides details on the time taken (Milliseconds) for encryption & decryption of 128 bit AES key and MD5 message digest using ECC and HECC.

Table 2: Time in Milliseconds for Encryption & Decryption of 128 bit AES key and MD5 message digest using ECC and HECC

	Encryption (*ECC*)	Decryption (*ECC*)	Encryptio n (*HECC*)	Decryption (*HECC*)
128 bit AES key	123	130	121	120
MD5 Message digest of the Ciphertext	102	134	100	120

The following figure gives the graphical output of the results.

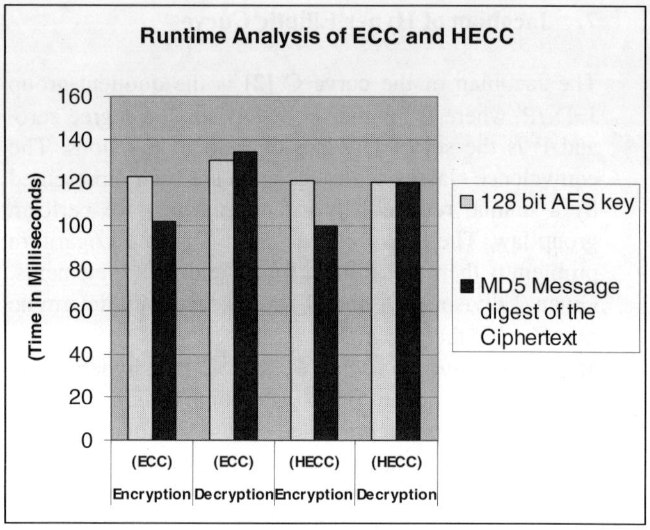

Figure 1: Runtime Analysis of ECC & HECC

Figure 1 clearly demonstrates that *HECC is better than ECC* for encryption and decryption processes.

12. Comparison between ECC and HECC

Many researches have been done using ECC and HECC. The working performances of these in the software and embedded (hardware) area have been compared. In this section we are highlighting that the performance of HECC is better than the ECC based on following statements. Roberto M.Avanzi **[5]** has stated that the performance of hyper-elliptic curves over prime fields is satisfactory enough to be considered as a valid alternative to elliptic curves, especially when large point groups are desired, and the bit length of the characteristic is close to (but smaller than) a multiple of the machine word length. Wollinger T's **[7]** contribution clearly shows that HECC - as equal alternative to ECC - can be the cryptosystem of choice for future embedded security applications.

13. Conclusion

In this paper, we have presented the fundamental concepts of Elliptic curve and hyperelliptic curve. Also, we have explained the working principle of ECC and HECC. Finally, we have analyzed the performance of both the ECC and HECC.

References

1. Christophe Doche and Tanja Lange, "Arithmetic of elliptic curves – chapter 13" from "Handbook of Elliptic and Hyper elliptic curve cryptography" by Henri cohen, Gerhard Frey, Chapman and Hall/CRC, Taylor and Francis Group.
2. Colm O Eigeartaigh, "A comparison of point counting methods for Hyper elliptic curve over prime fields and field of characteristics of 2", School of computing, Dublin City University, Dublin, Ireland
3. Roberto M.Avanzi and Henri Hohen, "Compositeness and Primality Testing Factoring – Chapter 25" from "Handbook of Elliptic and Hyper elliptic curve cryptography" by Henri cohen, Gerhard Frey, Chapman and Hall/CRC, Taylor and Francis Group
4. Roberto M.Avanzi and Tanja Lange, "Introduction to Public key cryptography – Chapter 1" from "Handbook of Elliptic and Hyper elliptic curve cryptography" by Henri cohen, Gerhard Frey, Chapman and Hall/CRC, Taylor and Francis
5. Roberto Maria Avanzi, "Aspects of hyperelliptic curves over large prime fields in software implementations", Institute for Experimental Mathematics (IEM), Ellernstrasse 29, D-45326 Essen, Germany, December 17, 2003.
6. Sylvain Duquesne and Tanja Lange, "Arithmetic of Hyper elliptic curves – Chapter 14" from "Handbook of Elliptic and Hyper elliptic curve cryptography" by Henri cohen, Gerhard Frey, Chapman and Hall/CRC, Taylor and Francis Group
7. Thomas Wollinger, Jan Pelzl, Volker Wittelsberger, And Christof Paar, "Elliptic & Hyperelliptic Curves on Embedded Microprocessor", ACM Special issue Security and Embedded Systems, March 2003.
8. Thompson SM, "An introduction to Elliptic curve cryptosystems", 1998, National Westminster Bank Plc.
9. Tong Jin, "Researching and Implementing on AKS Algorithm", University of Bath, May 2005
10. William Stallings, "Cryptography and Network Security, Principles and Practice", 2nd Edition, Pearson Education.

VOIP IN WIFI : QOS ENHANCEMENT BY CODEC SWITCHING

RAJINA M A RAJ MOHAMED, OSMAN MOHD SAID, KHONG NENG CHOONG, CHENG SUAN LEE, NURHAIZI HAMZAH

IMS Lab, Wireless Communication, MIMOS Berhad, Technology Park Malaysia
Kuala Lumpur, 57000, Malaysia

The rapid growth of internet technology and its infrastructure leads to high demand of VoIP. With a multitude of wireless access technologies such as GPRS, WiFi, WiMAX and 3G, the internet-based services such as VoIP can be experienced while being mobile. However, despite the telcos and service providers continue to upgrade their network capacity and accessibility (i.e. by introducing WiFi access points in some urban areas), it is still insufficient to support the high demand of multimedia traffic due to traffic congestion. And, since VoIP packets are delay sensitive, traffic congestion could easily affect the performance of a VoIP session. To address such issue, VoIP application should be enhanced with the capability of switching codec where each codec operates at different bitrate as to stay functional at different traffic conditions. In this paper, we describe a SIP-based traffic congestion scenario in a WiFi network and explain how codec switching helps users to stay connected on their calls with less VoIP performance degradation.

1. Introduction

The rapid growth of internet technology and its infrastructure leads to high demand of VoIP. With a multitude of wireless access technologies such as GPRS, WiFi, WiMAX and 3G, the internet-based services such as VoIP can be experienced while being mobile. Customers able to continue accessing VoIP regardless of location, terminal and independent of network access.

One of the main issue need to addressed in deploy of VoIP is how much bandwidth which is available, which will affect the choice of voice codec, packetization period, and where to use compression to best meet the service goals [10]. Since VoIP is delay-sensitive application, traffic congestion could easily affect the performance of VoIP sessions. Traffic congestion means high bandwidth utilization. Hence, it is crucial to provide good codec switching mechanism and this can be achieved by having the ability to switch codec at multiple rates at different traffic conditions.

In this paper we describe a codec switching procedure for VoIP under traffic congestion to maintain good VoIP session calls. The remainder of this paper is organized as follows. Sections two discuss the related works, section three we explain on the Codec Switching. Finally we discuss about the conclusion.

2. QoS: Provisioning

QoS provisioning for VoIP is of paramount importance in deploying VoIP in both wired and wireless network. There can be many levels of QoS that can be experienced by a user. For VoIP users, QoS is all about guaranteeing that voice traffic not delayed or dropped due network congestion. Many factors can degrade voice quality over IP such as latency, packet loss and network jitter and it leading to distorted audio and even will breakdown the VoIP communication. Thus, VoIP traffic requires minimum QoS guarantee from the network to meet its stringent bandwidth, delayed and jitter requirement [6]. Quality of Service (QoS) must be maintained across wired and wireless networks to ensure that delay-sensitive VoIP receives consistent and high priority end-to-end communication to provide optimal call quality.

As wireless networks are prone to channel error [12], maintaining a good QoS level for VoIP is not an easy process. The challenges must be tackled in delivering a framework to support efficient and effective switching in maintaining quality of services:

- The switching must be intelligently triggered to ensure that an application-specific QoS is not significantly affected.
- Thought must be given on determining which type of switching to take place at different conditions, i.e. considering the network traffic status as well as the user/application preferences.

There have been a few previous studies focusing on switching scheme and handover to ensure QoS maintain in good level for VoIP services. [8], introduced a mobile adaptive terminal architecture as an interface for flexible use of various network resources. [12], had implemented end-to-end based QoS, provisioning approach for all an-IP networks in order to provide users with a better quality of conversation and better utilization of network resources. [9], analyzed the handover performance of VoIP sessions in wireless overlay 802.11 WLAN and GPRs/UMTS networks when mobility is when mobility is handled at the application layer by SIP. [4], Introduce CapProbe to switch media codec when needed to enjoy real time communication although when they face resource heterogeneity. Two important criterias need to count into consideration in VoIP deployment:

2.1. *Codec Selection*

In VoIP, a COder-DECoder (also known as encoder/decoder or Compresion-decompression) is necessary. The network needs a way to be able to convert the voice into format that it can transport [14]. VoIP transmits voice data packets in a compressed form, so that the transmission of data packet is more lighter and thus improve the service performance. Table 1 lists some of the more important encoding standards covered by the International Telecommunications Union (ITU). Notice the tradeoff that the standards make between encoding efficiency, reduced bandwidth consumption and increased conversion delay

Table 1. ITU Encoding Standards [12].

ITU Standard	Description	Bandwidth (Kbps)	Conversion delay (ms)
G.711	PCM	64	<1.00
G.721	ADPCM	32, 16, 24, 40	<1.00
G.728	LD-CELP	16	~2.50
G.729	CS-ACELP	8	~15.00
G.723.1	Multirate CELP	6.3, 5.3	~30.00

2.2.*Network Congestion*

Network congestion occurs when too many hosts simultaneously try to send too much data through a network [2]. Various factors such as capacity, bandwidth and network topology play an important role in contributing to traffic congestion. In wireless communication, elements such as volume of calls, type of services and network architecture contribute the network congestion [7]. Protocols and algorithm to mitigate congestion at high traffic densities in both wired and wireless communication networks can be of practical importance.

3. Codec Switching Scheme

3.1. *Introduction*

In VoIP, codec switching can be adapted to retain voice quality to users. Through codec switching, users still can continue an audio communication without terminating a session even users not aware of the changing of the codec.

The selection of suitable codec is useful for efficient bandwidth utilization. Generally, in codec switching, the codec is switch from high bit rate to the low bit rate when the bandwidth utilization is high and is will change back to the high bit rate if the bandwidth is less utilized. This is to guarantee the audio packet is not dropped. Besides, it is fair to users to get a better or the best audio quality due to the less traffic congestion. A high bit rate codec get better performance than a lower bit rate codec in various traffic aggregates [13]. A common benchmark used to determine the quality of sound produced by specific CODECs is the mean opinion score (MOS), [9]. With MOS, a wide range of listeners judge the quality of a voice sample (corresponding to a particular CODEC) on a scale of 1 (bad) to 5 (excellent). Usually the assessment of VoIP is carried out using the subjective quality measure called Mean Opinion Score (MOS). MOS scales from 1 (lowest quality) to 5 (highest quality). Different coding techniques for telephony and voice packets are standardized by the ITU-T such as G.723.1, G.729, G.729A and etc [2].

3.2.*Scenario*

To illustrate how codec switching can be adapted, refer to Figure 1. By registering to SIP server, client 1 is having a conversation with client 2 using a laptop which equipped with WiFi connection. As there are a number of people accessing the WiFi connection at the same time, so the network bandwidth consumption increases. This results to a degrading voice quality. Nonetheless, the codec switching that's also equipped in the laptop improves the conversation by switching to a different codec. The conversation is maintained without any degradation and disruption. Finally, when the crowd which accesses the access point has reduced, the bandwidth has fewer loads. The codec system now switches back to the previous codec and remain the online conversation.

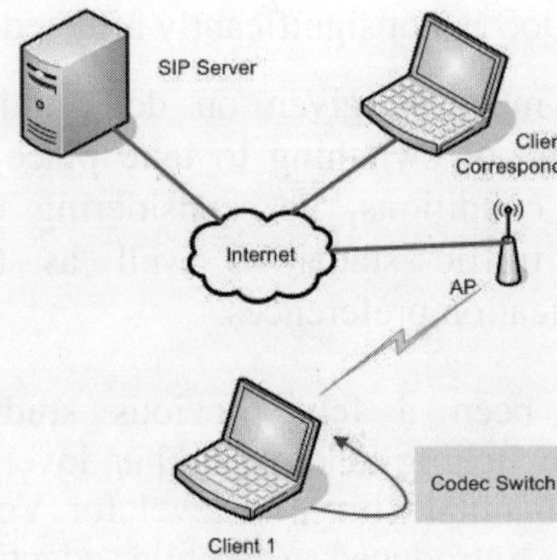

Figure 1. ©2009 MIMOS BERHAD. All Rights Reserved
Codec Switching Scenario

3.3. *SIP Flow Process*

Session Initiation Protocol (SIP) [5] is signaling protocol to establish, modify and terminate the sesion between two end-points . It can invites users to join the already existing session and also remove the participants and supports mobility. SIP can working together with Session Description Protocol (SDP) [10], to describe a session such as time network bandwidth and media format, address as well as ports. SIP enable users to be identified by their SIP URI (e.g. Kathy@abc.com). SIP signaling messages comprises client and SIP Proxy server.

Refering to Figure 2, depictes the SIP message flow when the session establish and the changing of codec during the realtime communication. It can be explained as follows :

- Process of online conversation has been established (1,2,3,4,5,6).
- At this point, SIP client 1 detects some audio quality degradation. Hence client 1 initiates the re-invite message (7,8). The message carries the new compatible parameter agreed by both client to have an online session, (9,10,11,12).

- The conversation with the new parameter is established
- SIP client 1 now detects that the traffic is less congested, so it re-invites messages (13,14). The codec is switches back to the higher bit rate codec and the conversation are remaining on (15,16,17,18).
- Ongoing VoIP session on Client 1 now trigger codec switching from low bit rate to high bit rate.

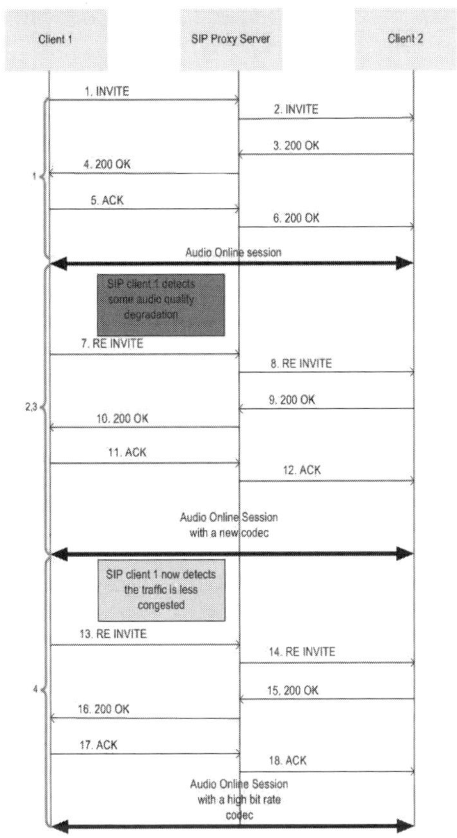

Figure 2. ©2009 MIMOS BERHAD. All Rights Reserved

SIP flow of codec switching.

3.4. *QoS Parameters*

QoS parameters can be identified by Table II [1]. We select packet loss as a parameter for QoS. The failure of packet delivery arrive at their destination is consider packet loss. The factor of packet loss : inadequate signal strength at the destination, natural or human-made interference, excessive system noise, hardware failure, software corruption or over burdened network nodes. Percentage of packet loss rate, y, can be calculated by:

$$y = \frac{a}{b} x \ 100 \qquad (1)$$

where,

a = number of packet loss

b = the number of RTP packets being transmitted

Table 2. Network QoS Parameters

Category	Parameters
Timeliness	Delay, Response Time, Jitter
Bandwidth	Systems-level data rate, Application-level data rate, Transaction time
Reliability	Mean time to failure (MTTF), Mean time to repair (MTTR), Mean time between failures (MTBF), Percentage of time available, Packet loss rate, Bit error

3.5. *Architecture and Flowcharts*

The setup of the propose architecture as depicted in Figure 3. It consists of :

- Ethernet and WiFi access point for fix-line and mobile access network.
- 3 laptops : 2 SIP clients and another laptop is configured as a traffic client.
- 2 machine servers for SIP server and Traffic Generator server.

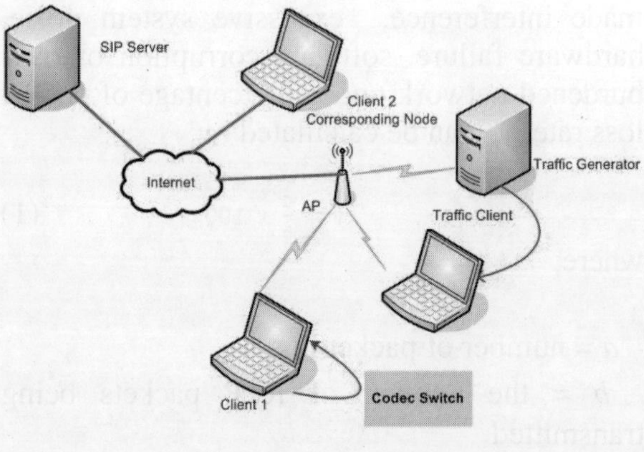

Figure 3. ©2009 MIMOS BERHAD. All Rights Reserved
Architecture of codec switching scenario.

Client 1 and Client 2 on laptop is installed with SIP-based VOIP application that enable to adjust the codec based on network bandwidth availability. It is connected to the WiFi AP whereas the SIP server is connected to the Ethernet. Client1 will be communicating with Client 2 by sending and receiving SIP signaling messages between SIP server and client. Two sample of codec with different bit rate will be used in the experiment. All clients need to register it with a SIP server in order to communicate to each other. The traffic generator is a traffic simulator meant to send packet to the traffic clients which also connected to WiFi access point to depict a heavy access to WiFi access point. This process can be referred to the flowchart in Figure 4 as shown below.

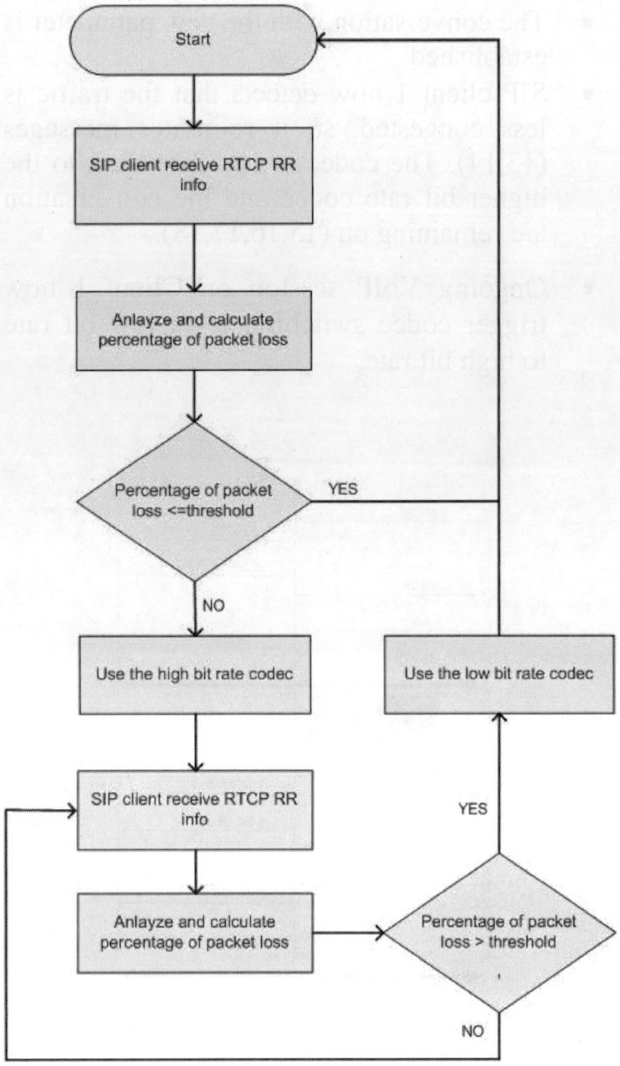

Figure 4. ©2009 MIMOS BERHAD. All Rights Reserved
Flowchart of codec switching.

The sending and recieving packets is gathered by RTP RR [15] – is a kind of RTCP message information collection at a certain time interval for QoS such as delay, jitter, packet. RTP RR data later will be analyzed to calcukate percentage of packet loss at that time. If the packet loss percentage is below or equal to the threshold value, the codec system will be triggered to the high bit rate codec. During the heavy traffic, on going VoIP session will be experience bad QoS and percentage of packet loss exceeds the threshold. Hence, Client 1 will switch a codec from high bit rate to the low bit rate, and later on will trigger to the high bit rate codec if the network traffic is less congested.

4. Conclusions

As availability of bandwidth is crucial in VoIP services and its bandwidth consumption typically relies on the codec used, there is a need to adjust the codec used to match the surging network traffic at that time. In this paper we present a switching scheme can help VoIP user to stay connected on their call while in traffic congestion. In this case we put traffic congestion in a WiFi network as a scenario.

References

1. A. M. Amin, "VoIP Performance Measurement Using QoS Parameters," The Second International Conference on Innovations in Information Technology, (2005).
2. B. K. Singh and N. Gupta, "Congestion and decongestion in a communication network," Physical Review E 71,(2000)
3. C. Gallon, "Quality of Services for Next generation Voice Over IP Network," www.msforum.org, (2003).
4. G. Marfia and K.D. Nguyen, "Rate Adaptation using SIP," http://www.comsoc.org/~mmc, Vol 3, No.2, (2006).
5. J. Rosenberg et al, " Voip Performance of Differentiated Services Enabled Network," IEEE International Conference, pp.419-423, (2000).
6. J.K. Mupalla et al, "SIP: Session Initiation Protocol," IETF RFC3261, (2002).
7. J. Fitzpatrick et al, "An Approach to Transport Layer Handover of VoIP over WLan," Consumer Communications and Networking Conference, Vol. 2, pp.1093-1097, (2006).
8. K. Ohta et al, " An Approach to Transport Layer Handover of VoIP over WLAN," Consumer Communications and Networking Conference, Vol. 1, pp.1093-1097, (2006).
9. M. Cardenete et al, "VoIP Perfromance in SIP-based vertical handovers between WLAN and GPRS/UMTS networks," IEEE Communication Society 2007 proceedings, pp.1973-1978, (2007).
10. M. Handley et al, "SDP: Session Description Protocol," IETF RFC 2327, (1998).
11. P. Drew, "Next-Generation VoIP Network Architecture," www.msforum.org, (2003).
12. S.L. Ng et al, "Effectiveness of Adaptive Codec Switching VoIP Application over Heterogenous Networks," Mobile Technology, Applications and Systems 2nd International Conference on, pp.7, (2004).
13. S. Burner et al, "Voice Over IP 101: Understanding VoIP Networks," www.juniper.net, USA, (2004).
14. S. Antoniou, "VoIP: How to effectively Encapsulate Voice in IP Packets," http://www.trainsignaltraining.com/cisco-voip-voice-encapsulation/2008-03-31/, (2008).
15. T. Koistinen, "Protocol Overview: RTP and RTCP," Nokia Telecommunication.

KNN AND LDA BASED DISCRETE HUMAN EMOTIONS CLASSIFICATION USING ELECTROENCEPHALOGRAM (EEG)

M.MURUGAPPAN, R.NAGARAJAN, AND S YAACOB

School of Mechatronic Engineering, Universiti Malaysia Perlis (UniMAP)
02600, Jejawi, Perlis, Malaysia

An electroencephalogram (EEG) signals based emotion recognition system is reported here. In principal, human emotions are easy to realize and difficult to detect. The combinations of surface Laplacian filtering, wavelet transform and linear classifiers (K Nearest Neighbor (KNN) and Linear Discriminant Analysis (LDA)) are used to detect the discrete emotions (happy, surprise, fear, disgust, and neutral) of human through EEG signals. A set of 20 subjects are used for analyzing the EEG signals on distinct emotions through 62 channels. An audio-visual induction based protocol has been designed for evoking the discrete emotions. The raw EEG signals are preprocessed through Surface Laplacian filtering method and decomposed into five different EEG frequency bands using Wavelet Transform (WT). In our work, "db4" wavelet function is used to derive the linear and non linear features for classifying the emotions. The validation of statistical features is performed using 5 fold cross validation. In this work, LDA outperforms KNN by offering a maximum average classification rate of 82 % on 62 channels, 75.652% and 72.391% on 24 channels and 8 channels respectively. Finally we present the average classification accuracy, individual classification accuracy and classification error of two different classifiers for justifying the performance of our emotion recognition system.

1. Introduction

The estimation of emotional changes from electroencephalogram (EEG) signals has recently gained attention among brain computer interface (BCI) and human computer interaction (HCI) researchers for developing the BCI/HCI devices. These devices are used for assisting physically disabled and immobilized people to interact with the real world. Several approaches have been reported by different researchers on finding the correlation between the emotional changes and EEG signals [1-3]. One of the major limitations on this area of research is "curse of dimensionality". The dimensionality of the data vectors extracted from the EEG data needs to be reduced because for most classification algorithms it is very difficult to reliably estimate the parameters of a classifier in high dimensions when only few training examples are available. In order to provide a simplified emotion recognition system, in our earlier work, we proposed asymmetric ratios based channel selection for reducing the number of channels from 62 to 8 and to 4 channels [4]. Since, the reduction of channels does minimize the physical burden, mental fatigue during electrode placement, computational time and complexity.

This work has three objectives: (1) to determine the best feature (either linear or non-linear) for classifying the emotions, (2) to determine the optimal number of channels required to achieve the better classification accuracy and (3) to determine the classifier which gives better average and individual classification rate. In our work, we have used audio-visual stimuli (video clips) for evoking five different emotions such as disgust, happy, fear, surprise and neutral. Both linear and non-linear features are derived using wavelet transforms over five different frequency bands (delta, theta, alpha, beta and gamma). These numerical features are classified using two different linear classifiers namely K Nearest Neighbor (KNN) and Linear Discriminant Analysis (LDA). Finally, we compared the classification rate of discrete emotions on different channel combinations over five frequency bands by combining wavelet features and linear classifiers.

2. Materials and Experimental Design

2.1.*EEG Data Acquisition*

This section describes the acquisition of EEG signals for emotion stimulation experiments. From our earlier experiment, we found that audio-visual stimulus is superior in evoking the discrete emotions than visual stimulus method [5]. Hence, we have used an audio-visual induction based protocol for eliciting the discrete emotions in this present work. The structural flow of emotion recognition using EEG signals is shown in Fig 1. A pilot panel study is conducted on 25 university students to select any 5 video clips (trials) for each emotion from 115 emotional video clips including from the international standard emotional clips (www.stanford.edu).

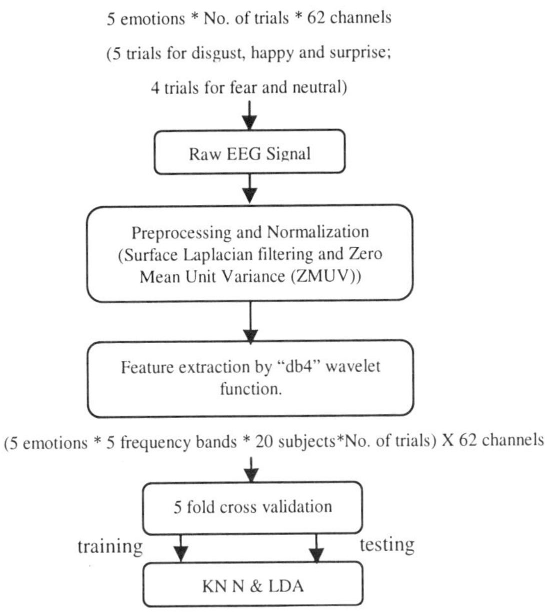

Fig.1. Systematic procedure of our work on emotion recognition using EEG signals.

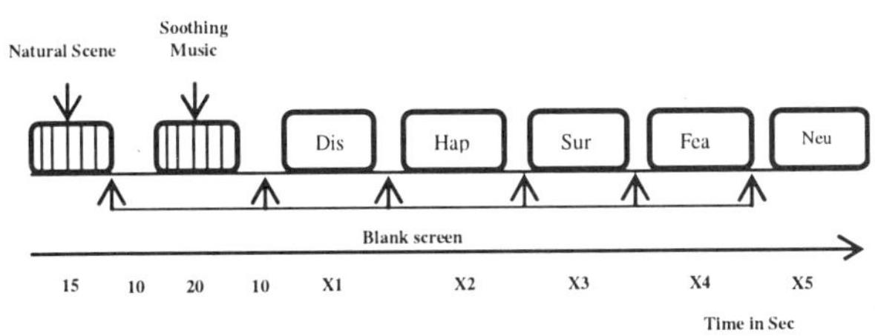

Dis = Disgust ; Hap = Happy ; Sur = Surprise ; Fea = Fear ; Neu= Neutral

Fig 2. EEG data acquisition protocol using audio-visual stimulus.

The selection of video clips is based on self assessment questionnaires mentioned in [6]. The subjects who have undergone for this panel study does not take part in the data collection experiment. The audio-visual stimulus protocol for Trial 1 of our experiment is shown in Fig. 2. From Trial 2 to Trial 5, the orders of the emotional video clips are changed in a random manner. X1 to X5 denote time periods of selected video clips. The time duration of video clips vary from one another. Three females and seventeen males in the age group of 21-39 years were employed as subjects in our experiment. Once the consent forms were filled-up, the subjects were given a simple introduction about the research work and stages of experiment. The recording of EEG signal has been done through Nervus EEG, USA with 64 channel electrodes at a sampling frequency of 256 Hz and band-pass filtered between 0.05 Hz and 70 Hz. All the electrodes are placed over the entire scalp using International standard 10-10 system. The impedance of the electrodes is kept below 5 kΩ. Between each emotional video clips, under self assessment section, the subjects were informed to answer the emotions they have experienced [6]. Finally, 5 trials for disgust, happy and surprise emotions and 4 trials for fear and neutral emotions are considered for further analysis.

2.2.*Preprocessing*

EEG signals recorded over various positions on the scalp are usually contaminated with noises (due to power line and external interferences) and artifacts (Ocular (Electroocculogram), Muscular (Electromyogram), Vascular (Electrocardiogram) and Gloss kinetic artifacts). The complete removal of artifacts will also remove some of the useful information of EEG signals. This is one of the reasons why considerable experience is required to interpret EEGs clinically [7, 8]. A couple of methods are available in the literature to avoid artifacts in EEG recordings. However, removing artifacts entirely is impossible in the existing data acquisition process.

In this work, we used Surface Laplacian (SL) filter for removing the noises and artifacts. The SL filter is used to emphasize the electric activities that are spatially close to a recording electrode, filtering out those that might have an origin outside the skull. In addition, it also attenuates the EEG activity which is common to all the involved channels in order to improve the spatial resolution of the recorded signal. The neural activities generated by the brain, however, contain various spatial frequencies. Potentially useful information from the middle frequencies may be filtered out by the analytical Laplacian filters. Hence, the signal "pattern" derived from SL filters is similar to "spatial distribution of source in the head".

The mathematical modeling of Surface Laplacian filter is given as

$$X_{new}(t) = X(t) - \frac{1}{N}\sum_{i=1}^{N} X_i(t) \tag{1}$$

where X_{new} : filtered signal ; X(t) : raw signal ; N: number of neighbor electrodes

2.3. *Feature Extraction*

There are two important aspects of feature extraction: (a) extracting the features using the most salient EEG channels (b) extracting the features only from the selected EEG channels. In the emotion recognition research using EEG signals, the non-parametric method of feature extraction based on multi-resolution analysis of Wavelet Transform (WT) is quite new. The joint time-frequency resolution obtained by WT makes it as a good candidate for the extraction of details as well as approximations of the signal which cannot be obtained either by Fast Fourier Transform (FFT) or by Short Time Fourier Transform (STFT) [9, 10].

The non-stationary nature of EEG signals is to expand them onto basis functions created by expanding, contracting and shifting a single prototype function ($\Psi_{a,b}$, the mother wavelet), specifically selected for the signal under consideration

The mother wavelet function $\Psi_{a,\,b}$ (t) is given as

$$\psi_{a,b}(t) = \frac{1}{\sqrt{a}}\psi\left(\frac{t-b}{a}\right) \tag{2}$$

where a, b ∈ R, a>0, and R is the wavelet space. Parameters 'a' and 'b' are the scaling factor and shifting factor respectively. The only limitation for choosing a prototype function as mother wavelet is to satisfy the admissibility condition (Eqn. 3),

$$C_\psi = \int_{-\infty}^{\infty} \frac{|\Psi(\omega)|^2}{\omega} d\omega < \infty \tag{3}$$

where ψ (ω) is the Fourier transform of $\psi_{a,\,b}$ (t). The time-frequency representation is performed by repeatedly filtering the signal with a pair of filters that cut the frequency domain in the middle. Specifically, the discrete wavelet transform decomposes the signal into an approximation coefficients (CA) and detailed coefficients (CD). The approximation coefficient is subsequently divided into new approximation and detailed coefficients. This process is carried out iteratively producing a set of approximation coefficients and detail coefficients at different levels or scales [11].

In this work, the multi-resolution analysis of "db4" wavelet function is used for decomposing the EEG signals into five different frequency bands (delta, theta, alpha, beta, and gamma). This wavelet function "db4" has been chosen due to their near optimal time-frequency localization properties. Moreover, the waveforms of "db4" are similar to the waveforms to be detected in the EEG signal. Therefore, extraction of EEG signals features are more likely to be successful [12]. In Table (1), A5, D5, D4, D3, and D2 represents the five EEG frequency bands. In order to analyze the characteristic natures of different EEG patterns, we used both linear (Recoursing Energy Efficiency (REE) [6], and power) and non-linear (entropy) statistical features for classifying the discrete emotions. These features are derived from the five frequency bands of EEG. Descriptions of these statistical features are given in Table 2. Table 1 also presents the bandwidth and the frequencies corresponding to different levels of decomposition for "db4" wavelet function with a sampling frequency f_s=256 Hz [11].

Table 1 Decomposition of EEG signals into different frequency bands with a sampling frequency of 256 Hz

Frequency Range	Decomposition Level	Frequency Bands	Frequency Bandwidth (Hz)
0 - 4	A5	Theta	4
4 – 8	D5	Delta	4
8 – 16	D4	Alpha	8
16 – 32	D3	Beta	16
32 – 64	D2	Gama	32
64 - 128	D1	Noises	64

A : Approximation coefficients D: Detail coefficients

Table 2 Statistical features used for emotion recognition and their description

Features	Description
Mean	Measures the mean value of electrodes potential
Power	Measures the amplitude of EEG signal
Entropy	Measures the useful information about the EEG signal for emotion from the intrusive noise.

2.4. *Classification*

In this work, we used two simple linear classifiers such as Linear Discriminant Analysis (LDA) and K Nearest Neighbor (KNN) for classifying the discrete emotions. Among these two classifiers, LDA provides extremely fast evaluations of unknown inputs performed by distance calculations between a new sample and mean of training data samples in each class weighed by their covariance matrices. A linear discriminant analysis tries to find an optimal hyper plane to separate five classes (here, disgust, happy, surprise, fear and neutral emotions).

In addition, KNN is also a simple and intuitive method of classifier used by many researchers typically for classifying the signals and images. This classifier makes a decision on comparing a new labeled sample (testing data) with the baseline data (training data). In general, for a given unlabeled time series X, the KNN rule finds the K "closest" (neighborhood) labeled time series in the training data set and assigns X to the class that appears most frequently in the neighborhood of k time series. There are two main schemes or decision rules in KNN algorithm, that is, similarity voting scheme and majority voting scheme [13]. In our work, we used the majority voting for classifying the unlabeled data. It means that, a class (category) gets one vote, for each instance, of that class in a set of K neighborhood samples. Then, the new data sample is classified to the class with the highest amount of votes. This majority voting is more commonly used because it is less sensitive to outliers.

Table 3 Average classification results among all statistical features over 3 different channels set using KNN and LDA

Channel	Class	Entropy	Power	Std Dev	Variance
62	KNN	80.04348	69.43478	69.8657	63.6087
	LDA	**81.4348**	52.17391	65.0896	51.8696
24	KNN	72.08696	71.73913	73	69.3478
	LDA	74.6087	**75.6522**	74.3782	70.3892
8	KNN	69.21739	70	60.2174	54.7101
	LDA	**71.4783**	56.26087	61.0869	49.3044

Table 4 Maximum Individual classification accuracy of discrete emotions over 3 different channels set

Channel	Features	Dis	Hap	Sur	Fea	Neu
62	Entropy	92	86	**68**	**76.25**	**95**
24	Power	92	84	47	76.05	85
8	Entropy	**92**	**88**	45	63.75	83.75

Dis = Disgust ; Hap = Happy ; Sur = Surprise ; Fea = Fear ; Neu= Neutral

Besides the training and testing samples, LDA does not require any external parameter for classifying the discrete emotions. However, in KNN, we need to specify the value of "K" closest neighbor for emotions classification. In this experiment, we try different "K" values ranging from 1 to 5. Finally, the value of "K" is selected as 2. This gives a maximum classification performance among the other values of K.

Table 5 The standard deviation of individual classification accuracy over different channels set

Channel	Classifier	Entropy	Power	Std Dev	Variance
62	KNN	**0.8559**	2.8076	2.2883	1.8989
	LDA	2.1444	4.9194	2.7352	1.6523
24	KNN	1.1565	1.0760	1.6726	0.7686
	LDA	1.2143	2.0566	1.0728	**0.6487**
8	KNN	2.1717	2.7498	4.1342	3.3698
	LDA	**1.2239**	5.3634	1.7391	1.6224

3. Results and Discussions

Among all twenty subjects, we sample and preprocess the total of 460 EEG epochs from five discrete emotions. The number of data points in each epoch depends on the time duration of video clips. In our experiment; the time duration of video clips vary from one another. The next stage is to train the KNN classifier with a best value of K while LDA classifier directly works for classifying the emotions. Among these two classifiers, LDA is of very simple but elegant approach to classify various emotions. The classification ability of a statistical feature set can be measured through classification accuracy and error rate by averaging five times over a *5 fold cross-validation*. The basic stages of 5 fold cross-validation includes: (a) total number of samples are divided into 5 disjoint sets (b) 4 sets are used for training and 1 set is used for testing (c) repeat stage (b) for five times and each time the data set is permuted differently.

From Table 3, we found that, LDA gives higher average classification accuracy than KNN on all different channels sets. The maximum classification accuracy of *81.4348 %* and *71.4783 %* is obtained using entropy feature on 62 channels and 8 channels respectively, and the power feature on 24 channels gives a maximum classification rate of *75.6522%*. Among the three different channel combination, entropy feature (non-linear) performs better than the other features (linear). Here, the entropy feature measures the regularity of different emotional EEG data. And so, each emotional EEG signals have its own regularity characteristics and it can be easily found out by using the entropy feature. Table 4 show the individual emotions classification rate of LDA classifier for the feature which gives the maximum average classification accuracy in three different set of channels in Table 3. From Table 4, we found that, the 8 channel EEG data gives the maximum individual classification rate in disgust and happy emotions compared to 62 and 24 channels respectively. In addition, 62 channels EEG data performs well on achieving higher classification rate on fear, neutral and surprise emotions than 8 and 24 channels. In Table 5 we present the standard deviation of classification accuracy in 5 different sets. All the programming was done in Matlab environment on a desktop computer with AMD Athlon dual core processor 2 GHz with 2 GB of random access memory.

4. Conclusion

This work addresses the classifiability of human emotions using EEG signals. The results presented in this paper indicate that the multi-resolution analysis based linear and non-linear features works well with the context of emotion classification. The experimental result on the performance of LDA is very encouraging. These results represent a possibility of determining the emotional changes of human mind through EEG signals. In addition, these results also confirm our hypothesis that it is possible to differentiate and classify the human emotions the linear and non-linear features. Compared to the linear features, non-linear feature (entropy) performs well on deriving the refined information on emotional changes from the EEG signals. The results of this study provide a framework of methodology that can be used to elucidate the dynamical mechanism of human emotional changes underlying the brain structure. In addition, the results can be extended to the development of online emotion recognition system.

Acknowledgments

This work is supported by the two grants of Ministry of Science and Technology

Innovation (MOSTI), Malaysia. Grant Code: 9005-00020 & 9005-00002.

References

1. Kim K.H, Band S.W., and Kim S.B. Emotion Recognition System using short-term monitoring of physiological signals, *Proceedings on Medical & Biological Engineering & Computing*, 42, 419-427, (2004).
2. Chanel, G., Karim, A.A. and Pun, T. Valence-arousal evaluation using physiological signals in an emotion recall paradigm, *Lecturer Notes in Computer Science*, Springer, 530 – 537, (2007)
3. Kazuhiko, T. Remarks on emotion recognition from bio-potential signals, *2nd International Conference on Autonomous Robots and Agents*, New Zealand, 186–191, (2004).
4. M.Murugappan, M Rizon, R.Nagarajan, and S Yaacob. Asymmetric Ratio and FCM based Salient Channel Selection for Human Emotion Recognition using EEG, *WSEAS Transactions on Signal Processing*, 10(4), 596-603, (2008).
5. M.Murugappan, M Rizon, R.Nagarajan, and S Yaacob. An Investigation on visual and audiovisual stimulus based emotion recognition using EEG, *Transactions on Medical Engineering and Informatics*, 1(3), 342-356, (2009).
6. M.Murugappan, M Rizon, R.Nagarajan, S Yaacob, D Hazry, and I Zunaidi. Time-Frequency Analysis of EEG Signals for Human Emotion Detection. *IFMBE Proceedings, Springer Book chapter,* 21, 262-265, (2008).
7. Jung T. Removing Electroencephalographic Artifacts by Blind Source Separation, *Journal of Psychophysiology*, 37(2), 163-178, (2000).
8. Gott P. S, Hughes E. C., and Whipple, Voluntary Control of Two Lateralized Conscious States: Validation by Electrical and Behavioral Studies, *Journal of Neuropsychological*, 22, 65-72, (1984).
9. Mallat S. G. A Theory for Multi-Resolution Signal Decomposition: The Wavelet Representation, *IEEE Transactions on Pattern Analysis and Machine Intelligence*, 11(7), 674–693, (1989).
10. Merzagora A.C, Bunce S, Izzetoglu M., and Onaral B. Wavelet Analysis for EEG Feature Extraction in Deceptive Detection. *IEEE Proceedings on EBMS*, 2434-2437, (2006).
11. Chethan P and Cox M. Frequency Characteristics of Wavelets, *IEEE Transactions on Power Delivery*, 17 (3), pp, 800-804, (2002).
12. Charles W.A. and Zlatko, S. Classification of EEG signals from four subjects during five mental tasks, *IEEE Proceedings on Engineering Application in Neural Networks*, 407–414, (1997).
13. Wanpracha A C, Ya-ju Fan, and Rajesh C S. On the Time Series K-Nearest Neighbor Classification of Abnormal Brain Activity, *IEEE Transactions on Systems, Man and Cybernetics – Part A:Systems and Humans* , 37 (6), pp, 1005-1016, (2007).

SECURED PATH REDUNDANCY ALGORITHM FOR HETEROGENEOUS SENSOR NETWORKS

P.SAMUNDISWARY
Department of Electronics and Communication Engineering
Sri Manakula Vinayagar Engineering College
Pondicherry-605107, India

PADMA PRIYADARSHINI and P. DANANJAYAN
Department of Electronics and Communication Engineering
Pondicherry Engineering College
Pondicherry-605014, India
pdananjayan@rediffmail.com

Abstract- Sensor networks consist of large number of nodes with limited energy, computation and transmission power. Since these nodes operate in a physically insecure environment, they are vulnerable to different types of attacks such as selective forwarding and sinkhole. These attacks can inject malicious packets by compromising the nodes. Furthermore, previous work on sensor networks mainly considered homogeneous sensor networks where all sensor nodes have the same capabilities. Generally homogeneous sensor networks have poor network performance limits and scalability. Hence, the network performance can be improved by deploying heterogeneous sensor networks. However, security mechanism is not explored in heterogeneous sensor network with limited memory against the above mentioned attacks. In this paper, a secured path redundancy algorithm is attempted to implement in heterogeneous sensor network by incorporating alternate path scheme in heterogeneous sensor networks. The simulation results prove that this algorithm has better network performance in terms of energy consumption, delivery ratio and delay than that of heterogeneous sensor networks in the presence of compromised nodes.

1. Introduction

Wireless sensor networks are expected to have applications in many areas, such as military, homeland security, environmental monitoring and healthcare systems. Most research work in sensor networks considered homogeneous sensor networks, where all sensor nodes are modeled to have the same capabilities in terms of computation, communication, energy supply, storage, reliability and other aspects [1]. Security is critical for sensor networks deployed in hostile environments to defend against attacks. Providing security and privacy to small sensor nodes is challenging, due to the limited capabilities of sensor nodes. However, only few of the routing protocols such as security protocols for sensor networks (SPINS) and path redundancy based security algorithm (PRSA) for wireless sensor networks address the security mechanism and authentication against the various attacks [2,3]. Moreover, secured homogeneous sensor networks suffer from poor fundamental limit and performance. To achieve better performance, a heterogeneous sensor network (HSN) model is adopted.

The HSN consists of a few powerful high-end sensors (H-sensors) and a large number of low-end sensors (L-sensors). Compared to a L-sensor, a H-sensor has better computation capability, larger storage and better reliability [4]. The sensor nodes may be captured by attackers and reloaded with malicious nodes. Some of the secured routing protocols of heterogeneous sensor networks can detect the malicious nodes and deliver the packets to the sink successfully. But these routing protocols increase the buffering requirements [5] and delay. In this paper, path redundancy based secured algorithm is extended for heterogeneous sensor network by including alternate path mechanism in HSN. This algorithm is simulated by using Glomosim for different coverage area of 300m×300m and 500m×500m in heterogeneous sensor network. The simulation results prove that path redundancy based security algorithm outperforms the heterogeneous sensor networks in terms of energy consumption, delivery ratio and delay even in the presence of malicious nodes.

2. Heterogeneous Sensor Networks

In the HSN model, H-sensors and L-sensors are randomly distributed in the field and clusters are formed. The cluster formation is shown in Fig.1, where L-sensors are the small squares, H-sensors are large rectangles, and the large square at the top-right corner is the base station (BS). It is natural to let powerful H-sensors serve as cluster heads The H-sensors have more energy supply, longer transmission range, higher data rate than L-sensors. All the H-sensors form a backbone in the network. H-sensors use multi-hop communications to reach the BS and L-sensors also use multi-hop communications to reach H-sensors [5]. H-sensors provide many advantages for designing better protocols, algorithms, and secure schemes in sensor networks. An efficient and robust cluster formation scheme with well organized routing protocol is adopted for HSNs.

2.1. *Routing in Heterogeneous Sensor Networks*

The primary functionality of a wireless sensor network is to sense the environment and transmit the acquired information to the BS for further processing. Since sensor nodes are small and unreliable devices, they are prone to failures. Thus, routing is an essential operation in sensor networks. A routing protocol should be robust to sensor failures and be able to find new paths when nodes fail. Security requirement adds new challenges to routing. Recent literatures have shown that routing protocols of HSNs can significantly improve the performance of sensor networks. The basic idea of routing in HSNs is to let each L-sensor sends data to its H-sensor. The H-sensors may aggregate data from multiple L-sensors and remove redundant data, and then send compressed data to the BS via the H-sensor backbone. Transmissions in the backbone have longer range and may use a different frequency than transmissions among L-sensors. Based on the above two layer communication architecture, an efficient routing protocol is implemented for HSNs. This consists of two types of routing: routing within a cluster (among L-sensors), and routing across clusters (among H-sensors) [6]. Each type of routing of HSN is discussed below.

2.2. *Intra- Cluster Routing*

Routing within a cluster (from an L-sensor to its cluster head) is referred to as intra-cluster routing which is illustrated in Fig.1. L-sensor sends its location information to the cluster head (H-sensor) during the cluster formation. The location of H is broadcasted to all L-sensors in the cluster. All the L-sensors in a cluster form a tree, rooted at the cluster head (denoted as H) so that each L-sensor sends packets to its H-sensor, when it generates packets. If data from nearby L-sensor nodes are highly correlated, then a minimum spanning tree (MST) can be adopted to approximate the least energy consumption case. A centralized algorithm created by H-sensor can be used to construct an MST. Then H disseminates the MST structure information to L-sensors, i.e., informing each L-sensor which node its parent is. If a data fusion is conducted at intermediate L-sensors nodes (two k-bit packets come in, and one k-bit packet goes out after data fusion), then MST consumes the least total energy in the cluster. If there is few or no data fusion among L-sensors in a cluster, a shortest-path tree (SPT) should be used to approximate the least total energy consumption. Similarly, the cluster head (H-sensor) can construct an SPT by using a centralized algorithm and the locations of L-sensors. Since L-sensors are small, unreliable devices, they may fail over time. Therefore robust and self-healing routing protocols are critical for routing among L-sensors. In the above route setup, each L-sensor may record two or more parent nodes. One parent node serves as the primary parent, and other parent nodes serve as backup parents. If the primary parent node fails, an L-sensor can use a backup parent for data forwarding. Further each L-sensor records one or more backup cluster heads during cluster formation. When a cluster head fails, L-sensors in the cluster send their packets to a backup cluster head.

2.3. *Inter-Cluster Routing*

Routing across clusters (from an H-sensor to the BS) is referred to as inter-cluster routing which is shown in Fig.1. After receiving data from L-sensors, cluster heads may perform data aggregation via the H-sensor backbone. Each cluster head exchanges location information with neighbor cluster heads. During route discovery, a cluster head draws a straight line L between itself and the BS, based on the locations of the BS and itself which is shown in Fig.1. Line L intersects with a serial of clusters, and these clusters are denoted as

C_0, C_1,..., Ck, which are referred to as Relay Cells. The packet is forwarded from the source cluster head to the BS via cluster heads in the Relay Cells. H-sensors are more reliable nodes than L-sensors. However, an H-sensor may also fail because of various reasons, such as harsh environment, or destroyed by an adversary. If any cluster head in the *Relay Cells* is unavailable, then a backup path is used. A backup path is set up as follows: The current cluster head (say *R*1) draws a straight line L' between itself and the BS, and line *L* intersects with several cells C'_1,..., C'_{k-1}, C'_k. If the next cell is the cell having the failed cluster head, *R*1 will use a detoured path to avoid the cell. The sequence cells C'_1,..., C'_{k-1}, C'_k will be the new Relay Cell and are used to forward the packet to the BS.

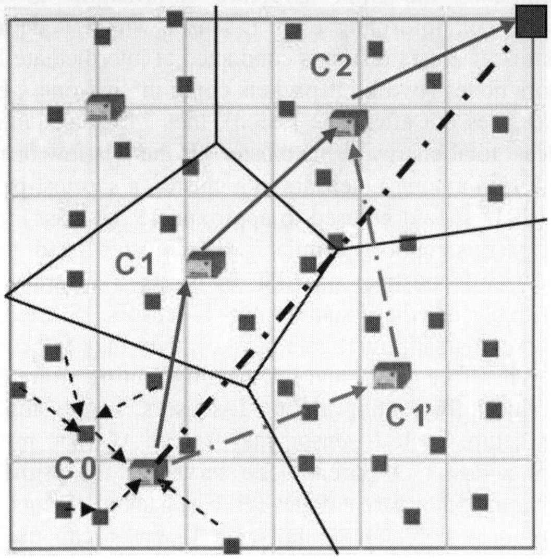

Fig.1. Heterogeneous sensor network model

3.Secured Path Redundancy Algorithm For Heterogeneous Sensor Networks

This algorithm may be applied for a network with various numbers of nodes; network capacity and attack type. The idea behind alternate path redundancy algorithm is to find secure multiple paths between the source and destination nodes in the presence of malicious nodes. This is achieved by removing one or more nodes that is suspected to be an active adversary node from the routing path [3]. Such nodes are identified by algorithm using a set of parameters that is usually reflecting the presence of adversary nodes. The parameters used are packet ID, no. of hop count and delay to reach the destination. This mechanism can defend against attacks such as selective forwarding attack and sinkhole attack.

4. Simulation Results

The secured heterogeneous sensor network is simulated for two different coverage areas (300m×300m,500m×500m) by varying the number of nodes from 100 to 500 nodes with two different values of malicious nodes (30 and 50) in Glomosim. The energy consumption, delivery ratio and delay are calculated for various numbers of nodes with two different coverage areas such as 300m×300m, 500m×500m having two values of malicious nodes (30 and 50). The parameters used in this simulation are

Table.1. Simulation Parameters

Simulation Parameters	Values
Number of nodes	100 to 500
Geographical area(m^2)	300×300,500×500
Packet Size	64 bytes
Traffic Type	CBR
Various number of malicious nodes	30,50
Simulation time(s)	600

4.1. *Energy Consumption*

The simulation results shown in Fig.2.a and Fig.2.b prove that there is a significant reduction in the energy consumption of secured heterogeneous sensor networks by increasing the numbers of nodes for different coverage area and different values of malicious nodes. When the number of nodes increases, the energy consumption of secured heterogeneous sensor networks reduces from 57% to 81.5% compared to heterogeneous sensor networks of malicious node 30 with coverage area of 300m×300m.

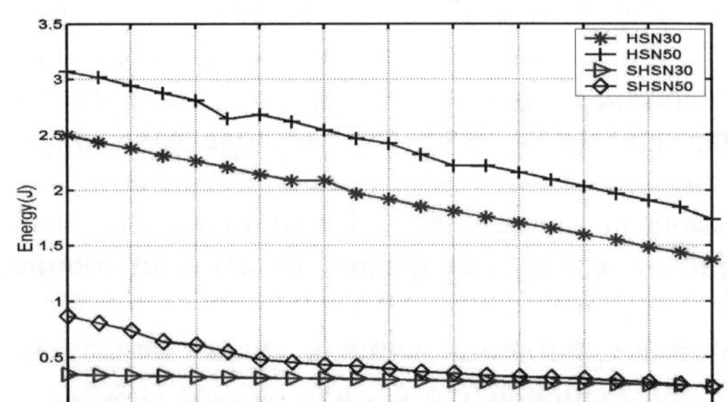

Fig.2.a. Energy consumption vs number of L-sensor nodes for coverage area 300m×300m

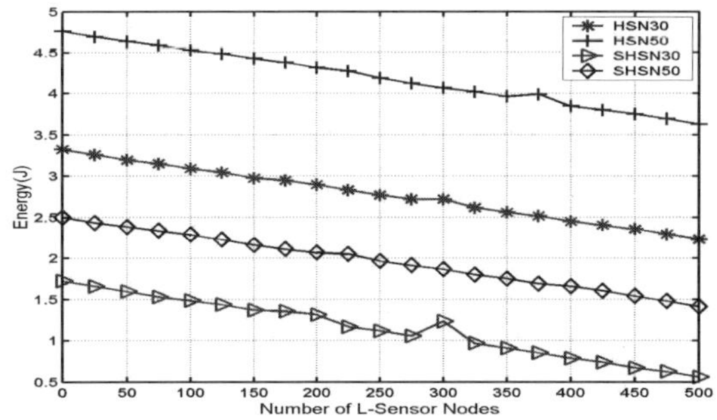

Fig.2.b.Energy consumption vs number of L- sensor nodes for coverage area 500m×500m

Even if the number of malicious nodes and coverage area increases, the energy consumption reduces by 49% to 67% with respect to heterogeneous sensor networks. Energy consumption of secured heterogeneous sensor networks is lesser than heterogeneous sensor networks because L-Sensors involve alternate shortest path even in the presence of malicious nodes

4.2. *Delivery Ratio*

Delivery ratio of secured path redundancy algorithm for heterogeneous sensor networks is higher than heterogeneous sensor networks which is shown in Fig.3.a and Fig.3.b. for different values of malicious nodes and different coverage area. The fact is that secured HSNs packets require less number of hop counts from the L-sensors to the cluster head than HSN. Moreover, the packet loss is reduced due to secured path from source to sink in secured heterogeneous sensor network

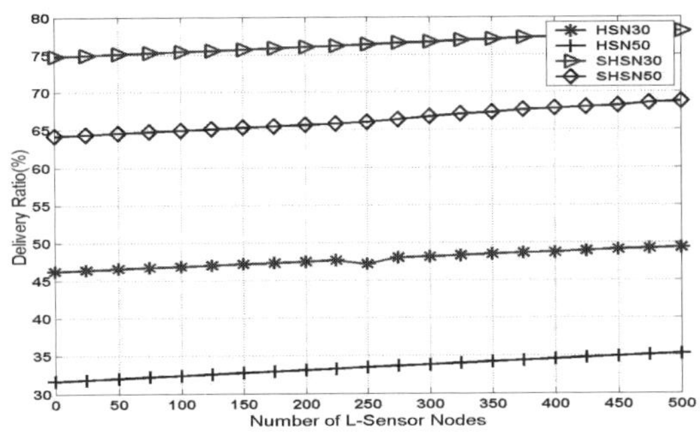

Fig.3.a.Delivery ratio with respect to number of L-sensor nodes for coverage area 300m×300m

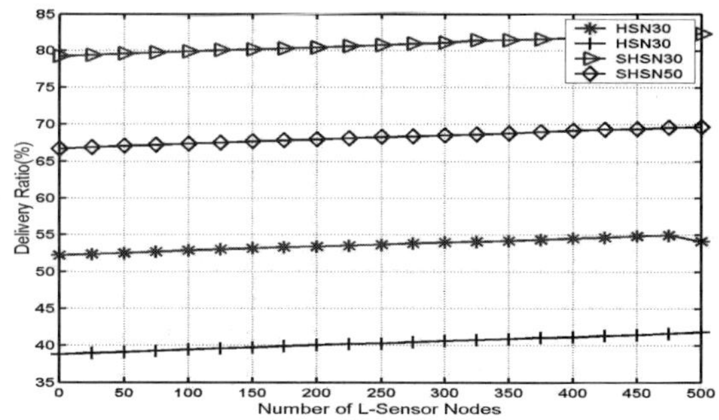

Fig.3.b.Delivery ratio with respect to number of L-sensor nodes for coverage area 500m×500m.

4.3. *Delay*

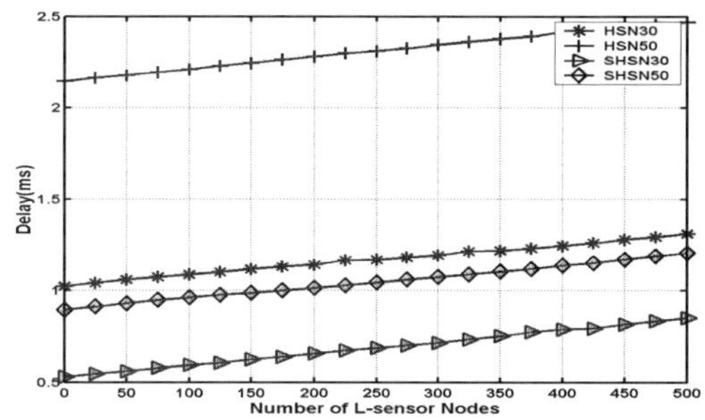

Fig.4.a. Delay with respect to number of L-sensor nodes for coverage area 300m×300m

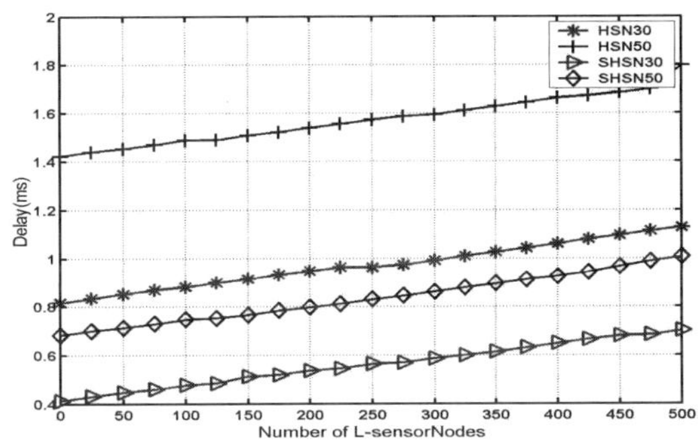

Fig.4.b.Delay with respect to number of L-sensor nodes for coverage area 500m×500m

The results illustrated in Fig.4.a and Fig.4.b show the delay for different coverage areas with 30 and 50 malicious nodes. From Fig.4.a it is proved that secured path redundancy algorithm for heterogeneous sensor network is lower than that of heterogeneous sensor network by 50% to 55%. Since packets of this algorithm use a path which requires less hop count to reach the sink even in the presence of malicious node.

5. Conclusion

The secured path redundancy algorithm for heterogeneous sensor network is simulated by varying the number of nodes from 100 to 500 with two different (300 m × 300 m, 500m×500m) coverage area scenarios for various numbers of malicious nodes (30 and 50). The simulation results prove that the above algorithm outperforms heterogeneous sensor networks by reducing the energy consumption. The results also demonstrate that the delivery ratio and end to end delay of secured heterogeneous network is better than the heterogeneous sensor network. The secured path redundancy algorithm for heterogeneous sensor network has better performance because it use path which involves less hop count and less packet loss to reach the destination node.

References

[1] Enrique J.Duarte-Melo, Mingyan Liu, "Analysis of Energy Consumption and Lifetime of Heterogeneous Wireless Sensor Networks", P*roceedings of IEEE GLOBECOMM 02*, Taipei, Taiwan, vol.1, pp.21-25, November 2002

[2] Dr.Sami, S. Al-Wakeel and A.Al-Swailem, "PRSA: A Path Redundancy Based Security Algorithm for Wireless Sensor Networks", *Proceedings of Wireless Communication and Networking Conference (WCNC 2007),* Hong Kong, March 2007.

[3]Adrian Perrig, Robert Szewczyk, Victor Wen, David Culler and J.D.Tygar, "SPINS: Security Protocols for Sensor Networks", *Proceedings of ACM Annual International Conference on Mobile Computing and Networking*, Rome, Italy, July 2001.

[4] Vivek Mhatre, Catherine Rosenberg, "Homogeneous vs Heterogenous Clustered Sensor networks:A Comparative Study", *Proceedings of IEEE International Conference on Communications (ICC'04)*, Paris, France vol.6, pp.3646-3651, June 2004.

[5] Xiaojiang Du, Sghaier Guizani, Yang Xiao and Hsiao-Hwa Chen, "A Secure Routing Protocol for Heterogeneous Sensor Networks", *Proceedings of IEEE GLOBECOM 2006,* San Francisco, California, December 2006

[6] Jeremy Brown and Xiaojiang Du, "Detection of Selective Forwarding attacks in Heterogeneous Sensor Networks", *Proceedings of IEEE International Conference on Communications (ICC 2008),* Beijing, China, May 2008.

Biblography

Samundiswary.P received the B.Tech degree (1997) and M.Tech degree (2003) in ECE from Pondicherry Engineering College, India. She is pursuing her Ph.D. programme in the Dept. of ECE, Pondicherry Engineering College, affiliated to Pondicherry University. She is currently working as Assistant Professor in the Dept. of ECE at Sri Manakula Vinayagar Engineering College affiliated to Pondicherry University, India. Her research interests include wireless communication and wireless sensor networks.

Padma priyadharsini received her B.Tech degree in ECE from Bharathiyar College of Engineering and Technology in 2007. She is pursuing her M.Tech degree in Pondicherry Engineering College, Pondicherry University, India..

P.Dananjayan received B.Sc. from University of Madras in 1979, B.Tech (1982) and M.E. (1984) from the Madras Institute of Technology, Chennai and Ph.D. degree from Anna University, Chennai in 1998. He is working as a Professor and Head of the Dept. of ECE, Pondicherry Engineering College, Pondicherry University, India. He has more than 60 publications in National and International Journals. He has presented more than 130 papers in National and International conferences. He has produced 6 Ph.D candidates and is currently guiding eight Ph.D students. His areas of interest include power electronics, Spread spectrum Techniques and Wireless Communication.

Session 6

A NOVEL BANDWIDTH UTILIZATION TECHNIQUE FOR CONVERGENCE NETWORK

R. SHANKAR
Sri Manakula Vinayagar Engineering College,
Madagadipet, Pondicherry

P. DANANJAYAN
Pondicherry Engineering College,
Pondicherry.
pdananjayan@rediffmail.com

Integration of different access technologies will result in high bandwidth connection for end users. The per flow bandwidth adaptation algorithm of reservation based QoS framework for integrated cellular and WLAN networks, decides how to adjust the QoS to maintain ongoing sessions at a satisfactory level with efficient use of the system resources. A QoS management scheme based on per class degradation provides better fairness than per flow bandwidth adaptation algorithm. In this paper per Group based Adaptation Algorithm (GAA) was proposed. Its performance has been compared with the previous proposed adaptation algorithms. The result shows that the new scheme generally performs better since it provides better fairness, faster calculation and can utilize the system bandwidth more efficiently.

1. Introduction

The demand for data communication paved the way for the migration of circuit-switched GSM systems to GPRS and 3G networks, which have the packet switched functionality. The ultimate aim is to provide a universal integrated all-IP platform which can provide much useful applications to the end users.

The all-IP platform can provide end users with benefits such as lower cost of transmission and higher bandwidth without losing the roaming features or pervasive aspects now emerging. Recent trend is that 3G networks like UMTS and WLAN technology integrate to provide the above benefits. WLAN systems provide high data rates at a relatively low cost compared to 3G networks, but it has a limited coverage area and less support for high speed mobility. WLAN have been widely deployed in places like airports, hotels, and campuses. Thus integrating WLAN and 3G networks offer benefits to the end users.

Many difficulties emerge when attempting to provide QoS solutions for integrated WLAN and cellular networks owing to the unbalanced capacity of the two systems; issues raised by handover between cells; handover between wireless access points; and handover between WLAN and cells caused by user mobility; as well as the unreliable communication of wireless media. To enable efficient use of the scarce resources provided by the cellular networks while maintaining strong QoS guarantees, a generic Reservation -based QoS model [1] has been proposed for the integrated cellular and WLAN network.

The per flow bandwidth adaptation algorithm [1], decides how to adjust the QoS to maintain ongoing sessions at a satisfactory level with efficient use of the system resources. A QoS management scheme based on per class degradation [2] provides better fairness than per flow bandwidth adaptation algorithm.

In this paper, per group based adaptation algorithm (GAA) is proposed and its performance is compared with the previous proposed adaptation scheme via simulation. The rest of this paper is organized as follows. Section 2 reviews the adaptive QoS framework. Section 3 presents the desirable features of the flow control algorithms. The per class adaptation algorithm is analyzed in Section 4. The features of proposed group based adaptation algorithm (GAA) is introduced and analysed in section 5. Section 6 describes the simulation setups and discusses the performance results. Finally section 7 summarizes this study and gives concluding remarks.

2. Adaptive QoS Framework

WLAN and UMTS networks have different transmission capacities; therefore handoff between the two systems makes the maintenance of a QoS connection very hard. One has to consider the significant difference in transmission capacity between the two systems especially when user handoff takes place. The second constraint is that WLAN operates on a free ISM band and has a lot of uncontrollable interference (i.e. microwave), like spread spectrum are used to reduce the interference. Such problems are beyond engineering control and hard QoS guarantee is very difficult or even impossible to achieve. To support QoS in packet switching networks there has to be some mechanisms to control network load, to keep it under a threshold, so that the system can achieve a satisfactory performance. The third problem is that the achievable QoS levels in WLAN and 3G cellular networks do not match each other. 3G cellular networks are very well designed with careful network planning and mature admission control algorithms. Therefore, the achievable QoS level is relatively high, while 802.11e WLAN works within a less controlled environment and it is difficult to achieve hard QoS. The previous proposed QoS framework [1] based on an adaptive approach for integrated WLAN and cellular networks addresses the above issues and provides practical and user-satisfied QoS.

3. Desirable Characteristics for Flow Control Schemes

The most important characteristic of the flow control scheme is fairness.

3.1 Fairness

When offered traffic load must be cut back in the adaptive approach, it is important to do so fairly. There are many notions of fairness by the presence of different session priorities and service requirements. In general, cooperation is required among the flows to allow equal access to network resources and those who are using up the resource more than its share should be cut off. An index [1] is used to measure the fairness among different flows. It is defined as:

$$\text{Fairness Index} = \frac{(\sum_{i=1}^{N} T_i)^2}{N(\sum_{i=1}^{N} T_i)^2}. \quad (1)$$

where N is the number of flows, T_i is the throughput of flow i. The higher the fairness index the better fairness the system can gain.

4. A Dynamic Bandwidth Management Scheme

Applying QoS means treating some traffic in preference to others, and this implies the ability to reject traffic. Especially in wireless mobile communication networks, uncontrolled error rate and users' mobility make us look for adaptation solutions. The use of degradation profile provides us a gradation between different QoS merits; therefore, negotiation between different network flows is an effective way to improve the overall system performance. The bandwidth adaptation algorithm as the key factor of the adaptive QoS framework decides how to adjust the QoS connections since mobile users should be able to seamlessly maintain their ongoing sessions at a satisfied level. This can be done in two ways. One is to adapt a flow to its corresponding level, when it migrates from one system into another. Ideally each call in the system should be allocated the maximum allowable bandwidth. However, WLAN and cellular networks have different transmission capacity; a session that consumes a moderate amount of bandwidth in WLAN system can be greedy and therefore could be rejected in the cellular networks. A connection switched from cellular networks to WLAN needs to level up its bandwidth otherwise it will lose the meaning of the integration. The other way is to adapt flows to use the system resource more efficiently in a single system or both to accommodate more new arrivals and handoff calls.

The method used in [1] degraded the longest calls in the system based on their state information with a good hope that those flows have a bigger probability to quit the system and leave fewer degraded connections in the system.

The management of the algorithm can be very complex as the CAC will need to search for the call each time. It can create unfairness because if the system state does not change frequently, you can have some connections degraded for long time while others are going at full or at least high speed. In the bandwidth adaptation scheme [2], which is based on per class degradation, When a new user arrives and there are no enough resources in the system, the system should ask all connections in the lowest priority level to degrade until they reach their minimum acceptable level and if the resources are still not enough continue with the next priority level (class). If all connections that have lower or equal priority to the new connection have degraded to their minimum and still there is no enough resource, this new connection will be rejected. By using this method would give better fairness between the connections of the same class and give high priority to the more sensitive classes so that their performance would not be affected by the lower priority classes. The above idea also can improve the scalability of the scheme and reduce the computation complexity.

5. Proposed Per Group Adaptation Algorithm

Although the previous bandwidth adaptation algorithm gives better fairness between connections, and better scalability, it does not utilize the system bandwidth in an efficient manner since it degrades all the connections in a class.

The proposed group based adaptation algorithm not only provides better fairness and scalability it also utilize the system bandwidth in an efficient manner. It is based on per group degradation. In this method the connections are grouped based on their state information.

When a new user comes and there are no enough resources in the system, the individual connections degraded one after another, after degrading certain no of connections in a group if enough resources are obtained for new connection then degrading other connections is stopped. Thus bandwidth is not wasted by degrading excess connection.

6. Performance Analysis

6.1 Simulation Model

This section uses simulation experiments to validate the proposed scheme. It is assumed that the call arrivals in the simulation follow an independent Poisson process and the session time of each connection is exponentially distributed.

It is well known that dropping an established communication is worse than rejecting a new call. Therefore cellular systems reserve a guard bandwidth for the handoff calls in order to reduce the handoff dropping probability. The reserved guard bandwidth can be either static or dynamic [3]. The dynamic approach often outperforms the static one at the expense of generating more control overheads [4]. However, the static approach is often attractive in practice owing to its design simplicity. In the simulation, a static guard bandwidth (i.e., 5% of the system capacity) is employed to deal with handoff calls.

Without loss of generality, the integrated network in the simulation consists of one cellular network and one WLAN hotspot. Since WLAN has a higher capacity and is cheaper than UMTS, it is assumed that the handoff probability from UMTS to WLAN is 5 times as much as that from WLAN to UMTS.

The system capacity for UMTS and WLAN is 2 Mb/s and 11 Mb/s respectively. The bandwidth requirement for each of four QoS classes {B1, *B*2, *B*3, *B*4} and their acceptable degradation level defined in degradation profile are assumed to be a portion of the system capacity listed in Table 1.

Table 1 Simulation parameters

Parameter	Value	Parameter	Value
UMTS Capacity (U)	2Mb/s	Session time	Exp(50)
WLAN Capacity	11Mb/s	Guard Band	5%
UMTS to WLAN Handoff	0.05	$\{B_1,B_2,B_3,B_4\}$	{5%×W,3%×W,5%×U,3%×U}
WLAN to UMTS Handoff	0.01	$\{D_1,D_2,D_3,D_4\}$	{4%×W,2%×W,4%×U,2%×U}
Reservation Signalling Cost	1%×W	Simulation Time	1000s

6.2 Experiment Results

This section presents the simulation results to demonstrate the effectiveness of the proposed scheme. To do so, the same traffic loads to two systems working under the normal operation condition and under the proposed framework, was assigned respectively. The performance of the new advanced adaptive algorithm with the previous one was compared. Each simulation experiment was run until the system reached its stable state. To measure the system performance merits, the normalized system utilization defined as the amount of data transmitted in the unit time normalized with the system capacity was examined first. QoS parameters: the call blocking probabilities and handoff dropping probabilities were considered. Finally, the fairness index and the overall system degradation are calculated.

Figure 1 compares the bandwidth utilization supported among the two schemes in the integrated network. From this diagram, it can be observed that the utilization increases as traffic loads increase. The reason that connections can better utilize the system bandwidth is that the proposed scheme allows the network to intelligently adjust each admitted QoS connection by its degradation profile and give sufficient resources for the new or handoff calls.

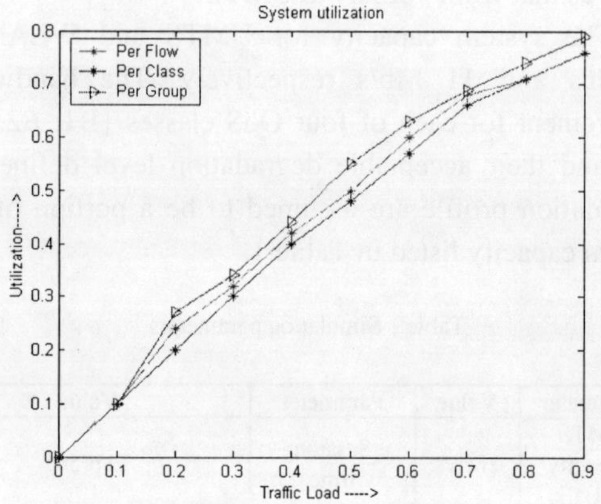

Figure 1 System utilization

It can also observe that at the low and moderate traffic load the per-flow method and our per group method uses the bandwidth more efficient than the per-class method, because where per-flow method only degrades one or several flows to release some bandwidth and our per group method degrades the connections based on the requirement of the new connection and every connections in a group are not degraded unlike the per class method which degrades all the flows in the lower priority class.

Figure 2 depicts the call blocking probability versus the traffic load.

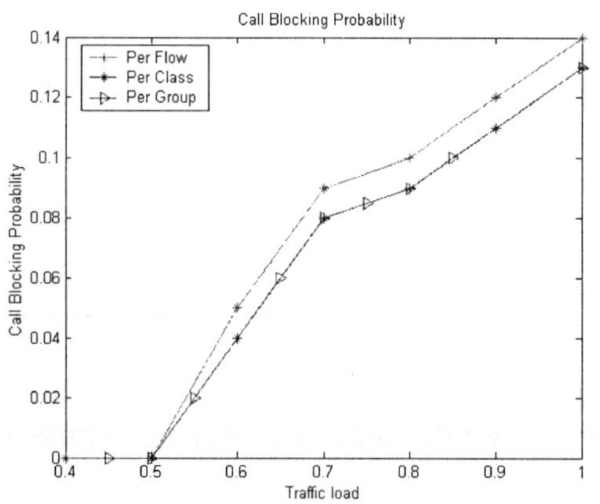

Figure2 Call blocking probability

From the result, it is observed that there is no call blocking probability for any of the methods with light traffic load. Particularly, we start to see the call blocking probability when the traffic loads reached 0.5.This clearly demonstrated the effectiveness of the proposed mechanism.

With further increment of the traffic load, the call blocking probability increases, since channel became more and more crowded. Per class and per group made no difference to provide more bandwidth for the new arrivals, since in the congested scenario they both degraded to the maximum allowable degree.

Figure 3 shows the degree of overall system degradation. This designed parameter can act as indicator to the network operators. When the overall system degradation parameter stays high for a certain period time, the network operator should think of installing more base stations or access point.

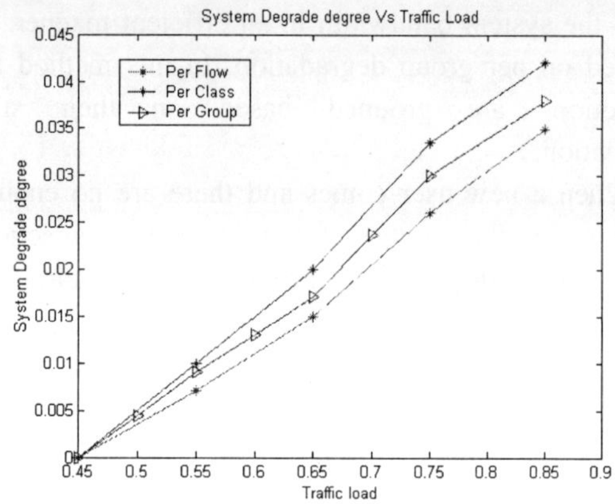

Figure 3 System Degrade Degree

From the figure, it is observed that the degradation degree for per class method and per group method increases nearly linearly with the increment of traffic loads, since with more users wanting to use the channel.

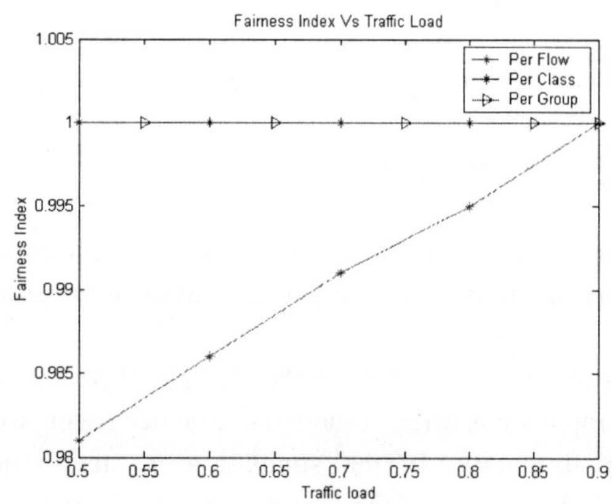

Figure 4 Fairness Index

As traffic load increases, the dividend between per class method and per group method is more evident, since per group method has the ability to degrade all flows in a certain group based on the requirement like per class method whereas per flow method degrades one or a few necessary flows.

Figure 4 shows that the fairness index for the per group method and per flow method. It is observed that per group method is fairer than per flow, since it degrades all the flow in a group and per flow method only degrades those needed. With more flows are degraded in the per group method, it reduces the difference between flows and it becomes fairer than the per flow method.

7. Conclusions

To design of a network architecture that can efficiently integrate WLAN and cellular networks with QoS support is a challenging task. The previously provided generic reservation-based QoS model for the integrated cellular and WLAN networks uses the dynamic bandwidth adaptation mechanism. In this paper, an advanced bandwidth adaptation algorithm based on per group degradation was proposed. We have compared the performance of the new approach with that of the adaptation method used in the previous study via simulation experiments. The results show that there are some tradeoffs between the two methods. Per group method generally performs better than per flow and per class method, since it has the ability to degrade all the flows in certain group and thus has better fairness than the per flow method. It also provides computation simplicity and executes faster, which is important to the admission control component. Per group method can also use the system resources more efficiently than the per class method since it degrade the connections based on requirement of the new connection. Simulation experiments also indicate that the proposed scheme outperform per class and per flow method while still maintaining acceptable QOS to the end users.

Acknowledgments

We would like to convey our acknowledgement to S. Arunkumar, E. Ashokkumar, M. Bremkumar, U. Ilamparithi and G. Karthik of Sri Manakula Vinayagar Engineering College (SMVEC), Pondicherry, India.

References

[1] Oliveira, C., J. B. Kim and T. Suda "Adaptive bandwidth reservation scheme for highspeed multimedia wireless networks." IEEE Journal on Selected Areas in Communications 16(6): 858- 874, 1998.

[2] Xin Gang Wang, Geyong Min, John Mellor and Khalid al-Begain "A QOS -based bandwidth management scheme in heterogeneous wireless networks" I.J. of simulation vol. 5 no 1-2, ISSN

[3] Ramanathan, P., K. M. Sivalingam, P. Agrawal and S. Kishore "Dynamic resource allocation schemes during handoff for mobile multimedia wireless networks." IEEE Journal on Selected Areas in Communications 17(7): 1270-1283, 1999.

[4] Wisely, D., P. Eardley and L. Burness IP for 3G, John Wiley 2002.

[5] Ahmavaara, K., H. Haverinen and R. Pichna "Integration of wireless LAN and 3G wireless - Interworking architecture between 3GPP and WLAN systems." Communications Magazine, IEEE 41(11): 74-8, 2003.

R. Shankar received the B.E., degree (2001) in Electronics and Communication Engineering (ECE) from A.V.C. College of Engineering, Bharathidasan University, Trichy and M.Tech degree (2006) in ECE from Pondicherry Engineering College, Pondicherry, India. He is pursuing his Ph.D. programme in the Department of ECE, Pondicherry Engineering College, Pondicherry. He is currently working as Assistant Professor in the Department of ECE at SMVEC affiliated to Pondicherry University, India. His research interests include wireless communication and convergence network.

P.Dananjayan received Bachelor of Science from University of Madras in 1979, Bachelor of Technology in 1982 and Master of Engineering in 1984 from the Madras Institute of Technology, Chennai and Ph.D. degree from Anna University, Chennai in 1998. He is working as a Professor and Head of the Department of Electronics and Communication Engineering, Pondicherry Engineering College, Pondicherry, India. He has more than 60 publications in National and International Journals. He has presented more than 130 papers in National and International conferences. He has produced 6 Ph.D candidates and is currently guiding eight Ph.D students. His areas of interest include power electronics, Spread spectrum Techniques and Wireless Communication.

VERTICAL HANDOFF DECISION ALGORITHM USING SYSTEM PERFORMANCE AND USER PREFERENCE

R. SHANKAR

Sri Manakula Vinayagar Engineering College, Madagadipet, Pondicherry

P. DANANJAYAN

Pondicherry Engineering College, Pondicherry.

pdananjayan@rediffmail.com

Future wireless networks must be able to coordinate services between diverse network environments. In this paper, vertical handoff is discussed which overcomes the disadvantage of traditional handoff, Several optimizations are proposed for the execution of vertical handoff decision algorithms, with the goal of maximizing the QoS experienced by each user. Performance analysis demonstrates that significant gains in the ability to satisfy user requests for multiple simultaneous services and a more efficient use of resources can be achieved from vertical hand off decision algorithm.

1. Introduction

A significant challenge for third generation (3G) and fourth generation (4G) wireless networks in figure 1 is to coordinate many types of networks being used for wireless communications. The third generation partnership project (3GPP) is currently developing standards for the inter-working of the Universal Mobile Telecommunications System (UMTS) with HiPerLAN, including the open issue of when, where and how to initiate handoff between a 3G cellular system and a WLAN.

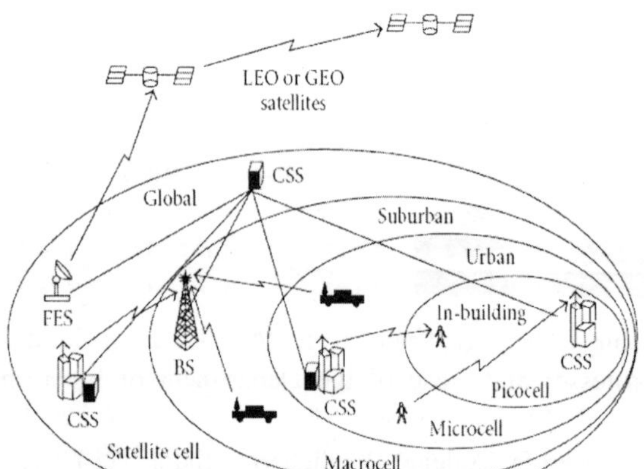

Figure 1: Diverse 3G and 4G wireless networks

Traditionally, handoff research has been based on an evaluation of the received signal strength (RSS) at the mobile nodes. Vertical or inter system handoff is the decision for a mobile node to handoff between different types of networks. Traditional handoff received signal strength are not sufficient to make a vertical handoff decision, as they do not take into account the various attachment options for the mobile user. A performance analysis demonstrates that significant gains in quality of service and a more efficient use of resources can be achieved from the proposed optimizations.

Using RSS based vertical handoff, a mobile device will handoff to another network when it cannot receive the minimum power from the original network. In case of vertical handoff a mobile user from a WLAN to WCDMA handoff can be done even though the achievable data rate from WLAN is much higher than WCDMA.

In this paper, a new vertical handoff decision algorithm using SINR instead of RSS as the handoff criterion is proposed. Analyses shows that SINR based vertical handoff provides higher average throughputs for end users comparing with the RSS based vertical handoff with various thresholds settings, and is better adaptive to different network conditions, such as different noise level and load factor.

The SINR based vertical handoff strategy describes analytical model used to evaluate the performance of different vertical handoff algorithms. The performance analysis and numerical results demonstrate the load-balancing advantages of the proposed technique, as well as the significant gains in satisfied user requests and a more efficient use of resources.

The rest of this paper is organized as follows Section 2 reviews the metrics such as system performance and user preference with their numerical results. Section 3 summarizes and concludes this analysis.

2. Services

In the case of vertical handoff, the policy database holds information regarding the metrics to be considered for a vertical handoff, where handoff metrics are the measured qualities that give an indication of whether or not a handoff is needed. As stated previously, in traditional handoffs, only RSS and channel availability are considered.

2.1 *System Performance and User Preferences*

To guarantee the system performance, a variety of parameters can be employed in handoff decision, such as the channel propagation characteristics, path loss, signal-to-noise ratio (SNR), and the bit error rate (BER), signal to interference plus noise ratio (SINR).

User preference can be added to cater to special requests for users that favor one type of system over another.

2.2 *SINR Based Vertical Handoff Strategy*

Using the RSS as the handoff indicator, the best possible performance of the integrated wireless networks is not achieved. To provide seamless handover between WLAN and WCDMA SINR based vertical handoff that can support multimedia QoS with adaptive rate is desirable. The new vertical handoff algorithm not only can support user with multimedia QoS and be capable of allowing the user achieving the maximum throughputs during vertical handoff, but also makes the load balancing between WLAN and WCDMA systems.

According to Shannon capacity, the maximum achievable rate R_{ij} is given by:

$$R_{ij}=W\log(1+\gamma_{ij}/\Gamma) \qquad (1)$$

where,

W is the bandwidth,

γ_{ij} is SINR received at user I when associated with AP_j or BS_j,

Γ is the gap between uncoded M-QAM and capacity, minus the coding gain.

Let R_{AP} and R_{BS} be the maximum downlink bandwidth available while user connected with WLAN and WCDMA.

From Shannon capacity,

$$R_{AP}=W_{AP}\log2\,(1+\gamma_{AP}/\Gamma_{AP}) \qquad (2)$$

$$R_{BS}=W_{BS}\log2\,(1+\gamma_{BS}/\Gamma_{BS}) \qquad (3)$$

where, γ_{AP} is the receiving SINR from WLAN, and γ_{BS} is the receiving SINR from WCDMA on High Speed Downlink Packet Access (HSDPA) channel. The relationship between required γ_{AP} and γ_{BS} while offering the same downlink bandwidth to user by WLAN and WCDMA is important.

Letting $R_{AP} = R_{BS}$, equation can be solved and get the relationship between γ_{AP} and γ_{BS} as

$$\gamma_{AP}= \Gamma_{AP}\,((1+\gamma_{BS}/\Gamma_{BS})\wedge W_{BS}/W_{AP}-1) \qquad (4)$$

The parameters in (4) are:

• The bandwidth for WLAN W_{AP} is 1MHz [1] and 5MHz for WCDMA W_{BS} [2].

• Γ_{AP} equals to 3dB for WLAN [1], and Γ_{BS} equals to 16dB for WCDMA [2].

Having the relationship between available bit rate and receiving SINR from both WLAN and WCDMA makes the SINR based vertical handoff method applicable, in which the receiving SINR from WCDMA γ_{BS} is being converted to the equivalent γ_{AP} *required* to achieve the same bit rate, and compared with the receiving SINR from WLAN.

Handoff is triggered while the user is getting higher equivalent SINR from another access network. It means that given the receiver end SINR measurements of both WLAN and WCDMA channel [3], the handoff mechanism now has the knowledge of the estimated maximum possible receiving bit rates a user can get from either WLAN or WCDMA at the same time within the handover zone, inside where both WLAN and WCDMA signal are available.

This gives the vertical handoff mechanism the ability to make handoff decision with multimedia QoS consideration, such as offer the user maximum downlink throughput from the integrated network, or guarantee the minimum user required bit rate during vertical handoff.

2.3 *Numerical Result*

SINR based vertical handoff algorithm is compared with the RSS based vertical handoff algorithm in terms of user's mean downlink throughputs while traveling through the integrated network. Various thresholds setting for RSS based vertical handoff: -90dBm, -85dBm and -80dBm are all tested together with the proposed SINR based vertical handoff.

The mean throughputs under different noise power of WLAN are shown in Figure 2. As it can be seen, the overall mean throughput becomes lower with higher noise power, since the maximum bit rate the user is getting from WLAN decrease while the interference level increases.

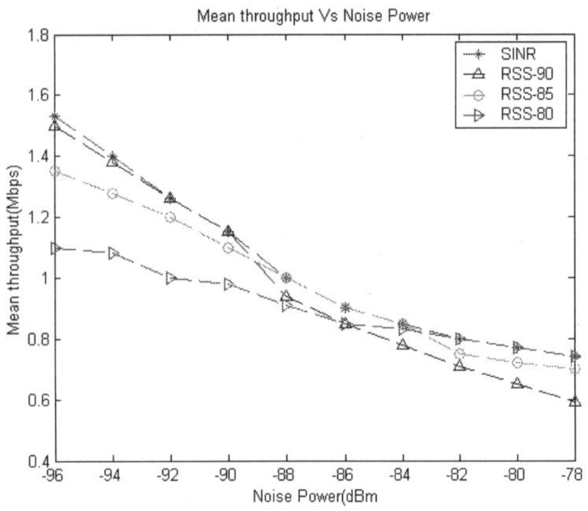

Figure 2 Mean throughput Vs Noise power

The performance of RSS based vertical handoff using different thresholds values varies under different network conditions. RSS based vertical handoff with lower threshold values perform better in low noise conditions than higher thresholds values, as they allow the user to stay connected with WLAN longer from which higher bandwidth is still available comparing with WCDMA. Comparing with the performance variations of RSS based vertical handoff using different thresholds values, the SINR based vertical handoff consistently offers the highest mean throughput under any noise level.

In real networks, interference power will be various depending on the user location as well as the density of users. Therefore, only the SINR based vertical handoff can guarantee multimedia QoS specifying the achieved date rate for end user inside vertical handover zone.

The average cells downlink load factor of WCDMA networks and the performance of different algorithms are varied and shown in Figure 4. In this comparison, the noise power of WLAN is fixed at its minimum value which allows the maximum available bit rate came from WLAN side. As the load factor of WCDMA networks increases, the downlink radio resource is getting scarce and decreases the maximum achievable bit rate of the channel. Therefore, the overall throughput becomes lower under higher load factor, with the performance variations of different RSS thresholds settings become more apparent.

2.4 *Performance Analysis*

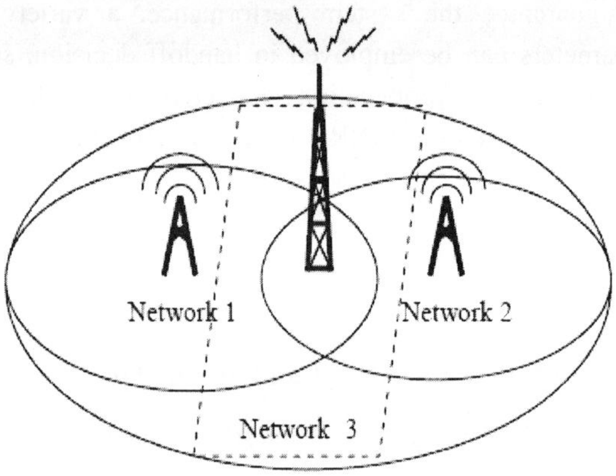

Figure 3 Overlay network of 3G cell

Simulations have been performed for the 3G cell overlay structure shown in Figure 3. In the figure, three networks of different data rates co-exist in the same wireless service area.

Network 1 and Network 2 represent WLANs. Network 3 is modeled as a GPRS network, which supports approximately 100 users simultaneously [4].

A user with active sessions that is located in the vicinity of all three networks must decide whether to execute a vertical handoff.

The decision is based on the use of two services, constant bit rate (CBR) and available bit rate (ABR).To highlight the effects of the vertical handoff procedure, only the users within the boundary cell area, which is bounded by the dashed square in Figure 3, are considered.

The load within the overlay cells is described by:

$$\rho = \lambda/\mu \quad (5)$$

where λ is the arrival rate and μ *is* the departure rate. Arrivals and departures are modeled as Poisson distributions.

Resources are assigned according to the type of call, where handoff calls are given a higher priority than new calls. For simplicity, a buffer-less handoff algorithm is used.

Each of the three networks in Figure 3 is modeled as an *M/M/1/Nn* queue system where *Nn* is the number of available channels in Network *n*. *Nn* is calculated:

$$N_n = B_n / D \quad (6)$$

where B_n is the total bandwidth of Network *n*, and *D* is the average data rate of each user.

For the blocking probability of Network *n*, P_{bn}, the blocking probability of an *M/M/1/Nn* queue is used when there are N_n users in system:

$$P_{bn} = \rho_n^{Nn}(1-\rho_n) / (1-\rho_n^{Nn+1}) \quad (7)$$

where ρ_n is the effective load experienced by Network *n*,

$$\rho_n = r_n\rho \quad (8)$$

and r_n is the percentage of total requests that will go to Network *n*.

2.5 *Numerical Result*

The user mobility, user requests, network acceptances and denials for the 3G/WLAN overlay system in Figure 3 were modeled and simulated using MATLAB, based on the system parameters. Each user can request a data rate up to a maximum of 500 kbps.

To gauge the response of the protocol to different traffic types, this data rate includes a combination of constant bit rate (CBR) services and available bit rate (ABR) services, where the CBR request per user is limited to a maximum of 50 kbps and the ABR request per user is limited to a maximum of 450 kbps. However, the objective is to gauge the ability of a combination of networks to satisfy as many user requests as possible. Thus, as data rates per network increase, the size of the data rate request may also increase, but the resulting trends for the given algorithms would remain the same.

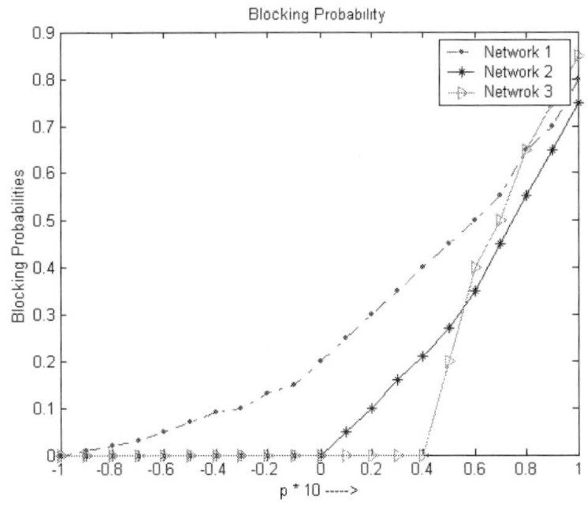

Figure 4. Performance Analysis

Figure 4 demonstrates the corresponding blocking probability of each network. An increase in blocking probability of Networks 1 and 2 earlier than Network 3 can be observed, which indicates that WLANs are favorite networks due to their relative larger available bandwidth to each use

Figure 5 shows APUSR and blocking probability versus user requests for the three handoff algorithms for the more demanding CBR requests.

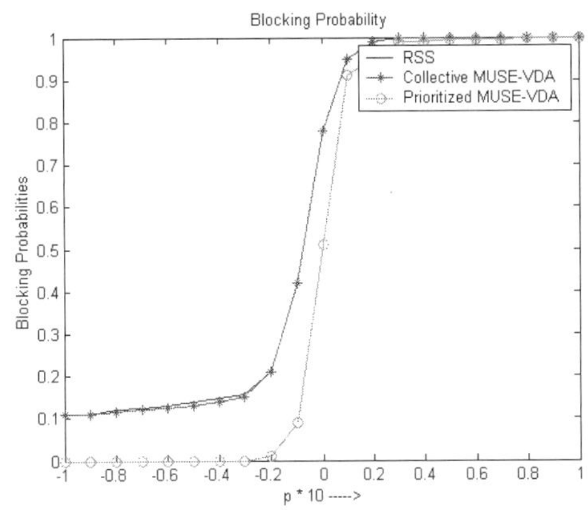

Figure 5: Blocking probability

In this case, Network 3 is eliminated in RSS-based and collective MUSE-VDA handoff algorithms, due to its limited data rate per user (less than 170 kbps). Thus, users will only be able to choose between Networks 1 and 2. This increases the APUSR in RSS-based algorithm in light traffic since users no longer join with Network 3. However, the APUSR in collective MUSE-VDA decreases, since Networks 1 and 2 cannot cover the whole area. On the other hand, all 3 networks can be used in prioritized MUSE-VDA, where the user's two sessions can be spread into multiple networks. If the bandwidth for one session cannot be satisfied, only one session will be blocked. This results in a higher APUSR and a lower blocking probability than the other two handoff schemes. Moreover, since users moving out of the limited coverage of Networks 1 and 2 cannot be served in RSS-based handoff algorithm and collective MUSE-VDA, a nonzero blocking probability can be observed all the time.

3. Conclusion

Expanding services through the use and coordination of diverse networks creates the challenge of developing a more complex, adaptive, and intelligent vertical handoff protocol. A performance analysis demonstrated significant gains in the ability to satisfy user's requests for multiple simultaneous services and a more efficient use of resources from the proposed optimizations. The new vertical handoff algorithm proposed in this paper using the receiving SINR from WLAN and WCDMA networks as the handoff criteria, which provides the knowledge of the achievable bandwidth from both access networks. Analysis results show that the performance of RSS based vertical handoff differs under different network conditions, for different thresholds setting. In contrast, the new SINR based vertical handoff algorithm is able to consistently offer the end user with maximum available throughputs during vertical handoff.

Acknowledgments

We would like to convey our acknowledgement to S. Lakshmidevi, T. Hemavathy, R. Lakshmi, and P. Maheswari of Sri Manakula Vinayagar Engineering College (SMVEC), Pondicherry, India.

References

[1] J. McNair and F. Zhu, "Vertical handoffs in fourth-generation multinetwork W.Wu,N.Banerjee, K. Basu, and S. K. Das, "SIP-based vertical handoff between WWANs and WLANs," IEEE Wireless Communications, vol. 12, no. 3, pp. 66–72, 2005.

[2] H. Badis and K. Al-Agha, "Fast and efficient vertical handoffs in wireless overlay networks," in Proccedings of IEEE International Sympopsium on Personal Radio communications (PIMRC '04), vol. 3, pp. 1968–1972, Barcelona, Spain, September 2004.

[3] J. Tourrilhes and C. Carter, "P-Handoff: a protocol for finegrained peer-to-peer vertical handoff," in Proceedings of the 13th IEEE International Symposium on Personal, Indoor, and Mobile Radio Communications (PIMRC '02), vol. 2, pp. 966–971, Lisbon, Portugal, September 2002.

[4] M. Salamah, F. Tansu, and N. Khalil, "Buffering requirements for lossless vertical handoffs in wireless overlay networks," in Proceedings of 57th IEEE Semiannual Vehicular Technology Conference (VTC '03), vol. 3, pp. 1984–1987, Jeju, South Korea, April 2003.

R. Shankar received the B.E., degree (2001) in Electronics and Communication Engineering (ECE) from A.V.C. College of Engineering, Bharathidasan University, Trichy and M.Tech degree (2006) in ECE from Pondicherry Engineering College, Pondicherry, India. He is pursuing his Ph.D. programme in the Department of ECE, Pondicherry Engineering College, Pondicherry. He is currently working as Assistant Professor in the Department of ECE at SMVEC affiliated to Pondicherry University, India. His research interests include wireless communication and convergence network.

P.Dananjayan received Bachelor of Science from University of Madras in 1979, Bachelor of Technology in 1982 and Master of Engineering in 1984 from the Madras Institute of Technology, Chennai and Ph.D. degree from Anna University, Chennai in 1998. He is working as a Professor and Head of the Department of Electronics and Communication Engineering, Pondicherry Engineering College, Pondicherry, India. He has more than 60 publications in National and International Journals. He has presented more than 130 papers in National and International conferences. He has produced 6 Ph.D candidates and is currently guiding eight Ph.D students. His areas of interest include power electronics, Spread spectrum Techniques and Wireless Communication.

APPLICATION RESEARCH OF WORKFLOW TECHNOLOGY IN COMPLEX PRODUCT DEVELOPMENT

CHENGLONG WANG

College of Mechanical and Electronics Engineering, Shandong University of Science & Technology Qingdao, 266510, China

ZENG QING-LIANG

College of Mechanical and Electronics Engineering, Shandong University of Science & Technology Qingdao, 266510, China

ZHANG XIN

College of Mechanical and Electronics Engineering, Shandong University of Science & Technology Qingdao, 266510, China

WANG ZAICHANG

College of Mechanical and Electronics Engineering, Shandong University of Science & Technology Qingdao, 266510, China

HE MING

College of Mechanical and Electronics Engineering, Shandong University of Science & Technology Qingdao, 266510, China

Application of workflow technology in complex product development is studied in this paper. Firstly the typical problems during the process of complex product development are analyzed. Secondly the requirement of using workflow technology is analyzed. A workflow model for complex product development and the method of using the model is given. Finally an instance is presented for application and validation.

1. Introduction

In this paper, the problems during complex product development are firstly analyzed from the viewpoint of authors in section 1. The method of overall using workflow technology in complex product development process is given in section 2. Finally an instance is presented for application and validation, which belongs to the development of YZ18JA-Vibration roller.

We will discuss them in detail in the following. Complex product, such as flying vehicles, automobile, railway vehicles and robotics etc., usually are complex large-scale systems. The development process for a complex product is a concurrent and collaborative design process involved with mechanics, electronics, software and other disciplines [1]. During the process of complex product development lifecycle, not only the distributed teams, interrelated activities and processes, but also all the data relevant to products need to be managed, so as to ensure that right information can be delivered to right person at right time and in a right way, which is a big challenge to the complex product development for the traditional Chinese manufacturing enterprises [2, 3].

2. Application research of workflow technology in complex product development

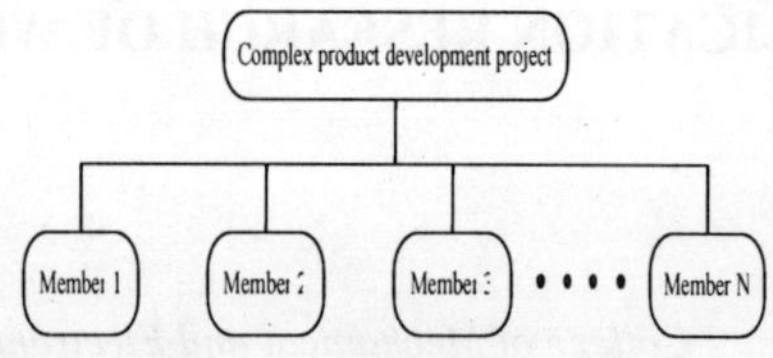

Figure 1 Organization model

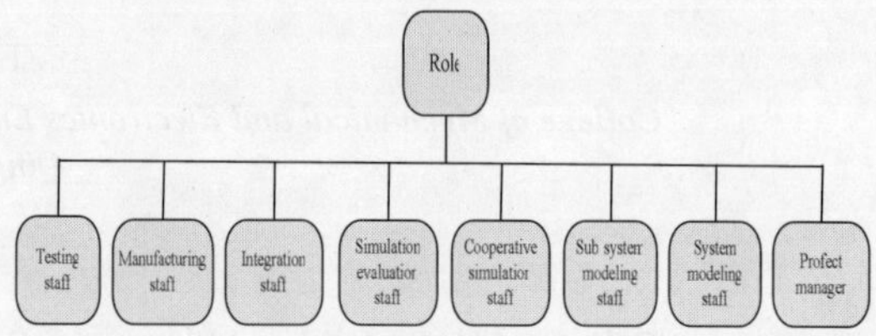

Figure 2 the role model

Workflow technology, which is one of the key technologies of collaborative work [4], can help to get a better control of work processes with better flexibility and efficiency. From the viewpoint of workflow, all activities during the product development process are composed of a series of workflows, including data flow and control flow. All these activities constitute a very complex workflow which is composed of many sub-workflows.

In order to make sure that the cooperation of multidiscipline teams can be successful and efficiently, the method of overall using workflow technology in complex product development is studied. According to the development process of complex product, workflow model is given, which includes team member management model and process model.

2.1. *Team member management model of complex product development*

Team member management model is also called "organizations - roles - authorities" model, which defines the organization, the role and the authority of team member involved in the process of complex product development. According to the definition of the team member management model, relevant members are enabled to work according to the expected workflow.

Organization model: According to the complex product development process, an organizations model is provided which is showed in Figure 1.In this model, member which is related to real person in real life, represents the staff who involved in the process.

Role model: Role is related to the responsibility of certain person. Because of the interrelationship and cooperation among different teams, team member will have multiple roles during the whole process. Here roles, which are showed in Figure 2, are defined as following:

Project manager: he is responsible for the management and monitoring of the whole process, the decomposition and distribution of tasks, and the management of roles and team members.

System modeling staff is responsible for system modeling. He will get tasks from his own working list which is given by project manager. After his work is finished, he will give the result to related sub-system modeling staffs.

Sub-system modeling staff is responsible for sub-system modeling and he will get tasks from system modeling staffs. After his work is finished, he will give the result to Cooperative simulation staff.

Cooperative simulation staff is responsible for cooperative simulation of the whole system. He will integrate the related simulation models and run the co-simulation. After his work is finished, he will give the result to Simulation evaluation staff.

Simulation evaluation staff is responsible for the evaluation of cooperative simulation with the help of evaluation system. He will evaluate the performance of the whole system. After his evaluation, the validity of the sub-system model will be given. If the sub-system models are acceptable, he will give the result to integration staff.

Integration staff is responsible for the review and the integration of the sub-system models with the aid of certain tools. After getting the result from simulation evaluation staff, he will review all the models and evaluate its assembling and manufacturing ability. If everything is ok, he will hand out all the related materials to manufacturing staff. At the same time, all the models will be checked into model data base. Manufacturing staff: he is responsible for the manufacturing and assembling of product. After this stage, a physical prototyping is given.

Testing staff is responsible for the testing of physical prototyping. After his evaluation testing, he will give the testing results to project manager.

Table1 Basic authority model

role	Working group	Controlled object	read	write	delete	modify
Project manager	Management	Whole project	Yes	Yes	Yes	Yes
System modeling staff	System modeling	System model	Yes	Yes	Yes	Yes
Sub-system modeling staff	Sub-system modeling	Sub-system model	Yes	Yes	No	Yes
Cooperative simulation staff	Cooperative simulation	Cooperative simulation model	Yes	No	No	No
Simulation evaluation staff	Simulation evaluation	Simulation evaluation model	Yes	Yes	No	No
Integration staff	integration	Evaluated system model	Yes	Yes	Yes	Yes
Manufacturing staff	manufacturing	Evaluated sub-system model	Yes	Yes	No	No

Authority model: In this model, the basic authority of all the roles is defined, which is showed on Table1. The controlled object of each role and the access to the controlled object is defined.

When these three models referred above are associated together, team member management model of the complex product development will be got, which is shown in Table 2.

Table 2 Team member management model

Group	User name	name	role
Management	Project manager	xxx	Project manager
System modeling	System designer	xxx	System modeling staff
Sub-system modeling	Sub-system designer	xxx	Sub-system modeling staff
Cooperative simulation	Cooperative simulation engineer	xxx	Cooperative simulation staff
Simulation evaluation	Simulation evaluation engineer	xxx	Simulation evaluation staff
integration	Integration engineer	xxx	Integration staff
manufacturing	Manufacturing engineer	xxx	Manufacturing staff

2.2. *Process model of complex product development*

Process model describes the general process of complex product development, which includes activities, roles related to activities and review rules in detailed. The workflow process model will be saved as a reference model which is called "workflow template", as showed in Figure 3.The entire process includes eight activities and three basic cycles. Only when the conditions of related cycle are satisfied, the next activity will be carried out.

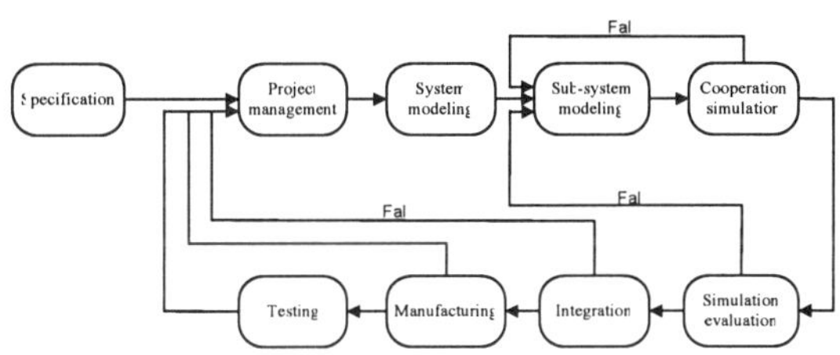

Figure 3 Process model

The first cycle model is mainly used to examine and check the correctness of sub-system model. When Sub-system modeling staff finished the work, he should submit the result to cooperative simulation staff. Cooperative simulation staff will run co-simulation. If the co-simulation does not work, Cooperative simulation staff will rejected the model and sends information to related Sub-system. Only when cooperative simulation staff accepts the results will this cycle be finished. The second cycle is used to optimize the sub-system model. After Simulation evaluation staff gets results from cooperative simulation staff, he will evaluate the performance of the whole system. After his evaluation, the validity of sub-system model will be given. If the sub-system models are not acceptable, he will give the results back to Sub-system modeling staff, and then the first cycle will be repeated. Only when simulation evaluation staff accepts the results will this cycle be finished. When these two cycles are finished, Integration staff will review the sub-system models and evaluate its manufacturing and assembling ability with the aid of virtual manufacturing and assembling tools. If something is wrong, he will send the information to project manager, the two cycles mentioned above should be repeated. If everything is ok, he will hand out all the related materials to manufacturing staff. At the same time, all the models, which are the final version in this process, will be checked into model data base. Until now the three cycles are finished.

After receiving materials from Integration staff, manufacturing staff will finish the manufacturing and assembly of product. At the end of this stage, a physical prototyping is given. Finally, testing staff will test physical prototyping, he will give the testing results to project manager, and then the whole process is finished.

2.3. *Implement the workflow model with the aid of workflow software*

According to the models set up in the section 2.1 and 2.2, the appropriate workflow software should be selected and the workflow will be implemented. In our research new workflow software is developed and used to implement the workflow model.

3. A case study:

The cooperative development of Vibration roller involves cooperation of multiple disciplinary teams, which are located in different places. How to manage and control the distributed teams, interrelated activities and all the data relevant to products efficiently is a key challenge. Workflow technology is used, which helps to improve the management and control of the whole process, shorten product development cycle, and reduce cost of this product. The detailed steps are as following:

Firstly, the team member management model of this case is given. (Figure 4).Secondly, the workflow process model of the cooperative development of Vibration roller is developed and implemented in the" Workflow Management System for Mechatronic System" (Figure 5).

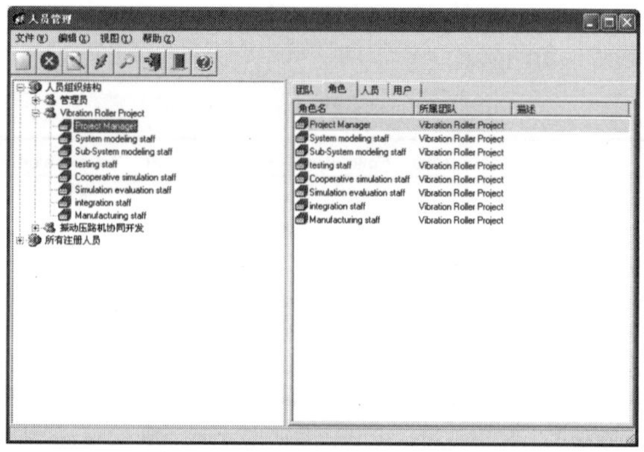

Figure 4 Team member management model

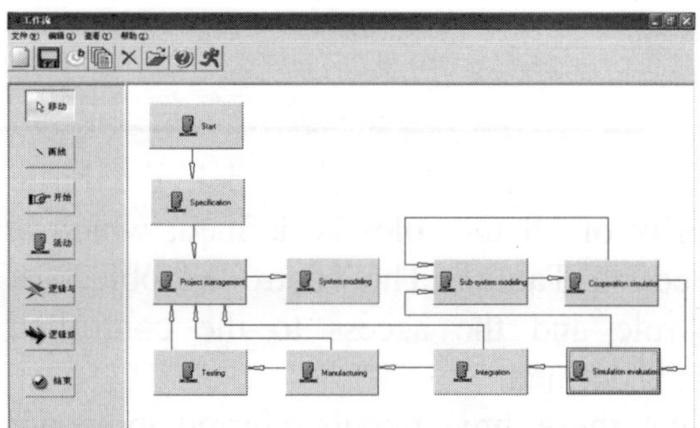

Figure 5 Implementation of workflow

Acknowledgments

The application reported in this paper is supported by the National Natural Science Foundation of China (No.50875158) , the National Key Technology R&D Program of China (No.2006BAB11B05) , Shandong Natural Science Foundation for Distinguished Young scholars of China (No. JQ200816) and Shandong Natural Science Foundation of China (No.Y2007G02)

References

1. Bohu Li and etc., The Research on supported environment techniques for complex product collaboration manufacturing, Computer Integrated Manufacturing System CIMS, Vol. 9, No. 8, Agu, 2003 (in Chinese)
2. Xiong, G., Zhang, H., and Li, B., 2000, Research and application of concurrent engineering in China, Computer Integrated Manufacturing Systems (CIMS), Vol. 6, No. 2, pp. 1-7.
3. Zhang, H. and Xiong, G., 2001, !An overview of concurrent engineering research and its industrial implementation in Chinese enterprises, High Technology Letters, Vol. 7, No. 1, pp. 42-46.
4. Xiong Guangleng. Concurrent Engineering Theory and Practice [M]. Beijing: Tsinghua University Press, 2000.

Design and Realization of Students' Comprehensive Information Management System Based on Database

Chang Haifeng
Tianjin Polytechnic University
Tianjin, China
pyy_jdxyh@sohu.com

***Abstract*—The target of building digital campus should be under the direction of new talent view, teaching view, scientific research view and management theory, seen from management, the digital campus-oriented students' information management system is a kind of solution of college student managers to digital environment challenges. As a relatively important part in digital campus, students' information management system should be one of the most fundamental management systems in digital campus and this paper mainly discusses business process, architecture and design, etc, of students' comprehensive information management system in the environment of digital campus and realizes partial functions of the system.**

Keywords-database; students' comprehensive information management system; digital campus

I. INTRODUCTION

Along with the development of technology and the change of objective demand, the researches and applications related to information system are also developing and changing continuously. Early computer was only used for scientific calculation and began to be used for commercial use from the 1950s and the application range was gradually extending to electronic data processing (EDP), transaction processing system (TPS) and information report system (IRS). In the 1960s, along with the maturity of database technology, when people could access to data immediately, management information system (MIS) was produced.

MIS system uses database technology to realize business management and carry out a mass of transaction processing work on a computer and its main purpose is to improve enterprise efficiency. After the middle period of the 1990s, along with the rapid development of network technology, the information technology synthesis combining computer, network, database and distributed calculation began to form into new browser/server (B/S) working mode to make information communication more convenient, rapid and accurate.

II. SYSTEM FUNCTION DESIGN

Students' comprehensive information management system is mainly involved in students' entrance (enrollment management system), students' training and management (school roll management system), students' various financial aids (scholarship, grant and loan system) and student graduation management (graduate management system), etc. Among these parts, graduate management system had been independent from students' comprehensive information management system and individually managed by employment guidance center in September, 2006.

The whole system is involved in every aspect of students in college, and therefore it includes a long time, many links and large data updating amount. The research and design of the system will basically realize the informatization of student management work. The informatization of student management work is, as it were, the realization of timely treatment and sharing of standard information by collecting and sorting out various data in student management work, establishing corresponding student management work databases, compiling related application software and normalizing student management work. According to the analysis of actual demand, the system can be divided into the following modules, namely enrollment management system, school roll management system, student aid system, graduate management system, system maintenance, user management, student area and system desktop. These modules include different functions and different users have different authorities.

TABLE I. FUNCTION STRUCTURE TABLE OF STUDENTS' INFORMATION MANAGEMENT SYSTEM

System Module	Function Module	Function Explanation
Enrollment Management System	Enrolment Information Release	Release of information, such as enrollment announcement, enrollment information in past years and enrollment policy and plan query, etc
	Online Registration	Examinees fill in registration information
	Achievement and Enrollment Result Query	Result query about art, music, sports, autonomous enrollment and common college entrance examination,

		etc
	Online Consultation	
	Freshman Register System	
School Roll Management System	Information Query	For various types of users to inquire about the related information
	Information Modification	Modify the wrong information in the system
	Information Downloading	Convert the data in the system into xls files and download
	Data Import	Import external information into system
Aid Management System	Rule Management	Manage various aid categories
	Application Status	Look over application status
	Aid Management	Look over, consider and audit students' aid applications
	Data Import	Import external information into system
Graduate Management System	Employment Information Release	Realize the release of information related to employment
	Employment and Agreement Management	Manage employment agreements
	Graduate Management on Leaving School	Manage graduates' information on leaving school
	Statistical Report	Count graduates' employment rate, etc
System Maintenance	System Setting	Set the related settings of the system
	System Backup	Time and manually back up databases
	Log Management	Set log action time and manage logs
User Management	User Management	Set user levels and authorities
	Add Users	Add new users to the system and set user levels and authorities
Student Area	System Announcement	Display various notices of the system
	Display and modify personal information	Basic Information
	Aid Application Information	Apply for aids and look over aid application status
System Desktop	System Announcement	Display various notices of the system
	User Information	Look over the current user information
	Common Link	Display links according to user type

III. DATABASE DESIGN

A. Data access design

The system is mainly developed by ASP and we adopt ADO (ActiveX Data Object) mode to access to data and realize the operations for table, such as increase, deletion, modification and query, etc, by database query language-SQL. Uses can finish the operations needed only according to prompts on Web pages, not needing to be concerned how these operations are realized completely.

B. Database structure design

Table 2, table 3 and table 4 are the detailed structure designs of partial tables in the system.

TABLE II. STRUCTURE DESIGN OF USER TABLE

Field Name	Field Type	Field Length	Null Value	Field Explanation
ID	Int	4	NO	Identification, increases 1 every time
User_Name	nvarchar	30	NO	User Name
User_Password	nvarchar	50	NO	User Password
Uset_TrueName	nvarchar	30	NO	User True Name
User_Sys	nvarchar	15	NO	User Module
User_Depart	nvarchar	15	NO	User Department
User_Level	nvarchar	15	NO	User Level
User_Purview	nvarchar	255	NO	User Authority
User_TimeLimit	nvarchar	30	YES	User Time Limit
User_Ip	nvarchar	15	YES	IP Address Allowed to Log in
User_No	int	30	NO	Unified Number in Digital Campus

TABLE III. SUBSYSTEM TABLE OF STUDENTS' INFORMATION MANAGEMENT SYSTEM

Field Name	Field Type	Field Length	Null Value	Field Explanation
ID	int	4	NO	Identification, increases 1 every time
Sys_Name	nvarchar	30	NO	Subsystem Name
Sys_No	int	10	NO	Subsystem Number
Sys_Run	bit	×	NO	Subsystem Switch
Sys_StartTime	datetime	8	YES	System Running Start Time
Sys_EndTime	dateime	8	YES	System Running End Time

TABLE IV. SUBSYSTEM FUNCTION MODULE TABLE OF STUDENTS' INFORMATION MANAGEMENT SYSTEM

Field Name	Field Type	Field Length	Null Value	Field Explanation
ID	int	10	NO	Identification, increases 1 every time
Module_Name	nvarchar	20	NO	Module Name
Sys_No	nvarchar	30	NO	Subsystem Number
Module_No	nvarchar	10	NO	Module Number
Module_Switch	bit	×	NO	Function Module Switch
Module_Switch	bit	×	NO	Module Switch

TABLE V. FRESHMAN INFORMATION TABLE

Field Name	Field Type	Field Length	Null Value	Field Explanation
ID	int	10	NO	Identification, increases 1 every time
xh	int	15	NO	Student Number
ksh	int	20	NO	Examination Number
zkzh	int	20	NO	Examination Admission Card Number
xm	nvarchar	15	NO	Name
xb	nvarchar	2	NO	Sex
zymc	nvarchar	30	NO	Specialty Name
yxmc	nvarchar	30	NO	College/Department Name
bz	nvarchar	4	NO	Undergraduate/Junior College
mz	nvarchar	10	NO	Nationality
csny	datetime	4	NO	Date of Birth
sf	nvarchar	15	NO	Province
lxdh	nvarchar	30	NO	Telephone Number
lxdz	nvarchar	60	NO	Address
qs	nvarchar	30	NO	Dormitory Number

bd	bit	1	NO	Register or not
bdsj	datetime	8	NO	Register Time
xxnum	int	6	NO	Register Ranking of the Whole University
yxnum	int	6	NO	Register Ranking of the Whole College
dang	bit	×	NO	Hand in the files or not

TABLE VI. STUDENTS' BASIC INFORMATION TABLE

Field Name	Field Type	Field Length	Null Value	Field Explanation
ID	int	10	NO	Identification, increases 1 every time
xh	int	15	NO	Student Number
ksh	int	20	NO	Examination Number
zkzh	int	30	NO	Examination Admission Card Number
xm	nvarchar	15	NO	Name
xb	nvarchar	2	NO	Sex
zymc	nvarchar	30	NO	Specialty Name
yxmc	nvarchar	30	NO	College/Department Name
bz	nvarchar	4	NO	Undergraduate/Junior College
mz	nvarchar	10	NO	Nationality
csny	datetime	8	NO	Date of Birth
sf	nvarchar	15	NO	Province
lxdh	nvarchar	30	NO	Telephone Number
lxdz	nvarchar	60	NO	Address
qs	nvarchar	30	NO	Dormitory Number

IV. AUTHORITY DESIGN

The system designs the following users of different grades to realize its classification management. Shown as Table 5, user level and authority are set as follows:

(1) Administrator: owns the administrative authority of the system.

(2) Advanced user: college/department administrator and various departments, etc

(3) Advanced user can be divided into three grades: first grade, second grade and third grade, among which administrator has all administrative authorities of the unit and the authority of increasing second-grade and third-grade users. First-grade user authority can not be modified and second-grade and third-grade user authorities can be set by administrators or first-grade users of the unit.

(4) Common user: student user, etc, and its authority can not be modified.

(5) Casual user: It is provided for extramural users, such as employing units, etc, and has time limit, its authority is set by first-grade users in advanced users and users of different grades have different authorities in different modules of the system. Table 6 is the relation between user levels and various modules of the system.

TABLE VII. COMPARISON TABLE OF USER ACCOUNT SETTINGS AND AUTHORITIES

User Level	User Classification	Authority Level	Time Limit	
Administrator	Administrator:	×	All	No
Advanced User	College/Department User	First Grade	This college or department	No
		Second Grade	This college or department is limited	No
		Third Grade	This college or department is limited	No
	Functional Department User	First Grade	This Department	No
		Second Grade	This department is limited	No
		Third Grade	This department is limited	No
Common User	Student User	×	Personal	No
Casual User	Casual User	×		Yes

TABLE VIII. COMPARISON TABLE OF USER AUTHORITIES OF VARIOUS MODULES

System Module	Administrator	College/Department User	Department User	Common User	Casual User
Enrollment Register System	All	Set	Set	No	Set
School Roll Management System	All	This college or department	Set	No	Set
Student Aid System	All	This college or department	Set	No	No
Graduate Management System	All	This college or department	This Department	No	Set
System Maintenance	All	×	×	×	×
User Management	All	This college or department	This Department	Personal	Personal
Student Area	×	×	×	Personal	×
System Desktop	Management Interface	×	×	×	×

V. SYSTEM SECURITY MECHANISMS

Students' information management system faces the whole internet application, and therefore security problem is an important aspect of system construction. In order to ensure the security of the whole system, we mainly adopt authentication mechanism, log mechanism, network security mechanism and backup mechanism, etc, when designing the system.

A. *Authentication mechanism*

Students' information management system identifies uses and prevents the login of illegal users and unauthorized users by authentication technology. This technology is mainly carried out from the following aspects:

(1) Identity and authority are strictly limited. For the user name and password submitted by a user to the server, we compare the record in the system with the record in the database and then judge if it is a legal user and the user's identity and authority, and finally we respond according to verification results. The system strictly limits user authority to prevent unauthorized operations.

(2) Limitation of verification code and wrong login frequency. The system checks the verification code generated randomly to prevent malicious login and reduce server burden. And meanwhile, user's login frequency per day is also limited. For example, if a user enters wrong passwords five times a day, he will be locked by the system automatically and can not log in to the system the same day. The locked user can be unlocked by the administrator manually or wait for being unlocked automatically next day.

(3) Login limitation in the specified IP address (or IP address segment). The system can set if users can only log in the specified IP address or IP address segment. After user

login IP address or address segment is designated, if the user enters correct user name and password within this range to log in, he is regarded as a legal user. If not, the system will refuse its login.

(4) Adopt SSL security communication standard. The system adopts SSL security communication standard to ensure that data is transmitted in the security channel constructed between the certificated browser and Web server.

(5) Character string anti-injection treatment

For the information submitted by the user to the server, the system will carry out anti-injection treatment if necessary. The transmitted data must be digital, such as student number and teacher number, etc, if it is not digital, we regard it as injection attack; for character string, the system uses user-defined function Safe Chock to filter illegal characters.

B. Log mechanism

The system provides complete log function to record each operation of the user in detail and use different colors to identify each operation according to operation type. Through log, the system can find the causes of problems rapidly, which is convenient for solving the problems.

C. Network security mechanism

We put up a firewall with powerful functions on the server of students' information management system and all connections should be examined to ensure the security of data server.

D. Backup mechanism

Students' information management system provides two kinds of backup modes, namely manual backup mode and automatic backup mode and it encrypts data and backs up the encrypted data to the local computer and remote backup server. In addition, the system uses the data backup strategy of SQL Server to carry out daily physical and logical backup of data regularly. Through these measures, we can ensure the integrity and security of data when the system is attacked or threatened by other factors. When data is modified in large quantity and changed frequently, the system can set stricter backup strategy.

In addition, backup mechanism also includes RAIDZ redundant data backup scheme adopted on the server to ensure the security of data on hardware.

VI. CONCLUSION

Along with the development of the society and the continuous expansion of college scale, students' information management also faces increasingly big challenges. The traditional manual operation modes can not meet the requirements of realistic development and the information exchange between colleges and students is also increasingly frequent, which require to establish an information management system to be convenient for students' information management and information transmission between colleges and students and achieve the goals, such as information sharing, long information preservation, timely information updating and rapid information exchange, etc. This paper discusses business process, architecture and design, etc, of students' comprehensive information management system in the environment of digital campus and realizes partial functions of the system.

REFERENCES

[1] Kyle Gabhart, J2EE pathfinder: J2EE technologies for the stateless network, IBM developer Works Java Technology Forum, 2003, http://www-128, ibm. com/developerworks/java/library/j-pj, 2ee 1 /index. Html

[2] James Goodwill. Mastering Jakarta Struts. Wiley US, 2002, 50-54

[3] Chuck Cavaness, Jakarta Struts. O'Reilly and Associates, 2002

[4] Malcolm Davis. Struts, an open-source MVC implementation (Manage complexity in large Web sites with servlets and JSP framework), IBM developerWorks Java Technology Forum, 2001, http://www-128. ibm. com/developerworks/java/library/j-struts/index, Html

[5] Fuzloklah Bijian, Adaptive decision Systems, 1 997,(20):297-315

[6] Chuang Ta-Tao, The development support systems [J].Decision Support of an adaptive decision

Research on A New Queuing Schedule Algorithm in the Wireless Communication Network

Wang Wen-cheng
Dept. name Business Management
Hwa Hsia Institute of Technology
Taiwan
wcwang@cc.hwh.edu.tw

***Abstract*—Along with the designation of wireless network and local area network standards and the progressive push-out of network card hardware and corresponding integrated circuits, the software of wireless networks with gradually declining price becomes mature day by day, combined with mobile Internet; its application prospect is wider. According to the characteristics of wireless network communication models, this paper designs a distributed packet fair queuing algorithm to solve the resource fair scheduling problem in packet networks. The distributed packet fair queuing algorithm is realized by changing the existing wireless local area network communication protocol---IEEE802.H accordingly and loading a proper fair scheduling algorithm.**

Keywords-wireless communication network; mobile internet; distributed; fair; queuing algorithm

I. INTRODUCTION

Compared to wired communication network, wireless communication network has a limited communication bandwidth (usually several kilobits per second) and multiple mobile hosts share a broadcast channel, in addition, it adopts competitive mechanism to access to the channel. Reducing the conflicts between hosts and providing a fair channel service for every host participating in competition is one of problems to be solved in the field of wireless communication nowadays. The distributed fair scheduling algorithm put forward in this paper can share the internal network of a wireless channel and schedule multiple packet streams on each mobile host to ensure that they can fairly use the resources of this shared channel within local and global ranges.

II. BASIC IDEA OF DISTRIBUTED FAIR SCHEDULING ALGORITHM (D—WFQ)

According to the communication characteristics of wireless network, this algorithm adopts a kind of fair scheduling strategy combining centralized scheduling with distributed scheduling to ensure the fair scheduling of packet streams in wireless network. The core of the algorithm is mainly to combine a mixed centralized packet fair scheduling algorithm with CSMA/CA of the existing distributed protocol---IEEE802.ll to carry out normal communication and fair scheduling of channel.

In the aspect of fair scheduling, we adopt two relatively typical centralized scheduling algorithms---weighted fair scheduling algorithm (WFS) and server-based fair scheduling algorithm (SBFA) and we use the characteristics that WFS algorithm can solve the short-term fairness of packet scheduling well and SB queue can ensure the long-term fairness of packet scheduling to realize the real fairness of packet scheduling.

Use CSMA to solve the conflict problem in distributed communication and control the normal communication between hosts of a shared wireless channel.

In order to prove the correctness of the algorithm, I design and develop a set of wireless distributed communication simulation environment to carry out an experimental comparative explanation.

The communication network model adopted by this algorithm is shown as the following diagram.

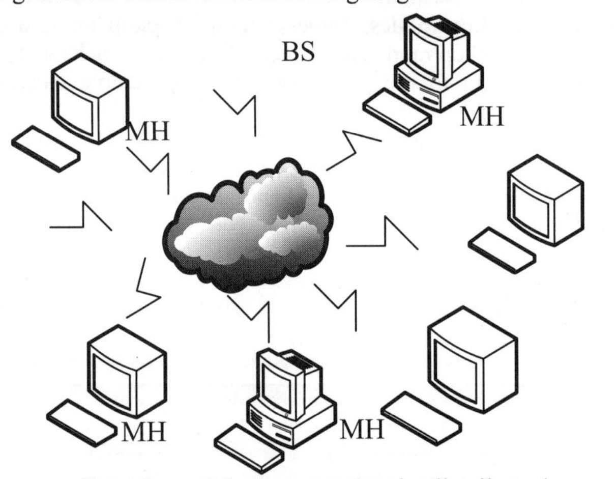

Position of the base station in distributed scheduling scheme in the network

Figure 1. Communication Network Model

III. COMMUNICATION MODEL OF DISTRIBUTED FAIR SCHEDULING PROTOCOL

In a cellular plot of the cellular network shown as Fig 1, the base station holds an important position when communicating and the information sent out by mobile hosts in the plot will be retransmitted by the base station.

In the distributed scheduling scheme, each mobile host independently schedules and monitors the state of the channel to communicate. In addition to the special function of communication retransmission, the base station has the equal status with other mobile hosts and it also monitors the state of the channel to communicate. This paper assumes that the base station adopts one broadcast frequency to carry out broadcast communication and another frequency to communicate with Internet in this plot.

If monitoring channel is idle, carry out RTS-CTS-DATA-ACK data communication, once a conflict happens in communication, adopt back-off mechanism to back off.

IV. FAIR SCHEDULING MODEL

In the distributed scheduling scheme, each mobile host self-schedules the sending of packets according to its own stream state, in the process of sending data, data conflicts will happen, according to the working principle of distributed coordination function (DCF) of IEEE802.ll, we need to adopt back-off mechanism (interceptive binary exponential back-off algorithm is commonly used).

This paper adopts a working mechanism similar to CSMA/CA, combined with the existing centralized packet fair scheduling algorithm, to realize the fair scheduling between various independent streams and this algorithm adopts a two-level fair scheduling model.

A. *First-level fair scheduling model---local fair scheduling model*

The first-level fair scheduling model refers mainly to that on each mobile host which can schedule independently, there may be multiple different streams and these streams need to share an input/output channel, we use an existing centralized fair scheduling algorithm to carry out fair scheduling to realize the local fairness of multiple streams on each mobile node in the whole element network.

B. *Second-level fair scheduling model---global fair scheduling model*

This scheduling model mainly uses the special position of base station (or mobile switching center) in the element network to carry out global fair scheduling. In the distributed scheduling scheme, each mobile host carries out independent stream scheduling. Compared to centralized scheduling scheme, base station (or mobile switching center) can only be responsible for these functions, such as communication data forwarding and routing, etc. Scheduling algorithm needs to maintain a stream information table (See Table 1) on the base station (or mobile switching center) and this information table records each mobile node which is communicating in the current element network, streams on each mobile node, packet transmission condition of each stream and packet numbers being transmitted, etc.

Initially, the stream information table is empty, when a certain mobile node i transmits packet information, because the communication in the element network is broadcast communication, the base station can also hear this packet information, get scheduler from the packet information and send address of packet mobile node, identification of packet stream, serial number of current packet, length of packet and number of packet of packet stream. Every time the base station hears a packet information it looks up the information table, if the information table doesn't contain the information of the packet stream, add the stream to the table, otherwise if the information table contains the information of the packet stream, update the packet number of the corresponding row in the table. When the packet number of a certain row is equal to the number of packet of the row, delete the row of data from the table.

TABLE I. STREAM INFORMATION TABLE

Serial number	Station address	Stream identification	Serial number of packet	Number of packet	Length of packet
1	A	1	1	30	500 (bits)
2	B	1	1	100	1000 (bits)
3	A	2	10	50	1000 (bits)
4	C	1	11	80	1000 (bits)
5	C	2	18	80	1000 (bits)
6	C	3	20	80	1000 (bits)

When communicating, the base station participates in the competition sharing channel, if the local data stream to be retransmitted is nonempty or the stream information table is nonempty, it will be monitoring the channel until the channel becomes idle, after a certain back-off time interval, it begins to use the channel. When using the channel, if the local data stream to be retransmitted is nonempty, give priority to sending the local data stream, otherwise hand the use right of the time slice of the channel to the mobile host corresponding to the stream which has the smallest packet number in the stream information table.

The concrete operation of base station handing the use right of the channel monitored by it to the stream on the mobile host getting the least services is as follows: the base station sends a modified CTS to the mobile host and this paper calls the modified CTS Single-Direction-Modify-CTS and then the mobile host with maximum lag receives Single-Direction-Modify-CTS, at this time the mobile host may be in two states: one is that the mobile host is in back-off state, i.e. back-off interval Bi is nonzero or Bi is just zero, when the mobile host is in this state, it sets Bi as zero immediately and carries out communication according to the transmission protocol of RTS-CTS-DATA-ACK to transmit the head packets of streams selected by the host according to centralized scheduling algorithm; the mobile host doesn't respond to the other state.

V. FIRST-LEVEL FAIR SCHEDULING MODEL---LOCAL FAIR SCHEDULING MODEL

On each mobile node computer, for multiple streams which may be transmitted, we need to adopt a fair scheduling algorithm to carry out communication scheduling to ensure the fair distribution of resources, this paper calls it local fair scheduling algorithm scheduling mechanism and the fair scheduling algorithm adopted by this mechanism is a variant of weighted fair scheduling algorithm (WFS). Its concrete principle is as follows:

For each stream to be transmitted with a weight ri, the calculation method of start mark and end mark of packet is as follows:

When each packet in the stream arrives at the head of the stream, we begin to calculate the start mark and end mark of packet. Initially, the start mark of packet is 0;

- Start Mark $S(P_i^k) = MAX\{V(A(P_i^k))\}$, $S(P_{i-1}^k)+(L_i^{k-1})+(L_i^{k-1})/r_i$;

  L_i^k is the length of the Kth packet of stream i;

  $A(P_i^k)$ is the arrival time of this packet; V(t) is the virtual time of time t.

  $S(P_i^k)$ is used to represent the services obtained by packet P_i^k.

- End Mark $F(P_i^k) = S(P_i^k)+(L_i^k)/r_i$;
- $dV/dt = C(t)/\sum_{i\in B(t)} r_i$;

  B(t) is the set of all streams in ready state at t; C(t) is the channel capacity at t.

- At each time t, for all streams in ready state, choose the stream with the minimum completion mark to schedule.
- The mark of a stream is the end mark of the stream head packet.

VI. FAIR BACK-OFF MECHANISM

Each mobile node schedules streams independently, and therefore conflicts will happen in communication, if conflicts happen, back off for some time at random. Along with the increase of the number of times conflicts happen, some streams need to back off many times, and within the time interval of back-off, some streams can successfully transmit their own packet information, thereby unfair phenomena arising. Because each stream on different mobile nodes is assigned a mark, we can use these marks used to identify the quantity of obtained services to schedule these streams, for the stream getting less services, make it have priority to getting services by reducing its back-off interval, for the stream getting more services, reduce its services by increasing its back-off interval to solve the above unfair phenomena.

From the above analysis we can know that we need to combine back-off time with service mark of stream to realize a fair scheduling.

Modify the above centralized fair scheduling algorithm, for a stream with a weight r, the calculation method of start mark and end mark of packet is as follows:

- When each packet in the stream arrives at the head of the stream, we begin to calculate the start mark and end mark of packet;
- For each packet, we use an end mark to identify it;
- V(t) is the virtual time of time t, used to represent the services obtained at t;
- Initially, the start mark of packet is 0;
- $S(P_i^k) = V(A(P_i^k))$; $A(P_i^k)$ is the arrival time of this packet; $S(P_i^k)$ is the end mark of the last packet;
- End Mark $F(P_i^k) = S(P_i^k) + Scaling\_factor*(L_i^k)/r_i$;

  $F(P_i^k)$ is used to represent the sum of services to be obtained by packet P_i^k:

  L_i^k is the length of the Kth packet of stream i;

  Scaling_factor is scaling factor, which allows choosing a mark suitable for scheduling;

- At each time t, for all streams in ready state, choose the stream with the minimum completion mark to schedule.
- Determination of back-off interval;

A stream with a small completion mark should have a small back-off interval, we adopt the exponential mapping scheme stated in〔18〕to determine back-off interval:

$$Bi = (\beta * Scaling\_fcator*(L_i^k)/r_i);$$

B is a random variable which is distributed in the interval [0. 9, 1. 1] normally and mainly used to reduce the possibility that conflicts happen.

Definition of $Bi = \lambda(Bi)$

$if \quad \Delta < threshold$ then

$\lambda(\Delta) = \Delta$

else

$$\left[Threshold + K1*\left(1-e^{-K2+(\Delta-Threshold)}\right)\right]$$

endif

Threshold, K1 and K2 are constant parameters and their values are 80, 80 and 0.0020 respectively.

Set the variable value of collision counter as 0.

- Conflict handling

When the back-off intervals of multiple mobile nodes are reduced to 0, they will send data information simultaneously. For the mobile node i which conflicts, a back-off time will be produced according to CSMA/CA back-off mechanism and its operation is as follows:

I. The variable value of collision counter increases 1;

II. Choose a new Bi and Bi is distributed in the interval $\left[1, 2^{CollisjopCounter-1}*CW\right]$ normally, CW is contention window and it is a constant parameter.

VII. MODIFIED VERSION OF CTS (51NGLE-DIREETION-MODIFY-CTS)

Use the format of IEEE802.11Frame shown as the following diagram, a reserved bit exists in Frame control field (dashed area in the diagram), we can assign a value to the field to define the modified CTS, when the value of Rsvd is 0, it is a normal CTS and when the value of Rsvd is 1, it is a modified CTS.

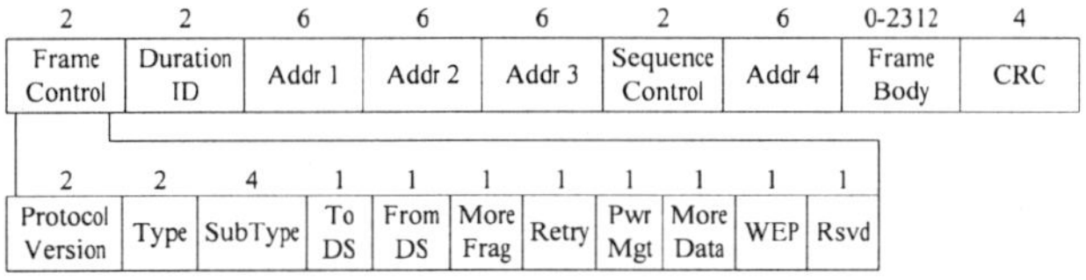

Figure 2. Format of IEEE802.11 Frame

This kind of modification is in accordance with RTS/CTS protocol of IEEE802.11. RTS/CTS protocol, namely request to send/clear to send protocol, is equal to a kind of handshake protocol and mainly used to solve "hidden stations" problems. "Hidden stations" refers to that mobile node A sends information to mobile node B, mobile node C has not detected A and it also sends information to B, so A and C sends signals to B simultaneously, which gives rise to signal conflict and finally leads to that all signals sent to B are lost. "Hidden stations" often occurs in large units (generally in outdoor environment), which will bring efficiency loss and need an error recovery mechanism. When a mass file needs to be transferred, we especially need to put an end to the occurrence of "hidden stations" phenomenon.

It can be seen that RTS/CTS protocol is mainly used to solve the possible conflict problem of hidden stations, a certain node A sends a RTS signal, which shows the request information sent by A for sending some data to a destination node B, after node B receives RTS, it sends a CTS signal to tell other mobile nodes that there will be data to be transmitted to make these nodes monitoring channels be in monitor wait state and not send data because the channels are monitored busy. The unilateral sending of CTS by base station also plays the above role, after the receiving of data is finished, base station broadcasts ACK acknowledgement frame to all mobile nodes, in this way, all mobile nodes can equally monitor and compete for channels again.

VIII. CONCLUSION

The problem studied in this paper is to try to avoid conflicts when mobile hosts communicate, provide a fair channel service for each mobile host participating in competition and solve the resources in mobile Internet according to the characteristics of wireless network communication models.

REFERENCES

[1] T. S. Eugene, 1. Stoica, Hui Zhang, Packet Fair Algorithms for Wireless Networks with Location-Department Errors, ACM, 1996.

[2] A. Demers, S. Keshav and S. Shenker, Analysis and simulation of a fair queuing algorithm, ACM, SIGCOMM'89, 1989.

[3] Songwu Lu, V. Bharghavan and R. Srikant, Fair Scheduling in wireless packet networks" , ACM SIGCOMM'97, 1997

[4] Songwu Lu, T. Nandagopal, and V. Bharghavan, Fair Scheduling in wireless packet networks, ACM MOBICOMM'98, 1998

[5] P. Ramanathan and P. Agrawal, Adapting Packet Fair Queuing Algorithms to Wireless Networks, ACM M08ILCOMM'98, 1998

[6] S. Floyd and V. Jacobson, Link-sharing and Resource Management Models for Packet Networks, IEEE/ACM Transactions on Networking, 1995.

[7] B. Bensaou, K. T. Chan and D. H. h. Tsang, Credit-Based Fair Queuing (CBFQ): A simple and feasible scheduling algorithm for packet networks, Hong Kong University of Science & Technology,1998

[8] Nitin H. Vaidya, Paramvir Bahl and Seema Gupta, Distributed Fair Scheduling in a Wireless LAN, ACM MOBILCOMM'2000, 2000.

Design and Research of an Information Service Subsystem

Zhang Xin-hua
Dept. of Information Management, Shangdong Economic University
Faculty of Economics and Management, Shangqiu Normal University
Jinan, China
zxh12778@163.com

***Abstract*—This paper proposes a resource information influx and release mode based on management domain and information nodes distributed in the domain, designs the hierarchical architecture of information service subsystem and gives detailed designs of various component modules of subsystem respectively. This information service subsystem is the concrete realization of grid information service in the particular grid environment. The design of subsystem combines practical resource distribution and management mode and adopts grid resource information influx and release mode based on management domain and collaborative buffer and management of information nodes distributed in the domain to unify the metadata description of resource information and improve the interoperability between various modules.**

Keywords-information service; information influx and release; resource management mode

I. Introduction

Grid is a new computing platform appearing after World Wide Web and it is a kind of infrastructure integrating scattered resources in geographical position. The dynamic property and distribution of resources in grid service system bring difficulty for grid users and related components to determine the current states of various resources and choose a suitable resource to finish the corresponding work. And therefore, we need a module which can provide true and real-time reflection of resource states in grid environment and finish the information management in grid environment to provide action basis for the whole grid service system and ensure the harmonious work of resources in the system. The information service subsystem in grid service system is proposed in view of this requirement and it is the core component of the whole system.

II. Basic Architecture

The software hierarchical structure and design information service subsystem general structure of the whole grid service system are shown as Fig 1:

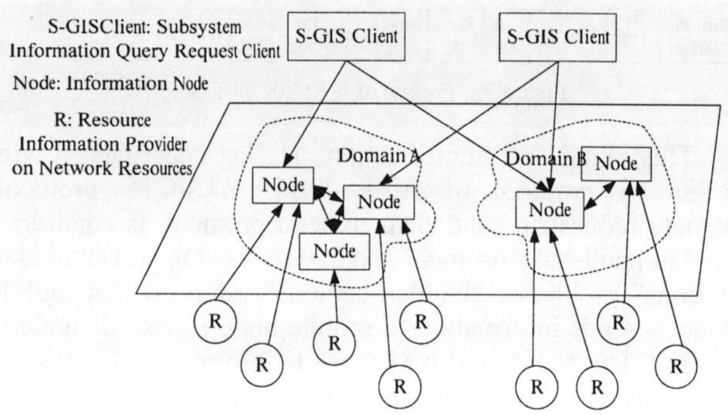

Figure 1. Basic Structure Framework of System

The relations among three main modules in the framework, namely information query request client, information node and resource information provider are as follows: The resources in management domain collect resource information on information nodes distributed in the domain. In addition to being responsible for storing and managing the state information of local resources registered on it, each information node also keeps partial information of perceptive resources and mapping relation information between resources and nodes in this domain. Information node receives various intra-domain resource information query requests from client.

III. Information Collector Module

A. *Division of function module*

Resource information collector module is resource information producer of the whole information service subsystem and this module is directly responsible for collecting bottom grid resource information, converting various state information of resources according to information representation Schema defined by the subsystem and registering the state information on resource controlled information nodes. When designing information collector module, we divide it into three main parts: sensor for collecting various information, sensor manager and information collector service. The call relations among its various components are described in Fig 2:

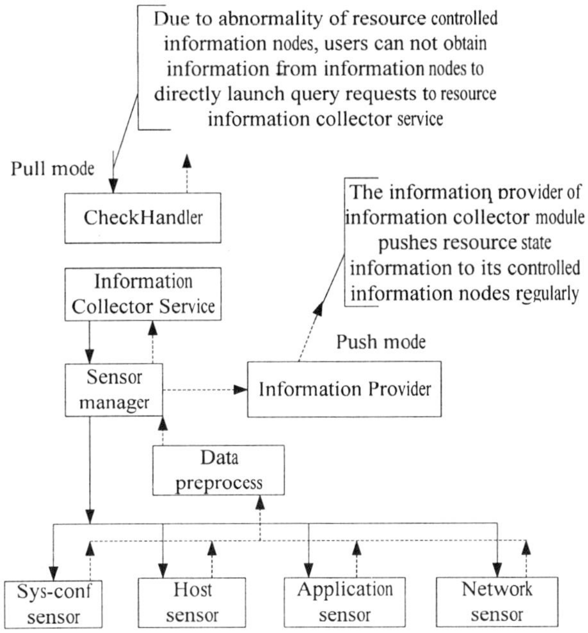

Figure 2. Call Relations among Components of Information Collector Module

B. *Information interaction mechanism*

In subsystem, various state information of resource needs to be collected to its controlled information node real-timely. The information interaction between information collector module and information node adopts two kinds of interactive means, namely regular "push" mode and active "pull" mode, regular "push" mode is the main mode adopted by the system and active "pull" method is a supplement. Regular "push" refers to that information provider regularly pushes information to information receiver and it is a kind of state detection mechanism, namely life cycle management mode. In information service subsystem, the resource information collector module deployed on resources uses SOAP messages to periodically send "update" messages to information nodes, update resource state information and inform that this resource is "normal", shown as Fig 3. Each "update" message sends two contents, namely TTL of this message (Time To Live) and latest state information of resource. Information node determines if resource state is good according to regular "update" message of waiting resource and updates the resource state information of its buffer according to message content.

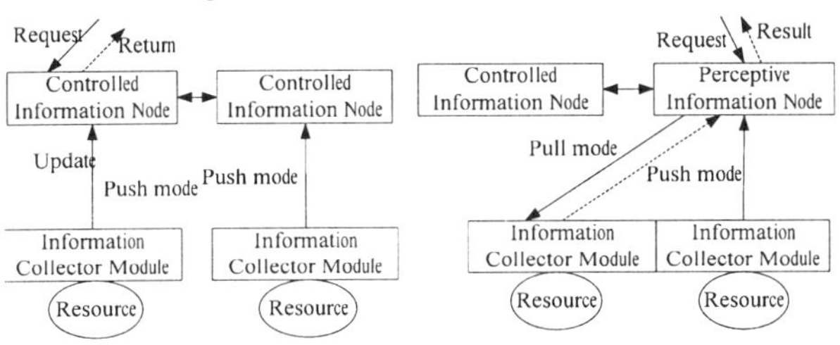

Figure 3. Soft State Register Modes of Active "Push" and "Pull" Modes

For passive pull mode, in view of robustness demand of information service subsystem, in order to avoid failure of controlled information node and invalidation of query function, information collector module also encapsulates information collection function into a Web service, namely information collector service. If necessary, we can access to this service through perceptive nodes of resources, the process of using active "Pun" mode (Shown as Fig 3, right) to obtain resource information is open to users.

In the system, as a supplement of "push" mode, "pull" mode provides certain fault-tolerant function. Its use opportunity is that: when a user needs to inquire about the detailed information of a certain assigned resource and the controlled information nodes of this resource go wrong, he can directly access to this resource and obtain resource information through service address of resource InfoCollectorService buffered by the perceptive nodes of the resource. As a supplement of regular "push" mode, "pull" mode not only improves the flexibility of system but also strengthens the fault-tolerant ability of the whole system.

IV. Design of Information Node Server Components

A. *Division of function modules*

Information node is located between portal layer and core layer in information service subsystem and it is a core component in subsystem, which collects the state information of multiple grid resources, completes the management of intra-domain resource information and provides convenient query service for upper layer. There are three Web services deployed on each information node by using Web Services technology and these Web services complete different functions according to different components or user needs. They are resource discovery service, note service and information register service respectively. Meanwhile, in order to effectively manage resource state data, information node uses native XML database to directly store resource state information represented in XML, which avoids the unnecessary data conversion work brought by using relational database to store information after data analysis and improves work efficiency.

B. *Register service*

The information register service on information node is used to provide register and update function for bottom resource information. It monitors the periodic information update message sent by information collector module on bottom resources and completes the real-time updating of information buffered by information node.

Add a new resource to grid service system, first we need to register the resource in grid, after the resource is registered, publish this resource through information service subsystem and grant the use right of the resource to a certain user through VO service subsystem module, after that the resource becomes a part of grid service system for grid user to use. The process of adding resources to grid service system can be divided into two parts, namely resource node access and resource state information registration.

C. *Note service*

Note service is an important service for providing interaction between information nodes. There is a note service and a note service client deployed on each information node. Note service is a Web service deployed on node, which is used for monitoring the access of other nodes; note service client is a Web service client program on node, which is used for launching the access to note services on other nodes.

In the system, interaction only occurs between information nodes in the same management domain to mutually notify the updating of local resource information. In information service subsystem, there are two interaction opportunities between information nodes through note service:

1. When the register service of information node receives resource state information register request and uses domain level update mode, this node needs to access to the note services of other information nodes in the domain and notify the updating of node perceptive resource state information after completing node level update.

2. When an information node recovers from a certain failure and restarts various services, it will use system service to automatically trigger the note service client of its node, send failure recovery message to the note services of other information nodes in the domain, check and update its global domain resource mapping relation table to keep the consistency of data.

D. *DiseoveryService*

Discovery service on information node is the most important service on node, which receives the access request sent by information service subsystem client and completes intra-domain resource discovery and information query function for users.

1) Access mode

When designing discovery service, we provide two types of query services according to requirements, namely information query access mode and resource discovery access mode:

2) Information state conversion of resource buffered by information node

The dynamic information data of resource buffered by information node is updated by information collector module on core layer in regular "Push" mode and we add two time tags, namely T_1 and T_2 to each update message in system, here:

T_1 represents resource information collection module on core layer and this resource information is valid from starting sending resource information update message to information node register service to T_2;

In addition, we use T_{1new} and T_{2new} to represent two time tags of a new update message and T_{1store} and T_{1store}, to represent two time tags of the latest resource information stored by the current information node; obviously, $T_{1store} \leq T_{1new}$ and $T_{2store} \leq T_{2new}$, additionally, we use T_{1first} and T_{2first} to represent two time tags of register message of the first resource state information and boundary to represent the current time of system.

In the following, we use finite state machine theory to describe the possible states of resource state information buffered by an information node and the conversion between various states. For the resource state information buffered by an information node, there may be the following four states:

1. Initial register state of resource S_0 (After resource is accessed to grid service system, establish the corresponding record on information node);

2. Valid state of resource information S_1;

3. There is resource information record in buffer, but the validity of current information is uncertain;

4. Resource cancellation S_3;

The state conversion of corresponding finite automation is shown as Fig 4, after a resource node is accessed to grid service system, it enters into initial state S_0;

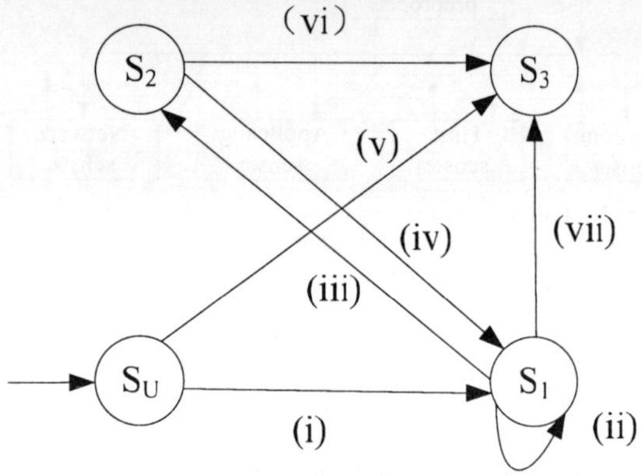

Fig 4 State Conversion Diagram of Node Buffer Resource Information

The state conversion conditions are as follows:

(i) $T_{1first} \leq T_c \leq T_{2first}$;

(ii) $T_c \leq T_{2store}$ and $T_{1store} < T_{1new} \leq T_c \leq T_{2new}$;

(iii) $T_{1new} \leq T_{2store}$ and $T_{2store} < T_c < T_{1new}$,

(iv) $T_c \leq T_{2store}$ and $T_{1new} \leq T_c \leq T_{2new}$。 、 ;

(v)(vi)(vii) Regular garbage collection or resource cancellation;

After an information node receives resource state register information, it will buffer the information for some time, during this time, the information is legal, if bottom resource node still has not updated its information after this time, the information node thinks this resource node go wrong (for example, down machine congestion or network transmission congestion, etc). Before information query and matching, the resource recovery service of information node should first determine that the current resource state information is valid, namely S_1 state in the above four states. For a certain query time T, we can easily judge if the current information stored is valid, i.e. when $T_{1store} \leq T \leq T_{2store}$, the current resource is normal and its state information is valid; when $T > T_{2store}$, the buffered state information is invalid and network or resource may go wrong. The validity time point of resource information T2 can be set by resource provider according to dynamic and static information respectively.

3) Security authentication

In the specific departments served by grid service system, there may be some business competition relations among various units in practical work. A unit accesses its own computing resources to grid service system, but for a certain consideration, the information of these computing resources is not wished to be understood and used by users of some departments. At this time, we need to control the access of query and access interface DiscoveryService provided by information service subsystem.

The authorization work for user resources is finished by another component in grid service system—VO service subsystem. After each user logs in to grid service system, he will be issued a user pass LP and a resource pass RP by VO service subsystem and use the private key of VO to sign. Before handling discovery service, the system will verify user identity and resource authorization conditions and the user can not use resource discovery service until he passes the verification. The process of verification can be divided into three steps:

- Verify the validity of user identity;
- Verify if user validity matches with user identity;
- Verify if user query resources are included in its legal resource list;

In order to ensure the control of user access, the series of work should be completed before accessing to service and realized by HandlierChain mechanism of Axis in the system.

V. CLIENT

Client is a unified entrance of subsystem and it is responsible for launching client program called by discovery service on the corresponding information node according to user request, user LP and RP. Meanwhile, it encapsulates preprocessing and fault-tolerant processing of abnormality:

- Preprocessing determines the URL of discovery service of pre-accessed information node and sets the corresponding access methods and parameters according to users' query parameters, query mode and logical addresses of authorized resources in user RP;
- Exception handling provides the function of automatically choosing other information nodes and launching calling again when the accessed information node service becomes invalid.

The access to client can be called directly by grid portal through RemoteObject in background Flex development tools or directly by other system components through class interfaces.

VI. CONCLUSION

When designing information service subsystem, we integrate the software architecture of the whole grid service system well, adopt the service-oriented architecture and closely combine with SOAP and XML technology, etc, in Web Services technology to provide convenient, effective and reliable resource information services for grid users and other components in the system. This paper introduces in detail the whole framework, related concepts and important parts of various layers of information service subsystem and describes how various parts interact and complete the specific functions.

REFERENCES

[1] YiLi Gong, FangPeng Dong, Wei Li et al, "VEGA infrastructure for resource discovery in grids", Journal of Computer Science and Technology, 2003,18(4): 413-422

[2] Xuehai Zhang, Jennifer M Schopf, "Performance Analysis of the Globus Toolkit Monitoring and Discovery Service MDS2", In: Richard Oliver(ed.). The International Performance Computing and Communications Conference (IPCCC), Phoenix, Arizona, April 2004, 843-849

[3] Deelman E, Singh G, "Grid-Based Metadata Services", In: H. Papageorgiou (ed.), Proceedings of 16th International Conference on Scientific and Statistical Database Management, Santorini Island, Greece, 21-23 June 2004, 393-402.

[4] Foster, I. Desselman, C.. Globus, "A metacomputing infrastructure toolkit", International Journal of Supercomputer Applications, 1997, 11(2):115-128.

[5] M.L. Massie, B.N. Chun, D.E. Culler, The Ganglia Distributed Monitoring System: Design, Implementation, and Experience", Parallel Computing, 2004,30(7): 817-840.

[6] Portable Batch System, Open PBS Release 2.3, Administrator Guide [EB/OL], http://www.Openpbs.org/, 2001.

Design and Realization of an Embedded Multimedia System Driver

Huang Lei
Depart. of Electrical and Electronics Information Engineering
Huangshi Institute of Technology
Huangshi, China
huangwglei@163.com

***Abstract*—Traditional multimedia transmission systems use analog signals to transmit voices and images, but analog signals are easy to be interfered, do not have safety assurance and lack control function. This paper studies the framework of audio/video system driver and carries out structured design for the driver: 1. Divide the driver into three modules, including control/configuration module, data transmission module and system control module; 2. Provide 4 interface functions for the upper layer; 3. Use two types of data buffers. Finally, it realizes driver codes. At present, the whole system operation is normal and stable.**

Keywords- embedded; multimedia system; interface function

I. INTRODUCTION

Along with the development of computer technology, maturity of digital audio/video compression algorithm and application of network technology and information security technology, using network to transmit clear multimedia data safely has become possible. At present, the research and development of network audio/video system are still in the start stage, many standards have just been completed or not been completed and the core technology is mainly in the hands of some foreign companies. And therefore, the research and development of network audio/video system are of great significance to the technology accumulation of our enterprises in this field and the competitiveness of our products with independent intellectual property in the international market. The network audio/video server designed by us is an independent embedded device which uses hardware coding technology to code the gathered analog audio/video data into MPEG4 format and transmit it to the client through network real-timely.

II. SOFTWARE STRUCTURE

The structure of network audio/video software system is shown as Fig 1:

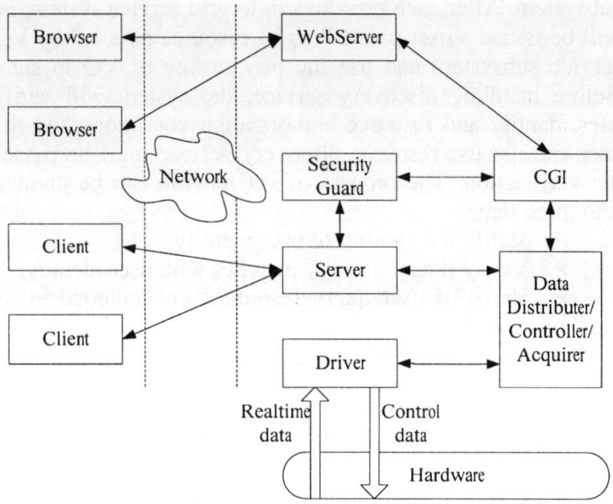

Figure 1. Software structure of network audio/video system

(1) Application layer module

Application layer module includes user browser, client program and server service program and web server. The software system has two parts, one uses B/S pattern and follows thin client principle. As long as special plug-ins are installed on the client, the client can receive the real-time audio/video data transmitted by the server. The web server on the server is used to realize web interface. User authentication, safety and access to real-time data are realized by http protocol and client reads and sets up system environmental parameters through CGI (Common Gateway Interface). Meanwhile, we provide another C/S pattern which can avoid the limitations of web server itself. Client can realize customization function according to needs conveniently. Server uses special programs to provide services for client. Authentication and safety are realized by security module.

(2) Driver module

Driver module is used to control hardware devices and transmit data to the upper layer.

(3) Data acquisition/ distribution/ control module

This module links with server module and driver module interacting with clients. It calls driver interface to get multimedia data and it is responsible for distributing data to the users who have requested for data, and meanwhile it is responsible for transmitting real-time MPEG4 coding parameter adjustment information to driver according to user feedback information.

III. DRIVER DESIGN

A. *Use of multimedia processing chip*

The uses of various kinds of multimedia processing chips are all different. Driver needs to be realized according to chip characteristics. The multimedia processing chip used by us contains multiple modules and its logical structure is shown as Fig 2:

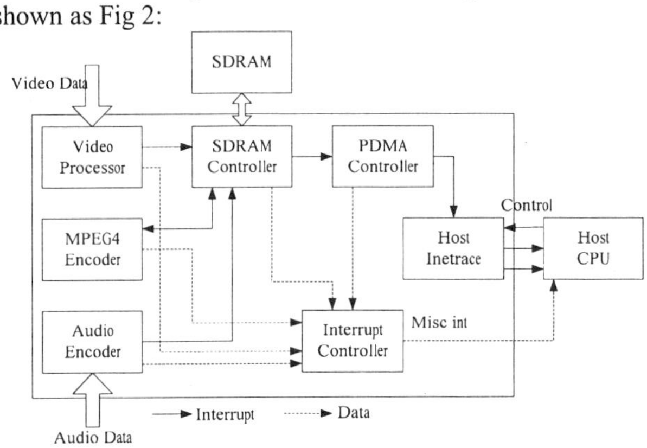

Figure 2. Structure of multimedia data processing chip

B. *Driver processing framework*

In the traditional design of Linux, multimedia processing chips, such as display card chip, sound card chip and LCD control device in embedded device, etc, most of these chips appear as character devices. Character device driver hides the complex control of multimedia chip and provides simple interfaces and perfect functions for the upper layer. Block device driver and network device driver are not suitable for multimedia processing chip driver.

Combined with chip characteristics, we divide the realization of driver into three main modules, use two types of data areas and provide four function interfaces. Shown as Fig 3:

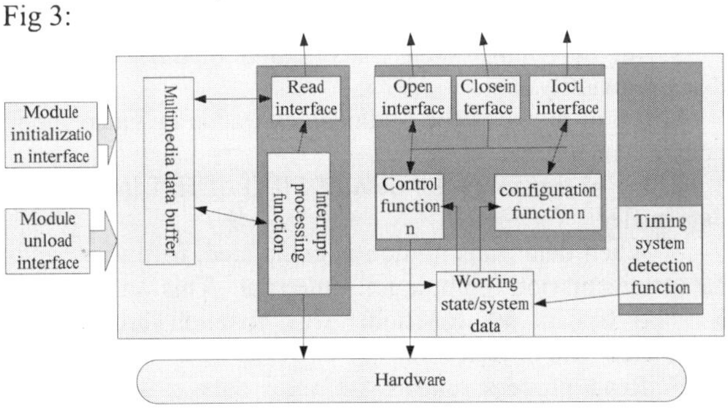

Figure 3. Streaming media driver framework

(1) Two types of data areas

Driver is responsible for acquisition, storage and transmission of two kinds of data. One kind is coded real-time multimedia data and the other kind is working state and configuration information data of the whole system.

(2) Three modules

Driver is divided into three modules, namely data acquisition module, system control/ configuration module and system monitoring module. The brief introduction about the three modules is as follows:

- Data acquisition module: When multimedia data coding is completed, it interrupts CPU. At this time, driver needs to distinguish data source (audio/video), keep coded data quantity information and then start data receiver function to obtain data. After completed, it starts obstructed read queue to submit the data to the application layer.
- System control/configuration module: This module is responsible for initializing system configuration data and setting hardware working state when the system starts up, and receiving the configuration and control information of application layer and setting up the system according to the requirements of system monitoring module during system operation.
- System monitoring module: Because video sources or audio sources may be disconnected or replaced during working, in order to increase system stability, system monitoring module is used to maintain system. This module mainly uses a time system detection function which detects the working states of various modules, calls the corresponding functions of system control/configuration module to modify system state data and reset hardware to make system hardware work normally when changed.

(3) Four interfaces

Application layer uses read function to obtain audio/video data. Call ioctl interface to realize system control and configuration and then ioctl interface calls various control functions and configuration functions on the bottom layer. Open function is used to realize system startup and initialization. Meanwhile, close function interface is provided for integrity.

IV. REALIZATION OF DRIVER

A. *System control/configuration module*

System control/configuration module is composed of two parts. One part is the interface provided to the application layer, mainly including ioctl and open. The other part includes two kinds of functions, namely control function family which is independent to control chips and configuration function family which operates system state and configuration information. Such a design can decrease system coupling degree and increase robustness and expansibility. Its configuration/control module call relation is shown as Fig 4:

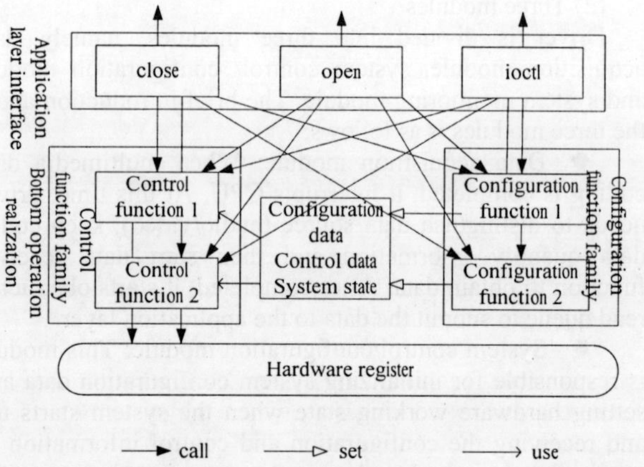

Figure 4. Multimedia processing chip driver configuration/control module call relation

1) Bottom operation realization

(1) Configuration function family

- System configuration setting int sys_cfg_set(struct sys_cfg*syscfg)
- System configuration acquisition int sys_cfg_get(struct sys_cfg*syscfg)
- System state acquisition int sys_status_get(struct sys_status*sysstatus)
- Video stream coding setting int v_mode_set(struct v_mode*vm)
- Audio stream coding setting int a_mode_set(struct a_mode*am)

(2) Control function family

- Coding start int code_start()
- Coding stop int code_stop()
- Chip reset int chip_reset()
- Data transmission void mpg_pdma_start()

(3) Other functions

- Buffer application int mpg_alloc_buffer()
- Buffer initialization int mpg_init_buffer()
- Buffer release int mpg_release_buffer()

2) Application layer interface

(1) Open operation flow

1. Buffer application: Audio block array structure, video frame array structure, audio buffer, video buffer
2. Data structure initialization
3. Set audio coding rate and start audio coding part
4. Obtain video type (PAL/NTSC), set resolution, frame rate and PI ratio and start video coding part
5. Initialization of other hardware modules
6. Start coding
7. Enable all interrupts of coding chips

(2) Close operation flow

1. Forbid all interrupts of coding chips
2. Stop coding
3. Buffer release: Audio block array structure, video frame array structure, audio buffer, video buffer

(3) Ioctl operation

The realization interface is static int mpg_ioctl(struet inode*inode,struct file*fllp,unsigned int cmd,unsigned long arg). General multimedia processing chip driver provides the following configuration options for application layer and application layer dynamically adjusts these parameters according to needs: audio enabling, video enabling, frame rate and I/P frame ratio, etc.

B. Data transmission module

Data transmission module mainly realizes the following functions:

- Transmit the coded data to main SDRAM buffer
- Submit the data in buffer to upper layer

The main functions are two interrupt service functions. One is interrupt service function special for receiving data; the other is other interrupt service functions. This module structure is shown as Fig 5:

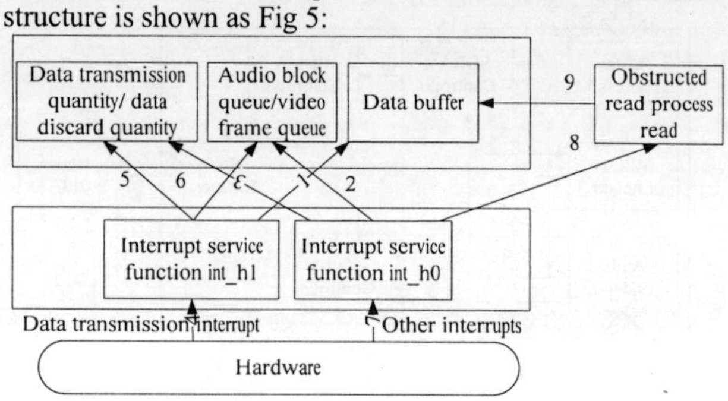

Figure 5. Streaming media driver data transmission module framework

Two interrupt service functions are the core of the module and they need to finish or assist in finishing the work indicated by nine arrows in the Fig. The flow is as follows:

1. When multimedia data is prepared, hardware produces audio/video data interrupt and int_h0 function is responsible for handling this type of interrupt.
2. Int_h0 obtains buffer use information according to audio block queue or video block queue first.
3. Int_h0 sets data transmission quantity and data discard quantity according to buffer use information (when buffer is not big enough) and starts hardware transmission data.
4. Hardware interrupts main CPU every time it transmits 256 bytes to FIFO of HPI interface. At this time, int_hl is responsible for handling this type of interrupt.
5. Int_hl obtains data transmission quantity and data discard quantity first.
6. Int_hl prepares the audio block queue or video block queue to be written.
7. Int_hl transmits the data of FIFO of HPI interface to data buffer.
8. When data transmission is completed, hardware sends data transmission completion interrupt. This interrupt is handled by int_h0 function. This function arouses the obstructed read process.
9. Read process returns the valid data in audio block queue or video frame queue to application layer.

C. System monitoring module

When audio sources or video sources are changed (for example, the connection is off and then connect up again), the system can not return to normal work mode, at this time, it needs to be reset automatically. Reset is realized by system monitoring module. The main part of system monitoring module is monitoring function void system_monitor(u_long arg).

(1) Monitoring module initialization and startup flow is as follows:

1. In order to monitor the system, first define timing execution queue statie struet timer_list timer_sys _mon.

2. Initialize this queue in open function init_timer(&timer_sys_mon)

Set the execution function of the queue timer_sys_mon.function=system_monitor

Set overtime (1 second at present) time_sys_mon.expires=jiffies+HZ;

3. After calling start-up system function, add monitoring function to timing execution queue

add_timer(&timer_sys_mon):, at this time, start working

(2) After the queue starts working, this module carries out one system state examination per second. If an abnormal condition occurs, then amend, if not, register itself into the timing queue again:

timer_sys_mon.expires=jiffies+HZ:

add_timer(&timer_sys_mon):

(3) When the system is abnormal, the work flow is as follows:

1. When video or audio device is abnormal, the chip interrupts main CPU; 2. Interrupt processing function obtains the cause of abnormality and sets the related configuration registers.

(4) When application layer requires driver to stop working, call in stop system function.

del_timer_sync(&timer_sys_mon);

5. Conclusion

This paper first introduces the software structure of embedded network audio/video system server and studies the driver framework suitable for streaming media, and then finishes design work and code realization, finally completes debugging work.

REFERENCE

[1] Rob Koenen, "Overview of the MPEG-4 Standard", 2002.5

[2] Ze-Nian Li, Mark S. Drew, "Fundamentals of Multimedia", English reprint edition, Published by Pearson Education Asia Limited and China Machine Press, 2004, 7

[3] Tom Shanley, Don Anderson, "PCI Architecture (4th edition)", Addison Wesley, 2000

[4] Yinyu Ye, Interior Point Algorithms: Theory and Analysis. John Wiley & Sons, 1997

[5] Herbert S. Wilf, Algorithms and Complexity, Prentice-Hall, 1986

[6] Vijay V. Vazirani, Approximation Algorithms, Springer-Verlag, 2001

[7] Robert E. Tarjan, "Data Structures and Network Algorithms", Society for Industrial and Applied mathematics, 1983

Optimized Program and Implementation of Oracle Database

Chen Yu, Cheng Pingguang
Dept. of Computer and Modern Education Technology
Chongqing Education College
Chongqing, China
teacherchenyu@126.com

***Abstract*—On the basis of the current database system research, according to the Oracle database system, in this paper a database optimization program is presented and implemented. Experimental results show that: the database optimization program can improve the disposing performance of the database and greatly accelerate the pace of its inquiries.**

Keywords-Oracle database; Optimize; Implementation; SQL

I. Introduction

At present, enterprises becoming more information-based, the production operations, electronic marketing, financial statistics all can be achieved through electronic means, which simplifies the complicated manual operation and greatly improves the efficiency and accuracy of the work.The various types of information data from the IT work is vital, such as the user data of the finance and insurance businesses, the card number data of the telecommunications companies, the plate number data of the department of transportation, the drug sales data of the medical and health department, and so on, are all the wealth and the lifeblood of the enterprises, once lost, the consequences would be unthinkable. At present, almost all enterprises use the database to store information, and the mass data storage can be achieved by large-scale relational database, through which users can search the related information according to their own needs, analyze the business operations on the basis of the data and frame rational development strategy. Therefore, the enterprise database is the core of the information-based enterprise operation system, the operation of the database has a direct impact on the enterprise production operations, so now all enterprises hope that their database can be more stable, more efficient and secure.

To stably and efficiently operate the database and achieve strong support to the enterprise operations needs constant and reasonable performance optimization on the database according to the business development. The unreasonable planning and configuration of the database will restrict the system fully use the hardware resources; the unreasonable database application design will make the system consume more resources and time. A large number of practices have proved that, the business system to enhance the overall performance, the effect of the hardware expansion can only account for 40%, and 60% is achieved through optimizing the database and business applications[3].Database optimization work should follow certain principles to avoid unnecessary adjustment or costing adjustment. In general, the order of "database configuration optimization -> database application optimization" is adopted. Through analyzing some database performance indexes, such as the involved response time, system throughput, availability of the database, success rate of the database, using efficiency of the EMS memory and the implementation efficiency of the application, the negative factors affecting the performance can be found and the reasonable optimization program can be designed, then according to this the database performance will be optimized.

II. DATABASE OPTIMIZATION TARGET AND FRAMEWORK

A. *Database system structure*

When without confusion, the database system is generally shortly called to be database. The database system structure is shown in figure 1[7].

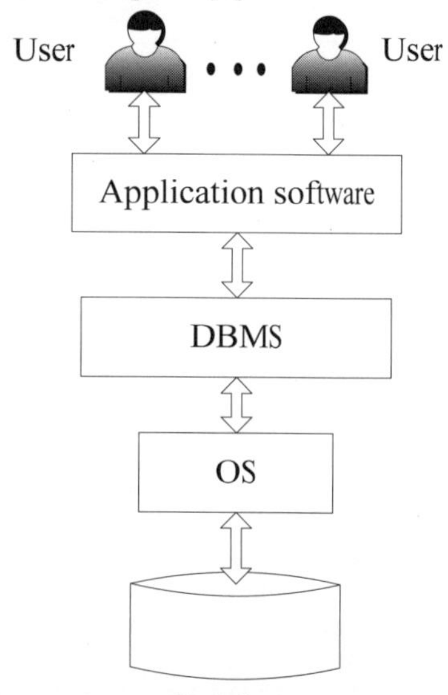

Figure 1. database system structure

From the above figure it can seen that the user does not directly operate the database, but through the application software and database management system to achieve access to the database. The application software is the middle software of the user interacting with the database management system, it switches the user operating instructions into the language and codes which can be understood by the database management system, then the database management system will operate the database and return the operating results data to the application software, and finally the application software will show the data to the user with a specific form[1] .

B. Database optimization framework

The database optimization mainly has four adjustment levels, as shown in figure 2. The first adjustment is the level of operation system and hardware platform, the second is database configuration level, the third is database design level and the final is SQL application level. Usually the entire performance of the database will be greatly improved by adjust and optimize the database according to the four adjustment levels. In the specific optimization implementation, it will determine which level should be the focus of the adjustment according to the state of business systems [2] . For example, the system in a stage of building will give more consideration to the adjustment of the database design level; the system in a stage of operation will give more consideration to the optimization of the database configuration SQL application levels, and so on.

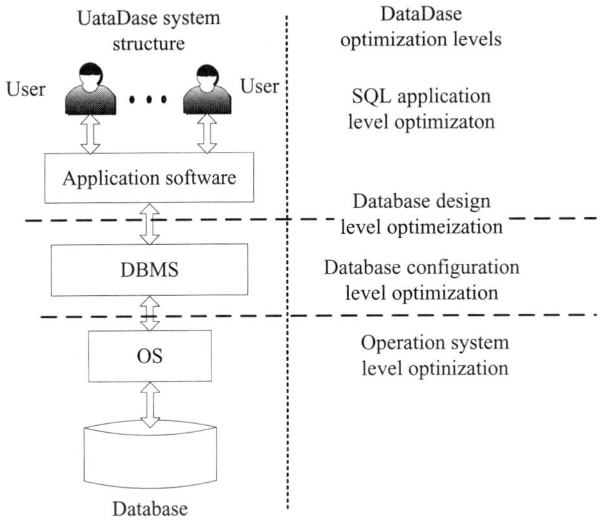

Figure 2. database optimization framework

Optimization implementation process generally uses the step of "performance data collection -> performance analysis -> optimization design -> optimization adjustment -> effect evaluation". Performance data collection refers to that through system order or related tools collect the system performance indexes such as CPU utilization, memory resource occupation, disk I/O operation frequency, waiting severity of the database incident, the response time of the database process, implementation efficiency of the SQL application and other indexes to be the data source of the optimization work; Performance analysis is to analyze the performance collecting data combining with the operation state of the business system, find that whether the factors affecting the system performance exist from the operating system, database configuration, database design, SQL applications, and then provide direction and ideas to the follow-up optimal adjustment work; optimization design is to coordinate the optimization project and design reasonable optimization process according to the discovered results from the performance analysis, which can reduce the adjustment effect on the business and the cost for the optimization; optimization adjustment is to achieve the purpose of improving system performance through the adjustment in the forms of operation system, database design and database application; effect evaluation is to embody the help of the optimization implementation to the performance advance of database and the operation improvement of business system, stand out the effect the optimization work obtained [4] .

III. ORACLE DATABASE OPTIMIZATION

A. Oracle database design optimization

An appropriate database logical design can not only improve the database application performance, but also simplify the database management process. Oracle database automatically creates a standard OFA table space when establishing [6] . In the OFA, the same used segment types are stored together; the data with similar number of users and affairs is also stored together; the data dictionary is separately stored in a table space, and there should be individual regions for exceptions, so that the conflict of the table space will be minimized.

In the database logic design the database is composed by a series of table space, if it is in physical design, to reduce the I/O conflicts between the data documents, it is best to store these data documents separately in different physical disks. But generally it is very difficult to achieve in actual hardware environment, so in the database physical design the distribution of data documents should follow some principles, for example, the table space of DATA and INDEX should be stored separately, the table space of RBS and DATS should be stored separately and the table space of SYSTEM and others in the database should be stored separately, and so on.In addition to the logic physical design, it is also should be considered that whether or not to use the partition function of the Oracle database, whether or not to establish index for the table often visited and which index should be established, and whether or not to establish materialized views for the static mass data [5] .

B. SQL optimization in Oracle application software

The implementation of the application programs will eventually boil down to the implementation of the SQL statement in the database, so the implementation efficiency of the SQL statement eventually determines on the Oracle database performance [8] . SQL language is a type of flexible language, in which the same function can be realized through using different statements. But the implementation efficiency of the statements is not the same, programmers can use the EXPLAIN PLAN statement to compare with the variety of realized programs and select the best realized program.Generally speaking, writing SQL statements must meet the rules as follows: to make full use of the index; to choose the joint order of the joint inquiry; in the sub-query to cautiously use IN or NOT IN statement but in favor of where (NOT) exists; to cautiously use the joint inquiry of the view, especially the joint inquiry between the more complex views, and the inquiries to the views should best be broken down into the direct inquiries to the data tables; in parameter document to set SHARED_POOL_RESERVED_SIZE parameter which will retain a continuous memory space in the SGA shared pool, and the continuous memory space is beneficial to store large SQL package.

C. *Oracle database configuration parameter optimization*

In Oracle database architecture the memory optimization is the key of performance optimization. Optimizing the memory is mainly to improve the system performance through optimizing the memory structure. Here the memory structure involved is mainly composed by the specific SQL, PL/SQL area, log buffer and high-speed buffer storage.

Because that the Oracle memory structure demand is closely related to the application, the memory structure should be optimized after the SQL statements and application programs optimization, as well as before the input/output (I/O) optimization [9] . Furthermore, the operation system should be firstly optimized and the private SQL and PL/SQL area should be considered before dealing with the share pool. System globe area (SGA) is a memory segment which is allocated to the Oracle and contains example control information of the Oracle database. SGA size may greatly affect the system performance, and its default parameter settings apply only to the computer with very low configuration, but not apply to the needs of existing equipment in actual system. If these parameters are not adjusted, the system resources will be caused a huge waste.

As a result, the system parameters should be readjusted and optimized according to the actual system. It is proposed that when setting the parameters lock_sga=true (in a different platform may be in a different way, in Windows platform, this parameter is invalid) should be mounted in the init.ora at the same time, which makes SGA be locked in physical memory rather than be placed in SWAP, so that the database efficiency will be improved. Generally the size of SGA is mounted as the half of the server physical memory.SGA includes the database buffer cache, log buffer cache, shared pool, big buffer pool and Java pool. In which the shared pool includes library cache and dictionary cache. In Oracle9i Server, the size of the database buffer cache and the shared pool can be dynamically changed to achieve dynamical adjusting its performance when database running.Following the three basic caches in SGA will be optimized and adjusted.

1) *Adjust database buffer cache*

Oracle reads and writes data to the database cache during running, goal means that the information has been in memory, and failure means the needs of Oracle for disk I/O operation. The key of maintaining the cache failure to minimum rate is to ensure the size of the cache. Initialization parameter db_cache_size controls the size of the database buffer cache. The goal percentage can be obtained through inquiring the V$SYSSTAT and so that whether the db_cache_size value will be increased can be confirmed. The goal percentage can be calculated by the formula of "1-physical reads/ (dbblock gets +consistent gets)". If it is less than 0.5, then the db_cache_size value should be increased.

2) *Adjust library cache*

Library cache includes the private and shared SQL areas and PL/SQL area. The important issue of adjusting SGA is to ensure the cache large enough, so that Oracle can keep analyzing and implementing the statement in the shared pool, improve the efficiency of statement analysis and implementation and reduce resource consumption. Its value is confirmed through comparing the goal percentage of the library cache, if sum (reload)/sum (pins) ≈0, then the successful rate of the library cache is suitable, and if it is more than 1 the shared_pool_size must be increased. (in which, pins refers to the cache goal percentage, reloads refers to the error of the SQL, PL/SQL and the visited objects occurred in the library buffer when defining burden, that is, the cache failure rate.)

3) *Adjust data dictionary cache*

Data dictionary cache includes the related database structure, users and entity information. The goal percentage of the data dictionary cache has great influence on the system.In the calculations of the goal percentage, getmisses means the number of failures and gets means the number of success.If (1-(sum (getmisses)/(sum(gets)+sum(getmisses))))*100 >90% , the goal percentage is suitable. Otherwise, the shared pool should be increased.

D. *System I/O optimization*

The reasons of impacting the disk I/O performance are mainly disk competition, overfull number of I/O and the allocation management of data block space [10] . The large table structure can be separated into several small table structures according to the application needs to reduce the amount of data need to be accessed in unit time. Table partition technology is to divide the large table and its index into a number of small, manageable small blocks in VLDB through the form of partition, and each partition can be further divided into smaller sub partitions which are transparent to the application. For the great tables with mass of data, they can be managed by using table partition technology and also can be stored separately from a number of small tables according to actual circs, so that the data can be applied more purposefully.

To avoid disk I/0 operation conflict, the data files should be created in different locations. Redo log file is written into the disk orderly, so as far as possible not to store it in same disk with the data files. If you had to store it in same disk with the data files, then the disk space should not belong to the SYSTEM table space, RBS table space, as well as DATA and INDEX table space. They will directly lead to contention with the redo log file.

The archives log file, system table space and the redo log files should be stored separately. In a large amount of data transaction processing, the database archiving function would lead to contention between it and redo log disk. And when the archives redo log file has not enough space, the database would be frozen. Therefore, the archives log file can not be stored in the same device with the SYSTEM table space, RBS table space or INDEX table space, and also can not stored in the same device with any online redo log files.

IV. OPTIMIZATION RESULTS ANALYSIS

The Oracle database system is optimized in two phases, which are system design phase and database operational phase. In the database concept design and the database design process, except the related analysis of the data, reducing the data redundancy to a minimum and establishing the main keywords and external keyword index, all the table designs strictly follow the standard paradigm in the third. In the design process of the database physical structure, as noted above, the table space and the data block of the database logical structure are monitor and optimize for emphasis.

In addition to adding the index, the database performance is adjusted according to former optimization strategy of the Oracle database. According to the experience from the application development process, some SQL statements with longer running time are rewritten and some database objects (tables, indexes, below) are optimized, then from ORACLE architecture and ORACLE storage structure, through adjusting ORACLE instance (that is, reasonable organizing and allocating the system and program whole area in the memory area, confirming a reasonable goal percentage, adjusting and selecting reasonable initialization parameters), database table space, data files and control file size, whether the line link and move occurred is tested. Through the above optimization and adjustment means orderly from the top to down, the Oracle database performance has been obviously improved, which is clearly embodied when accessing to the application modules of a few database tables with mass data. Here the selection and inquiry program is selected to be the example, on many occasions in the comparison before and after the optimization of the database response time, the relative values obtained as shown in the following table:

TABLE I. ORACLE DATABASE RESPONSE TIME COMPARISON TABLE

STEP	Optimization mean	Responsge tiom(S)
1	nothing	246
2	Database design iptimization	127
3	SQL optimization in application software	76
4	Database configuration parameter optimization	43
5	System I/O optimization	29

After the optimization of the database design, SQL in the application software, the database configuration parameter and the system I/O, the system response time is obviously reduced and the running speed is rapidly improved. Practice has proved that the design and optimization mean is effective and has achieved the expected results.

V. CONCLUSION

With the development of computer applications and the widely used of enterprise information system, database has gradually become the base and core of computer information system and computer application system, and the importance of the database performance is also growing concern. As the largest database, Oracle database has been widely applied at home and abroad. Therefore, in-depth researching the performance issues of Oracle database system, presenting specific methods and measures aimed at Oracle database performance adjustment and optimization play a key role to ensure the stability and efficient operation of the database, and also has certain guidance and very good theory and application value. Combining with using experience of Oracle database, in this paper the adjustment and optimization of the Oracle database performance were roundly, systematically analyzed and researched, the experiment results have proved that the optimization program presented in this paper could obviously improve the database query speed.

REFERENCES

[1] Du Qingfeng, Zhang Weishan. Performance Optimization Analysis Based on Oracle Database Application System[J].Computer Engineering,2005,(16):155～157.

[2] Clifton Nock. Data Access Patterns: Database Interactions In Object-Oriented Application [J].Addison-Wesley Professional, 2003.1-400.

[3] Thomas Kyte. Expert Oracle Database Architecture: 9i and 10g Programming Techniques and Solutions. American:Apress,2005.

[4] Edward Whalen. Oracle Performance Tuning and Optimization. Macmillan Computer Publishing, 1996,(4):400～401.

[5] Oracle Real Application Clusters 10g, [EB/01]. http://www.oracle.com/lang/cn/technologies/grid/index.html,2006-1.

[6] Murali Vallath. Oracle real application Clusters [M]. USA digital press, Oct 22, 2003

[7] Robert Freeman. Oracle database 10g new features [M].USA Osborne Oracle press series, 2004.

[8] Mike Ault, Madhu Tumma. Oracle 10g Grid & Real Application Clusters [M]. USA. Rampant tech press, May 1, 2004.

[9] Kevin Loney. Oracle database 10g: the complete reference [M].USA. Osborne Oracle press series. May 5, 2004.

[10] PL/SQL User's Guide and Reference Release 2(9.2), [EB/01]. http://downloadwest. oracle.com/docs/cd/B10501_01/appdev.920/a96624/05_colls.htm#28178, 2006-4

Design of Production Line Temperature Control System Based On Neural Network PID

Zhang Dingqun
Department of Electric and Electrical Engineering,Nanyang Institute of Technology
zhangdingqun@163.com

***Abstract*—After more than ten years' development, the neural network PID control technology, combining intelligent control technology and traditional control theories, has got remarkable achievements both in theory and use. This paper designs the whole production line temperature computer control system; production line crystallization process temperature control adopts multilayer network approximate PID controller based on BP algorithm, which verifies the validity of the control method after simulation comparison; finally, this paper discusses the feasibility of using VB language to realize the control process in RSView32.**

Keywords- temperature control system; neural network; PID

I. INTRODUCTION

Process control usually refers to the automatic control in industrial processes, such as petroleum, chemical, metallurgy, light industry and building materials, etc, and it has a very important place in national economy. Along with the development of industry and modern science and technology, production process becomes increasingly complex and the requirements of people for the overall performance of industrial process are also improving constantly. It is very difficult to accurately describe any physical phenomenon and motion state of complex objects and systems, and therefore traditional control methods founded on object accurate model are often difficult to meet the requirements of closed-loop optimal control. How to improve the quality of process control by economical and effective means has a very important practical significance.

II. SYSTEM CONFIGURATION

According to three main principles of automatic integrated control system design, namely standardization and openness, economical efficiency and energy saving property, reliability and easy maintenance, after the analysis of control task and considering the compatibility with old system, finally this system uses the following hardware configuration, network structure and software configuration.

A. Hardware configuration

The system uses SLC500 series module and 1797 series explosion-proof module of ROCKWELL Company and 2711-T10C8 touch screen of AB. Its processor uses 11 SLC5/04 (1747-L543C) CPU (including 4 CPU after the original system is upgraded). Considering the characteristic that various process sections are as independent of each other as possible on control, the system uses the principle that independent process sections and suitable data quantity to distribute processors. In addition, reaction kettle process section is the core part of the whole production and its production situation directly determines output, moreover this process section has the characteristics of complex working conditions (high temperature, high pressure and high sealing) and strict field requirements (fire and leak proof), and therefore we configure scanner module 1747-SN and Ex (intrinsic safety) series remote I/O adapter 1794-ASB for 4 reaction kettle control systems and they realize the distributed intrinsically safe explosion proof of the system together with other Ex series modules. This paper takes the control system of one reaction kettle as an example to give the configuration diagram of its system, shown as Fig 1.

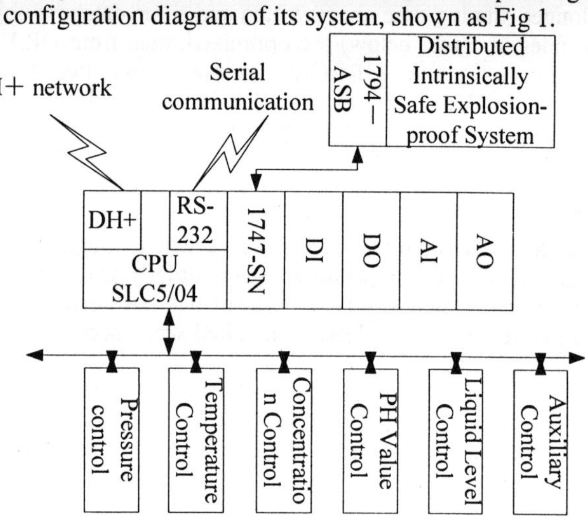

Figure 1. System Configuration of Reaction Kettle Process Section

B. Network structure

This system includes 11 PLC nodes, 4 touch screen nodes and 5 operation station nodes. 11 control cabinets, 5 monitoring PC computers and 2 servers are distributed in 3 different control rooms and 4 touch screens are distributed on the spot. According to the system's characteristics of wide node distribution and large data exchange capacity, combined with system hardware configuration, this system adopts three-layer network framework, shown as Fig 2. Upper management layer net is constructed according to ethernet protocol and it can link the computers on the platform with switch through ethernet card to form local area network, thereby realizing multi-microcomputer monitoring and management; the second layer-control layer (control net) uses DH+ network, configures one DH+ communication card 1784-PKTX (D) for 5 upper monitoring PCs respectively as the communication driver device between operation station and control station and provides corresponding communication interfaces. Bottom device net includes field transducer, instrument and third party device.

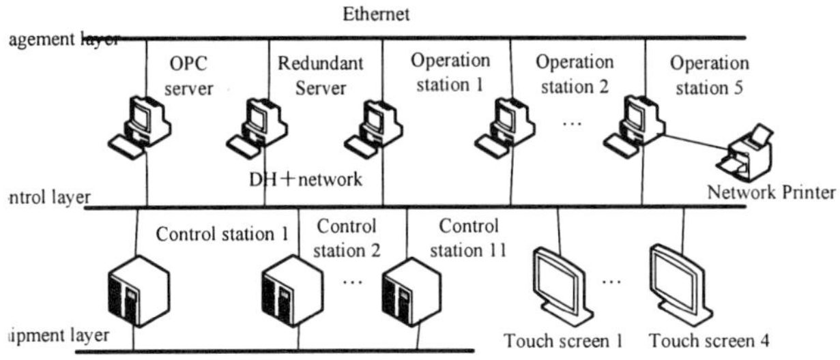

Figure 2. Structure Diagram of Control System Network

As the core layer of the control system, DH+ network simultaneously realizes the communication between PLC and PLC and between programming terminal and PLC in the mode of a physical bus and it has a very high reliability, uses the same communication parameters, thereby saving the investment in engineering. One DH+ link can connect a maximum of 64 nodes (intelligent equipment). However, considering communication speed, we should limit the number of nodes on the network as possible to meet the requirements of the system for real-time performance. The backbone of DH+ network is connected by screened coaxial cable or twisted pair line, and therefore its communication rate can reach 57. 6kpbs (it is three times faster than the communication rate of the original DH-485 network) and its transmission distance can reach 3048m. Facts show that these performance indexes completely meet the requirements of the system.

C. *Software configuration*

The design and realization of a large PLC automatic control system software system is the key link which measures if the system can be realized, its operation effect and automation level. A good PLC automatic control system software system not only can make the administrators and operators of this system understand and grasp the operation conditions of various process flows, changes of process parameters and results of process control in time but also should have the functions of optimizing process parameters, improving operation management level, reducing production cost and making system run steadily for a long time to reach the best benefit. After analysis and comparison, finally the system selects the following software configuration:

Its operating system software selects Microsoft Windows 2000 of American Microsoft; its network communication software selects RSLinx, which provides the communication driver from PLC control layer to OPC client and realizes network configuration; PLC programming software selects RSLogix500, namely special programming software of SLC500 series PLC; touch screen edit software selects PanelBuilder32, namely general programming software of AB-PanelView; upper configuration software selects RSView32 development edition, all the above software selects the software products developed matching with hardware of Rockwell Company except operating system software, such a configuration is favorable for realizing the seamless integration between hardware and software and between software and software and provides a premise guarantee for secure, stable and reliable operation of system.

III. Design and Realization of Temperature Control System

A. *Control scheme design*

From production practice, we can know that in order to reach higher production quality requirements, apart from accurate design and standard operation of other process sections, there are also strict requirements for crystallization process section, especially the material temperature of crystallization process should be strictly ensured to change within a certain range and it can not be too high or too low. The temperature control of crystallization process is closely related to product quality and production efficiency of the whole production line and it has a relatively important place in the whole production process. Through the analysis of thermal process of crystallization process section, we can know that there are many factors influencing crystallization temperature, including steam flow, material weight, material composition and external temperature, etc. Among these factors, steam flow is the main factor, it has a good controllability and its size can be controlled by adjusting the opening of steam regulating valve. And therefore, the temperature control design of crystallization process is shown as the control system in Fig 3, in the figure, Tr is set temperature of material, the material temperature Tc of crystallization process is controlled parameter, the output θ of regulator is control quantity, namely opening signal of regulating valve and T0 is external temperature as disturbance factor.

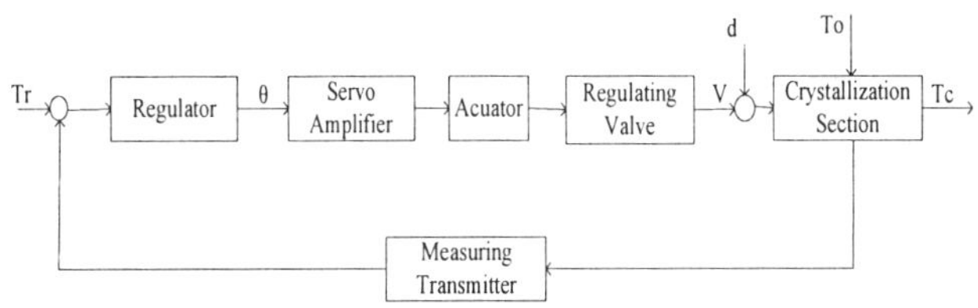

Figure 3. Structure Diagram of Crystallization Process Temperature Control System

Due to comparatively complex crystallization process, relatively large capacity lag and many disturbances, modeling by any methods can not completely describe its dynamic characteristics, and meanwhile the influences of external environment on process and the changes of object characteristics in operation will introduce uncertainty into controlled object, and therefore it is difficult to get relatively satisfactory control effects by using traditional PID control. Considering extensive application of traditional PID control in industrial process and characteristics of neural network control technology, combined with characteristics of crystallization process, system performance requirements and simplicity of control realization, we use multilayer net approximate PID controller (LPNC) to design a crystallization process temperature controller to meet the requirements of good system dynamic performance, good disturbance-rejection performance and a certain adaptive capacity.

B. *Mathematical model of controlled process*

According to practical experience, crystallization process has characteristics of large inertia, large lag and time variation, etc, and therefore it is difficult to establish an accurate mathematical model of controlled object, but for the needs of verifying the feasibility of fuzzy PID control and system simulation, we will use test method to establish an approximate model of controlled object.

There are many test methods for modeling and this paper uses measured step response to determine approximate transfer function. This method is carried out in two steps:

1. Acquisition of step response

The principle of measuring step response is very simple, but doing this kind of test in practical industrial process faces many practical problems, for example, we can not disturb normal production due to test and should also try to reduce the influence of random disturbance and nonlinear consideration in system, etc. In order to exert relatively large disturbance amplitude and not seriously disturb production, we can use rectangular pulse input to replace usual step input, namely immediately removing the large amplitude step disturbance after it is exerted for a short time. Although such moral rectangular pulse response is different from normal step response, there is a close association between the two responses and we can obtain the step response needed according to superposition principle.

2. Determine approximate transfer function according to step response

According to measured step response, we can fit it to an approximate transfer function. First, we should determine the form of transfer function, namely model structure of mathematical model to be established. Typical industrial process transfer functions can be in various forms (first-order, second-order or multi-order inertia plus time delay) and we select second-order inertia plus time delay form according to practical experience.

$$G(s)=\frac{Ke^{-\tau s}}{(T_1 s+1)(T_2 s+1)} \tag{1}$$

Next, we should determine parameters K, τ, T1 and T2 in formula 1. Gain K is determined by the ratio of steady state input value to steady state output value. And then determine parameter τ according to the unresponsive stage when step response curve breaks away from initiation and the moment it begins to change. After that, the remaining problem is to use the following transfer function to fit the non-dimensional step response $y^*(t)$ whose delay part has been taken off:

$$G(s)=\frac{1}{(T_1 s+1)(T_2 s+1)}, T_1 \geq T_2 \tag{2}$$

The step response corresponding to the above formula should be:

$$y^*(t)=1-\frac{T_1}{T_1-T_2}e^{-\frac{1}{T_1}}-\frac{T_2}{T_2-T_1}e^{-\frac{1}{T_2}} \tag{3}$$

According to the above formula, we can use the data of two points on step response $\left[t_1, y^*(t_1)\right]$ and $\left[t_1, y^*(t_2)\right]$ to determine parameters T_1 and T_2.

$$\begin{cases} \frac{T_1}{T_1-T_2}e^{-\frac{t_1}{T_1}}-\frac{T_2}{T_1-T_2}e^{-\frac{t_1}{T_2}}=0.6 \\ \frac{T_1}{T_1-T_2}e^{-\frac{t_2}{T_1}}-\frac{T_2}{T_1-T_2}e^{-\frac{t_2}{T_2}}=0.2 \end{cases} \tag{4}$$

The approximate solution of the above formula is:

$$T_1+T \approx \frac{1}{2.16}(t_1+t_2) \tag{5}$$

$$\frac{T_1T_2}{(T_1+T_2)} \approx \left(1.74\frac{t_1}{t_2}-0.55\right) \tag{6}$$

After calculation, K=16.5, τ=35, T_1=124 and T_2=84. And therefore, the approximate mathematical model of crystallization process is as follows:

$$G(s)=\frac{16.5e^{-35_N}}{(124s+1)(84s+1)} \tag{7}$$

This approximate mathematical model is built on the premise of assumption of constant steam pressure, temperature and room temperature, and therefore it is not very accurate, but the inaccuracy is inevitable to a large extent. Just because of this, the requirements for controller are higher, especially adaptive capacity and anti-interference capacity of controller should be strong when model parameters change. If we use a traditional PID controller, it is very difficult to meet the requirements when maintaining controller parameters unchanged.

C. *Realization scheme of control system*

In practical production line computer control system, in order to realize the automatic control of crystallization process temperature, we need to carry out programming and configuration in upper computer. Concrete control algorithms and operation processing programs are edited in global script editor. The global script editor of RSView32 provides standard Visual Basic language program operation environment and we can use the function libraries provided by it, such as project function library and standard function library, etc, to carry out programming and debugging conveniently.

In the process of system running, upper computer collects process data and sends out a control command according to control algorithm under the condition of meeting automatic control. The control command is sent out by process variable and transformed into the value which matches with the data format of PLC through linear calibration, and then it is transformed into a current signal whose value is between 4 and 20 mA by AO module and finally the current signal is sent to manual operator and servo amplifier for controlling the opening of field regulating valve to achieve the goal of regulating crystallization process temperature by adjusting steam flow. Convenient for operation and control, we configure an automatic control operation window in RSView32, by which we can real-timely monitor process parameters, choose automatic or manual control mode and adjust the set value of controlled variable or the opening of given valve to make the output of system approach set value. Meanwhile, we edit a parameter setting window to switch two kinds of automatic control modes and set controller parameters in running environment conveniently.

In the global script of RSView32, we can conveniently use VB language to realize the control algorithm of crystallization process temperature control system. Set the scan period of program, foreground scan period is set as 0.5s and background scan period is set as 0.2s. The script runs in the background, and therefore the program circulates once 500ms when conditions are met, the detailed program flow chart is shown as Fig 4.

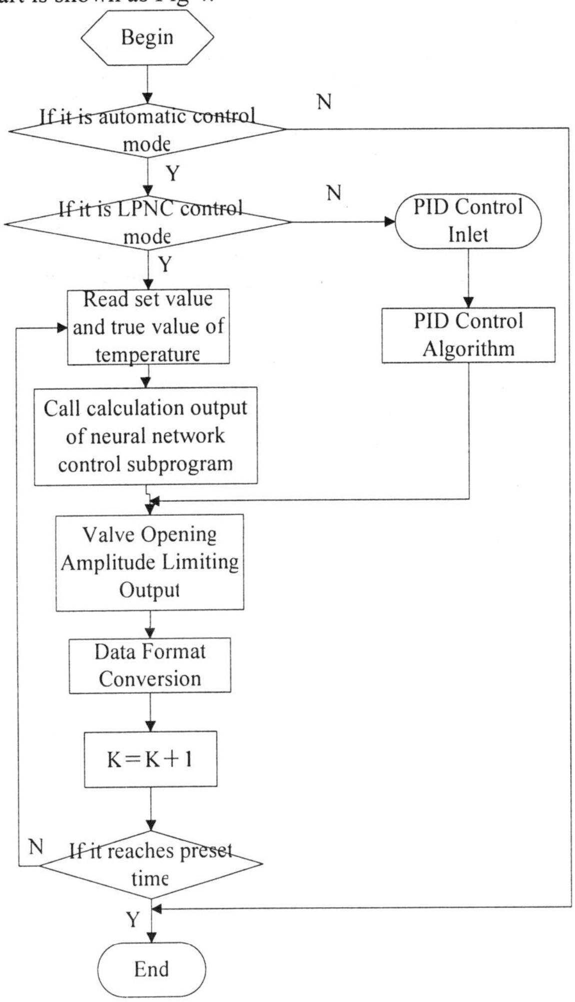

Figure 4. Flow Chart of LPNC Algorithm Main Program

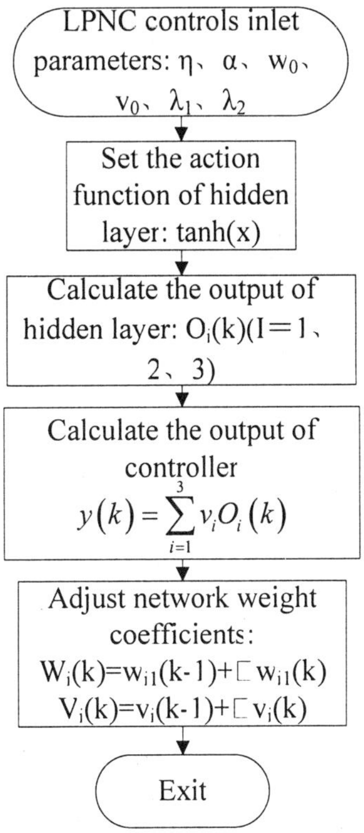

Figure 5. Flow Chart of Neural Network Control Subprogram

IV. CONCLUSION

This paper applies neural network PID control to the temperature control of crystallization process in the automatic control system project of production line, verifies its validity and applicability through simulation comparison and uses VB language to realize the automatic control process of temperature in RS View.

REFERENCES

[1] W.S. Mclulloch, W.Pitts,A Logical Calculus of the Ideas Immanent in Nervous Activity, Bulletin of Mathematical Biophysics, 1943(5):115-133

[2] D.O.Hebb, The Organization of Behavior Wiley, New York, 1949

[3] F.Rosenblatt, The Perceptron: A Probabilistic Model for Information Storage and Organization in the Brain, Psychological Review, 1958(65):386-408

[4] D.Rumelhart, J.McCelland, Parallel Distributed Processing, MIT Press, 1986

[5] B .Widrow, M.Hoff, 1960 IRE WESCON Conr. Record, 1960:96-104

[6] J.Moody, C.Darken, Fast Learning in Networks of Locally-Tuned Processing Units, Neural Computation, 1989, 1(2):281-294

[7] J.S.Albus, A New Approach to Manipulator Control: The Cerebellar Model Articulation Controller(CMAC), Trans. Of ASME Journal of Dynamic Systems Measurements and Control, 1975(9): 220-227

[8] J.J·Hopfield, Neural Networks and Physical Systems with Emergent Collective Computational Abilities, PNAS, USA, 1982(79):2554-2558

Advanced Manufacturing Technology Implementation Evaluation Tool (AMTIET)

Sara Saberi, Rosnah M.Y[1], Eliza Dianna
Department of Mechanical and Manufacturing Engineering
Faculty of Engineering
Universiti Putra Malaysia
43400 UPM Serdang, Selangor

[1] - corresponding Author

Abstract- The Advanced Manufacturing Technology Implementation Evaluation Tool (AMTIET) is an analytical tool that brings together management and technology research concepts to help company's managers and operational engineers make technology implementation and application decisions. AMTIET integrates research and data from an extensive literature sources to facilitate users conducting implementation analyses of technology implementation. With AMTIET, companies seeking AMTs will be able to find their strength/weakness points in technical and organizational structures. This tool is programmed in PHP environment and has equipped with Neural Network prediction ability to forecast the level of performance in company based on their condition.

Keywords; assessment tool, advanced manufacturing technology

1. Introduction

The globalization of the economy is forcing many enterprises to change in order to survive. To compete in these global markets, many small and medium-sized enterprises (SMEs) in manufacturing part need to develop new business strategies and employ new advanced manufacturing technologies (AMTs) [1].

AMT has potential to bridge the chasm between choosing either low-cost dedicated production, or high-variety differentiation [2]. Therefore, AMT has been viewed as a strategic weapon to gain competitive advantage, to improve productivity and performance, to improve flexibility of production [2, 3], and to improve product and service [4, 5].

It has been found that expectations of AMT will not be brought to fruition unless a holistic approach is taken to planning, acquiring, implementation and exploitation [6]. The manufacturing literature suggests that firms need to invest in both structure (e.g., process or information technology) and infrastructure (e.g., management, people and procedures) to build the capabilities required to meet these benefits besides adopting new technologies [7]. This dramatically increases the complexity of the adopting manufacturing system especially in SMEs where usually have poor human and financial resources and are therefore likely to be less prepared and less able to change [1]. The choice of technology, for which many options exist, must be driven by, and closely aligned with, the structure and infrastructure of the firm. However, despite the abundance of information, manufacturing companies often rely on marketing data, trial and error, and anecdotal information to make technology purchasing/ implementing decisions [8]. Therefore for implementing AMTs, it is essential to have a detailed assessment of what is required and what is available to satisfy those requirements. A more analytically sound basis for decision making is essential.

To respond to this need, we are going to introduce a new assessment tool to help managers in evaluating their companies in relation to advanced manufacturing technology implementation to get most benefits from adopting theses technologies in their companies. Since failure to meet the technical/manufacturing benefits will almost invariably result in failure on the performance bases, it is extremely important that assessment of AMT implementation should include related factors from background of companies [9, 10], the levels of AMT investment [7, 11], structures and infrastructures such as organizational structure/culture, workforce and management practices and integration [12-14], and obstacles and benefits [9, 15, 16]. Another critical reason for early assessment of the technical/manufacturing level of firms is that it can provide an early signal of technology incompatibility or technology implementation problems [17]. It can be applied as a better understanding of the ways in which SMEs adopt and implement new advanced technologies/practices besides improving the way of managing information in SMEs. This research, conducted in Malaysian manufacturing SMEs, was designed to provide an in-depth understanding and explanation of the relative levels of success in advanced manufacturing technology adoption and use.

2. Assessment Tool Concept

This assessment tool (AMTIET) is internet-based software and a multi-attribute decision tool applicable to all manufacturing firms. The base of analysis in this tool is related to results of analyzing responses from a survey. The survey is done by means of questionnaire which is sent to a big group of SMEs in Malaysia. The questionnaire includes the most important factors in AMT implementation based on literatures.

Before starting to build this assessment system, we had to:

- Define a full set of criteria for technology implementation, combining technical and organizational criteria.
- Choose technologies to be included in the questionnaire as well as in database
- Identify a number of influencing variables, which can be represented by 5-point Likert scale, which will form the basis for our decision.
- Develop a generic, multi-paradigm intelligent support framework that combines analysis with artificial intelligence in such a way that it could be reused for a wide range of manufacturing.

3. Assessment Tool Model Structure

After considering all above criteria, developing this tool follows these steps (figure 1):

- Step1: Preparing a questionnaire contains factors influence implementation of AMT, and sending it to SMEs in Malaysia, implementing AMT. the questions are rated based on 5-point Likert scale.

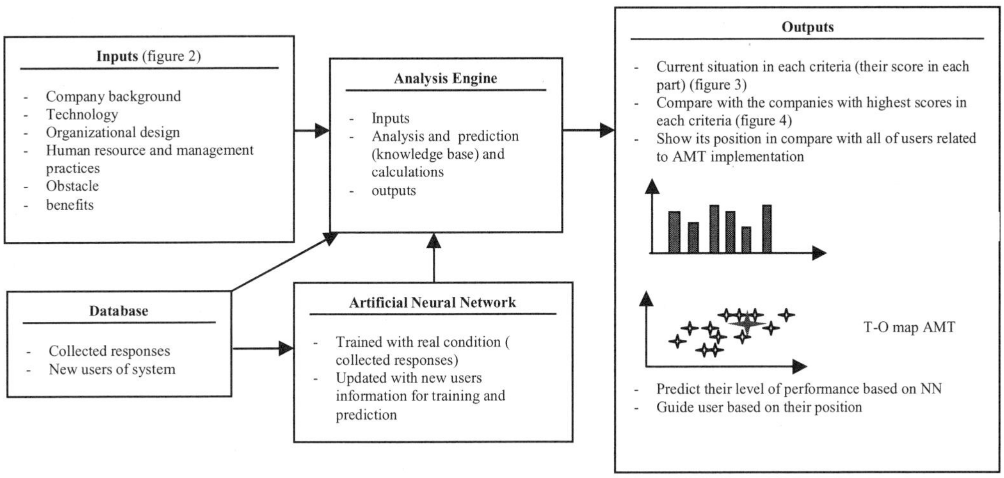

Figure 1: schematic structure of Assessment System

- Step2: Preparing the interface for this internet-base tool with PHP (based on questionnaire questions) and matching it with Navicat MySQL Admin Tool to manage database in system. This interface plays input role for the system (figure 2).
- Setp3: analyzing data from collecting responses with statistical tools such as:
  - Regression: to find the relationship between benefits and other factors;
  - Cluster analysis: to separate and specify different AMT users and also different level of performance gained after implementing AMT.

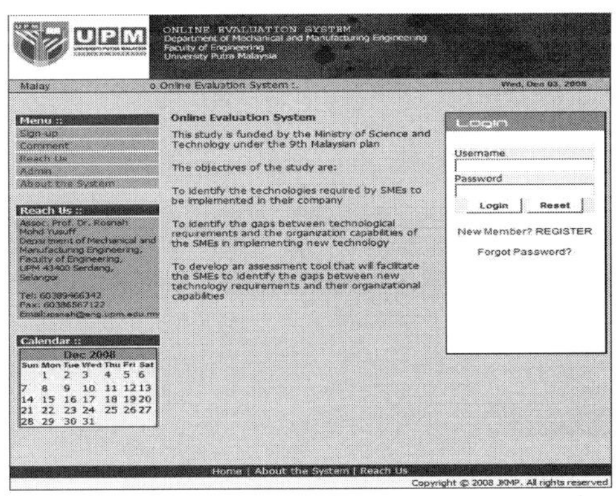

Figure 2: interface of system (main page)

- Step 4: developing an Artificial Neural Network (ANN) and train it with analyzed data. The NN will be used for predicting the situation of the

assessment tool (e.g. for the performance level of their company based on company condition and AMT investment level).

- Step 5: the output of system will provide the users with some graphical results about the firm and guide them into their weakness/strength point and compare them with others to show their position in comparison with the other manufacturer.

4. System Input

At first, any user will be provided with an ID and Password to be sure about their information confidence. Therefore they have the ability of using this system not for first time, but to use it any time to evaluate themselves after any change. System presents users with a variety of input criteria. To see total result for prediction and comparison with others, all of parts are mandatory to be filled, but if user is going to evaluate only especial part to see its current condition, that part should be filled. By doing so, system will mentioned the empty parts to be filled. Figure 3 illustrates three examples of user input: background, the investment level of technologies, and benefits.

The dialog box on the middle of Figure 3 shows how the user identifies the information about its level of investment in AMT. Since AMT usage data are the main focus of study, this is an important input parameter. The user ranks the level of applying each technology. The importance levels of focus on any other criteria are used to get the average for the results and also for regression. All criteria have some degree of limitation about the items included in each one, because the questions is based on our survey questionnaire, and by adding more questions, it may make responses less precise.

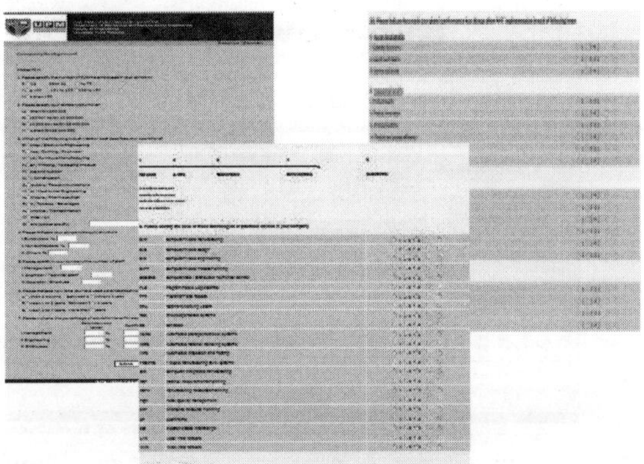

Figure 3: three examples of system input criteria

5. Analysis Engine

The "engine" of the model is a combination of equations and formulas within PHP environment, in addition to JavaScript codes and Navicat MySQL Admin Tool. The PHP code serves major purposes. The user interface (menu selections, parameter choices (multi answer questions) and output results and figures) is built from PHP code. MySQL code controls the flow of the data through the database, and manages tables. For some system errors and pop up windows, JavaScript code is used. The data analyzing is arranged into the following steps:

- assemble the data
- Conduct analyses and calculations
- Call prediction function
- Produce output

Data are assembled based on three criteria: the level of investment on technologies, the level of importance emphasis on technology requirement and the intensity of performance changes after AMT implementation. It was suggested that companies with different taxonomy of technologies differ in terms of Contextual factors [18-20]. For instance, some taxonomy may affect operational performance more, and others may relate to especial strategies. The types of analyses and calculations incorporated into the model include mean weighted average for technical, organizational, performance and comparing the criteria scores with other companies and use in graphical output beside use of trained Neural Network (NN) for prediction. The networks used in this study are called *feedforward networks* as long as the arcs do not form a circuit, in that as one travels from a node following the direction of the arcs, one cannot return to the starting node. The NN is developed in MATLAB and trained there with collected data. NN predicts the level of company performance according to user inputs. Assessment tool generates output in both documentation and graphical forms.

6. System Output

The output of system falls into the three categories of graphical, prediction, and documentation. The graphical data mostly used for comparison between users whereas documentation and prediction explain situation and tries to make the figures and graphs clear in details. These results give the user an idea of how much attention is needed to put in weakness points to overcome them. Figure 4-6 show three types of output results.

The Score

The score for section ORGANIZATION DESIGN are displayed below

Company structure	Your Score	Average
Centralization	3.00	2.92
Formalization	3.33	2.99
Complexity / Specialization	3.33	2.95
Structure		

Company culture	Your Score	Average
Group Value System	2.00	3.50
Developmental	2.00	3.41
Hierarchical	2.00	3.39
Rational	2.00	3.30
Flexibility		
Control		

Show graph of company's score for each area of focus.

Figure 4: output of system (current score)

In Figure 5, the graph compares the cumulative score for organizational criteria with company with highest score in this part. This could be used to benchmark the user among its competitors.

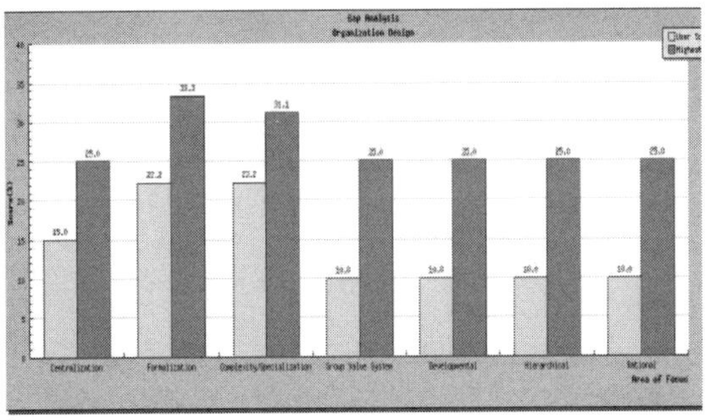

Figure 5: output of system (compare with highest score)

Figure 6 shows two-dimensional map of three important dimensions. The O-T map quantitatively analyzes aggregated indexes on organization, technology, and performance. This information-map could be used to describe the organization and technology and performance in dynamic manner as the speed of organizational/technical innovation is represented by the slope (dO/dT). The map can declare that if companies are shifting toward technical (more emphasize on level of technology), organizational (focus more on organizational criteria), or in balanced situation (have an equilibrium stress on both technology level and organizational criterion).

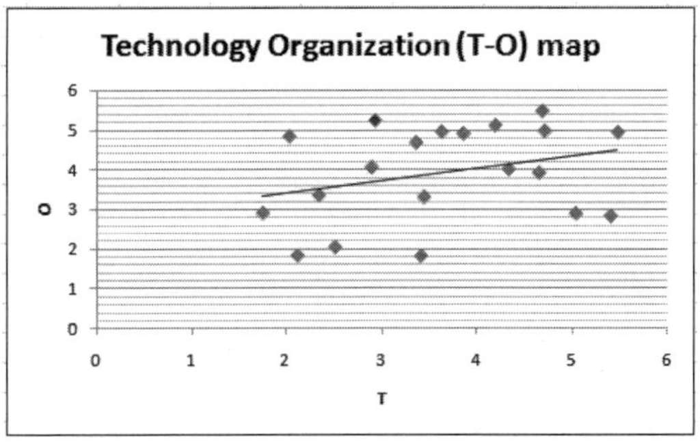

Figure 6: output of system (two-dimensional map)

7. Summary

Applying Advanced manufacturing technologies are not as easy as signing a cheque for their purchasing. Although the rate of technology growth is astounding, implementing these technologies and evaluating the benefits of them is not straightforward. For companies which are seeking to use any of these AMTs, they will require a tool to assess different technologies and provide information regarding the requirements and benefits. AMTIET is an internet-base analytical model to assist managers and operational engineers with technology acquisition and implementation decision-making. AMTIET continues to provide companies the information about their position in compare with other manufacturers whether in their industrial sector or in general, beside to predict the level of performance according to current situation. It can be used as a powerful tool for sharing and managing information about new technologies among companies.

References

1. Caldeira, M.r.M. and J.M. Ward, "Using resource-based theory to interpret the successful adoption and use of information systems and technology in manufacturing small and medium-sized enterprises", European Journal of Information Systems, 2003. 12: pp. 127–141.
2. Efstathiades, A., S. Tassou, and A. Antoniou, "Strategic planning, transfer and implementation of Advanced Manufacturing Technologies (AMT). Development of an integrated process plan", Technovation, 2002. 22(4): pp. 201-212.
3. Zhao, H. and H.C. Co, "Adoption and implementation of advanced manufacturing technology in Singapore", Int. J. Production Economics, 1997. 48: pp. 7-19.
4. Preece, D., Organisation and technical change. 1995 London: Routledge.
5. Ghani, k.A. and v. Jayabalan, "advanced manufacturing technology and planned organizational change", the journal of high technology management research, 2000. 11(1): pp. 1–18.
6. Sohal, A.S., "Assessing AMT implementations: an empirical field study", Technovation, 1996. 16(81): pp. 377 384.

7. Small, M.H. and M.M. Yasin, "Advanced manufacturing technology: Implementation policy and performance", Journal of Operations Management, 1997. 15: pp. 349-370.
8. Cooper, W., J. Dukovich, and J. Bouffard. "The Corrections and Law Enforcement Technology Assessment System (CLETAS)". in *Engineering and Technology Management, 1998. Pioneering New Technologies: Management Issues and Challenges in the Third Millennium. IEMC '98 Proceedings. International Conference on*. 1998. 419-424.
9. Swamidass, P.M. and S. Kotha, "Explaining manufacturing technology use, firm size and performance using a multidimensional view of technology", Journal of Operations Management 1998. 17: pp. 23–37.
10. Millen, R. and A.S. Sohal, "Planning processes for advanced manufacturing technology by large American manufacturers", Technovation, 1998. 18(12): pp. 741–750.
11. Small, M.H. and M.M. Yasin, "Developing a framework for the effective planning and implementation of advanced manufacturing technology", International Journal of Operations & Production Management, 1997. 17(2): pp. 468-489.
12. GUPTA, A., I.J. CHEN, and D. CHIANG, "Determining Organizational Structure Choices in Advanced Manufacturing Technology Management", Omega, Int. J. Mgmt Sci, 1997. 25(5): pp. 511-521.
13. Chang, P.-L. and Scott S C Lung, "Organizational changes for advanced manufacturing technology infusion: An empirical study", International Journal of Management, 2002: pp. 206.
14. Malhotra, M.K., M.L. Heine, and V. Grover, "An evaluation of the relationship between management practices and computer aided design technology", Journal of Operations Management 2001. 19 pp. 307–333.
15. Shapira, P. and T. Rephann, "New Technology Adoption in West Virginia Implications for Manufacturing Modernization Policies", Environment and Planning C - Government and Policy, 1996. 14: pp. 431-450.
16. Hofmann, C. and S. Orr, "Advanced manufacturing technology adoption—the German experience", Technovation, 2005. 25 pp. 711–724.
17. Small, M.H., "Assessing manufacturing performance: an advanced manufacturing technology portfolio perspective", Industrial Management & Data Systems, 1999. 99(6): pp. 266-277.
18. Boyer, K.K., P.T. Ward, and G.K. Leong, "Approaches to the factory of the future An empirical taxonomy", Journal of Operations Management, 1996. 14 pp. 297-313.
19. Dıaz, M.S., J.A.D. Machucaa, and M.ı.J. Álvarez-Gil, "A view of developing patterns of investment in AMT through empirical taxonomies: new evidence", Journal of Operations Management 2003. 21 pp. 577–606.
20. Jonsson, P., "An empirical taxonomy of advanced manufacturing technology", International Journal of Operations & Production Management, 2000. 20(12): pp. 1446-1474.

TURN-ON TIME DELAY OF DEGRADED BULK UNCOOLED SEMICONDUCTOR LASER DIODES

MOHAMMAD SYUHAIMI AB-RAHMAN
syuhaimi@vlsi.eng.ukm.my

MAZEN R. HASSAN
mrhassan@vlsi.eng.ukm.my

Computer & Network Security Research Group
Faculty of Engineering & Built Environment
Department of Electrical, Electronic and Systems Engineering,
University kebangsaan Malaysia (UKM)
43600 Bangi, Selangor, Malaysia.

In this paper, a full analytical and exact expression form of turn-on time delay, t_{on}, of degraded bulk uncooled laser diode (DBUSLD) has been presented in terms of nonradiative, A_{nr} , radiative, B_r , Auger recombination coefficients, C_{auger}, cavity dimensions, threshold carrier density, N_{th},, injection current, I_{inj}, number of "0" bits preceding the considered bit, N_{bit}, bit-rate, Brate and temperature of operation, T. Also we included, in addition to the mentioned parameters, dark defect (DD) parameters, i. e. number of DD, n_{DD} and width of DD, w_{DD}. In addition, an exact and full analytical expression form of carrier density, N, corresponding to the current flowing through laser active region, I, and in term of all the above mentioned parameters has been derived which can be used to determine any value of N corresponding to I exactly, therefore, the temperature dependence (TD) of threshold carrier density of DBUSLD (which is used in ton calculation) is calculated corresponding TD of threshold current of the device. Simulation results show that worst case of DBUSLD is when operates with large n_{DD} and at high temperature degree.

1. Introduction

Semiconductor laser diodes (SLD's) are most important for various applications such as material processing, medical surgery, photodynamic therapy, pumping of solid-state lasers and fiber lasers, and for space applications. Latter include communication terminals, light detection and ranging (LIDAR) and the laser interferometer space antenna (LISA), for example [1]. In such systems, the reliability of the SLD is a crucial factor. Device failure can lead to serious system downtime and high repair costs, so the reliability of the SLD's weights heavily in the system specifications. [1-5]. A rapid decrease in optical power was very often observed within a few hundred of hours after the LD is starting to operate under a constant output power [3]. This is due to dark defect (dark line defects (DLD's) growth from dark spot defect (DSD) in the active layer of LD)) as shown in Fig. 1 [1] where it shows the images of three laser stripes, (a) after gradual degradation, (b) after freak failure and (c) sudden failure after gradual degradation.

The images indicate dark spots in case of gradually degraded devices (a and c). A dark line loop along the laser stripe is observed in the freak device (b), but there are no dark spots. The suddenly failed device (c)

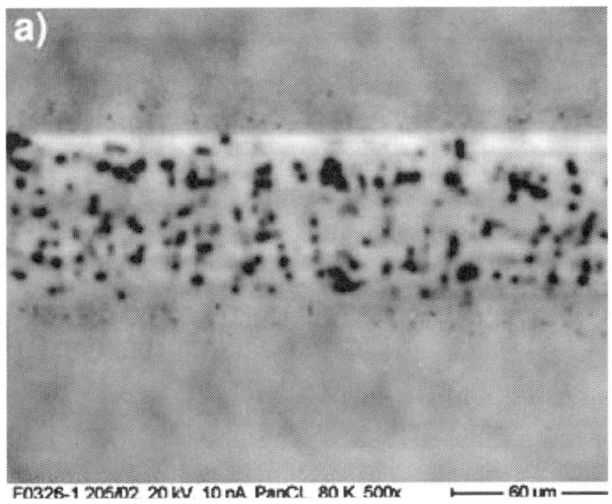

(a) After gradual degradation

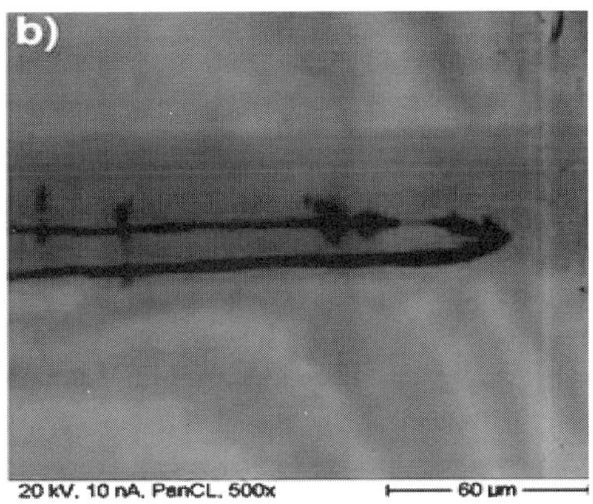

(b) After freak failure

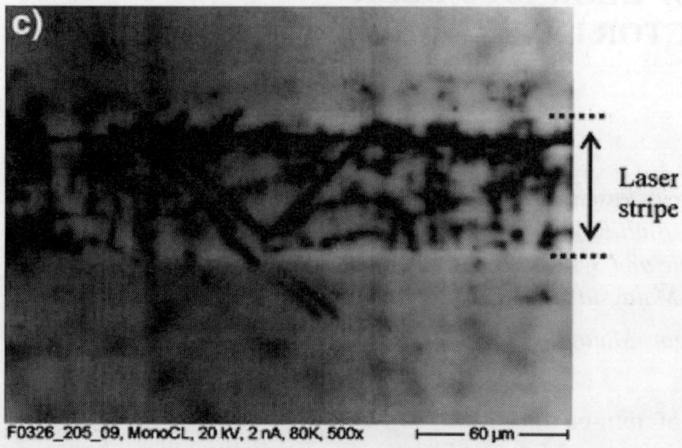

(c) Sudden failure after gradual degradation

Fig. 1 Top view CL images of (a) gradual degradation, (b) freak failure, and (c) sudden failure after gradual degradation [1].

indicates dark lines along the laser stripe. The dark spots are known to originate from dislocation loops [1, 2]. The DLD causes the internal absorption losses to increase and the injected carrier lifetime to be shortened because of the increase in nonradiative recombination. These result in an increase in the lasing threshold current and a decrease in the external differential quantum efficiency [4]. The dependence of threshold current, I_{th}, increase on the number of DD's is explained in terms of a model which includes effects due to the DD's, as well as changes in the regions outside the DD's [2]. The latter is found to be responsible for the major part of I_{th} increase [2]. From the measurements of I_{th} of degraded SLD, threshold carrier density, Nth can be calculated accordingly.

From other hand, it is known that the performance of high-speed, intensity modulated, direct detection systems is critically dependent on the characteristics of SLD [7]. The turn–on time delay, t_{on}, and its jitter plays a significant role in determining the system performance of SLD and has been studied both experimentally and theoretically. To our best knowledge, all the previous studied depended on either experimental or approximated calculations of ton [7-12]. However, In [13], we derived for the first time a full analytical and exact expression form of ton in terms of nonradiative, A , radiative, B , Auger, C_{auger}, recombination coefficients, cavity dimensions, threshold carrier density, N_{th}, (and in turn threshold current density, I_{th}), the device injection current, I_{inj}, and temperature of operation, T. In this paper, we will include, in addition to the mentioned parameters, the main DD parameters, i. e. n_{DD} and w_{DD}. We think that it is the first time of which the influence of DD's of DBUSLD on t_{on} is determined exactly and analytically corresponding to exact and analytical value of N_{th}. In addition, the improvements in laser manufacture allow today operating uncooled direct modulated SLD over abroad temperature range. Given that, a strong cost reduction in optical systems can be achieved by eliminating costly laser temperature control. Uncooled SLD's have been considered as a key technology for future optical network systems [14-15]. The aim of this paper is to study the influence of DD's on ton of DBUSLD in the presence of temperature of operation. The influence of DD on ton will be studied corresponding to its influence on N_{th}, which is calculated analytically and exactly from known value of I_{th}. This will give the designer the chance to determine the exact value of N_{th} from any experimental measurements or proposed model of I_{th} and then determine ton accordingly. It should be noted that we assumed that (1) temperature of operation does not affect DD's themselves and (2) $I_{inj} = u.\ I_{th}(To)$, To=25°C and u =2, in all results corresponding to SLD without degradation, i.e. I_{inj} is independent of temperature and DD. This assumption is made according to the normal operation of laser source. In other words, the current source supplies a fixed value of injection current.

2. Mathematical description

2.1. *Threshold carrier density*

In [2], the authors proposed analytical model of total threshold current, I_{th}^{total} , of DBSLD. In this section we aim to obtain an analytical model of total threshold carrier density, N_{th}^{total} , of DBUSLD in the presence of temperature of operation, $N_{th}^{total}(T)$. To realize that, we will consider Nth (of normal "good region") in [2] as function of T in order to obtain an expression of I_{th}^{total} as function of T, $I_{th}^{total}(T)$ correspondingly. Then in order to obtain the corresponding threshold carrier density we will derive full and exact analytical expression form of carrier density in term of laser cavity parameters and current flowing through the SLD active region.

In the time period ($0<t<t_{on}$), the stimulated emission rate can be neglected and the carrier density rate equation of single mode semiconductor laser can written as [11]

$$\frac{dN}{dt}=\frac{I}{qV}-N(AN+BN^2+C_{auger}N^3) \qquad (1)$$

Where q is the electron charge and V is the volume of active region. The steady state solution can be obtained by setting $\frac{dN}{dt}=0$, so Eq. (1) can be re-written as

$$N^3+\frac{B}{C_{auger}}N^2+\frac{A}{C_{auger}}N-\frac{I}{qVC_{auger}}=0 \qquad (2)$$

The three root solutions of the above Eq. can be written as

$$N_1=\frac{1}{6}N_{r1}-6\frac{N_{r2}}{N_{r1}}-\frac{1}{3}B_c \qquad (3a)$$

$$N_2=\left[\frac{-1}{12}N_{r1}+3\frac{N_{r2}}{N_{r1}}-\frac{1}{3}B_c\right]+j\left[\frac{\sqrt{3}}{2}\left(\frac{1}{6}N_{r1}+6\frac{N_{r2}}{N_{r1}}\right)\right] \qquad (3b)$$

$$N_3=\left[\frac{-1}{12}N_{r1}+3\frac{N_{r2}}{N_{r1}}-\frac{1}{3}B_c\right]-j\left[\frac{\sqrt{3}}{2}\left(\frac{1}{6}N_{r1}+6\frac{N_{r2}}{N_{r1}}\right)\right] \qquad (3c)$$

where

$$\mathrm{N_{r1}}=\left[36\mathrm{A_cB_c}+108\mathrm{I_{qv}}-8\mathrm{B_c^3}+12\left(12\mathrm{A_c^3}-3\mathrm{A_c^2B_c^2}+54\mathrm{A_cB_cI_{qv}}+81\mathrm{I_{qv}^2}-12\mathrm{I_{qv}B_c^3}\right)^{\frac{1}{2}}\right]^{\frac{1}{3}} \qquad (4a)$$

$$\mathrm{N_{r2}}=\frac{1}{3}\mathrm{A_c}-\frac{1}{9}\mathrm{B_c^2} \qquad (4b)$$

and

$$A_c=\frac{A}{C_{auger}},\ B_c=\frac{A}{C_{auger}}\ \text{and}\ \mathrm{I_{qv}}=\frac{I}{qVC_{auger}}.$$

Interesting only with real root solution , i. e. Eq. (3a), a full analytical and exact expression form of N in term of all appeared parameters will be obtained i. e. $N=N_1$. The value of N corresponding to any value of I can be obtained from Eq. (3a), therefore, we can obtain the expression of N_{th}^{total}(T) by substituting $I_{th}^{total}(T)$. In [2] the authors presented analytical model of I_{th}^{total} and we modified it by considering it as function of temperature corresponding to TD of N_{th}

$$I_{th}^{total}(T)=\frac{qVN_{th}(T)}{\tau_e(T)}\left[1+(C-1)\frac{w_{DD}}{L}n_{DD}\right] \qquad (5)$$

where $C\approx 2$ [2], $\tau_e(T)$ is TD of carrier lifetime, τ_e, corresponding to the TD of threshold carrier density in good region, $N_{th}(T)$, and may be written as

$$\tau_e(T)=\frac{1}{A_{nr}+B_{nr}N_{th}(T)+C_{auger}\left(N_{th}(T)\right)^2} \qquad (6a)$$

and $N_{th}(T)$ can be written after modifying [10, 11] as

$$N_{th}(T)=N_t(T)+\frac{1}{\Gamma v_g\, g_o(T)\tau_p(T)} \qquad (6b)$$

where Γ is the optical confinement factor of laser cavity , $N_t(T)$, $g_o(T)$ and $\tau_p(T)$ are the TD's of carrier density at transparency, N_t, differential gain, g_o, and photon lifetime, τ_p, and they can be expressed respectively as [13, 14]

$$N_t(T)=\frac{T}{T_o}N_t(T_o) \qquad (7a)$$

$$g_o(T)=\frac{T_o}{T}g_o(T_o) \qquad (7b)$$

$$\tau_p^f(T)=\frac{1}{v_g\alpha_{total}(T)} \qquad (7c)$$

where $\alpha_{total}(T)$ is the TD of total cavity losses of SLD, v_g (= $Clight/n_g$)) is the group velocity and ng is the group refractive index. $\alpha_{total}(T)$ of distributed feedback (DFB) laser can be written, with assumption that the mirror loss is dominate, as [14]

$$\alpha_{total}(T)=\alpha_{int}(T)+\frac{1}{2L}ln\frac{1}{r_1 r_2} \qquad (7d)$$

Where L is the cavity length and $r1$ and $r2$ are field reflectiveties of the laser facets and $\alpha_{int}(T)$ is the TD of internal cavity losses, α_{int}, which can be written as [13, 14]

$$\alpha_{int}(T)=\alpha_{int\,o}\frac{T}{T_o} \qquad (7e)$$

where $\alpha_{int\,o}$ is internal cavity losses at room temperature, To. By substituting Eq. (5) in (3a) we will obtain a very flexible expression which describes threshold carrier density of DBUSLD in the presence of temperature of operation i. e. $N_{th}^{total}(T)=N_1\big|_{I=I_{th}^{total}(T)}$.

Notes:

1. At room temperate, To = 25oC, $N_{th}^{total}(T)\big|_{T=T_o}=N_1\big|_{I=I_{th}^{total}(T_o)}=N_{th}(T_o)$ and the resulted expression of $Nth(To)$ is as given in [2].

2. When n_{DD}=0, then $N_{th}^{total}(T) = N_1\big|_{I=I_{th}^{total}(T)}\big|_{n_{DD}=0} = N_{th}(T)$ and the resulted expression of $N_{th}(T)$ as given in [13] and $N_{th}(To) = 1.837\times10^{18}\, cm^{-3}$ (according to the typical values)

2.2. *Turn-on time delay*

In [13], we derived a full analytical and exact expression form of t_{on} which can be written as

$$t_{on} = \left[f(R,N)\big|_{R=R_1} + f(R,N)\big|_{R=R_2} + f(R,N)\big|_{R=R_3}\right]\Big|_{N=N_{th}} - \left[f(R,N)\big|_{R=R_1} + f(R,N)\big|_{R=R_2} + f(R,N)\big|_{R=R_3}\right]\Big|_{N=N_i} \tag{8}$$

where

$$f(R,N) = \frac{-R}{C_{auger}}.ln\left[\left(6A_{nr}C_{auger}Q - 2B_r{}^2Q\right)R + 3QC_{auger}{}^2\right]N + \left(-QA_{nr}B_r - 9IC_{auger}\right)R + QB_rC_{auger}\Big] \tag{9}$$

where R_i is the ith (i =1, 2, 3) root of $G(Z)$ which can be written as

$$G(Z) = \left[\left(4Q^2A_{nr}^3C_{auger}\right) - \left(Q^2B_r^2A_{nr}^2\right) + \left(18QI_{inj}A_{nr}B_rC_{auger}\right) - \left(4QI_{inj}B_r^2\right) + \left(27I_{inj}{}^2C_{auger}^2\right)\right]Z^3 + \left[\left(-3Q^2A_{nr}C_{auger}^3\right) + \left(Q^2B_r{}^2C_{auger}{}^2\right)\right]Z - \left[C_{auger}^4Q^2\right] \tag{10}$$

The roots of $G(Z)$ can be written as

$$R_1 = G_1 + G_2 \tag{11a}$$

$$R_2 = \frac{-G_1 - G_2}{2} + j\frac{\sqrt{3}}{2}(G_1 - G_2) \tag{11b}$$

$$R_3 = \frac{-G_1 - G_2}{2} - j\frac{\sqrt{3}}{2}(G_1 - G_2) \tag{11c}$$

where

$$G_1 = \frac{\left(\sqrt[3]{12}\right)C_{auger}}{6}\frac{F_1}{D_1} \tag{11a}$$

$$G_2 = \frac{1}{6}Q^2\left(3A_{nr}C_{auger} - B_r{}^2\right)\frac{\left(\sqrt[3]{12}\right)^2C_{auger}}{F_1} \tag{11b}$$

and

$$F_1 = Q^2\left[9C_{auger} + \sqrt{3}\left(\frac{D_2}{D_1}\right)^{\frac{1}{2}}D_1{}^2\right]^{\frac{1}{3}} \tag{12a}$$

$$D_1 = 27C_{auger}^2I_{inj}^2 + 4C_{auger}A_{nr}^3Q^2 + 18I_{inj}QA_{nr}B_rC_{auger} - A_{nr}^2B_r^2Q - 4I_{inj}QB_r^3 \tag{12b}$$

$$D_2 = \left(9A_{nr}B_rC_{auger}Q\right)^2 - 36Q^2A_{nr}B_r^4C_{auger} + 4Q^2B_r^6 + 729C_{auger}^4I_{inj}^2 + 486C_{auger}^3I_{inj}QA_{nr}B_r - 108I_{inj}QB_r^3C_{auger}^2 \tag{12c}$$

where N_i is the initial carrier density. In our work we modified the expression of N_i given by [12] by considering τ_e as a function of $N_{th}(T)$ and may be written as

$$N_i^{total}(T) = N_{th}^{total}(T)\cdot e^{\frac{\frac{N_{bit}}{B_{rate}}}{\tau_e(T)}} \tag{13}$$

where N_{bit} is the number of "0" bits preceding the considered bit and $\tau_e(T)$ is already given in Eq. (6a). Substituting $N_{th}^{total}(T)$ and $N_i^{total}(T)$ instead of N_{th} and N_i respectively in Eq. (8), we obtain a full analytical and exact expression form of t_{on} in terms of laser cavity parameters, temperature of operation, T, and corresponding degradation's parameters (i.e. w_{DD} and n_{DD}).

Note: we used N_{th} rather I_{th} in order to give more physical form and that will be useful to complete the analysis further to include the next two stages (not indicated here). However, one simply can substitute $N_{th}^{total}(T) = \frac{I_{th}^{total}(T).\tau_e(T)}{qV}$ in order to calculate t_{on} in term of $I_{th}^{total}(T)$.

3. Results and discussion

Parameter values of SLD at room temperature can be found in Table 1. The effect of temperature of operation, T, and the number of dark defects, n_{DD}, on the $I_{th}^{total}(T)$ and $N_{th}^{total}(T)$ is shown in Fig. 2a and Fig. 2b respectively. According to the mathematical model of I_{th}^{total} presented in [2] and after the modification (considering the TD of I_{th}^{total}, i. e. $I_{th}^{totald}(T)$, we note at

Table 1. Parameter values used in calculations

Parameter	Description	Value	Unit
d	Active region thickness	0.2	μm
W	Active region width	5	μm
L	Cavity length	500	μm
A	Nonradiative recombination coefficient	5.10^8	sec^{-1}
B	Radiative recombination coefficient	1.10^{-16}	m^3/sec
C	Auger recombination coefficient	3.10^{-41}	m^6/sec
g_o	Differential gain	$2.5.10^{-20}$	m^2
Γ	Confinement factor	0.3	
α_{int}	Internal loss	40	cm^{-1}
v_g	Group velocity	$7.5.10^9$	cm/sec
C_{light}	Speed of light	3.10^{10}	cm/sec
q	Charge of electron	$1.6.10^{-19}$	C
N_o	Carrier density at transparency	$1.\ 10^{18}$	cm^{-3}
n_g	Group refractive index	4	
r1, = r2	Field reflectivetics of the laser facets	0.566	
I_{inj}	Injection current	$2\ I_{th}(T_o)$	A

Fig. 2a the increasing of I_{th}^{total} (T) with T and n_{DD} due to increasing of $N_{th}(T)$ and I_{th}^{total} respectively. In Fig. 2b, $N_{th}^{total}(T)$ increases with T due to increasing of carrier density at transparency, N_t, decreasing of gain coefficient, g_o, and increasing of cavity internal loss, $\alpha_{i..}$ and also, $N_{th}^{total}(T)$ increases with the increasing of n_{DD} according to Eq. (5) [2]. Here we combined the influence of both T and n_{DD} by considering, the TD of N_{th} of the normal "good" SLD active region, in the I_{th}^{total} model given by [2]. The worst case of N_{th} is when the DBUSLD operates at higher temperature degrees and with large n_{DD}, for instance (as a comparison), at T = 25°C (room temperature) and n_{DD} =0 (no degradation), N_{th} = $1.837\times10^{18}cm^{-3}$ while it increases

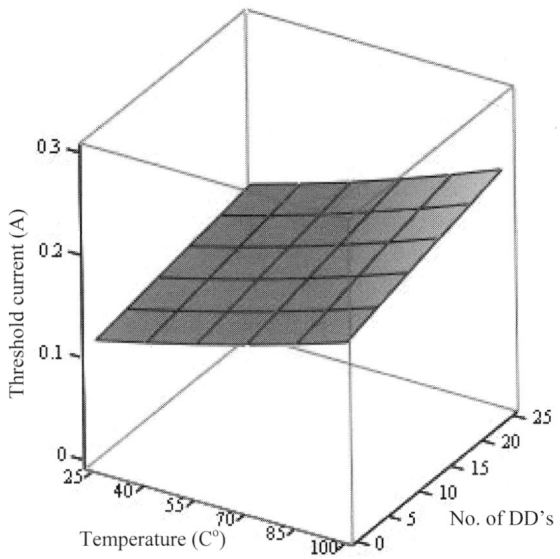

Fig. 2a Threshold current vs. the temperature of operation and number of DD's for DBUSLD.

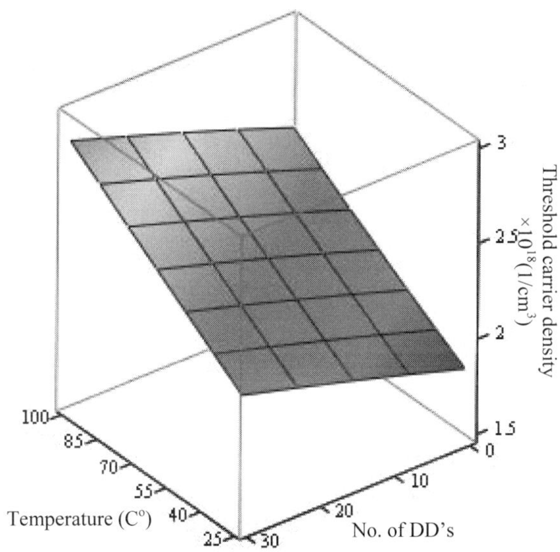

Fig. 2b Threshold carrier density vs. the temperature of operation and number of DD's for DBUSLD.

To $2.814\times10^{18}cm^{-3}$ at T = 100 °C and n_{DD} = 25.

Fig. 3 shows the calculated t_{on} as a function of T and n_{DD} for bit-rate, B_{rate}=4 Gb/s, and different values of N_{bit}. It is noted that t_{on} increases with the increasing of T and n_{DD} due to increasing of N_{th} and N_i. In addition, when N_{bit} increases the whole graphs moves up, i. e. t_{on}

increases, because physically, N_{th} (which will be as N_i for the next "one" pulse) has enough time between the pulses to decrease (diminish) to low level values before the next "one" bit. Also we note that t_{on} takes higher values when n_{DD} is large especially at high temperature degrees. Finally, Fig. 4 is the same of Fig. 3 but for N_{bit} = 1 and different values of bit-rates (B_{rate} = 1, 4 and 7 Gb/s). We note that when B_{rate}, i. e. bit time decreases, N_i increases then in turn t_{on} decreases correspondingly. Physically, N_{th} which will be as N_i for the next "one" pulse has no enough time to decrease; therefore, it still has a relatively high significant value.

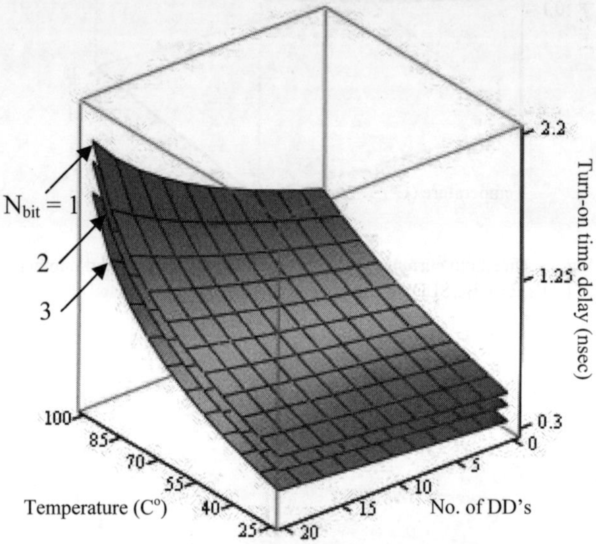

Fig. 3 Turn-on time delay vs. the temperature of operation and number of DD's for B_{rate}= 4 Gb/s and different values of N_{bit}.

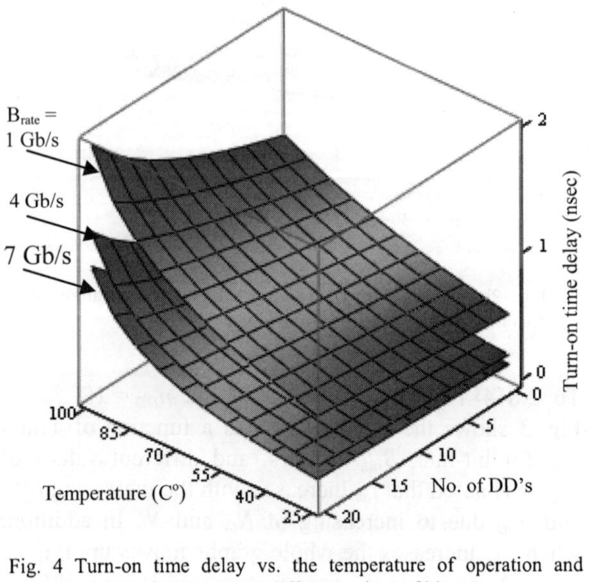

Fig. 4 Turn-on time delay vs. the temperature of operation and number of DD's for N_{bit}=1 and different values of bit-rates.

4. Conclusion

In this paper we studied the influence of temperature of operation of degraded bulk semiconductor laser and the number of dark defects by considering the threshold carrier density as function of temperature then inserted it in a total threshold current model of degraded bulk SLD presented in [2] to obtain the TD one. In order to obtain the corresponding threshold carrier density we derived full and exact analytical expression form of carrier density in term of laser cavity parameters and current flowed through the SLD active region.. In addition, the effect of dark defects on the turn-on time delay is calculated in the presence of temperature of operation using a full and exact analytical expression form. It is noted that t_{on} increases with the increasing of n_{DD} and T. The analysis can be extended further to include the transient response of degraded bulk uncooled SLD.

Reference

1. K. Hausler, U. Zeimer, B. Sumpf, G. Erbert, G. Trankle, J. Mater Sci: Mater Electron, ©Springer Science + Business Media, **LLC** (2008).
2. T. Kallstenius, J. Backstrom, U. Smith, and B. Stoltz, J. of Lightwave Technol., **17**, 12, (1999).
3. M. Fukudas. Norwood, MA: Artech House (1991).
4. M. Fukuda, Elsevier Science Ltd., Microelectronics Reliability, **42**, 679 (2002).
5. M. Fukuda, Elsevier Science Ltd., Microelectronics Reliability, **46**, 263 (2006).
6. M. Fukuda, Elsevier Science Ltd., Microelectronics, Reliability, **47**, 1619 (2007).
7. T. Stephens, K. Hinton, T. Anderson, and B. Clarke, J. of Lightwave Technol., **13**,4 (1995).
8. P. Pepeljugoski, D. Kuchta and j. Crow, IEEE Photon. Technol. Lett. **8**, 461 (1996).
9. K. Obermann, S. Kindt and k. Petermann, IEEE Photon. Technol. Lett. , **8**, 31 (1996).
10. M. Ming and K. Liu, McGraw-Hill companies, Inc (1996).
11. G. P. Agrawal and N. K. Dutta, New York: Van Nostrand Reinhold (1986).
12. D. M. Curter and K Y. Lau, IEEE Photon. Technol. Lett. **7**,4 (1995).
13. M. R. Hassan, European Phys. J. Appl. Phys, **41**, 41 (2008).
14. J. P. Morgado and A. T. Cartaxo, IEEE J. Select. Topic Quantum Electron., **9**, 1315 (2003).
15. T. Peng, Y. Huang, C. Yang, K. Huang, F. Lee, C. Hu, M. Wu, and C. Ho, IEEE Photon. Technol. Lett., **18**, 12 (2006).

DESIGN OF VEHICLE WARNING AND CONTROL SYSTEM BASED ON GIS [1]

ZHU YONGSHENG

School of Mathematical Science, Harbin Normal University
Harbin,Helongjiang,150025, China
e-mail: qinyuan168@163.com

SHAO HUIHUA

Library of Harbin Normal University
Harbin,Helongjiang,150025, China

JIANG CHUNMAO †

School of Computer, Harbin Normal University
Harbin,Helongjiang,150025, China

PAN HAIJING

School of Mathematical Science,Harbin Normal University
Harbin,Helongjiang,150025, China

Abstract—This paper studies a vehicle speed intelligent warning system, designs a vehicle safe running and intelligent control system with dynamic recognition and automatic control functions and establishes the architecture of the intelligent control system. This system judges the safe state of a vehicle automatically by comparing its real-time running speed with safe driving speed limit and then gives the vehicle driver a clue by releasing the vehicle speed warning information and finally controls the running speed by vehicle control module.

Keywords— intelligent control; vehicle speed warning; GIS; GPS; road safety

1. Introduction

Along with the quickening of expressway construction, the information which needs to be handled in management work, such as road safety, monitoring, communication and maintenance, etc, becomes larger and larger and manual information processing can not meet actual requirements. Thereafter, various countries begin to pay attention to the construction of road traffic real-time and dynamic information system. How to set the dynamic safety speed limit value and real-timely monitor the vehicle running speed according to these factors, such as vehicle type, road conditions and climatic conditions, etc, thereby actively controlling the safe running speed of vehicle and effectively improving the traffic safety situation of expressway is of important theoretical and practical significance. This paper emphatically introduces the design of a vehicle warning and intelligent control system.

2. Vehicle speed safety warning system

2.1. *Overall structure of warning system*

A vehicle speed safety warning system includes monitoring center, vehicle warning system and information transmission system and it is the core of the whole vehicle speed intelligent control system, its overall frame structure is shown as Fig 1. The system has many functions, such as vehicle real-time monitoring, vehicle speed warning, assistant decision-making, GIS map and vehicle speed safety prompt, etc.

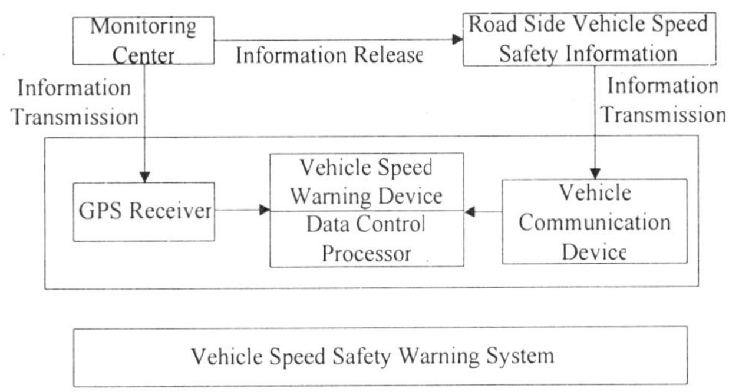

Figure 1. Structure of Vehicle Speed Safety Warning System

[*] This work is supported by the Science and Technology Research Projects of Education Office of Heilongjiang Province
[†] Corresponding author.

Monitoring center

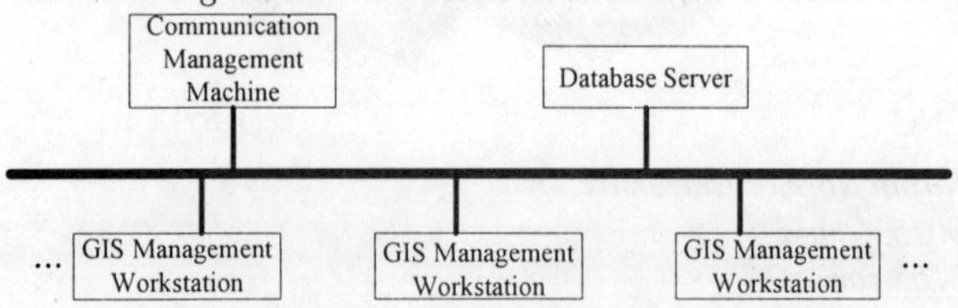

Figure 2. Frame Diagram of Monitoring Center

Monitoring center is a vehicle position and status display, query, analysis and processing system established on the basis of GIS software platform and its frame diagram is shown as Fig 2. It is responsible for receiving and displaying vehicle position, status and alarm information, etc, and carrying out parameter setting and control of system and vehicle unit. The functions of monitoring center include vehicle information receiving, system and vehicle station parameter setting, monitoring acceptance, map display, comprehensive information query, vehicle track storage and playback and database maintenance, etc.

2.1.1 Vehicle warning system

Vehicle warning system is responsible for the communication with monitoring center and wireless transmission of target vehicle position and vehicle speed safety warning status information, etc. And meanwhile, it can receive control instructions from monitoring center to control the vehicle running speed. Vehicle warning system is mainly composed of GPS information receiver, vehicle speed warning device, data control processor and vehicle wireless communication device, etc, and its functions include timing vehicle speed information transfer, vehicle running speed changing, vehicle speed emergency alarm and vehicle control, etc.

2.1.2 Road side vehicle speed safety information

Road side vehicle speed safety information release, such as real-time traffic, weather, road condition or other vehicle speed information, etc, released by monitoring center, can assist in vehicle running safety well, at present, commonly used safety information release ways include variable speed limit sign, vehicle speed display board and radiobroadcast, etc.

2.2. *Design of vehicle warning system*

The main routine design flow of vehicle speed safety warning system is shown as Fig 3 and its working principle is as follows: read the data in integrated GIS comprehensive management database according to real-time vehicle speed data collected by GPS and vehicle feature data obtained by video detection and calculate by vehicle speed safety evaluation, judge and handle the current driving safety status and give processing results, and then monitoring center real-timely displays the speed safety situation of target vehicle by information release, if the vehicle speed is in an unsafe state, monitoring center will give a corresponding alarm so that the driver could change the vehicle running speed.

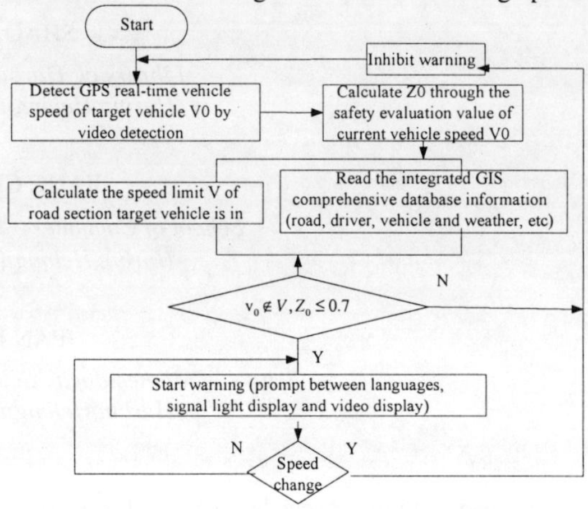

Figure 3. Main Routine Design Flowchart of Vehicle Speed Warning System

Where, the hardware structure of vehicle terminal warning system can be set by referring to Shenzhen Wufeng vehicle structure and its hardware structure is shown as Fig 4.

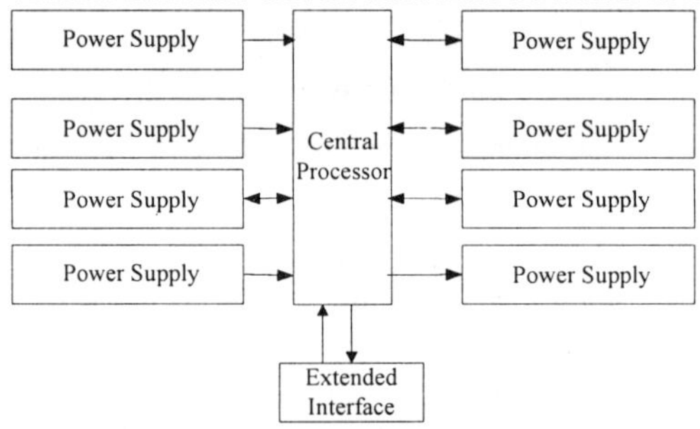

Figure 4. Hardware Structure of Vehicle Terminal Speed Warning System

3. Integrated design of vehicle speed intelligent control system

The integration of traffic safety technologies is the objective need of ITS development and its feasibility mainly embodies in technical composition, including geographic information system of traffic, vehicle positioning technology and wireless communication technology, etc. The core of safety technology integration consists in that GIS can act as a fundamental information system platform and it has the advantages of visualization, geographic and spatial analysis and unified database management, etc; vehicle positioning technology can real-timely obtain the position information of target vehicles with different precisions according to concrete application requirements; wireless communication technology can realize the data transmission within a large range and it is of great significance to the commanding, scheduling, monitoring and management of information system. The integration of the three technologies can effectively realize the real-time and dynamic monitoring, analysis and assistant decision-making of traffic information.

The frame structure of integrated design of vehicle speed intelligent control system is shown as Fig 5. From Fig 5 we can see that vehicle running speed intelligent control system platform is the core platform of expressway traffic guidance center and the design requires taking geographic information comprehensive database and electronic map as the main interface support of working platform and traffic guidance center computer network as a carrier, integrating road traffic management information system (vehicle management, driver management, violation management and accident treatment), GPS vehicle positioning system, TV monitoring system, over-speed detection system, over-speed warning system, information release system and wireless communication system, etc, to realize the integration, further treatment and value added service of various traffic management information, make the vehicle driver have a comprehensive grasp of the traffic conditions of monitored road sections, amend the traffic plan in time and maintain a reasonable running speed, thereby ensuring the safety and smoothness of traffic.

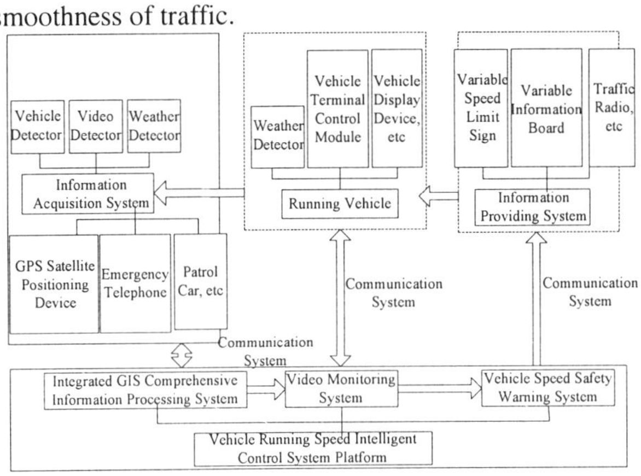

Figure 5. Frame Structure of Integrated Design of Vehicle Speed Intelligent Control System

3.1. System integration platform: *geographic information system of traffic (GIS-T)*

As a tool for obtaining, storing, analyzing and processing traffic geographic data, GIS-T technology integrates many kinds of geographic data in different levels to form a real world model and therefore it has strong spatial data management, geographic and spatial analysis abilities. GIS system is the framework of the whole system, various function displays of the system are all organically integrated in the display function of GIS and target location and query are both finished by GIS system. System functions include over-speed case management, electronic map system (GIS), TV monitoring, dynamic and static data acquisition and management, vehicle, driver and weather information, video detection, vehicle speed violation scheduling and commanding, vehicle speed warning and information statistics and query, etc.

3.2. *Integration of GPS and GIS*

Vehicle GPS system is composed of vehicle receiving and display system, radio communication system and ground control center, etc. As long as the GPS receiver installed at vehicle terminal receives the signals sent by more than four satellites, the position, time and motion state of GPS receiver can be reported after calculation and the current longitude, latitude, time, speed and course of the vehicle can be worked out through triangle location principle. The driver can take reasonable traffic action in time according to the traffic safety conditions displayed on the vehicle display device.

3.3. *Integration of electronic map*

Compare the position estimation outputted by positioning system (GPS) with the road position information provided by map database (GIS) and determine the current road section the vehicle runs on and the accurate position of the vehicle in the road section through proper pattern match and recognition process, thereby improving positioning accuracy.

Realize the integration of TV monitoring system, detection system and warning system and use the vehicle management base, driver management base and weather base information, etc, of system database server to realize the integration of over-speed violation detection system, over-speed violation warning system, vehicle and driver management system and weather base system, which can inquire about the running information conditions of the vehicle very easily. The organic integration of over-speed violation detection, over-speed violation warning, vehicle and driver management and weather information management can not only ensure the unity and integrity of data but also directly display on GIS electronic map, thereby improving the processing efficiency of over-speed events and enhancing the running safety of vehicles on the expressway.

3.4. *Integration of TV monitoring*

Through the integration of various subsystems, TV monitoring device can know the violation details of over-speed vehicles conveniently and in time, release danger signals to vehicle drivers and provide strategies through automatic switching of large screen or video wall, thereby effectively improving the safety consciousness of vehicle drivers.

GIS can make special map layers for traffic TV monitoring system. Through database, the position of each monitoring camera can be got and use camera symbols to carry out graphic identification in the electronic map. After the operator clicks on a certain camera in the map, he will command the platform software system to provide the status information of monitor or display the information of monitoring system according to the information in the database or to automatically switch to the corresponding camera and display its image through video matrix. And by controlling the matrix, he can directly use a keyboard to realize cloud platform control, camera control, monitoring mode control and monitoring parameter control of monitoring end, such as change of the direction of remote cloud platform, focusing, zooming and aperture adjusting of a camera and brightness and contrast adjustment according to weather situation, etc.

3.5. *Integration of video detection*

The installation of video detection and vehicle GPS devices through road section can real-timely detect the vehicle running conditions of the current road section, such as target vehicle and real-time running speed tracking. Operators of monitoring center can monitor the speed safety of running vehicles through large screen or video wall. The system integration of video detection is mainly realized by system database. Detection system transmits the shot picture and text record information to the database server through network. And the control and setting of video devices need the coordination between the subsystem and integrated system, thereby ensuring the consistency of protocols.

Integration of vehicle speed warning system

The over-speed violation prediction scheme, etc, can be edited through a friendly interface. Use real-time data to replace the predefined macros in the prediction scheme to realize the real-time traffic data release. And meanwhile, automatically display the recommended coping schemes of over-speed violation events on GIS according to the pre-edited prediction scheme base and by prediction scheme selection to improve users' emergency ability of over-speed events, shorten reaction time and serve vehicle drivers faster and better.

3.6. *Integration of radio communication system*

Realize the information interaction between running vehicles and monitoring center. Users of monitoring center can obtain the detailed data needed from the system database rapidly by inputting simple personal or vehicle information; vehicle drivers can transmit the real-time vehicle speed information to the system database according to the vehicle running information obtained by GPS and video detection devices and through high-speed wireless network, such as GPRS, etc, thereby realizing data updating and integration.

Various statistical data can be got very easily through the calculation function of relational database. GIS information release platform uses the statistical data whose forms are different figures, diagrams and reports to provide the most visual, effective, simplest and practical analysis tools for customers.

4. Application of vehicle speed intelligent control system

After the comprehensive analysis of vehicle speed information acquisition, information management and warning, we apply the existing ITS technology, integrated idea and cooperative control theory to expressway vehicle speed control, which can effectively monitor the running state of vehicles and improve vehicle speed safety level. Its application frame structure is shown as Fig 6.

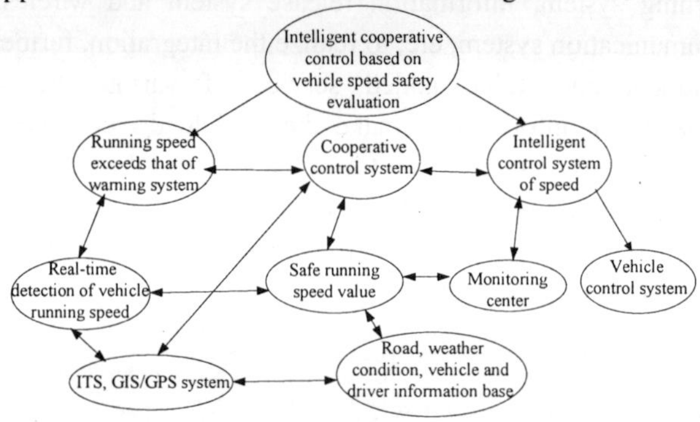

Figure 6. Application Frame Structure of Vehicle Speed Intelligent Control System

According to the previous evaluation and analysis results, choose road section 1 to design a vehicle speed intelligent control scheme, shown as Fig 7.

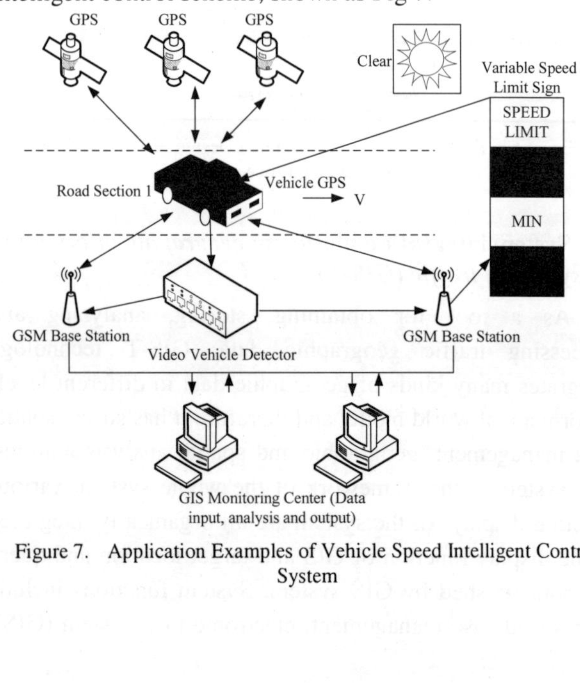

Figure 7. Application Examples of Vehicle Speed Intelligent Control System

Where, use video detector and vehicle and driver information base to obtain vehicle and driver index data; use GPS and GIS to obtain the road section information of target vehicle and dynamic information of vehicle speed; use monitoring center and integrated GIS comprehensive database management center to carry out fusion processing, data analysis and safety evaluation of information to get the safety situation of vehicle speed; use road side variable speed limit sign board to real-timely display the speed limit values of road sections and variable speed limit sign display value can be divided into various display modes, such as speed limit by road section, speed limit by traffic lane, speed limit by vehicle type and speed limit by time period, etc; use GSM public network to transmit vehicle speed safety commands in time in GSM short message.

5. Conclusion

The vehicle speed limit designed in this paper is a comprehensive method by vehicle type, time period and road section, this paper carries out an integrated design of the control system and the vehicle speed safety warning system composed of vehicle GPS, warning device, road side dynamic speed limit sign, communication system and monitoring center can induce and control the vehicle running speed safety well and has practical theoretical value and application guidance value.

References

1. George YANNIS, John GOLLAS, George KANELLAIDIS, A Comparative Analysis of the Potential of International Road Accident Data Files [J], IATSS Research, 2000, 124(2):111-120
2. Solomon D, Accidents on main rural highways related to speed, drivers, and vehicle [R], Washington: Bureau of Public Roads, 1964
3. Federal Highway Administration. Synthesis of Safety Research Related to Speed and Speed Limits[R], Publication No, FH-WA-RD-98-154, 1999
4. FILDES B N, RUMBOLD G, LEENING A, Speed behavior and drivers attitude to speeding [R], Sydney: Monash University, 1991
5. BARUYA A, Speed-accident relationships on different kinds of European roads [R].London: Transportation Research Laboratory, 1998

A NEW APPROACH FOR VOICE SPECTRUM ANALYSIS (VSA): SUITABLE FOR PERVASIVE COMPUTING USING MATLAB

PROF. VIJAY KUMAR CHAUDHARI
CSE Department, Madhya Pradesh Bhoj University, Bhopal (M.P.), India
E-mail: vijay_ashish@yahoo.com

DR. R. K. SINGH
Director, MATS University, Raipur (C.G.), India
Email: vcrks@rediffmail.com

DR. DINESH VARSHNEY
Regional Director, Madhya Pradesh Bhoj (Open) University-Bhopal (M.P.), India
Email: vdinesh33@rediffmail.com

SHIV KUMAR
Department of IT, Technocrats Institute of Technology, Bhopal (M.P.)-462021, India
E-mail: shivksahu@rediffmail.com

ABSTACT- In this paper, Voice Spectrum Analysis (VSA) is a methodology which defined the evaluation in between constitutional and unconstitutional voice with the help of various parameters of Digital Signal Processing (DSP). Average pitch value of recorded .wav file, vector differences in between formant peaks value of each file etc… are main parameters of DSP, for example. Pitch value define the frequency of the sound, perfect pitch refers to the ability of some persons to recognize the pitch of a voice note without any discernable pitch standard. Formant analysis calculates the peak points of power spectral density for a selected .wav file. This work is useful for many small devices for security purpose. For example, if a device is bolted with voice parameters then it can unbolt only when bolted device is recognized the same DSP parameters from the .wav warehouse. For do this .wav file is used to bolt and unbolt that device.

KEYWORDS- MatLab6.0, DSP Toolbox, .wav warehouse, Algorithms

1. Introduction

In this paper, It is reported the programming methods by using MatLab6.0 with DSP Toolbox using mathematical technique Fourier transforms. The Fourier Transform breaks down time signals into frequencies, which can then analyze. We are analyzing the VSA using MatLab Toolbox. Spectrum is a function we used frequently in MatLab to look at the spectral envelope of a recorded sin wave. Spectrum takes numbers of vectors from a .wav file and the sampling frequency of that file. The function outputs of FFT of the .wav file is plotted in graph format. Background noise was removed up to maximum extent from a signal by the application of a 3rd order Butterworth filter. A code was then developed to compare the pitch spectrum and formant of a known speech file to N bit unknown speech files and chooses for top 4 matches. The sorting routines performed to sort and compare the average pitch of the reference file with all other files, compare the formant vector of the reference file to all .wav files, sort for the top 4 average pitch correlations and then sort these files by formant vectors, and finally sort the top 2 formant vector correlations and then sort these by average pitch.

The development of the speaker identification system began as early as the 1960s with exploration into voiceprint analysis, where characteristics of an individual's voice were thought to be able to characterize the uniqueness of an individual much like a fingerprint.

In this paper, we identify that which one .wav file is constitutional and which is unconstitutional. Speaker record the voice and stores it in the .wav warehouse. Now two .wav file will be same if both file is recorded with same sentences by the same speaker otherwise difference must identify by the pitch value & frequency spectrum. This paper is the part of voice comparison system.

2. Problem Identification For Proposed Work

In the referenced paper, there is no consideration for N bits long parameters for security of devices.

Shaleena Jeeawoody, "Voice Analysis and Recognition as a Car Theft Deterrent", California State Science Fair 2008, Project No: J1307, Ap2/08 http://www.USC.edu/CSSF/Current/Projects/J1307.pdf

To get N-bits long security parameters, different DSP parameters are used:

1. Speech Enhancement
2. Pitch Analysis
3. Single Echo
4. Multiple Eco
5. FIR Reverb
6. IIR Reverb
7. Flat Response Reverb
8. Formant Analysis
9. Flange
10. Fade-In
11. Fade-Out
12. Wavelet Comparison

2.1. *Speech Enhancement*

The file recorded with slower speech and noise in the background was found from the ordered list of speakers, this is defined in Figure-1. Recorded voice signal is then converted to the frequency domain through the use of a shifted FFT and correctly scaled frequency vector.

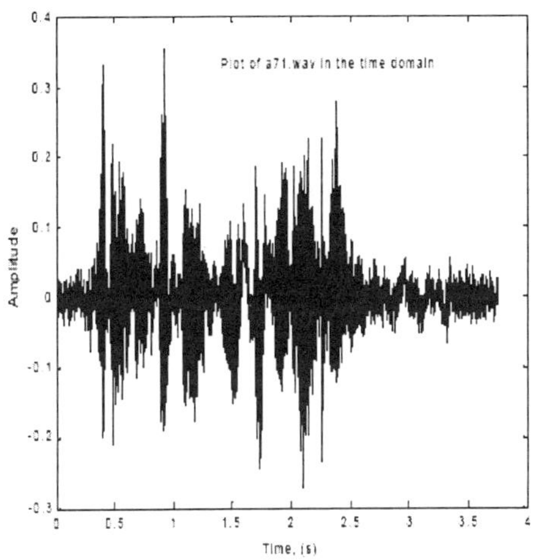

Figure-1: Speech Enhancement

The higher frequency noise components were then removed by application of a 3rd order Butterworth low pass filter with the cutoff chosen to remove as much of the noise signal as possible while still preserving the original signal. Cutoff frequency is that frequency where the magnitude response of the filter is $(1/2)^{1/2}$. To calculate Butterworth low pass filter output, following equation is used in MatLab:

$$[b, a] = \text{butter}\,(n, w_n) \ldots (1)$$

Equation (1) is used to design an order n lowpass digital Butterworth filter with normalized cutoff frequency Wn. It returns the filter coefficients in length n+1 row vectors b and a, with coefficients in descending powers of *z*.

$$H(z) = \frac{B(z)}{A(z)} = \frac{b(1) + b(2)z^{-1} + \cdots + b(n+1)z^{-n}}{1 + a(2)z^{-1} + \cdots + a(n+1)z^{-n}} \quad \ldots.(1)$$

The Butterworth filter is a reasonable choice to use as it more closely approximates an ideal low pass filter as the order n is increased. The resulting filtered signal & the original noisy signal was then scaled and plotted and to get the final comparison.

2.2. *Pitch Analysis*

Pitch is the representation of a sound wave frequency (the number of cycles per second).The file recorded with slower speech was found from the ordered list of speakers. Pitch analysis was conducted and relevant parameters (Low Pitch & High Pitch) were extracted. The average pitch of the entire wav file was computed and found to have a value of 154.8595 Hz. The graph of pitch contour versus time frame was also created to see how the pitch varies over the wav file in Figure-2.

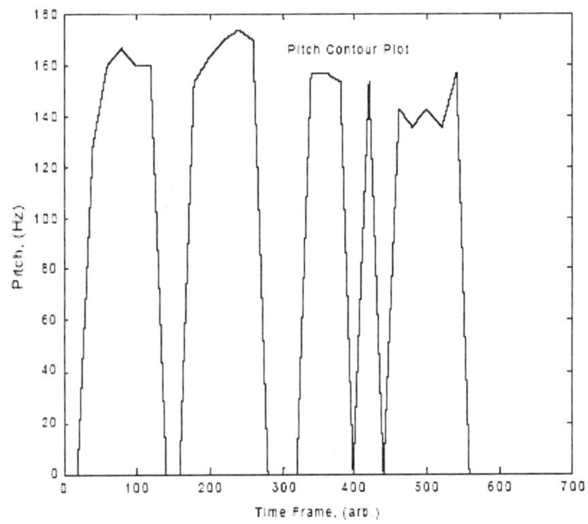

Figure-2: Pitch contour plot

The results of pitch analysis can be used in voice recognition, where the differences in average pitch can be used to characterize a voice file. Pitch Analysis is defined in figure-2. Pitch defines two parameters:

i) Low pitch
ii) High Pitch

This is modulation standard that the frequency from 440Hz to 880Hz, depending on the octave. Low pitch is an effect in which the frequency of wave becomes down to a certain value. High pitch is an effect in which the frequency of wave becomes high to a certain value.
If two wave file have the frequency A = 440 Hz and B = 547 Hz respectively then A belong to low pitch and B belong to high pitch standards.

2.3. ***Single Echo***

The single echo is nothing but editing a delay in to input signal. An FIR filter can use to edit the delay in input signal. According the need, delay can be increase & decrease for the desired result. This is a MatLab function that makes a rough calculation of a room's impulse response. The output can then be convolved with an audio clip to produce good and realistic sounding reverb. The effect of delay is achieved when a signal is played and then a modified version of that signal is played back after a period of time, either one time or multiple times, resulting in an echoing effect. The simplest version of delay is an FIR filter through which a signal is played back only one time. This is called simple delay. Delay time and relative amplitude (and hence relative intensity) for the echoes are two parameters that can be specified.

2.4. ***Multiple Echo***

The multiple echoes are nothing but editing a delay in to input signal. A COMB filter can use to edit the delay in input signal. Comb filters are essentially notch filters with deep notches equally spaced in a band of frequencies. The periodic, deep notches make comb filters ideal for applications that need to eliminate specific frequency components. A comb filter can be designed by placing zeros equally spaced around the unit circle at the desired notch locations. However, the resulting FIR notch filter will exhibit relatively large bandwidth at each notch, which will result in the attenuation of desired frequency components.

2.5. ***FIR Reverb***

Reverberation, or reverb, is a slightly more complex FIR form of delay. FIR reverberation is defined as the combined effect of multiple sounds reflections within a room. Reverb is used to digitally simulate a surrounding by modeling echoes that would naturally be present in that environment. The reverberation characteristics of a room are affected by several factors: the shape and size of the room, the materials of which the room is constructed, and the materials present in the room.

Filters are electronic circuits that respond to impulses, processing signals by enhancing certain aspects reducing certain aspects. There are several different types of filters. A finite impulse response (FIR) filter is one in which the output signal goes to zero in some finite amount of time. An FIR filter will take as input the current sample in addition to some previous sample An FIR filter has not internal feedback.

2.6. ***IIR Reverb***

Reverberation, or reverb, is a slightly more complex IIR form of delay. IIR reverberate involves saving the past values of the output instead of the input values. An infinite impulse response (IIR) filter may run for an arbitrarily long period of time and never have the output go to zero. IIR filter is recursive; i.e., an IIR filter will take its previous output and use it as input for the next output. Reverb is used to digitally simulate a surrounding by modeling echoes that would naturally be present in that environment. An IIR filter create internal feedback

2.7. ***Flat Response Reverb***

Flat-response reverb has a flat response for all values of frequencies. For an all-pass filter the gain is ideally unity for all values. The flat response filter is derived from the all-pass filter for which the poles and the zeros are conjugate reciprocals of each other.

2.8. ***Formant Analysis***

Formant analysis is performed on slow recorded voice file. The first five peaks in the power spectral density were returned and the first three can be seen in Figure-3. The vector position of the peaks in the power spectral density is calculated and can be used to characterize a particular voice file. This technique is used in the waveform comparison section. Power Spectrum is just another mathematical tool for analyzing the signal.

2.9. ***Flange***

Flange is used to filter the original signal and try to remove maximum noise from the signal. Noise is the unwanted bits that are edited in between the data. With the help of FLANGE Effect, we want to reduce maximum noise from the data.

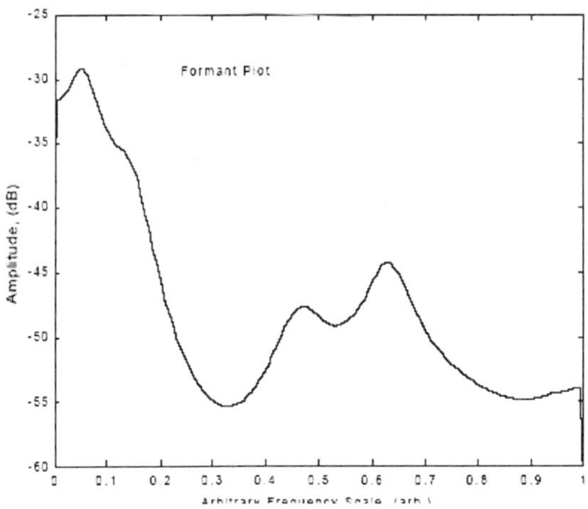

Figure-3: Plots of First Few Format

2.10. *Fade-In*

This is effect in which the soundness of wav becomes low to high. We can analyze the .wav spectrum from low to high. This effect is used when we want to analyze spectrum from low to high.

2.11. *Fade-Out*

This is effect in which the soundness of wav becomes high to low. We can analyze the .wav spectrum from high to low. This effect is used when we want to analyze spectrum from high to low.

2.12. *Waveform Comparison*

Using the results and information learned from pitch and formant analysis, a waveform comparison code was written. Speech waveform files can be characterized based on various criteria. Average pitch and formant peak position vectors are two such criteria that can be used to characterize a speech file. The slow speech file was used as a reference file. For sorting routines were then written to compare the files. The sorting routines performed to sort and compare the average pitch of the reference file with all other files, compare the formant vector of the reference file to all .wav files, sort for the top 4 average pitch correlations and then sort these files by formant vectors, and finally to sort for the top 2 formant vector correlations and then sort these by average pitch.

3. Conclusion

In this paper, it is proposed to evaluate (comparison) in between constitutional & unconstitutional voice. It was found that comparison based on pitch compute most accuracy. So if compute voice signals according to DSP parameters then selected voice may produce best result for comparison of constitutional & unconstitutional voice of N-bit signals. DSP parameters are single Eco, Multiple Eco, FIR Reverb, IIR Reverb, Flat Response Reverb, Flange, Fade-In, Fade-Out, etc... On the basis of these Parameters different result computes of given input signal & their delays can give better result for desired output.

4. Future Work

Recorded voice may contain N-bit signals in the form of .wav file, so if recorded file is compressed first with same extension (.wav to .wav file) then compared with one compressed file with another, then it may compute better result in very short time.

The N-bit .wav file may contain more background noise that may be reduced by some better algorithms.

References

1. Shaleena Jeeawoody, "Voice Analysis and Recognition as a Car Theft Deterrent", California State Science Fair 2008, Project No: J1307, Ap2/08 http://www.USC.edu/CSSF/Current/Projects/J1307.pdf
2. Khalid Saeed, "Sound and Voice Verification and Identification a Brief Review of Töeplitz Approach", Znalosti 2008, pp. 22-27, ISBN 978-80-227-2827-0.FIIT STU Bratislava, .stav informatiky a softvÈrovÈho inæinierstva, 2008. http://znalosti2008.fiit.stuba.sk/download/articles/znalosti2008-Saeed.pdf
3. Maria Markaki, Andre Holzapfel, Yannis Stylianou "Singing Voice Detection using Modulation Frequency Features", Computer Science Department, University of Crete, Greece http://www.sapa2008.org/papers/122.pdf
4. Engin Avci, "An Automatic System for Turkish Word Recognition Using Discrete Wavelet Neural Network Based on Adaptive Entropy", International Conference-Elazig, Turkey-Dec 06, 2007, the Arabian Journal for Science and Engineering, Volume 32, Number 2B.

http://www.kfupm.edu.sa/publications/ajse/Articles/322B_P.04.pdf

5. Frank A Russo, Lola L Cuddy, Alexander Galembo, William Forde Thompson, "Sensitivity to tonality across the pitch range", Perception, 2007, volume 36, pages 781-790, DOI: 10.1068/p5435, ISSN 0301-0066 (print) http://www.perceptionweb.com/perception/fulltext/p36/p5435.pdf

6. Murtaza Bulut, "Mult-level emotional speech analysis resynthesis", Proposed thesis for Ph.D. in Electrical Engineering, University of Southern California (USC), Los Angeles, CA, (graduation expected in November 2007). http://sail.usc.edu/~mbulut/pdfs/murtaza_bulut_CV_Oct2007.pdf

7. Michael I Mandel, "Recognition and Organization of Speech and Audio (LabROSA)", Ph.D. candidate in the department of Electrical Engineering at Columbia University, Proposed work for 2009 (Jan) exp. http://mr-pc.org/cv.pdf

8. Sarantos Psycharis "The Didactic Use of Digital Image Lossy Compression Methods For The Vocational Training Sector", University of Agean, Proceeding of Current Developments in Technology-Assisted Education 2006(FORMATEX 2006) http://www.formatex.org/micte2006/pdf/2065-2069.pdf

9. Graziano Bertini, Federico Fontana, Diego Gonzalez, Lorenzo Grassi, Massimo Magrini "Voice Transformation Algorithms With Real Time Dsp Rapid Prototyping Tools", Proceeding In International Conference –Eusipco 2005 http://www.eurasip.org/Proceedings/Eusipco/Eusipco2005/defevent/papers/cr1227.pdf

10. Marcos Faundez-Zanuy, "Non Liner speech Processing", Proceeding in ISCpad 66, 19-22 April-2005, Barcelona, Spain http://www.isca-speech.org/escapads/pad67.text

11. Keikichi HIROSE, "Speech Prosody 2004", Proceeding in ISCApad 56, International Conference: Speech Prosody 2004 on March 23 -26, 2004-Japan, http://www.gavo.t.u-tokyo.ac.jp/sp2004

12. Kyogu Lee,"Pitch Perception: Place Theory, Temporal Theory, and Beyond", IEE 391 Special Report (Autumn 2004), Center for Computer Research in Music and Acoustics (CCRMA), Music Department, Stanford University http://ccrma-www.stanford.edu/~kglee/pubs/klee_ee391_fall04.pdf

13. Bal´azs Bank, Federico Avanzini, Gianpaolo Borin, Giovanni De Poli, Federico Fontana, Davide Rocchesso, "Physically Informed Signal Processing Methods for Piano Sound Synthesis: A Research Overview", EURASIP Journal on Applied Signal Processing 2003:10, 941–952, ©2003 Hindawi Publishing Corporation http://home.mit.bme.hu/~bank/publist/jasp03.pdf

14. Douglas A. Reynolds, Larry P. Heck, "Automatic Speaker Recognition" Presented at the AAAS 2000 Meeting Humans, Computers and Speech Symposium 19 February 2000, Nuance Communications United States Air Force. http://www2.imm.dtu.dk/~lf/Automatic%20Speaker%20Recognition.pdf

15. Matti Karjalainen, Tero Tolonen,"Multi-Pitch and Periodicity Analysis Model for Sound Separation and Auditory Scene Analysis", Laboratory of Acoustics and Audio Signal Processing-Helsinki University of Technology http://www.ee.columbia.edu/~dpwe/papers/KarjT99-pitch.pdf

16. Ganesh K Venayagamoorthy, Viresh Moonasar, Kumbes Sandrasegaran, "Voice Recognition Using Neural Networks",Institute of Information Science and Technology (IIST), Massey University, New Zealand, Published in IEEE in 1998, Val. No. 0-7803-5054-5.0029 http://acil.mst.edu/documents/voice_recognition_using.pdf

17. Brett A. St. George, Ellen C. Wooten, , Louiza Sellami "Speech Coding and Phoneme classification Using MATLAB and NeuralWorks" Department of Ellectrical Engineering,U.S. Naval Academy-Annapolis, MD 21402 http://file.engrng.pitt.edu/fie97/papers/1037.pdf

18. Audio Signal Processing and Coding "Andress Sparias Ted Painter Venkatraman http://www.amazon.com/Signal-Processing-Coding-Andreas-Spanias/dp/0471791474